Inside the Apple Macintosh®

Jim Heid
Peter Norton

Brady

New York

BRADY

Simon & Schuster, Inc.
15 Columbus Circle
New York, NY 10023

DISTRIBUTED BY PRENTICE HALL TRADE

Manufactured in the United States of America

1 2 3 4 5 6 7 8 9 10

Library of Congress Cataloging-in-Publication Data

Heid, Jim.
    Inside the Apple Macintosh / Jim Heid, Peter Norton.
        p.   cm.
    ISBN 0-13-467622-X
    1. Macintosh (Computer)   I. Norton, Peter, 1943–   . II. Title.
QA76.8.M3H39   1989
004.165—dc20   89-22378
                                                CIP

Contents

Contents iii

Acknowledgments vii

Read This First ix
Welcome to Macintosh ix
What's Inside x
Whom This Book is For x
What Isn't Inside xi
A Roadmap for Using This Book xi
A Word About System Versions xii
A Final Note xiii

Section I   *Introducing the Mac* 1

1 Computer Fundaments 3
A Joint Effort 3
Dealing With Data 5
A Closer Look At Hardware 8
Types of Software 12
Chapter Summary 14

2 A Standard is Born 17
The Dawn of Mac 17
Interacting With Computers 18
Chapter Summary 30

3 The Macintosh Interface 31
The Bit-Mapped Display 32
The Machine of Metaphors 35
Interacting With The Mac 39
The Finder 49
The Mac's Filing System 55

MultiFinder   60
System Disk Basics   66
The Clipboard   71
Desk Accessories   71
Color in the Mac Interface   81
Sound in the Mac Interface   82
Chapter Summary   83

4   The Macintosh Family   85
Mac Categories and Capabilities   86
Assessing Your Needs   86
The Mac Family   90

5   System Folder Details   109
System Version Numbering   110
The Primary Players   112
Miscellaneous Files   129
Keeping Up to Date   131
The Evolution of the Mac System   135
Chapter Summary   143

6   Macintosh Video   145
Video Recap   146
Bit-Mapped Versus Character-Based Displays   146
Video Details   147
Mac II Video   151
Color Architectures   160
Chapter Summary   163

Section II   *Mastering the Mac*   165

7   Fonts   167
Font and Type Basics   167
Mac Font Basics   172
Font Structure   172
Font Details   185
Chapter Summary   194

8   Printing   197
Mac Printing Overview   197
The ImageWriter Family   202
Laser Printers   211
Chapter Summary   250

9   Setup and Operating Tips   251
System Folder Setup   251
Operating Tips   257
Hardware Setup Tips   305

10 Customizing Tips   313
Resource Details   313
Customizing Projects   326
Customizing With Accessories   369

Section III   *Exchanging and Sharing*   379

11 Exchanging Data   381
Clipboard Details   382
Exchanging Data With Disk Files   390
Exchanging Files With an MS-DOS Computer   401
Using Transferred Files   415
Chapter Summary   424

12 Networking   427
Why Network?   428
Network Concepts   430
A Network Scenario   439
Chapter Summary   497

Section IV   *How the Mac Works*   499

13 Hardware Details   501
Hardware Concepts   502
Under The Hood   506
Memory Details   519
Expansion Slots   526
The Mac's Microprocessors   529
The Start-up Process   533
Chapter Summary   536

14 Input and Output   539
The Keyboard and Mouse   539
Sound Details   546
SCSI Details   554
The Serial Ports   562
Chapter Summary   567

15 Disk Details   569
Disk Basics   570
Hard Disks   576
Removeable-Media Drives   577
Shopping For Storage   581
How the Mac Saves Files   585
Disk Troubleshooting   591
Chapter Summary   599

Appendix A: Mac Applications Glossary   601

Appendix B: For More Information   605

Index   615

Acknowledgments

We're deeply indebted to everyone who helped make this book a reality. At Apple Computer, Frank Casanova always found time to provide encouragement and technical insights. We also relied on the assistance and expertise of Steve Goldberg, Jim Gable, Donn Denman, Mark Lentczner, Neil Cormia, Mark Orr, and Scott Darling. Martha Steffen also provided cheerful assistance, and Jackie Perez answered frequent pleas for photographs.

At Norton Computing, Marvin Carlberg, Gary Amstutz, and John Socha provided enthusiastic support and technical assistance, and Kevin Goldstein offered editorial and technical suggestions that were often so good they stung. Thanks also to Linda Brent at Xerox's Palo Alto Research Center and to the staff of the Computer Museum in Boston.

Also taking time from busy schedules to discuss technie details were Joel West, Dennis Cohen, Richard Hill, and Erik Smith. Diane Whittaker of Diversified Computers in Keene, NH proved herself an able logic board juggler as she kept Macs healthy and customers happy. And Jeffrey Thompson was absolutely, positively there when we needed him.

At Brady Books, Milissa Koloski, Michael Mellin, and Mia McCroskey supported us with humor and good company. They got the book off the ground, while Burt Gabriel saw to it that it landed on time. (Well, almost on time.) Tom Dillon expertly kept track of the project even as last-minute changes spilled out of express envelopes and FAX machines. And the Brady Books production staff together with Carol Barth and the rest of the gang at Modern Design put it all together.

Finally, Jim Heid would like to extend a special thanks to his colleagues and friends at Macworld magazine, who patiently endured missed deadlines as the book came together, and whose guidance and support over the years have been an inspiration. And he can't begin to thank Maryellen Kelly, his loving and lovable wife, who edited pages, listened to rages, and had the good sense, when it was all over, to say, "Let's move to California."

Limits of Liability and Disclaimer of Warranty

Trademarks

Read This First

WELCOME TO MACINTOSH

It's that start-up message—and the smiling Mac that precedes it—that clue you in to the fact that the Apple Macintosh is a different kind of computer. It's an approachable computer that hides its complexities behind a facade of pull-down menus, sharp graphics, trash cans, and desktops. Rather than giving you the job of memorizing and typing arcane commands, the Macintosh invites exploration. Go ahead, point to something. What's in that menu? With a Mac, you don't feel like a stranger in a strange land; you feel like an explorer embarking on a new adventure.

But behind the Mac's facade is a sophisticated machine that, in some ways, is more complex than a room-sized computer. Eventually, you'll encounter those complexities. Maybe you'll want to add or remove some fonts. Or you'll wish a certain menu command had a keyboard shortcut. Or you might want to share information with other computers in your office. Or, as you decide how to best equip your Mac, you'll want to know how it creates screen displays, how its memory can be expanded, or how it accesses external add-ons.

At times like those, *Inside the Apple Macintosh* will be there. This book is your guide to mastering the Mac and understanding the technology behind it. Some people use the phrase "power user" to describe someone who knows the nooks and crannies of a machine. To us, a power user is a person who gets an electric bill each month. A knowledgeable user is someone whose understanding goes beyond the basics needed to make the computer work. After all, knowledge, not power, is what separates novice from master.

WHAT'S INSIDE

The road to mastery begins with the basics, and so does this book. In Section I, "Introducing the Mac," we'll look at the basics of how computers operate and at the people and events that made the Mac possible. We'll look at how you interact with the Mac and we'll explore the software that allows the Mac to run. We'll examine the Mac's family tree and note the differences between each member of the Macintosh family, and we'll see how the Mac creates screen displays.

In Section II, "Mastering the Mac," we'll take a hands-on look at tips and techniques that can help you use the Mac more efficiently. We'll showcase the Mac's typographic talents by looking at how Macintosh fonts and printers operate, and we'll present tips for getting the most from your printer. We'll look at ways to efficiently issue commands and navigate between programs, at how to get the most out of your Mac's memory and disk storage space, and at ways to customize the Mac to fit your working style.

In Section III, "Exchanging and Sharing," we'll look at the fine points of exchanging information between programs and between the Mac and other computers. We'll look at how you can tie the Macs (and other computers) in your office together into a *network* to share information and expensive add-ons such as laser printers. We'll show how a network can unite two or more computers to allow coworkers to efficiently communicate and share expensive add-ons such as laser printers.

In Section IV, "How the Mac Works," we'll look under the hood. We'll build on previous sections and explore Macintosh technology in greater detail. We'll take a close look at how the Mac accesses external add-ons, how it produces sound, and how it stores and retrieves information on disks. And because the worst *does* happen to the latter, we'll present some tips for diagnosing problems and recovering information from damaged disks.

WHOM THIS BOOK IS FOR

We wrote this book with three types of readers in mind:

- Macintosh users who want to master the Mac's workings, who want to understand how the Mac operates, and who want practical information on customizing, troubleshooting, and exchanging information with Macs and other computers.

- Experienced business users of the IBM PC and other MS-DOS computers who are buying Macs or using them at work. If you're in this group, our look at Mac and PC networking and data-exchange issues will be of special interest to you.

- Potential Macintosh programmers looking for a technical primer on Macintosh technology. This book doesn't teach how to program the Macintosh, but it does provide the technical background you'll need to read and get the most from books that do (we'll list some of them in Appendix B, "For More Information").

WHAT ISN'T INSIDE

It may seem odd to begin a book by stating what it *doesn't* cover, but we think it's only fair to tell you.

We don't examine each category of application software (word processing, data base management, presentation graphics, and so on). Appendix A, "Mac Applications Glossary" provides brief definitions of the ways Macs are used, but generally, we assume you already know that a diverse array of business, entertainment, personal improvement, and educational software is available for the Mac. Phrased another way, we prefer to describe the "how" and "why" of the Macintosh world rather than the "what."

To that end, we generally avoid describing specific software or hardware products in detail. Companies update and improve their products regularly, and detailed product descriptions would probably be outdated by the time you read them. Generally, we'll mention specific products only to illustrate the differences in approach within a given product category, or to show how various programs can exchange information with each other. The product discussions that we do provide aren't endorsements, nor does a products' absence imply that it's under par. The best sources for current information on specific products are user groups, magazines, and knowledgeable dealers.

A ROADMAP FOR USING THIS BOOK

Because this book is divided into four sections, you shouldn't feel obliged to read it from front to back, especially if you're already familiar with the Mac or other computers. Here are a few guidelines to aim you in the direction you're most interested in.

If you're just getting started with computers, start at the beginning. Chapter 1 provides an overview of how computers operate, and introduces common computer acronyms and jargon such as *CPU, RAM, ROM, mass storage,* and *system software.*

If you've had some experience with the Mac, skim the first few chapters and read over the summaries at the end of each one. If you encounter new terms or concepts, leaf back to the appropriate sections. If you're more interested in hands-on tips and customizing information than in theory and background, start with Section II, then refer back to Section I if you encounter unfamiliar concepts.

If you've used a computer other than the Mac, start with Chapter 2, but concentrate on Chapters 3 and 4, which describe the members of the Mac family and the visual traits that give the Mac its operating style.

To allow you to locate information quickly, the chapters (and many sections within them) begin with a short summary paragraph and a bulleted list, like this one:

- Bulleted lists summarize the information in a section or a chapter.

- Each chapter also ends with a bulleted list that summarizes the chapter's contents.

When we introduce a new term, it appears in italic type. We also use italic in the hands-on exercises to indicate text you're supposed to type. For example, the instruction "Type *sample* and press Return" is telling you to type the word *sample*, and then press the keyboard's Return key.

A WORD ABOUT SYSTEM VERSIONS

While we were writing this book, Apple announced System 7.0, a major revision in the fundamental software that allows the Mac to run. System 7.0 is scheduled to be released in 1990, but the current version of the Mac's system software—System 6.0—is expected to live on for some time after System 7.0 appears.

System 7.0 will give the Mac many significant new features. To give you an accurate picture of where the Mac family is heading, we've included information on System 7.0 in this book. This information is based on preliminary Apple technical documents and on interviews with Apple programmers and product managers. But because System 7.0 was still in development at this writing, some things may change by the time it's released.

Finally, you'll frequently encounter the phrase "in System 6.0 and earlier versions." Unless otherwise noted, this phrase refers to all the versions of the Mac's system software that begin with the number "6;" in other words, 6.0.1, 6.0.2, 6.0.3, and so on.

A FINAL NOTE

Even though this book is about the Macintosh, it contains numerous references to the IBM family of microcomputers. If you're familiar with the PC and are just getting up to speed with the Mac, these references will allow you to apply your PC knowledge to the Mac. If you've never used a PC and never plan to, you can ignore references to it without missing any new Mac-related information.

If you're a Macintosh zealot who believes "IBM" stands for "I bought Macintosh," you'll have to suffer through (or skip over) our discussions of Mac and PC data exchange and networking concepts. We don't play the us-versus-them game. We don't believe that the Mac and the PC represent different schools of thought or opposing corporate philosophies. They're just tools, and like many people, we use both.

That said, let's start exploring the Macintosh.

Jim Heid

Peter Norton

Section I

Introducing the Mac

1

Computer Fundamentals

In this chapter, we'll lay the foundation of your computer knowledge by examining the basic components and concepts around which all computers are built. We'll look at:

- how hardware and software work together
- how computers deal with numbers
- the types of memory computers use
- the role played by storage devices such as disk drives
- how computers receive information
- the differences between system software and application software.

Most of the concepts discussed here are covered in greater detail in later chapters.

A JOINT EFFORT

The operation of a computer is the result of an expertly choreographed joint effort between *hardware* and *software*. The common definition of hardware is that it's the stuff that breaks when you drop it. More specifically, hardware comprises a computer's physical components—its circuitry, disk drives, keyboard, video screen, and so on.

Software is the less tangible member of the duo, but it's what brings the hardware to life. Software is a series of detailed, stepwise instructions that programmers assemble in order to control the hardware and turn it into a tool for specific tasks, everything from writing memos to drawing floor plans. Software is *stored* by hardware (on disks, for example), but the instructions themselves are invisible. You can't look at a disk and tell whether it contains software any more than you can determine what someone knows by looking at his or her brain.

A variation of software is *firmware*—software instructions that are permanently frozen into hardware, rather than loaded from disk. As we'll see in later chapters, firmware plays an essential role in the Macintosh.

The Central Processing Unit

Software and hardware work together much like your brain and body do. A person's brain handles the cerebral work—assimilating information and making decisions—and uses the body to interact with the outside world. In a computer, the *central processing unit*, or *CPU*, follows the software's instructions—shuttling information, performing calculations, and making decisions—and uses the hardware to interact with you, receiving your instructions from the keyboard and mouse and supplying responses using the screen or a printer.

In minicomputers and mainframe computers, the workhorses of business and scientific computing, central processing units comprise many separate electronic components—often more than exist in an entire Macintosh. In a personal computer like the Mac, however, the CPU is a one-piece affair. The Mac is built around a *microprocessor*—a single component that performs the same basic jobs as the CPU in a larger computer.

A microprocessor is an *integrated circuit*, also called an *IC* or *chip*. The latter term is a tribute to the substance from which ICs are made—minute wafers, or chips, of silicon. A single IC contains the electronic equivalent of thousands— in many cases, millions—of separate electronic components. It's an entire circuit that would have filled a gymnasium thirty years ago—miniaturized to fit on a head of a thumbtack. From our perspective as computer users, the development of the IC was the most significant advance in electronics since the dawn of transistors marked the dusk of vacuum tubes.

From the outside, an IC chip looks like a multilegged bug, a rectangular piece of plastic with between four and 80 or more legs on opposite sides. Remove the plastic case and put what's left under a microscope, and the view becomes more interesting. An IC looks like an aerial view of a midwestern city, with myriad streets and avenues running in straight, precise lines, interconnecting infinitesimally small components. You've probably seen such views: phone companies like to show them in commercials, with animated bolts of current zapping down their silicon avenues for dramatic effect.

The CPU chip in most Macs is called a *68000*, the number bestowed on the chip by its designer and manufacturer, Motorola Corporation. The Mac II contains the 68000's successor, the Motorola *68020*. The Mac IIx, IIcx, and SE/30 contain the 68020's successor, the 68030. As these numbers show, Motorola, like most microprocessor manufacturers, groups related chips under the umbrella of a "family" number, and then numbers the members within that family. Macs use the 68000 family of microprocessors, sometimes referred to as *680xx*, since those final two numbers change with each new generation of CPU chip. For example, the 68030's successor, which at this writing is still in development, will be the 68040.

Bits and Bytes

A CPU is often described as a computer's brain. When you consider the CPU's role as decision maker and information mover, that description seems accurate. But technically speaking, it's more accurate to call a CPU the computer's central switching station. In addition to being able to perform calculations, the CPU gives a computer the ability to store, retrieve, and manipulate information. It earns that talent by being able to read and change the on-off settings of millions of electronic switches in the computer's *memory*.

Each of these switches represents one *bit*—the smallest piece of information a computer can work with. A group of eight bits is a *byte*—the real workhorse of information storage. Some background on bits and bytes and on how computers represent numbers appears below. You can go far in exploring the Mac without having to know about these concepts, so don't feel like you need to come to grips with them now. Feel free to skip on to the section "A Closer Look at Hardware," later in this chapter.

DEALING WITH DATA

You've probably heard or read the term *binary*, and you've probably heard the phrase "ones and zeros" thrown around. These terms refer to the fundamental way in which information is represented within a computer. Without slogging through blackboards filled with mathematics theory, let's see how.

Numbering Systems

In our daily lives, we work with numbers using the decimal numbering system. By "*decimal*," we mean "ten:" all of the numbers we work with are based on arrangements of ten symbols—0, 1, 2, 3, 4, 5, 6, 7, 8, and 9. When we need to represent a number larger than 9, we combine symbols. For example, to represent the number "ten," we put a 1 in the "tens" place and zero in the "ones" place. We use the same basic techniques to work with larger numbers. The value 5,480, for example, is represented by a 5 in the "thousands" place, a 4 in the "hundreds" place, an 8 in the "tens" place, and a zero in the "ones" place. Because our numbers are based on units of ten, our numbering system is called *base ten*.

But there's no law of mathematics stating that numbers must be represented in base ten. That's simply the system we use—just as Americans measure distance using inches, feet, and miles, while Europeans use centimeters, meters, and kilometers. Numbers can be represented with fewer than ten symbols. If we want to use base eight, for example, we simply forget that the numeral 9—the symbol itself, not the value—exists. When we need to represent the value nine, we combine two symbols, putting a 1 in the "eights" place and a one in the "ones" place. We can represent other values by following this scheme:

Table 1-1. Examples of base eight mathematics.

Value	Representation	Description
nine	11	one "eight" and one "one"
eleven	13	one "eight" and three "ones"
sixteen	20	two "eights" and no "ones"

Using these same techniques, we can represent values in base six, base three—or base two. Even if we forget that the numerals 2 through 9 exist, we can still represent any number by using the numerals 0 and 1. To represent the value two, we write 10: one "two" and no "ones." The value three becomes 11: one "two" and one "one." Representing values greater than three means adding additional places, like this:

Table 1-2. Examples of binary mathematics.

Value	Representation	Description
four	100	one "four," no "twos," no "ones"
five	101	one "four," no "twos," one "one"
nine	1001	one "eight," no "fours," no "twos," one "one"

Larger values require still more places: in binary, a base-ten value of 87 is written as 1010111: one "sixty-four," no "thirty-twos," one "sixteen," no "eights," one "four," one "two," and one "one." Obviously, base two is not a convenient way for people to represent numbers. You would need an awfully wide check to spell out most amounts.

Base Two and Computers

Base two may not be convenient for people, but it happens to be extremely convenient for a machine containing millions of electronic switches. Why? Because a switch can represent one of two values. We can say that when the switch is off, it reflects a value of zero, and when it's on, it reflects a value of one. By combining switches, we can represent larger values. If we combine eight switches, for example, we can represent any value between 0 and 255.

This base-two numbering system is called *binary*, and the two symbols in binary numbering, 1 and 0, are called *binary digits*. To chop out a few syllables, computer scientists shortened the phrase "binary digit," coining the term *bit*. A bit, then, is a one or a zero, and is the smallest piece of information a computer can work with.

We just mentioned that computers can represent larger values by combining bits. We used eight as an example, and for a good reason. Because a group of eight bits is able to represent 255 different values, it makes a versatile building block for representing program instructions and information. These eight-bit building blocks are called *bytes*. Just as writers combine letters into words, computers combine bits into bytes.

Bragging About Bits

As you peruse computer magazines or brochures, you'll often see a computer described as being an eight-bit computer, or a 16-bit or 32-bit computer. These phrases refer to how many bits of data the computer can process at a time. Generally, the ability to process more bits at once makes the computer faster—just as a steam shovel whose bucket holds three tons of dirt can dig a hole faster than one that holds only one.

The first mass-produced microcomputers—the Apple II and the Radio Shack Model I—were 8-bit computers. The IBM PC was the first mass-produced 16-bit computer. Its ability to move data in two-byte chunks (called *words*), combined with generally faster circuitry, made it a swift machine in its day. Today's top-of-the-line PCs, built around Intel's 80386 microprocessors, are 32-bit computers—as is the Mac II. These machines can work with information in 32-bit chunks.

Apple used to describe the original Macs as 32-bit computers, but technically speaking, they were hybrids of 16- and 32-bit computers. Some portions of the 68000 microprocessor can work with only 16 bits of data at once, while others can work with 32. The original IBM PC's 8088 microprocessor was similar, except it straddled the 8- and 16-bit fence instead of the 16- and 32-bit fence.

A CLOSER LOOK AT HARDWARE

We've already defined hardware as the stuff that breaks when you drop it. Now let's take a closer look at the different types of hardware you'll find in the Macintosh.

Memory: The Mac's Storage Space

A computer's CPU is a central switching station, but a switching station isn't worth much if it isn't connected to something. A CPU is connected to many components, but one of the most important is *memory*, the computer's storage area for software and for *data*—the information you're creating and storing, whether a letter, a name-and-address list, or a picture.

The Mac's memory consists of a set of chips, each containing thousands of electronic switches, each of which, as we now know, represents one bit. The CPU reads and changes the settings of these switches as it stores the bits that comprise the programs you use and the information you create.

Addressing and Accessing Memory

A CPU must be able to keep track of what's stored where. If it were to use memory indiscriminately, it might load a program into an area that already contains a program, or worse, your own data. Thus, each location in memory—each group of eight switches—has its own *address*, the computer memory equivalent of post office box numbers. By keeping track of memory addresses, the CPU is able to determine where things are, and equally important, how much unused memory, or *free memory*, is available for new data or more programs.

In the early days of computers, CPUs had to access memory sequentially, one byte after another. To keep our post office box analogy alive, it was as if, in order to retrieve your mail, you had to go through all the boxes with lower numbers first. Needless to say, a sequential approach to accessing memory wasted the CPU's time and slowed the computer's performance. These problems were solved with the development of *random-access memory*, or *RAM*—memory whose addresses the CPU could access in any order. With RAM, the

CPU can go directly to a given memory address—just as postal patrons go directly to their post office boxes.

An important point to remember about RAM is that it retains its contents only while the computer is turned on. In computer jargon, RAM is *volatile.* Computers contain other kinds of memory that isn't volatile. This second category of memory (there are several) helps give the Mac its unique operating style.

ROM: Memory that Doesn't Forget

This second type of memory is called *read-only memory,* or *ROM.* ROM plays a different role from RAM, but an equally important one. The Mac's ROM chips store software that enables the computer to operate—to check its hardware for problems when you first switch it on, for example, and to look for a disk. We'll look more closely at the work ROM performs later in this chapter.

In ROM chips, the electronic switches that represent ones and zeros are "glued" in place. The contents of a computer's ROM are recorded permanently when the ROM chips are created, and can't be erased or changed (except by bolts of lightning and other electrical mishaps). Because its contents are permanent and don't have to be restored each time the computer is turned on, ROM is an ideal place to store the fundamental software a computer needs to operate. (As mentioned before, this low-level software is often called *firmware* because it performs very basic, but vital, tasks.)

Technically speaking, ROM is random-access memory, too. That is, a computer doesn't have to access the fixed addresses in a ROM chip in sequential order. So, the term "random-access memory" and the acronym RAM are a bit outdated and somewhat misleading. Indeed, many people prefer to describe RAM as *read/write memory,* a phrase that more accurately describes what it does. In this book, we use the term "memory" when it's obvious that we're talking about RAM; when there might be some confusion, we use "RAM" or "ROM."

Measuring RAM and ROM Capacity

RAM and ROM chips have finite storage capacities which are determined by the number of electronic switches built into the chip. These capacities are measured in units of 1,024 bytes called *kilobytes,* usually abbreviated with the letter *K* or the letters *KB.* 1,024 kilobytes form a *megabyte* (*M* or *MB*), or roughly one million bytes.

You might wonder why kilobytes are formed by 1,024 bytes instead of a nice, round number such as 1,000. The answer is simple if you think in binary terms. 1024 equals 2 raised to the tenth power. So, in binary, 1024 *is* a round number—just as, in the decimal numbering system we're used to working with, 10 to the third power (1000), is a round number.

Storage

Because RAM loses its contents when the power goes, computers need a way to store the information they work with. The answer is a *mass-storage* device such as a floppy disk drive. Floppy disks, and their faster and more copious cousins, *hard disks*, operate by translating the ones and zeros that make up software or data into magnetic patterns on a circular spinning disk. With your data, this translation process occurs when you save your work; at that time, the Mac copies the data from RAM to the disk. When the Mac needs to read the stored information, the drive's magnetic recording head interprets the magnetic patterns and translates them back into ones and zeros, which the CPU stores in memory.

Because floppy and hard disks contain mechanical parts, they're far slower than all-electronic memory. Still, they're quite a bit faster than the mass-storage devices computers used to have. Early microcomputers, for example, used cassette tapes to store programs and data. Just loading a single program could take several minutes.

Storing programs and data isn't the only role disks play. In addition to acting as a safe haven for programs and data, disks can act as an extension of your computer's memory. Using a technique called *virtual memory*, the computer can treat a disk as if it were memory. Most word processing programs use this technique to allow you create documents larger than would otherwise fit into memory. The word processor keeps only the portion of the document you're working with at the moment in memory, and "swaps" the rest of the document to and from the disk.

Input and Output

For a computer's information storage and manipulation skills to be useful, it must be able to get information and instructions from you and to show you the fruits of its labor. The circuitry and devices responsible for interacting with you form the computer's *input/output*, or *I/O*, section. A Mac's *input devices* are the keyboard and the mouse, and you can use both to either issue instructions or create data.

With the mouse, you can choose commands and click on options. These tasks fall into the "issuing instructions" category. But you can also use the mouse to draw an image. In that case, you're using the mouse to create data.

With the keyboard, you can issue instructions by using the *keyboard shortcuts* that many programs provide. And, of course, you can create data by typing text.

The Mac's primary *output device* is, obviously, its video screen. The speaker also qualifies as an output device. It allows the Mac to aurally inform you of a problem or to get your attention before performing an operation that would result in data loss, such as quitting a program without saving your work. Other output devices are printers such as Apple's ImageWriter and LaserWriter, which allow you to commit your work to paper.

Although you don't use it to choose commands or view responses, a disk drive is also an input/output device. A disk drive is an I/O device for the Mac itself; it lets the Mac read (input) information into its memory, and write (output) information from memory to disk.

Ports—Serial and Parallel

Input/output devices attach to the computer by means of sockets called *ports*. The word "port" may sound like jargon at first, but when you think of a shipping port—a point where ships can "connect" with a city to discharge and take on cargo—you can see how the term applies to input/output devices. In its manuals, Apple doesn't use the term "port," but instead, calls these I/O sockets *connectors*, since that's what you see on the outside of the machine.

We'll explore the Mac's ports of call in later chapters. For now, let's look at the underlying concepts behind how they transport data. The ways in which a computer moves bits from place to place are straightforward, and they lend themselves nicely to real-world comparisons. Understanding them will help you understand why some ports can move data faster than others.

Two major but different data-transporting techniques exist: *parallel* and *serial*. With parallel transmission, the eight bits that form each byte move alongside each other, each in its own wire. With serial transmission, each bit in a byte travels in single file, one behind the other. Now imagine the wires on which bits travel as lanes on a roadway. With parallel transmission, you have eight lanes; with serial, you have just one. You don't have to be a computer scientist to figure out which method can move data faster.

And if you've ever driven in rush hour traffic, you've experienced the frustration of whizzing along an 8-lane freeway, but slowing to crawl on a one-lane exit ramp. Data can fall victim to the same bottleneck. The circuits that carry bits within the CPU and between the CPU and memory are parallel ones, but if the data's final destination is a device that requires serial transmission, transmission speed decreases when the data begins moving serially.

TYPES OF SOFTWARE

The final stop on our tour of computer fundamentals is a look at the two basic types of software a computer needs. We've briefly defined both types already, and if you've used a Mac, you've already encountered them yourself. The first type is *system software*, also called *operating system software*. System software is the fundamental software that transforms a box of chips and parts into a working computer. The second type is *application software* such as word processors or drawing programs. Application software is the software we encounter more directly because it represents the instructions that show the Mac how to perform specific computing tasks.

One way to understand the difference between system and application software is to think of system software as the Mac's basic education, and application software as its college education. When the Mac loads its system software at start-up time, it learns the basics. When you run an application program, its software instructions give the Mac a specialized education, turning it into a job specialist that can manipulate text, calculate numbers, organize names and addresses, and so on.

System Software

Because system software teaches the Mac the basics, let's look at it first. As we said before, some rudimentary system software is stored in the Mac's ROM. But most of a computer's system software is stored on disk and loaded into memory at start-up time; this approach allows a manufacturer to add features or fix problems by supplying a new disk instead of manufacturing and distributing new ROM chips.

In the IBM PC family, ROM contains a very small amount of system software. In the Mac, ROM plays a much larger role. It stores the software that application programs tap into to create the visual elements that give the Mac its unique operating style. Because a ROM chip's contents are permanent, Apple stores in ROM those elements of the Mac's system software that are the least likely to change.

Bypassing Bugs

All programmers—even ones who write the software that becomes frozen in ROM chips—are fallible. Program errors, or *bugs*, do occasionally rear their ugly heads. To take that possibility into account, computer manufacturers design ROMs so that their software can be bypassed and replaced with corrected or improved software that's loaded into RAM at start-up. This process, called *patching*, involves loading the replacement software into RAM and erecting a detour sign at a key memory address. When the CPU reaches that address, it dutifully executes the patch instead of the original software. The replacement software often consists of short snippets of software instructions that perform small specialized tasks, such as allowing the Mac to draw a character on the screen. In computer jargon, these software snippets are often called *routines*.

(Incidentally, the story behind the term "bug" is one you might find amusing. In the 1940s, Grace Hopper, a pioneering computer scientist in the United States Navy, was troubleshooting a problem with a prototypical computer. Peering into the bowels of the beast, she saw that a moth had wedged itself between the contacts of a mechanical switch. She extracted the intruder, pasted it into her notebook, and next to it wrote, "Found bug in computer today." The term—and the moth, no doubt—stuck.)

Patching is a convenient way to correct ROM bugs or improve performance, but it's only effective up to a point. After all, if you fill the Mac's RAM with patches and enhancements to the operating system, you won't have any memory left to store programs or data. To avoid that, Apple periodically introduces new ROM chips. Many new Mac models bring expanded ROMs containing corrected and improved system software. In later chapters, we'll spotlight the key differences between ROMs in each member of the Mac family, and we'll see how Apple has managed to keep the Macintosh family compatible while its system software evolves.

The majority of the disk-based portion of the Mac's system software is stored in the disk file named System. This software, which the Mac loads into RAM at start-up time, rounds out the machine's operating system by providing patches that fix or enhance ROM routines, as well as entirely new routines that Apple chose to leave out of ROM in the interest of flexibility.

Application Software

The combined efforts of the disk- and ROM-based system software allow a computer to run the second kind of software: *application software*. Application software—usually called *applications* or, more simply, *programs*—give the computer specific capabilities. A word processor like Microsoft Word, for example, teaches the Mac how to manipulate and store large passages of text. A graphics program such as MacDraw teaches the Mac how to translate mouse movements into an on-screen image.

Applications work closely with the Mac's system software, relying on the system routines to display and format text and transfer information between programs. Many routines act as a liaison between the application and the Mac's hardware, allowing the application to access disk drives, printers, and other I/O devices.

Another set of routines lets the application acquire memory in which to run. When you start an application, it requests a chunk of free memory from the operating system. Because a Mac using MultiFinder is capable of storing more than one program in memory at once, the operating system must rule with an iron fist, doling out memory as needed and making sure that one application doesn't clobber another program or a chunk of data.

When Applications Misbehave

If you belong to a user's group or read Macintosh magazines, you might occasionally hear an application described as "ill behaved" or as "violating Apple's guidelines." Such an indictment can mean two things. The application's developer may have bypassed certain operating system routines in the interest of faster performance. Or, it could mean that the application doesn't use the Mac's pull-down menus, dialog boxes, and other personality traits in the way that Apple prescribes.

The second violation is the more serious of the two. A program that strays from Apple's *user-interface guidelines*—its rules for how Mac programs should look and work—may take you longer to learn, since you won't be able to apply your knowledge of existing Mac programs to it.

As for the first violation—bypassing certain system routines—it's probably more common than the second. Many application developers bend the rules to get better performance or work around a problem known to exist in a specific routine. As we'll see later, however, this rule-bending can sometimes cause a program to not run properly when Apple revises its system software or releases a new Macintosh model.

CHAPTER SUMMARY

- A computer's operation is the result of an expertly choreographed joint effort between hardware (the computer's physical components) and software.

- The central processing unit (CPU) follows the software's instructions—moving information, calculating, and acting on input—and uses the hardware to interact with you. The Mac's CPU is a microprocessor, an integrated circuit containing the electronic equivalent of millions of separate electronic components.

- The smallest unit of information a computer can work with is a bit. Computers combine bits into groups of eight to form bytes, which are used to represent program instructions and data.

- The Mac uses random-access memory (RAM) to store software and the data you create. RAM is volatile—it loses its contents when the power is shut off. RAM is sometimes referred to as read/write memory.

- The Mac also contains another type of memory: read-only memory (ROM). ROM holds a large percentage of the software that enables the Mac to run and gives it its unique operating style.

- Because the CPU must be able to keep track of what's stored where, each byte of RAM and ROM has its own address.

- Because RAM is volatile, computers provide mass-storage devices such as disk drives, which use non-volatile magnetic disks to hold software and the documents you create.

- The Mac's keyboard and mouse are input devices for issuing commands and supply information. The Mac's video screen and printer are output devices that allow you to see your work.

- Input and output devices attach to the Mac by means of rear-panel sockets called ports. These ports transfer data using one of two transmission methods: serial or parallel. With serial transmission, bits travel in single file. With parallel transmission, the bits that form each byte travel alongside each other, each in its own wire. Serial transmission is generally slower than parallel transmission.

- The Mac uses two types of software: system software, which enables the Mac to operate; and applications software, which "educates" the Mac in specific tasks, such as word processing or data base management.

- A large percentage of the Mac's system software is stored in ROM. Because the contents of ROM are permanent, computer manufacturers design ROM-based software so that any bugs can be bypassed, or patched.

- Apple has published reams of technical documentation describing how the Mac's system software operates and how application programs should access it. When you hear an application program described as being "ill behaved" or "misbehaved," it means the program's designers have violated Apple's guidelines. That could cause the program to not run properly on future versions of the Mac's system software.

2

A Standard is Born

In this chapter, we'll look at the events that led to the development of the Macintosh, and at the advantages of the Mac's way of operating. We'll examine:

- the ways people can interact with computers
- the Mac's forerunners
- the breakthroughs in computer design that made the Mac possible
- the development of the Mac itself.

THE DAWN OF MAC

In the *laissez-faire*, survival-of-the-fittest world of computing, establishing a standard isn't easy. No government body exists to tell hardware and software manufacturers, "You must develop products for this machine." Instead, a computer has to prove itself by surviving a financially risky game of Catch-22: people won't buy it unless a reasonable selection of hardware and software is available, but hardware and software developers won't make products for a computer until it's popular enough to make their efforts pay off. A computer isn't considered a standard until it attains that combination of popularity and *third-party support*—the availability of products from independent manufacturers.

That goal is even more difficult to reach when a standard already exists—especially one created by the largest computer company in the world. When the Mac appeared in 1984, the IBM PC was a red-hot star around which revolved a solar system of software developers and hardware manufacturers. Many of the latter were making *clones*—computers that ran PC software and accepted PC add-ons. But despite those obstacles and a rocky start, the Mac has established itself as the second standard in microcomputing. Today, the Mac is at the center of its own solar system—and it's exerting a strong gravitational pull on IBMs.

Perhaps the most remarkable thing about the Mac's success is that Apple succeeded in bending the rules of the Catch-22 game. Thousands of people bought Macs in the first months after the machine's release, a time when you could have counted the number of Macintosh products on two hands. What's more, the original Mac was woefully underpowered, a Porsche body with a team of chipmunks under the hood.

How did Apple do it? Some might say good marketing—Apple's pioneering "the Mac will save the world from IBM" commercials were controversial and award winning—but more likely, what sold the Mac in 1984 was the promise held in the the Mac's unique and appealing operating style.

INTERACTING WITH COMPUTERS

Next to the phrase "available soon," the word "revolutionary" is the most abused set of letters in the computer industry. But the word does apply to the Macintosh. The Mac represents a revolution in the design of a microcomputer's *user interface*—the way in which it accepts commands and interacts with you.

The Macintosh represented the public's first opportunity to afford a computer built around a mouse-based *graphical* user interface, which uses sharp graphics and pictures to make learning and using a computer a more familiar process. To appreciate the significant advantages of the Mac's operating style, let's step back and look at the methods in which people can interact with computers.

Types of User Interfaces

The most spartan user interface (and the kind still used on many IBM PCs) is the *command-line* interface. With a command-line interface, you type commands in response to a *prompt*—a character such as a question mark or ">" symbol that the computer's operating system uses to say, "I'm ready for a command." To view a list of the files on a disk, for example, an IBM PC user

lllBradyLine

Insights into tomorrow's technology from the authors and editors of Brady Books.

You rely on Brady's bestselling computer books for up-to-date information about high technology. Now turn to BradyLine for the details behind the titles.

Find out what new trends in technology spark Brady's authors and editors. Read about what they're working on, and predicting, for the future. Get to know the authors through interviews and profiles, and get to know each other through your questions and comments.

BradyLine keeps you ahead of the trends with the stories behind the latest computer developments. Informative previews of forthcoming books and excerpts from new titles keep you apprised of what's going on in the fields that interest you most.

- Peter Norton on operating systems
- Jim Seymour on business productivity
- Jerry Daniels, Mary Jane Mara, Robert Eckhardt, and Cynthia Harriman on Macintosh development, productivity, and connectivity

Get the Spark. Get BradyLine.

Published quarterly, beginning with the Summer 1988 issue. Free exclusively to our customers. Just fill out and mail this card to begin your subscription.

Name _____

Address _____

City _____ State _____ Zip _____

Name of Book Purchased _____

Date of Purchase _____

Where was this book purchased? *(circle one)*

    Retail Store   Computer Store   Mail Order

FREE

Mail this card for your free subscription to BradyLine

Place
First Class
Postage
Here
Post Office
Will Not
Deliver
Without Postage

Brady Books
One Gulf+Western Plaza
New York, NY 10023

types "*dir*" (short for *directory*) and presses the Enter key, as shown in Figure 2-1. The PC's original operating system, *MS-DOS*, doesn't provide any hints as to what command you must type to see a file listing. The job of remembering which commands the computer needs and their correct spelling is up to you. (IBM's new operating system, *OS/2*, provides a friendlier interface, but still offers a command-line option.)

Figure 2-1. Issuing a command with a command-line user interface.

Command-line interfaces place a mammoth obstacle on the path toward computer proficiency. It's difficult enough for a novice to come to terms with a computer's psuedo-intelligence; having to memorize and type cryptic commands in response to a machine that won't even provide a hint makes it harder still.

Command-line interfaces are throwbacks to the days when a computer's primary output device was a typewriter-like terminal that clattered the computer's responses onto a sheet of paper. As video screens replaced typewriter-like *terminals*, user interfaces improved. Being able to quickly display a full screen of information allowed a computer to display *menus*—lists of available commands, each with a corresponding letter or number, as shown in Figure 2-2. With a *menu-driven* user interface, choosing a "directory" command might involve pressing the D key. By listing available options, menus take the mystery out of issuing commands, and they eliminate error messages caused by clumsy typing or misspelling.

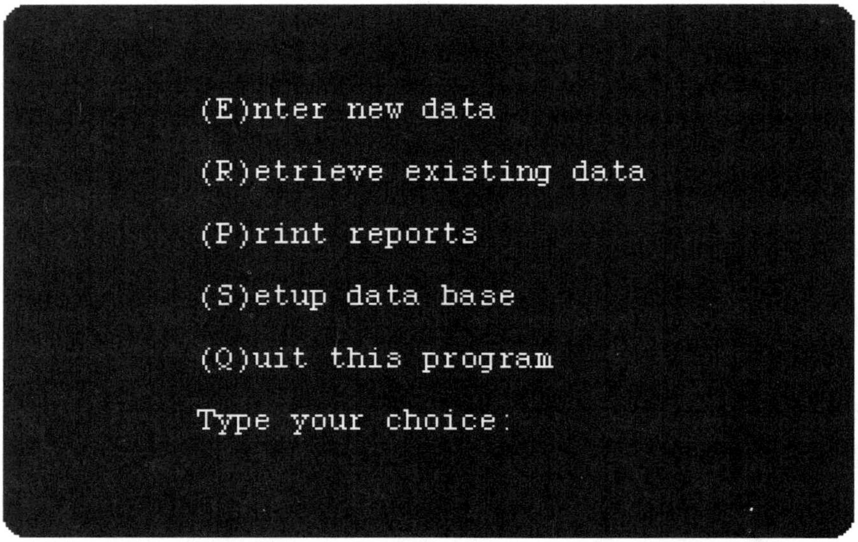

```
(E)nter new data

(R)etrieve existing data

(P)rint reports

(S)etup data base

(Q)uit this program

Type your choice:
```

Figure 2-2. A typical menu-driven user interface.

Menus are a vast improvement over command-line user interfaces, but what if every software firm has its own ideas of how menus should be presented and structured? One might think it's best to assign each command a number for you to type. Another might want you to type the letter corresponding to the first character in a command. Still another might think you should use the arrow keys to point to the command you want. Each time you buy a new program, you must learn a new method of interacting with your computer. That isn't an efficient way to use a computer—imagine if you had to learn to drive again each time you got a new car.

The Macintosh changed all that by being the first personal computer in its price range to provide a consistent user interface, one that doesn't vary from program to program. The Mac's ROM chips contain routines that programmers can use to create the user interface elements you see in Macintosh programs. These routines are grouped according to the jobs they perform, with each group referred to as a "manager." (The Menu Manager, for example, contains the routines that create pull-down menus.) Because they contain tools for building programs with a consistent interface, the Mac's managers are referred to collectively as the *toolbox*.

Apple provides guidelines for the use of the Mac's toolbox in several phone book-sized volumes, the *Inside Macintosh* series (published by Addison-Wesley). By following these guidelines, software developers can create programs that look and work like other Macintosh programs. The advantage? Once you learn one Mac program, you have a head start in learning others.

But consistency is only one of the strengths of the Mac's user interface. The others are the pervasive use of graphics and the mouse. Those concepts trace their beginnings to a time long before before Apple's founders, Steve Jobs and Steve Wozniak, formed the company in a garage in Cupertino, California.

The Mac's Forerunners

If you want to remember where the Mac's user interface concepts were born, remember fourteen letters: ARPA, MIT, SRI, and PARC. ARPA is short for the Advanced Research Projects Agency, a government-funded research hotbed formed in the late 1950s. It was the age of the space race and the Jetsons, a time when the United States was enamored of all things scientific and modern, and it led to some significant breakthroughs (aside from tailfins).

The first person to head ARPA's Information Processing Techniques division was J. C. R. Licklider. In 1960, Licklider wrote a paper called "Man-Computer Symbiosis." In his paper, he proposed that a new relationship between people and computers was necessary. People should be able to "think in interaction with a computer," he said. To make his vision a reality, he and his successors began pioneering the concepts behind *time-sharing*. With time-sharing, multiple users, each at his or her own typewriter terminal, could access a central computer, with the computer dividing its time between the users to give each the illusion that he or she alone was interacting with the machine. Before time-sharing, people supplied instructions to computers on punched cards, and waited hours or days until their cards were able to be processed—a computing technique that was as far from interactive as you could get.

ARPA also made a somewhat more dubious contribution to the computer world: in 1962, someone attached a video tube to a DEC PDP-1 computer and programmed the world's first computer game: Spacewars, in which you blasted a moving blip with torpedoes. ARPA never officially acknowledged Spacewars, but there was no doubt that those who played it realized the significant contribution a video screen made to interactive computing.

From ARPA we jump to MIT, the Massachusetts Institute of Technology. At MIT, a graduate student named Ivan Sutherland created a program called Sketchpad, which used a video screen and light pen to allow users to draw and alter geometric shapes, as shown in Figure 2-3. With Sketchpad, users could change the size of shapes, attach them to each other, move them on the screen, and store them in the computer's memory for later recall. Sketchpad was a primordial drawing program that foreshadowed a new era in which people would interact directly with computers. As for Ivan Sutherland, he would later succeed J. C. R. Licklider at ARPA.

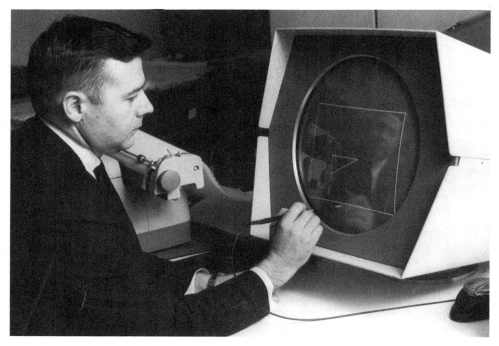

Figure 2-3. Ivan Sutherland operating Sketchpad, circa 1963 (*photo courtesy of the Computer Museum, Boston*)

SRI stands for the Stanford Research Institute, where, in 1964, Douglas Englebart invented the "X-Y Position Indicator for a Display System." Shown in Figure 2-4, U.S. Patent #3,541,541 is now called a mouse. Englebart invented the mouse in the course of SRI's research into advanced office-automation systems that augmented the traditional keyboard with specialized input devices.

The word "augment" figured prominently in Englebart's work: In 1962 he wrote a paper, "Experimental Results of Tying a Brick to a Pencil to 'De-Augment' the Individual." In that experiment, Englebart timed how long it took a person to write the same sentence with a normal pencil, with a pencil tied to a brick, and with a typewriter. This experiment was designed to illustrate—in a tongue-in-cheek way—Englebart's view that future innovations would make a typewriter seem as cumbersome as trying to write with a pencil attached to a brick.

Englebart's group at SRI made significant progress in designing computer systems whose augmentations—the mouse and a unique five-key keyboard called a *chord keyset*—proved that the traditional typewriter keyboard was not necessarily the best way to interact with a computer.

Figure 2-4. The first mouse: Douglas Englebart's "X-Y Position Indicator for a Display System" (photo courtesy of Douglas Englebart)

Alan Kay, PARC, and Larry Tesler

This concept intrigued another visionary computer scientist, a University of Utah graduate student named Alan Kay. Kay, too, wanted to make computers more approachable and accessible. His vision was of a $1000 computer small enough to fit in a bookbag, but with the power of a room-sized mainframe computer. He called this still unrealized dream machine the Dynabook. In 1967, Kay and a hardware designer named Edward Cheadle began designing a computer that would provide sharp graphics and windowing features, and in 1969, they completed work on a computer they dubbed FLEX.

After building FLEX, Kay joined the research group where the previous years' advancements in interactive computing and augmentation were to gel: Xerox's Palo Alto Research Center, or PARC. Xerox formed PARC in 1970, giving it free rein to conduct research and development, with no obligation to produce commercial products. PARC combined an academic atmosphere with the deep pockets of a large corporation—a combination that attracted many of the best computer scientists of the day.

Xerox hired an ARPA administrator named Bob Taylor to head PARC's Computer Sciences Lab. Taylor's team included Alan Kay, Charles Simonyi (now a chief software engineer at Microsoft), Chuck Thacker (who helped develop Ethernet, a networking and communications technology that remains one of the industry's standards), Butler Lampson (a timesharing pioneer), and Larry Tesler (a software engineer).

In 1971, a dozen PARC researchers headed by Kay formed the Learning Research Group. One of their first projects was to create a programming language called Smalltalk, which was designed to be the centerpiece of an easy-to-use computer employing sharp graphics and a mouse or other pointing device.

Smalltalk made its way into a Xerox computer called Alto, shown in Figure 2-5. Alto was to be PARC's version of the office-automation system Douglas Englebart helped create at SRI. It combined Smalltalk, sharp graphics, a mouse, and the Ethernet networking system, which allowed a group of interconnected Altos to communicate and share each other's resources.

What was especially significant about the Alto, however, was the way its software worked. After working with Englebart's system, Larry Tesler saw that it was fast and responsive, but difficult to learn. The problem was that the system required users to memorize a large number of abbreviated commands. To delete a word, for example, users had to type a command, point to the word with the mouse, and then press the mouse button to confirm the command. Tesler's solution was to reverse the procedure: users would first point to the information they wanted to change, and the software would respond with a list of commands.

This "select, then act" procedure is at the center of the Mac's operating philosophy. To delete a word, for example, you select the word and press the Delete key. To quote from *Inside Macintosh*, the bible of Macintosh programming mentioned earlier, "Selecting the object of an operation before identifying the operation is a fundamental characteristic of the Macintosh user interface, since it allows the application to avoid *modes*."

In the software world, a mode is a state in which the range of tasks you can perform is restricted. For example, an overly modal word processing program might require you to enter a text-entry mode to type new text, an editing mode to edit existing text, and a printing mode to print text. When you're typing new text in such a program, you can't edit or print. This operating style is contrary to the way people work, and reinforces the computer's reputation as an intimidating, unnatural machine. Avoiding modes was another key concept born at PARC.

Figure 2-5: Xerox's Alto computer (*photo courtesy Xerox Corporation*)

The Alto's developers also believed that sharp graphics were a key factor in making a computer easy to use. Sharp graphics allowed the Alto to accurately show on screen how a document would appear when printed, taking the guesswork out of formatting a document and eliminating trial-and-error print runs. This operating style has come to be called "what you see is what you get," and abbreviated as *WYSIWYG* (pronounced *wizzy-wig*).

Equally significant was the Alto's use of small, on-screen pictures, or *icons*, to represent real-world objects such as file folders and sheets of paper. Alan Kay strongly believed that these metaphors for real-world objects made computers easier to use because they replaced unfamiliar concepts (such as transmitting work to another computer) with familiar concepts (such as putting a piece of paper in an "out" basket).

If all these software innovations took place in the 1970s, why didn't they show up on desktops until the early 80s? Several reasons. PARC researchers, from their vantage point in the ivory tower of R&D, failed to realize that people were anxious for any kind of personal computer, even if it didn't embody every PARC breakthrough. Xerox was hesitant to enter the microcomputer field, and when it did in 1981, its offering—the 820—used an aging operating system, CP/M, and an aging 8-bit microprocessor chip, the Z80. The 820 was technologically uninspiring, and when IBM announced its much more powerful PC later that year, the 820 died a quiet death. These events failed to convince Xerox that microcomputers were a great new frontier for profits.

Another reason was that the memory and circuitry required to build a computer with high-resolution graphics were costly. Xerox supplied several government agencies with Altos, but the computer was never a commercially marketed product—only 2000 were built. In 1981, Xerox announced the Star, an office system that used the Alto's breakthrough technology (see Figure 2-6). But with a price of $16,595, the Star wasn't a personal computer, either. Nor did Xerox try to sell it as one; the Star was marketed through Xerox's national sales force, not computer stores.

Figure 2-6. The Xerox Star (*photo courtesy Xerox Corporation*)

No, it wasn't Xerox that would bring PARC concepts to the masses. It was Apple.

Steve Jobs' Field Trip

In 1979, Apple began work on a computer whose destination was vaguely described as "the office market." The machine was code-named Lisa. The Lisa was to use Motorola's then brand-new 68000 microprocessor—arguably the most powerful microprocessor available at the time.

As it worked on the Lisa project, Apple began looking for additional financial backing (its first public stock offering was a year away), preferably from a corporation with a presence in the office market. Apple cofounder Steve Jobs approached Xerox and offered its investment arm, the Xerox Development Corporation, a deal: Apple would sell Xerox a million dollars worth of stock if Xerox would part the curtain and show Apple what was going on at PARC. The trade press had reported that big things were happening there, and Jobs wanted a closer look. Xerox agreed, and later that year, Steve Jobs, Bill Atkinson (an Apple graphics programmer), and several other members of the Lisa team went to PARC.

By then, Larry Tesler had become PARC's personal computer expert and proponent. A neighbor of Tesler's had dragged him to some meetings of the Homebrew Computer Club, a band of build-it-yourself computer hobbyists, a few years earlier. Initially, Tesler was skeptical, but eventually he saw the potential and increasing momentum of personal computers. Because he was one of the few researchers at PARC who felt that way, he was assigned to show Jobs and his entourage the Alto.

The Apple contingent was awed. They loved the way the Alto's sharp graphics allowed it to mimic a desktop and the documents on it. They loved how the mouse and icons supplanted the keyboard for issuing commands. Bill Atkinson, who was working on the graphics routines that drove the Lisa's display, gazed at the screen from a distance of a few inches. Jobs was impressed, and decided that Apple would build an Alto for the masses.

Tesler, too, was impressed, and believed that Apple could do it. He liked the enthusiasm the Apple people expressed toward the Alto. He liked the questions they asked. And he liked the fact that they wanted to take PARC's advancements out of the labs and put them on people's desktops. A few months later, Larry Tesler was working for Apple.

The Lisa was to be Apple's Alto, but a variety of reasons—including Apple's desire to weigh it down with features and to write a complete set of application software for it—detoured it from its destination of "the masses." The Lisa grew from a $2,000 computer to a $10,000 one when it was finally released in 1983. Critics were wowed, but accountants winced. The Lisa never sold well and it attracted only a few software developers.

The Lisa for The Rest of Us

Meanwhile, another new computer was taking shape within Apple: the Macintosh. Jeff Raskin, who originally came to Apple in 1977 to head the company's documentation group, dreamed of producing an "appliance" computer—a sealed box that you could turn on and use without fussing with cables, circuit boards, or operating system commands. He led a small group that was working on the machine, which he code-named Macintosh—an imperfect speller's tribute to the apple.

The Macintosh project was a small, obscure effort in a company whose primary focus had become the Lisa. The project came close to being cancelled on several occasions. All that changed in the beginning of 1981, when Steve Jobs made the Macintosh his project.

Jobs liked the notion of an appliance computer. Under his influence, the Macintosh's software direction changed. The machine was to be a "little Lisa." Programmer Bud Tribble, Bill Atkinson's best friend, was put in charge of the

Macintosh software, and began lobbying for the use of a 68000 in the Mac. Basing the Mac on a 68000, he said, would allow it to use Bill Atkinson's graphics routines, called *LisaGraf*. Burrell Smith, the Macintosh team hardware designer, reworked his prototype to use the 68000. By Christmas of 1980, Smith, a self-taught hardware specialist who started in Apple as a service technician, had designed a compact circuit that ran twice as fast as the Lisa and used far fewer parts.

The goal was for the Macintosh and the Lisa to ship at the same time. But the Macintosh project was two years behind the Lisa. Jobs drafted Andy Hertzfeld, then a programmer in the Apple II group, to convert Bill Atkinson's LisaGraf routines to run on the Mac. It was decided that the machine must have a detachable keyboard and take up no more desk space than a telephone book, an edict that meant giving the Mac an unheard-of vertical orientation. Burrell Smith refined the Mac's hardware accordingly. The ROM code that would form the basis of the Mac's personality slowly came together.

The Macintosh that was taking shape bore little resemblence to the machine Jeff Raskin envisioned, except for its "sealed box" design. Jobs was against giving the Macintosh internal expansion slots, which can accept add-on circuit boards and which helped make the Apple II and IBM PC such versatile and successful machines. One of his arguments was that the variety of boards available for Apple IIs and IBM PCs made it difficult to write software that would run on every possible machine configuration. By casting the Mac's hardware traits in stone, software developers could be assured that their wares would run on every machine, and users wouldn't have to fuss with running "installation programs" to specify what hardware they had. This argument had some merit, but overall, the sealed-box design would prove to be the Mac's ball and chain in its early days.

In 1981, Jobs met with Bill Gates, chairman of Microsoft Corporation, one of the largest microcomputer software firms—and the company that supplies the IBM PC world with its operating system software, MS-DOS and OS/2, as well as many important application programs. Jobs wanted Microsoft to commit to writing software for the Macintosh, and to have several packages ready for the machine's 1984 release. At a demonstration at Apple's Cupertino offices, Burrell Smith explained the hardware and Andy Hertzfeld detailed the software, with its toolbox in ROM whose routines developers could use to create a consistent user interface.

Gates saw the Mac's potential, and agreed to become involved. Microsoft completed two products—its Multiplan electronic spreadsheet and BASIC programming language—in time for the 1984 release. Numerous other products followed, and Microsoft quickly became a leading Macintosh software developer.

The Macintosh Unveiled

The next few years were tumultuous. The Mac's introduction was postponed regularly, as deadlines fell to the daunting technical tasks involved in creating the Mac's system software. The growing Mac team slaved on the fledging machine days, nights, weekends, and holidays. They saw themselves as pirates who would steal the market from IBM and change the world. A pirate's flag was hoisted over the Macintosh headquarters. Specifications—even such basic ones as the size of the screen—were changed in midstream. Programmers sweated to complete the word processor and painting program that would be included with the machine.

Finally, toward the end of 1983, the first Macs were shown to journalists in a series of "sneaks." Everyone in attendance was required to sign nondisclosure forms prohibiting news about the Mac from appearing until after January 24, 1984—the date when the Mac would be unveiled at Apple's annual shareholder meeting in San Francisco. But Apple's public relations firm, Regis McKenna, knew (or at least hoped) that word would leak out. It did, creating a sense of anticipation that grew so strong that when the Macintosh was announced, the ABC, CBS, and NBC television networks carried the story on their evening news programs.

And the rest, as they say, is history. The Mac stumbled along for a while, with too little memory and too few programs and hardware add-ons to choose from. But subsequent Mac models were to shed the sealed box design, provide more memory, and better performance. The Mac had attained that combination of popularity and product availability that makes a computer a standard.

CHAPTER SUMMARY

- The Mac represents a revolution in the design of a microcomputer's user interface—the way in which it accepts commands and interacts with you.

- The Mac's graphical user interface is easier to use than a command-line interface, with which you must remember and type awkward commands.

- The Mac's user interface basics are consistent from one program to the next, making it easier to learn new programs.

- Many of the concepts behind the Mac's user interface originated at Xerox's Palo Alto Research Center (PARC).

- Three cornerstones of the Mac's interface are that programs should not impose distinct modes on the user; that users should work with information or objects using a "select, then act" technique; and that a computer is less intimidating and easier to learn if it relies on graphical, iconic metaphors for real-world objects such as trash cans and desktops.

3

The Macintosh Interface

We've covered the basics of how computers operate, and we've seen how advances in user interface design have made them easier to use. Now it's time to meet the Mac face-to-interface. In this chapter, we'll set the stage for our journey inside the Mac by examining:

- the Mac's approach to creating screen displays

- the elements that form the Mac's user interface

- the Finder, which you use to start programs and manage the contents of your disks

- MultiFinder and how it works with the Finder to let you run more than one program at once

- the basic concepts behind start-up disks

- the Clipboard, which lets you move information between programs

- the desk accessories Apple includes with the Mac

- the roles of color and sound in the Mac interface.

If you're just starting out with a Mac, this chapter will teach you basic Macintosh terminology that we'll use throughout the rest of our trek. If you're a veteran Mac user, you probably know many of the terms and concepts discussed here, but you may still want to skim this chapter.

This chapter also contains some tips for navigating within the Mac, but it doesn't provide step-by-step instructions for using Finder or the Mac's desk accessories here. That information appears in your Mac's manuals. In later chapters, we'll pass along some tips for using and customizing the Finder and desk accessories.

THE BIT-MAPPED DISPLAY

Prior to the introduction of Apple's Lisa, microcomputers generally used one of two operating modes to create screen displays. In *text mode*, the computer displayed text by retrieving the appearance of each character from a *character-generator chip*. In *graphics mode*, the computer displayed graphics by selectively turning on or off the dots on the screen—the *picture elements*, or *pixels*. Because the computer used different modes to display text and graphics, it was difficult to create programs that combined text and graphics, and it limited the variety of type styles the computer could display on its screen.

The Lisa, like Xerox's Alto and Star, operated in graphics mode all the time. It created text in the same way it created circles or lines—by "drawing" it on the screen, rather than retrieving character descriptions from a character-generator chip. This approach gave the Lisa an attractive, WYSIWYG display that made working with the computer far less tedious.

The Mac also operates in graphics mode all the time. It, like the Lisa and Xerox's pioneering machines, uses a *bit-mapped display*, in which each screen pixel corresponds to a bit in the computer's memory. A bit with a value of 1 creates a black dot; a bit with a value of 0 creates a white dot.

On the Mac, everything you see on the screen is created by a library of fast graphics routines named *QuickDraw*. QuickDraw is what allows the Mac to easily mix text and graphics on the same screen. And it's what allows the Mac to display a variety of type styles, or *fonts*. Instead of having to gaze at a boring, computer like font, Mac users can choose from thousands of attractive fonts— the same ones graphic designers use for books and magazines.

The Mac's bit-mapped display and its ability to combine attractive fonts with graphics are vital cornerstones that have helped make the Mac a leader in the desktop publishing and presentation graphics worlds. The Mac has even influenced the IBM world to begin adopting bit-mapped displays. You'll see bit-mapped displays in Microsoft's *Windows* and Digital Research's *GEM* operating environments, and in the OS/2 Presentation Manager.

Font Basics

Thanks to the Mac's bit-mapped display, fonts play a large part in the Mac world. Most Mac programs let you take advantage of the Mac's typographic prowess by altering the appearance of the text in your documents. For this reason, understanding of the Mac's approach to fonts is an important step in mastering the machine.

We'll explore the Mac's font features in detail in later chapters. For now, all you need to remember are these five points:

- The Mac comes with an assortment of fonts, each of which has a name such as Chicago, New York, Helvetica, and Times. You can add additional fonts or remove unused fonts easily.

- Using mathematic formulas, the Mac can simulate bold, italic, bold italic, outlined, underlined, and shadowed type styles, as shown in Figure 3-1. When you specify italic, for example, the Mac slants the upright, or *Roman*, version of the font to simulate italics. This simulation of a typographic style has important ramifications for graphic designers and desktop publishers (we'll discuss them in Chapter 7).

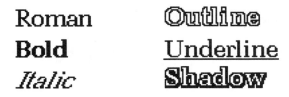

Figure 3-1. Type styles the Mac creates by altering the Roman version of a font.

- The Mac uses the Chicago font in its menus and in many other user interface elements.

- Most fonts include several different *point sizes*. A *point* is a printer's unit of measurement; there are 72 points in an inch. Several different point sizes of the Times font appear in Figure 3-2.

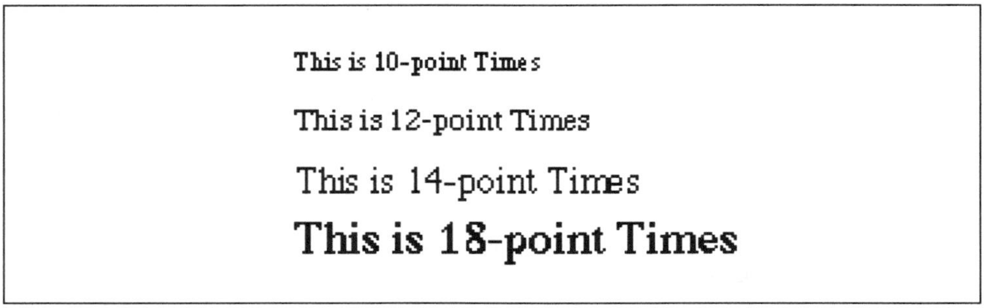

This is 10-point Times

This is 12-point Times

This is 14-point Times

This is 18-point Times

Figure 3-2. Several point sizes of Times.

- You can tell which point sizes are available in a given font by examining your application's Font or Size menus. When a specific point size exists, that size appears in outlined type. If you choose a size that doesn't appear in outlined type, the Mac must simulate that size by *scaling* an existing size. This process causes characters to appear distorted on the screen, as shown in Figure 3-3. Whether the final, printed results appear distorted, however, depends on your printer. (We'll explore this point in detail in Chapter 8.)

This is 12-point Helvetica.

This is 18-point Helvetica—scaled.

Figure 3-3. Distorted text (*bottom*) results when the Mac scales an existing font size (*top*).

It's important to note that the last two points apply to Mac's running System 6.0 or earlier versions. System 7.0, in development at this writing and due for release in 1990, gives the Mac significant new font features. We'll examine these enhanced font features in Chapter 7.

Mouse Basics

Another essential part of the Mac's operating style is the mouse. As you move the mouse on your desk, an on-screen *pointer* moves accordingly. This pointer is usually shaped like an arrow, but it can assume other shapes, depending on the program you're using or on what the Mac is doing. For example, when the Mac is performing a time-consuming operation such as copying a disk, the pointer looks like a wristwatch.

Moving the mouse around simply moves the pointer. The action begins when you press the mouse *button*. There are three basic mouse button manuevers you can perform:

Clicking. The most common manuever, *clicking* involves simply pressing the mouse button and then releasing it.

Double-clicking. The *double-click*—two clicks in rapid succession—has many uses. Usually, it's a shortcut that lets you perform a two-step job in just one step.

Dragging. *Dragging* involves holding down the mouse button while moving the mouse. One use of the dragging technique is to move things around on the Mac's screen.

THE MACHINE OF METAPHORS

The Mac's bit-mapped display is only a medium—a means to an end. Whether any medium is successful depends on how it's used. The secret to the Mac's easy operating style isn't the bit-mapped display or even the mouse. It's the metaphor. Instead of creating an alien environment in which you memorize and type commands to perform tasks, the Mac's designers created on-screen versions of things people use every day: desktops, push buttons, volume controls—and trash cans.

The Desktop, Icons, and Windows

The Mac's *desktop* is the gray-patterned area that the Finder creates and that appears behind open windows, as shown in Figure 3-4. But in some books and manuals you may hear the term applied slightly differently. Sometimes, it's used to refer to the screen itself, as in "move the window to the bottom half of the desktop." At other times, it's used instead of "Finder." For example, the instruction "return to the desktop," means "return to the Finder." At still other times, it's used to describe a program's on-screen work area, as in "A few moments after you start GollyCalc, its desktop appears." In this book, we use "desktop" to mean the gray-patterned background that appears behind open windows.

Upon the desktop rest icons for disks and the Trash can. You may remember from the previous chapter that, in the world of graphic user interfaces, icons are small pictures that represent objects (such as disks) or functions (such as the Finder's Trash can).

Figure 3-4. The Macintosh desktop.

The Finder uses icons to represent disks, applications, documents, the Trash, and disk *folders* (which can hold programs and documents). *Application icons* usually have a diamond shape (Apple recommends that developers use the basic diamond shape, but it's up to the developer to design the icon). *Document icons* represent documents you create with applications. They usually look like a piece of paper with its upper-right corner folded over. Most document icons also have additional graphic flourishes that visually relate them to their corresponding applications' icons, as shown in Figure 3-5.

You access whatever an icon represents—that is, you run a program, load a document, or view the contents of a disk or folder—by *opening* the icon. As Figure 3-5 shows, when you open a disk or folder icon, a *directory window* appears showing the contents of that disk or folder.

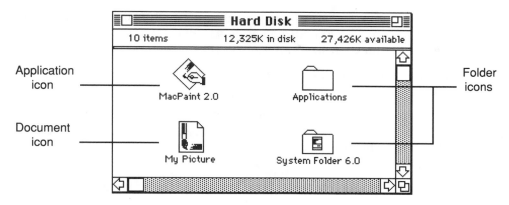

Figure 3-5. A typical directory window.

Window Controls

Directory windows have standard *controls* that let you move them on the screen, change their size, close them, and *scroll* through them to see portions of the directory that don't fit within the window. The *document windows* that applications create to display your open documents have these same controls, which are shown in Figure 3-6.

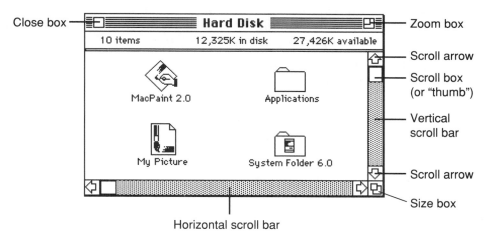

Figure 3-6. Standard window controls.

You can *close* a window—make it disappear—by clicking within the *close box*. The *size box* lets you *resize* a window to make it larger or smaller. The *zoom box* lets you quickly resize a window to fill the screen.

A scroll bar has several components, each of which scrolls the window in a different way.

- Clicking the up or down scroll arrow causes the window to scroll a small amount. A word processor, for example, usually scrolls one line at a time when you click on a scroll arrow. Pointing to a scroll arrow and holding down the mouse button causes the window to scroll continuously.

- Clicking the shaded area above or below the *scroll box*—the white box within the scroll bar's shaded area—causes the window to scroll by the windowful. Holding the mouse button down while pointing to the shaded area causes the window to scroll continuously until the scroll box reaches the spot where you're pointing.

- Dragging the scroll box up or down (or left or right) causes the window to scroll quickly in that direction. You can move to the top or bottom of a window by dragging the scroll box to top or bottom of the scroll bar. (Incidentally, you may also hear the scroll box called the *thumb* or the *elevator*.)

The Mac can display many open windows at once, but only one window is *active* at a given time. The active window is the frontmost window; it's the window you're currently working with. As Figure 3-7 shows, an active window has horizontal stripes running across its title bar; an inactive window doesn't.

You activate a window by clicking once within it. In Figure 3-7, for example, you could activate the window named Inactive Window by clicking on any part of it.

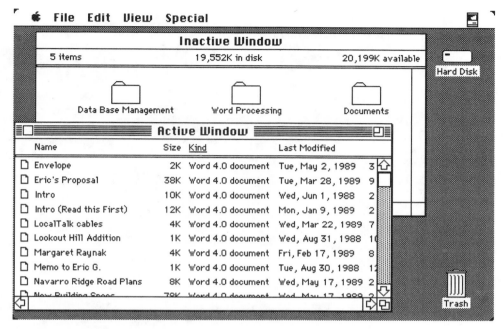

Figure 3-7. Active and inactive windows.

INTERACTING WITH THE MAC

You control the Mac by using the mouse or keyboard to choose *commands*, and by selecting options and supplying information in special windows called *dialog boxes*.

Menus and Commands

The key to controlling the Finder and the applications you use is the *menu bar*, which appears across the top of the screen, as shown in Figure 3-8. The leftmost menu is the *Apple menu*, represented by an apple icon. The Apple menu is generally available in all applications. Some small applications that perform simple tasks may not have a menu bar and thus lack Apple menus.

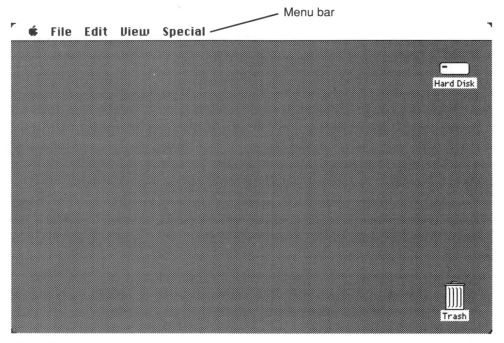

Figure 3-8. The menu bar.

The first command in the Apple menu is the *About command*. When you choose it, a message appears describing the application you're currently using, as shown in Figure 3-9. Some applications use the About command as the gateway to their on line help systems. Below the About command is a list of currently available *desk accessories*, small programs you can access at any time. We'll look at desk accessories again shortly.

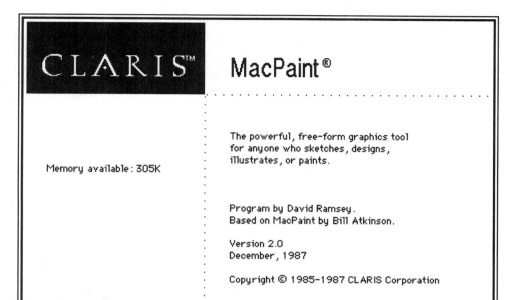

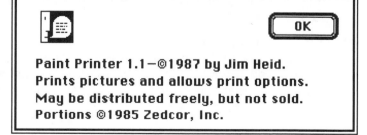

Figure 3-9. Some sample About messages.

When you start a program, it takes over the menu bar, replacing the Finder's menus with its own. A typical menu appears in Figure 3-10. This menu—the File menu from Microsoft Word—is a good example because it has elements you'll find in most menus, including:

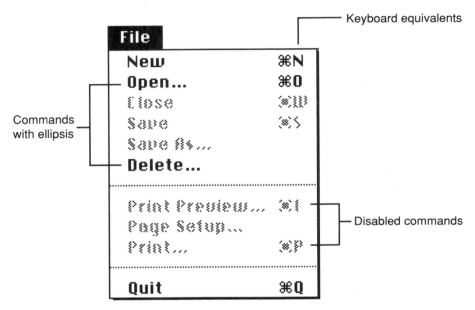

Figure 3-10. A typical menu.

Keyboard equivalents. When a command has a keyboard equivalent, you can use the keyboard to choose the command by holding down the Command key and then pressing the letter that appears next to the Command symbol. Some keyboard equivalents require you to press additional *modifier keys*, such as Option or Shift, along with the Command key. Keyboard equivalents are often called *Command-key shortcuts*.

Commands with ellipsis. When you see a command that ends with ellipsis (...), it means you'll need to supply additional information after choosing the command. For example, after you choose the Print command, you're asked to specify additional information about the print job, such as the number of copies you want to print.

Disabled commands. A command is *disabled* when it wouldn't make sense for you to choose it or when you've reached a limitation of the program. For example, if a program can have only one document open at a time, its Open command is disabled when a document is already open. When a command is disabled, it appears gray. You can move the mouse over a disabled command, but the command won't be highlighted. It's also possible for an entire menu to be disabled. In a drawing program, for example, the Font menu might be disabled unless you're currently typing or editing text. You can pull down a disabled menu to view its commands, but all of them appear gray.

Hierarchical Menus

A special type of menu, the *hierarchical menu*, is finding its way into more and more Mac applications. A hierarchical menu is a menu within a menu. When you select a hierarchical menu title, an additional menu called a *submenu* appears. A hierarchical menu is denoted by a right-pointing triangle adjacent to the menu item, as shown in Figure 3-11. You don't need to point to this triangle to open a submenu; the submenu opens automatically after a very brief delay. This delay is built into the Mac's Menu Manager. Without it, making your way through a menu with more than one hierarchical menu would be tedious, since each submenu would open briefly as the mouse pointer passed through its title.

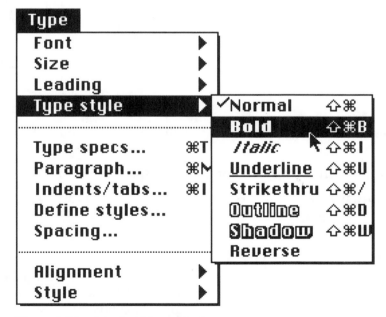

Figure 3-11. A typical hierarchical menu.

As Figure 3-11 shows, a submenu can have its own keyboard equivalents, and can even have submenus of its own. Hierarchical menus allow programmers to cram more commands into their programs' menus, but they can be awkward to use, especially if a submenu contains submenus of its own. If you see a program that uses hierarchical menus with reckless abandon, evaluate it carefully before buying; awkward design may crop up in other areas of the program as well.

Dialog Boxes

Programs constantly need information from us. What document do you want to open? How many copies do you want to print? What text do you want to search for? With the Macintosh, you supply such information using *dialog boxes*. A dialog box is a special kind of window that appears when a program needs more information—often after you've chosen a menu command. As Figure 3-12 shows, within a dialog box are controls that let you supply that information with a minimum of typing.

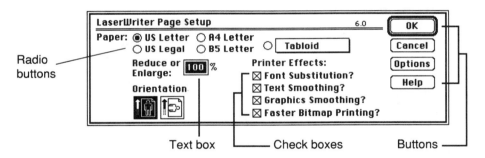

Figure 3-12. The Page Setup dialog box

The Page Setup dialog box contains almost all the controls you will see in a dialog box, including:

Check boxes, which let you select or deselect a specific option.

Radio buttons, which let you select only one option out of a list of options. Radio buttons are so named because they work like the station-changing buttons on a car radio.

Text boxes, which let you supply typed values.

Buttons, which let you confirm your choices by clicking a button labeled OK, or cancel them by clicking a button labeled Cancel. Some buttons, such as the Help and Options buttons in the Page Setup dialog box, may lead you to additional dialog boxes.

The distinction between check boxes and radio buttons is an important one. With check boxes, you can select any or all options in a group of options. But with radio buttons, only one option within the group can be active. If you click a different option within that group, the previously selected option is deselected (see Figure 3-13).

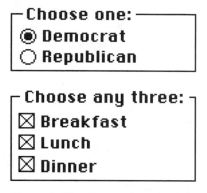

Figure 3-13.   Comparing check boxes and radio buttons.

Dialog boxes are almost always *modal*. When a program's modal dialog box is open, you can't perform any other tasks until you either confirm or cancel the dialog box.

Pop-Up Menus

Dialog boxes can contain menus of their own called *pop-up menus*. A pop-up menu normally displays the currently selected option. When you point to the option and click, the menu "pops up," revealing additional options, as shown in Figure 3-14. When you choose a different option and release the mouse button, the pop-up menu closes and the new option becomes the visible one.

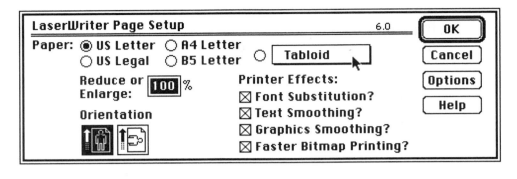

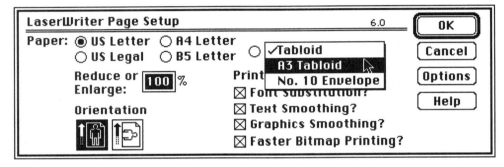

Figure 3-14. A pop-up menu.

Typing Values in Text Boxes

The text box is the only place within a dialog box where you'll have to type a value. Figure 3-15 shows just a few of the ways you might use text boxes: to type a name for a new document, to specify search-and-replace text in a word processor, and to specify the number of copies to print.

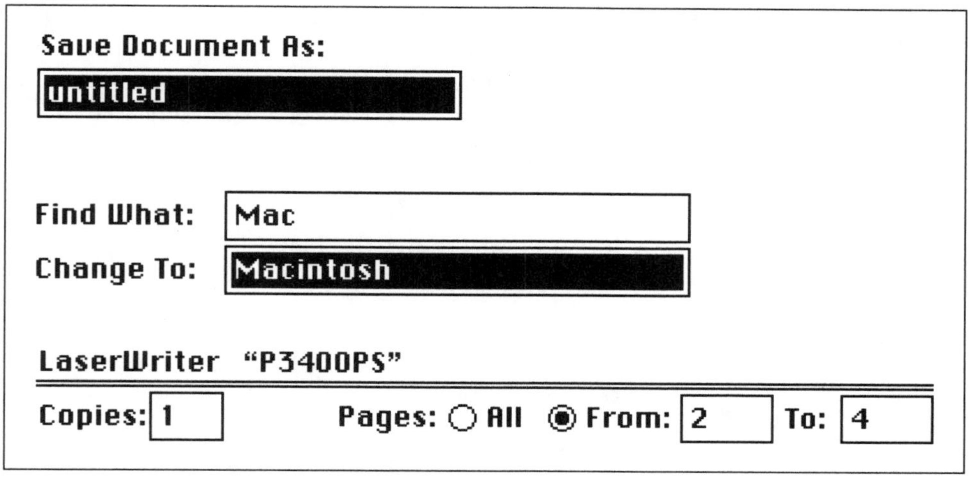

Save Document As:
untitled
Find What:
Mac
Change To:
Macintosh
LaserWriter "P3400PS"
Copies: 1
Pages: All From: 2 To: 4

Figure 3-15. Some typical text boxes.

In a dialog box containing more than one text box, you can move from one text box to the next by pressing the Tab key, as shown in Figure 3-16.

Copies: 1
Pages: All From: 2 To: 4
Copies: 1
Pages: All From: 2 To: 4
Copies: 1
Pages: All From: 2 To: 4

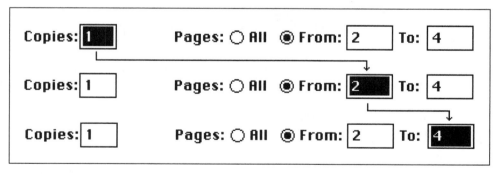

Figure 3-16. Press the Tab key to move from one text box to the next.

The Insertion Point and the I-Beam Pointer

While we're talking text entry, let's cover two terms you'll encounter throughout this book and in most Mac programs. In the IBM PC world, the blinking underline that appears at the point where you're typing is called the *cursor*. In the Macintosh world, the point at which your typing appears is called the *insertion point* and is represented by a blinking vertical bar.

To control the position of the insertion point, you use the *I-beam pointer*. The arrow-shaped mouse pointer assumes an I-beam shape when you move the pointer to an area where text can appear. In a word processing program, the I-beam pointer appears when you're pointing at the page area. It *may* also appear within a text box in a dialog box. (It's up to the application's developer to change the pointer shape when it enters a text box. Some developers don't bother; in these cases, the pointer remains an arrow when it's in a text box.) Figure 3-17 shows the I-beam pointer and the insertion point.

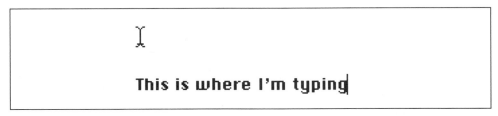

Figure 3-17. The I-beam pointer (*top*) and insertion point (*bottom*).

Selecting Text

The Mac offers standard text-selecting features that work in all programs as well as in the text boxes that appear in dialog boxes. (Many programs also provide additional text-selection shortcuts; we'll sample some of these shortcuts in Chapter 9.)

Dragging. The most common technique for selecting text, dragging involves moving the mouse pointer to the location that marks the beginning of passage you want to select, and then dragging until you've reached the last character you want to select. As you drag, the Mac highlights the text you've selected.

Double clicking. When working with text, double clicking selects words. If you double click and then drag, the Mac continues to select text in one-word increments.

Shift-clicking. Shift-clicking involves pressing the Shift key while clicking the mouse pointer elsewhere in the document. (This technique is sometimes called *extending a selection*.) Shift-clicking is especially useful for selecting a large portion of text. Simply move the insertion point to the start (or end) of the text you want to select. Next, use the mouse and the window's scroll bar to locate the point that marks the end (or start) of the passage you want to select. Finally, press and hold down the Shift key while clicking at that point. It's much faster than dragging—and yawning—while the document window scrolls.

Incidentally, when you've selected some text as a prelude to replacing it with new text, don't bother pressing the Backspace or Delete key before typing the new text. Simply begin typing; the first character you type will clear the selected text.

THE FINDER

The first place you encounter the user interface elements we've just described is the *Finder*, the Mac's file- and disk-management software. Many people erroneously describe the Finder as "the Mac's operating system." The Finder is actually an application—like Microsoft Word or MacPaint. Unlike these applications, however, the Finder runs immediately after you start your Mac and also takes over when you quit an application. And instead of letting you process words or paint with pixels, the Finder helps you manage disks, applications, and documents.

If you've used the IBM PC, you might think of the Finder as a very sophisticated, college-educated version of MS-DOS' COMMAND.COM command processor, which displays the DOS prompt and interprets your typed commands. If you've used the Microsoft Windows operating environment under MS-DOS, there's a closer parallel: the Finder performs for the Mac many of the same jobs that the MS-DOS Executive performs for Windows. The Finder's parallel in the OS/2 world is the Presentation Manager.

Because the Finder is a special application that the Mac runs, it's possible to replace the Finder with other file- and disk-management software. Several companies have created "Finder surrogates" that work more quickly than the Finder or provide useful features the Finder lacks; we'll discuss the best of them in Chapter 10.

The Finder's Jobs

Let's look briefly at the jobs the Finder performs and how it performs them.

Displaying the contents of disks and folders. It isn't named the Finder for nothing. The Finder's primary job is to let you view the contents of disks and folders in any of six viewing methods, as shown in Figure 3-18. In System 6.0 and earlier versions, the Finder performs this job by creating and maintaining an invisible file named DeskTop on every disk you use. (An *invisible* file doesn't appear on the desktop; that's to keep us users from trying to open it or throw it away.) The DeskTop file performs several important behind-the-scenes jobs that we'll look at later in this chapter.

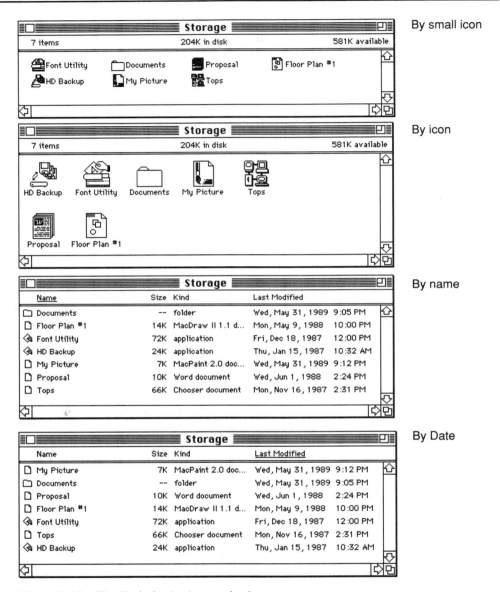

By small icon

By icon

By name

By Date

Figure 3-18. The Finder's viewing methods.

Storage			By Size
Name	Size	Kind	Last Modified
Font Utility	72K	application	Fri, Dec 18, 1987 12:00 PM
Tops	66K	Chooser document	Mon, Nov 16, 1987 2:31 PM
HD Backup	24K	application	Thu, Jan 15, 1987 10:32 AM
Floor Plan #1	14K	MacDraw II 1.1 d...	Mon, May 9, 1988 10:00 PM
Proposal	10K	Word document	Wed, Jun 1, 1988 2:24 PM
My Picture	7K	MacPaint 2.0 doc...	Wed, May 31, 1989 9:12 PM
Documents	--	folder	Wed, May 31, 1989 9:05 PM

Storage			By Kind
Name	Size	Kind	Last Modified
Font Utility	72K	application	Fri, Dec 18, 1987 12:00 PM
HD Backup	24K	application	Thu, Jan 15, 1987 10:32 AM
Tops	66K	Chooser document	Mon, Nov 16, 1987 2:31 PM
Floor Plan #1	14K	MacDraw II 1.1 d...	Mon, May 9, 1988 10:00 PM
My Picture	7K	MacPaint 2.0 doc...	Wed, May 31, 1989 9:12 PM
Proposal	10K	Word document	Wed, Jun 1, 1988 2:24 PM
Documents	--	folder	Wed, May 31, 1989 9:05 PM

Figure 3-18. (*continued*)

Opening applications and documents. When you double click on a program's icon, the Finder starts that program. When you double-click on a document, the Finder determines which application created it, and it starts that application and passes the document's name to it. The DeskTop file is a key player in allowing the Finder to determine which application created which document. (Incidentally, some people use the term *launch* to describe the process of starting a program, as in, "I launched MacWrite.")

Organizing documents and applications in folders and on the desktop. The Finder works together with the Mac's system software to allow you to create a filing system that efficiently holds your documents and applications. You can also move document and application icons around on the desktop and within disk and folder windows to create a personalized workspace where everything is where you want it.

Managing application and document files. The Finder helps you manage the contents of disks. With it, you can:

• copy a file to a different disk by dragging its icon to that disk's icon or window

• duplicate a disk by dragging its icon to a different disk's icon

- delete a file by dragging it to the Trash

- make a copy of a file by selecting it and choosing Duplicate from the File menu

- use the Get Info command to find out information about files, "attach" brief descriptive phrases to them, and alter the memory requirements of applications (we'll look at the latter option in detail in Chapter 9)

- print a document by selecting it and choosing Print. Doing so causes the Finder to start the document's application, tell it to print the document, and then quit.

Specify your startup options. With the Special Menu's Set Startup command, you can specify whether you want your Mac to start up running Multi-Finder, the Finder, or an application, as shown in Figure 3-19. If you choose to start up under MultiFinder, you can specify that MultiFinder open multiple applications and/or desk accessories upon start-up.

Figure 3-19. The Set Startup dialog box.

Selecting Multiple Files at Once

You can perform many of the previous file-management tasks on more than one file at a time by selecting each file. You can also open two or more documents in one step by selecting them and choosing Open. (The documents must be created by the same application for this to work.) You can select multiple files using either of two methods:

- By drawing a selection marquee around the files, as shown in Figure 3-20.

- By Shift-clicking—holding down the Shift key while clicking on each file, as shown in Figure 3-21.

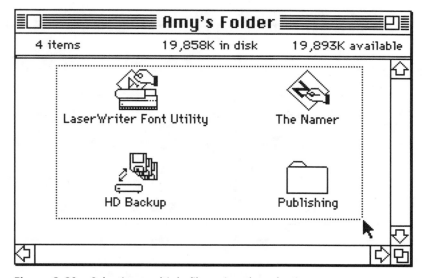

Figure 3-20. Selecting multiple files using the selection marquee.

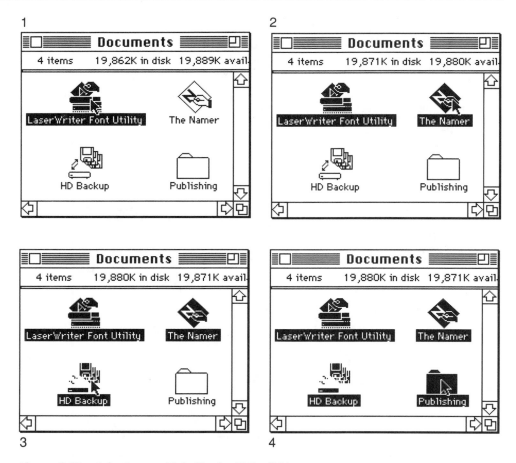

Figure 3-21. Selecting multiple files by Shift-clicking.

It's also possible to combine both techniques. You might, for example, use the selection marquee to select files located next to each other, and then scroll to a different part of the window and Shift-click on additional files.

THE MAC'S FILING SYSTEM

Floppy disks can hold hundreds of files; hard disks can hold thousands. The Mac provides a way to efficiently organize the contents of your disks. It's called the *Hierarchical File System*, or *HFS* for short.

With HFS, organizing your disk files is much like organizing paperwork within a filing cabinet. The disk compares to the filing cabinet—it's the outermost level of the storage hierarchy. Disk folders compare to the paper folders nested in the file drawers, and can hold both applications and documents. And just as you can place paper folders within other paper folders, you can place disk folders within other disk folders. (We'll look at a few filing strategies in Chapter 9.)

The folder icons that appear in disk directory windows are another example of how the Mac uses metaphors for objects people encounter every day. While you're working with disk folders, the Mac is working with a *directory*—a special area of the disk that acts as a table of contents for the disk. The directory allows the Mac to keep track of where files are located on the disk, and of how much free space is available for new files. When you use the Erase Disk command in the Finder's Special menu, one of the jobs the Finder performs is to create a blank directory on the disk that you're erasing.

Directory Dialog Boxes

We've seen how the Finder lets you keep track of documents by storing them in folders. But how do you save a new document or retrieve an existing one? With computers that lack a consistent user interface, you often have to learn many methods of saving and retrieving documents. The Mac provides standard dialog boxes called *directory dialog boxes* for these often-performed tasks. Shown in Figure 3-22, these dialog boxes offer buttons for switching between disks, ejecting disks, and cancelling the Open or Save command. Both also provide *list boxes* that list the documents on the current disk or in the current folder.

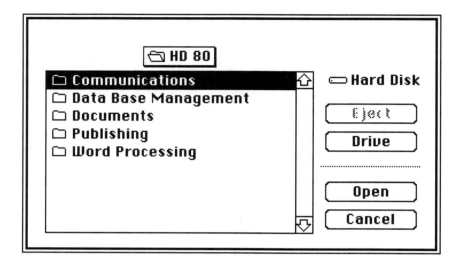

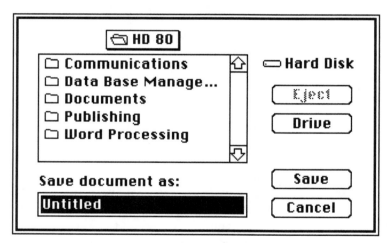

Figure 3-22. Open and Save directory dialog boxes.

Accessing Folders in Directory Dialog Boxes

When you're opening or saving documents, you often have to maneuver within the HFS storage hierarchy to access a specific folder. Figure 3-23 shows a simple storage hierarchy: a disk named Storage containing a folder named Documents, which contains a folder named Letters.

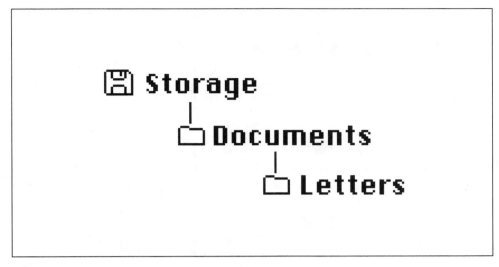

Figure 3-23. A simple storage hierarchy.

Let's say you're writing a letter using your word processor, and you decide to save it in the Letters folder. As Figure 3-24 shows, doing so is a three-step process:

1. Open the Documents folder by double-clicking it (or by selecting it and clicking Save, or by selecting it and pressing Return). Notice that the pop-up menu above the list box changes to reflect the currently open folder.

2. Open the Letters folder. Again, the pop-up menu above the list box changes to show that the Letters folder is open.

3. Type a name for the document and click the Save button or press Return.

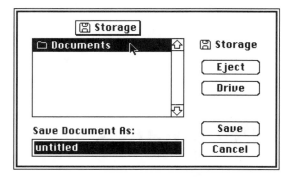

1. Open the Documents Folder

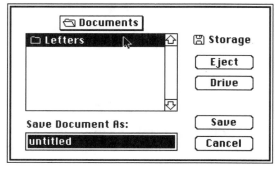

2. Open the Letters Folder

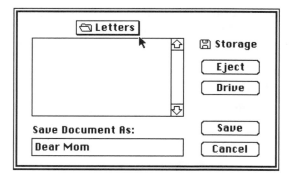

3. Type the document name

Figure 3-24. Saving a document in a folder that's inside another folder.

Now, you've finished your letter and have started working on that overdue proposal, which you want to save in the Documents folder. When you choose the Save command, however, the pop-up menu at the top of the Save dialog box indicates that the Letters folder is the current folder. To save the proposal in the Documents folder, you must move up one level in the hierarchy by using the pop-up menu to select the Documents folder, as shown in Figure 3-25.

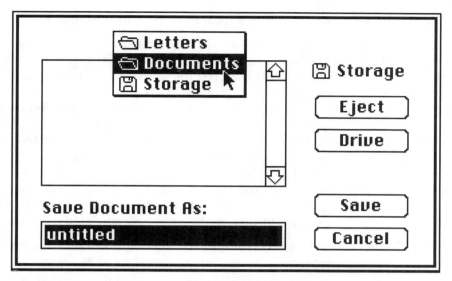

Figure 3-25. Moving up one level in the storage hierarchy.

These same techniques also apply to the Open dialog box. To sum them up:

- A disk is always at the outermost level of the storage hierarchy, and folders are within it.

- To move deeper into your storage hierarchy, double-click on the folder you want to open, or select the folder and click the Open button, or select the folder and press the Return key.

- To move out toward the desktop, use the pop-up menu above the list box to select the desired folder name (or select the disk name to move to the outermost level). Alternatively, you can move one folder at a time by clicking on the disk name that appears above the Open (or Save) and Eject buttons.

The DeskTop File

Let's take a closer look at the DeskTop file—the invisible file the Finder creates and maintains on each disk you use. The DeskTop file contains a number of things the Finder uses as it works, including:

The application list. A list of all the applications on the disk. The Finder uses the information in the application list to start the appropriate application when you double-click on a document. The Finder modifies the application list when you add applications to the disk or remove them. (We'll look at the application list again in Chapter 15.)

The Get Info comments. These appear in the Get Info window.

The location of the icons and disk windows on the desktop. When you move document or application icons within a directory window, the Finder records the icons' positions in the DeskTop file so that the icons appear in the same positions the next time you insert that disk or return to the Finder. The Finder also records the position and size of disk or folder windows. When you insert a disk or when you return to the Finder by quitting an application, the Finder consults the DeskTop file to determine whether any disk or folder windows were open, and recreates the window arrangement accordingly. For example, let's say you've sized and moved a disk window so that it appears in the lower-left corner of the desktop, and then you eject that disk. When you reinsert the disk, the Finder reads the DeskTop file and learns that the disk's window was previously open and located in the lower-left corner of the screen.

The way the contents of disks and folders are displayed on the desktop. The Finder's View menu lets you view the contents of a disk or folder in any of six ways; just as the DeskTop file stores window-position information, it stores your viewing preferences so that the disk or folder windows appear in the way you previously chose.

The icons for each application, and for the documents the application creates. Because the DeskTop file also stores the icons for the documents an application creates, the Finder is able to display a document icon properly even if the document's application isn't on the disk.

Remember, the Finder uses a DeskTop file only on Macs running System 6.0 or earlier versions. In System 7.0, the Mac will use a new manager, the *Desktop Manager*, to keep track of icons, Get Info comments, and viewing preferences.

MULTIFINDER

MultiFinder builds on the foundation laid by the Finder to give the Mac additional capabilities. That's an important point: MultiFinder doesn't replace the Finder, it works with it. This has some important ramifications that we'll discuss in later chapters. For now, let's step back to get the big picture of what MultiFinder does.

Running multiple programs simultaneously. With the Finder, you must quit one program before you can start the next. That isn't the case with Multi-Finder. While a program is running, you can return to the desktop with a single mouse click and start another program—or as many as programs as will fit in memory.

Managing background tasks. The Mac is fast, but many things still take time. Printing to a LaserWriter, transferring a large file to another computer, sorting a huge database, calculating a complex spreadsheet—these are tasks that make you drum your fingers instead of type with them. When running under MultiFinder, you can start or switch to another application and resume working while the time-consuming process continues. When you do, the time-consuming process is said to be *running in the background*. The currently active program—the one you've switched to—is called the *foreground application*. (We'll discuss the technicalities behind MultiFinder's approach to running multiple programs in Chapter 7, and we'll take a closer look at background printing in Chapter 8.)

Allocating memory. MultiFinder adds an additional text box to the Get Info window that lets you allocate how much memory a given program should get, as shown in Figure 3-26.

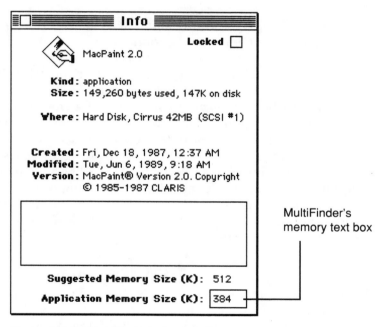

Figure 3-26. MultiFinder's Get Info box.

MultiFinder and Multitasking

On the surface, MultiFinder seems to be able to run several programs simultaneously. In reality, MultiFinder runs only one program at a time. "But," you might ask, "what about when something is going on in the background, such as when I'm printing to a LaserWriter or transferring a large file over a telephone modem?" Even then, MultiFinder is running only one program at a time. It's simply switching between each so quickly that it appears to be doing several things at once.

There are a few multitasking-related terms you may encounter as you work with the Mac, and each deals with how a computer provides the illusion of running several programs simultaneously. One is *context-switching*. Context-switching is the simplest kind of multitasking; it involves simply putting Program A on hold and activating Program B. When you use MultiFinder to switch from, say, MacWrite to MacPaint, you're using its context-switching features.

Another term you might hear is *cooperative multitasking*. This is the type of multitasking MultiFinder uses to perform background operations. With cooperative multitasking, a computer gives each program a chance to run, and each program turns control of the machine over to the next, in round-robin fashion. With cooperative multitasking, it's up to each program to not monopolize the computer to the point where other programs don't get a chance to run. Each program is like a guest at a banquet: The tray of food gets passed from one guest to the next, and it's up to each guest to take only as much as he or she needs, and then pass the tray along to the next guest. If one guest takes too much, the others don't get a chance to eat. Worse, if one guest passes out at his chair, the tray stops moving entirely. Cooperative multitasking is sometimes called *non-preemptive* multitasking, since the computer's operating system never interrupts, or preempts, a program. Microsoft Windows, a Mac-like operating environment for MS-DOS computers, also uses this multitasking technique.

The third type of multitasking has been used by big computers for some time, but is just making its way to the desktop. Called *preemptive* multitasking, it's found in IBM's OS/2 operating system, but isn't expected to be available for the Mac until the early 1990s. With preemptive multitasking, a system software component called a *task manager* doles out chunks of time to each program, and exercises a great deal of control over how much time each program gets. It's as if a strict waiter has arrived at the banquet and dishes out each serving himself, instead of letting each guest take as much as he or she wants.

Operating systems that provide preemptive multitasking usually also provide *memory protection* features that prevent one crashed program from bringing down all the other programs that might be running. To return to our banquet analogy, if one guest passes out, the waiter takes over to ensure that the tray keeps moving.

Multitasking gurus often deride non-preemptive operating systems such as MultiFinder, claiming they don't provide "true" multitasking. The fact is, however, the non-preemptive approach works well, provided that programs are written to behave within its round-robin operating style. MultiFinder may not offer the "true" multitasking that OS/2 provides, but it does allow programs to print, transfer files, and perform other time-consuming tasks in the background.

Switching Between Applications

MultiFinder lets you switch between applications in several ways.

Choosing the application name from the Apple menu. MultiFinder places the name and icon of each running application in the Apple menu, after the list of desk accessories, as shown in Figure 3-27. You can move to a different application or to the Finder by choosing its name. If you have several applications open, this technique is usually the fastest.

Figure 3-27. Application names in the Apple menu.

Clicking the icon at the right end of the menu bar. Under MultiFinder, the icon of the currently active application appears at the right end of the menu bar, as shown in Figure 3-28. This icon lets you "page through" the open applications, activating each one in turn. If you have several applications open, this technique is more cumbersome than using the Apple menu. It's like leafing through a book to find something instead of using the table of contents to get there in one step.

Figure 3-28. MultiFinder's menu bar icon.

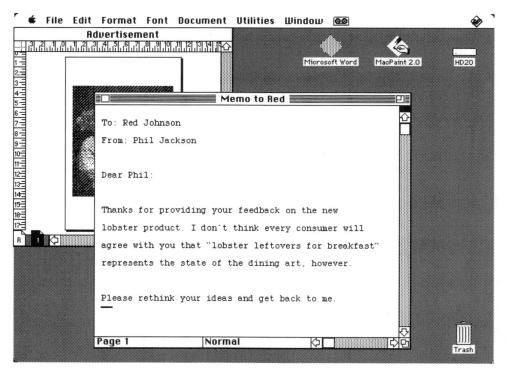

Figure 3-29. MultiFinder runs each application in its own layer.

Clicking "behind" the foreground application. MultiFinder runs each application—including the Finder—in its own *layer*, as shown in Figure 3-29. Unless the foreground application's window completely fills the screen, you can usually see the applications beneath it. Beneath your Microsoft Word document, for example, you might be able to see part of the Finder's Trash icon, or part of a picture you're drawing with MacDraw.

You can switch to the Finder or a different application by clicking on that visible portion, as shown in Figure 3-30. If the active application's window fills the screen, you can close the window or drag it to the side in order to see applications beneath it.

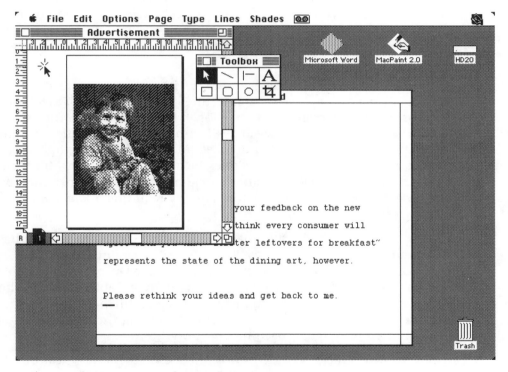

Figure 3-30. You can activate a different application by clicking one of its components.

Double-clicking dimmed application icons. The Finder dims the icons of applications that are running. You can return to a given application by double-clicking its dimmed icon.

MultiFinder and Memory

When a computer is running multiple applications, it must be able to manage memory so that applications don't step on each other's toes. Multi-Finder helps the Mac manage and allocate memory to allow programs to coexist peacefully.

Exactly how many programs can you run at once? That depends on two primary factors:

- The size of the programs you run. Some programs have a bigger appetite for memory than others; generally, the more fancy features a program has, the more memory it requires. The larger the programs you run, the fewer you'll be able to fit into your Mac's memory at once. Here's where MultiFinder's Get Info box can help: by carefully fine-tuning the amount of memory you give to applications, you increase your chances of being able to run more of them at once.

- The amount of RAM your Mac has. A Mac with only one megabyte of RAM will usually have room for one "full-featured" application such as Microsoft Excel or Word, and might also have enough free RAM left over for a smaller application. Even so, two megabytes is a much more realistic minimum memory configuration for MultiFinder. Memory-devouring applications such as Ashton-Tate's FullWrite Professional can't run under MultiFinder on a one-megabyte machine, and are cramped even on a two-megabyte one. System 7.0 will up the memory ante by requiring a *minimum* of two megabytes.

Using MultiFinder efficiently is like packing for a trip: Your suitcase has a finite amount of space, and only by choosing and arranging your clothes and toiletries carefully can you squeeze everything you need into that space. We've been speaking in general terms here because many variables influence how many programs you can pack into memory using MultiFinder. In Chapter 9, we'll present some guidelines and scenarios for getting the most out of—or, more accurately, into—your machine's memory.

As mentioned earlier, System 7.0 will provide *virtual memory* features that will allow certain Macs to treat a hard disk as an extension of memory, thus dramatically increasing the number of programs you can run simultaneously.

SYSTEM DISK BASICS

You may recall from Chapter 1 that some of the Mac's system software is stored in ROM, and the rest is stored on disk and loaded into memory during start-up or as you use your Mac. This disk-based system software is stored in several files located in a folder named System Folder. A disk that contains a System Folder is called a *system* disk.

The files in the System Folder contain:

- routines that Apple has updated since creating the Mac's ROM chips
- the Finder's software
- the fonts that appear in your applications' Font menus and dialog boxes
- the desk accessories that appear in the Apple menu
- the auxiliary files used by the Chooser and Control Panel desk accessories
- the text or graphics that you've pasted into the Scrapbook desk accessory.

The Startup Disk

Another important concept that's directly related to the System Folder is that of a *start-up disk*. The start-up disk is the disk (hard or floppy) whose System Folder is in use. "In use" simply means that the Mac occasionally accesses the files within the System Folder as it runs. For example, when you start an application, one of the first tasks the application performs is to access the System Folder to determine which fonts are available so that it can display their names in its Font menu or dialog box.

The Finder always positions the start-up disk's icon in the upper-right corner of the desktop (although you can drag the icon elsewhere on the desktop). You can eject a start-up disk using the Finder's Eject command (in the File menu), but you may have to reinsert the disk, depending on the tasks you perform next. You cannot eject the start-up disk *and* remove its icon from the desktop by dragging the disk's icon to the Trash can. If you do drag the start-up disk's icon to the Trash, the Finder acts as though you chose Eject: it ejects the disk, but it leaves its icon visible on the screen, and it dims the icon to signify that the disk is ejected.

Now here comes the potentially confusing wrinkle: The start-up disk may *not* necessarily be the disk you started your Mac with. You can switch from one system disk to another by starting an application on the second system disk, as shown in Figure 3-31. This process is called *switch-launching*. If you don't have a hard disk, but instead swap floppies as you move between applications, it's very likely that you'll switch-launch from one start-up disk to another while using your Mac. If you have a hard disk, but occasionally run a program from a floppy, it can happen to you, too.

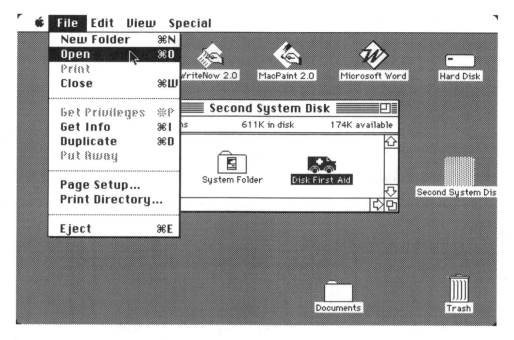

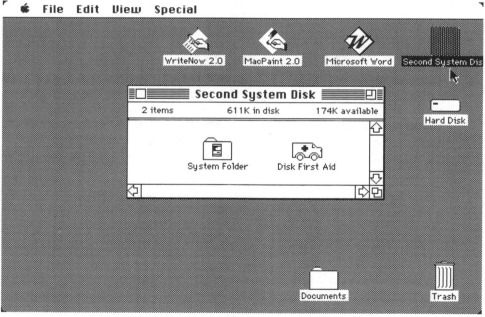

Figure 3-31. Switch-launching from one system disk to another.

Forcing a Switch-Launch

Here's another confusing wrinkle: Starting an application on a different system disk *doesn't guarantee* that the Mac will switch-launch to that disk's System Folder. There are times when the Mac will start the application on the second disk, but still use the System Folder on the first disk. So, to force the Mac to switch-launch, you need to perform one of the following special procedures.

- Hold down the Option key, and then double-click on an application stored on the second system disk.

— or —

- Open the second disk's System Folder, and then hold down the Command and Option keys while double clicking on the file named Finder.

When You Can't Switch-Launch

There are times when the Mac will never switch to a different system disk, even if you try to force a switch-launch. This refusal to switch occurs:

- When you're running under MultiFinder. Because applications that are running are already relying on a specific System Folder, the Mac will never switch-launch when you're running under MultiFinder. If you try to force a switch-launch under MultiFinder, the Mac displays the alert box in Figure 3-32.

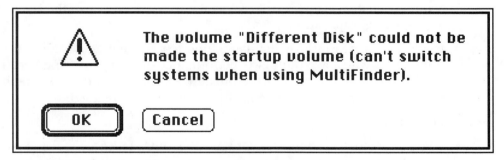

Figure 3-32. You can't switch-launch under MultiFinder.

- When the second disk's System Folder contains earlier versions of the Mac's system software. Apple adds many new routines to each system version, and if you switched to an earlier version of the system, certain routines wouldn't be available when the Mac needed them. If you try to force a switch-launch to an older system version, the Mac displays the alert box in Figure 3-33.

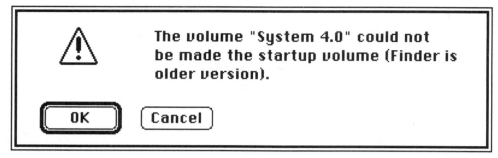

Figure 3-33. You can't switch-launch to an earlier version of the system.

The Pros and Cons of Switch-Launching

Switch-launching from one system disk to another can be useful at times, but it can also cause headaches. First, let's look at why switch-launching can be undesirable:

- It causes the Mac to switch to a different set of fonts, and the second set might not contain the same fonts as the first.

- It causes the Mac to switch to a different set of desk accessories, which may not contain the same ones as the first set.

- It causes the Mac to use a different Scrapbook, which will not contain the same data as the first. If you paste some data from Application A into the Scrapbook, and then start Application B from a different system disk, your Scrapbook data will appear to have vanished when you open the Scrapbook after starting Application B.

- If you use a hard disk, switch-launching to a System Folder located on a floppy disk will slow your Mac's performance dramatically. And because a hard disk can hold more fonts, more desk accessories, and more Scrapbook data than a floppy, the problems mentioned above are magnified.

But switch-launching can be desirable, too:

- If you know that a system disk contains the fonts, desk accessories, or Scrapbook data that you need for a given task, you can switch-launch to that disk to make them available.

- If you accidentally start the Mac with an earlier version of the system, you can switch-launch to a later version without having to restart your Mac.

THE CLIPBOARD

The Mac's *Clipboard* lets you move data created in one application into another application. Using the Clipboard, you can illustrate a report with charts or drawings, move large passages of text from one document to another, or include financial data retrieved over the phone from your company's central computer in a spreadsheet document.

The key to the Clipboard is the Edit menu and its Cut, Copy, and Paste commands.

- **The Cut command.** Removes what you've selected from the document and places it on the Clipboard, replacing the Clipboard's previous contents.

- **The Copy command.** Places what you've selected on the Clipboard, replacing the Clipboard's previous contents, but doesn't remove the selection from the original document.

- **The Paste command.** Adds the contents of the Clipboard to the currently active document. That document might be the same document you cut or copied the data from, or it may be a different document created by the same program, or it may be a document created by an entirely different program. In any case, the data remains on the Clipboard, so you can paste the same information over and over again by repeatedly choosing Paste.

Many applications include a Show Clipboard command that displays the contents of the Clipboard. The Show Clipboard command is usually in the Edit menu, but may also appear in a menu named Window. (In most Microsoft programs, Show Clipboard is in the Window menu.)

Moving information between programs is usually a straightforward process, but there are some subtle points you might want to be aware of. They're described in Chapter 11.

DESK ACCESSORIES

Even without MultiFinder, the Macintosh provides a way to run multiple programs simultaneously: desk accessories, those small programs whose names appear in the Apple menu. As we'll see in Chapter 9 and 10, desk accessories are an easy and popular way to enhance and customize your Mac. When you choose a desk accessory's name, the Mac runs the desk accessory, opening its window and adding any menus it provides to the menu bar. You can open a desk accessory whenever the Apple menu is available, provided that enough memory remains free to load the desk accessory and that no modal dialog box (the kind you can't click outside of) is open.

The desk accessories included with System 6.0 include:

Alarm Clock. This desk accessory, shown in Figure 3-34, displays the current time and date as stored by the Mac's built-in, battery-powered clock and calendar. True to its name, Alarm Clock also provides an alarm feature. At the time you've set, the Mac beeps once and the Apple menu flashes until you reset the alarm.

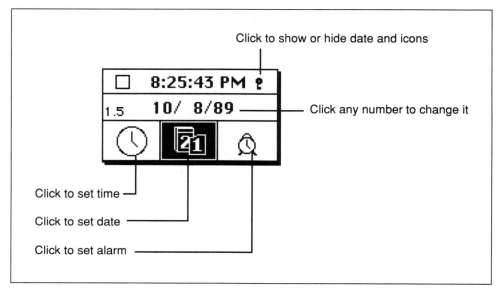

Figure 3-34. The Alarm Clock desk accessory

Calculator. This desk accessory, shown in Figure 3-35, mimics a simple and convenient four-function calculator—the kind that cost almost as much as a Mac when they first came out. You can click the on-screen buttons or "press" them using the keyboard's number keys or the numeric keypad present on the Mac Plus and later machines.

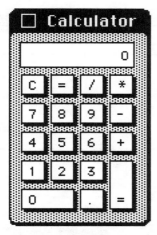

Figure 3-35. The Calculator desk accessory.

Chooser. The Chooser lets you select and switch between devices such as printers. If you have just one Mac and one printer, you may never have to use the Chooser at all; on the other hand, if your office has many Macs and laser printers interconnected on a network, you may use the Chooser many times a day for such tasks as:

- switching from one laser printer to another

- activating or deactivating MultiFinder's background printing option

- connecting to a central network storage disk, called a *file server*

- connecting to a network electronic mail system for communicating with other members of your network.

When you open the Chooser, it examines the contents of your System Folder for files designed to control printers and access network devices. As Figure 3-36 shows, the icon for each such file appears in the list box on the left side of the Chooser's window.

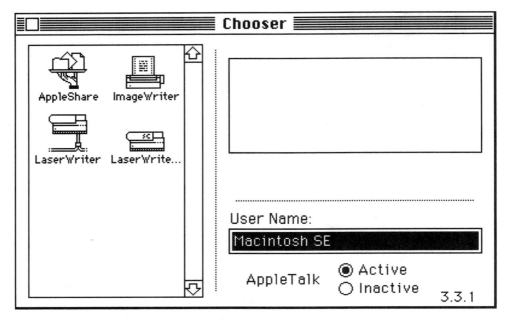

Figure 3-36. The Chooser desk accessory.

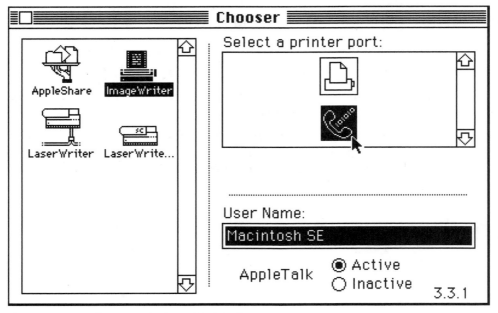

Figure 3-37. Selecting a device with the Chooser.

To select a given device, you click on its icon, and the Chooser modifies the right side of its window to display any options appropriate to the device you choose, as shown in Figure 3-37.

Control Panel. This desk accessory, shown in Figure 3-38, lets you adjust numerous system settings, from simple ones such as the current time and date to more complex ones—like the number of colors you want to display on a Mac II. Like the Chooser, the Control Panel uses auxiliary files located in the System Folder. When you open the Control Panel, it displays those files' names and icons. Selecting each icon lets you control a different aspect of the Mac's operation.

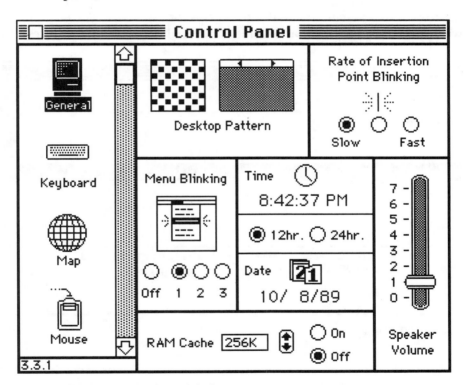

Figure 3-38. The Control Panel desk accessory

Many of the Control Panel's settings are stored in a special area of memory called the *parameter RAM*. The parameter RAM is powered by the Mac's battery, so its settings are retained even when the Mac's power is off.

The Control Panel provides access to so many settings that we won't describe them all here. You'll find more information on specific Control Panel settings in Chapter 5 and in Chapter 9.

Find File. The Mac's Hierarchical File System makes organizing files easy, but it makes misplacing them easy, too. The Find File desk accessory helps you locate misplaced files. Type all or part of the file name in the Search For box, press Return or click the Search icon, and Find File examines the current disk, including any folders. If it locates any files whose names contain what you typed, Find File displays their names in its window (Figure 3-39). Click on a file, and Find File displays its location in the lower-right portion of its window, and some information about the file in the lower left. Find File also adds a menu to the menu bar. The Search Here command lets you switch to a different disk if you have more than one inserted. The Move to Desktop command moves a file within a folder to the outermost level of the disk hierarchy—the desktop. In later chapters, we'll provide tips for using Find File efficiently and we'll spotlight products that provide additional file-searching features.

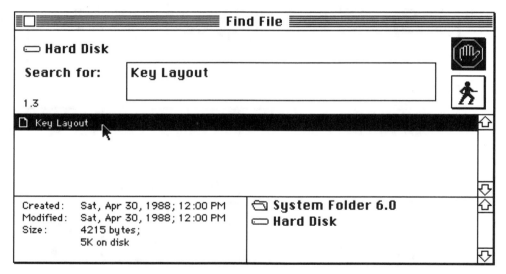

Figure 3-39. Using the Find File desk accessory.

Key Caps. The Mac's fonts include a wider range of characters than those of most computers. In addition to the standard alphabet, numerals, and math symbols all computer fonts provide, the Mac's *character set* includes special characters such as accents, typographic opening and closing quotes, math symbols, copyright and trademark symbols, and more. You summon these special characters by holding down the Option key (and, sometimes, the Shift key) and pressing another key. This other key is often related to the character you want; for example, pressing Option-N and then typing "n" summons an "n" with a tilde over it: ñ.

Remembering which Option-key sequence summons which character is difficult, and that's where Key Caps can help. Key Caps's window is an on-screen keyboard, shown in Figure 3-40.

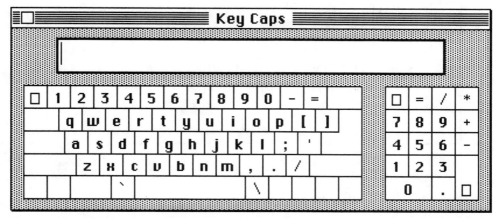

Figure 3-40.   The Key Caps desk accessory.

If you press a key on your Mac's keyboard, Key Caps highlights that key in its window. If you press the Shift or the Option key (or both), Key Caps changes its on-screen keyboard to reflect the characters accessible with those keys pressed, as shown in Figure 3-41. You can use Key Caps to find out which keyboard sequence accesses which special characters.

Key Caps also adds a menu to the menu bar that lets you change the font in which the on-screen keys appear. Choosing the right font is important, since some special characters don't appear in all fonts.

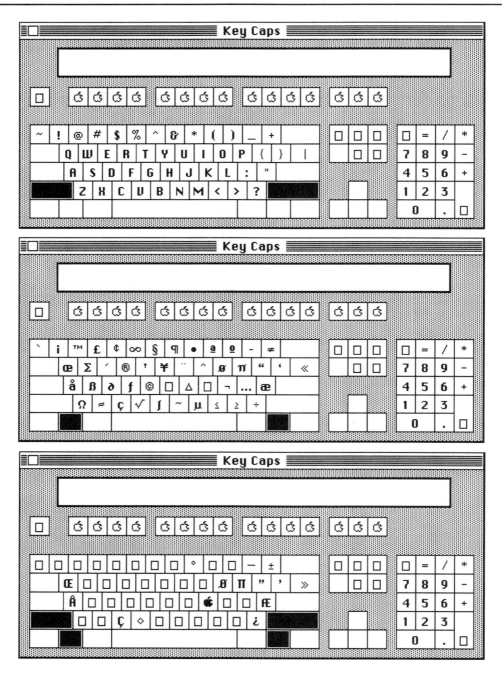

Figure 3-41. Key Caps with Shift pressed, with Option pressed, and with Shift and Option pressed.

Scrapbook. The Mac's Clipboard stores only one piece of information at a time; when you use the Cut or Copy commands, the Clipboard's previous contents are replaced. The Scrapbook desk accessory works along with the Clipboard to allow you to save cut or copied data for future use. When you open the Scrapbook and choose Paste from the Edit menu, the Mac adds a new "page" to the Scrapbook and pastes the contents of the Clipboard into the new page, as shown in Figure 3-42.

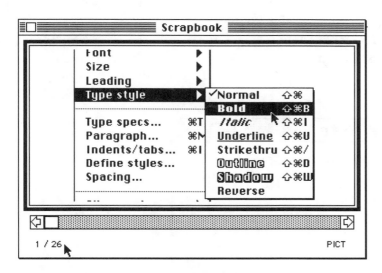

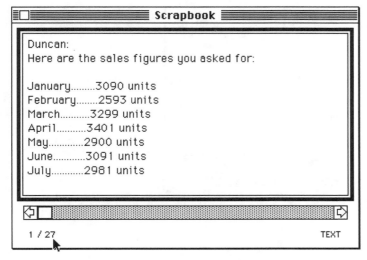

Figure 3-42. Choosing Paste adds a page to the Scrapbook.

You can flip through the Scrapbook by using the horizontal scroll bar at the bottom of the Scrapbook window. The Scrapbook can hold as many pages as disk space allows. We'll look at the Scrapbook again in Chapter 11.

Optional Desk Accessories

The following two desk accessories also come with the Mac, but because a single disk doesn't have room for all of the available desk accessories, these two aren't installed in the Apple menu.

Note Pad. The Note Pad desk accessory lets you type and store up to eight "pages" of notes. Each page holds 256 characters. To move to the next or previous page, click the dog-eared corner of the current page as shown in Figure 3-43.

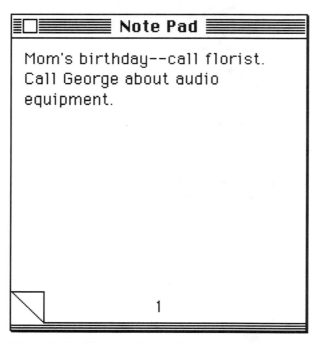

Figure 3-43. The Note Pad desk accessory.

Puzzle. The Puzzle desk accessory creates an on-screen version of the classic kid's puzzle in which you try to arrange the tiles in numeric order (Figure 3-44). The only difference between Puzzle and the real thing is that you can't rip the tiles out of the desk accessory in a moment of frustrated rage.

Figure 3-44.   The Puzzle desk accessory—unsolved.

In the System Update 6.0 package, these two desk accessories are stored in a Font/DA Mover document called Desk Accessories, located in the Font/DA Mover Folder on the Utilities 2 disk. To use these desk accessories on a Mac running System 6.0 or an earlier version, you must install them using the Font/DA Mover utility. (Details on the Font/DA Mover appear in Chapter 7.)

COLOR IN THE MAC INTERFACE

As we'll see in the next chapter, many Macs provide color display capabilities. A color Mac can display startlingly detailed photographic images as well as color graphs, charts, text, and more.

Color also plays a role in the Macintosh interface, but it's a small role. Apple takes a conservative approach to color in the user interface. One obvious reason is that thousands of Macs lack color capabilities. A less-obvious but perhaps equally important reason is because color is a powerful communication tool, and Apple's user interface engineers feel strongly about not overwhelming users with a rainbow of colors in scroll bars, menus, and other user interface elements.

For these reasons, the screen of a color Mac looks very similar to that of a monochrome one. In fact, the only differences between the two are:

- The Apple menu appears in color on a color Mac

- On color Macs, the Finder has an additional menu, Color, that lets you assign one of eight colors to disk, folder, and file icons

- On color Macs, the Finder's View menu provides an additional command, By Color, that lets you view a disk's or folder's contents sorted according to their icons' colors.

- On color Macs, a Control Panel option called Colors lets you change the color in which selected (highlighted) text appears.

Colorizing Your Interface

Although Apple doesn't provide a way to change the color of menus, scroll bars, buttons, and other interface elements, the ROMs of color Macs do support color interface elements. Using Palomar Software's Colorizer accessory kit, you can customize your interface to include color user interface elements. We'll look at Colorizer in Chapter 10.

SOUND IN THE MAC INTERFACE

Historically, sound has played a minor role in the microcomputer world. Most games produce grating squawks and tinny musical effects, and some programs beep at you if something goes wrong. Beyond that, microcomputers (and, for that matter, minicomputers and mainframes) haven't taken advantage of the power of sound.

That's slowly changing, thanks in part to the Mac. In addition to being able to produce the same tinny music and error beeps as other microcomputers, the Mac can play back digitally recorded sounds. On Macs running System 6.0 or later versions, you can choose from a number of digitally recorded sounds, from a screeching monkey to a springy "boing." HyperCard can also play back digital sounds. Many HyperCard stacks take advantage of this feature; an educational stack called Bird Anatomy II, for example, plays bird songs. Apple has even experimented with (but never released) a number of "sonic Finders," which produce wooshing sounds when windows are opened or closed and when files are thrown in the Trash.

In Chapter 14, we'll explain how Macs play back digital sound. We'll also show how you can record sounds, and we'll look at the differences in the sound circuitry in each Mac model.

CHAPTER SUMMARY

- The Mac's bit-mapped screen lets it display a variety of fonts as well as icons.

- Icons are pictorial representations of real-world objects such as disks, push buttons, documents, the trash can, and volume controls.

- Macintosh windows have standard components that let you move them, scroll through their contents, resize them, and close them.

- You interact with the Mac by issuing commands using the mouse or keyboard, and by choosing options and supplying information using dialog boxes.

- The Mac provides standardized directory dialog boxes that all applications use for opening and saving documents. Within a directory dialog box are buttons and pop-up menus for accessing other disks and folders.

- The Finder is an application that you use to manage disks and start application programs.

- On Mac's running System 6.0 and earlier versions, the Finder keeps track of a disk's contents by creating and maintaining an invisible file called the DeskTop file.

- MultiFinder extends the Finder's capabilities by allowing you to run multiple programs simultaneously.

- The disk-based portion of the Mac's system software is stored in a folder named System Folder. A disk whose System Folder files are currently is use is called the startup disk.

- Under certain circumstances, you can switch from one startup disk to another, a process called switch-launching.

- The Clipboard lets you cut or copy information from one document for subsequent pasting into another document or another application.

- The Apple menu contains a list of desk accessories, small programs that are always available. Some simple programs that lack menu bars don't provide access to desk accessories.

- Color plays a small role in the overall Mac interface, but you can use utility programs such as Colorizer to add color to user interface elements such as menus and scroll bars.

- On Mac's running System 6.0 and later versions, you can choose from a number of digitally recorded beep sounds.

4

The Macintosh Family

All Macs provide the same user interface elements described in the last chapter, but in the hardware department, there are significant differences between each Mac model. If you're in the market for a new Mac, knowing these differences can help you select the Mac that's best for you.

In this chapter, we'll climb the Mac's family tree and spotlight the differences between each member. We'll look at:

- the current members of the Mac family—the Macintosh Plus, the Mac SE, and SE/30; and the Mac II, IIx, and IIcx

- factors to consider when shopping for a Mac

- the discontinued Macs—the 128K, 512K, and 512K Enhanced

- the upgrade options Apple offers to allow you to keep pace with the evolving Mac family.

If you're already familiar with the Mac family, you may want to just skim this chapter.

MAC CATEGORIES AND CAPABILITIES

Apple divides the Mac line into two categories: the *compact* Macs, those with the original, vertically oriented case and built-in screens; and the *modular* Macs, which lack built-in screens. We'll follow this terminology in this book, and we've organized this chapter according to these categories.

But size isn't the only thing that differs from one Mac to the next. There are more important differences, including:

Speed. Some Macs are faster than others, and are therefore better equipped to handle jobs that require extensive calculations. In the microcomputer world, processing speed is determined in part by the type of microprocessor used and its *clock rate*—the speed at which it runs. Clock rates are measured in millions of cycles per second, or *megahertz (MHz)*.

Expandability. Some Macs can accept a wider range of hardware add-ons than others.

Video features. Some Macs display only black and white pixels; in computer jargon, these Macs have *monochrome* displays. Other Macs can accommodate color displays and *gray-scale* displays, which show true shades of gray instead of simulated gray shades.

System 7.0 support. All Macs from the Plus on will be able to run System 7.0, but some Macs are better equipped than others to take full advantage of System 7.0's features.

ASSESSING YOUR NEEDS

Determining which Mac is best for you involves assessing your present and future computing needs and balancing those needs against your budget. You probably wouldn't buy a house or a car without first determining the features you need and don't need. By applying the same strategy to your computer purchases, you'll increase your chances of buying the hardware that will serve you now—and later.

Who Needs Speed?

In one sense, everyone does. No matter how you use or plan to use a Mac, chances are you'd prefer hardware that responds instantly to your commands instead of leaving you twiddling your thumbs. After all, no one likes to wait.

But speed costs. While you might want the speed of the fastest Macs—the SE/30 and the II family—you may not be able to justify the higher price tag. Some applications do demand the fastest Macs, but many tasks are well within the processing abilities of the Mac Plus and SE. If the jobs you plan to perform are in this second group, it might make sense to buy a Plus or SE and either pocket your savings or spend it on software or hardware add-ons.

To help you decide what level of speed you need, Table 4-1 lists some typical applications and divides them into three categories:

Speed is essential. These applications all but require the fastest Macs. You may be able to perform some of these jobs on slower Macs, but you're likely to spend a lot of time looking at the wristwatch pointer.

Speed is beneficial. These applications don't require the fastest Macs; if your budget is tight, you can use a Plus or SE without worrying about cobwebs forming between you and the screen. But a fast Mac's extra speed won't be wasted on these jobs; if your budget permits, consider springing for the extra horsepower.

Speed is not critical. With the applications in this category, the Mac's speed isn't a large variable; a slower Mac can handle the task almost as well or equally as well as a faster one.

These categories aren't carved in stone. Use them as starting points in deciding how much speed you need. (If you aren't familiar with the applications listed below, you'll find some brief definitions in Appendix A.)

Table 4-1: Speed considerations of common applications.

Speed is Essential	Computer-aided design and drafting (CAD)
	Animation
	Complex spreadsheet and statistical analysis
	Color illustration and image processing
	Professional-level digital audio recording
	Advanced database management (multiuser, large databases)
	File serving to large network
Speed is Beneficial	Desktop publishing
	Advanced word processing (for example, large documents with automatic indexing)
	Presentation graphics
	Database management
	Creating and using HyperCard stacks
	General-purpose spreadsheet analysis
	File serving to small network
	Gray-scale image processing
Speed is Not Critical	Telecommunications
	Simple word processing
	Monochrome drawing
	MIDI sequencing and patch editing
	Simple filing

Room to Grow

Not only is it important to assess your present computing needs, you also need to anticipate your future requirements. One way to anticipate those needs is to buy a Mac that offers *expansion slots*—internal connectors that accept plug-in *expansion cards*, also called *boards*, containing additional hardware.

Expansion slots allow Apple and other manufacturers to create specialized hardware that lets you tailor the Mac to your needs. Camera buffs will appreciate this benefit: Like a camera that accepts different lenses, flash units, and film holders, a computer that accepts expansion boards is more versatile and less prone to obsolescence.

Some of the boards expansion slots can accommodate include:

Accelerator boards. These boost the Mac's performance by replacing the Mac's original microprocessor with a faster one. Accelerator boards are available that make an SE much faster than a Mac IIcx, and that make a Mac II faster than many minicomputers.

Specialized video boards. These control *large-screen monitors* that show one or two full pages at once; color monitors that display images with photographic realism; or gray-scale monitors that display true shades of gray.

Coprocessor boards. These contain specialized microprocessors that work together with the Mac's CPU to improve performance with specialized tasks, such as recording and playing back sound.

Communications boards. These allow the Mac to communicate with other computers.

Data-acquisition boards. These allow the Mac to connect to laboratory equipment and accept and store incoming data.

The Mac SE and SE/30 each contain one expansion slot. The Mac II and IIx contain six, while the IIcx contains three. As we'll see later, the slots in the Mac II family are more sophisticated than those in the SE and SE/30.

Video Features

Do you need a color or gray-scale display or will a monochrome display suffice? And how large a screen do you need? The answers to these questions depend on how you'll use your Mac. Table 4-2 lists some common applications and the video hardware that's best for them.

Table 4-2: Matching video hardware to the application.

Color/Gray-scale	Monochrome	Large Screen
Image processing/scanning	Word processing	Word processing
Desktop publishing	Database management	Desktop publishing
Presentation graphics	Monochrome drawing	Advanced drawing and drafting
Animation	Music	
Color drawing (CAD, 3-D, illustration)	Spreadsheet and statistical analysis	
	Telecommunications	
	HyperCard work	
	Programming	

There are other factors you may want to consider. For example, monochrome displays tend to be sharper than color displays, and they're less expensive. Also, for technical reasons that we'll examine in Chapter 6, monochrome displays are generally much faster than color or gray-scale ones. And of course, many applications for which a gray-scale display is preferable are still possible on a monochrome display. You can use a monochrome monitor for color desktop publishing or gray-scale image processing—you just won't see colors or accurate shades of gray.

The Mac Plus and SE are monochrome Macs. The SE/30 contains a monochrome screen, but its expansion slot lets you attach an external color display. The Mac II family lacks built-in displays; you purchase a video card and external display. As we'll see later in this chapter, a Mac II, IIx, or IIcx can use more than one monitor at the same time. For one of these Macs, you might consider buying more than one monitor, and switching between them as you switch tasks.

Taking Full Advantage of System 7.0

System 7.0 will provide a virtual memory feature that will let the Mac treat a hard disk as an extension of RAM, allowing you to run programs that otherwise wouldn't fit into RAM—or to run more programs at the same time. System 7.0's virtual memory feature will work only on Macs containing special *paged memory management* hardware. Those Macs include the SE/30, IIx, IIcx, and, with the addition of a single chip, the Mac II. The Plus and the SE will not support paged memory, although they'll still be able to run System 7.0 and take advantage of its other enhancements.

What does this mean to you? If you anticipate running many programs simultaneously using MultiFinder, you might want to consider a Mac that will support virtual memory. But don't base a buying decision on this factor alone. After all, if you add a few megabytes of RAM to a Plus or SE, it, too, will be able to accommodate several programs simultaneously.

(We'll look at virtual memory and paged memory concepts again in Chapter 13.)

THE MAC FAMILY

Now let's look at each member of the Mac family. First, we'll cover the common ground—the features and expansion connectors that all currently manufactured Macs provide, and then we'll look at what makes each machine unique.

The Common Ground

All Macs provide some common features:

- All include a minimum of one megabyte of RAM. Some Macs are available in more powerful and more expensive configurations that include more RAM. You can expand the RAM in any Mac using small, plug-in boards called *SIMMs*, short for *single in-line memory modules*. (Chapter 13 contains more information on RAM chips and SIMMs.)

- All include two serial ports, the *printer port* and the *modem port*. You can attach many types of serial add-ons to these ports, but generally, you use the printer port to attach the Mac to an Apple ImageWriter printer or to a network, and you use the modem port to attach an external *telephone modem*, which lets the Mac communicate with other computers over the phone lines.

- All include a fast expansion connector for attaching external hard disks, scanners, and other add-ons. This port is based on an expansion standard called the *Small Computer System Interface*, or *SCSI* (commonly pronounced *scuzzy*). The SCSI port gives all Macs a degree of hardware expandability.

- All contain at least one internal floppy disk drive. Some Macs can accommodate two internal floppy drives, and some also provide a port for an external drive. Also, the floppy drives on some Mac models store much more than those of other models.

Introducing SCSI

Before looking at the members of the compact Mac family, let's take a brief look at the SCSI port and its benefits.

A SCSI port attains its superior performance by transferring data in parallel, eight bits at a time. The Mac's serial modem and printer ports are limited to a maximum speed of roughly 29,000 bytes per second; the SCSI port can transfer more than 320,000 bytes per second. Which port would you rather attach a hard disk to?

Another of SCSI's benefits is that it lets you connect several add-ons to one port using a wiring technique called *daisy-chaining*. Every SCSI device has two connectors. You can attach two SCSI devices to the Mac by plugging the first device into the Mac's SCSI port, and then attaching the second device to the first. To add a third, you plug it into the second. You can continue daisy-chaining devices in this way until the total length of all the SCSI cables reaches 20 feet. SCSI interfaces can't reliably transmit data over cable distances longer than that.

We'll take a closer look at how SCSI works and at how to connect SCSI devices in Chapter 14.

The Compact Macs

Now that we've covered the common ground, let's look at what makes each Mac unique. First, we'll start with the compact Macs—the Plus, SE, and SE/30.

The Macintosh Plus

The Mac Plus was an exciting machine when it debuted in April 1986. In terms of technological sparkle, the Plus has since been overshadowed by newer Macs. But it remains a workhorse, able to run nearly all Mac software. And the Plus is the least expensive Mac; it's often discounted as low as $1200.

The Plus contains the same 68000 processor as the original Macs, and it runs at the same clock rate—8MHz. The Plus is significantly faster than the Macs it succeeded, however, thanks largely to its extra RAM and its improved ROM-based system software.

The Plus' biggest limitation is that it lacks internal expansion slots, eliminating many categories of expansion. Some accelerator boards and internal hard disks are available for the Plus, but they must be attached directly to the 68000 using a special clip. This back-door expansion technique can be less reliable than using expansion slots. And because the Plus wasn't designed to accommodate internal add-ons, its power supply may be stressed and overheated, even if you add a fan. The bottom line is that the Plus isn't the machine to buy if hardware flexibility is important.

But not everyone needs an accelerator board or large-screen display. And many users prefer external hard disks; an external hard disk is easy to move from one Mac to another, and if it breaks, you don't have to part with your Mac while it's in the shop. If your needs are simple, a Plus may be ideal for you. What's more, the Mac Plus has held its value well. If you do outgrow one, you'll probably be able to sell it for a price that will help pay for your next Mac.

The Macintosh SE

Introduced in March 1987, the SE (short for "system expansion") was the first Mac in the original-sized case to offer a built-in expansion slot for accepting add-on boards. The SE is a good choice if your needs are simple now, but you want the flexibility to add more sophisticated hardware later.

The SE uses the same 68000 process as the Plus, and it runs at the same 8MHz clock rate. But the SE houses 256K of ROM, versus the Plus' 128K. Apple used the extra space in the 256K ROMs to cast in stone (more accurately, silicon) certain routines and elements of the Mac's user interface that, in the Plus, are loaded into RAM at start-up time. Apple also refined the routines that control the SE's SCSI port, allowing the SE to transfer data via SCSI roughly twice as fast as the Plus. This improvement makes the SE much faster than the Plus when accessing a hard disk. Hard disk accesses aside, the SE is about 20 percent faster than a Plus.

In the mass-storage department, the base-model SE includes two internal 800K floppy drives, providing a total of 1.6 megabytes of floppy disk space. The SE also has a connector for an external drive, making it the only Mac that can have three floppy drives for a total of 2.4 megabytes of floppy disk storage.

Figure 4-1: The Macintosh SE. (*photo courtesy of Apple Computer*)

The SE is also available with one floppy drive and a variety of Apple internal hard disks. Prior to the SE's release, the only internal hard disks you could buy for a Mac were made by other manufacturers; General Computer's HyperDrive was popular (if sometimes quirky) in its day. You can also buy a base-model SE and replace its second floppy drive with an internal hard disk from a different manufacturer. And because the SE has a SCSI connector, it can connect to external hard disks, too.

Its faster performance and ability to house two disk drives are significant, but the most important improvement in the SE is its expandability. The machine contains one 96-pin expansion slot into which you can plug add-on boards. In order to accommodate the power requirements of two disk drives and possibly an expansion board, Apple gave the SE a new, beefed-up power supply and a fan.

The SE provides another means for expansion called the *Apple Desktop Bus*, or *ADB*. ABD is a relatively low-speed bus designed primarily for input devices like the keyboard and mouse. (Such devices don't require blazing transmission speeds because even their slow speeds can keep up with our typing or mouse movements.) Apple created the bus so that it would have a consistent hardware interface for input devices that it could use on all its computers. With the exception of the Plus, all other currently manufactured Macs use ADB ports, as does the Apple IIGS. (Apple's LaserWriter IINT and NTX laser printers also have ADB ports that can attach to special high-capacity paper feeders.)

Like SCSI, the ADB allows you to daisy-chain hardware add-ons, plugging one into the next, and the first into the Mac itself. The SE's rear panel contains two ADB ports. You can plug the mouse into one and the keyboard into the other, or you can plug the keyboard into one, and the mouse into the keyboard's second ADB connector. (Many SE users have reported smoother mouse movements when the mouse is connected directly to the Mac rather than to the keyboard's ADB port, but we've never noticed a significant difference.) You can attach up to 16 devices to ADB. We'll look at how ADB operates in Chapter 14.

While the SE has the same basic dimensions of earlier Macs, the case itself is different. The ventilation slots on the top of the case are gone, probably because people often defeated their purpose on earlier Macs by placing things on them. The fan and new ventilation slots on the front of the machine, below the screen, make up the difference. The Mac's speaker is behind the front panel slots, moved there from the left side of the machine to improve sound quality and projection.

The Mac SE/30

Introduced in January 1989, the SE/30 is a powerful but petite package that combines the portability of the compact Macs with the speed and color capabilities of the Mac IIx. In fact, the SE/30 has so much in common with the IIx that some industry jokesters dubbed it the "SEx" shortly after its release.

The SE/30 contains Motorola's 68030 microprocessor and 68882 *math coprocessor*, a special microprocessor whose sole purpose is to perform math calculations. (We'll look at math coprocessors in Chapter 13.) These are the same two chips that power the modular Macintosh IIx and IIcx. Both chips run at the same 16MHz clock rate that the IIx and IIcx use. The SE/30 is slightly faster than a Mac II, but slightly slower than a IIx or IIcx.

In the memory department, the SE/30's logic board contains eight SIMM sockets, versus the SE's four. Its extra SIMM sockets allows the SE/30 to accommodate a maximum of 8MB of RAM using 1MB SIMMs. Apple designed the SE/30's SIMM sockets to accommodate high-density, 4MB SIMMs. When they become available, the SE/30 will be able to accommodate up to 32MB of RAM.

As for ROM, the SE/30 contains 256K of ROM, mounted on a SIMM as in the IIx. The ROMs are similar to those of a Mac IIx, containing *Color QuickDraw* software that allows an SE/30 to use an external color monitor.

For mass storage, the SE/30 contains Apple's *FDHD* (*floppy drive high density*) floppy disk drive, which provides 1.44MB of storage space—nearly twice the 800K capacity of previous Mac floppies. When used with the Apple File Exchange program (which accompanies the Mac), the FDHD drive can also access disks created by MS-DOS, OS/2, and *ProDOS*, an Apple II operating system. Unlike the standard Mac SE, however, the SE/30 cannot accommodate a second internal floppy disk drive. There simply isn't enough room in its case. You can attach an external floppy drive, however.

The SE/30 is available with a 40MB or 80MB internal hard disk. The 80MB configuration includes 4MB of RAM.

Like the SE, the SE/30 provides one expansion slot. The slot itself, however, differs from the SE's. The SE/30's 030 Direct Slot, as Apple calls it, contains 120 pins, versus the 96 pins of the SE's slot. The *030 Direct Slot* provides access to the 68030's 32-bit data pathways and all 68030 signals. These extra signal lines contribute to the SE/30's ability to control an external color monitor. (We'll explore the concepts of data pathways and microprocessor signals in Chapter 13.)

Compact Mac Summary

Table 4-3 lists the specifications of the compact Mac line.

Table 4-3: Compact Mac family specifications.

	Plus	SE	SE/30
Processor	68000	68000	68030
Memory Management Unit	none	none	in CPU
Math coprocessor	none	none	68882
Clock speed	8MHz	8MHz	16MHz
Maximum RAM with 1MB SIMMs	4MB	4MB	8MB
ROM size	128K	256K	256K
ROM configuration	socketed	socketed	SIMMs
Expansion slots	none	one 96-pin	one 120-pin
Internal floppy drives	one	two	one
External floppy drive port	yes	yes	yes
Supports FDHD floppy drive	no	yes[1]	yes
Video display	internal; 9-in. b&w	internal; 9-in. b&w	internal; 9-in. b&w
Supports color/gray monitors	no	no	yes
Sound output	mono	mono	stereo
Power requirements	105-125VAC; 50–60Hz	(1)	(1)
Dimensions (inches)	13.6x9.6x10.9	13.6x9.6x10.9	13.6x9.6x10.09
Footprint (square inches)	104.6	104.6	104.6
Weight (pounds)	16.5	17–21	19.5

(1) Self-adjusting world-wide power supply.

[1] As of August 1, 1989. An FDHD upgrade will be available for older SEs.

The Modular Macs

If expandability is more important to you than portability, consider a modular Mac—the Mac II, IIx, or IIcx.

The Common Ground

Like all compact Macs, all modular Macs have two serial connectors and one SCSI connector. And like the SE and SE/30, all modular Macs provide two ADB ports. But the modular Macs part company with their compact cousins in two key areas:

They're more expandable. The members of the Mac II family contain not one expansion slot, but three or six (depending on the model). The slots use an Apple variation of a hardware standard called *NuBus*, which was created by Texas Instruments, AT&T, MIT, and others, under the auspices of the Institute of Electrical and Electronic Engineers (IEEE). We'll explore NuBus in Chapter 13; for now, it's enough to say that the NuBus standard dictates how signals travel from the Mac II's CPU to the NuBus expansion boards you've installed. The NuBus standard also spells out the basic physical characteristics of a NuBus board, such as the position and number of pins on its connectors.

They lack built-in video screens. With a modular Mac, you purchase a plug-in video board and display combination from Apple or another hardware manufacturer. This flexibility lets you tailor the machine to your display requirements.

Being able to choose your own display system by adding a video board is nothing new; Apple II users have done it for years, as have IBM PC and AT users. But what *is* new about the Mac II's display talents is that it can control several screens *at once*, even ones of different sizes and color capabilities. You can drag a window from one screen to another, or even resize a window so that it spans several screens (see Figure 4-2). Several of the Mac II's managers work together with Color QuickDraw to make these remarkable feats possible.

The Macintosh II

The Mac II, also introduced in March 1987, was a Mac of many firsts. It was the first Mac to use a microprocessor other than the 68000, the first to offer color capabilities, the first to work with a variety of monitors, and the first to offer a large number of internal expansion slots. And, as one glance reveals, the Mac II was the first Mac to depart from the original, everything-in-one-box case design. The Mac II, shown in Figure 4-3, was the first modular Mac.

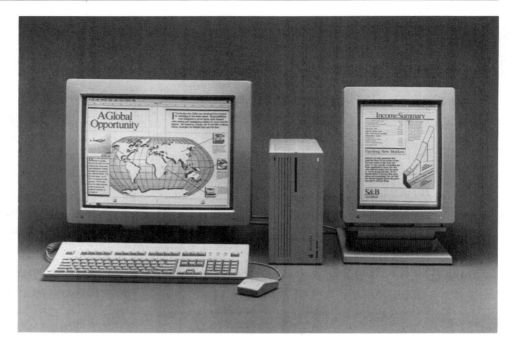

Figure 4-2: A Mac IIcx with multiple displays. (*photo courtesy of Apple Computer*)

Under the Mac II's hood are a Motorola 68020 and 68881 math coprocessor. Both chips run at a 16MHz clock rate. But because the 68020 and 68881 aren't as fast as the newer 68030 and 68882, the Mac II is slightly slower than the SE/30, IIx, and IIcx.

In its least-expensive configuration, the Mac II contains one megabyte of RAM. Its main system board has sockets that accept SIMMs similar (but not identical) to those of a Mac Plus or SE. If you use 256KB SIMMs (currently the most popular kind, but quickly being supplanted by higher-capacity SIMMs), you can expand the II's memory to up to two megabytes. When equipped with SIMMs containing 1MB RAM chips, a Mac II can house up to eight megabytes of RAM on its system board. When RAM chips with even higher capacities become available in the early 1990s, a Mac II may be able to house up to 128 *megabytes* on its system board. (You can also plug additional memory boards into the Mac II's NuBus expansion slots.)

As for mass storage, the Mac II lacks a connector for an external floppy disk, but it does have room for two internal 800K floppy disk drives and an internal hard disk. The base model Mac II, however, comes with only one floppy disk drive—not a particularly copious configuration. Most users opt for a machine equipped with one of Apple's 20-, 40-, or 80-megabyte hard disks. Numerous other hardware manufacturers also offer internal hard disks for the II, and some of their drives are faster and store more than Apple's. You can also attach an external hard disk to the Mac II's SCSI port.

The Mac II was a revolutionary Mac when it was introduced, but today, it's showing its age a bit. The II is slightly slower than the IIx and IIcx, but more important, it lacks a key chip needed to support System 7.0 virtual memory feature. You can add that chip, a Motorola 68851 *paged memory-management unit (PMMU)*, after you purchase your II, but it costs several hundred dollars.

Figure 4-3: The Mac II, the first modular Mac. (*photo courtesy of Apple Computer*)

If you haven't yet bought a Mac and you're in the market for a fast one, consider a IIx or IIcx instead of a II. But if you own a Mac II, don't feel obligated to sell it and buy a IIx or IIcx instead. The performance differences between a II and its successors are minor. And when equipped with a PMMU chip, a II can take full advantage of System 7.0.

The Macintosh IIx

In September 1988, Apple introduced the Mac IIx. The IIx contains the successor to the 68020, Motorola's 68030. The 68030 helps make the IIx roughly 15 percent faster than the II. More important, the 68030 contains built-in paged memory management hardware, which will support System 7.0's virtual memory feature. The IIx also contains a newer and faster math coprocessor, the 68882.

The IIx includes 4MB of RAM as standard equipment. Like the Mac II, you can expand the IIx's memory to 8MB using 1MB SIMMs, to 32MB using 4MB SIMMs, and to far more than that using NuBus memory boards. Also like the II, the IIx contains 256K of ROM. However, the ROMs themselves are slightly different. Physically, they're mounted on SIMMs for easy replacement. Internally, the ROMs contain new software that supports the IIx's FDHD floppy disk drive.

If there's a drawback to the Mac II and IIx, it's that all their horsepower and flexibility don't fit in a petite package. The II and IIx are big microcomputers; if they had legs, they'd make fine end tables. The girth of these machines matches that of an IBM AT, the former industry leader when it came to devouring desk space. The Mac II and IIx are larger than all of IBM's current microcomputers, except the PS/2 Models 60 and 80—which, unlike the II and IIx, are designed to stand upright on the floor. The position of the ventilation slots in the II and IIx prohibit floor-standing operation without a special stand (described in Chapter 9).

The Macintosh IIcx

You want NuBus slots but you don't want to give up half your desk to get them? Meet the Mac IIcx, the smallest member of the Mac II family, shown in Figure 4-4. Introduced in March 1989, the IIcx straddles the fence between the large Mac IIs and the compact Macs. It provides the performance and expandability of the former, and the small footprint of the latter.

The IIcx base configuration includes 1MB of RAM; a 4MB configuration is also available. The IIcx logic board contains eight SIMM slots, and thus, can house up to 8MB of RAM using 1MB SIMMs. When 4MB SIMMs become widely available, the IIcx will be able to accommodate 32MB of RAM.

The IIcx uses the same 256K ROM chips as the SE/30 and IIx, but the chips are soldered to the logic board, rather than mounted on SIMMs, as they are in the SE/30 and IIx. The IIcx has a separate set of SIMM slots to accommodate future ROM upgrades.

Figure 4-4: The Macintosh IIcx. (*photo courtesy of Apple Computer*)

Like the IIx and SE/30, the IIcx contains a 1.44MB FDHD high-density floppy drive. Like the SE/30, the IIcx has room for only one floppy drive, but it does offer a floppy drive connector for attaching an external drive. As for internal expansion, the IIcx provides three NuBus slots—half the number the Mac II and IIx provide, but more than enough for most users.

The IIcx offers several interesting features that its predecessors lack:

- Its power switch can be locked in the "on" position, which causes the machine to automatically restart itself in the event of a power failure. This feature is valuable for IIcxs that will be used as network file servers described in Chapter 12.

- All critical ventilation slots are located on the front and back of the machine, allowing you to position the computer on its side without a special stand.

- The computer's internal construction is highly modular. Pop the lid, and you can disassemble the computer into its five major components—logic board, disk chassis, power supply, fan, and speaker—within minutes. This modular construction style is similar to that of IBM's PS/2 series of computers, and contrasts sharply with the internal layout of the large Mac IIs, which often require you to remove the hard disk or other internal components to perform simple jobs such as installing a RAM upgrade.

Modular Mac Summary

Table 4-4 summarizes the specifications of the currently available members of the modular Mac family.

Table 4-4: Modular Mac family specifications.

	II	IIx	IIcx
Processor	68020	68030	68030
Memory Management Unit	optional	in CPU	in CPU
Math coprocessor	68881	68882	68882
Clock speed	16MHz	16MHz	16MHz
Maximum RAM with 1MB SIMMs	8MB	8MB	8MB
ROM size	256K	256K	256K
ROM configuration	socketed	SIMMs	soldered; replaceable
Expansion slots	6 NuBus	6 NuBus	3 NuBus
Maximum internal floppies	two	two	one
External floppy drive port	no	no	yes
Supports FDHD floppy drive	no	yes	yes
Video display	external	external	external
Supports color/gray monitors	yes	yes	yes
Sound output	stereo	stereo	stereo
Power requirements	(1)	(1)	(1)
Dimensions (inches)	5.5x18.7x14.4	5.5x18.7x14	5.5x11.9x14.4
Footprint (square inches)	269.3	269.3	171.4 or 79.2[2]
Weight (pounds)	16.5	17–21	19.5

(1) Self-adjusting worldwide power supply.

[2] Depending on horizontal or vertical orientation.

Mac Keyboards

The Mac's keyboards have evolved along with the machines they're attached to. The Mac Plus keyboard, shown in Figure 4-5, was the first Mac keyboard to include arrow keys and a calculator-like *number keypad* for quick entry of figures. The arrow keys allow you to move the blinking insertion point in a word processor or a text-entry box. Arrow keys are standard equipment on most computers, but Steve Jobs felt that cursor-movement should be performed with the mouse, and vetoed them for the first Mac. User outcry, however, made Apple see the error of its ways.

Figure 4-5: The Mac Plus keyboard. (*photo courtesy of Apple Computer*)

The ADB Keyboards

When Apple introduced the SE and II in 1986, it also introduced two new keyboards, all of which use the Apple Desktop Bus. Both keyboards, shown in Figure 4-6, have a very different key design that eliminates the "echo" that annoyed many users of the old keyboards. (With the old keyboards, each keystroke seemed to reverberate within the keyboard.) On the negative side, the keys on the new keyboards have a relatively short travel—the distance the key moves when you press it—that can lead to hand fatigue. (We speak from experience.) If it bothers you, you can buy an alternative keyboard such as Datadesk's Mac-101.

Figure 4-6: The ADB keyboards: the standard Apple Keyboard (*top*) and the Apple Extended Keyboard (*bottom*). (*photos courtesy of Apple Computer*)

The layout of the standard Apple Keyboard is similar to that of the Mac Plus keyboard. The Apple Extended Keyboard has 105 keys. The extended keyboard requires more desktop real estate, but it gives a great deal in return, including:

- A row of 15 horizontally arranged *function keys*. Some programs use function keys as shortcut keys for menu commands or other functions that would normally require a trip to the mouse. You can also use keyboard-enhancement software to "program" the function keys to perform certain tasks. Such programs (described in Chapter 10) allow you to tailor the function keys to the tasks you perform most often.

- An arrow-key cluster that's arranged more logically than that of the standard Apple Keyboard

- Navigation keys labeled Page Up, Page Down, Home, and End. Most word processors let you use these keys to quickly move the blinking insertion point or scroll through documents without having to use the mouse.

- Two sets of Control, Option, and Command keys, one on either side of the space bar. The Control keys are most often used with telecommunications programs; we looked at the role of the Option and Command keys in the previous chapter.

- A layout identical to that of the IBM extended keyboard that ships with IBM's Personal System/2 series of computers. You'll find this layout useful if you equip your Mac with an *MS-DOS coprocessor* board such as Orange Micro's Mac286, which allows the Mac to run MS-DOS and IBM PC software.

The Discontinued Macs

The earliest Macs—the 128K, 512K, and 512K Enhanced—are no longer made, but they often show up in classified ads and college dorm bulletin boards. What are their limitations? Should you buy a used one? We'll look at these issues in this section.

The 128K Macintosh

The original Mac was the machine that simultaneously convinced the computer world of two things: first, that graphics-and-mouse-based user interfaces represented the future of microcomputing; and second, that such interfaces needed far more memory and faster disks than the Mac provided.

These days, the original Mac is called the "128K Mac" in honor of the paltry amount of RAM it contained. In the early 1980s, 128K of RAM was quite a bit—no pun intended. The IBM PC shipped with 64K in 1981, and people looked at *that* as a vast expanse. But the Mac's graphical user interface demanded more. Apple worked around the constraints by creating system software routines that would allow programmers to *segment* applications—to divide a program into chunks that could be loaded into and out of memory as necessary. Segmentation allowed the 128K Mac to run some relatively sophisticated programs, but at a snail's pace; loading program segments means making disk accesses, and the Mac's disk drive was no speed demon. (The 128K Mac contained one floppy disk drive capable of storing 400K. An external 400K floppy drive was also available.)

Although the 128K Mac lacked a SCSI port, some brave hardware manufacturers introduced hard disks for the machine. The hard disks were faster than floppies and stored more, but had problems of their own. Because the 128K Mac wasn't designed with hard disks in mind, you couldn't start it directly from the hard disk—you had to "jump start" it with a floppy, and then switch to the hard disk. Another problem was that the original *Macintosh File System* (*MFS*) could only keep track of only about 128 files on one disk—and a hard disk can hold thousands. (The Hierarchical Filing System described in the last chapter didn't appear until the Plus was introduced.) Most hard disks worked around this problem by creating software that would allow you to *partition* the hard disk—divide its capacity into a number of smaller chunks, each of which the Mac could treat as a separate disk.

If you did suffer through using a hard disk with the 128K Mac, you attached it to the modem port. But because serial ports are slower than parallel ones, the first Mac hard disks were saddled with a performance-crippling bottleneck in addition to their other handicaps.

The Macintosh 512K

Apple released the 512K Mac—the Fat Mac, as it was often called—in November of 1984, a few months ahead of schedule, but not a moment too soon. The 512K Mac offered four times the RAM of the first Mac. This larger workspace meant that programs didn't have to rely so heavily on the Mac's segment-loading features. More of the application could reside in memory at once, and as a result, the Mac ran faster.

A more significant benefit came with the release of Andy Hertzfeld's Switcher, a program that allowed you to run more than one application and switch between them with a keystroke. A 512K Mac running Switcher could run two or three applications at once, depending on their size. Switcher was useful (if quirky) in its day; it's since been relegated to the history books by MultiFinder.

In the ROM and mass storage department, the Fat Mac didn't offer any improvements. However, its extra memory did make possible a storage related trick. Using special software, you could set aside some memory as a RAM disk. The software would trick the Mac into thinking that part of its memory was a disk that could hold files just as a real disk did. Many people used RAM disks to hold their System folders and one or two programs (there wasn't room for more than that). Because the Mac accessed memory far faster than even a hard disk, a RAM disk boosted the Mac's performance dramatically. It also allowed people who didn't have a second floppy drive to avoid the dreaded disk swap. RAM disks are still useful; we'll look at them again in Chapter 9.

The Macintosh 512K Enhanced

When Apple introduced the Plus, it also introduced a lesser-known Mac that walked the line between the 512K and the Plus: the 512K Enhanced. This Mac retained the 512K Mac's memory configuration, offering 512K of RAM with none of the RAM-expansion flexibility of the SIMMs used by the Mac Plus. But unlike the 512K Mac, the 512K Enhanced contained the same 128K ROMs as the Mac Plus, giving it the same performance benefits and the new HFS disk-management software. Also like the Plus, the 512K Enhanced included an 800K floppy disk drive.

The 512K Enhanced lacked the Plus' SCSI port, prohibiting it from exploiting the new generation of SCSI hard disks and other add-ons. Several hardware companies, however, quickly introduced SCSI port kits that allowed you to add a SCSI port yourself. Such kits are still available from firms such as Dove Computer.

The 512K Enhanced was a stepping stone to the Plus. You could buy one, and then upgrade to a Plus later for $799. If you had an unenhanced Mac 512K, you could "enhance" it for $299, and still retain the option to boost it to a Plus later. Apple no longer manufactures the 512K Enhanced, although Apple's 512K Enhanced upgrade kit may still be available at some dealers.

Should You Buy a Discontinued Mac?

We don't recommend buying a used 128K Mac. None of today's popular programs will run within its cramped confines. Even if you found one for a few hundred dollars, you would spend almost $1000 upgrading it to a Plus—and at that price, you can almost buy a brand-new Mac Plus.

Nor do we recommend buying a used 512K Mac, especially if you plan to use it on a network with other Macs. As we'll see in Chapter 8, you can encounter problems when trying to share a laser printer between a 512K Mac and a newer model.

Of the discontinued Macs, the 512K Enhanced is the least obsolete. Because it has the identical ROMs of the Mac Plus, it's able to run many of today's application programs—provided they'll fit within its limited RAM. Add a non-Apple SCSI port and a memory upgrade, and you'll have the equivalent of a Plus. The down side is that, after you've added these items, you may have spent more than a new Plus costs.

In the end, approach the purchase of a discontinued Mac carefully. Be sure the hardware is good condition (look for obvious signs of abuse, such as scratches or cracks in the case). And take a close look at your needs. If the price is right and your needs are simple, a discontinued Mac may serve you well. But in most situations, opt for a new model instead.

Macintosh Upgrades

Apple offers numerous upgrade kits that allow you to keep pace with the Mac family's advancing technology. In this section, we'll describe the upgrades available as of summer 1989. All of the following upgrades require dealer installation, and require you to trade in existing components (such as logic boards or floppy disk drives).

Upgrades for the 128K and 512K Macs

If you have a 128K or 512K Mac, you can upgrade it to a Mac Plus using the following three upgrades:

- Macintosh Plus Disk Drive Kit. Includes an 800K floppy disk drive, 128K ROM chips, and Macintosh Plus System Tools Disk. If you purchase only this kit and install it in a 512K Mac, you'll have a 512K Enhanced.

- Macintosh Plus Logic Board Kit. Includes a Mac Plus logic board with 1MB of RAM and a new back panel to accommodate the Mac Plus' rear-panel connectors. If you purchase this kit, you must also purchase the disk drive kit described above.

- Macintosh Plus Keyboard Kit. Includes the Mac Plus keyboard.

Upgrades for the Mac SE

You can upgrade a Mac SE to an SE/30 using the following two upgrades:

- Macintosh SE/30 Logic Board Kit. Includes SE/30 logic board and chassis.

- FDHD Upgrade Kit. Includes 1.44MB high-density internal floppy disk drive.

Upgrades for the Mac II

You can upgrade a Mac II to a Mac IIx using the following two upgrade kits:

- Macintosh IIx Logic Board Upgrade Kit. Includes IIx logic board.

- FDHD Upgrade Kit. Includes 1.44MB high-density internal floppy drive and SWIM disk-controller chip.

5

System Folder Details

By storing some of the Mac's system software on disk, Apple can add features, fix bugs, and improve performance—without requiring users to buy new ROM chips. The Mac's disk-based system software has seen many revisions. A new Mac model often brings a new version of the system, one that can take advantage of the new Mac's features while retaining compatibility with other Macs. Apple may also release a revised system when introducing a new hardware add-on or software product.

Knowing what goes on in the System Folder can help you diagnose problems, fine-tune your system for better performance, use disk space more efficiently, and remain up to date with the latest system software. In this chapter, we'll open the System Folder and examine its contents. We'll look at:

- Apple's system version-numbering scheme

- the purpose of each file in the System Folder

- the role printer drivers play in the Macintosh

- the Control Panel and how it operates

- Init files and their role

- the software Apple provides for updating your System Folder

- the key differences between recent system software releases.

Two points before we start: The information in this chapter is current through System version 6.0.3. As we've mentioned before, System 7.0 will add significant new features to the Mac's system software.

Second, throughout this chapter and this book, you'll sometimes see the word *system* appearing with an initial capital letter ("System"), and sometimes in all lowercase letters. That isn't a raging inconsistency. The phrase "the Mac's *system* files" refers to all of the files in the System Folder. By contrast, the phrase "the System file" refers to the one file named System.

SYSTEM VERSION NUMBERING

Like all software developers, Apple uses version numbers to differentiate between each generation of its software. You can find out which version of the system software your Mac has in two ways:

• By choosing About the Finder from the Apple menu when the Finder or MultiFinder is active. This opens a window listing one or more version numbers. In older versions of the Mac system (such as those used by 512K Macs), this window lists the version number of the Finder only. In more recent versions, it reports the version numbers of both the Finder and System, as shown in Figure 5-1.

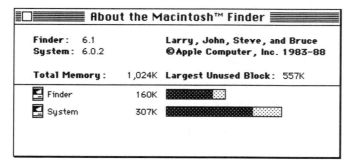

Figure 5-1: The About the Finder window: an older version (*top*) and a recent version (*bottom*).

- By selecting the files named System and Finder in the System Folder and then choosing Get Info from the Finder's File menu. As Figure 5-2 shows, the version numbers appear in different places, depending on which version of the system you're using. In older versions, they appear as Get Info comments. In recent versions, they appear in the upper portion of the Get Info window. (In the oldest versions of the system, version numbers may not appear at all.)

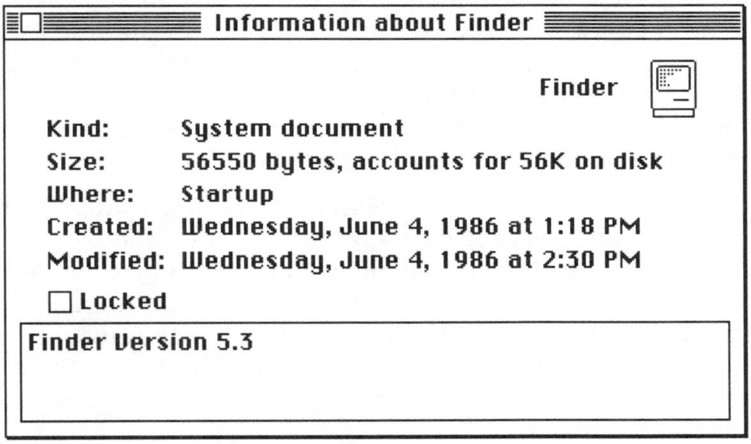

```
▤▢▦▦▦▦▦ Information about Finder ▦▦▦▦▦▦

                                          Finder    ▣

    Kind:     System document
    Size:     56550 bytes, accounts for 56K on disk
    Where:    Startup
    Created:  Wednesday, June 4, 1986 at 1:18 PM
    Modified: Wednesday, June 4, 1986 at 2:30 PM

    □ Locked
 ────────────────────────────────────────────────
 Finder Version 5.3


```

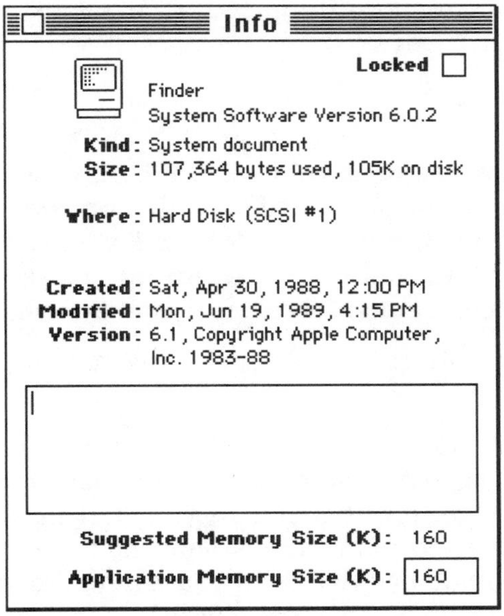

```
▤▢▦▦▦▦▦▦▦ Info ▦▦▦▦▦▦▦▦

      ▣                      Locked □
           Finder
           System Software Version 6.0.2
      Kind: System document
      Size: 107,364 bytes used, 105K on disk

     Where: Hard Disk (SCSI #1)


   Created: Sat, Apr 30, 1988, 12:00 PM
  Modified: Mon, Jun 19, 1989, 4:15 PM
   Version: 6.1, Copyright Apple Computer,
            Inc. 1983–88
 ┌──────────────────────────────────┐
 │ |                                │
 │                                  │
 │                                  │
 │                                  │
 └──────────────────────────────────┘
     Suggested Memory Size (K):  160
   Application Memory Size (K): │ 160 │
```

Figure 5-2: Version numbers in Get Info windows: an older version (*top*) and a recent version (*bottom*).

As you can see, the version numbering scheme uses a number with a decimal portion. When Apple makes a major revision to the system, the number to the left of the decimal point increases. When Apple makes minor changes or fixes bugs, the number to the right of the decimal point increases. If a new release contains very minor changes (often bug fixes), you might find two decimal points, as in 6.0.3.

Another potentially confusing point is that all the files in the System Folder may not have the same version number. Apple may make major revisions to some files, but no changes to others. To avoid confusing people with a slew of different version numbers, Apple groups the files under the umbrella of a "system tools" or "system update" number. For example, the "System Tools 5.0" package included Finder 6.0, MultiFinder 1.0, and System 4.2. "System Update 6.0" included Finder 6.1, MultiFinder 6.0, and System 6.0.

Although System Tools or System Update numbers represent Apple's official numbering scheme, many users and developers still refer to system versions in "System/Finder" style, as in "this program requires System 4.2/Finder 5.0." When you see such a phrase, it simply means you need the system update that contained version 4.2 of the System file and version 5.0 of the Finder file. You might also encounter the phrase "requires System 4.x or later." That simply means you need any System version beginning with 4 (the decimal doesn't matter) or any greater number.

Now that we've demystified system version numbering, let's look at the individual files in the System Folder.

THE PRIMARY PLAYERS

The exact number of files inside your System Folder depends on which Mac you have, on the hardware you've attached to it, and on which version of the system you're using. With version 6.0.3, the average System Folder contains about a dozen files. Of these, three files are the key players in the disk-based portion of the Mac's operating system: Finder, MultiFinder, and System.

Finder. This file, as you can probably guess, holds the software that forms the Mac's Finder.

MultiFinder. This file, present in System Tools 5.0 and later versions, contains the software that allows the Mac to run more than one program at once. The Finder and MultiFinder files work together. When you start up under MultiFinder, the MultiFinder file *extends* the Finder to provide the capability of running more than one program simultaneously. So, if you always use Multi-Finder, don't assume you can free up some disk space by throwing away the Finder file; if you do, you won't be able to start your Mac from that disk. You can, however, perform the opposite: if you never use MultiFinder, you can throw away its file and others (see Chapter 9 for details).

System. The Finder and MultiFinder files are your link to the file named System. The System file performs a dual role, as shown in Figure 5–3. It contains portions of the system software that aren't in ROM, and it contains *system resources* such as fonts and desk accessories. These resources are generally available to all applications. When you start a program—a word processor, for example—the program checks the resource area of the System file to see which fonts are available, and then lists those fonts in its Font menu. Similarly, when you start up the Mac, the Finder checks the System file for desk accessories, and lists each one in the Apple menu. As we'll describe in Chapter 7, you can install and remove fonts and desk accessories using Apple's Font/DA Mover program.

System

System software (patches, RAM-based routines)	Resources (fonts, FKEYs, desk accessories)

Figure 5-3: A block diagram of the System file's contents.

The System file can also accommodate a cousin to the desk accessory, the *function key*, or *FKEY*. FKEYs, like desk accessories, are small programs that are generally available in any application. Unlike desk accessories, FKEYs aren't listed in the Apple menu. To run an FKEY, you type a Command-Shift keyboard sequence. The standard Mac System file includes four FKEYs:

- Command-Shift-1 and Command-Shift-2 eject the disk in the internal or external floppy disk, respectively. (On a two-floppy Mac SE, Command-Shift-1 ejects the disk in the lower drive and Command-Shift-2 jettisons the disk in the upper one; on a two-floppy Mac II or IIx, Command-Shift-1 ejects the disk from the left-hand drive and Command-Shift-2 ejects the disk from the right-hand one.)

- Command-Shift-3 creates a screen *snapshot*, a file of whatever is displayed on the screen when you press the key sequence. We'll look at snapshot files in Chapter 9.

- Command-Shift-4 prints the contents of the active window on an ImageWriter printer. If you press the Caps Lock key and then press Command-Shift-4, the FKEY prints the contents of the entire screen.

A third type of System file resource, the *driver*, isn't as visible as a font, a desk accessory, or an FKEY, but is important nonetheless. Drivers are routines that allow the Mac to access or control external devices. One important driver in the System file works with the Mac's Print Manager to control printers.

The Printer Drivers

The driver mentioned above is a low-level one; it communicates with the Mac's Print Manager, which communicates with *printer resource files*, more commonly called *printer drivers*. As Figure 5-4 shows, printer drivers act as intermediaries between a program that has something to print and the printer itself. The driver translates the commands that describe a document's appearance into the specific commands required by a given printer. As mentioned in Chapter 3, you use the Chooser desk accessory to select the driver for your printer.

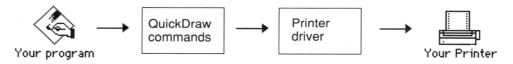

Figure 5-4: How a Macintosh program prints.

In the System Update 6.0 package, the Printing Tools disk contains six printer drivers:

ImageWriter. For printing to the ImageWriter and ImageWriter II printers connected to the Mac's printer or modem port.

AppleTalk ImageWriter. For printing to ImageWriter II printers equipped with Apple's optional *AppleTalk* board. This board and driver work together to allow Macs attached to a network to share an ImageWriter II printer.

LQ ImageWriter. For printing to the ImageWriter LQ printer connected to the Mac's printer or modem port.

LQ AppleTalk ImageWriter. For printing to ImageWriter LQ printers equipped with Apple's optional AppleTalk board.

LaserWriter. For printing, via a network, to LaserWriters and other printers equipped with the PostScript page-description language.

Laser Prep. Technically speaking, Laser Prep isn't a printer driver, but a *prep file*. When you begin printing to a PostScript printer that has just been switched on, the Mac transmits the contents of the Laser Prep file to the printer, which stores it in its own memory. It's this process that produces the "Status: Initializing printer" message you may see at the beginning of your first print job of the day.

LaserWriter IISC. For printing to Apple's LaserWriter IISC printer, connected to the Mac's SCSI port.

Chapter 8 contains more information on these printers and their drivers.

The Control Panel Devices

The Control Panel desk accessory, which lets you view and adjust system settings, shows a row of icons along its left edge. Each icon corresponds to a particular system setting (see Figure 5-5).

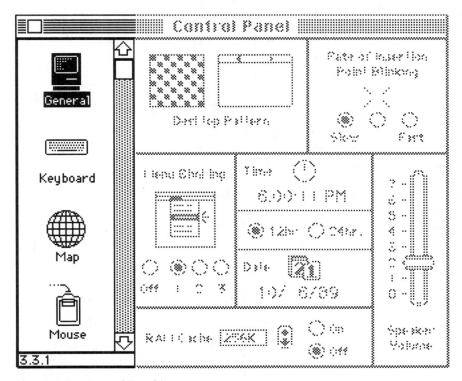

Figure 5-5: Control Panel icons.

Each icon corresponds to a file in the System Folder called a *control panel device*, or *cdev* (pronounced *see-dev*). When you click on a cdev's icon, the cdev takes over, changing the right-hand side of the Control Panel window as necessary. This usually means displaying buttons and other controls that you'll use to adjust the settings the cdev provides.

The Control Panel hasn't always worked this way. Prior to the release of System version 4.0, the Control Panel consisted of one window that was the same on every Mac (see Figure 5-6). The newer, modular approach gives the Control Panel the flexibility required to act as a control center for each member of the Mac family, automatically adapting itself to each model's features. For example, the Colors cdev doesn't appear in the Control Panel window of a Mac SE or Plus, since they lack color capabilities.

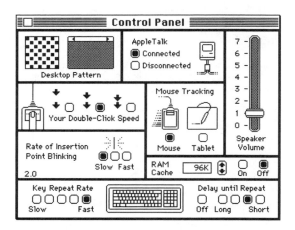

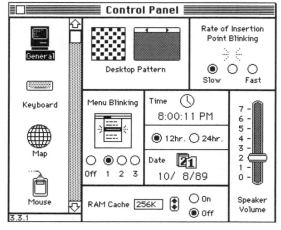

Figure 5-6: An old Control Panel (*top*), and the newer, modular Control Panel (*bottom*).

Another benefit of the modular Control Panel is that hardware manufacturers can include cdevs with their products that allow you to adjust settings using the Control Panel. This allows the Control Panel to be your primary source for system-related settings, and it helps eliminate having to run an "installation program" to adjust a fancy new add-on—a familiar chore to IBM PC users.

Let's look at each of the cdevs that accompany the System Update 6.0 package, and find out which Macs each is intended for.

General. This appropriately named cdev, shown in Figure 5-7, lets you change basic system settings: the date, time, speaker volume, number of times a menu command flashes after you choose it, the current desktop pattern, the speed at which the insertion point blinks, and the *RAM cache*. (The RAM cache option lets you improve performance by decreasing the frequency of disk accesses. We'll explore it in Chapter 9.)

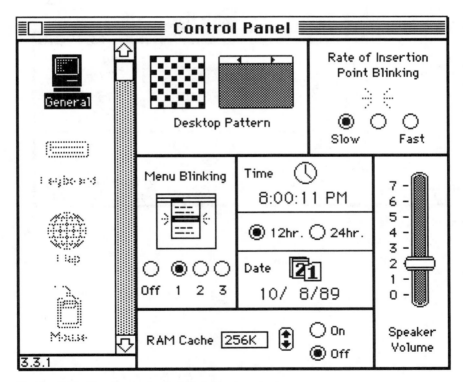

Figure 5-7: The General cdev's icon and controls.

CloseView. The CloseView cdev lets you enlarge a portion of the Mac's screen image up to 16 times (see Figure 5-8). CloseView's primary purpose is to make the Mac's screen easier for visually impaired users to read, but it's also useful in precision drawing or desktop publishing applications, since it lets you zoom in for a closer view.

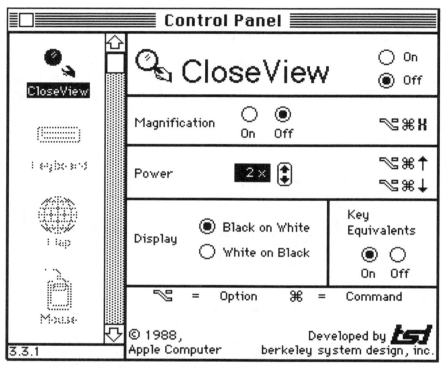

Figure 5-8: The CloseView cdev.

Color. The Color cdev, which appears on Macs with color capabilities, lets you change the color in which selected text appears (see Figure 5-9). If you'd rather see selections in shocking pink than black, this is the cdev for you.

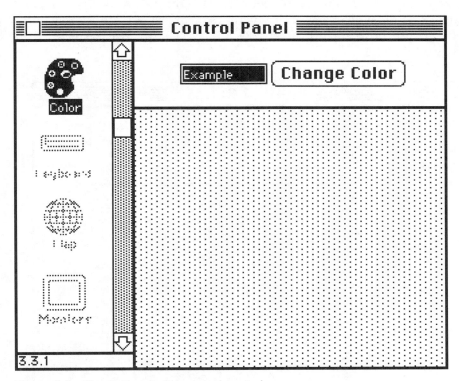

Figure 5-9: The Color cdev's icon and controls.

Keyboard. When you hold down a key, the Mac repeats that key's character. The Keyboard cdev, shown in Figure 5-10, lets you change the *keyboard repeat rate*, the speed at which a key repeats. With a slow keyboard repeat rate, a small amount of time elapses between each repetition. With fast repeat rates, there's no delay between each repetition. The Delay Until Repeat setting lets you govern how much time elapses after you've pressed a key until the key begins to repeat.

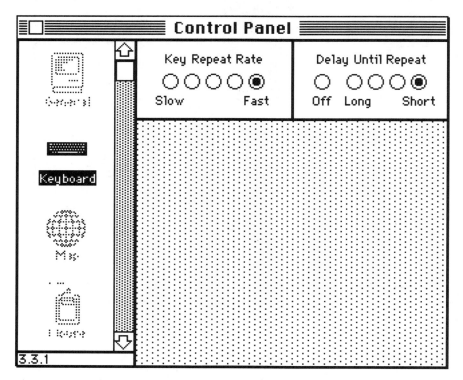

Figure 5-10: The Keyboard cdev's icon and controls.

Mouse. This cdev, shown in Figure 5-11, lets you adjust mouse settings. The mouse-tracking settings let you control how the Mac's on-screen pointer responds to mouse movements. When you choose the Tablet setting, the pointer moves at a snail's pace—too slow for convenient navigation, but potentially useful for detailed drawing. The Tablet setting is intended for use with a *graphics tablet*, an input device that consists of a flat tablet and a pencil-like stylus. Graphics tablets are popular for electronic drafting and drawing applications.

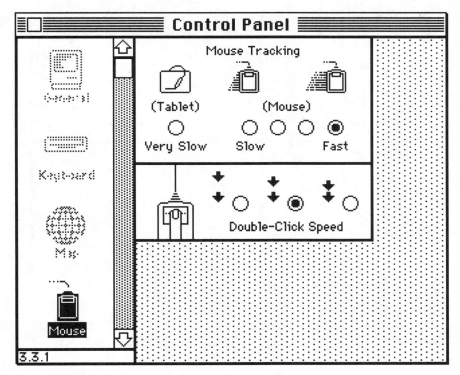

Figure 5-11: The Mouse cdev's icon and controls.

The remaining tracking options are for use with a mouse, and control the relationship between mouse movement and the pointer's on-screen movement. The faster settings are useful if you have a large screen or if you don't have a lot of free desk space. The slower settings are ideal for extra precision when you're drawing or moving items using a desktop publishing program. (For more background on mouse tracking, see Chapter 14.)

Sound. The Sound cdev lets you choose one of four sounds as the current *alert sound*—the tone you hear when you click outside of a dialog box or commit some other no-no. This cdev, shown in Figure 5-12, takes advantage of the Mac's Sound Manager to let you choose sounds that are a little more interesting than a simple tone. And why not? If mistakes are a little less frustrating when you're notified by a squawking monkey, you can have the option of hearing one.

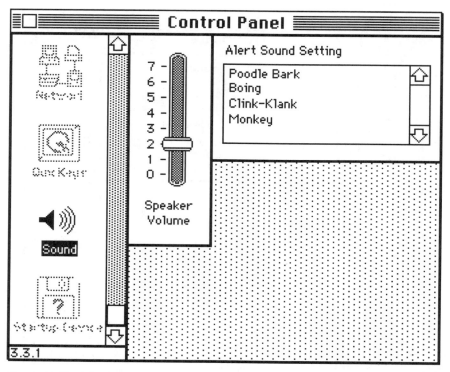

Figure 5-12: The Sound cdev's icon and controls.

Startup Device. This cdev works only with the Mac SE and later machines, and it's useful only if you have more than one SCSI storage device. If you do, you can use the Startup Device cdev to specify which SCSI device the Mac should "start up from" the next time you restart. When you restart a Mac, it scans the drives connected to it in search of a disk containing a System Folder. The Startup Device cdev lets you override the order of that scanning process. (A drive must contain a System Folder in order for the Mac to start from it.) When you click on the Startup Device icon, the Control Panel displays an icon for each SCSI storage device in your system, highlighting the currently selected startup device, as shown in Figure 5-13. To choose a different device, click its icon. To deselect a device, press Command while clicking its icon. (Chapter 14 contains more details on SCSI and the start-up-scanning process.)

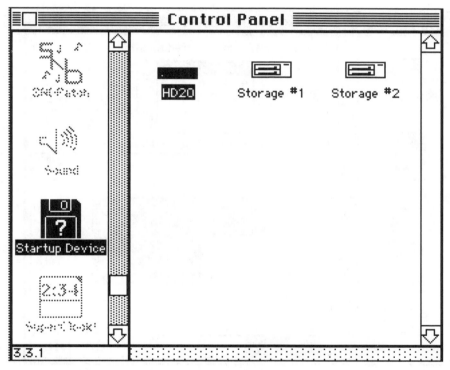

Figure 5-13: The Startup Device cdev's icon and some typical SCSI storage-device icons.

Monitors. Apple's video board for color Macs has several operating settings. It can create displays in black-and-white with 2, 4, 16, or 256 simultaneous shades of gray, or in color with 2, 4, 16, or 256 simultaneous colors (You need the optional video card memory-expansion kit for 256 gray shades or colors; unexpanded cards can generate a maximum of 16 gray shades or colors.) The Monitors cdev, shown in Figure 5-14, lets you view and change the current setting. If you've connected more than one monitor to your Mac, you can use Monitors to designate one monitor as the *main monitor*—the one on which the menu bar appears. You can also reposition the monitor outlines to correspond to the actual location of the monitors on your desk. (Chapter 6 describes how color Macs keep track of multiple monitors. Chapter 9 contains some tips on using the Monitors cdev more effectively.)

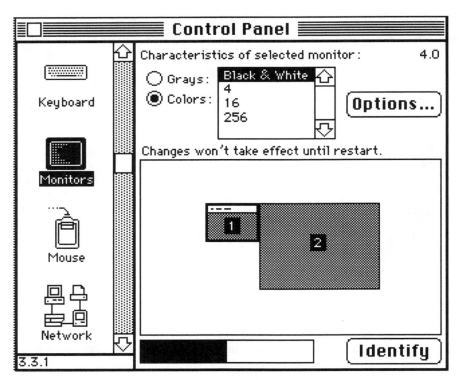

Figure 5-14: The Monitors cdev depicting two monitors.

Map. This interesting cdev, shown in Figure 5-15, lets you reset the Mac's clock when you move the Mac from one time zone to another, and it lets you determine the distance and time difference between your location and others.

If you live in a major city, you can specify your location by typing its name, clicking Find, and then clicking Set. (The flashing dots on the map display represent places that Map knows about.) Map stores your choice in the Mac's parameter RAM, the battery-powered memory area that also holds the time, date, and other Control Panel settings.

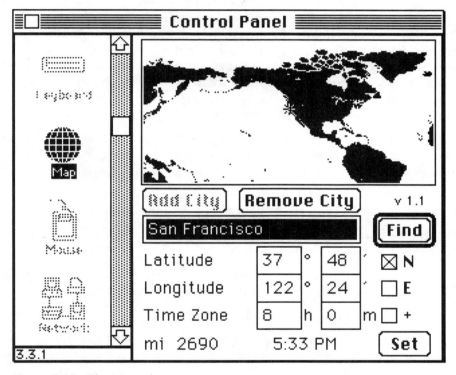

Figure 5-15: The Map cdev.

If the Mac beeps when you click Find, it doesn't know about your city. Don't be offended; Apple's selection criteria for which U.S. cities got "on the map" seems a bit arbitrary to us, too. (Heid thinks the omission of his home town of Pittsburgh is inexcusable, especially since pint-sized Cupertino, California—Apple's home—is listed.) In any case, you can add a city to Map's internal list by typing its name, latitude, and longitude, and then clicking Add.

If you move your Mac to a different time zone, use the Find button to locate a city in that time zone (or add the city as described above), then click Set. The Map cdev will reset the Mac's clock to reflect the time zone you've moved to. (Tips: To see an enlarged view of the world, press the Option key while clicking on the Map cdev. To see the time difference instead of the time zone, click on the words "Time Zone" below the Map display.)

Init Files

Beginning with System version 3.2, Apple devised a method for the Mac to load small, system-modifying software routines during the start-up process. Shortly after displaying the "Welcome to Macintosh" message, the Mac looks in the System Folder for a type of file called an Init (short for *initialization* resource), also called a startup document. If it finds one, it loads its software, and adjusts some key values in memory to ensure that the Init's turf isn't invaded by other programs. If the System Folder contains more than one Init, the Mac loads them in alphabetical order.

The workings of an Init generally span applications; that is, instead of being "use and put away when you're finished" programs such as desk accessories, Inits perform tasks you can use in any application. This kind of file might include:

- Software that lets you create your own keyboard shortcuts.

- Software that customizes your Mac, for example, by displaying the current time in the Mac's menu bar

- An *electronic mail* package that notifies you—regardless of what application you're using—when someone on your network has sent you mail

- Software that controls a hardware add-on.

In the IBM PC world, a rough equivalent to Inits would be terminate-and-stay-resident programs such as Borland International's SuperKey. If you've been exposed to the world of TSRs, as they're abbreviated, you know how tricky using several of them can be. Loading several TSRs can cause memory conflicts and system errors. The Macintosh's Init mechanism is designed to avoid software anarchy by providing a clean, orderly method of loading system-modifying software upon start-up.

Unfortunately, Inits aren't an ironclad defense against software anarchy. They can sometimes conflict with each other, causing system errors during the start-up process. When this happens, you have to endure a troubleshooting routine that involves renaming Inits to change their loading order or pulling certain ones out of your System Folder to see if they're the troublemakers. It's a sad fact that, as the Macintosh becomes more complex, it becomes prone to some of the same hassles that IBM PC users face.

The standard System Folder includes three Init files: CloseView, Easy Access, and MacroMaker.

CloseView. We peered at CloseView earlier in this chapter; it's the cdev that lets you enlarge the Mac's screen image. CloseView is also an Init: during start-up, it loads its screen-enlarging code into memory, where it's ready to be summoned by the cdev.

Easy Access. This Init modifies the Mac's keyboard driver to allow you to type multikey sequences (such as Command-Q or Shift-Option-G) with one hand and also to control the mouse pointer from the keyboard. As indicated by its wheelchair-on-the-screen icon, Easy Access is designed to assist physically challenged users who might have trouble typing multikey sequences and moving the mouse. It's also useful for making precise adjustments in the pointer's position.

Easy Access's *Sticky Keys* feature simplifies multikey sequences. To activate Sticky Keys, press the Shift key five times. When Sticky Keys is active, you can type multikey sequences by typing their keys sequentially. For example, instead of pressing Command and S simultaneously, first press Command, and then S.

Easy Access's *Mouse Keys* feature lets you use the keypad to move the mouse pointer. (It's important to emphasize that Mouse Keys controls the mouse pointer, not the blinking insertion point that appears when you're typing or editing text. Many word processors use the keypad's 2, 4, 8, and 6 keys to move the insertion point down, left, up, and right.) To activate Mouse Keys, press Command-Shift-Clear. Subsequently, the keypad's keys move the pointer as shown in Figure 5-16. Pressing the 5 key is like clicking the mouse button. Pressing 0 (zero) is like holding the button down, while pressing the decimal point key is like releasing the button. Pressing Clear deactivates Mouse Keys and restores the keypad to normal operation.

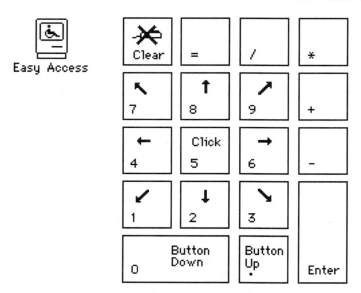

Figure 5-16: The Easy Access Init's icon and legend for the Mouse Keys feature.

MacroMaker. This Init, authored by veteran Mac team member Donn Denman, debuted with System Update 6.0. MacroMaker, shown in Figure 5-17, lets you record keystrokes and mouse movements, and then play them back with a single key sequence. These recorded events are called *macros*. Apple's primary reason for creating MacroMaker was to enable users of the 105-key Apple Extended Keyboard to use that keyboard's 15 function keys. But MacroMaker is invaluable regardless of which keyboard you have, since it also lets you assign macros to any modifier-key sequence. Some of the things you can do with MacroMaker include:

- Adding keyboard shortcuts to commands that lack them or changing existing keyboard shortcuts to suit your tastes.

- Storing and recalling frequently used text, from passages of legal jargon to finger-twisting scientific terms to your name and address.

- Automating frequently performed tasks that require several steps, such as copying text to the Clipboard, opening the Scrapbook desk accessory, and then pasting the text into the Scrapbook.

Chapter 10 contains more information on MacroMaker and on some programs that provide more keyboard-customizing features.

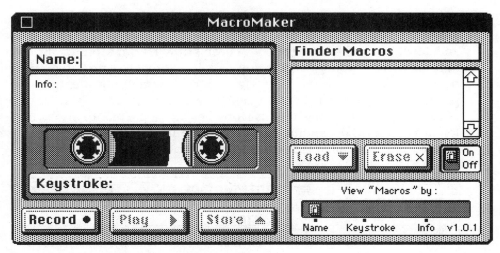

Figure 5-17: The MacroMaker window.

Remember, CloseView, Easy Access, and MacroMaker aren't the only Inits a System Folder can contain. Many software developers and Mac programming hobbyists have created Inits that perform some very useful jobs (and in some cases, provide some amusing diversions). We'll look at some of these Inits in Chapter 10.

MISCELLANEOUS FILES

The rest of the files in the System Folder don't fall into the Init, cdev, or printer driver categories, but perform important jobs nonetheless. Let's continue our tour of the System Folder by looking at them.

Backgrounder. One of MultiFinder's most useful features is its ability to print to a PostScript-based printer (such as the LaserWriter IINT and NTX) in the background. The Backgrounder file works with MultiFinder and the Print Monitor file (described below) to make background printing possible. Backgrounder is a small application that's active whenever the Chooser's Background Printing option is turned on. Backgrounder constantly scans a folder within the System Folder, called Spool Folder, looking for a printer *spool file*, which is created when you use the Print command after activating the background printing option. A spool file represents the contents of the document you're printing—it contains the data that would otherwise go directly to the printer if background printing were not turned on. When Backgrounder finds a spool file, it starts Print Monitor.

Print Monitor. Print Monitor communicates with the printer in the background, sending it spool files, downloading fonts, reporting error messages, and deleting spool files after they've been printed. Print Monitor also provides options that let you defer printing to a later time and rearrange or remove pending print jobs, as shown in Figure 5-18. If something goes wrong during printing—the paper jams or someone turns the printer off—Print Monitor can get your attention by flashing its icon over the Apple menu, displaying a dialog box, or both, depending on your preferences. Print Monitor uses a set of toolbox routines called the Notification Manager to get your attention.

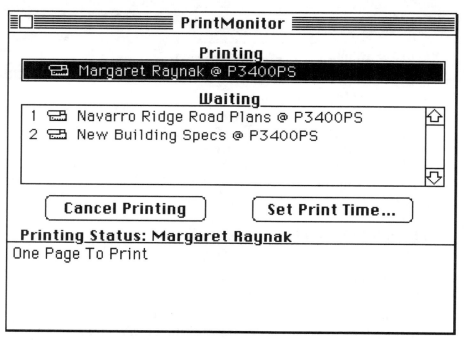

Figure 5-18: Print Monitor's window.

Finder Startup. When using the Finder or MultiFinder, you can choose the Special menu's Set Startup command to specify that certain applications be opened at startup time, and to designate whether or not the Mac should run MultiFinder after starting up. The Mac stores your choices in the Finder Startup file. (Chapter 10 contains a tip for switching between Finder Startup files.)

DA Handler. Here's another file that works with MultiFinder. As you may recall from Chapter 4, MultiFinder runs all desk accessories within a single "layer." DA Handler creates that layer, and it provides Edit menu commands for cutting and pasting from and to desk accessories, and a File menu whose Close and Quit commands let you close the currently active desk accessory or all open desk accessories.

Key Layout. This file works along with the Key Caps desk accessory, which graphically depicts the Mac's keyboard so you can locate special characters. The availability of different Mac keyboards required Apple to create a more flexible Key Caps accessory, one that could show the layout for any of the keyboards that might be attached to a Mac. That's where the Key Layout file comes in. When you open Key Caps, it looks in the System Folder for the Key Layout file, and reads its contents to determine which keyboard is attached to your Mac.

Clipboard File. This file, which may not always be present in your System Folder, can contain the contents of the Mac's Clipboard. When you cut or copy a large amount of data, an application can optionally store it on disk instead of in the Mac's memory. If it elects to store it on disk, it saves it in the Clipboard File.

Scrapbook File. This file contains the contents of the Mac's Scrapbook.

Note Pad File. This file contains the "pages" that you create with the Note Pad desk accessory.

KEEPING UP TO DATE

In this section, we'll look at what's involved in keeping your System Folder up to date, and we'll examine the key differences between recent versions of the Mac's system software.

Updating Your System

Why should you bother keeping your system up to date? For two reasons. First, upgrading your system to the latest version is the least expensive way to add new features to your Mac and improve its performance. Apple's system upgrade packages, which include disks and manuals describing the new version, usually cost about $50 at dealers. Even better, many dealers or user groups will let you copy the new system disks at no cost if you provide your own disks, and Apple encourages this policy.

The second and more important reason to keep your system current is to ensure that you can run the latest software. When Apple releases a revised system with new features, software manufacturers quickly take advantage of those new features in their programs. If you don't upgrade your system to keep pace, you may not be able to run that new whiz-bang program you just bought.

The Installer

In the Mac's early days, updating to a newer version of the system involved simply copying the new system files to the hard disk or floppies you used to start your Mac. This method had its drawbacks. Because fonts and desk accessories are stored in the System file, replacing your old System file meant installing your favorite fonts and desk accessories all over again. And because some add-ons required you to install software drivers directly into the System file, updating your system meant installing those drivers again, too.

Apple wisely realized that updating would be easier if users weren't forced to reinstall fonts, desk accessories, and software drivers. Thus, a utility called Installer was born. Installer comes with several special documents called *scripts*, each of which is tailored to a specific model of Macintosh. You choose the script that matches your Mac, Installer reads it to determine how to modify your System Folder, and then makes the modifications.

Another extremely important part of Installer's job involves adding certain system routines to your system disk's System file, a process called *patching*. During start-up, the Mac loads the patches into a special area of memory called the *system heap*. Patching the System file is a technique Apple uses to ensure that, from the system software standpoint, all Macs have a consistent set of basic features and capabilities.

Why bother? Consider the alternative: Apple introduces a new Mac containing expanded ROM chips with new system routines that greatly enhance the user interface. Developers would like to create software that uses these new routines, but if they do, thousands of older Macs that lack the new routines won't be able to run the new software. Thus, they don't take advantage of the new routines—or they slash their potential market by programming for the new machine only.

The patching process avoids this nightmare. It allows Apple to continue improving the Macintosh and expanding its ROM chips without leaving older Macs out in the cold. It assures developers that the programs they write will run on any Macintosh, and it allows owners of older Macs to run software that uses the newest system enhancements without having to upgrade their ROM chips. Basically, patching creates a common ground that exists across the Macintosh family.

Well, almost. There are limits to what patching can do. It can't, for example, add color capabilities to a black-and-white Mac. Nor does it add system routines designed to control expansion slots to a Mac that doesn't have slots. Installer's patching job is always appropriate to the machine you have—provided you choose the proper Installer script before updating a disk. If you don't, you can end up with a System Folder containing superfluous files—such as a Colors cdev in a monochrome Mac's System Folder.

Scaled-Down Systems

As the Mac system evolves, it gets larger. The System 6.0 files barely fit on a single 800K floppy disk. So that users of floppy-only Macs can update their systems, the System Update 6.0 package includes a set of *minimal scripts* that create the smallest possible System Folder. For example, the minimal Mac SE script accompanying System 6.0 installs only the Control Panel and Chooser desk accessories, and just a few fonts. These minimal scripts also perform minimal patching jobs—indeed, they craft the System Folder so carefully that you can't use a system disk they create to start up a different model of Mac. If you try to start a Mac II with a minimal system disk intended for a Mac SE, an error message appears.

Which System for Which Mac?

The growing size of the Mac system has another important ramification. Because patches are loaded into memory during start-up, they reduce the amount of memory available for programs. 512K Macs—whether enhanced or not—just don't have enough memory to hold the required patches and still leave enough memory left over to run programs. A 512K or 512K Enhanced Mac can go no further than Finder 5.5 and System 4.1.

Actually, a 512K Enhanced Mac *can* run System 6.0, but it leaves only a small cubbyhole of memory free for running programs. How small? When we started a 512K Enhanced with a System 6.0 floppy disk, only about 170K remained free—enough to run MacPaint at a snail's pace, but not much more. This shows the wisdom of using the system version that Apple recommends for your model of Macintosh. Table 5–1 shows which versions of the system will run on which Macs. A plus sign (+) indicates the version Apple recommends for that Mac.

Table 5-1: Recommended Finder and System files for each Macintosh model.

System/ Finder	512K	512K Enhanced	Plus	SE	SE/30	II	IIx	IIcx
3.2/5.3	+	+	•					
3.3/5.4	+[3]	+[3]	•[2]					
3.4/6.1		+[3]						
4.0/5.4		•	•	•				
4.1/5.5		•	•	•		•		
4.2/6.0[1]			•	•		•		
6.0.2/6.1[2]			+	+		+[4]		
6.0.3/6.1[2]			+	+	+	+	+	+

[1] These versions are part of the "System Tools 5.0" release.
[2] These versions are part of the "System Update 6.0" release.
[3] These versions are recommended for these machines when they are used with Apple's Appleshare file server software (described in Chapter 12).
[4] To use a 24-bit color board with a Mac II, you must use System 6.0.3 or a later version.

Tips for Updating Your System

Generally, updating your system to the latest version is a straightforward process. But there are ways for flies to enter the ointment. Here are some tips for keeping that ointment fly-free.

Use the Installer. Don't just use the Finder to drag files from the update disks to your System Folder. If you do, your System file won't be properly updated, and your Mac will probably not startup properly—or it may crash during use.

Don't copy the Installer and its scripts to your startup disk. If you have a hard disk, you might be tempted to do this so that the Installer will run faster. Resist the urge. To copy the proper files and patches to your startup disk, the Installer needs to access the System Folder of the disk it came on. What's more, the Installer can't modify the System Folder of the current start-up disk. Always run the Installer from its original disk (or, better yet, from a backup copy of its original disk).

Make backups first. If you don't have a hard disk, you'll be updating your floppy system disks. In case something goes wrong during the updating process, make a backup copy of each system disk you plan to update. If you're using a hard disk, make a backup copy of your System and Finder files. The easiest way is to use the Finder to copy the files to one or more floppy disks. If you have a huge System file laden with fonts and desk accessories, it may not fit on a floppy. If that's the case—and if your hard disk has sufficient space—make a duplicate of the System file (not the entire System Folder); select it and choose the Duplicate command from the Finder's File menu.

Disable font and desk accessory extenders. Two popular Init programs, Fifth Generation Systems' Suitcase II and AlSoft's Font/DA Juggler, let you use fonts and desk accessories without having to install them in the System file. Because these products modify the workings of the Mac's system software, using the Installer while one of them is running can cause problems. If you're using these or similar products, disable them by dragging their files out of the System Folder and then restarting the Mac.

Start up with the Installer disk. For the Installer to work, its disk must be the start-up disk. Although you can switch-launch to the Installer's disk to make it the start-up disk, doing so is asking for trouble. Any Inits you've loaded or applications you've run before switch-launching may have put your system in a state that could cause problems during the updating process. The best way to ensure accurate updating is to shut your Mac off, insert the Installer's floppy disk, then turn the Mac on.

THE EVOLUTION OF THE MAC SYSTEM

How has the Mac's system software improved? What are the limitations of earlier versions? In this section, we'll explore the primary differences between each major system update. This discussion is more than just a trip down memory lane: by examining the differences between each version of the Mac system, you can get an accurate picture of how the Mac family has evolved and get some hints as to where it's heading.

Still, the information in this section isn't essential to using the Mac. If you're just starting out with the Mac, or if you simply aren't interested in knowing the differences between system versions, feel free to skip this section and move on.

The improvements in the Mac system fall into five basic categories.

- Finder—changes you can see in the Finder's menus, dialog boxes, or on the desktop

- System—changes involving the addition or alteration of software in the System file

- Accessories—the addition of new utility programs, Inits, desk accessories, or cdevs

- Printing—improvements in the Mac's printer drivers that give it better printing capabilities

For convenient reference, we've organized this section according to these categories.

We'll begin our look into the past with Finder 5.3 and System 3.2—the last versions recommended for use on unenhanced 512K Macs.

Finder 5.3 and System 3.2

When Apple introduced the Mac Plus and 512K Enhanced in January 1986, it also released Finder 5.1 and System 3.0. In the six months that followed, Apple fixed some bugs and made some minor enhancements, and in June 1986, the Mac world settled into Finder 5.3 and System 3.2.

The most significant aspect of this release was a new method of managing files on a disk: the Hierarchical File System, or HFS, discussed in the last chapter. The software that implements HFS is stored in the ROMs of all Macs except the 128K and unenhanced 512K. Still, the introduction of a new file system required major changes in the System and Finder files.

Finder. The most noticeable interface change in Finder 5.3 was the addition of a new File menu command called New Folder. Previous versions of the Finder used an awkward mechanism for creating folders. Every disk automatically contained one folder named Empty Folder. To create a new folder, you selected Empty Folder and duplicated it. The New Folder command made creating a new folder a process similar to creating a new document in an application program, and thus took some of the mystery out of working with folders.

Another small but useful improvement was the debut of zoom boxes, which, as Chapter 3 mentioned, let you quickly resize a window to fill the screen. The 128K ROMs contained new software that allowed windows to have zoom boxes, and the new version of the Finder was the first place users encountered them.

System. We've already detailed the most significant change in the System, the new File Manager and its ability to work with the HFS code in ROM. There were other improvements, too, however.

- The Init mechanism for loading routines during start-up debuted.

- The Control Panel's disk cache option appeared.

Accessories. Finder 5.3 included a time-saving *MiniFinder* feature that first debuted in an earlier Finder, version 4.1. The MiniFinder was a tiny application that allowed you to bypass the Finder at start-up time and when moving between applications, allowing you to perform both tasks more quickly. The MiniFinder displayed a window containing the icons for the applications and documents you used most (see Figure 5-19). You could "install" up to 12 icons by selecting them using the Finder, and then choosing the Use MiniFinder command in the Finder's Special menu. Next to the icons were buttons that let you eject disks, shut down, and start applications whose icons didn't appear in the window. The MiniFinder didn't let you copy files or disks; to perform those tasks, you clicked the Finder button to run the "full Finder." (Incidentally, some Mac magazines and books incorrectly refer to the list of files you see when you choose an application's Open command as "the minifinder." Don't be confused by this misuse of Mac terminology.)

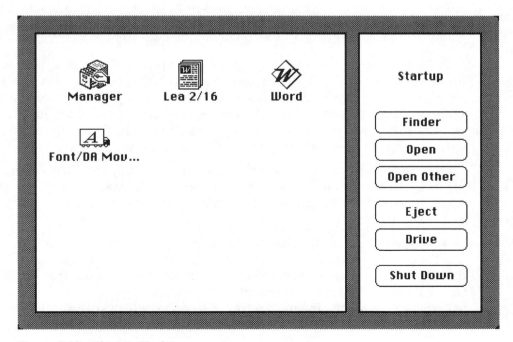

Figure 5-19: The MiniFinder.

Printing. Finder 5.3/System 3.2 included version 3.1 of the LaserPrep and LaserWriter duo, and version 2.3 of the ImageWriter driver.

Finder 5.3/System 3.2 were the last versions of the system that ran on every Macintosh model available at that time, from an unenhanced 512K with two floppy drives to a Mac Plus with a hard disk. When running on a machine with the original 64K ROMs, Finder 5.3/System 3.2 used MFS, and thus, treated folders as mere cosmetic niceties. On a 512K Enhanced or a Mac Plus, the system used HFS.

Finder 5.4/System 4.0 and Finder 5.5/System 4.1

When Apple introduced the Mac SE and II in April 1988, the path of the Mac system's progress diverged. The System and Finder chugged toward the future, leaving the 512K Mac waving from the platform of the station. Finder 5.3 and System 3.2 comprised the last system upgrade that unenhanced 512K Macs would ever see. That wasn't because Apple was trying to make 512K Macs obsolete—some fine software still runs on them. (A HyperDrive-equipped 512K Mac still serves us reliably—we're thinking of getting classic license plates for it.)

The improvements in Finder 5.4 and System 4.0 (and in their successors, Finder 5.5 and System 4.1, which shipped in April 1987), accommodated the hardware expandability of the Mac SE and II and made the Mac better equipped to handle the demands of businesses applications.

Finder. Finder 5.4 included features that worked with Apple's *AppleShare* file-server software. (AppleShare turns a hard-disk equipped Mac into a central storage repository for a network.) And there were little cosmetic touches: the Trash can bulged when it contained files. The Restart command debuted in the Finder's Special menu. The wording and workings of the Clean Up command changed depending on whether any icons were selected.

System. System 4.0 contained new routines that supported the enhanced ROMs of the Mac SE. System 4.1 added support for the Mac II. System 4.1 also added patches that, from the system software standpoint, made a Mac Plus look more like an SE.

Accessories. System 4.0 was the first version to include the modular Control Panel with its cdevs. It contained an improved Chooser desk accessory that had more room to display icons for the many printers and other devices a large network might have. It brought the modular Key Caps desk accessory, with its Key Layout file that tells the desk accessory which keyboard you have.

Printing. With the improved Finder and System files came improved printer drivers for PostScript printers. Version 4.0 of the LaserPrep and Laser-Writer files were much faster than their predecessors and offered new printing options. These options allowed you to specify that documents be flipped horizontally or vertically, or inverted (black turned into white), and were aimed at improving the Mac's ability to control PostScript typesetters such as the Linotronic 100 and 300. Other options allowed you to change the way the printer's memory was used to allow you to print images closer to the edges of the page. These options exist in today's PostScript drivers; Chapter 8 describes many of them in greater detail.

System Tools 5.0 (Finder 6.0 and System 4.2)

In October 1987, Finder 5.5 and System 4.1 surrendered to Finder 6.0 and System 4.2. With this release, Apple began grouping the system files under the umbrella of a "system tools" number. Finder 6.0 and System 4.2 were part of the System Tools 5.0 update. The big news in System Tools 5.0, however, was MultiFinder 1.0, which gave the Mac world its first glimpse of multitasking. Because the Finder and MultiFinder files work together, the new Finder features that we describe here also apply to MultiFinder.

Finder. Finder 6.0 offered several new niceties:

- An improved About the Finder command that, when chosen, displayed a bar graph showing how much memory was being used by the system (which included memory taken up by Inits) and how much remained free. Under MultiFinder, the graph also showed how much memory each open application used.

- A new progress dialog box appeared when you copied a disk or some files, informing you of the status of the copy operation and containing a Cancel button.

- An improved Set Startup command, which let you choose between running under the Finder or MultiFinder. You could also designate that one or more applications would be opened under MultiFinder at start-up time.

- A new menu, Color, which allowed users of Mac IIs—the only color Mac available then—to choose colors for icons and folders.

It's worth noting that the birth of MultiFinder meant the death of the MiniFinder, that small application used for switching between programs without using the Finder. It's true that the MiniFinder would have been useful for those times when you weren't running under MultiFinder, but getting people to run under MultiFinder was an important goal for Apple, since MultiFinder represented the future of the Mac system. Finder 6.0 did not support the Mini-Finder.

System. Several of the system files described earlier in this chapter—Backgrounder, PrintMonitor, and DA Handler—first appeared in the System Tools 5.0 release. All three work along with MultiFinder—Backgrounder to look for LaserWriter spool files, PrintMonitor to print spool files in the background, and DA Handler to give desk accessories a MultiFinder layer in which to run.

Accessories. The EasyAccess Init made its appearance in this update.

Printing. Thanks to MultiFinder, PrintMonitor, and Backgrounder, System Tools 5.0 was the first system release that provided background printing for LaserWriters and other PostScript printers.

System Update 6.0 (Finder 6.1 and System 6.0)

Software is rarely perfect in its first release, and MultiFinder 1.0 proved it. MultiFinder had a quirk that earned quite a bit of criticism: If you double-clicked on a document created by an application that was already open, Multi-Finder didn't switch to the application and open the document. Instead, it displayed a dialog box telling you that you should use the application's Open command.

Apple fixed that quirk in April 1988 by releasing System Update 6.0. In keeping with its somewhat random approach to version numbering, Apple boosted MultiFinder's version number from 1.0 all the way to 6.0. The version number for the System file took an upward leap, too, from 4.2 to 6.0. The version numbering was bizarre, but the end result was welcome. In MultiFinder 6.0, when you double-clicked on a document whose application was open, MultiFinder switched to that application and opened the document.

Finder. Besides fixing the problem mentioned above, System Update 6.0 included other Finder-related improvements:

- An enhanced Get Info command. When you chose Get Info for an application, the window displayed the application's version number by reading it from a special resource stored in the application file.

- An enhanced Erase Disk command. When you initialized a new disk, the Finder would display a dialog box warning that you were about to erase the disk and giving you a Cancel button to back out. If you proceeded to erase the disk, a new status dialog box appeared during the initialization process.

System. System Update 6.0 took one more step towards giving the Mac a complete multitasking operating system. The Notification Manager, the mechanism that allows background applications to get your attention by flashing their icons over the Apple menu and displaying dialog boxes, made its first appearance.

System 6.0 also included a revised Sound Manager, the portion of the Mac's operating system that lets it play digitally recorded sounds. The Sound Manager first appeared in System 4.1, but only on Mac IIs. Beginning with System 6.0, the Sound Manager existed on Mac Pluses and SEs, as well. By giving all three machines equal sound-oriented system routines, Apple simplified life for developers creating sound-oriented software. And there was a side benefit: Mac SE and Plus users could choose the same entertaining alert sounds that II users had been enjoying all along.

Another improvement in System 6.0 allowed Mac IIs to display color graphics more quickly. In 1987, pioneering Mac team member Andy Hertzfeld wrote an Init called QuickerGraf and distributed it free of charge through user's groups and online information services. QuickerGraf replaced certain Color QuickDraw routines in the Mac II with ones that performed the same tasks in less time. Users embraced it, and Apple, concerned that an important part of the Mac II's system software had been created by an outside party, licensed it and made it part of the System file.

(Incidentally, in defense of Color QuickDraw's original programmers, it's worth noting that QuickerGraf didn't contain any routines that Apple's own programmers couldn't have created. QuickerGraf's creation was a case of someone who wasn't on a daunting deadline being able to improve on the work of people who were. There's a parallel in the publishing world: a good editor can, in a few days, refine a manuscript that took weeks to write. Editors—and programmers—can step back and see where a completed project can be improved.)

Accessories. Also making their maiden voyages in System Update 6.0 were the MacroMaker and CloseView Inits, and the Map cdev, all of which were described earlier. Apple also made a minor but welcome change in the way that the Alarm Clock, Calculator, Chooser, Scrapbook, and Find File desk accessories operated. When you closed one of these desk accessories, it "remembered" the position of its window and appeared there when reopened.

A new version of the Font/DA Mover utility shipped with System Update 6.0 that had significant ramifications for font hounds. Version 3.8 was the first version of the Font/DA Mover to support a new internal format for representing fonts. We'll discuss the ramifications of this format, called NFNT (short for *new font-numbering table*), in Chapter 7.

Printing. And there were improvements in the printer drivers. Apple's LaserWriter drivers added support for tabloid-sized (11 by 17 inches) paper, allowing all Mac applications to work with such printers as the Varityper VT-600W and the Dataproducts LZR-2665. Prior to System Update 6.0, application developers needed to supply their own PostScript printer driver to offer tabloid printing.

Another improvement that made its appearance in this release was the LaserWriter Page Setup dialog box's Unlimited Downloadable Fonts option, which changes the way the printer's memory is used in order to allow an unlimited number of downloadable fonts in a document. Also making its debut was the Text Smoothing option, which smooths the edges of non-LaserWriter fonts such as Geneva, Chicago, and New York.

System revisions are a kind of proving ground that measures how well developers adhere to Apple's programming guidelines. Applications that bend the rules are more likely to snap when a new system is released. That was the case with System 6.0. Many mainstream applications—including Microsoft Excel, Ashton-Tate's FullWrite, and Acius's 4th Dimension—crashed or did unexpected things when run under System 6.0.

But some of these problems were caused by bugs in System 6.0 itself. Thus, in September 1987, Apple released System 6.0.1. In addition to fixing over 50 bugs, System 6.0.1 brought a faster Palette Manager, the portion of the operating system that allow applications running on color Macs to switch between different sets of colors and provide other color-related features. The system saw two more minor revisions in subsequent months, settling into version 6.0.3 with the release of the Macintosh IIcx.

The Color Disk and LaserWriter 6.0

In May 1989, Apple released an update called the Color Disk. The contents of the Color Disk represent an intermediate advance of the Mac's system software—not as major a leap as from System 5.0 to 6.0, but an interim improvement. The Color Disk contains:

- Version 6.0 of the LaserWriter printer driver and LaserPrep PostScript dictionary. This driver provides improved support for color PostScript printers, and also allows Mac applications to produce halftones of gray-scale and color images on PostScript printers. Chapter 8 contains more information on LaserWriter 6.0.

- A file called 32-Bit QuickDraw, which loads patches into RAM to allow color Macs to support certain color video boards. Chapter 6 contains details on 32-bit QuickDraw and color boards.

The LaserWriter 6.0 driver operates with System 6.0 through 6.0.3. The 32-Bit QuickDraw file, however, requires System 6.0.3. When System 6.0.3 starts up, it looks in the System Folder for the 32-Bit QuickDraw file. If found, it loads its software. This process occurs just before the system begins looking for and loading Inits.

CHAPTER SUMMARY

- The System Folder has evolved since the Mac's introduction, with each new version offering additional features and support for advances in the Mac's hardware.

- Apple indicates improvements in system files by advancing their version numbers. Generally, major enhancements are indicated by an increment in the number before the decimal point (for example, System 4.0 to System 5.0) while minor revisions are indicated by an advancing number after the decimal point (for example, System 4.0 to System 4.1).

- System files fall into several categories: the main players such as the System and Finder files; start-up documents (Inits) like Easy Access and Macro-Maker; Control Panel devices (cdevs) such as General, Monitors, and Keyboard; printer drivers like ImageWriter and LaserWriter; and miscellaneous files such as Print Monitor and Finder Startup.

- Apple's Installer utility updates the contents of a System Folder. Installer also uses a technique called patching to create a common ground of software features that exist across the Macintosh family.

- As the Mac's system software has evolved, earlier machines such as the 512K and 512K Enhanced have been left behind because they lack sufficient RAM to hold the patches necessary to run the latest system versions.

6

Macintosh Video

The Mac has many unique features, but the one you notice first is its razor-sharp video screen. Because graphics play such a large role in the Macintosh world, it's important to understand how the Mac creates screen displays. This chapter summarizes the video-related information we've touched on in previous chapters, and describes in greater detail how the Mac creates screen images. We'll examine:

- how the Mac's video circuitry works

- the differences between the video circuitry in monochrome and color Macs

- how color Macs create color or gray-scale displays.

Because the Mac's screen reflects what you'll see when you print a document, an understanding of its video concepts will also help you understand the Mac's approach to fonts and printing. We'll explore those topics in the next two chapters.

Unless noted otherwise, this discussion applies to the entire Macintosh family.

VIDEO RECAP

First, let's review the three key points about Mac video that we've mentioned already.

- Unlike many microcomputers, which have separate display modes for creating text and graphics, the Mac's display circuitry has only one display mode: graphics. It's this trait that allows the Mac to display its vast variety of type fonts and sizes.

- The Mac uses a bit-mapped display. In a monochrome (black and white) Mac, each screen dot, or pixel, corresponds to—or *is mapped to*—one bit in the Mac's memory. In compact Macs (the Plus, SE, and SE/30), about 22K of RAM is required for this memory area, called the *screen buffer*. As we'll see later in this chapter, creating displays with color or shades of gray requires the Mac to assign more than one bit to each pixel.

- To create screen displays, application programs use a library of ROM-based graphics software called QuickDraw. QuickDraw provides routines for drawing text and shapes, filling shapes with patterns, and inverting shapes (turning white pixels black and vice versa). QuickDraw provides the foundation of the Mac's display capabilities. Other components of the Mac's system software, such as the Menu Manager, Font Manager, and Window Manager, rely on QuickDraw routines to do their work.

(As you may recall from Chapter 3, the Mac has shown the IBM world that graphical user interfaces can be superior to character-based, command-line user interfaces. The leading graphical operating environments in the IBM PC world—Microsoft Windows and OS/2 Presentation Manager—switch the PC into an all-graphics, bit-mapped display mode. These environments also provide QuickDraw-like libraries of graphics routines.)

BIT-MAPPED VERSUS CHARACTER-BASED DISPLAYS

If you've ever seen a computerized scoreboard at a sports stadium, you've seen how text and images can be created by turning some lights on and others off. Bit-mapped displays work in the same way, except they use pixels instead of light bulbs.

As for the old-fashioned scoreboards that stadiums used to have, they compare accurately to character-based video displays. With a character-based scoreboard, a cigar-chomping curmudgeon inserts numbers into holes as the game progresses. With character-based video, a character-generator chip "inserts" characters into invisible holes on the computer screen.

We may be swimming against the tide of progress, but we'll take the charm of an old-fashioned scoreboard over its computerized counterpart any day. But there's nothing charming about a video screen that displays the same monotonous typeface all day long. Where computers are concerned, there's nothing like that bit-mapped look.

VIDEO DETAILS

It's time to leave the ballpark and take a closer look at how the video circuitry operates in the Mac.

Like all microcomputers and consumer video equipment, the Mac uses a *raster display*—its screen images are comprised of hundreds of horizontal lines created by a beam of electrons on the inside surface of the video tube. This surface is coated with *phosphor*, a material that glows briefly when struck by electrons. The electron beam is guided by a magnetic field created by the video tube's *yoke*, a series of wire coils that encircles the neck of the video tube like a gaudy necklace. (*Raster* is a Latin word meaning *rake*. Imagine the electron beam raking a series of equally spaced lines across the video tube, and you can understand why pioneering television engineers of the 1930s coined the term.)

To rake an image into the phosphor, the electron beam begins at the upper-left corner of the screen and scans across the screen from left to right. As it moves from left to right, the beam pulses off and on to create black and white pixels as needed. When the beam reaches the right edge of the display, the Mac's video circuitry shuts it off momentarily, and then returns it to the left edge of the screen, but down one pixel. The beam is then switched back on to paint another *scan line*. On compact Macs, this scanning scheme repeats until the beam has drawn 342 scanning lines. At that time, the video circuitry shuts the beam off again, aims it at the top-left corner, and repeats the entire process. Figure 6-1 summarizes this process.

This screen-painting process sounds time-consuming, but it's nearly instantaneous. On a compact Mac, the beam scans the entire screen in about 1/60 second. The speed with which a video system creates a complete screen is called its *frame rate*. Compact Macs have a frame rate of 60.1 Hertz; that is, a compact Mac redraws, or *refreshes*, its entire display 60.1 times per second. The Apple video card for the Mac II refreshes the entire display 66.67 times per second.

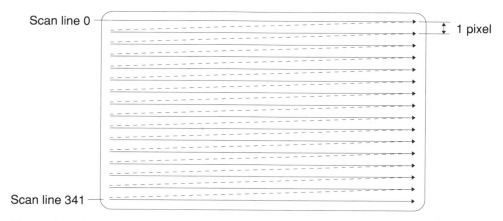

Figure 6-1: Creating a screen display.

And when we say the *entire* display, we mean it. Unlike television sets, the Mac repaints *every* scan line during each refresh cycle. Televisions use a screen-painting technique that involves drawing all the even numbered scan lines during one pass, and then all the odd numbered ones during the next pass. This scheme, called *interlacing,* can result in noticeable screen flicker. By combining *non-interlaced* video with a fast refresh rate, the Mac provides an image with much less flicker than a conventional television.

Resolution versus Pixel Count

The word *resolution* is often used to describe the number of pixels a computer's screen can display. Technically, resolution is the number of pixels *per inch* a video screen can display. The total number of horizontal or vertical pixels a screen can display determines its *pixel count.*

We've already mentioned that a compact Mac's screen contains 342 horizontal scan lines. Because a scan line is one pixel wide, the compact Mac's screen has a vertical pixel count of 342 pixels.

Compact Macs have a horizontal pixel count of 512 pixels. It's worth noting that this value isn't determined by the number of scan lines on the screen; instead, it's determined by how quickly the electron beam can flick on and off as moves from left to right to create a scan line.

As for resolution, a compact Mac's video screen provides a resolution of approximately 74 pixels per inch. This is quite close to a standard unit of measurement in printing and typesetting, the *point,* of which there are 72 per inch. The AppleColor and Apple Monochrome monitors available for modular Macs have a resolution of approximately 80 pixels per inch. They display 640 pixels horizontally and 480 vertically.

Table 6-1 summarizes the resolution and pixel counts of the Mac family's standard video hardware.

Table 6-1: Resolution and pixel counts of Apple video hardware.

Video Hardware	Resolution (dpi)	Pixel Count[1]	Screen Size[2]
Compact Macs	74	512 by 342	9, L
Apple Monochrome Monitor	80	640 by 480	12, L
AppleColor Monitor	80	640 by 480	13, L
Two-Page Monochrome Monitor	77	1,152 by 870	21, L
Macintosh Portrait Display	80	640 by 870	15, P

[1] Pixel counts appear with the horizontal value first followed by the vertical.

[2] In inches, measured diagonally. "L" indicates a landscape (wider than tall) orientation; "P" indicates portrait (taller than wide) orientation.

Simulating Shades of Gray

The Mac Plus and SE can display any color pixel you want, as long as it's black or white. Because each pixel in a monochrome Mac is mapped to one bit, and because a bit can have only one of two values (zero or one; white or black), monochrome Macs can't display color or shades of gray.

They can, however, simulate gray shades by using patterns of white and black pixels, a process called *dithering*. Two common examples of dithering in the Mac interface are the Mac's gray desktop pattern and the gray pattern you see inside scroll bars.

Figure 6-2 shows how a dithered gray compares to a true shade of gray. It shows an image created by a scanner and displayed by Letraset's ImageStudio electronic retouching program. The top screen shows how the image appears on a monochrome Mac SE. The bottom screen shows how the same image appears on a Mac II configured to display 256 shades of gray. Which machine would you prefer for electronic retouching?

Figure 6-2: Dithered gray (*top*) versus true gray (*bottom*).

As you may recall from Chapter 4, the phrase gray scale is often used to describe hardware or software that can work with true shades of gray. For example, the phrase "a gray-scale monitor" refers to a monitor that can display shades of gray. If you plan to work with scanned images, you'll encounter gray-scale issues frequently. Details on printing gray-scale images appear in Chapter 8. For information on exchanging gray-scale images with IBM PCs, see Chapter 11.

MAC II VIDEO

Where video is concerned, the members of the Mac II family have much in common with their pint-sized cousins. Like compact Macs, the Mac II family uses non-interlaced, bit-mapped displays driven by QuickDraw graphics commands. Beyond this, however, are some significant video-related differences:

- As mentioned in Chapter 4, the Mac II family lacks built-in monitors and video circuitry. They use external monitors controlled by plug-in NuBus expansion boards. This design allows you to match your Mac's video hardware to your needs.

- The Mac II family can accommodate multiple video cards, and thus can drive multiple monitors at the same time.

- The Mac II family (and the Mac SE/30) use a special version of QuickDraw, Color QuickDraw, that offers additional commands and features for creating color displays.

The following sections explore these differences in greater detail.

Color and Gray-Scale Video

Let's start out by taking a look at how the Mac II family displays color and gray-scale images. This information also applies to Mac SE/30s containing color or gray-scale video hardware.

When you look closely at a color Mac's monitor, you can see that each color pixel is actually comprised of three much smaller patches of red, green, and blue light. These three colors are *primary colors*, the basic building blocks of white light. Because these *triads* of colored light are too small to see individually, the eyes merge them into a single, colored pixel.

Each pixel's triads of red, green, and blue light are created by three electron guns (one for each color) in the video tube's neck. The tube's inside surface is coated with red, green, and blue phosphor dots. By controlling the stream of electrons from each gun as the guns create each pixel, the Mac's video circuitry controls each pixel's color. (Some video monitors, such as Sony's, use just one electron gun that fires at all three types of phosphors.)

Storing and Representing Color

So a color monitor creates color pixels under the direction of the Mac's video circuitry. But how does the Mac keep track of colors internally? And how does it know how much red, green, and blue light is required to create a given color?

In the world of bit-mapped video, the secret to storing color information is to assign more than one bit to each pixel. These additional bits convey information about the pixel's color or shade of gray. By assigning two bits to each pixel, color Macs can display four colors. Four bits can represent 16 colors, and eight bits can represent 256. A fully expanded Apple Video Card can assign up to eight bits per pixel. Without the memory-expansion kit, the card can assign up to four bits per pixel.

As Figure 6-3 shows, you use the Control Panel's Monitors cdev to specify how many bits are assigned to each pixel.

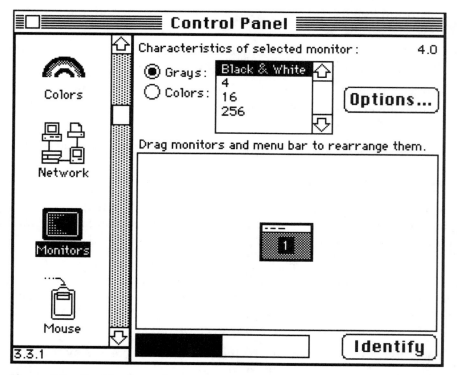

Figure 6-3: The Monitors cdev.

How can two bits represent four colors, or eight, 256? Each pixel's bits can be on or off in different combinations. For example, in the two-bits-per-pixel mode, four on/off combinations exist:

- bit #1 is on and bit #2 is on

- bit #1 is off and bit #2 is off

- bit #1 is on and bit #2 is off

- bit #2 is on and bit #1 is off

Thus, the Mac's first step in creating a color pixel is to determine the value of the bits assigned to that pixel. This results in a number that the Mac uses to retrieve a color description that specifies how much red, green, and blue light will be needed to create that color. That description comes from a special table of data, stored in the video board's memory, called a *color look-up table*.

Color Look-up Tables

Look-up table sounds like a typically technical computer term. But a look-up table is simply a set of data structured in a way that lets you locate an unknown piece of information by looking up a known piece of information. A telephone directory is one example: by looking up a person's name, you can find his or her phone number or address. Those cursed government tax tables are look-up tables: you look up your income to find out how much tax you owe.

The Mac's color look-up table tells the Mac how much red, green, and blue light to mix in order to create a given color. In a way, a color look-up table is like a paint-mixing chart at a paint store: just as the store employee uses the chart to find out what pigments to mix to create a certain color, the Mac uses a color look-up table to find out how much red, green, and blue light to mix to create pixels of a given color.

Figure 6-4 summarizes this discussion, showing steps the Mac performs to create a single, colored pixel.

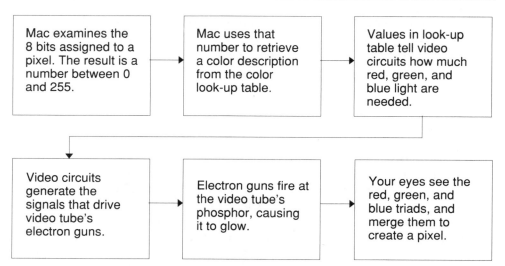

Figure 6-4: Creating a color pixel.

Switching Look-up Tables

Unlike numbers in a phone book or values in a tax table, the color recipes in a color look-up table aren't permanent. They're stored in RAM, and because of that, the Mac can load different look-up tables into RAM as needed.

This point is significant: it means that a pixel's resulting color number—the value the Mac obtains by examining the pixel's bits—never corresponds to a specific color, such as barn red or sky blue. The bits that are assigned to a given pixel might always result in a color number of, say, 2, but the color you see on screen depends on the color recipe that's assigned to the fifth entry in the look-up table (color numbering begins at zero). Figure 6-5 illustrates this point.

This ability to load different color look-up tables makes it possible to tailor the Mac's color features to specific tasks. For example, portrait artists might replace the blues and oranges in the Mac's palette with a larger selection of flesh tones. Similarly, a poster artist might prefer to replace the subtle pastels with some brilliant, Day Glo hues. Two parts of the Mac's Toolbox, the Palette Manager and the Color Manager, control the Mac's palette-customizing features.

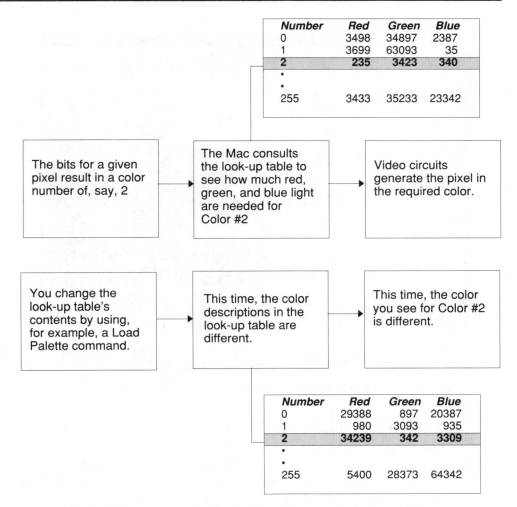

Figure 6-5: Switching color recipes by loading different color look-up tables.

Many programs take advantage of the Mac's palette-swapping talents. One example is SuperMac Software's PixelPaint color painting program. Choosing its Colors command reveals a dialog box that lets you choose from several built-in palettes, as shown in Figure 6-6. PixelPaint also lets you modify the colors in each palette, and as well as save and load different palettes to and from disk.

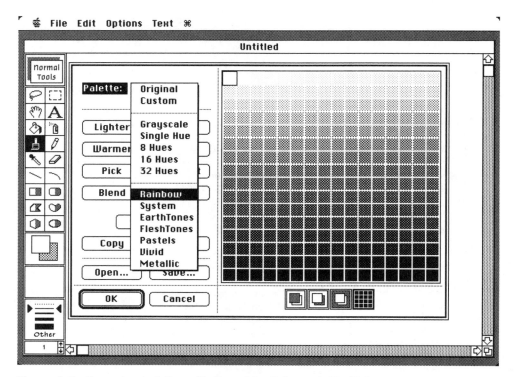

Figure 6-6: Swapping palettes with SuperMac Software's PixelPaint.

Controlling Multiple Monitors

As mentioned earlier, the Mac II family can drive more than one monitor at the same time. In these NuBus-equipped Macs, each monitor has its own video card, which contains RAM for the screen buffer, a *configuration ROM*, which describes the board's display capabilities, and other support circuitry. (We'll look at NuBus in greater detail in Chapter 13.)

The Mac's ability to drive multiple monitors lets you mix and match monitors offering different color and gray-scale features. However, when you have monitors with different color or gray-scale features attached to one Mac, the Mac must keep track of each monitor's color or gray-scale capabilities. To do so, the Mac stores separate color look-up tables for each monitor and display board combination. Because it maintains a separate color look-up table for each board and monitor, you can mix and match different types of displays without worrying about each one being in the same display mode. By referring to each monitor's color look-up table, the Mac can adjust the way it renders the image on each monitor.

Are 256 Colors Enough?

The 256 colors that an expanded Apple Video Card provide seem like a large enough number for any task. But, while 256 colors are more than adequate for color charts and graphs, artists striving for photographic realism or smooth, airbrush like color gradations require a larger rainbow of hues. The eye can discern between thousands of different colors or gray shades; 256 aren't enough for photographic realism. By dithering (combining patterns of colored pixels), a color Mac can simulate more than 256 colors, but even this technique isn't adequate for rendering color images with photographic realism.

For such applications, the answer may be a *24-bit color board*. By assigning 24 bits to each pixel, such boards give you direct access to over 16 million colors. SuperMac, RasterOps, and Jasmine are just a few of the firms selling 24-bit color boards for NuBus-equipped Macs and for the Mac SE/30. These boards use Apple's 32-bit Color QuickDraw. (What about the eight-bit difference between 24-bit boards and 32-bit QuickDraw? Those extra eight bits, sometimes called an *alpha channel*, can be used by application developers for specialized purposes, such as assigning transparency information to images.)

To use a 24-bit color board, you need:

- Apple's 32-Bit QuickDraw file, which shipped in May 1989 as part of the Color Disk update, discussed in the previous chapter.

- System 6.0.3. This version of the Mac's system software looks for the 32-Bit QuickDraw file during start-up, and loads it into memory. (32-bit Quick-Draw will be an integral part of System 7.0; when you upgrade to System 7.0, you won't need the 32-Bit QuickDraw file.)

- A Mac with at least 2MB of RAM. 1MB Macs lack sufficient memory to accommodate the 32-Bit QuickDraw code and still leave enough free RAM to run color applications.

Color Video and Memory

It's obvious that color and gray-scale video require more video memory than monochrome video. All those extra bits you're assigning to each pixel have to come from somewhere. In color Macs, that "somewhere" is video RAM located on the video card. The Apple Video Card includes 256K of memory. The Video Card Expansion Kit, required for 256 colors or grey shades, doubles that amount to 512K. Yes, a fully expanded Apple Video Card provides four times as much RAM for video alone as the original Macintosh provided for video and everything else.

(Knowing that—and knowing that RAM chip prices have decreased while their storage density has increased—you can see how economics prevented Apple from building color capabilities into the original Mac. Of course, performance was another reason: the original 8MHz, 68000-based Macs lacked the processing punch to manipulate the large amount of data involved in representing color.)

Color and Compatibility

We've mentioned that color Macs use a beefed up version of QuickDraw called Color QuickDraw. The fact that different members of the Mac family use different versions of QuickDraw—one with advanced color features, and one without—imposes some compatibility concerns that the Mac world had been spared until the Mac II's debut.

Color-related incompatibilities can surface in three areas:

- A program designed specifically for a color Mac will not run on a monochrome one

- You may not always be able to use a monochrome Mac to open or print a color image

- Some older Mac applications may produce strange screen displays when run on a color Mac.

The first incompatibility level is an obvious one: You can't run color painting program such as SuperMac's PixelPaint on a monochrome Mac. A monochrome Mac can, however, run many other types of programs that support color, including desktop publishing programs such as QuarkXpress and Aldus PageMaker; spreadsheet programs such as Microsoft Excel and Ashton-Tate's FullImpact; word processors such as Microsoft Word; and even some drawing and drafting programs, including Adobe Illustrator 88, VersaCAD, and Claris' MacDraw II. You won't see colors on the screen when you run one of these programs on a monochrome Mac, but you will be able to use their color-formatting features.

The second level of potential incompatibility can arise when you attempt to use a monochrome Mac to open or print a color image. If your monochrome Mac is running System 4.1 or a later version, you can open a Color QuickDraw image, but all non-white areas will appear black. Worse, you may have trouble printing the image. Obviously, a monochrome Mac is not the place to open your latest multihued masterpiece.

You're susceptible to this problem if you have a number of Macs networked together and you routinely exchange data between them. For example, a publishing-oriented office might use a color Mac to create color illustrations, and a monochrome Mac for page layout. If this describes your office, beware.

The third type of incompatibility is shown in Figure 6-7. These strange multiple images can appear when you run an older application on a color Mac configured to display more than two colors. We've encountered this problem with two painting programs: Ashton-Tate's FullPaint 1.1 (shown in Figure 6-7) and Silicon Beach Software's SuperPaint 1.0.

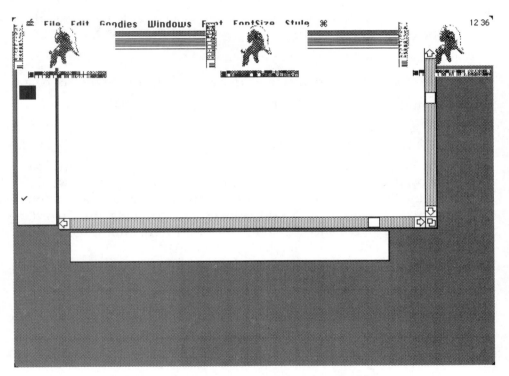

Figure 6-7: Older applications may not run properly on a color Mac.

The problem occurs because the applications' developers, in the interest of faster performance, strayed from one of Apple's programming guidelines: instead of using QuickDraw routines to draw screen images, they manipulate the Mac's video memory directly. Because these applications predate color Macs, they assume they're running on a one-bit-per-pixel Mac. When you run such a program on a color Mac, the application accesses multiple bits for each pixel it tries to draw, and thus, it draws several small images—one for each bit. The solution is to switch the Mac into two-color (one bit per pixel) mode.

COLOR ARCHITECTURES

We've said that color Macs get their color capabilities by assigning multiple bits to each pixel. Now let's see how those bits are arranged in the Mac's video memory. Several methods, or *architectures*, exist for arranging and storing the bits in a color or gray-scale board's video memory. You don't have to understand these architectures in order to use a color Mac, but some background will help you shop intelligently for color video hardware—especially if you plan to purchase a 24-bit color board.

The three most common color video architectures are:

- The *chunky* architecture, used by Apple's video cards and most other video boards

- The *planar* architecture, not used in the Mac world

- The *chunky-planar* architecture, used by some early 24-bit color boards

Strange names, aren't they? Let's demystify them.

The Chunky Architecture

The chunky architecture, also called the *packed pixel* architecture, is the most common color video architecture in the microcomputer world. Besides being used by most Macintosh video boards, the chunky video architecture is also used by most IBM PC video hardware, including the Color/Graphics Adaptor (CGA), Enhanced Graphics Adaptor (EGA), Multi-Color Graphics Array (MCGA), and Virtual Graphics Array (VGA).

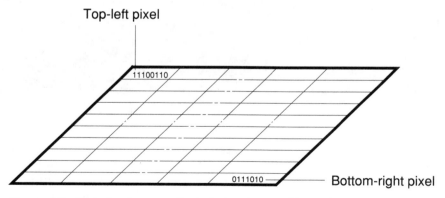

Figure 6-8: The chunky, or packed pixel, color graphics architecture.

In the chunky architecture, the bits assigned to each pixel are packed alongside each other in video memory, as shown in Figure 6-8. The bits are stored sequentially, starting with the top-left pixel and ending with the bottom-right one.

Apple's versions of Color QuickDraw support only the chunky architecture. As mentioned earlier, the bits stored in the video board's memory serve as an index to a color look-up table, which tells the video board how much red, green, and blue light to use in order to create the required color.

The Planar Architecture

The planar architecture isn't used in the Mac world, but we'll take a brief look at it because the chunky-planar architecture, discussed next, borrows some concepts from it.

With the planar architecture, the bits that form each pixel are arranged in separate *bit planes*, as shown in Figure 6-9. Think of each bit plane as a see-through plastic overlay; the screen image is produced by combining the contents of each bit plane.

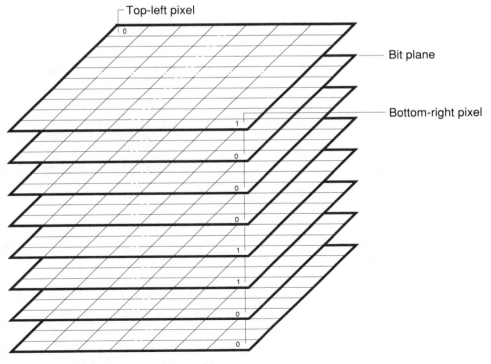

Figure 6-9: The planar graphics architecture.

The Chunky-Planar Architecture

What do you get when you combine the sequential-bit organization of the chunky architecture with the bit planes of the planar architecture? That's right: chunky-planar, a hybrid architecture that borrows from both the chunky and planar architectures. Like the planar architecture, chunky-planar uses bit planes. However, instead of providing one bit plane for each bit assigned to a pixel (as does planar), chunky-planar video boards provide just three bit planes: one each for red, green, and blue. Within each bit plane, the bits that describe how much red, green, and blue are required to create the color are packed sequentially—as they are in the chunky architecture.

This hybrid architecture was popular among pioneering 24-bit video boards such as RasterOps' ColorCard 1/104. Because the original version of Color QuickDraw could not work with more than eight bits of information per pixel, the developers of the 24-bit color boards provided software that coerced Color QuickDraw to work with 24 bits of information.

The secret behind this coercion was to divide the 24 bits of information into three eight-bit chunks: one each for red, green, and blue. Each of these three eight-bit values acted as an index to three separate color look-up tables, as shown in Figure 6-10.

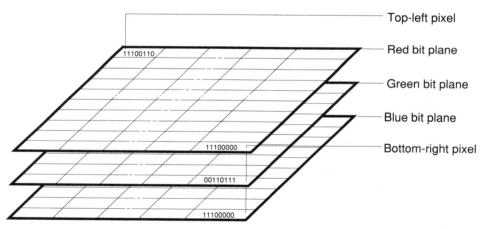

Figure 6-10: The chunky-planar architecture.

To create a 24-bit color image, a chunky-planar video board drew three screen images: first the red "layer," then the green layer, then the blue layer. With some chunky-planar 24-bit Mac II color boards, you could see each layer being drawn. Other boards used graphics coprocessors to speed the display process.

Direct-Chunky Boards

When Apple released its 32-Bit QuickDraw driver in May 1989, the Mac world saw a new generation of *direct-chunky* 24-bit video boards such as SuperMac's Spectrum/24. (Direct-chunky boards are also referred to as *full chunky*, *direct color*, and *true color boards*.) Like the original crop of chunky video boards, direct chunky-boards store the bits that describe each pixel's color sequentially in video RAM. Unlike original chunky video cards, however, direct-chunky boards do not require color look-up tables. Instead, they directly drive the circuitry that controls the monitor's red, green, and blue electron guns, as shown in Figure 6-11.

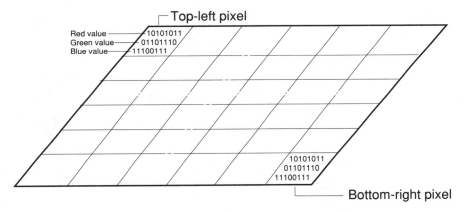

Figure 6-11: Direct chunky boards eliminate color look-up tables and drive electron guns directly.

CHAPTER SUMMARY

- Unlike television sets, the Mac uses non-interlaced video—it repaints the entire screen during each refresh cycle, rather than just the odd or even numbered scan lines. Non-interlaced video provides a steadier image with less flicker.

- The term *resolution* refers to the number of pixels per inch a video screen can display. The total number of horizontal or vertical pixels a screen can display determines its pixel count.

- Monochrome Macs can simulate shades of gray by using a technique known as dithering. Macs equipped with gray-scale or color video cards can display true shades of gray, making them preferable for image retouching and processing applications.

- Color cards operate by assigning multiple bits to each pixel. The bits that describe a given pixel act as an index to a color look-up table, which tells the card how much red, green, and blue light to mix to create a given color.

- The Mac II family and the SE/30 can drive multiple monitors, even if each monitor provides a different mix of color or gray-scale features.

- Several methods, or architectures, exist for arranging and storing the bits in a color or gray-scale board's video memory. Apple's video cards use the chunky architecture.

Section II

Mastering the Mac

7

Fonts

Understanding the Mac's approach to fonts can help you use its typographic features more effectively and get the best results from your printer. In this chapter, we'll look at the Mac's font features. We'll examine:

- basic typographic terminology

- the basics of Mac fonts

- how to add and remove fonts

- how the Mac's fonts are structured

- how the Mac's font features differ between System 7.0 and earlier versions.

This look at the Mac's typographic talents will set the stage for the next chapter's tour of the Mac's printing features.

FONT AND TYPE BASICS

Like any specialized field, the typesetting world has its own language. This section describes the terminology you'll encounter as you work with fonts. If you're familiar with such terms as *typeface*, *ascender*, and *x-height*, you may just want to skim this section or skip on to the section "Mac Font Basics," later in this chapter.

Typefaces versus Fonts

First, let's clarify the difference between the terms *typeface* and *font*. A typeface is a unique design of uppercase and lowercase characters, numerals, punctuation marks, and symbols. A font is the implementation—in one size—of a typeface. Figure 7–1, which shows Times Roman in four different sizes, depicts one typeface, but four fonts.

This is 12-point Times Roman.

This is 14-point Times Roman

This is 18-point Times Roman

This is 24-point Times Roman

Figure 7-1: One typeface, four fonts.

In the days of hot metal type, when different molds were required to cast different sizes of type, the distinction between typeface and font was important. Today, the terms are often used interchangeably.

Typefaces are often grouped together in *families*. In the Mac world, a type family usually contains four *styles*:

- Roman, the upright version of the typeface. On the Mac, the Roman style is called *normal* or *plain*.

- *Italic*, a calligraphic variant often used for emphasis. This book uses italic to emphasize new terms.

- *Bold*, a heavier version of the roman style, often used for headings.

- *Bold Italic*, a bold version of the italic style.

You may also encounter a style called *oblique*, a slanted version of the Roman style. That sounds similar to italic, but there's a significant difference. As Figure 7-2 illustrates, an italic style is a completely different rendering of a typeface, while an oblique style is simply a slanted version of the Roman or bold style.

This is Times Italic

This is Times Oblique

Figure 7-2: Times Italic versus Times Oblique.

Understanding the difference between the italic and oblique styles is important because of the technique the Mac uses to display italic text. The Mac can use similar techniques to simulate other type styles, such as outlined and shadowed type. We'll elaborate on these points later in this chapter.

Character Components

Figure 7-3 shows the primary components that form characters. It's the shape and combination of these and other components that give each type style its unique appearance and personality.

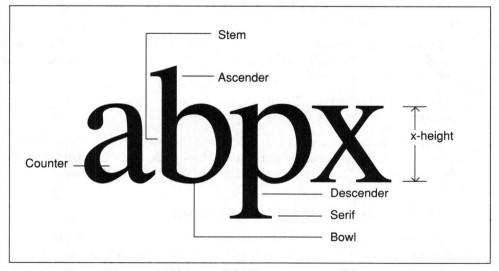

Figure 7-3: Components and characteristics of type.

These components and characteristics include:

Ascender. The portion of a character that extends above the tops of lower-case characters.

Bowl. The round portions of characters such as b, p, and d.

Counter. The white space within a character that helps to define the character's shape.

Descender. The portion of a character that extends below the *baseline*, the imaginary line upon which characters rest.

Serif. Ornamental embellishments attached to the edges of characters that serve to lead the eye across a line of type. A typeface whose characters have serifs (such as Times) is called a *serif typeface*; a typeface that lacks serifs (such as Helvetica) is described as *sans-serif* (without serifs). Serif typefaces are generally considered more legible and superior for lengthy passages of text.

Stem. The vertical portion of a character.

x-height. The height of the lowercase characters (specifically, of the lower-case x) in a given typeface.

Measuring Type and Line Spacing

The typographic world also has its own units of measurement. These measurements include:

Point. A unit equal to 1/72 inch. (Technically, a typographer's point is equal to .351 millimeters, so there are 72.27 points per inch. Apple, however, defines a point as *exactly* 1/72 inch.)

Pica. A unit equal to 12 points. Picas are often used to specify the width of columns.

Em. A unit of horizontal space equal to the square of the type size. For example, in 10-point type, an em is 10 points wide and 10 points high. In the typesetting world, em spaces are often used to specify the size of paragraph indents.

En. A unit of horizontal space equal to half of an em space.

Of these common measuring units, the point is the most important. Points are used to specify the vertical size of type. In a 72-point typeface, for example, there are 10 points of space between the lowest descender and the highest ascender, as shown in Figure 7-4.

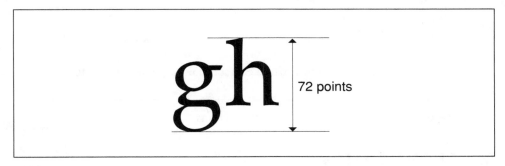

Figure 7-4: How type size is measured.

Points are also used to specify *leading*—the amount of vertical space be-tween lines. Leading (pronounced *ledding*) is measured from baseline to baseline, as shown in Figure 7–5. The term comes from the days of hot metal type, in which strips of lead were used to add space between lines.

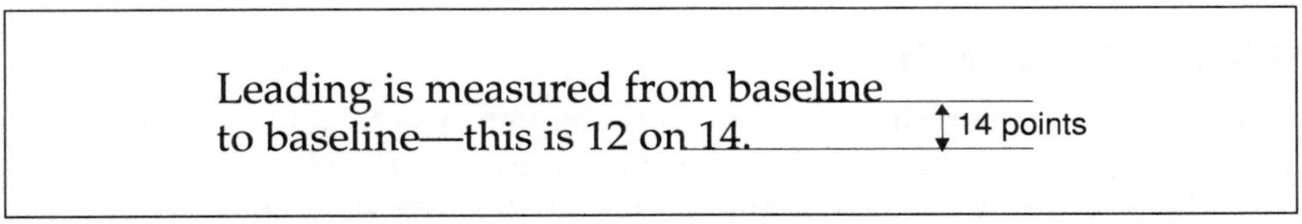

Leading is measured from baseline
to baseline—this is 12 on 14.   ↕ 14 points

Figure 7-5: Leading is measured from baseline to baseline.

When specifying type size and leading, typesetters and designers write a fraction in which the type size is the numerator and the leading, the denomi-nator. In Figure 7-5, the text uses 12-point type and 14 points of leading. This combination is written as *12/14* and pronounced *twelve on fourteen* or *twelve over fourteen*.

Monospaced versus Proportional Fonts

On a typewriter, every character has the same width: a lowercase *i* uses as much horizontal space as an uppercase *M*. Fonts whose characters are spaced in this way are called *monospaced* or *fixed-width* fonts.

Fixed-width fonts are fine for mechanical typewriter mechanisms, but they aren't as legible as *proportional* fonts—fonts whose character widths vary. Pro-portional fonts are easier to read and are preferred for publishing applications. Figure 7-6 shows compares fixed-width and proportional fonts.

```
This is Courier, a fixed-width font.
```

This is New Century Schoolbook, a proportional font.

Figure 7-6: Fixed-width versus proportional fonts.

MAC FONT BASICS

With a knowledge of type terms under our belts, we're ready to explore how fonts work in the Mac world. This section describes:

- how fonts are structured in System 6.0 and earlier versions
- the advantages and disadvantages of the Mac's approach to fonts
- how to add fonts to, and remove them from, your system.

FONT STRUCTURE

As you may recall from previous chapters, the Mac's fonts are a type of resource—a collection of data that programs can use when they're running. In this section, we'll take a closer look at the two ways font resources can be structured.

Bit-mapped versus Outline Fonts

The best way to think of a font resource is as a description—a kind of recipe—that tells the Mac how to draw a given typeface in a given size and style. These font descriptions can take one of two forms: *bit maps* or *outlines*. Macs running System 6.0 and earlier versions use bit-mapped fonts to display text on the screen, but most Mac-compatible laser printers use outline fonts to produce hard copy. Thus, you're likely to encounter both types of fonts as you use the Mac. What's more, System 7.0 will dramatically change the Mac's approach to fonts by providing outline fonts for the screen. For these reasons, it's important to understand both approaches in order to use and choose fonts effectively.

In a bit-mapped font, the font description specifies the exact arrangement of pixels that will form a given character *in a given size*. With bit-mapped fonts, a separate description is required to accurately render each size. As you may recall from Chapter 3, if a program needs a size for which no description exists, the Mac must create that size by altering, or scaling, an existing size. The results of that scaling process aren't very attractive. It's in your eyes' best interest to install the specific sizes you use most often.

With outline fonts, the font description is a mathematic recipe that describes the characters' properties: their proportions, the size of their stems, ascenders, descenders, and other components. The advantage of outline fonts over bit-mapped fonts is that an outline font doesn't require a separate font description for each type size. Instead, one outline font description can be used to create characters of any size.

To appreciate this difference, imagine that you've been given the job of describing the letter O using toy wooden blocks. First, you arrange the blocks in the shape of an O, and then you note the arrangement and quantity of blocks required to form the letter. If you need an O of a different size, you must assemble a completely different arrangement of blocks. This analogy compares to the bit-mapped approach; the wooden blocks are pixels, as shown in Figure 7-7.

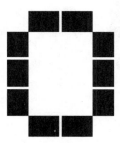

Figure 7-7: Describing an "O" using a bit-mapped approach.

Now let's assume you've been given the task of describing an O using the outline approach. This time, your tool isn't a set of blocks, but a pair of rubber bands. Because the rubber bands describe the properties of the O—they're round—you don't need to create a separate description for each size. To create a larger O, you simply stretch the rubber bands proportionally. To create a stretched or compressed O (in type jargon, an *expanded* or *condensed* O), you simply stretch the rubber bands more in one direction than in the other.

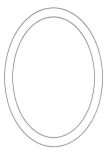

Figure 7-8: Describing an "O" using an outline approach.

It's obvious that the outline approach is more flexible, but there's a catch. Because video screens and laser printers are raster devices, ultimately the character must be described as a bit map. Thus, as Figure 7-9 shows, rendering a character from an outline description is a two-step process: First, the device consults the outline description to learn the character's properties; and second, the device constructs a bit map from that description to create a character of the required size and proportions.

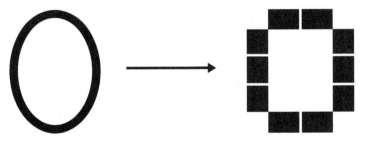

Figure 7-9: Rendering a character from an outline is a two-step process.

If outline fonts require a two-step process to be displayed or printed, why use them? Two reasons:

- Outline font descriptions are *resolution independent.* Unlike bit-mapped descriptions, they aren't tied to a specific number of dots per inch. The character isn't described as a bit map until moments before it's printed or displayed. This flexibility allows one font description to work on any device, regardless of its resolution, and to take maximum advantage of that resolution. It's what allows you to use the same font on a 300-dots-per-inch Laser-Writer or a 2540-dpi Linotronic typesetter. We'll look at the benefits of resolution independence in more detail in the next chapter.

- Outline fonts can create sharp characters in a virtually unlimited range of type sizes. A device that uses outline fonts can generate text in virtually any size. To put it another way, outline fonts are as flexible as rubber bands.

Summing Up Bit Maps versus Outlines

The wood block-versus-rubber band example oversimplifies the technicalities behind bit-mapped and outline fonts. But it does show the basic differences between the two approaches, and it illustrates the ramifications of each, which are:

- Bit-mapped fonts require more storage space, since a separate description is needed for each size.

- Outline fonts are far more flexible; one description can generate a character of any size and proportion.

- Outline fonts are resolution independent; unlike bit-mapped fonts, they aren't tied to a specific number of dots per inch.

- Because an outline must be converted to a bit map before it's displayed or printed, outline fonts can be slower to use than bit-mapped fonts. Whether this is true, however, depends on many technical factors, including the method used to describe the outline.

Adding and Removing Fonts

You can add fonts to, and remove them from, the System file by using Apple's Font/DA Mover utility. You may want to add fonts when you acquire a new printer or want to spice up your typographic life. You may want to remove some fonts when you're running low on disk space or if you're simply tired of a given typeface.

This section provides step-by-step instructions for adding and removing fonts on Mac's running System 6.0 and earlier versions. With System 7.0, you will install fonts by dragging them to the System Folder.

- A copy of the current version of the Font/DA Mover utility; at this writing, version 3.8. In the System 6.0.2 update package, the Font/DA Mover is located in a folder called Font/DA Mover Folder on the disk labeled Utilities 2.

- A font file containing a font that you can add to your System. (If you aren't sure what a font file is, you'll find an introduction in the next section, "A Font/DA Mover Overview.") If you have the Utilities 2 disk we just mentioned, you're all set: a file named Fonts, located in the Font/DA Mover Folder, contains additional fonts you can add. If you don't have any font files, just follow along. Directions for creating new font files and adding fonts to them appear later in this section.

- A start-up disk containing a System file, to which you will add the fonts. Your start-up disk must have at least 10K of free space to accommodate the new font. (Note: If you've never used the Font/DA Mover before, you may want to make a backup copy of the System file. If your System file will fit on a single floppy disk, use the Finder to make a backup copy on the floppy. If you have a hard disk and a huge System file, you may just want to create a backup on the hard disk. Be sure your hard disk has enough free space to accommodate the backup, then open the System Folder, select the System file, and choose Duplicate from the Finder's File menu. This creates a file named Copy of System. If something happens to your original System file, you can rename this duplicate to *System* and be back in business. Remember that you'll need to start your Mac with a different system disk in order to throw away your original System file and rename the duplicate.)

Finally, when you're adding or removing fonts or desk accessories, it's a good idea to not run under MultiFinder. If you're using MultiFinder now, use the Finder's Set Startup command to specify that your Mac start up with the Finder, then choose Restart from the Special menu. To verify that you aren't running under MultiFinder, check the right end of the menu bar and verify that no icon appears there.

A Font/DA Mover Overview

The Font/DA Mover lets you perform three basic tasks:

- Add fonts or desk accessories stored in separate files to the System file
- Remove fonts or desk accessories from the System file
- Copy fonts or desk accessories from the System file into a separate file or to a second System file located on a different disk.

As for those "separate files," Apple calls them *font files* and *desk accessory files*, but many Mac users call them *suitcase files* because their icons resemble suitcases, as shown in Figure 7-10.

The term *suitcase files* accurately describes their role. Like a real suitcase, a suitcase file is packed with baggage—one or more fonts, or one or more desk accessories. And like a suitcase, a suitcase file acts as a temporary carrying case, a place to hold baggage until it arrives at its destination—a System file.

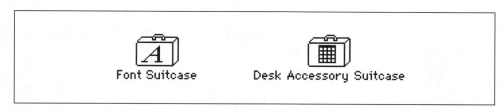

Figure 7-10: Suitcase files for fonts (left) and desk accessories (right).

And who does the unpacking? The Font/DA Mover. When you add a font, the Font/DA Mover copies it from the suitcase file into the System file. (Notice, though, that the Font/DA Mover's approach to unpacking differs from a business traveler's: when you add a font to the system file, the Font/DA Mover doesn't actually remove it from the suitcase file; it reads the font description and then *copies* it into the System file.)

Adding a Font

The following steps describe how to add a font from a suitcase file to the System file. If you have the suitcase file called Fonts from the Utilities 2 disk, you can follow these instructions to add the Athens font to your System file. If you're adding a different font, substitute that font's name each time you see Athens.

1. Start the the Font/DA Mover by double-clicking its icon.

   After a few moments, the Font/DA Mover screen appears. Notice that the Font/DA Mover has opened the System file for you; the names of its fonts appear in the left list box, as shown in Figure 7-11 (your font names may differ). Each entry you see represents a separate bit-mapped font description for a given point size. This illustrates the point made earlier: with bit-mapped fonts, each size requires its own description.

2. To open a suitcase file containing the font you want to add, click the Open button under the right list box, and then locate and double-click the name of the suitcase file.

   A list of the font descriptions contained in the suitcase file appears in the right list box, as shown in Figure 7-12. Notice, too, that the Open button now reads Close.

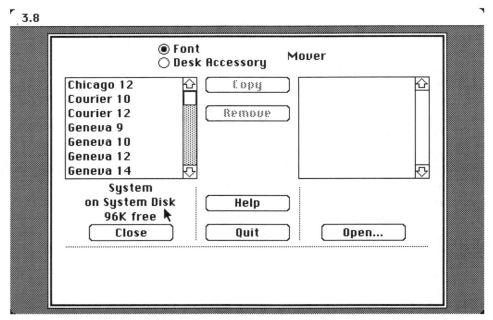

Figure 7-11: The Font/DA Mover window with the System file open (*at left*).

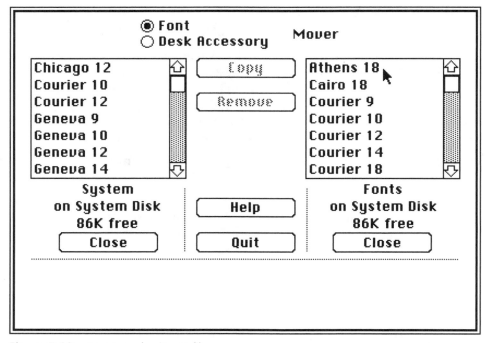

Figure 7-12: An opened suitcase file.

3. Locate the entry *Athens 18* in the right list box, and select it by clicking once on its name.

The Copy and Remove buttons located between the two list boxes are now active (previously, they were inactive). Also, the Font/DA Mover has displayed the size of the font and a sample sentence, as shown in Figure 7-13.

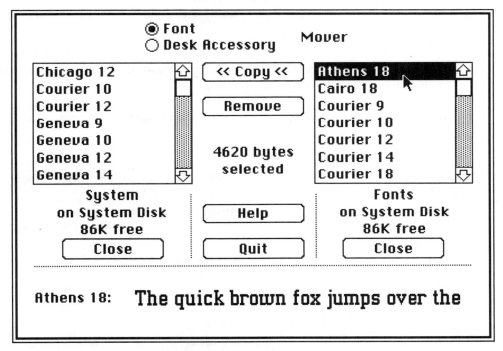

Figure 7-13: A selected font, ready to be copied.

4. Click the Copy button to add the font to the System file.

The wristwatch pointer appears to let you know the Mac is busy moving the font. After a few moments, the entry *Athens 18* appears in the left list box, indicating that the font is now installed in the System file.

5. To quit the Font/DA Mover, click the Quit button.

If you like, you can start an application and check its Font menu or dialog box to verify that the font is installed. Or simply open the Key Caps desk accessory and check its menu.

Adding Multiple Fonts

You can also add more than one font at a time. To do so, substitute the following step for Step 3 in the preceding instructions.

3. Select the first font you want to add, and then hold down the Shift key while clicking on other fonts. If you select a font by mistake, you can deselect it: continue to hold the Shift key, and then click on the font to deselect it. (Incidentally, this is another example of how the Mac lets you extend a selection by Shift-clicking.)

When you select more than one font, no sample text appears at the bottom of the window, but the total space required by all the selected fonts still appears below the Remove button, as shown in Figure 7-14.

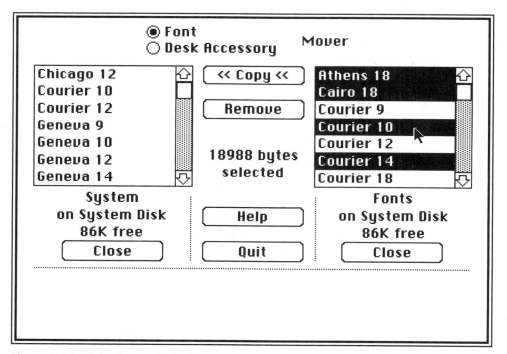

Figure 7-14: Selecting multiple fonts.

Removing a Font

Removing a font isn't too different from adding one. The following steps describe how to remove Athens 18, the font you added in the previous exercise. If you want to remove a different font, substitute its entry for *Athens 18*.

1. Start the Font/DA Mover by double-clicking its icon.

   The Font/DA Mover automatically opens the System file and displays its fonts.

2. In the left list box, locate the entry *Athens 18*, and select it by clicking on it once.

   To remove more than one font, Shift-click on the subsequent fonts as described in the previous section, "Adding Multiple Fonts." Notice that the Copy button is inactive; that's because no second file is open (the right list box is blank, and the button below it reads Open).

3. To remove the font, click the Remove button.

   The Font/DA Mover asks if you want to remove the selected items. You can cancel the operation by clicking Cancel or pressing Return.

4. To verify the operation and remove the font, click OK.

   The wristwatch pointer appears as the Font/DA Mover removes the font. After a few moments, the list box is updated to reflect the font's demise.

   It's worth mentioning that you can't remove the Chicago 12, Geneva 9, and Monaco 9 fonts. The Mac uses Chicago for menus, dialog boxes, buttons, and other controls, and it uses Geneva 9 to label icons in the Finder. If you try to remove one of these fonts, the Font/DA Mover displays a message stating, "Sorry, the font <name> is reserved for system use and will not be removed."

Creating a New Suitcase File

As mentioned previously, the Font/DA Mover also lets you create new suitcase files and add fonts to them. There are several reasons why you might want to create and "pack" your own suitcases:

- To create a backup copy of the font and size combinations in your System file (a good idea)

- To store one or more fonts that you plan to remove from the System file, but may want to restore later.

- To create a file that you will use on a different Mac to recreate the font and size combinations of your own System file.

   Let's see how to create a new suitcase file and copy two fonts—Geneva 9 and Monaco 9—into it. (These fonts were chosen because they're present in every System file. To copy different fonts into a suitcase file, substitute their names.)

1. Start the Font/DA Mover by double clicking its icon.

   The Font/DA Mover opens the System file and displays its fonts.

2. Click the Open button below the right list box.

   An open dialog box appears, as shown in Figure 7-15.

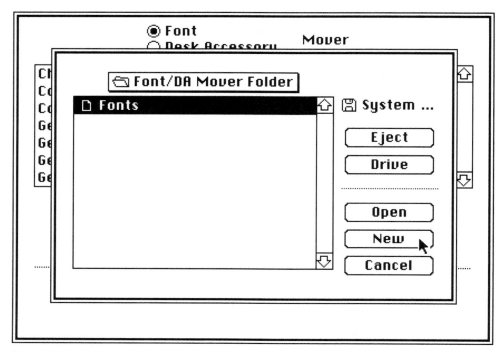

Figure 7-15: The Font/DA Mover's Open dialog box.

3. In the Open dialog box, click the New button.

   A dialog box appears asking for a name for the new font file, as shown in Figure 7-16.

4. If necessary, click the Drive button until the name of the disk on which you want to create the font file appears above the Eject button. If you want the font file in a specific folder, open that folder.

5. Type a name for the new font file—let's use *My Suitcase*—and click the Create button or press Return.

   The Font/DA Mover creates and opens the suitcase file, as shown in Figure 7-17.

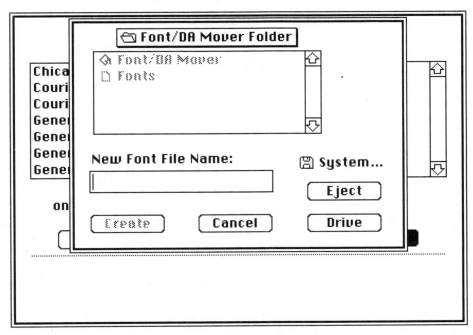

Figure 7-16: Dialog box for creating a new font file.

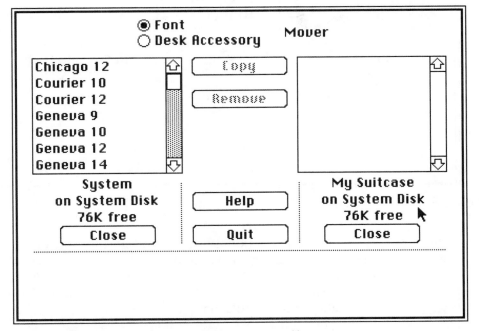

Figure 7-17: Newly created—but empty—suitcase file.

6. In the left list box, locate the entry *Geneva 9* and select it.

7. Hold down the Shift key, and then locate the entry *Monaco 9* and select it.

The Copy button is enabled and is surrounded by right-pointing arrows, indicating the Font/DA Mover is ready to copy the selected fonts into the suitcase file. Because you selected more than one font, no sample text appears at the bottom of the window. If the sample text does appear, you didn't press Shift before selecting the second font.

8. Click the Copy button to copy the fonts into the new suitcase file.

The wristwatch pointer appears and after a few moments, the copied fonts appear in the right list box, as shown in Figure 7-18.

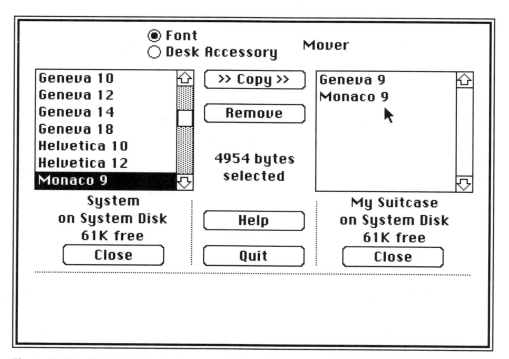

Figure 7-18: Copied fonts in the new suitcase file.

From here, you can copy additional fonts to the suitcase file, or you can close the suitcase file by clicking the Close button that appears beneath its name. After quitting the Font/DA Mover, you can remove the file *My Suitcase* by dragging it to the Trash. Note that by doing so, you aren't throwing away the 9-point Geneva and Monaco fonts in the System file; you're simply throwing away the copies you added to the suitcase file.

The preceding example illustrates another important point: A suitcase file can contain more than one typeface. Some people miss this point, and create separate suitcase files for each typeface (Geneva, Monaco, Times, and so on). There are times when this one-face-per-suitcase approach is desirable—such as when you want to install your Times family on a different Mac—but there are also times when you want to move numerous typefaces in one fell swoop. For those occasions, remember that a suitcase can hold any combination of type-faces. When you're packing for a trip, you don't have to use separate suitcases for your pants, shirts, and socks. Similarly, when you're packing suitcase files, you don't have to use separate files to hold different typefaces.

What About Desk Accessories?

It's worth mentioning that you can install and remove desk accessories us-ing the same basic techniques described in the previous exercises. Simply click the Desk Accessory button at the top of the Font/DA Mover's window to switch from its font mode to its desk accessory mode. Or use this undocu-mented tip: Hold down the Option key while the Font/DA Mover is loading. Doing so causes it to start up with the Desk Accessory button selected.

One more point: While you can mix and match typefaces in a single suit-case file, you can't mix fonts and desk accessories in a single suitcase. As their different icons indicate, they're two different kinds of suitcase files.

FONT DETAILS

The Mac makes switching fonts, sizes, or styles as easy as choosing a com-mand. Under the hood, however, a complex set of events occurs. In this sec-tion, we'll examine:

- what happens when you choose a specific font, style, and size
- how the Mac's bit-mapped font resources are structured
- some font-related problems that can occur
- how System 7.0's outline font resources are structured.

Understanding the technicalities behind Mac fonts isn't necessary for using them, but it can help you install and choose fonts better, and it can help you troubleshoot the font-related problems that can occur when you move a docu-ment to a Mac that has different fonts. You may be especially prone to font troubles if you move documents between Macs on a network or if you send documents to a service bureau for laser printing or typesetting (a subject we'll discuss in the next chapter).

If you'd rather learn about the Mac's printing features now, feel free to skim or skip the rest of this chapter. When you want to learn more about fonts—or if you fall victim to font difficulties—you can return to it.

Bit-mapped Fonts, QuickDraw, and the Font Manager

Displayed text is the result of a joint effort between four participants: an application, QuickDraw, the Font Manager, and the Resource Manager. When you choose a font-formatting command, QuickDraw requests the desired font, size, and style from the Font Manager. QuickDraw doesn't ask for the font by name; instead, it uses a unique ID number that's assigned to each font and stored in the System file. Table 7-1 lists the ID numbers assigned to the fonts included in the System 6.0.2 update package.

Table 7-1: Apple's fonts and their ID numbers.

Font Name	ID Number
Athens	7
Cairo	11
Chicago	0
Courier	22
Geneva	3
Helvetica	21
London	6
Los Angeles	12
Mobile	24
Monaco	4
New York	2
San Francisco	8
Symbol	23
Times	20
Venice	5

When QuickDraw requests a given font, it also requests a specific style (plain, italic, bold, and so on) and a specific size. The Font Manager takes this information and uses the Resource Manager to load the appropriate font into memory. However, if the specific size or style isn't available—that is, if no bit map description for it exists—the Font Manager must simulate, or *derive*, the font by altering the description of a font that does exist. Figure 7-19 illustrates the often unattractive results.

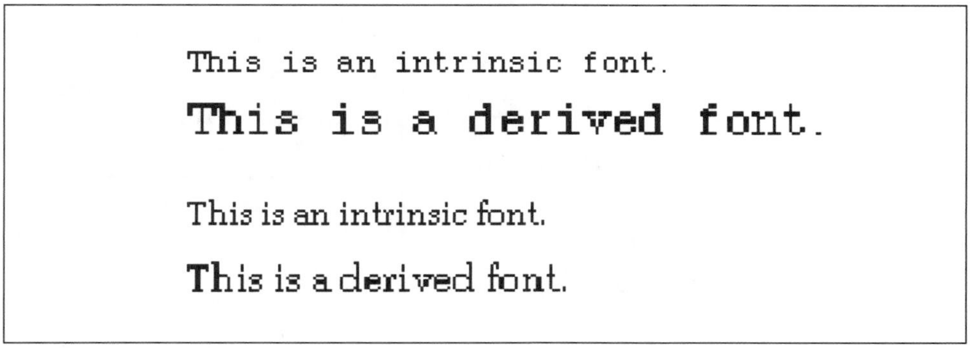

Figure 7-19: Intrinsic fonts versus derived fonts.

Deriving a font size is the Font Manager's responsibility, but deriving a font *style* is QuickDraw's. Many fonts (including New York and Geneva, to name only two) don't contain descriptions for such stylistic variants as italics and bold. When you choose a style for which no intrinsic definition exists, Quick-Draw derives the style by altering the intrinsic style. To create italics, for example, QuickDraw shifts the bits in the font to slant its characters. The bits above the baseline are skewed to the right, while bits below the baseline are skewed to the left.

Because derived styles will never look as good as their intrinsic counterparts, it's in your best interest to install the specific styles you use most often. The fonts that accompany the Mac don't include descriptions for various styles, but fonts sold by font vendors such as Adobe Systems, Bitstream, and Compugraphic usually do include them.

Accessing Other Styles

When you install a font family that includes stylistic variations, your Font menus list each style. Figure 7-20 shows a Font menu after the New Baskerville family has been installed. Note that the three stylistic variants of New Baskerville—italic, bold, and bold italic—appear in the menu along with New Baskerville itself. As Figure 7-20 shows, the characters *I*, *B*, and *BI* appear before the family name to allow you to differentiate between styles in programs that display fonts in list boxes (which aren't always wide enough to show the entire font name) instead of menus.

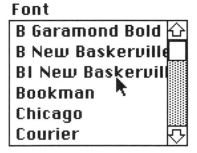

Figure 7-20:   Style variations in a Font menu and list box.

When you've installed the stylistic variants of a typeface, there are two ways to access a given style:

- You can choose its name, for example BI New Baskerville Bold Italic—from the Font menu or dialog box

- You can choose the desired combination of styles—for example, Bold and Italic—from the Style menu. When you use this method, the Mac first looks for the intrinsic style. If one doesn't exist, the Mac derives the style using the techniques we've described.

Why does the Mac offer two ways to access the same style? And wouldn't it make more sense to *not* list each style variant in the Font menu? That way, you wouldn't have all those different styles cluttering up the font menu.

Yes, it would make more sense to choose different styles by simply choosing commands from a Style menu. And yes, that approach would eliminate cluttering the Font menu with style variations. In the ideal world, font styles would be grouped together under the umbrella of a family name, such as Palatino or Bookman. Only the family name would appear in the Font menu, but when you chose a different style, the Mac would know to retrieve its definition from the System file.

This ideal world does exist—sort of. The problem is that the original version of the Mac's Font Manager didn't support the approach of grouping styles under the umbrella of a font family. Today's Font Manager does support this approach, but not all font manufacturers do, nor do all Mac applications. The Macintosh font world is still evolving, and Apple and font manufacturers are taking a slow and steady course to avoid leaving users of older Macs or older applications out in the cold. (If you want to do something about it now, you can; Chapter 10 presents some tips for uncluttering Font menus.)

To see how the Mac's Font Manager groups font styles together into font families, let's step back and look at how font resources are structured.

FONDS, FONTS, and NFNTs

Three different types of resources play a role in the Mac's font-handling capabilities: *FONT*, *NFNT*, and *FOND*. This section briefly introduces each type of resource.

FOND. The name FOND stands for *font family descriptor*. A FOND resource acts as an electronic table of contents for a given font family. The System file contains one FOND resource for every font family you have installed. For example, if you have five fonts installed—Times, Helvetica, Geneva, Courier, and Monaco—your System file contains five FOND resources. When an application program tells the Mac, "I need 24-point Times Italic," the Mac consults the FOND for the Times family in order to locate the font's resource ID—that unique font-identifying number mentioned earlier. QuickDraw and the Resource Manager use this number to retrieve the font's bit map description.

Knowing this, you can see how a FOND resource compares to a table of contents: Just as you use a table of contents to locate a specific subject in a book, the Mac uses a FOND resource to locate a specific font in the System file. And like each page of a book, each font has a unique number that identifies it.

FONT and NFNT. The FONT and NFNT resource types hold the bit map descriptions that tell QuickDraw how to draw a given typeface. The FONT resource was the original resource structure for fonts; the NFNT resource (commonly pronounced *en-font*) is a newer resource type; it appeared when the Mac Plus was introduced. Both resource types perform the same end result—they tell QuickDraw how to draw a given font—but their internal structures are different.

The most significant difference is in the way fonts are numbered. Apple's original font-numbering technique allowed for approximately 128 font ID numbers. That seems like a large amount, but remember that each style requires a separate number. Thus, if you install 10 font families, you actually use

40 ID numbers. In the Mac's early days, fonts rarely included intrinsic styles (that is, true italics and bolds rather than derived ones), so this limitation wasn't serious. As font vendors began supplying more and more font packages (each including its own intrinsic styles), it became clear that 128 ID numbers weren't enough. Many font vendors were forced to reuse ID numbers. The NFNT resource type uses a different numbering scheme that allows for roughly 16,000 ID numbers.

Multi-Bit Fonts

NFNT resources also allow font developers to create *multi-bit fonts* for use with Macs that have gray-scale or color monitors. Multi-bit fonts can make large sizes of text look far sharper; technically speaking, they can improve the *apparent resolution* of text. They do so by displaying subtle shades of gray around a character's edges. At normal viewing distances, these gray shades serve to smooth the jagged character edges that appear when a font is displayed on the Mac's screen.

Alas, the only place you can see multi-bit fonts is in Letraset's LetraStudio typography program. Version 3.8 of the Font/DA Mover is not able to install multi-bit fonts, nor are any offered by font vendors. (LetraStudio uses its own fonts rather than the Mac's.)

So NFNT resources actually provide more potential than the current versions of the Mac's system software are able to exploit. It's another example of how the Mac's font-handling features are still evolving.

Summary of Font Technicalities

Let's summarize the swamp of technicalities we just waded through:

• FOND and NFNT resources work together to allow the Mac to support stylistic variations (such as italic and bold) within a font family.

• All Mac models beginning with the 512K Enhanced support the approach of listing only the family name in a menu, rather than listing every style. But 128K and 512K Macs don't support this approach, nor do some older Mac applications.

• Some font vendors still distribute their fonts in FONT, rather than NFNT, format. Thus, if you install all four styles of a given family, you're stuck with cluttered Font menus that list all four styles.

Leading, Width, and Kerning Information

In addition to storing family names and bit map descriptions, font resources contain components that tell the Mac what degree of vertical spacing (leading) and horizontal spacing to apply to the font.

The *auto-leading* portion of a font tells the Mac how much vertical space to place between baselines when an application's auto-leading option is active. Most applications let you override the auto-leading option by specifying how much space you want between lines.

The *width table* lists the spacing for the characters in the font. The Font Manager supplies the information in the width table to QuickDraw, which uses the width data to space the characters properly.

The *kerning table* contains information that applications can use to improve the spacing of certain letter pairs, such as To, Yo, and Ay. (*Kerning* involves removing space between two characters to improve their appearance.) Many applications (particularly desktop publishing programs) provide *automatic kerning* options that use kerning tables to determine how much space to re-move between characters. Judicious use of an application's automatic kerning features can give a professionally typeset look to your documents. Several font utility programs are available that let you alter a font's kerning tables to suit your kerning preferences. Four such utilities include Edco Services' LetrTuck, ICOM Simulations' MacKern, Software Shop's Kern Rite, and Kerningware Marketing's Kerningware.

Fractional Character Widths

Now let's examine a term you've probably encountered in the Page Setup or Preferences dialog boxes of your applications: *fractional character widths*. Beginning with the 128K ROMs of the Mac Plus and 512K Enhanced, Apple gave the Font Manager the ability to use fonts that express character widths using frac-tional values rather than whole numbers. For example, instead of stating that a given character is 16 units wide, the width table might state that it's 16.5 units wide.

Fractional character widths improve the spacing of text printed by a laser printer or typesetter, and they improve the Mac's WYSIWYG qualities by al-lowing QuickDraw to position text so that it more accurately reflects how a document will look when printed.

Along with that second advantage comes a drawback. Pixels don't have frac-tional portions—the Mac can't draw a letter 5.5 pixels wide. Thus, when an application uses fractional character widths, character spacing on the screen may appear irregular or tighter than it does when fractional widths are dis-abled. These irregularities are more apparent with small text sizes.

When Fonts Conflict

You've created a document that uses several fonts, and you've taken it to someone else's Mac so that you can print it on his or her laser printer. Or perhaps you've taken the document to a service bureau for high-resolution typeset output. In any case, when you open the document on the other Mac, it appears in different fonts. What's happened?

You've fallen victim to font numbering conflicts. When you install a font whose ID number is already in use by a different font, the Font/DA Mover assigns a new number to the font you're installing. By itself, this renumbering process doesn't cause the problem. The problem occurs because many application programs store font numbers, rather than font names, in the documents they create. For example, assume you create a document that uses the fonts Korinna and New Baskerville. Assume further that on your Mac, those fonts have ID numbers of 197 and 205, respectively. (These are the actual ID numbers assigned to Adobe Systems' Korinna and New Baskerville fonts.) When you save the document, the application stores those ID numbers, not the names *Korinna* and *New Baskerville* in the document file.

Now assume that you're about to open the document on a different Mac. On this second Mac, Korinna and New Baskerville have different ID numbers because the numbers 197 and 205 were already in use by two other fonts—let's call them Sloppy and Tasteless. When you open your document, the application program requests font numbers 197 and 205; thus, your document appears not in Korinna and Baskerville, but in Sloppy and Tasteless.

Avoiding Font Conflicts

There are several ways to avoid the conflicting fonts problem:

- When you move your document to a different Mac, take your System file with it. This approach isn't an ideal one, however. If your System file is chocked full of fonts and desk accessories, it may be too large to fit on a floppy disk. What's more, the owner of the second Mac probably won't be receptive to having you replace his or her System file with your own.

- Use only one manufacturer's fonts. When you mix and match fonts from a variety of sources, the chances of ID number conflicts increase, since each manufacturer doesn't know what numbers other vendors have used. Apple requests that font vendors register ID numbers with Apple's Developer Technical Support department to avoid duplication, but some developers may not. If you stick with one firm's fonts, ID conflicts can still occur, but are less likely.

- Use applications that store font names, not ID numbers, in the documents they create. Apple recommends this procedure to avoid font conflicts, but not all developers have followed the recommendation. The following applications are among those that store font names rather than ID numbers:

  Aldus PageMaker and FreeHand

  Claris MacDraw II

  Letraset Ready,Set,Go 4.5 and StandOut

  Microsoft PowerPoint 2.0 and later versions

  QuarkXpress 2.0 and later versions

  You can expect more applications to work this way in the future, as developers revise their programs' approach to fonts.

- Use a program that can resolve font ID number conflicts, such as Font Harmony, which is included with Fifth Generation Systems' Suitcase II, discussed in Chapter 10.

System 7.0 and Outline Fonts

System 7.0 will provide the most significant typographic enhancements the Mac has ever seen. System 7.0 will provide outline fonts that the Mac will be able to use to create text in any size without the distortion that occurs when a bit-mapped size is scaled to different size. Bit-mapped fonts from earlier system versions will still be useable in System 7.0. What's more, Apple is making its outline font format available to many font developers, with the goal of having a large library of outline fonts available after System 7.0 is released.

System 6.0 and earlier versions are limited to a maximum type size of 127 points. That isn't the case with System 7.0. Figure 7-21 shows a 500-point character created by a prerelease version of an Apple outline font, as displayed by Claris' MacDraw II. Notice, too, that all of the sizes in the Size menu are outlined, indicating that all the sizes are available.

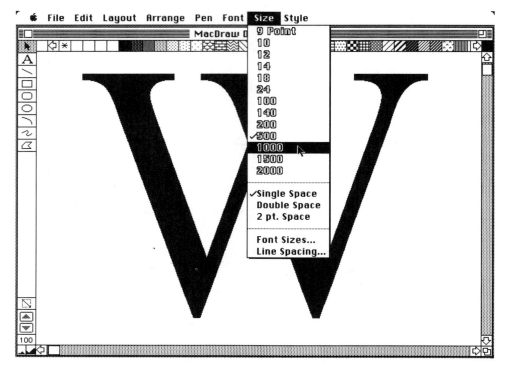

Figure 7-21: A 500-point "W" from a prerelease version of an Apple outline font.

Another benefit of outline screen fonts will surface in programs that let you view documents in varying degrees of magnification. (Different magnification views are most common in desktop publishing, presentation graphics, and drawing programs.) Because outline fonts will allow the Mac to create any size it needs, programs that offer different magnification scales will be able to display sharp, distortion-free text in all their viewing scales.

System 7.0's outline fonts use a new font resource format called *sfnt*, short for *spline font*. The basic building block of System 7.0's outline fonts are *quadratic B-splines*—that's mathematic jargon that refers to how the curves and end points that form each character are described by the font outlines.

CHAPTER SUMMARY

- A typeface is a unique design of uppercase and lowercase characters, numerals, punctuation marks, and symbols. A font is the implementation, in one size, of a typeface. In digital typography, the terms *typeface* and *font* are often used interchangeably.

- Mac font families usually contain four styles: plain, italic, bold, and bold italic.

- An important unit of typographic measurement is the point, equal to approximately 1/72 inch.

- The vertical space between two lines of type is called leading.

- Most Mac fonts are proportionally spaced rather than fixed-width fonts. (In a fixed-width font, all characters have the same width.)

- Fonts can be described for a computer or printer as bit maps, which require a separate description for each size, or as outlines, which are mathematic descriptions of each character's components. Macs running System 6.0 and earlier versions use bit-mapped fonts for their screen displays.

- Outline fonts, used in LaserWriters and other PostScript printers, are more versatile, but can impose additional processing time on the device that uses them.

- You can add fonts to, and remove them from, your System file using Apple's Font/DA Mover utility.

- Every font has a unique ID number that the Mac uses to load the font into memory.

- When the Mac needs to display a size or style of text for which no intrinsic definition exists, the Font Manager and QuickDraw can derive the size or style by modifying an existing size or style.

- A newer type of font resource called NFNT provides support for intrinsic style definitions (for example, true italic instead of obliqued plain). However, not all font vendors support the NFNT resource type.

- Font resources also contain width tables that govern character spacing, and kerning tables that allow applications to improve the appearance of letter pairs such as To and AY.

- Activating an application's fractional character width option results in better spacing when a document is printed by a laser printer or typesetter, but can make the text less legible on screen.

- When you open a document on a Mac containing a different System file, the document may appear in different fonts. This problem occurs when the font ID numbers in the second System file differ from those of the System file you used when creating the document.

8

Printing

The Mac's sophisticated typographic capabilities would be worthless if you couldn't get your work from screen to paper. Fortunately, the Mac's printing features are up to the challenge. In this chapter, we'll tour the Mac's pressroom to examine:

- the basics of Macintosh printing

- how the ImageWriter family of printers operates

- how LaserWriters and other laser printers operate

- factors to consider when shopping for a laser printer

- ways to use an ImageWriter or LaserWriter more effectively.

The information in this chapter applies to System 6.0 and earlier versions. At the end of the chapter, we'll note how printing processes will differ in System 7.0 and later versions.

MAC PRINTING OVERVIEW

On computers without graphical operating environments, displaying a document and printing a document are two very different processes. With a graphical environment, however, displaying and printing are closely related. Because the screen accurately depicts what a document will look like when printed, the processes required to display a document are similar to those required to print it. This is true in the IBM world with Microsoft Windows and OS/2 Presentation Manager.

And it's true in the Mac world. When you print a document, your application performs many of the same processes involved in displaying the document on screen. QuickDraw and the Font Manager work hand in hand to calculate character widths and display text, and the application uses similar (in many cases, identical) QuickDraw commands to position text and graphics.

Printer Drivers

With printing, another component of the Mac's system software enters the picture: the printer driver. Chapter 5 introduced printer drivers by saying they act as intermediaries between an application and a specific printer. While printing, an application uses QuickDraw commands to specify a document's appearance, and a printer driver translates those QuickDraw commands into the codes and commands that a specific printer requires.

During this process, an application uses another component of the Mac's system software, the *Printing Manager*. The Printing Manager serves as a liaison between the application and a printer driver. The application uses QuickDraw routines to specify the document's appearance, and the Printing Manager passes those routines to the print driver you've selected using the Chooser desk accessory. Figure 8-1 summarizes this process.

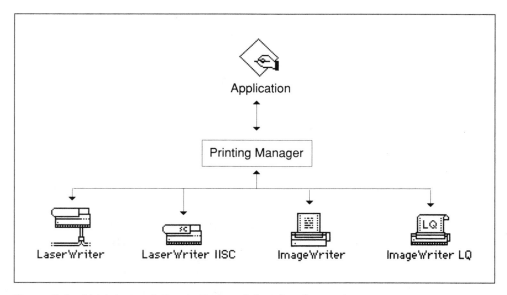

Figure 8-1: Macintosh printing in System 6.0 and earlier versions.

This division of labor approach eliminates the need for applications to contain program code tailored to a specific printer. An application can use the same routines to print a document on an ImageWriter, a laser printer, a film recorder, or typesetter—each of which produces images in different ways, using different internal commands.

One way to understand this approach is to imagine yourself as an ambassador at a United Nations session. You have to address a group that speaks dozens of different languages. You can't learn each one, so you speak the language you know, and interpreters translate your words into ones the attendees can understand.

In this scenario, the ambassador is the Mac, the attendees are a variety of different printers, and the interpreters are printer drivers. The Mac speaks in the language it knows—QuickDraw—and printer drivers translate the commands into ones that the printers can understand.

In addition to communicating with a printer in its native tongue, a printer driver provides another, more visible role: It allows you to use the Page Setup and Print commands to specify print options that are appropriate to the printer you've chosen. Figure 8-2 shows the Page Setup dialog boxes for the ImageWriter and LaserWriter drivers; Figure 8-3 shows the Print dialog boxes for both drivers.

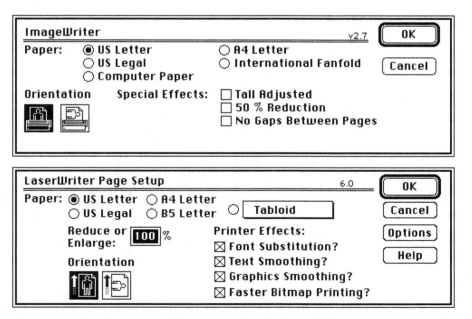

Figure 8-2: The Page Setup dialog boxes for the ImageWriter driver (*top*) and the Laser-Writer driver (*bottom*).

Notice that the available options differ depending on which printer is selected. In the subsequent sections of this chapter, we'll describe how both types of printers operate, and we'll see why print options differ between printers.

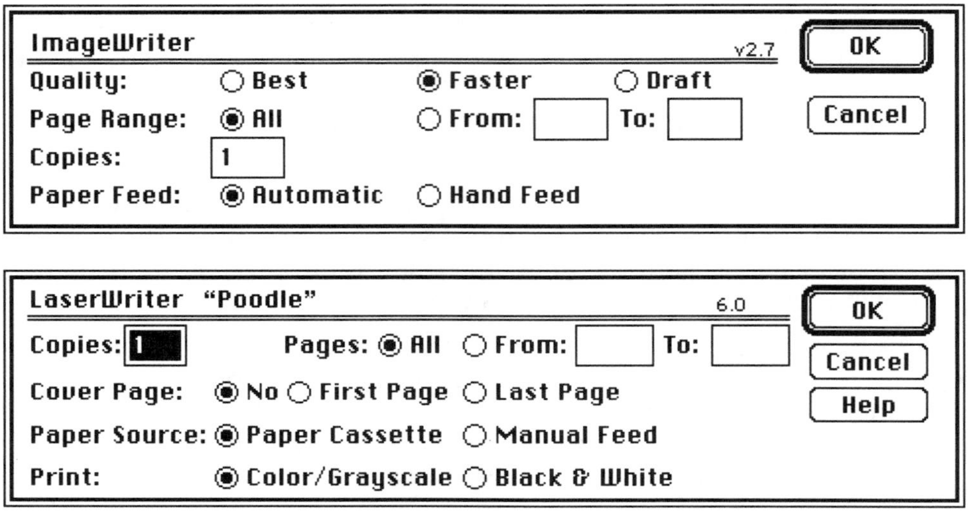

```
┌─────────────────────────────────────────────────────────────────┐
│ ImageWriter                              v2.7    ┌──────────┐     │
│ Quality:      ○ Best        ● Faster    ○ Draft  │    OK    │     │
│ Page Range:   ● All         ○ From: [    ] To: [    ]              │
│ Copies:       [1 ]                               ┌──────────┐     │
│ Paper Feed:   ● Automatic   ○ Hand Feed          │  Cancel  │     │
└─────────────────────────────────────────────────────────────────┘
```

```
┌─────────────────────────────────────────────────────────────────┐
│ LaserWriter  "Poodle"                      6.0   ┌──────────┐     │
│ Copies:[█]        Pages: ● All ○ From: [   ] To: [   ]  OK         │
│ Cover Page:    ● No ○ First Page ○ Last Page     │  Cancel  │     │
│ Paper Source: ● Paper Cassette ○ Manual Feed     │   Help   │     │
│ Print:         ● Color/Grayscale ○ Black & White                  │
└─────────────────────────────────────────────────────────────────┘
```

Figure 8-3: The Print dialog boxes for the ImageWriter driver (*top*) and the LaserWriter driver (*bottom*).

Screen Fonts versus Printer Fonts

Before examining specific printers in detail, let's draw an important distinction between *screen fonts* and *printer fonts*. The relationship between screen fonts and printer fonts will change under System 7.0; we've noted the key differences at the end of this chapter.

In System 6.0 and earlier versions, screen fonts are the bit-mapped fonts the Mac uses to display text on its video screen; as we saw in the previous chapter, you install and remove screen fonts using the Font/DA Mover. Screen fonts are only reasonable facsimiles of true typographic fonts; the limited resolution of the Mac's screen makes it impossible to convey the delicate serifs and subtle strokes of true typographic fonts.

Printer fonts are separate font descriptions that don't play a role in display-ing text on the screen. Instead, they swing into action when you print a docu-ment, describing for the printer what various typefaces look like. As you may recall from the previous chapter, LaserWriters and other PostScript printers use outline fonts; these outline fonts are printer fonts.

Printer fonts are usually stored on ROM chips within a printer, although as we'll see later in this chapter, they can also be stored on a Mac's hard disk and transferred to the printer when needed. Apple's LaserWriter IINT and NTX each contain 35 printer fonts.

Here's another important point: Not all printers require printer fonts. In-stead, some printers rely on the Mac's screen fonts to tell them how to create text. Apple's ImageWriter dot-matrix printers and its LaserWriter IISC laser printer are in this group.

When you use an ImageWriter or any printer that lacks separate printer fonts, the screen fonts tell the printer how to create the typefaces in the docu-ment. The printer creates text based on the bit map font descriptions stored in the System file.

When you use a printer containing corresponding printer fonts, the screen fonts play a different role. They still allow you to see on screen how the docu-ment will appear when printed, and they still control the spacing of the printed text. However, they don't appear in the final output; instead, the printer uses its printer fonts. Thus, a screen font is like an understudy who plays an actor's part during rehearsals, but defers to the star in the final per-formance. Figure 8-4 shows some bit-mapped screen fonts and their corre-sponding laser printer fonts.

As you can see, screen fonts are important to the printing process regardless of what kind of printer you use. What's important to remember, however, is that when you use a printer that contains corresponding printer fonts, the screen fonts aren't used to generate the final text. We'll explore the screen-versus-printer fonts issue in greater detail later in this chapter.

This is 12-point Times

This is 12-point Helvetica

This is 18-point Palatino

This is 18-point Palatino Italic

This is 12-point Times

This is 12-point Helvetica

This is 18-point Palatino

This is 18-point Palatino Italic

Figure 8-4: Screen fonts (*top*) and corresponding printer fonts (*bottom*).

THE IMAGEWRITER FAMILY

Apple's ImageWriter printers are sturdy scribes that are as adept at printing graphics as they are at printing text. LaserWriters, with their quiet operation and near-typeset text, may grab the glory, but the ImageWriters are the affordable workhorses of Apple's printer line. And they remain the preferred printers for certain jobs, such as printing mailing labels and printing on multipart forms.

This section is dedicated to giving the ImageWriter family its due. We'll examine:

- the key differences between each ImageWriter model

- how ImageWriters operate

- how to get better performance and print quality from an ImageWriter.

Dot Matrix Basics

All ImageWriter printers are *dot matrix* printers. Printers in this category produce images by striking an inked ribbon with minute, moveable pins, also called *print wires*. Located in the printer's *print head*, these pins are grouped together in a matrix; each pin, when it strikes the ribbon, produces a single dot. The printer produces images by controlling which pins strike the ribbon and which ones remain stationary, as shown in Figure 8-5.

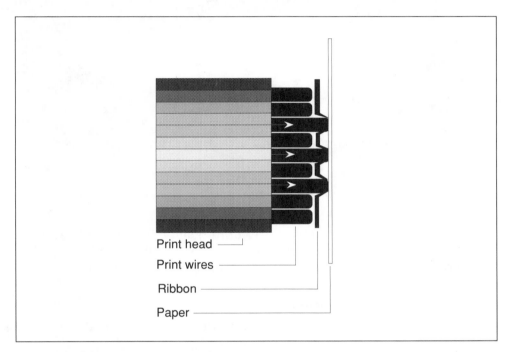

Figure 8-5: A dot matrix printer's pins strike a ribbon.

As we'll see shortly, a dot matrix printer's resolution depends partially on the number of pins in its print head and on the size of the pins.

The ImageWriter and ImageWriter II

The ImageWriter was the Mac's first printer. In January 1986, the Image-Writer was replaced by the ImageWriter II, which offers faster speed, more reliable paper handling, and higher resolution (both printers have nine-pin print heads, but the the ImageWriter II's pins are smaller). The ImageWriter II, shown in Figure 8-6, also contains a single expansion slot into which you can install an AppleTalk board that allows multiple Macs to access one printer over a network.

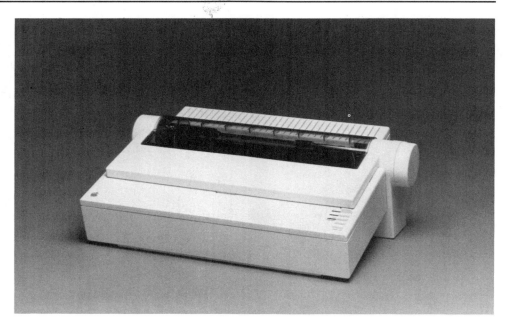

Figure 8-6: The ImageWriter II dot matrix printer. (*photo courtesy of Apple Computer*)

When you've selected the Faster print-quality option, the ImageWriter II's resolution is 72 dpi horizontally and 80 dpi vertically. In the Best quality print mode, its resolution doubles to 144 horizontal dpi and 160 vertical dpi.

Differences in Print Modes

The ImageWriter printer driver offers three printing modes: Draft, Faster, and Best.

Draft. In Draft mode, the Mac doesn't send to the printer bit map descriptions for fonts or graphic images that a document may contain. The printer receives only character codes and spacing information, and prints using its internal fonts, which have a decidedly "computer printer" look to them. As Figure 8-7 shows, when you print a proportionally spaced font in Draft mode, word spacing is irregular. Apple designed the Draft mode so that each word still begins where it will appear when printed in higher quality modes. If you hold a page of draft-printed output over the Mac's screen, you can see that words appear at roughly the same locations on both the screen and the printed output.

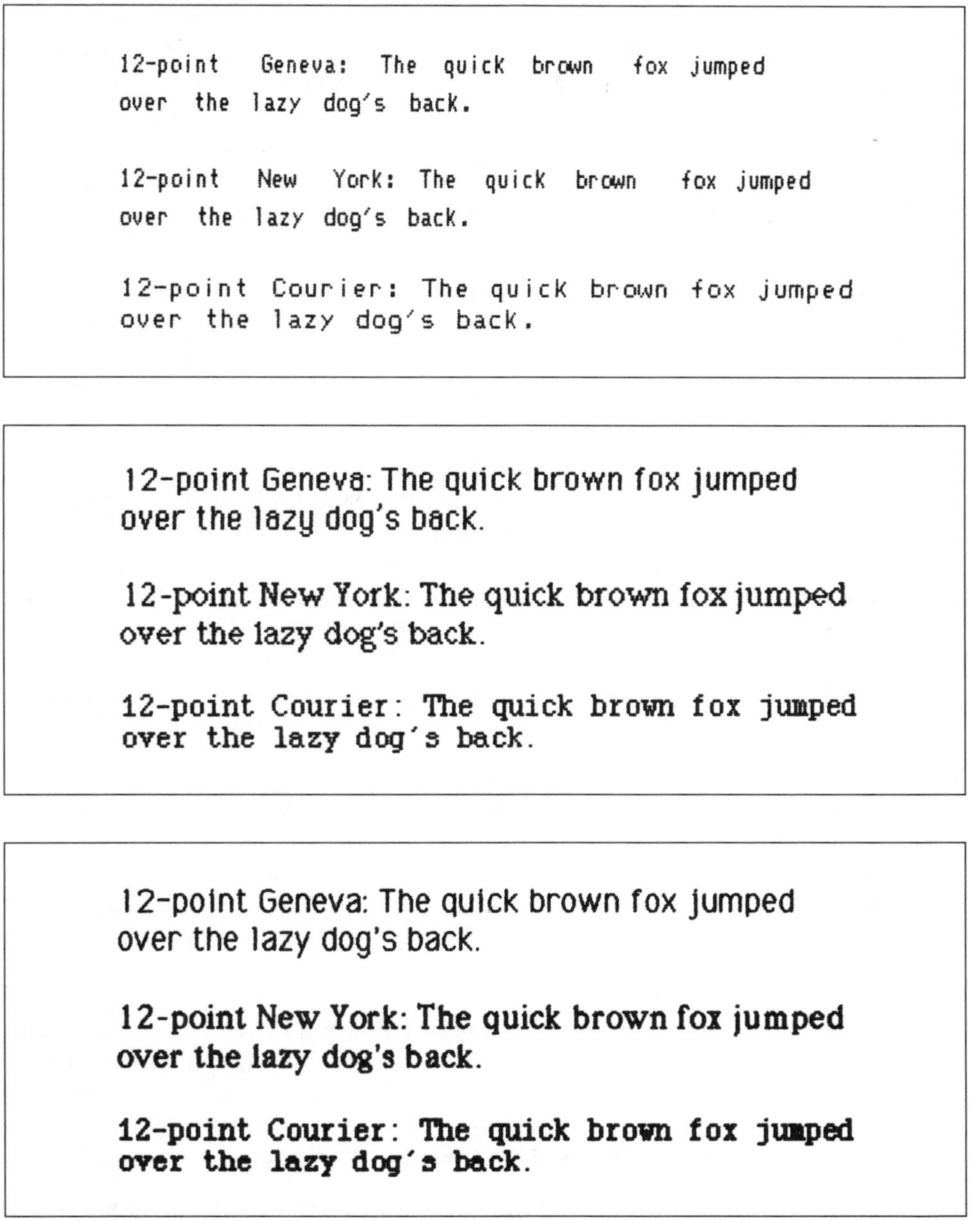

12-point Geneva: The quick brown fox jumped
over the lazy dog's back.

12-point New York: The quick brown fox jumped
over the lazy dog's back.

12-point Courier: The quick brown fox jumped
over the lazy dog's back.

12-point Geneva: The quick brown fox jumped
over the lazy dog's back.

12-point New York: The quick brown fox jumped
over the lazy dog's back.

12-point Courier: The quick brown fox jumped
over the lazy dog's back.

12-point Geneva: The quick brown fox jumped
over the lazy dog's back.

12-point New York: The quick brown fox jumped
over the lazy dog's back.

12-point Courier: The quick brown fox jumped
over the lazy dog's back.

Figure 8-7: ImageWriter output three ways: Draft (*top*), Faster (*middle*), and Best (*bottom*).

Faster. In the Faster print mode, the Mac *does* send font and graphic bit maps to the printer. When printing in this mode, a Mac application creates a bit map of the page in the Mac's memory, and then transmits this bit map to the printer. Because a bit map image of a full page would use too much of the Mac's memory, the Mac's Printing Manager creates the bit map in stages: it creates a bit map for part of the page, transmits it to the printer, discards that bit map, and then repeats the process for the next portion of the page. This printing technique is called *banding*.

Best. Best quality mode is similar to Faster mode in that the Mac uses banding to create and transmit a bit-mapped image of the page. In Best mode, however, the Mac creates a bit map that's twice the size of the page, and then "plays back" the bit map at half that size. Because larger bit maps require more memory, the Mac must divide the page into more bands—47, to be exact.

This double-then-reduce approach requires the Mac to handle fonts differently. When you print in Best mode, the Mac looks in the System file for a point size twice the size of the text on the page, and then it reads that bit map description and reduces (shrinks) the text by 50 percent. Because larger font sizes can convey typographic subtleties more accurately, this results in improved text quality. If a size twice the required size isn't in the System file, the Mac looks for a size four times the required size. If it strikes out there, too, the Font Manager continues to look for the next best size, and scales it appropriately.

Another factor that improves quality is that the print head makes twice the number of passes to print the document. Before printing the second pass, the printer rolls the paper up slightly (about half a dot's worth). This causes the dots to overlap slightly, filling in the edges of characters and improving the appearance of text.

The ImageWriter LQ

The ImageWriter LQ, shown in Figure 8-8, is a faster, higher resolution dot-matrix printer with a wide (15-inch) carriage. The LQ offers resolution of 216 dpi, thanks to its 27-wire print head. At 216 dpi, ImageWriter LQ output isn't much coarser than the 300-dpi resolution of laser printer output. The overall difference in print quality is still significant, however.

Like the ImageWriter II, the LQ accepts an optional single-sheet feeder and an AppleTalk board that lets you share the printer on a network.

Figure 8-8: The ImageWriter LQ dot-matrix printer. (*photo courtesy of Apple Computer*)

The ImageWriter LQ driver offers the same print quality options as the standard ImageWriter driver but, behind the scenes, it approaches the Best printing option differently. In Best mode, the driver looks for and scales a font three times, rather than two times, larger than the size you're printing. For example, to print a document containing 12-point Times, your System file should contain 36-point Times.

Knowing that font bit maps increase in size along with the point size, you can see that outfitting a System file with a suitable range of font sizes for Best quality printing devours disk space. That's just one of the drawbacks to using bit-mapped font descriptions. A more significant drawback is that you're restricted to just those sizes that exist in the System file. Print a different size, and you'll get unacceptably ragged-looking characters.

Under System 7.0 these drawbacks will vanish. You'll be able to use the same font outlines that produce text on the screen to produce ImageWriter LQ output, and you'll have a virtually unlimited range of sizes to choose from.

Ten Tips for ImageWriters

Here are ten tips to help you get more out of an ImageWriter.

When to use the Tall Adjusted option. If you print documents containing pictures pasted from MacPaint or other painting programs, you may notice that the images appear to be stretched vertically. This problem occurs because the vertical resolution of the printer and screen don't match: the screen's vertical resolution is 72 dpi, but the printer's is 80 dpi. Choosing the Tall Adjusted option in the Page Setup dialog box fixes the problem, but introduces a side effect: the printed document is approximately 13 percent wider than its screen counterpart. For example, a line of text that's six inches wide on the screen will be roughly 6 3/4 inches wide when printed. However, selecting the Tall Adjusted option also causes ImageWriter output to more closely match LaserWriter output. (Later in this section, we'll provide another tip for using the ImageWriter to proof documents destined for a laser printer.)

Use fixed-width fonts for Draft printing. When you want the fastest text printing, format a document in a fixed-width font such as Monaco, and then print the document in Draft mode. Using a fixed-width font helps avoid the irregular word spacing that usually occurs in Draft mode. In our experience, 14-point Monaco produces the best-looking draft copy. But because it isn't terribly attractive on screen, you may want to type and edit your document in a different font, save it, and then switch to Monaco just before printing.

Use uniform-stroke fonts for Best quality printing. Fonts with uniform stroke widths, such as Geneva, Monaco, and Courier, produce better results in the Best quality mode than do fonts whose stroke widths vary, such as New York. That's because uniform-stroke fonts are easier for the Mac to scale to the appropriate size. When the Mac scales varying stroke-width fonts, the characters can take on a lumpy look.

Install the proper font sizes for Best quality printing. Because the Mac looks for and reduces larger type sizes to print in Best mode, be sure your System file contains the sizes you'll need for best results. Table 8-1 shows the sizes required for Best quality printing on an ImageWriter I, II, and LQ. (Remember that this applies only to Macs running System 6.0 and earlier versions.)

Table 8-1: Font sizes required for Best quality printing.

To print this size...	ImageWriter Model I, II	LQ
	You need this size...	
9	18	27
10	20	30
12	24	36
14	28	42
18	36	54
20	40	60
24	48	72
32	48	96

Where to shop for fonts. Compared to that of PostScript laser printers, the selection of fonts available for ImageWriters is paltry. An ImageWriter can print any screen font, but LaserWriter fonts such as Palatino and Bookman produce poor results. These fonts are intended to approximate the appearance of the real thing; they're designed for on-screen proofing and formatting, not ImageWriter printing. For the best results, shop for fonts designed specifically for an ImageWriter's limited resolution. Bitstream and Casady & Greene sell numerous high-quality ImageWriter fonts. Another font to consider is Boston II, which is available free through user's groups.

You can specify custom paper sizes. If you frequently print on non-standard paper stocks such as index cards, consider modifying your ImageWriter driver to recognize the non-standard sizes you use. For instructions, see the section "Creating Custom Paper Sizes" in Chapter 10.

How to get faster printing in Faster mode. This tip applies to the Image-Writer II only. You can get faster printing in the Faster mode by pressing the Caps Lock, Shift, and Option keys while clicking the Print dialog box's OK button. Doing so causes the printer to print bidirectionally; normally, the printer prints in one direction only in the Faster mode. Some ImageWriter IIs may lack sufficient mechanical precision to print bidirectionally in Faster mode, however, and will produce slightly skewed output. Note: The Mac "remembers" this setting by storing it in the printer driver; to revert to the normal Faster printing mode, press the Command key while clicking the Print dialog box's OK button.

You *can* use an ImageWriter for PostScript proofing. You may have heard that you can't use an ImageWriter to proof documents intended for a PostScript laser printer because the Mac's screen fonts print with different spacing. That's true, but one desktop publishing application—Aldus PageMaker 3.0—is designed to take the spacing differences into account. Figure 8-9 shows a PageMaker document printed on an ImageWriter and on a PostScript laser printer. As you can see, PageMaker alters the word and letter spacing in the ImageWriter version to compensate for differences in font spacing. You can lay one printout over the other, and see that the ImageWriter's line endings match the LaserWriter's.

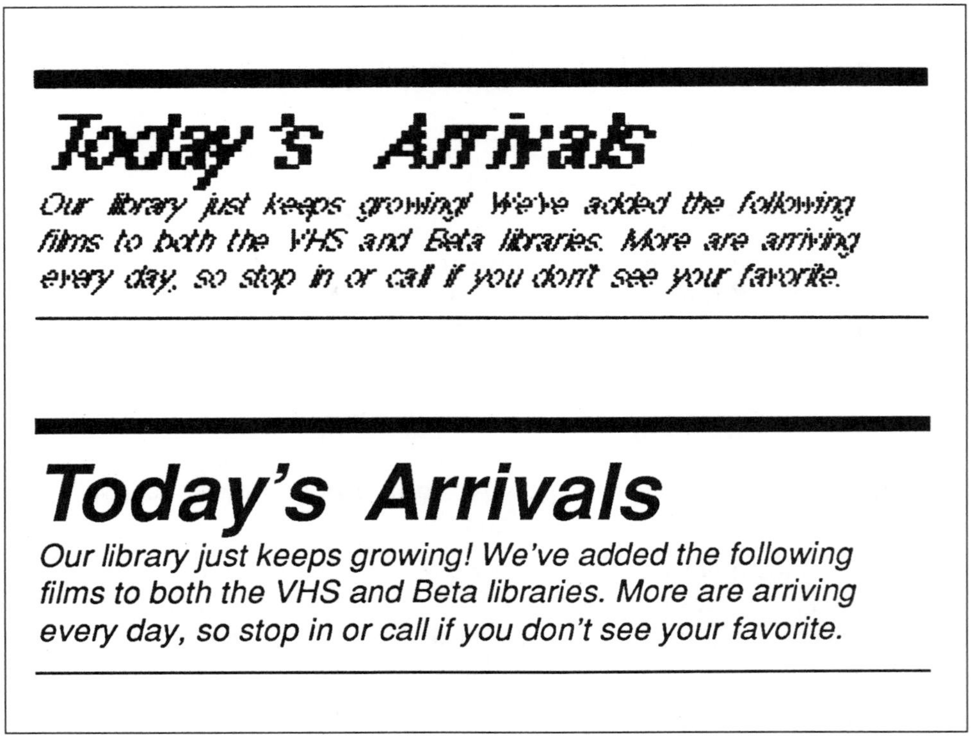
Today's Arrivals

Our library just keeps growing! We've added the following films to both the VHS and Beta libraries. More are arriving every day, so stop in or call if you don't see your favorite.

Today's Arrivals

Our library just keeps growing! We've added the following films to both the VHS and Beta libraries. More are arriving every day, so stop in or call if you don't see your favorite.

Figure 8-9: PageMaker output on an ImageWriter (*top*) and LaserWriter (*bottom*).

Avoid lengthy Best printing sessions. Because of the extra passes required for Best printing, the ImageWriter's print head can overheat and be damaged. The original ImageWriter is especially prone to this problem. To avoid it, print only a couple of pages at a time in Best quality mode, and give the printer a rest for a minute or two between each run.

Use older ribbons for Best quality printing. Because Best quality printing requires two passes of the print head, a new ribbon can produce text that's too dark, with the round portions of characters such as *e* and *a* filled in. Because an old ribbon contains less ink, it can often produce cleaner type in Best mode, as shown in Figure 8-10. Many ImageWriter users like to "rotate" their ribbons: Use a new ribbon for Draft and Faster quality, then reserve it for Best quality mode as it ages. Store unused ribbons in zip-top plastic bags to keep their ink from drying out. And because inked ribbons dry out over time, don't stockpile ribbons; buy only a few at a time.

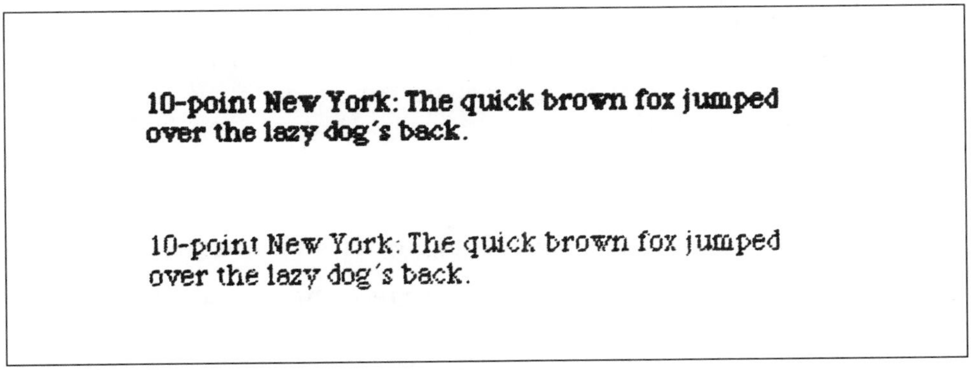

10-point New York: The quick brown fox jumped
over the lazy dog's back.

10-point New York: The quick brown fox jumped
over the lazy dog's back.

Figure 8-10: Best quality with a new (*top*) and old (*bottom*) ribbon.

Incidentally, several companies sell ribbon re-inking kits that allow you to squeeze more mileage out of a ribbon. Some readers will disagree with us, but we recommend against re-inking ribbons. You may save a few dollars on ribbons, but you risk damaging the printer's print head as the ribbon wears and lint and dust from it collect on the print wires.

LASER PRINTERS

If ImageWriters are workhorses, laser printers are show horses. By printing 300 dots per inch (instead of an ImageWriter's 80), a laser printer can more accurately render the subtleties of typographic fonts, as well as produce tack-sharp graphics from drawing and graphing programs. Laser printers are also faster than dot-matrix scribes, and they're blissfully quiet. Instead of gritting your teeth as an ImageWriter carriage whines from left to right, you hear only a ventilation fan and a few unobtrusive *thunks* as sheets of paper travel through the printer's photocopier-like mechanism.

This section examines the world of laser printers. We'll explore:

- the basic concepts behind laser printing

- the components of a laser printer

- the types of laser printers available for the Mac

- how to get more out of a laser printer.

First, a note about terminology: Laser printers earned their name because their print mechanisms contain a laser. However, some 300-dpi printers are conceptually identical to a laser printer, but don't actually contain lasers. Technically, the term *page printer* is more accurate than *laser printer* these days. But because the vast majority of page printers available for the Mac do contain lasers—and because far more users are familiar with the term *laser printer*—we'll stick with the familiar.

Laser Printer Basics

Two components work together to give a laser printer its talents:

- the print *engine*, the photocopier-like mechanism that feeds the paper and produces images on it

- the *controller*, the brains of the duo, the component that accepts an application's printing instructions and governs the print engine accordingly in order to produce the document.

In nearly all laser printers, the controller and engine are housed within the same case. But some low-cost printers, which include GCC Technologies' Personal LaserPrinter and Apple's LaserWriter IISC, use the Mac as the controller. As we'll see shortly, this reduces the printer's cost, but at the expense of versatility and performance.

Print Engines

A print engine translates the controller's instructions into hard copy. The print engine's design determines several factors:

- The printer's resolution—the number of dots per inch the printer can produce. Engines with greater mechanical precision *can* produce more dots per inch. (Whether they actually *do* produce more dots per inch depends on additional factors, however.)

- The output quality. Variations in engine design can have a significant impact on print quality.

- The printer's *duty cycle*—the number of pages you can print before having the printer overhauled.

Notice that we didn't list printing speed as a factor determined by the print engine. The Mac world relies heavily on graphics and a variety of type styles and sizes; because reproducing typefaces and creating graphics requires a printer's controller to perform complex calculations, the print engine has little bearing on print speed. Unless you're printing typographically simple documents or multiple copies of a single page, the speed of most Mac-compatible laser printers is determined by the performance of the controller, not the engine. We'll discuss performance issues in greater detail when we examine printer controllers.

Print Engine Components

The primary components of a laser printer's engine include:

- A light-sensitive rotating drum or belt. In most laser printers, the drum or belt is disposable; you replace it after several thousand copies. Some expensive laser printers, particularly ones with resolutions higher than 300 dpi, use a non-disposable, precision-machined drum.

- A low-power laser assembly, aimed at the photosensitive drum or belt through a series of lenses and mirrors.

- A reservoir containing a supply of *toner*, a fine plastic powder. Toner is coated with a polymer that causes it to acquire a negative electric charge. Some expensive printers use a two-component system comprising toner and another powder called *developer*.

- Wires called *charging coronas*, which carry high voltages and electrically charge the drum as it rotates, and the paper as it travels through the engine. As we'll see shortly, this charging process allows the toner to be transferred to the paper.

- A *fusing assembly*, which uses heat to melt the toner particles and adhere them to the paper.

Print Engine Quality

Many engine-related factors influence the appearance of laser output, but the most important factors are:

- the resolution of the print engine

- the print engine's imaging method

- the techniques used by the printer's controller to produce fonts

We'll examine the third factor later. In this section, we'll examine the first two factors and provide some guidelines for assessing laser print quality.

Resolution

We've said it before, but it bears repeating: the more dots per inch a printer produces, the better. More dots per inch allow a printer to more accurately render the subtleties of typographic fonts and to minimize the "jaggies" when printing graphics. Figure 8-11 illustrates this point. On the top is 300-dpi output; on the bottom is 600-dpi output produced by a Varityper VT-600. In particular, notice the relative absence of the "jaggies" in the italic text, which is especially prone to showing this undesirable stair-stepping effect.

Figure 8-11:   300-dpi output (*top*) versus 600-dpi output (*bottom*).

Print resolution is governed by several factors:

- The precision of the engine's imaging components. As mentioned earlier, printers that print more than 300 dpi generally have non-disposable, precision-machined print drums as well as more precise laser mechanisms. This greater precision helps allow them to position more dots on the page, with greater accuracy.

- The size of the toner particles. Smaller toner particles allow for smaller printer dots, and that means more dots per inch. High-resolution laser printers that produce 400 to 600 dpi use finer toner particles than do 300-dpi printers.

- Memory economics. In printers that use the PostScript page-description language (and in the QuickDraw-based LaserWriter IISC), one bit of printer memory is required for each dot on the page. Thus, the more dots the printer produces per inch, the more memory the printer's controller must contain. And the amount of memory required increases dramatically as resolution climbs—and the printer's price tag climbs along with it.

Imaging Methods

The method a printer's laser uses to expose the white and black areas of a page influences the appearance of text (especially at small point sizes) and also helps determine whether solid black areas of a page really do appear solid black.

Two imaging techniques exist: *write-black* and *write-white*.

Write-black. A write-black engine exposes those areas of the drum or belt that will appear black in the final output. At printing time, the toner powder adheres to these areas. Write-black engines are used in Apple's LaserWriter series, as well as in printers from QMS and GCC Technologies.

Write-white. In a white-write print engine, the laser exposes those areas of the drum that will appear white in the final output. The toner is then attracted to the areas that the laser did not expose. Write-white engines are used in AST's TurboLaser/PS, Texas Instruments' OmniLaser 2108 and 2115, and Qume's ScripTen.

In the next section, we'll examine the merits of each approach.

Judging Print Quality

The output of any laser printer looks far better than dot-matrix output. But laser print quality can vary dramatically, even among printers that print the same number of dots per inch. Some engines simply produce better-quality output than others.

But what does "better quality" really mean? Asked another way, what constitutes good-looking laser output?

Sharply formed characters, especially at small sizes. At 300 dpi, creating sharp text in small sizes (10 point and smaller) is a challenge that some printers meet better than others. As a general rule, write-black engines such as those used by Apple, GCC, and QMS handle small text better than write-white engines. With write-white engines, small text often appears too dark, with the enclosed portions of letters such as e and a appearing filled in.

Fine line strokes that don't run together. If you print illustrations containing fine lines, you'll want a printer that can print those lines accurately. Generally, write-black engines produce finer lines and screens (gray-shaded areas) than do write-white engines. Figure 8-12 shows a portion of an Adobe Illustrator image printed by a write-black LaserWriter IINT and a write-white AST TurboLaser. Notice that the write-black engine renders the delicate strokes of the drawing more accurately; in the write-white output, the strokes run together as they converge.

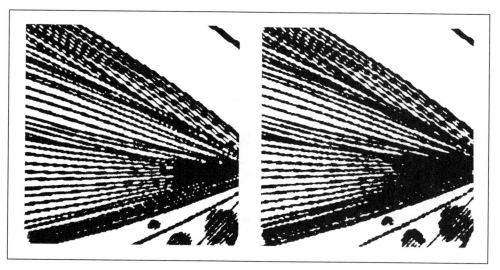

Figure 8-12: Write-black output (*left*) contains finer line strokes than write-white output (*right*).

Rich, solid black areas. The appearance of solid black areas can be important if you're printing illustrations, bar or pie graphs, and reverse type (white type against a black background). As a general rule, write-white engines produce superior blacks. With many write-black engines, solid blacks can appear gray. Upon close examination, you can even see the individual scan lines created by the printer's laser. This shortcoming was especially apparent in the original LaserWriter and LaserWriter Plus. The LaserWriter II printers produce much more solid blacks, although they still use a write-black engine.

As you can see, the write-white and write-black imaging methods each have their own advantages. To summarize them:

- Write-black engines generally produce better fine lines and small text, but less solid black areas.

- Write-white engines tend to produce dark, heavy-looking text, but more solid blacks.

In the end, your preferences should dictate the imaging method you choose. Create some representative documents, then seek out printer dealers who will let you print them on each type of engine.

A Print Engine Sampler

Dozens of laser printers are available for the Mac, but many of them use print engines made by two manufacturers: Canon and Ricoh. This section describes the most popular print engines and spotlights some printers that use them. We'll also look at some alternative print engines that use components other than lasers to produce their images.

Canon CX. The first mass-produced laser printer engine, the Canon CX is at the heart of the original LaserWriter and LaserWriter Plus. Other CX-based printers include the Hewlett-Packard LaserJet and LaserJet Plus and the QMS PS-800 and PS-800 Plus. The Canon CX uses a disposable cartridge that contains both the imaging drum and toner supply.

Canon SX. The Canon SX engine replaced the CX, and is used in all three of Apple's LaserWriter II printers, as well as in the Hewlett-Packard LaserJet Series II and the QMS PS-810. The QMS PS-820 uses Canon's TX engine, which provides two paper trays. Like the CX engine, the SX uses a disposable cartridge containing the imaging drum and toner supply. The cartridges themselves, however, are not interchangeable.

Ricoh 4081. The Ricoh 4081 is used in Texas Instruments' OmniLaser 2108 and AST's TurboLaser/PS. The 4081 is the most common write-white engine. Instead of using a drum (as do Canon's engines), it uses a disposable *organic photo conductor (OPC)* belt. Its toner is stored in a separate hopper.

Ricoh 4150. This engine is the big brother to the 4081, and is used in the Texas Instruments OmniLaser 2115 and QMS' PS-1500. Like the 4081, it's a write-white engine that uses an OPC belt rather than a drum. The 4150, however, provides two paper trays and prints faster.

Ricoh 1060. The Ricoh 1060 is a compact engine designed for lighter duty use than the 4150 and 4081. You'll find this engine in GCC Technologies' Personal LaserPrinter and Business LaserPrinter, IBM's Personal Page Printer II, and Texas Instruments' OmniLaser 2106. The 1060 departs from the write-white and OPC belt design found in Ricoh's 4081 and 4150; it's a write-black engine that uses a disposable drum. Its toner is held in a separate hopper.

Casio LCS-130. This engine is another compact, light-duty engine; it's used in Qume's CrystalPrint series of printers, as well as in Jasmine's DirectPrint and La Cie's Panther PDX. (The latter two printers are identical to Qume's Crystal-Print Publisher; Jasmine and La Cie sell it under their own labels.)

The LCS-130 engine uses *liquid-crystal shutter (LCS)* technology instead of a laser. In an LCS engine, the light source is a halogen lamp; pulses of electricity open and close an array of over 2,000 liquid-crystal shutters, each 1/300 of an inch in diameter, to expose the drum. Proponents of LCS technology say it's superior because it requires fewer moving parts (it doesn't require a rotating mirror) and provides greater precision and sharper images at the edges of pages. In reality, LCS printers haven't been around long enough to prove claims of superior reliability, and in our experience, their sharpness advantage can be seen only through a magnifying loupe.

NEC 890. The NEC 890 is used in NEC's SilentWriter 890 PostScript printer. The NEC 890 is another engine that doesn't use lasers. Its light source is an array of 2,400 light-emitting diodes (LEDs) that flash on and off to expose the image. Like LCS engines, LED engines contain fewer moving parts and offer—in theory, at least—greater reliability and precision.

Table 8-2 summarizes the specifications of the engines discussed here. By mentioning these engines, we're not implying that they're the best or only print engines available. They're simply the ones you'll encounter most often in the consumer laser printer field.

Table 8-2: Specifications of common print engines.

	Canon SX	Ricoh 4081	Ricoh 4150	Ricoh 1060	Casio LCS-130	NEC 890
Writes white or black	black	white	white	black	black	black
Rated engine life (pages)	300,000	600,000	1.5 million	180,000	300,000	600,000
Consumable components	drum/toner cartridge	toner, belt	toner, belt	toner, drum, cleaning unit	toner, drum	toner, drum
Number of paper trays	1	1	2	1	1	1
Capacity of paper tray (sheets)	200	250	250 (each)	150	100	250 (each)

Laser Printer Controllers

Without a controller, a laser printer is little more than a mutant photocopier. The engine moves the paper, but the controller is in the driver's seat.

In the Macintosh world, a laser printer's controller plays a large role in determining a printer's text- and graphics-printing capabilities. This section examines laser printer controllers. We'll discuss:

- the types of controllers used in Mac-compatible laser printers

- how a controller's design influences printing capabilities, networking features, and performance.

Controller Basics

As you may recall from earlier chapters, the Mac and most other computers use a raster display, in which screen images are composed of hundreds of horizontal lines. Laser printers work similarly. Instead of inscribing scan lines on a video monitor, however, a laser printer draws them on the photoconductive surface of the engine's drum or belt. A letter-sized page of 300-dpi laser printer output contains over 3300 scan lines. Because laser printers are raster devices, their controllers are often called *raster-image processors*, or *RIPs* for short.

A controller's job is to accept printing commands from an application program and control the the engine's exposure and paper-handling mechanisms accordingly. The most basic difference between controllers concerns the type of commands they use:

PostScript printers such as the LaserWriter IINT and NTX use Adobe System's PostScript page-description language. In a PostScript printer, the controller is a powerful computer unto itself, containing a 68000 or 68020 microprocessor, two or more megabytes of memory, and ROM chips containing printer fonts stored in outline form. The controller and engine are usually housed in the same case.

QuickDraw printers such as the LaserWriter IISC and GCC Technologies' Personal LaserPrinter use QuickDraw commands. These printers use the Mac as the controller; when you print a document, the Mac performs many of the tasks that a PostScript printer's controller performs. This approach has important performance ramifications that we'll discuss later in this chapter.

PostScript Controllers

In the Mac world, most laser printers use controllers built around Adobe System's PostScript page-description language. You'll find PostScript lurking within Apple's LaserWriter IINT and NTX, QMS's PS-810 and 820, AST's TurboLaser/PS, Dataproduct's LZR-1260, GCC Technologies' Business Laser-Printer, and NEC's SilentWriter LC-890, to name just a few. All of these printers are completely compatible with the Mac.

But what is PostScript? At its foundation, PostScript is a programming language. But unlike general-purpose programming languages such as BASIC and Pascal, PostScript was designed specifically for describing the appearance of printed pages. A variation of PostScript called *Display PostScript* is designed for describing the appearance of screen displays.

PostScript was created by Adobe Systems' founders John Warnock and Charles Geschke. The language is similar to another language Warnock helped design at Xerox PARC called JaM (short for John and Martin; Martin Newell worked on the language with Warnock). A variation of JaM eventually became Interpress, Xerox's page-description protocol. Warnock and Geschke founded Adobe Systems in 1982; the first printer to use PostScript was the Apple Laser-Writer, introduced in January 1985.

How a PostScript Printer Works

Each time you print a document to a PostScript printer, a complex series of events occurs. The following steps summarize how a Mac running System 6.0 and earlier versions access a PostScript printer.

1. The Mac establishes a communications link with the printer; during this process, you see the "Looking for LaserWriter" message. (If you're running under MultiFinder with background printing activated, you don't see this or the following messages unless Print Monitor's window is open.)

2. The Mac checks to see if the printer contains Apple's custom PostScript dictionary, which is stored in the system file called Laser Prep. Laser Prep adds new functions to the PostScript language that allow it to work better with QuickDraw. Laser Prep also reprograms the printer to accept instructions from the LaserWriter driver, which transmits not standard PostScript commands, but a special "shorthand" that takes less time to transmit over an AppleTalk network. If the printer doesn't contain the Laser Prep dictionary, the Mac transmits it, and displays the "Status: Initializing printer" message.

3. After the printer is initialized, the print job begins. The Mac's Print Manager works together with your application and the LaserWriter driver to translate the QuickDraw commands that describe the page's appearance into the PostScript shorthand that the printer has been programmed to recognize. This shorthand represents a computer program that the printer will execute in order to create the page. During this process, you see the "Status: Processing job" and "Status: Preparing data" messages. If the page contains bit-mapped graphics such as MacPaint drawings or scanned images, the LaserWriter driver transmits the bytes that represent the graphics.

4. Meanwhile, within the printer's controller, the *PostScript interpreter* reads the program, interprets its instructions, and then creates a bit-mapped image for the entire page in an area of the printer's memory called the *page buffer*. During this process, the interpreter may need to read the ROM-based printer font outlines in order to generate font bit maps in the sizes required for the page. (We'll take a closer look at how PostScript handles fonts shortly.) This process of converting the PostScript program into a bit map is called *scan conversion*.

5. The controller uses the resulting bit map to govern the engine's imaging mechanism. After the page is printed, the bit map and the PostScript program are discarded.

Figure 8-13 summarizes this complex process.

Step 1: If the printer has just been turned on, the Mac transmits the LaserPrep PostScript dictionary, which configures the printer for subsequent PostScript shorthand.

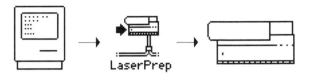

Step 2: Your application works with the Printing Manager and LaserWriter driver to translate the document's appearance from QuickDraw into PostScript shorthand.

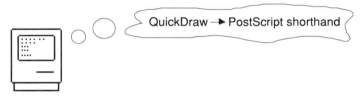

Step 3: Within the printer's controller, the PostScript interpreter creates a bit-mapped image of the page and stores it in the printer's page buffer.

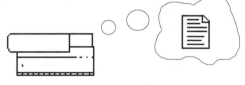

Step 4: The controller uses the bit map to govern the engine's imaging mechanism to print the page.

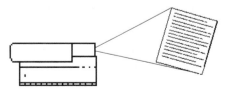

Figure 8-13: How a PostScript printer operates.

Why use a programming language to describe the appearance of a page? Couldn't the Mac simply create the bit map in its own memory, and then send it to the printer? ImageWriters work that way; why can't laser printers?

Actually, they can. But as we'll see in the next section, PostScript's approach gives it far more printing flexibility.

PostScript's Advantages

The PostScript approach—having the host computer create a program which is then interpreted by the PostScript controller—has several advantages:

Device independence. Because the Mac transmits PostScript to the printer rather than a bit map for the page, your application programs need not know the resolution of the printer you're using. That means you can use the same application programs to print the same documents on any PostScript printer, from a 300-dpi LaserWriter to a 600-dpi Varityper VT-600 to a 2540-dpi type-setter. With a few minor exceptions, the only difference will be increasingly sharper copy. (For information on those minor exceptions, see the section "Differences Between PostScript Printers" later in this chapter.)

Lower hardware overhead. Creating a bit map for an entire page requires time and memory (for the latter, about eight million bits, or one megabyte, for an 8 1/2 by 11-inch page). By handling the scan-conversion process and pro-viding its own page buffer, a PostScript printer frees the Mac's processor for other tasks and eliminates the need for the Mac to store huge bit maps in memory or on disk.

Sharing potential. Because the PostScript interpreter and page buffer reside in the printer, you can attach multiple machines to the printer—a good way to make an expensive device earn its keep. Every PostScript printer contains ROM-based *print server* software that allows up to 32 machines to tap its tal-ents. This print server software is what communicates with the Mac during the printing process.

Wide support. PostScript is supported on computers ranging from the Mac to the IBM PC to minicomputers and mainframes. If you equip your office IBM PCs with LocalTalk network boards (described in Chapter 12), your PCs and Macs can access the printer using one network.

Flexibility. Because PostScript is a full-fledged programming language, it can be enhanced, or *extended*, to provide new features and functions. Using appropriate software, you can even alter PostScript fonts to create new type-faces, as shown in Figure 8-14.

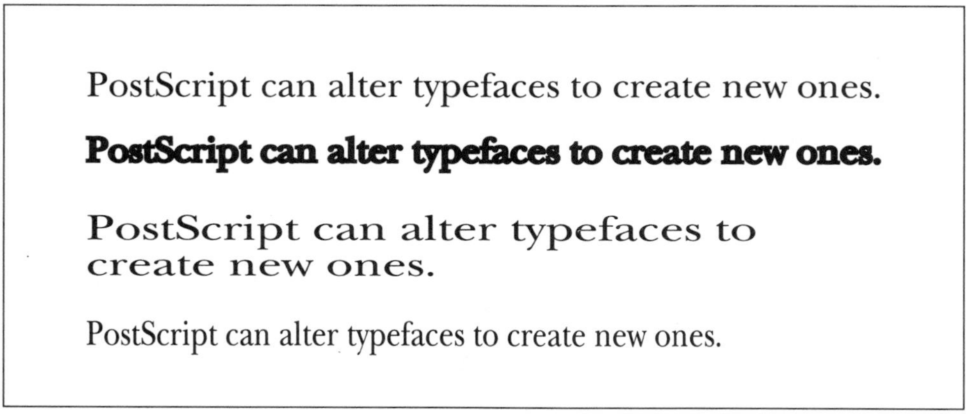

PostScript can alter typefaces to create new ones.

PostScript can alter typefaces to create new ones.

PostScript can alter typefaces to create new ones.

PostScript can alter typefaces to create new ones.

Figure 8-14:   PostScript can alter existing fonts to create new ones.

PostScript's Drawbacks

For all their strengths, PostScript printers do have some drawbacks.

Cost. A PostScript controller is a powerful computer in its own right. Its microprocessor and all those RAM and ROM chips don't come cheap. And Adobe Systems charges licensing and royalty fees for its PostScript interpreters and outline fonts. The end result: a Hewlett-Packard LaserJet Series II, which contains an extremely simple controller by PostScript standards, sells for under $2,000. By contrast, a LaserWriter IINT, which contains the identical Canon SX engine, retails for $4,999.

Performance. A PostScript printer imposes fewer processing demands on the Mac, but it nevertheless takes some time to process pages in the printer itself. PostScript has always been criticized as being slow; today's PostScript interpreters are far faster than the original LaserWriter's, but few interpreters can keep up with their engines.

PostScript and Fonts

This section takes a closer look at how PostScript printers use fonts. We'll look at:

• the fonts built into PostScript printers

• how you can supplement a printer's built-in fonts

• how PostScript controllers manipulate fonts internally.

Built-in Fonts

The built-in outline fonts stored in ROM chips on a PostScript printer's controller board are called *resident* typefaces. Most PostScript printers, including the LaserWriter IINT and NTX, contain 35 resident typefaces in 11 font families:

- Helvetica with oblique, bold, and bold oblique (remember from the previous chapter that the oblique style is a slanted variation of the upright, or Roman, style)

- Times with italic, bold, and bold italic

- Courier with oblique, bold, and bold oblique

- Symbol

- New Century Schoolbook with italic, bold, and bold italic

- Palatino with italic, bold, and bold italic

- ITC Bookman Light with light italic, demi, and demi italic

- ITC Avant Garde Gothic Book with oblique, demi, and demi oblique

- Helvetica Narrow with oblique, bold, and bold oblique

- ITC Zapf Chancery Medium Italic

- ITC Zapf Dingbats

The original LaserWriter and some older printers, such as QMS's PS-800, contain only the first three font families and the Symbol font. Some printers contain the aforementioned fonts and add additional ones. IBM's Personal Page Printer II, for example, also contains the Korinna, Garamond, Helvetica Black, and Helvetica Light families. Compugraphic's P3400PS includes 73 fonts.

Downloadable Fonts

You can supplement a PostScript printer's resident fonts with *downloadable fonts*—outline fonts stored in your Mac's System Folder and transferred, or *downloaded*, into the printer's memory before use. A vast selection of downloadable fonts is available from Adobe Systems, Bitstream, Compugraphic, Casady & Greene, and others.

Downloadable fonts can be automatically or manually downloaded. With automatic downloading, the LaserWriter driver shuttles the fonts into the printer's memory during the print job; you need perform no special steps to use the fonts. One font takes roughly 20 to 30 seconds to download. After the print job, the LaserWriter driver removes, or *flushes*, the fonts from the printer's memory.

With manual downloading, you use a special utility program to transfer the fonts into memory, as shown in Figure 8-15. That requires effort on your part, but it has an advantage: manually downloaded fonts aren't flushed from the printer's memory after the print job. Thus, if you plan to use a specific font extensively, you can manually download it and save 20 to 30 seconds on each subsequent print job containing that font.

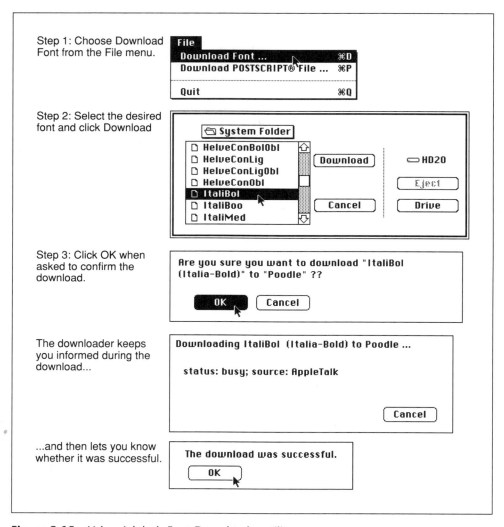

Step 1: Choose Download Font from the File menu.

File
Download Font ...   ⌘D
Download POSTSCRIPT® File ...   ⌘P

Quit   ⌘Q

Step 2: Select the desired font and click Download

🗁 **System Folder**

□ HelveConBolObl
□ HelveConLig   **Download**   ▭ HD20
□ HelveConLigObl
□ HelveConObl   Eject
□ **ItaliBol**
□ ItaliBoo   **Cancel**   **Drive**
□ ItaliMed

Step 3: Click OK when asked to confirm the download.

Are you sure you want to download "ItaliBol (Italia-Bold)" to "Poodle" ??

OK   Cancel

The downloader keeps you informed during the download...

Downloading ItaliBol (Italia-Bold) to Poodle ...

status: busy; source: AppleTalk

Cancel

...and then lets you know whether it was successful.

The download was successful.
OK

Figure 8-15: Using Adobe's Font Downloader utility.

Downloadable font files have names assigned to them by the font developer. For example, Adobe's American Typewriter Bold downloadable font is named AmeriTypBol. *Never change these names.* If you do, the LaserWriter driver won't be able to download the font automatically.

Downloadable Fonts and Memory

Downloadable fonts are stored in a reserved area of printer memory called *virtual memory*, or *VM*. A PostScript printer has a finite amount of VM available for downloadable fonts. The original LaserWriter offered approximately 200K of VM, room enough for about four downloadable fonts. Today's PostScript printers offer more memory and use that memory more efficiently. A printer with 2MB of RAM, for example, offers between 400K and 500K of VM and can hold approximately eight downloadable fonts. (We say "approximately" in each case because the size of downloadable fonts varies according to the complexity of the typeface. And incidentally, don't confuse a PostScript printer's virtual memory with the virtual memory features that System 7.0 will provide; they're completely different entities.)

If you have Adobe's Font Downloader utility, you can find out how much VM your printer provides by choosing the Printer Font Directory command from the Special menu. The amount of VM available appears at the bottom of the font directory display, as shown in Figure 8-16.

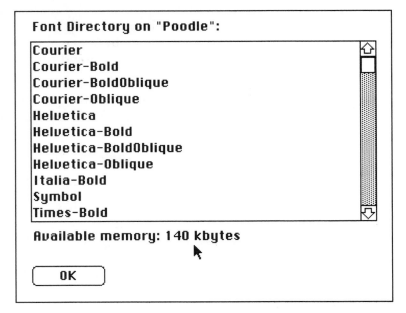

Figure 8-16: Determining available VM using the Adobe Font Downloader.

How PostScript Uses Fonts

We've mentioned before that PostScript fonts are stored as mathematic formulas called outlines. We've also stated the primary benefit of font outlines: they allow the printer to create fonts in virtually any size, they use less storage space than a large selection of bit-mapped sizes, and they allow the printer to create special text effects, such as condensed, expanded, and even rotated type, by simply interpreting the font outlines differently.

But the final step in printing a page involves creating a bit map of the entire page in the printer's memory. Thus, when you print a document, the PostScript controller must translate font outlines into bit maps that match the required type size and the resolution of the printer's engine. This outline-to-bit map conversion process is among the most complex tasks a PostScript controller performs. Simplified somewhat, it works as follows.

1. When a page calls for a character in a given size and orientation, the controller reads the outline description and generates a bit map of the character in that size. During this process, the controller tweaks the shape of the character, adding and removing printer dots as needed, to produce the best-looking character possible at the engine's resolution. Each outline font contains special routines called *hints* that make this optimization process possible.

2. The controller then stores the bit map in a reserved area of printer memory called the *font cache*. The font cache keeps the character bit map on the sidelines, so to speak. If that character is needed again later, the controller retrieves its bit map from the font cache. According to Adobe, retrieving a character bit map from the font cache is roughly a thousand times faster than recreating the bit map from the original outline.

3. The controller adds the bit map to the page buffer, and continues interpreting the page description, generating font bit maps as needed, and retrieving already built bit maps from the font cache when they exist.

More About Font Caching

The font cache plays an important role and dramatically improves the controller's performance at printing documents containing a large variety of fonts, sizes, and styles. When the font cache fills, the controller discards characters on a "least recently used" basis. The larger the controller's font cache, the more room there is for font bit maps. When other factors such as engine speed and processor type are equal, a printer with larger font cache will be faster than a printer with a smaller one.

As PostScript has evolved and grown more memory-efficient, the size of font caches has grown accordingly. For example, the LaserWriter Plus had a relatively small 160K font cache. The LaserWriter IINT has a 200K font cache, while QMS' PS-810 has a 279K font cache. A LaserWriter IINTX containing its maximum of 12MB of memory has a whopping 1200K font cache.

The ROM chips of most PostScript printers also contain prebuilt bit maps of commonly used fonts and sizes. The LaserWriters, for example, contain the full ASCII character set in 10-point Courier, as well as letters, numbers, and common punctuation in 12-point Times and Helvetica. If a document requires these sizes, the controller retrieves the prebuilt outlines from ROM.

Most printers also build bit maps for other sizes of Times and Helvetica in their spare time; that is, when they aren't processing a print job. This technique is called *idle-time font-scan conversion*. Font bit maps created using this technique are stored in the font cache, just as if they had been generated for a specific document. Some high-performance printers containing more memory build bit maps for additional fonts. For example, Dataproducts' LZR-1260 creates bit maps for the aforementioned fonts and also for New Century Schoolbook Roman, Helvetica Narrow, Palatino, Avant Garde, Gothic Book, and Bookman Light.

More About Hints

We've mentioned that part of a PostScript controller's job is to optimize the appearance of each character to match the engine's resolution. Within each font outline are mathematic formulas, often called *hints*, that make this optimization possible. (You might also hear this optimization process referred to as *grid-fitting*.)

What we haven't mentioned, however, is that an Adobe PostScript interpreter will only use hints created in Adobe's own format. If you use downloadable PostScript fonts from firms such as Bitstream on a printer containing an Adobe interpreter, small text sizes are likely to have a "chunky" appearance to them, especially on printers with 300-dpi resolution. On higher resolution printers such as Varityper's VT-600, this problem is far less noticeable. When printed on high-resolution typesetters, non-Adobe fonts generally look as good as Adobe fonts. (At least from the standpoint of character shape; many other factors influence the quality of a font, and not all font developers take as much care as Adobe in crafting their typefaces.)

All of this can be summarized as follows:

- Adobe fonts contain hints that the controller uses to optimize the appearance of each character to match the printer's resolution.

- Hints are especially important at relatively low resolutions, such as 300 dpi. As printer resolution grows, hints become less important.

SCSI Font Storage

Some PostScript printers offer a SCSI connector that allows you to attach a SCSI hard disk to the printer. A hard disk adds two benefits to a PostScript printer.

- It holds downloadable fonts. When you store downloadable fonts on a printer's hard disk, they need not be transmitted over AppleTalk. Thus, printing times for documents containing downloadable fonts decrease significantly. Also, downloadable fonts stored on a printer's hard disk are available to all Macs on a network. Each Mac need not waste disk space storing the printer fonts.

- It makes the font cache larger. When the printer's font cache fills, the controller stores the characters that would otherwise be purged on the hard disk. Only when the disk-based font cache fills are its least-recently used characters purged. Generally, a PostScript printer divides a hard disk's capacity in half, using half for downloadable fonts and the other half as an extension of the font cache. Thus, if you attach a 20MB hard disk to a printer, you give the printer the equivalent of a 10MB font cache.

The following printers are among those that accept an optional hard disk: Apple's LaserWriter IINTX, GCC's Business LaserPrinter, and Dataproducts' LZR-1260. Printers that include a hard disk as standard equipment include Agfa/Compugraphic's CG-400PS and P3400PS, Varityper's VT-600 and VT-600W, and the Linotronic series of typesetters.

Note that not all SCSI storage devices work with PostScript printers. Table 8-3 is a partial list, compiled from information supplied by Apple and GCC Technologies, of SCSI drives that are and are not compatible with PostScript printers.

Table 8-3: SCSI drives that are and aren't compatible with PostScript printers.

Compatible Drives	Incompatible Drives
GCC HyperDrive FX/20, FX/40, FX/60, FX/80	GCC HyperDrive FX/40 (early versions only; no front-panel light)
Apple HD20SC	
Everex EMAC 20HD	AST 2000
Jasmine DirectDrive 80	MDIdeas HD20
Seagate ST225N	SuperMac DataFrame 20 and DataFrame XP series
Rodime 650 series (RO651, (RO652, RO751, RO752)	
MiniScribe 8425-SCSI, 8051S	

PostScript's Typographic Capabilities

PostScript printers take advantage of the flexibility of font outlines to allow you to create text in virtually any size and orientation. PostScript can create text in any size from 1 point up to, according to Adobe, a character the size of the state of Rhode Island. (Rhode Island residents need not fear an invasion by such a colossal character. This upper limit represents PostScript's theoretical limits; no printer exists that could create it!)

The Mac's Font Manager supports type sizes ranging from 4 point to 127 point. The formatting menus of some programs contain a fixed set of type sizes in common "graphic arts" sizes, such as 8, 10, 12, 14, 18, 20, and 24 point. More flexible programs allow you to type your own size values into a dialog box. If you choose a size for which no screen font exists—such as 19-point—the text will appear ragged on screen (at least in System 6.0 and earlier versions), but thanks to the versatility of outline fonts, it will appear tack-sharp in your final output, as shown in Figure 8-17.

Some programs also support fractional font sizes (such as 12.5 point), and some support type sizes above 127 point. The QuarkXpress desktop publishing program is one such package; it supports sizes from 2 to 500 point. Quark-Xpress also lets you take advantage of PostScript's ability to stretch and condense existing typefaces to create new ones.

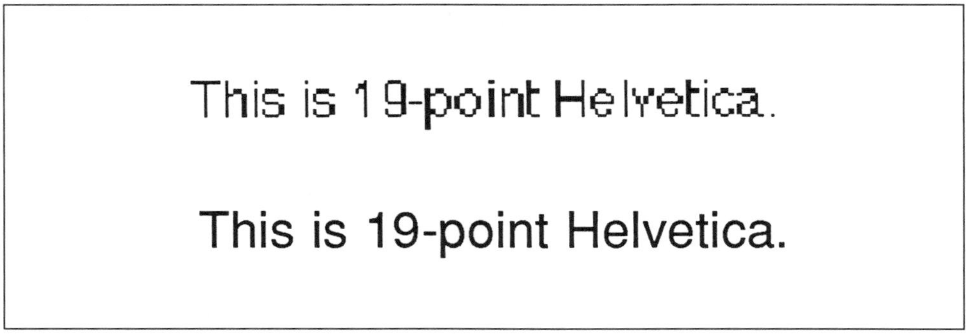

This is 19-point Helvetica.

This is 19-point Helvetica.

Figure 8-17: A derived 19-point screen font (*top*) and the resulting PostScript output (*bottom*).

Like the Mac itself, PostScript treats all elements of a page—text and images—as graphics. PostScript also provides a sophisticated array of commands, called *operators*, for rotating, scaling, shading, and otherwise manipulating graphics. Because text in PostScript is simply a type of graphic, PostScript printers can apply these operators to text to produce some remarkable effects. The most common PostScript effects are shown in Figure 8-18.

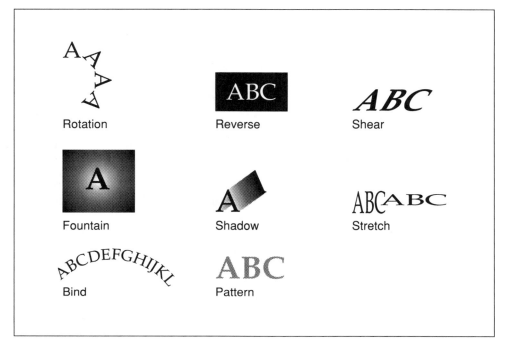

Figure 8-18: Common PostScript text effects.

Differences Between PostScript Printers

All PostScript printers are compatible with the Mac and with each other. By saying that all PostScript printers are compatible with each other, we mean that you can print a given document on any PostScript printer and get the same results.

Well, almost. The fact is, there are differences between PostScript printers. The most significant differences include the following.

Processor. Some PostScript printers contain 68000 processors, while others contain 68020s. This difference shows up only on your stopwatch; 68020-based printers are generally much faster than their 68000-based counterparts.

PostScript versions. Adobe continues to improve its PostScript interpreters, and different printers contain different versions of PostScript. As a general rule, the later the version (that is, the higher its version number), the faster and more memory efficient the printer is.

Memory configuration. The original LaserWriter contained only 1.5MB of RAM; today's PostScript printers come with a minimum of 2MB, and some (such as the LaserWriter IINTX) can hold up to 12MB. This disparity can work against you if you use downloadable fonts extensively. For example, assume your office contains one printer with 4MB of memory, and another with only 2MB. If you create a document using numerous downloadable fonts, you may be able print it on the 4MB printer, but not on the 2MB one. If you prefer the output quality of the 2MB printer, you'll need to redesign the document and substitute resident fonts for some of the downloadable ones. The moral: When choosing fonts for a document, always work within the memory limitations of the printer that will produce the final copy.

Font configuration. If you will print final copies of a document on a printer other than your own, verify that the final printer contains the same resident fonts as yours, or that the resident fonts it lacks are available in downloadable form. Again, the best policy is to design documents for the printer that will produce the final copy.

Engine resolution. Differences in print resolution can cause unexpected results when you print documents containing shaded areas, called *screens*, and fine lines, called *hairline rules*. A screen consists of a collection of dots; the more dots within the screened area, the darker the shade appears. The problem is that printers with different resolutions produce different-sized dots. A 300-dpi printer produces a dot 1/300 inch in diameter; a 2,540-dpi Linotronic typesetter produces a dot 1/2540 in diameter. The result: when you print a screened area on a Linotronic, it appears much lighter than it does when printed by a 300-dpi printer. Hairline rules, which are one dot wide, also appear lighter on Linotronic output for the same reason. The easiest way to avoid this problem is to use programs such as Aldus PageMaker and QuarkXpress, both of which compensate for differences in printer resolution when printing screens and rules.

Bit map smoothing capabilities. Of all PostScript printers, only Apple's LaserWriters contain routines for smoothing the rough edges of bit-mapped (MacPaint-type) graphics. These smoothing routines can improve the appearance of some bit-mapped graphics, as shown in Figure 8-19. Some application programs, including Aldus PageMaker, include their own smoothing routines, allowing them to print smoothed bit maps on any PostScript printer. However, if you use applications that don't provide built-in smoothing, and if you prefer the smoothed look, consider an Apple PostScript printer.

Figure 8-19: A smoothed bit map (*top*) and unsmoothed bit map (*bottom*).

Halftoning capabilities. Like a printing press, a laser printer can't print shades of gray. To reproduce a photograph, the printer must use a printing industry technique called *halftoning*, in which the image is converted into dot patterns, with larger dots representing darker grey shades, and smaller dots representing lighter ones. Halftones are described in terms of lines per inch (lpi); the more lines per inch a halftone contains, the less apparent the dots become, and the better the image appears. Newspaper halftones generally contain 65 lpi; high-quality magazine halftones usually have 120 or more lpi.

A laser printer produces halftones by combining printer dots into larger groups called *cells*. The greater a printer's output resolution, the better the quality of halftones the printer can produce, since each halftone cell can be smaller. The practical upper limit for a 300-dpi printer is a 53-lpi halftone; a 600-dpi printer can produce high-quality 71-lpi halftones. Linotronics and other high-resolution laser typesetters can produce 120-lpi halftones. Figure 8-20 shows 53-lpi and 71-lpi halftone, created by a 300-dpi PostScript printer and a Varityper VT-600, respectively.

Figure 8-20: A 53-lpi halftone (*left*) and 71-lpi halftone (*right*).

Emulation modes. Most PostScript printers can imitate popular non-Post-Script printers. The most common *emulation mode* allows the printer to act like a Diablo 630 daisy wheel printer. Some printers, including the LaserWriter IINTX and QMS PS-810 and 820, can also imitate the Hewlett-Packard LaserJet. IBM's Personal Page Printer II can also emulate an IBM ProWriter, while the printers in Texas Instruments' OmniLaser series include emulation modes for the Texas Instruments 855. Because these non-PostScript printers lack Post-Script's versatility, an emulation mode will always turn a PostScript printer into something with inferior text and graphics printing features. Still, if you use IBM PC software that doesn't support PostScript, emulation modes will at least let you take advantage of the printer's sharp copy and fast print engine.

Interfaces. All PostScript printers provide a LocalTalk connector for use with Mac networks, and an RS-232C serial connector for use with other computers. Some printers also provide a Centronics parallel port for use with IBM PCs.

Paper-handling features. Some printers provide dual paper trays that let you mix and match paper sizes and types. Linotronic typesetters don't use single sheets of paper, but instead use rolls of photographic film or paper. To allow users to take advantage of specific printer features, Adobe developed *Adobe printer descriptions* (*APDs*), files that contain information about a printer's features, from the number of paper trays it provides to its output resolution. Most printers that offer unusual paper-handling features or resolutions other than 300 dpi include an APD file. Application programs can read an APD and adjust their Page Setup and Print dialog boxes to reflect that printer's features. If the printer's resolution is other than 300 dpi, applications can also adjust the way they print hairline rules, screens, and halftones.

Unfortunately, at this writing, only a few applications—Aldus' PageMaker and FreeHand and Adobe Illustrator 88—support APDs. Some programs, such as QuarkXpress, contain internal coding that allows them to recognize special paper trays or output resolutions. This approach lacks the flexibility of APDs, however; when a new printer is released, the software developer must release a new version of its software in order to support it.

Table 8-4 lists the specifications of four popular PostScript printers.

Table 8-4: A comparison of several PostScript printers.

	Apple LaserWriter IINT	Apple LaserWriter IINTX	GCC Business LaserPrinter	IBM Personal Page Printer II
Processor type and speed	68000, 12MHz	68020, 16MHz	68000, 12.5MHz	68000, 16MHz
PostScript version	47	47	49.2	50.5
Number of resident fonts	35	35	39	41
Accepts font-storage hard disk	no	yes	yes	no
Size of font cache (kilobytes)	200	200-1200[1]	230[1]	238K[1]
Amount of RAM	2MB	2MB	2MB	2MB
RAM expansion options	none	to 12MB	to 4MB	to 4MB
Emulation modes	Diablo 630	Diablo 630, HP LaserJet Plus	none	HP LaserJet Plus, IBM Pro Printer XL
Interfaces[2]	L, R, ADB	L, R, ADB, SCSI	L, R, P	L, R, P

[1] For standard RAM configuration; font cache size increases when RAM is expanded.

[2] Interfaces: L, LocalTalk; R, RS-232C; ADB, Apple Desktop Bus; SCSI, Small Computer System Interface; P, parallel

PostScript Clones

In 1989, a new wrinkle formed in the issue of PostScript compatibility when several firms released printers containing non-Adobe PostScript interpreters. In these so-called *PostScript clones*, the interpreter is designed to act just like an Adobe PostScript interpreter—just as, in the IBM PC world, a Compaq or Tandy computer is designed to act like an IBM.

It may surprise you, but IBM computers are far easier to clone than a Post-Script interpreter. As the previous sections have shown, PostScript is an extremely complex language in which myriad factors interact in countless ways to produce a page of output. The only way for a clone developer to judge a PostScript clone's compatibility is run test after test, making adjustments in the interpreter as needed. If you're a clone developer, the tricky part is determining when you've run enough tests. Every document is different, and thus creates a different state within the controller. A hundred documents may print perfectly, but as we've seen in our own work with PostScript clones, the hundred and first may crash the interpreter.

One measure of compatibility that clone developers use is to say their interpreters are *red book compatible*. This means that the interpreter acts like an Adobe interpreter, as described in the red-covered book, *PostScript Language Reference Manual* (Addison-Wesley, 1985). Red book compatibility is desirable, but it isn't a guarantee that a PostScript clone will print every document thrown at it.

The red book aside, PostScript clones share one glaring incompatibility: they can't use Adobe downloadable fonts. Adobe's fonts are stored in an encrypted format that only an Adobe PostScript interpreter can read. Non-Adobe interpreters can, however, use a special type of downloadable font called the *Type 3* font. Several font vendors, including Bitstream, Compugraphic, and Casady & Greene, supply their fonts in Type 3 format. Thus, PostScript clone users can still choose from a large selection of downloadable fonts, but are locked out of the Adobe library, which many desktop publishers and designers regard as the finest.

Some clone developers have announced that they've "cracked" Adobe's encryption scheme, but at this writing, no clones that can use Adobe fonts are available. If you're considering a clone that claims to support Adobe fonts, print some test pages at small type sizes (12-point and smaller) and compare them to the output of an Adobe interpreter.

What advantages does a PostScript clone offer? Clones are often much faster than printers that use Adobe interpreters. Clones such as Qume's CrystalPrint Publisher use special processors called *reduced instruction-set computers*, or *RISCs* for short. RISC processors are streamlined to perform common tasks more quickly than conventional processors such as the 68000 and 68020.

But PostScript clones aren't always faster. In particular, they tend to be slower at printing bit-mapped graphics such as MacPaint drawings and scanned images. Adobe has optimized the way its interpreters handle bit-mapped graphics so that even a RISC-equipped clone can't keep up.

You're also unlikely to notice the extra performance of a PostScript clone if you primarily print simple, text-oriented documents such as manuscripts or legal contracts and briefings. When printing simple text documents, the printer's print engine becomes the most important performance-determining factor. An Adobe PostScript printer with a 10-page-per-minute engine will print a text-only document more quickly than a clone with a 6-ppm engine.

PostScript clones also tend to cost less, although that isn't always the case. At least two Adobe PostScript printers—GCC's Business LaserPrinter and NEC's SilentWriter LC-890—sell for prices comparable to many PostScript clones'. Neither is as fast at printing typographically complex documents, but both offer the assurance of a true Adobe interpreter and the ability to use Adobe downloadable fonts.

We feel that the jury is still out on PostScript clones. Initial offerings have had technical problems and limitations. As these wrinkles are ironed out, PostScript clones may become as viable and popular as IBM clones. For now, however, if your needs dictate a PostScript printer, you're probably better off with one containing a true Adobe interpreter.

Finally, we'd be remiss if we didn't mention a unique approach to PostScript cloning: a software product called Freedom of Press, from Custom Applications, Inc. Freedom of Press is a software-based PostScript-compatible interpreter; that is, the interpreter and its outline fonts reside on your hard disk, not in a printer. You produce documents by creating print files (which we'll describe later), and then running Freedom of Press and telling it to interpret the print files. The Freedom of Press interpreter then produces output on any of numerous printers, including Hewlett-Packard's LaserJet laser printers and DeskJet ink-jet printers, a variety of dot-matrix printers, and even some color printers.

Freedom of Press isn't as convenient or as fast as a PostScript printer, but it's ideal for users who need only occassional PostScript output, or who want to get more use out of a LaserJet or other non-PostScript printer. It's also an excellent choice for users who need color PostScript output, since non-PostScript color printers cost far less than color PostScript printers. Freedom of Press has been available for IBM machines since late 1988. At this writing, the Macintosh version was scheduled to be released during 1989.

Ten Tips for PostScript Printers

Here are ten tips for using LaserWriter IINTs, NTXs, and other PostScript printers.

Disabling the start-up page. All PostScript printers print a start-up page listing details such as resident fonts, memory configuration, and current operating mode. In addition to listing vital statistics, the start-up page shows that the printer's controller and engine are operating properly. However, it also wastes a sheet of paper each time you switch on the printer, and it lengthens the printer's start-up process by the amount of time taken to describe and image the start-up page. The easiest way to disable the start-up page is to pull the printer's paper tray out an inch or two before or after you power up the printer. When the printer's activity light stops flashing, you can push the tray back in.

If you want to disable the start-up page permanently, use a word processor to type the two-line PostScript program shown in Figure 8-21. Proofread it carefully, then save the program in text-only format. Next, use the Adobe Font Downloader to transmit the file to your printer. To send the file, choose Download PostScript File from the program's File menu.

```
serverdict begin 0 exitserver

statusdict begin false setdostartpage end
```

Figure 8-21: PostScript program for disabling start-up page.

The program disables the start-up page by setting PostScript's **dostartpage** value to "false." This value is stored in a non-volatile area of memory called the *status dictionary*. To restore the start-up page, replace the word *false* in the second line of the program to *true*, then download the program again.

Avoid non-PostScript fonts. You'll always get the best results by using screen fonts that have either resident or downloadable printer counterparts. Avoid fonts such as New York, Geneva, and Monaco. These fonts don't have PostScript counterparts. When you print a document containing them, one of two things will happen, depending on whether the Page Setup dialog box's Font Substitution option is selected.

If font substitution is activated, the Mac substitutes Helvetica for Geneva, Times for New York, and Courier for Monaco. Because these fonts' spacing doesn't match that of Geneva, Times, or Monaco, however, the printed output will appear irregularly spaced.

If font substitution is disabled, the Mac transmits bit-mapped versions of the fonts to the printer. The resulting text appears ragged, as if printed on an ImageWriter. If you have an Apple PostScript printer, you can improve the appearance of the text by choosing the Text Smoothing option in the Page Setup dialog box.

Creating a print file. You can create a disk file containing the commands that the LaserWriter driver transmits to the printer. To do so, press Command-F within one second after okaying the Print dialog box. To include the Laser Prep PostScript dictionary in the print file, press Command-K instead of

Command-F. The Mac names the resulting file PostScript0. If you create additional print files, they're named PostScript1, PostScript2, and so on. You can download the resulting print files to a printer using the Adobe Font Downloader's Download PostScript File command.

One use for this print-to-disk technique is to create a print file for subsequent printing at a typesetting service bureau. Before using this technique, however, check with your service bureau for instructions on how to prepare documents for typesetting. Some bureaus prefer to work with original documents rather than print files.

Changing the printer's name. Using an Apple utility called The Namer, you can change your printer's name, which appears in the Chooser and on the start-up page. If you have more than one printer, use The Namer to give each one a descriptive name, such as "1st Floor Printer" or "Accounting Printer." Printer names can be up to 31 characters long, but cannot contain the colon (:) or "at" sign (@) characters.

Avoiding Laser Prep conflicts. If you share a PostScript printer on a network, be sure that all Macs are using the same version of the LaserPrep and LaserWriter drivers. If they aren't, your network's users will frequently see error messages telling them that the printer will need to be restarted and reinitialized because it was initialized with an incompatible version of the Laser Prep software. If all Macs on your network use the same version of LaserPrep and LaserWriter, this problem will not occur.

Unfortunately, if your network contains one or more 512K Macs, you'll be forced to mix different versions of LaserPrep and LaserWriter. The 512K Mac must use version 3.1 or earlier versions of LaserPrep and LaserWriter; it can't use versions 5.2 or later.

When System 7.0 becomes available, you *will* be able to mix its LaserWriter driver with earlier versions on the same network. That's because System 7.0's LaserWriter driver will not rely on a separate LaserPrep file; instead, the driver will initialize the printer during the actual print job, transmitting only those portions of the PostScript dictionary necessary to print the job.

Using the Precision Bitmap Alignment option. When you print a 72-dpi bit-mapped graphic (such as a MacPaint image) that you've pasted into another application, the LaserWriter driver scales it up to 300 dpi. Because 300 dpi isn't an even multiple of 72 dpi, the graphic can appear distorted. To avoid this distortion, choose the Page Setup command, click the Options button, and then choose the Precision Bitmap Alignment option. This option reduces the entire page by four percent (to 288 dpi), thus avoiding bit map distortion. Figure 8-22 shows the results.

Figure 8-22: A bit-mapped image printed without Precision Bitmap Alignment (*left*) and with it (*right*).

Using more downloadable fonts. Tired of running out of printer memory when using downloadable fonts? If you don't mind longer printing times, you can use an unlimited number of downloadable fonts in a document. Choose the Page Setup command, click the Options button, and then choose the Unlimited Downloadable Fonts in a Document option. When this option is active, the LaserWriter driver flushes each downloadable font from the printer's memory when that font is no longer needed.

Sharing downloadable fonts on a network. We've mentioned that adding a laser printer hard disk eliminates the need to store downloadable fonts in every Mac's System Folder. If you use network file server software such as AppleShare or TOPS, there's another way to avoid storing downloadable fonts on every Mac: Tactic Software's FontShare. FontShare lets all the Macs on a network access downloadable printer fonts stored on the file server. FontShare instructs the Mac to look for downloadable fonts in the file server volume you specify if the fonts aren't found in your System Folder.

Printing envelopes. Look in many laser printer-equipped offices, and you'll probably notice a typewriter tucked in the corner with a stack of envelopes next to it. Most laser printers that have manual feed slots can accept envelopes, but formatting text for an envelope often seems like more trouble than it's worth.

The easiest way to print envelopes is to use a $5 shareware desk accessory called Kiwi Envelopes, available from on line information services and through user's groups, or direct from Kiwi Software (see Appendix B for its address). With Kiwi Envelopes, you simply type (or paste from the Clipboard) the return address and addressee's address; Kiwi Envelopes automatically formats the text appropriately. (Version 3.0 of Kiwi Envelopes is no longer a shareware product; it's a commercial program, and it offers additional features, including a page-preview option and the ability to print postal service bar codes on envelopes.)

If you laser-print envelopes extensively, you might consider using James River Corporation's Laser Envelopes, distributed by Pro-Tech of Ludlow, MA. Laser Envelopes are specially made to fit into a laser printer's letter-sized paper tray; the envelopes are designed so that the pocket and open flap measure 8 1/2 by 11 inches. The flap is not folded, so it doesn't create the irregular surface that often causes marred type with conventional envelopes—and the heat of the laser printer's fusing assembly doesn't glue it shut.

Choosing paper. Laser printer engines are close cousins of photocopier engines, so you can generally use any paper designed for photocopiers. However, you'll get better results by choosing a paper designed for high-quality laser printer output, such as Hammermill Laser Print or Laser Plus. Both papers are identical, with one exception: Laser Plus contains a *wax hold-out*, a special coating on the paper's reverse side that lets you apply rubber cement, spray adhesive, or graphic arts wax without it soaking through.

You can also print mailing labels on a laser printer if you choose your label stock carefully. Use labels designed to be run through photocopiers. Other types of labels can peel off as they travel through the print engine, or their adhesive can melt under the heat and pressure of the fusing rollers. Either way, you'll develop a new appreciation for the phrase "gumming up the works." Avery offers a large selection of laser-compatible label stocks. We're especially fond of Avery's full-sheet labels (Avery part number 5455), an 8 1/2 by 11-inch peel-and-stick label stock. With this versatile label stock, you can print everything from multiple columns of mailing labels (cut them apart with a paper cutter) to videocassette labels.

You can also print 8 1/2 by 11-inch transparencies using Avery's transparency stock, code number 5282 (20 sheets) or 5182 (50 sheets). Table 8-5 lists the specifications of several other varieties of Avery label stock.

Table 8-5: A sampling of Avery label stock for laser printers.

Label Size[1]	Layout on Page[2]	Labels Per Sheet	Avery Code
1 by 2 5/8	3 by 10	30	5260
1 by 4	2 by 10	20	5261
1-1/2 by 4	2 by 7	14	5262
1/2 by 1 3/4	4 by 20	80	5267
2 by 4	2 by 5	10	5163
3 1/3 by 4	2 by 3	6	5164
1 2/3[3]	4 by 6	24	5293
2 1/2[3]	3 by 4	12	5294
3 1/3[3]	2 by 3	6	5295

[1] In inches, height by width.
[2] Number of labels across by number of labels down.
[3] These labels are round.

Can I Quote You?

An easy way to make your laser-printed documents look professionally typeset is to use the typographer's quotes and dashes that the Mac provides. These characters, shown in Table 8-6, are available whether you're using an ImageWriter, PostScript printer, or QuickDraw printer.

Table 8-6: Typesetter's characters and how to type them.

Character	Key Sequence
Open single quote (')	Option-]
Closed single quote (')	Shift-Option-]
Open double quote (")	Option-[
Closed double quote (")	Shift-Option-]
Em dash (—)	Shift-Option-minus (-)
En dash (–)	Option-minus (-)

The em dash is generally used where you'd normally type two hyphens, as in "George is late—again." The en dash is often used in place of the word "to," as in "I'm on the San Francisco–Pittsburgh flight." Single opening and closing quotes are generally used to set off a quote that appears within a quote, as in "He said, 'Can I help you?'"

Most word processors and desktop publishing programs provide a smart quotes feature, which automatically creates the proper opening and closing quotes for you as you type (or, with most publishing programs, when you open a word processor file). You can also add smart quote features to any program by using one of two free startup documents (Inits): Curlers, by Tom Phoenix; and Laser Quotes, by Deneba Software. We don't know of any programs that automatically insert em dashes for you when you type two hyphens, however.

Tip: If you're using a word processor to type a message that you'll transmit on a communications service such as MCI Mail, disable the smart quotes feature before typing the message. Communications services generally can't interpret the Mac's typesetter's quotes, and substitute other characters in their place.

QuickDraw Laser Printers

PostScript printers don't have a monopoly on the Mac laser printer world. Two laser printers are available that don't use PostScript, but instead, rely on QuickDraw, the Mac's built-in library of graphics routines. They are GCC Technologies' Personal LaserPrinter and Apple's LaserWriter IISC.

GCC Personal LaserPrinter

GCC's Personal LaserPrinter (PLP, for short) was the first non-PostScript laser printer offered for the Mac. Although it isn't a PostScript printer, the PLP shares much in common with PostScript printers:

- It uses outline fonts, giving it the ability to create a virtually unlimited range of sizes and type orientations

- It uses a font-caching mechanism similar to that of a PostScript printer

- It includes a selection of prebuilt font bit maps for often-used fonts and sizes.

Step 1: The PLP driver reads font outlines from the hard disk and constructs bit maps in the sizes required for the page.

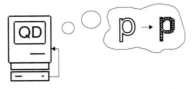

Step 2: The PLP driver works with QuickDraw to produce a bit-mapped image of the page in the Mac's memory.

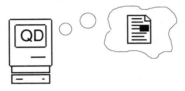

Step 3: The PLP driver stores the bit map on disk as it's being prepared.

Step 4: The PLP driver transmits the bit map to the printer over the SCSI bus, timed to match the rotation of the drum in the printer's engine.

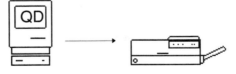

Step 5: The PLP's engine prints the page.

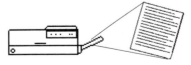

Figure 8-23: How the GCC Personal LaserPrinter operates.

The big difference between the PLP and a PostScript printer, however, is where the processing takes place. The PLP uses the Mac's memory and processor to perform the tasks that, in a PostScript printer, occur within the controller—tasks such as generating font bit maps from the original outlines, caching font bit maps, and generating the commands that control the print engine. Because the Mac handles these jobs, the PLP doesn't require its own processor and memory chips. Thus, it costs far less than a PostScript printer, while offering nearly the same typographic versatility. Figure 8-23 summarizes how the PLP processes print jobs. (These steps may differ when a version of the PLP driver is released for System 7.0.)

The PLP does have some drawbacks. It tends to be slow, since its software must share processor time and memory with the program you're running. The faster your Mac, and the more memory it contains, the faster the PLP operates. On Macs containing only 1MB of memory, the PLP often requires a two-step printing process which involves creating a disk file containing the print instructions, and then running a separate application program to produce the document. Also, because the PLP attaches to the Mac via its SCSI connector, multiple Macs can't share a PLP over a network. To share the PLP, you need GCC's PLP Share, a $499 hardware add-on.

Finally, while the PLP's outline fonts theoretically allow it to create expanded, condensed, and rotated text, few application programs can create these effects on the PLP. These limitations make the PLP a second-best alternative to a PostScript printer. Still, if your budget prevents the purchase of a PostScript printer, the PLP deserves consideration. As your needs grow, you can have the printer upgraded to the PostScript-based Business LaserPrinter.

Apple LaserWriter IISC

The LaserWriter IISC is the least expensive and least capable printer in Apple's LaserWriter II line. The best way to understand how the IISC operates is to think of it as an ImageWriter that prints 300 dots per inch. Like an ImageWriter, the IISC uses the Mac's bit-mapped screen fonts for final output. Like the ImageWriter driver, the IISC's driver looks for larger-sized fonts, and then reduces them to obtain better resolution.

But while the ImageWriter driver needs a two-times larger font and the ImageWriter LQ driver needs a three-times larger font, the IISC driver requires a four-times larger font. Table 8-6 lists the font sizes required to print common sizes on an LaserWriter IISC.

Table 8-6: Font sizes required for LaserWriter IISC printing.

To print this size...	You need this size...
9	36
10	40
12	48
14	56
18	72
24	96

The LaserWriter IISC's reliance on bit-mapped fonts makes it quite fast, but imposes even greater font storage demands than an ImageWriter. Moreover, the IISC's fonts generally lack the quality of PostScript and Personal LaserPrinter fonts. For these reasons, the IISC is more suited to printing simple text documents than to desktop publishing and advanced graphics applications.

When System 7.0 appears, the IISC will receive a tremendous shot in the typographic arm, thanks to System 7.0's outline fonts. With the ability to create high-quality typographic fonts in a virtually unlimited range of sizes, the IISC will become a much more viable printer for desktop publishing applications. However, if you need to share a printer on a network or you plan to print final output on PostScript-based typesetters, you'll still be better served by a PostScript printer.

Printing and System 7.0

Although many of the concepts we've discussed in this chapter will still apply to System 7.0, there will be some important differences.

- As mentioned in the last chapter, System 7.0 will provide outline fonts that the Mac will be able to use to create sharp text in any size and on any output device whose printer driver is compatible with System 7.0.

- Under System 7.0, the ImageWriter drivers will still offer Faster and Best modes. In Best mode, the driver will still reduce a larger font for better quality—the standard ImageWriter driver will use a font twice the required size, while the ImageWriter LQ driver will use a font three times the required size. And here's the good news: Thanks to System 7.0's outline fonts, the driver will always "find" the size it needs. If you print 29-point text in Best mode on an ImageWriter, the driver will use the outline fonts to create a 58-

point font, and then reduce it by half. By using the No Breaks Between Pages option, you'll be able to produce huge banners with tack-sharp text.

- When you print to a PostScript printer using System 7.0, the LaserWriter driver will still use a printer font if one exists. For example, if you format a document in Times, the LaserWriter driver will use the Times printer font built into the printer. In such a case, System 7.0's outline fonts will play a role similar to their role in System 6.0 and earlier versions: they'll act as stand-ins that appear on screen, but not in the final output.

- You will be able to use Apple-format outline fonts to produce high-quality PostScript output, but you will first need to convert the fonts into downloadable PostScript fonts by running an Adobe Systems translator utility. At this writing, the utility was still in development, and its final name, price, and availability date had not been determined.

- System 7.0 will bid farewell to the Laser Prep file. The Mac will no longer transfer the entire PostScript dictionary to the printer at the beginning of the first print job; instead, it will initialize the printer "on the fly" during each print job, sending only those portions of the dictionary necessary to print the current job. This should result in more efficient use of the printer's memory. As mentioned earlier, it will also allow you to mix System 7.0 and earlier versions on the same network without Laser Prep conflicts—a problem that currently plagues networks mixing System 6.0 and earlier versions.

- System 7.0 will provide new Toolbox managers for printing and positioning text. These new managers should improve document fidelity between different types of printers; that is, you should be able to print documents on a variety of different printers without differences in letter spacing and line breaks.

- For System 7.0, Apple will provide printer developers with a toolbox of routines they can use to create printer drivers for their hardware. By using this toolbox, developers will only need to write code that handles features specific to their hardware (such as color capabilities, dual paper bins, two-sided printing engines, and so on). This is expected to make it easier for printer developers to enter the Mac market; thus, a wider range of printers should become available. However, this may also introduce new compatibility wrinkles. The new printing architecture may make it easier for printer developers to enter the Mac market, but there's no guarantee that every new printer will provide the same degree of compatibility and the same ease of use (in terms of error messages, easy-to-understand Page Setup and Print dialog boxes, and so on) that current Mac-compatible printers provide.

CHAPTER SUMMARY

- Because of the Mac's graphical operating environment, printing and creating screen displays are closely related. When an application prints a document, it uses many of the same QuickDraw commands and Font Manager routines that it uses to display a document.

- To print to a specific printer, you need a printer driver for that printer. The driver acts as a liason between the Mac and the printer; it accepts QuickDraw commands and translates them into the specific commands required by the printer.

- PostScript printers and GCC's Personal LaserPrinter use separate font descriptions called printer fonts. When you use a PostScript printer, the Mac's screen fonts don't appear in the final output unless a corresponding printer font is unavailable.

- ImageWriters and the LaserWriter IISC use the Mac's bit-mapped screen fonts to produce text by reducing larger sizes to obtain sharper output. This approach requires more storage space and limits the selection of available type sizes. System 7.0's outline fonts will greatly enhance the typographic capabilities of these QuickDraw-based printers.

- Laser printers rely on two components: an engine, which shuttles paper and applies toner powder; and a controller, which communicates with the printer driver and governs the engine's imaging mechanism.

- You can supplement a PostScript printer's built-in (resident) fonts with downloadable fonts, which are stored on the Mac and transferred to the printer's memory before use.

9

Setup and Operating Tips

One of the things that separates novice from master is a knowledge of the little subtleties, the tips and techniques that help you get the most from a computer. This chapter is a collection of those tips and techniques, divided into three broad categories:

- setup tips for your System Folder

- operating tips for your daily computing routine

- hardware-oriented setup and operating tips.

SYSTEM FOLDER SETUP

This section contains tips for setting up your System Folder. The techniques described here can help you conserve memory and disk space—two scarce commodities on many Macs.

Saving Memory and Disk Space By Removing Start-up Documents

Chapter 5 described the start-up documents, or Inits, that accompany the Mac's System Update 6.0 package. These startup documents include:

- CloseView, for magnifying the screen image

- Easy Access, for simulating mouse movements using the numeric keypad

- MacroMaker, for assigning keyboard shortcuts and automating repetitive tasks.

Each of these start-up documents performs a useful task, but none are vital to the Mac's operation. You can save memory by dragging one or more of them out of the System Folder, and then restarting. If you never plan to use them, you can throw them in the Trash and save some disk space, too. (Just be sure you have copies elsewhere before throwing them away.) Table 9-1 shows how much memory and disk space each uses.

Table 9-1: Memory and disk space used by startup documents.

Init Name	Memory Used	Disk Space Used
Closeview	36K	21K
Easy Access	1K	4K
MacroMaker	50K	35K
Total	**87K**	**60K**

In this day of multimegabyte Macs and hard disks, 87K of RAM and 60K of disk space aren't much. Still, there are times when every little bit—or kilobit—helps, especially if your Mac has only 1MB of RAM and/or no hard disk.

It's easy to forget that each start-up document you use nibbles away at your RAM. And many start-up documents use far more RAM than the ones we've described here. For example, the TOPS network software (described in Chapter 12) uses 92K of RAM. If you use TOPS or other similarly RAM-hungry start-up documents, remember that you can recover their RAM by dragging the start-up documents out of the System Folder, and then restarting. An easy way to temporarily disable a start-up document is to drag it to the desktop (the gray-shaded area on which the Trash icon and disk icons rest). To put it back into the System Folder, simply select it and choose Put Away from the Finder's File menu. You can also use the Find File desk accessory to locate and remove a start-up document from the System Folder. (For information on Find File, see the section "Finding Files," later in this chapter.)

You might also consider creating a folder within the System Folder for temporarily storing Inits. Or, you might want to use an Init-management cdev such as Init or CE Software's Aask (both are described in the next chapter).

Saving Disk Space by Streamlining the System Folder

The previous tip mentioned that you can recover some disk space by throwing away unneeded start-up documents. This technique applies to many other files in the System Folder, too. Many System Folder files are candidates for the Trash. In particular, you should do away with any printer drivers that aren't applicable to your system. Table 9-2 lists the disk space used by the printer drivers in the System Update 6.0 package.

Table 9-2:   Disk space used by System Update 6.0 printer drivers.

Driver	Disk Space Used
ImageWriter	38K
AppleTalk ImageWriter	44K
LQ ImageWriter	46K
LQ AppleTalk ImageWriter	55K
Laser Prep[1]	28K
LaserWriter	64K
LaserWriter IISC	59K
Total	**334K**

[1] Don't throw this file away if you have a LaserWriter.

Other candidates for the silicon landfill include Control Panel documents, or cdevs, that aren't applicable to your hardware. For example, if you have a Mac SE, you don't need the cdevs that pertain to a Mac II, such as Color and Monitors. If you bought a preformatted hard disk, however, your System Folder may contain these cdevs. You won't see them when you open the Control Panel, because the Control Panel shows only those cdevs that apply to your Mac. But the cdevs themselves may be in the System Folder, taking up disk space. Table 9-3 lists the disk space used by the System Update 6.0 cdevs.

Table 9-3: Disk space used by System Update 6.0 cdevs.

Cdev Name	Disk Space Used
Monitors	16K
Color	2K
Sound	4K
Startup Device	3.3K
Mouse	4K
Keyboard	4K
General	14K
Map	22K
CloseView	21K
Total	**90.3K**

You probably wouldn't want to throw away every cdev listed in Table 9-3, unless you're trying to cram a System Folder and some applications onto one floppy disk for use on a Mac without a hard disk. If you do remove all the Control Panel devices and then try to open the Control Panel, the Mac displays an error message saying that no Control Panel files were found.

Finally, remember that you can save a considerable amount of disk space by removing unneeded fonts from the System file. You can clean out your electronic type foundry in two ways: by removing entire typefaces you don't use, or by removing only those font sizes you don't use. For example, if you use Courier for writing manuscripts, you wouldn't want to remove the 12-point size, but you could purge the larger sizes. The larger the font size, the more disk space it uses.

If you have an ImageWriter, LaserWriter IISC, or other QuickDraw-based printer, however, don't remove any sizes that the printer's driver requires to produce high-quality output. For example, don't remove 24-point Courier if you plan to print 12-point Courier in the ImageWriter's best quality mode. If you use a PostScript printer, you can still get excellent results when printing with the larger sizes, even though the derived sizes will look jagged on screen.

Living without MultiFinder

Another effective way to save RAM and disk space is to remove the system files associated with MultiFinder. Removing MultiFinder-related files from a system disk prevents you from using MultiFinder with that disk, but if your Mac has only 1MB of memory, you may not get much use out of MultiFinder anyway. (Indeed, even a 2MB Mac lacks sufficient RAM to run several large applications simultaneously.) Table 9-4 lists the MultiFinder-related files you can remove and the disk space each uses. These values apply to the System Update 6.0 package, which includes MultiFinder 6.0.1.

Table 9-4: Disk space used by MultiFinder-related files.

File Name	Purpose	Disk Space Used
MultiFinder	Contains multitasking software extensions	49K
PrintMonitor	Allows background printing to PostScript printers	37K
Backgrounder	Allows background printing to PostScript printers	5K
Total		**91K**

And here's a less drastic variation on the MultiFinder purging theme: If you want the option to use MultiFinder but you never plan to use its background PostScript-printing option, remove only the PrintMonitor and Backgrounder files, leaving the MultiFinder file intact.

If you have a hard disk, saving RAM is probably more important than saving disk space. In that case, don't throw away any MultiFinder-related files. Instead, use the Finder's Set Startup command to specify that your Mac run under the Finder, not MultiFinder, as shown in Figure 9-1. Restart the Mac after using the command to put the changes into effect.

How much memory will you gain by not running under MultiFinder? A 1MB Mac SE running MultiFinder 6.0.1 reports roughly 540K free when you choose About the Finder. With MultiFinder disabled, however, the Finder reports over 800K free—an increase of over 50 percent, and enough to run an application that might not otherwise be able to run.

Step 1:
Choose Set Startup
from the Special
menu.

Step 2:
Select the Finder
button and click OK.

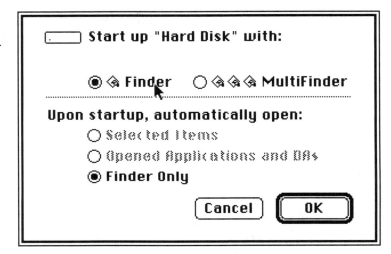

Figure 9-1: Using Set Startup to disable MultiFinder.

You'll find more tips for saving memory and for working with MultiFinder later in this chapter.

System 7.0 and Virtual Memory

For some Macs, System 7.0 will ease the memory crunch by providing a *virtual memory* feature. Virtual memory allows the system to treat a hard disk as an extension of memory, *swapping* programs from memory to the hard disk and vice versa as needed. However, to take advantage of System 7.0's virtual memory features, your Mac will need at least 2MB of RAM and a 68030 chip, or 2MB and a 68020 chip with the optional paged memory-management unit (PMMU). If yours is a 1MB Mac without an 030 or PMMU, you'll need to stick with System 6.0—and the memory-saving tips provided here—until you upgrade.

While System 7.0 will ease the memory crunch for certain Macs, it still won't eliminate the need for memory expansion. Apple's preliminary recommendation is that you should add as much memory as needed to accommodate the most memory-hungry application you plan to use.

OPERATING TIPS

This section presents tips you can apply to your daily computing routine. Topics discussed include:

- navigation techniques to improve your proficiency with the Mac and its software

- inexpensive ways to improve the Mac's performance

- how to get the most out of your Mac's memory

- Finder and MultiFinder shortcuts

- memory-saving alternatives to MultiFinder

- techniques for managing disks and files efficiently.

Navigation Techniques

One of the best ways to improve your Mac's performance is to master the Mac's navigation techniques—the mouse movements and keystroke combinations that control the Mac and its applications. There's a parallel in the sports world: A new pair of skis won't help inexperienced skiers thread their way through a slalom, but some guidance from a seasoned veteran will. Let's head for the slopes, shall we?

Selection Strategies

The act of selecting is one of the most common activities you perform when using the Mac. You can't run a program, delete a word, move a graphic, or copy a file without first selecting. Because selecting is such a cornerstone of Mac navigation techniques, it's important to master the Mac's various selection options.

Chapter 3 described the three basic techniques for selecting text: dragging (to select a range of characters), double-clicking and then dragging (to select text in one-word increments), and Shift-clicking (to extend a selection). Now let's look at some other selection strategies.

Shift-clicking in drawing and publishing programs. Shift-clicking is a common selection technique in drawing programs such as MacDraw II and in desktop publishing programs. Figure 9-2 shows an Aldus PageMaker window in which three elements have been selected using the Shift-click technique. As the figure shows, most graphics-oriented Mac applications indicate selected items by placing black boxes called *handles* at the corners of each item. In most programs, you can resize a selected element by dragging the handle—just as you can resize a window by dragging its size box.

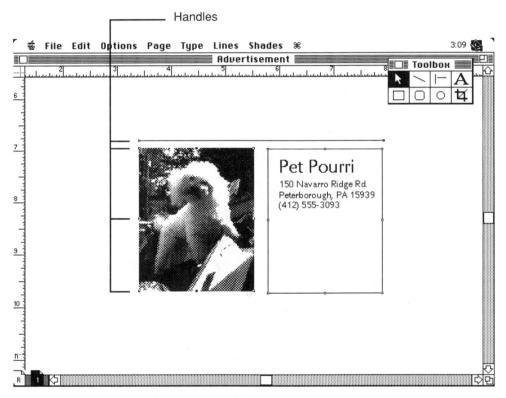

Figure 9-2: Three selected elements in Aldus PageMaker.

When you're working with files in the Finder, you can Shift-click to select additional files. If you want to throw away five files, for example, click on the first file, and then Shift-click on the remaining four files. You can also use this technique to open multiple documents at once. For example, to open three Microsoft Word documents, select all three by clicking on the first and Shift-clicking on the second and third, and then choose Open from the Finder's File menu. The Mac will start Microsoft Word, which will then open the documents.

Selection marquees. Here's another graphics-oriented selection technique. The Finder and many drawing and publishing programs let you select multiple items (or rectangular portions of an image) by enclosing them within a *selection marquee*, a dotted rectangle whose dotted lines move like the lights on a theater marquee.

In drawing, painting, and publishing programs that provide tool palettes, you may have to activate a specific tool in order to draw a selection marquee. Icons can vary among programs. In MacPaint and HyperCard, for example, the selection tool icon looks like a small selection marquee. In MacDraw II and Aldus PageMaker, the arrow-shaped pointer tool must be active before you can draw a selection marquee. Figure 9-3 shows both icons.

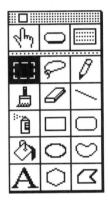 

Figure 9-3: The selection tool icons in HyperCard (*left*) and PageMaker (*right*).

The workings of the selection marquee may vary between programs. With the Finder, for example, the marquee need touch only part of an icon in order for that icon to be included in the selection. With Aldus PageMaker and MacDraw II, however, an item must be completely enclosed within the marquee in order to be included in the selection.

Select All commands. The Finder and many applications provide Select All commands in their Edit menus. Choosing Select All is the easiest way to select everything in the window or document you're working with. Some applications lack a Select All command, but provide a keyboard key sequence that performs the same result. In Microsoft Word 4.0, for example, pressing Command-Option-M selects the entire document. (In Word, you can also select the entire document by moving the pointer to the selection bar—the area between the left margin and the left edge of the document window—and pressing Command while clicking.)

Combining Selection Techniques

You can combine many of the selection techniques we've just examined. For example, you might use a selection marquee to select Finder icons that are adjacent to each other, and then Shift-click to include icons that aren't adjacent to the ones you selected using the marquee. Figure 9-4 illustrates this process.

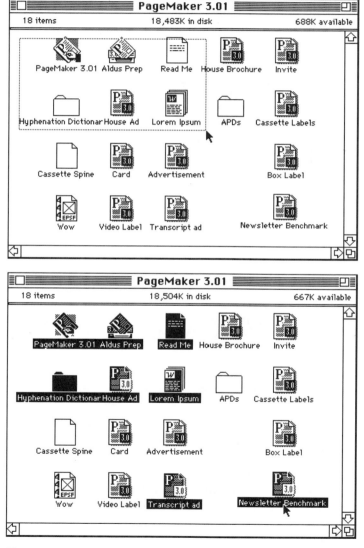

Figure 9-4: Combining selection techniques to select adjacent and non-adjacent files: First, select with the marquee (*top*); then, Shift-click to add files (*bottom*).

Spreadsheet Selection Techniques

The selection techniques we've just described are generally available in all Macintosh applications. Spreadsheet programs such as Microsoft Excel, Ashton-Tate's Full Impact, and Microsoft Works provide some specialized selection techniques of their own—techniques that apply to the row-and-column world of the electronic spreadsheet. Consult your spreadsheet program's manual to see if it supports the following techniques.

Selecting an entire row or column. You can select an entire row or column by clicking the mouse within the row or column heading, as shown in Figure 9-5. To select multiple rows or columns, drag across their headings.

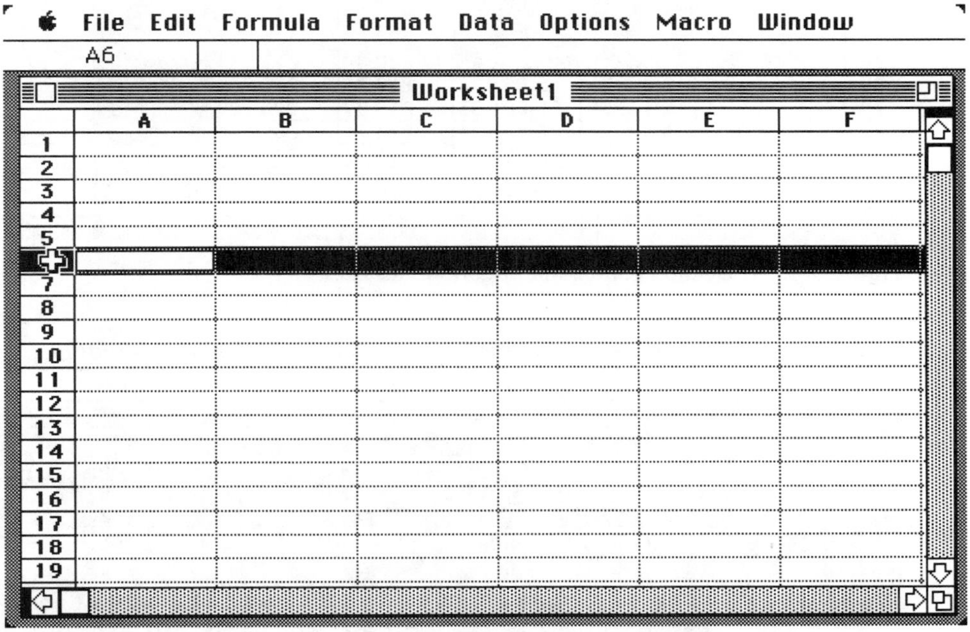

Figure 9-5: Selecting an entire spreadsheet row by clicking in its heading.

Selecting discontinuous cells. You can select cells that aren't physically adjacent to each other by using the Command key. First, select the first cell or range of cells. Next, press the Command key while clicking within another cell or dragging across a range of cells. The resulting selection resembles Figure 9-6.

Selecting the entire worksheet. To select the entire worksheet, click the box at its upper-left corner, as shown in Figure 9-7. (Microsoft Works 2.0 does not support this selection technique. To select an entire Works spreadsheet, choose Select All from the Edit menu.)

File   Edit   Formula   Format   Data   Options   Macro   Window

| G23 | | =D23-F23 |

LOAN3

	A	B	C	D	E	F	G	H
13		Payment	Payment	Beginning			Ending	Cumulativ
14		no.	dates	balance	Interest	Principal	balance	interest
15		1	Sep-87	30,000.00	243.75	250.42	29,749.58	243
16		2	Oct-87	29,749.58	241.72	252.45	29,497.13	485
17		3	Nov-87	29,497.13	239.66	254.50	29,242.62	725
18		4	Dec-87	29,242.62	237.60	256.57	28,986.05	962
19		5	Jan-88	28,986.05	235.51	258.66	28,727.39	1,198
20		6	Feb-88	28,727.39	233.41	260.76	28,466.63	1,431
21		7	Mar-88	28,466.63	231.29	262.88	28,203.76	1,662
22		8	Apr-88	28,203.76	229.16	265.01	27,938.74	1,892
23		9	May-88	27,938.74	227.00	267.17	27,671.58	2,119
24		10	Jun-88	27,671.58	224.83	269.34	27,402.24	2,343
25		11	Jul-88	27,402.24	222.64	271.53	27,130.71	2,566
26		12	Aug-88	27,130.71	220.44	273.73	26,856.98	2,787
27		13	Sep-88	26,856.98	218.21	275.96	26,581.03	3,005
28		14	Oct-88	26,581.03	215.97	278.20	26,302.83	3,221
29		15	Nov-88	26,302.83	213.71	280.46	26,022.37	3,434
30		16	Dec-88	26,022.37	211.43	282.74	25,739.63	3,646
31		17	Jan-89	25,739.63	209.13	285.03	25,454.60	3,855
32		18	Feb-89	25,454.60	206.82	287.35	25,167.25	4,062

Figure 9-6: A selection containing discontinuous cells.

File   Edit   Formula   Format   Data   Options   Macro   Window

| A13 | | |

LOAN3

	A	B	C	D	E	F	G	H
13		Payment	Payment	Beginning			Ending	Cumulativ
14		no.	dates	balance	Interest	Principal	balance	interest
15		1	Sep-87	30,000.00	243.75	250.42	29,749.58	243
16		2	Oct-87	29,749.58	241.72	252.45	29,497.13	485
17		3	Nov-87	29,497.13	239.66	254.50	29,242.62	725
18		4	Dec-87	29,242.62	237.60	256.57	28,986.05	962
19		5	Jan-88	28,986.05	235.51	258.66	28,727.39	1,198
20		6	Feb-88	28,727.39	233.41	260.76	28,466.63	1,431
21		7	Mar-88	28,466.63	231.29	262.88	28,203.76	1,662
22		8	Apr-88	28,203.76	229.16	265.01	27,938.74	1,892
23		9	May-88	27,938.74	227.00	267.17	27,671.58	2,119
24		10	Jun-88	27,671.58	224.83	269.34	27,402.24	2,343
25		11	Jul-88	27,402.24	222.64	271.53	27,130.71	2,566
26		12	Aug-88	27,130.71	220.44	273.73	26,856.98	2,787
27		13	Sep-88	26,856.98	218.21	275.96	26,581.03	3,005
28		14	Oct-88	26,581.03	215.97	278.20	26,302.83	3,221
29		15	Nov-88	26,302.83	213.71	280.46	26,022.37	3,434
30		16	Dec-88	26,022.37	211.43	282.74	25,739.63	3,646
31		17	Jan-89	25,739.63	209.13	285.03	25,454.60	3,855
32		18	Feb-89	25,454.60	206.82	287.35	25,167.25	4,062

Figure 9-7: Selecting the entire worksheet.

Other Application-Specific Selection Techniques

Spreadsheet programs aren't the only applications that provide their own selection techniques. In addition to supporting standard Mac selection techniques, many applications provide their own selection options. What follows are some specialized selection techniques for today's most popular application programs. Even if you don't use the programs described here, you will probably find that these or similar techniques apply to the programs you do use.

Aldus PageMaker. When editing text in PageMaker (and several other programs), you can select an entire paragraph by triple-clicking within it. You can continue selecting text in one-paragraph increments by dragging across it immediately after triple-clicking. Another PageMaker selection technique lets you select items that are behind other items, such as a rule that appears behind a text block. To select an item that's behind another item, press the Command key while clicking on the item you want to select. If several items are stacked on top of each other, you can select each one in turn by Command-clicking on the stack of items. If you press Shift while Command-clicking, each one is added to the selection.

WordPerfect. In WordPerfect, you can use the Select submenu (in the Edit menu) to select a sentence, paragraph, page, column, or entire document. Or, by choosing the Select command from the Select submenu, you can select text without having to drag across it or press a Shift key. To do so, choose Select On, then use the arrow keys to select text. You can also select text from the keyboard by pressing Shift and using the arrow keys.

Microsoft Word. Word provides numerous selection options; its mouse-oriented ones are listed in Table 9-5.

Table 9-5: Microsoft Word selection options.

To select this...	Do this...
A sentence	Press Command and click within the sentence.
One line of text	Click in the selection bar to the left of the line.
A paragraph	Double click in the selection bar to the left of the paragraph.
The entire document	Press Command and click within the selection bar.

Word also provides several techniques for selecting text from the keyboard. One unique technique is the *extend-to* technique, which lets you extend a selection from the insertion point's current position to any character you type. To use this technique, position the insertion point to the left of the first character to be included in the selection, then press Command-Option-H. The text "Extend to" appears in the page number area at the bottom-left corner of the screen. Press a character, and Word searches ahead of the insertion point for that character, and then extends the selection to include it. For example, to select everything from the insertion point to the end of a sentence, press Command-Option-H and type a period (.).

Like WordPerfect, Word also lets you select text from the keyboard by pressing Shift and using the arrow keys as well as the document-navigation keys on the Apple Extended Keyboard.

QuarkXpress. This popular desktop publishing program offers several selection shortcuts, listed in Table 9-6.

Table 9-6:   Selection shortcuts in QuarkXpress.

To do this...	Do this...
Select a line	Triple-click within it.
Select a paragraph	Quadruple-click within it.
All text in a chain	Quintuple-click within it.

FileMaker II and other data managers. Claris's FileMaker II data base manager provides form-design features that work similarly to a desktop publishing program to let you create forms. In FileMaker's form-layout mode, you can select a group of objects (such as fields or field titles) by Shift-clicking on each or by using a selection marquee. These techniques also work in several other data managers, including Microsoft File 2.0 and Ashton-Tate's dBASE Mac.

Deselecting and Cancelling a Selection

When you're selecting multiple items using a marquee or the Shift-click technique, you may occasionally select an item you didn't mean to select. Rather than begin the selection process from scratch, you can simply deselect the item by Shift-clicking on it.

Finally, there are times when you've finished working with a selection and want to deselect everything. In a drawing or publishing program, you can deselect everything by clicking the pointer elsewhere within the document window, in an area where there are no elements to select.

In a word processor (and in the text-editing areas of any program), the easiest way to cancel a selection is to simply click the mouse button to create a blinking insertion point. If you selected the text in order to replace it with new text, simply begin typing. You don't have to press Delete or Backspace first; your first keystroke causes the Mac delete the selected text.

The Power of the Double Click

Let's turn our attention from selecting to issuing instructions. The most common way to tell the Mac what to do is to choose a command from a menu. But the Finder and many Mac applications also respond to another form of command: the double click.

Where navigation is concerned, the double click is a shortcut that usually eliminates having to choose a menu command. In the Finder, for example, you can open an application or document by double-clicking its icon, instead of selecting it and then choosing Open from the File menu. The Finder offers several double-click shortcuts: You can open a directory window by double-clicking a disk or folder icon, and you can open the Trash by double-clicking its icon. Most people master these shortcuts quickly; they're much faster and more convenient than the two-step, select-and-choose-Open routine.

But once away from the Finder, some people forget about the power of the double click. It's still there. Most applications that have tool palettes offer double-click shortcuts. Double-click on a tool, and the application performs a task related to the tool, but usually a notch above its normal purpose. In HyperCard, for example, double-clicking on the eraser tool erases the entire card or background. (This same shortcut applies to MacPaint and other painting programs.) Figure 9-8 shows the other double-click shortcuts that HyperCard's Tools menu provides.

In Claris' MacDraw II, double-clicking on a palette tool causes that tool to remain active after you've finished using it (to draw a line or shape, for example). When you activate a tool with a single click, MacDraw II deactivates the tool and reactivates the pointer tool after you've used the tool. Another double-click shortcut in MacDraw II involves the pattern palette at the top of the document window. Double-clicking a pattern causes MacDraw II to display the Patterns dialog box, as if you had chosen Patterns from the Layout menu. And double-clicking on the Corner/Center control (located above the layer arrows near the bottom of the tool palette) displays the Preferences dialog box.

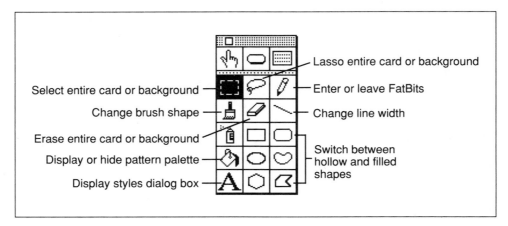

Figure 9-8: Double-click shortcuts in HyperCard's Tools menu.

You'll also find double-click shortcuts in Adobe Illustrator 88. Double-clicking on the hand tool, for example, lets you see the full 14 by 14-inch work area, as if you had chosen the Fit in Window command. If you double-click on the hand tool while holding down the Option key, Illustrator 88 switches to its actual-size view.

As the previous examples have shown, you're most likely to encounter double-click shortcuts in graphics-oriented programs that contain tool palettes. But that doesn't mean double-click shortcuts don't exist elsewhere. Microsoft Word 4.0 has a remarkable array of double-click shortcuts. Within Word's document window are numerous "hot spots" where you can double-click to perform various tasks. Figure 9-9 shows these hot spots.

The double click also plays a role in Word's dialog boxes and in the dialog boxes of Word's cousin, Microsoft Excel. In both programs, you can choose a radio button option and okay the dialog box by simply double-clicking on the radio button. For example, in Word's Index dialog box, you can double-click on the Nested or Run-in radio buttons to choose the type of index you want and begin the indexing process. In Microsoft Excel's Alignment dialog box, you can double click on an alignment option to choose that option and okay the dialog box. In Excel's New dialog box, you can choose the type of new document you want (worksheet, chart, or macro sheet) and create the document by simply double-clicking on the document type's radio button. This technique of double-clicking a radio button to both choose the option and okay the dialog box is available in many Mac programs.

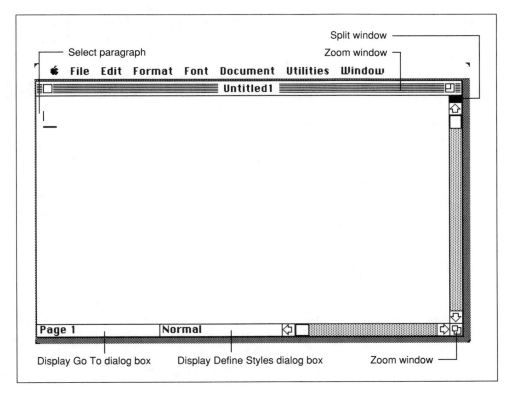

Figure 9-9: Word 4.0 double-click hot spots.

The Power of the Option Key

Another key to mastering Mac navigation techniques is, quite literally, a key. We're referring to the Option key, whose normal role is to allow you to access special characters such as accents and symbols. In the Finder and in many applications, pressing the Option key while choosing a command or clicking the mouse performs a special variation of the command or mouse click. (In some cases, you must press both Option and Command.)

In HyperCard, MacPaint, and many other painting programs, pressing Option while dragging a selection causes the program to duplicate the selection, leaving the original where it was. Press Command-Option while dragging a selection, and the program makes copy after copy, leaving a trail of duplicates in the pointer's wake.

Many programs also use the Option key to modify the workings of a menu command, palette tool, key sequence, or mouse movement. In MacDraw II, for example, pressing Option while clicking on the drawing surface lets you select an object on a different drawing layer. In Aldus PageMaker, pressing Option while clicking within the document window turns the pointer into a hand that lets you scroll in any direction. Many other graphics-oriented programs also provide this scrolling shortcut.

In Ashton-Tate's FullWrite Professional word processor, pressing Option-Delete removes the previous word, and Option-arrow moves the insertion point in one-word increments. The Option key alters the workings of many FullWrite Professional menu commands. For example, pressing Option changes the Print command to read Print Page, and the Index Entry command to read Index Selection.

The Finder provides numerous Option and Command-Option shortcuts. They're listed later in this chapter, in the section "Finder and MultiFinder Shortcuts."

A Command Key Reminder

You probably already know about this navigation shortcut, but it's significant enough to warrant repeating. All Mac applications provide Command-key shortcuts—key sequences that let you choose menu commands from the keyboard by pressing the Command key along with another key. While shortcuts can often vary between programs, there are numerous shortcuts that are found in nearly every program. They're listed in Table 9-7.

Table 9-7: Common Command-key shortcuts.

Key Sequence	Command Equivalent
Command-A	Select All
Command-C	Copy
Command-D	Duplicate
Command-F	Find
Command-G	Go to page
Command-I	Get Info
Command-N	New
Command-O	Open
Command-P	Print
Command-Q	Quit
Command-S	Save
Command-V	Paste
Command-W	Close
Command-X	Cut
Command-Z	Undo

Remember that these sequences may not apply to every program. Some programs, for example, use Command-P to summon the plain-text style, not the Print command. Fortunately, it's easy to find out what your favorite programs' Command-key shortcuts are: just pull down the menus and look.

Application-Specific Shortcuts

In addition to the generic navigation techniques we've discussed, many programs provide their own keyboard navigation shortcuts. Microsoft's programs started this trend shortly after the Mac's release, and other software developers have followed suit. Today, many applications let you use the keyboard to choose dialog box options and "click" buttons.

Microsoft's current offerings continue the trend. In Microsoft Word, for example, you can "click" a button in a dialog box by pressing Command and the button's first letter. For example, when the Character dialog box is open, you can activate or deactivate the Bold option by typing Command-B. In Word's Save As dialog box, you can specify an alternative file format by typing Command-F. In the Define Styles dialog box, you can "click" the Define button by typing Command-D. When faced with a "Save changes before closing?" dialog box, you can answer yes, no, or cancel by pressing the Y, N, or C keys. (For a complete description of Word 4.0's keyboard shortcuts, see page 144 in the *Reference to Microsoft Word* manual.) Microsoft Excel provides similar keyboard shortcuts.

Some keyboard shortcuts can seem convoluted at first—Word's Command-Shift-Option-S sequence, which opens the Footnote window, is one example. But even a finger-twister like this can become second nature if you use it often enough. Our advice: Check your programs' manuals for shortcuts that apply to your work, then memorize them or make a "cheat sheet" for the ones you want to use.

Shortcuts for Directory Dialog Boxes

The Mac provides several standard shortcuts for navigating within directory dialog boxes. Mastering these shortcuts will save time when opening or saving files.

Locating a file or folder. You can locate a file or folder in an Open dialog box by using the up or down arrow keys or quickly typing the item's name. We say "quickly" because if you pause too long between keystrokes, the Mac assumes that the first keystroke after the pause represents a new name, not a continuation of the old one. For example, if you quickly type *l-e-t-t-e-r*, the Mac selects a file or folder beginning with *letter*. However, if you type *l-e-t* (pause) *t-e-r*, the Mac attempts to select a file or folder beginning with *ter*.

Using Return to confirm the dialog box. After you've located the desired file or folder, you can open it by pressing Return—you don't need to reach for the mouse to click the Open button. If you selected a file, pressing Return opens it. If you selected a folder, the Mac opens the folder and displays its contents in the dialog box.

Opening and closing folders. To close a folder—that is, to move up one level in the storage hierarchy—press Command-up arrow. To open a folder, either select it and press Return as described above, or select it and press Command-down arrow.

Moving up one level in the hierarchy. To use the mouse to quickly move up one level in the storage hierarchy, simply click once on the disk name that appears in the directory dialog box. Each click moves you one level closer to the desktop level.

Using Tab to switch disks. If you have more than one disk on your desktop, you can switch between them by pressing the Tab key instead of clicking the Drive button.

Cancelling the dialog box. If you decide not to open or save a document, you can cancel the directory dialog box by pressing Command-period (.) instead of clicking the Cancel button.

Remember, these shortcuts are built into the Mac's system software, so you can use them with any program.

Making Reference Cards and Taking Snapshots

We've mentioned that one way to remember the various navigation options a program provides is to make a cheat sheet. The System file contains an FKEY that saves the screen image as a MacPaint document when you press Command-Shift-3. You can use this feature to take "snapshots" of your programs' palettes and dialog boxes, and then combine them and annotate them using a Paint program.

Here are a few tidbits to keep in mind about the snapshot FKEY.

- The Mac names snapshot documents Screen 0, Screen 1, Screen 2, Screen 3, and so on, through Screen 9. If all ten names exist when you press Command-Shift-3, the Mac beeps. To create additional snapshots, throw away or rename one or more existing snapshots.

- If you have the standard Apple Video Card installed on any member of the Mac II family, snapshots appear sideways (in landscape orientation) on the page. If you want the final image to contain just a portion of the screen, cut or copy that portion, paste it into a new document, and then use your paint program's Rotate command to reorient it.

- The Command-Shift-3 FKEY doesn't work if your Mac II or SE/30 video card is in color or gray-scale mode. Use the Monitors cdev (described later in this chapter) to put the Mac in one-bit-per-pixel mode. FKEYs are available that let you take snapshots of a color or gray-scale display; see the section "Showing Your True Colors" in Chapter 10 for details.

- Because of the way the Mac responds to the mouse button, the Command-Shift-3 FKEY will not allow you to take a snapshot of a menu that's pulled down, or of any event that involves the mouse button being down. If you need to take snapshots of open menus or other mouse-down events, use a desk accessory called Camera (by Keith Esau). When you choose Camera from the Apple menu, a dialog box appears allowing you to specify a time delay before the snapshot is taken. You then click OK, open the desired menu, and wait for the snapshot to be taken.

Another way to take snapshots of mouse-down events is to add an Init called MenuPicture to your System Folder. MenuPicture, by Douglas Wyatt, patches a ROM routine so that the Command-Shift-3 FKEY works when the mouse is down. In our experience, MenuPicture tends to be more reliable than Camera on 68020- and 68030-based Macs.

Both Camera and MenuPicture are available free through user's groups and on line information services such as CompuServe. (If you download them from an information service, you will have to pay its normal connect-time charges. Only the files themselves are free.)

The Importance of Backing Up

The Mac is generally very reliable, but hardware and software can fail, and when they do, they can take your work with them. So, regardless of how you use your Mac, one of the most important things you can do is to make backup copies of your disks at regular intervals.

Floppy disks are easy to back up, especially if your Mac has two floppy drives. If it does, first lock the original disk (slide the plastic tab in the corner of the disk so that you see through the small square hole), and then drag its icon to a second floppy disk. When the Mac asks if you want to replace the contents of the second disk with those of the first, answer OK.

If your Mac has one floppy drive and a hard disk, you can back up floppies in two ways:

- If the hard disk has enough free space on it, you can use the hard disk as an intermediary. First, copy the original floppy disk's contents to the hard disk by dragging the floppy's icon to the hard disk. When you do, the Mac creates a new folder on the hard disk and stores the floppy's contents within it.

Next, eject the original floppy, insert the backup floppy, and copy the contents of the new folder to the backup. Finally, you might want to throw away the new folder on the hard disk to free up space.

• If you can't or don't want to use the hard disk as an intermediary, you can still back up a floppy on a one-floppy drive system, but you'll need to do some disk-swapping. First, insert the backup disk, and then select its icon and choose Eject from the Finder's File menu. The Finder dims the disk's icon to show that it's ejected but that the Finder still "knows" about it. Next, lock the original disk, insert it, and drag its icon to the backup disk's dimmed icon. When asked if you want to replace the backup disk's contents, click OK. During the backup process, you'll be asked to swap disks as needed.

To backup a hard disk, use a backup utility program such as HD Backup, which comes with the Mac. You might also consider a more fully featured backup utility such as SuperMac's DiskFit or Fifth Generation Systems' Fast-Back. These programs let you be more selective about which files you want to back up; you can, for example, choose to back up only applications or only documents.

If your hard disk holds more than 20 or 30 megabytes, hand-feeding floppy after floppy can become tedious. For backing up large-capacity hard disks, you might consider another storage device such as a *tape drive*, which uses special tape cartridges to store the contents of a hard disk, or a *removeable media* drive such as an Iomega Bernoulli Box or Mass Micro DataPak. These cousins to hard disks store between 20 and 45 megabytes on removeable cartridges; they're much faster than tape drives, and you can use them for general-purpose storage along with your hard disk. We'll look at these drives in Chapter 15.

How often should you back up? That depends on how much you use your Mac. Use this rule of thumb: Back up when you reach the point where you wouldn't want to recreate lost work if the worst happened. And because fire and thieves don't discriminate between backups and originals, it's a good idea to store your backup disks separately from the originals—in a safe-deposit box, for example.

Finally, for additional insurance against lost work, you might consider using a disk utility package such as the Norton Utilities or First Aid Software's 1stAid Kit. These products contain specialized software that allow you to resurrect damaged or accidentally deleted disk files and recover disks that you accidentally erased. They can't replace a diligently followed backup routine, but they can help you recover a disk or file that's damaged in between backup sessions.

Performance Tips

This section is a collection of tips and insights for getting maximum performance out of your Mac's hardware. Topics we'll discuss include:

- switching between color and monochrome modes on a color Mac

- using disk caches and RAM disks to boost performance

- how to get the most out of your Mac's memory when using MultiFinder

- how to manage disks and files efficiently.

Matching the Video Mode to the Task

Many users of Macs equipped with color video boards and monitors leave their machines in color mode all the time. If you're in this group, you aren't getting the maximum performance out of your Mac. It takes time for the Mac to manipulate the extra memory required to create color screens—time that could be better spent on other tasks.

A better operating approach is to match the current video mode to the task at hand. For example, if you're using a word processor and don't need color, switch into black-and-white mode. (By "black and white," we're referring to the one-bit-per-pixel mode.) What kind of performance gain can you expect? A big one. In one test we performed, a Mac II running Microsoft Word 4.0 took 109 seconds to scroll through a 14-page document with the Mac in 256-color (eight bits per pixel) mode. When the Mac was in black-and-white mode, however, the same test took only 27 seconds. Is a full-color Apple menu really worth a 400-percent decrease in performance?

You'll notice significant performance differences in any program that performs extensive screen drawing. In another test we performed, Aldus Page-Maker required 6 seconds to redraw a two-page spread with the Mac in 256-color mode. In black-and-white mode, however, the time dropped to 3 seconds.

The moral? Don't use the Mac's color or gray-scale modes—especially the 256-color/grays mode—unless your application requires it. Using the Control Panel's Monitors cdev to switch between modes doesn't take that long, and the time you spend doing it will be paid back with interest by the Mac's faster performance.

A Faster Way to Switch Video Modes

Although it doesn't take that long to summon the Control Panel and use the Monitors cdev, there is a much faster way to switch video modes. It's an FKEY called Switch-A-Roo, created by Bill Steinberg, Mac programmer extraordinaire. Switch-A-Roo is available free from user's groups and on line information services.

You install Switch-A-Roo into your System file using Apple's ResEdit. Or, you can leave it out of the System file and access it with a system extender utility such as Suitcase II. (Both ResEdit and Suitcase II are described in the next chapter.) In either case, once you install it, you use it to specify your two favorite video modes, as shown in Figure 9-10. After that, you can switch between the two modes by simply pressing Command-Shift-9. The time saved compared to using the Control Panel is significant.

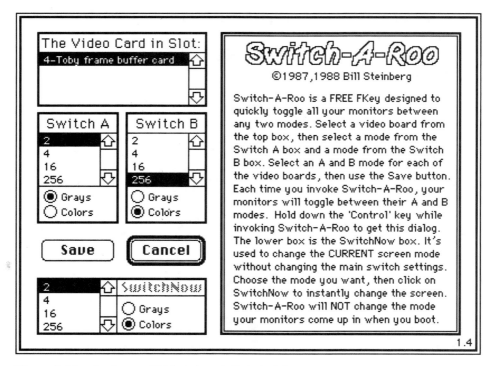

Figure 9-10: Setting up Bill Steinberg's Switch-A-Roo.

After you set up Switch-A-Roo the first time, it creates a file in your System Folder called Roo File, which stores the results of your setup. To specify different operating modes, invoke Switch-A-Roo by pressing Control-Command-Shift-9. Or, simply throw the file Roo File in the Trash.

Disk Caches and RAM Disks

Disks—even hard disks—are slow when compared to memory. Within memory, data moves at the speed of light. With disks, its speed is restricted by the mechanical nature of the rotating disk and the drive's read/write heads. For this reason, you'll always get better performance when you keep as much application code or document data in memory as possible. Phrased another way, you'll get better performance when you minimize disk accesses.

There are two primary ways to minimize disk accesses:

• use the *disk cache* option available in the Control Panels of all Macs beginning with the Mac Plus

• use a *RAM disk*, a pseudo disk drive that you create in memory using special software.

Differences Between Disk Caches and RAM Disks

On the surface, a disk cache and a RAM disk provide the same benefit: they lessen the frequency of disk accesses by storing code and data in memory. But beneath the surface, these two performance-boosting options work quite differently.

A disk cache operates by saving the most recently accessed program code and data in memory, in the likely event that it will be required again later. If it is, the cache supplies it from RAM, eliminating the need for a slow disk access. As the cache fills, older code and data are replaced by more recently accessed code and data. (Conceptually, this process works similarly to the font cache in a PostScript printer.)

On the other hand, a RAM disk is far less dynamic; that is, unlike a disk cache, its contents don't change to match the way you use the Mac. *You* determine which files or applications the RAM disk will contain. If you run an application from a RAM disk, it will run at top speed.

Which should you use, and when? That depends on how much memory you have, and also on how you use your Mac.

Cache Advantages

A disk cache will provide better performance under the following circumstances:

• When you frequently switch between two applications while running under MultiFinder. In this case, parts of each application will be stored in the cache, reducing disk accesses when you switch between them.

- When you're sorting a large database or editing a large word processor document. In this case, parts of the database or document will be stored in the cache. (Many database managers provide their own internal caching; with such programs, using the Mac's disk cache won't improve sorting and data-retrieval performance, but it is likely to improve other aspects of the program's operation, such as displaying large dialog boxes or switching between form-layout and data-retrieval modes.)

- When you use a large, complex program extensively. In such cases, you probably hear or see your disk drive activating frequently as the Mac swaps code segments into and out of memory. By keeping portions of those code segments in the disk cache, complex programs such as PageMaker or 4th Dimension will run faster.

- When you regularly repeat certain tasks during a work session.

The degree of improved performance you can expect from a disk cache depends on the speed of your Mac and its disk drives. On a Mac Plus or SE with no hard disk, a disk cache will make a significant improvement. As a test, we set up a 1MB SE with no hard disk to use a 256K disk cache, then we started Microsoft Word from a floppy disk, quit to the Finder, and then repeated the process. Table 9-8 shows the difference that the disk cache made when we repeated the process. As the table shows, Word took half the time to load when we started it the second time.

Table 9-8:   Performance gain of 256K disk cache on a stock 1MB SE without hard disk.

Action	Seconds Required
Start Word 4.0	22
Quit to Finder	9
Start Word 4.0 again	11
Quit to Finder again	6

On a fast Mac with a fast hard disk, the performance improvement will still be there, but will be less noticeable. We ran the same test on a Mac SE equipped with a Radius Accelerator 25 and Cirrus 40MB hard disk—a combination that provides faster performance than a Mac IIcx. Table 9-9 shows the results.

Table 9-9: Performance gain of 256K disk cache on 1MB SE equipped with Radius Accelerator 25 and Cirrus 40MB hard disk.

Action	Seconds Required
Start Word 4.0	5
Quit to Finder	3
Start Word 4.0 again	3
Quit to Finder again	2

In this second test, the cache still improves performance, but saving two seconds isn't exciting enough to give us goosebumps. More to the point, it isn't significant enough to warrant giving up 256K of RAM to the disk cache. (What this test really illustrates is how well an accelerator board such as the Radius Accelerator 25 improves an SE's performance.)

So how large a disk cache should you use? As a general rule, the larger the cache, the better the performance increase, until the cache size equals roughly 25 percent of your total amount of RAM. For example, on a 1MB machine, you shouldn't create a cache larger than 256K. In the end, there are no carved-in-stone rules regarding disk cache size. You need to balance the benefits of the disk cache against its disadvantages.

Cache Disadvantages

The Mac's disk cache does have some drawbacks:

- It uses memory that could otherwise be used to run programs. On a 1MB machine, not using a disk cache can make the difference between being able to run a large program and not being able to run it.

- Its performance improvement is minimal if your computing routine is haphazard rather than repetitive. If you jump between different programs to perform different tasks, much of the code and data that are squirrelled away in the cache may not be needed again.

RAM Disks

When the 512K Mac debuted late in 1984, RAM disks enjoyed a burst of popularity. Because of several factors, including the increasing girth of the Mac's system software, they're less practical than they used to be. Still, they do have their proponents and they certainly can boost performance, so we'll give them their due.

A RAM disk isn't actually a disk at all; it's an area of memory that the Mac *thinks* is a disk. You can store system files and/or applications on a RAM disk, and run them at top speed.

You create a RAM disk by running a special utility program. Several free or inexpensive RAM disk programs are available through user's groups and on line information services. The most popular are RAMStart (by George Nelson) and RamDisk+ (by Roger Bates). The process usually involves specifying the RAM disk's size and then choosing the files you want to store on the RAM disk. Most programs remember your settings, so once you specify them, you can create a RAM disk by simply starting the program. If you use the Finder's Set Startup command to designate the RAM disk utility as the start-up application, you can have a fresh, fully loaded RAM disk created for you each time you start up.

RAM Disk Advantages

The primary advantage of a RAM disk over a disk cache is that its performance-boosting benefits surface immediately. By comparison, a disk cache's performance improvements surface over time, as you use the Mac.

What kind of performance gains do RAM disks provide? Table 9-10 shows the results of some tests we performed on a 1MB Mac SE using MacWrite 5.0. Because you can configure a RAM disk to contain either applications or system files or both, we performed the test four different ways. We measured the time required to start MacWrite from a floppy disk with a floppy start-up disk (in other words, with no RAM disk), from a floppy disk with a RAM disk start-up disk, from a RAM disk with a floppy start-up disk, and from a RAM disk with a RAM disk start-up disk.

Table 9-10: A RAM disk's effect on performance.

Action	Seconds Required
Start from floppy (floppy start-up disk)	22
Start from floppy (RAM disk start-up disk)	15
Start from RAM disk (floppy start-up disk)	12
Start from RAM disk (RAM disk start-up disk)	7

As the table shows, we saw a performance increase of more than 300 percent when the RAM disk contained both the application and the System and Finder files. Performance still improved dramatically, however, when only the application was stored on the RAM disk.

You may have noticed we performed this test using MacWrite, rather than Microsoft Word 4.0, which we used for the disk cache tests. That's because Word 4.0 wouldn't fit on the RAM disk. The largest RAM disk we could reliably create on a 1MB SE provided 576K of free space—too little to hold the Finder, a stripped-down System file, and the Word 4.0 application.

And this illustrates the primary limitation of RAM disks: A 1MB Mac doesn't have enough memory to create a RAM disk that can hold the latest Finder and System files as well as a large application.

A Mac with 2MB of RAM can accommodate a more useful RAM disk. A 1MB RAM disk can accommodate the Finder and System files, a printer driver, and a MacWrite-sized application. (The MacWrite 5.0 application file requires 171K of disk space; with its spelling checker dictionaries, it needs 298K.) Only when you have more than 2MB of RAM can you create a RAM disk that can hold system files and larger applications such as Microsoft Word.

Based on this and on the results in Table 9-10, we don't recommend trying to cram system files and an application into a modest-sized RAM disk. Instead, we recommend storing only applications on a RAM disk. You'll still get a dramatic performance improvement, and you won't have to laboriously craft a stripped-down System Folder.

RAM Disk Disadvantages

Although RAM disks boost performance, they have several serious drawbacks.

- They lack the "intelligence" of a disk cache. A RAM disk contains only what you put in it. If you need a program that isn't on the RAM disk, you must run it from a floppy or hard disk, or copy it to the RAM disk.

- They're ephemeral. When the power goes, a RAM disk's contents go with it. This has two implications: first, you should *never* store documents on a RAM disk; and second, the process of copying applications or other files to the RAM disk actually lengthens the time it takes to start up your Mac.

A RAM disk's transitory nature also has some subtle ramifications. Even if you only store applications on a RAM disk, you can fall victim to its fragile existence. Many applications store your working preferences within the application file itself. If you change a working preference when running the application from a RAM disk, those changes won't be permanent unless you copy the application file from the RAM disk to a floppy disk. Other applications store working preferences in separate disk files, which are usually kept in the System Folder. If you run such an application from a RAM disk containing a System Folder, you'll need to copy the preferences file to a floppy to avoid losing your latest preference specifications.

A Memory Balancing Act

This section has shown that a disk cache or RAM disk can boost performance by minimizing disk accesses. We've also provided some guidelines for determining how large a cache or RAM disk you should create. But these guidelines are just starting points. To determine how to best use your Mac's RAM, you must weigh the memory requirements of the applications and Inits you use against the performance benefits provided by a cache or RAM disk. The best way to establish an ideal balance is through experimentation.

MultiFinder and Memory

All this talk about disk caches and RAM disks leads us to another memory-related topic: MultiFinder. In theory, MultiFinder lets you run numerous programs simultaneously and switch between them with a mouse click. In practice, the number of programs you can run simultaneously depends on their size and on how much memory your Mac has. If your Mac has just 1MB or even 2MB of RAM, you probably see the message "Try quitting from another application to increase unused memory" frequently.

The obvious solution is to expand your Mac's memory. But memory is expensive, and you might prefer to spend your computing dollars on software or more mass storage. (Indeed, if you don't have a hard disk now, buying one should be your first priority. If you haven't bought a Mac yet, consider buying a hard disk when you do make your purchase.)

There is no magic shoehorn to help you squeeze more programs into your Mac's memory, but there are techniques for getting the most out of the memory you do have. In this section, we explore these techniques by examining:

- how MultiFinder uses memory

- how to configure your system and your applications to use your Mac's memory efficiently

- how to interpret MultiFinder's free-memory display.

The following information applies to the versions of MultiFinder that accompany System 6.0.3 and earlier versions.

How MultiFinder Uses Memory

We'll set the stage for our tour of MultiFinder memory issues by first examining how MultiFinder uses the Mac's memory. When you start a program under MultiFinder, the program requests a specific amount of memory. If the amount requested is available, the Mac sets it aside for the application, and then starts the application.

The chunk of memory an application requests must be *contiguous*. Recall from Chapter 1 that each byte of memory has its own address. When an application requests a chunk of memory from MultiFinder, it's requesting a continuous range of addresses. To return to the post office box analogy we used in Chapter 1, it's as if a large postal customer says, "I need 10 post office boxes, and they all have to be sequentially numbered and adjacent to each other. Don't try to give me boxes 1 through 5, then 11 through 16." (We know that people rarely request more than one post office box at a time; we're bending reality a bit to create a more effective analogy.)

When a postmaster grants a customer a range of post office boxes, those boxes aren't available to any other customers. Similarly, once MultiFinder gives an application a chunk of memory, that memory isn't available to other programs. When you quit the application, the memory it used becomes available—just as when a resident moves elsewhere, his or her post office boxes become available to new residents.

The amount of memory an application requests is initially determined by the program's developer. You, however, can determine how much memory a program actually receives by using the Finder: Select the program's icon and choose Get Info from the File menu. The program's memory information appears at the bottom of the Get Info window, as shown in Figure 9-11.

As Figure 9-11 shows, the Get Info window provides a text box labeled Application Memory Size. Above that, another value appears next to the text Suggested Memory Size. The Suggested Memory Size is the minimum amount of memory the developer recommends. The Application Memory Size is the preferred amount—the "if I had my druthers" amount. With some applications, both values are the same. More often, however, the Application Memory Size value will be higher—sometimes much higher.

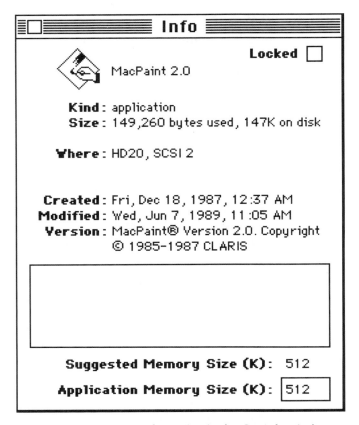

Figure 9-11: Memory information in the Get Info window.

You can use the Application Memory Size box to change the amount of memory an application requests. By carefully altering this memory value, you can use your Mac's memory more efficiently. We'll discuss this point in detail shortly.

Fragmented Memory

As you start and quit applications under MultiFinder, the Mac's free memory becomes *fragmented*—divided into chunks scattered throughout the total range of memory addresses. Why does this happen? Think about the post office: When one resident leaves town, his or her post office boxes become available to new residents. But some residents stick around, and their boxes remain in use, as shown in Figure 9-12. As some residents move in while others move away, the post office's set of boxes become increasingly fragmented.

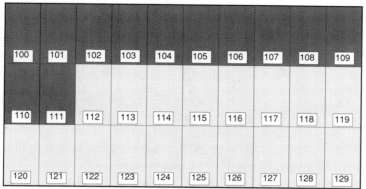

You start a program that uses "boxes" 100 through 111. Boxes 112 through 129 are available.

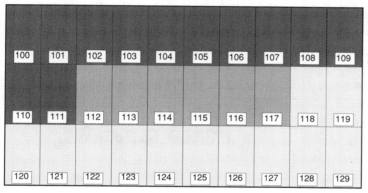

You start a second, smaller program, which uses boxes 112 through 117. Now, only boxes 118 through 129 are free.

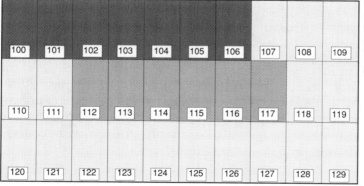

You quit the first program, and then start another small program, which uses boxes 100 through 106. The free boxes are now fragmented.

Figure 9-12: How memory becomes fragmented under MultiFinder.

A similar situation occurs with MultiFinder. When you quit one program, its memory is freed. But if other programs are still running, their memory is in use. As you quit some programs and run others, the Mac's memory becomes increasingly fragmented.

When memory becomes fragmented, the largest program you can run is limited by the largest free block of memory. For example, assume your Mac contains 700K of free memory, scattered throughout its total memory in several chunks, the largest of which is 400K. In this case, you can run a program only if it requires 400K or less—even though a total of 700K may be free.

You can find out how much space exists in the largest free block of memory by choosing About the Finder from the Apple menu when MultiFinder is active. MultiFinder reports how much total memory exists in your machine, and also lists the size of the largest unused block of memory, as shown in Figure 9-13. We'll examine the graph again later in this chapter.

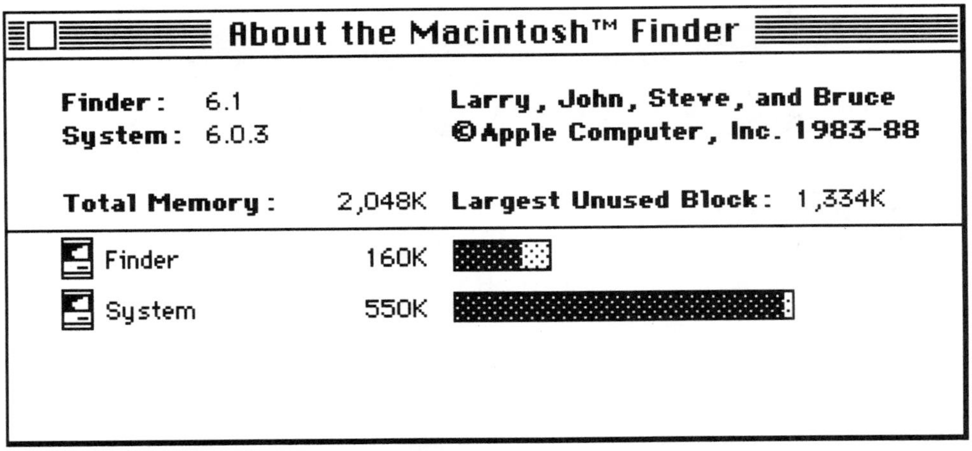

Figure 9-13: MultiFinder's free memory display.

The solution to fragmented memory is to quit all the applications you're running. You can then restart the applications you want to use, and the Mac will assign memory in contiguous blocks. To return to the post office once more, quitting all applications is the equivalent of the postmaster unassigning *all* the post office boxes. The postmaster can then assign post office boxes in contiguous blocks, with no fragments—until someone moves, of course, starting the fragmentation process all over again.

Fine-Tuning Application Memory Requirements

We mentioned that when running under MultiFinder, you can use the Get Info command to view and increase or decrease an application's memory requirements. But under what circumstances might you want to change memory requirements? And by how much should you change them?

You may want to change an application's memory requirements for two basic reasons:

- to decrease the amount of RAM used by the application in order to squeeze more programs into memory or to have some memory left over for a disk cache

- to increase the amount of RAM used by the application in order to improve its performance or, with applications that store documents entirely in RAM, to be able to create larger documents or open more document windows at once.

As for how much of a change you should make in an application's memory appetite, that's a bit more difficult to determine. Your first step should be to consult the application's manual for memory recommendations. Unfortunately, you're likely to strike out there: A survey of our software shelves revealed that few developers include information on changing their applications' MultiFinder memory requirements.

If you strike out with the documentation, you might consider calling the developer's technical support department for recommendations. Or you might want to just experiment. You can't damage an application by experimenting with its memory requirements, although you might create a situation that will cause the program to crash, taking any unsaved documents with it. To be on the safe side, perform your experiments on a backup copy of the application and save your work often. (Saving often is a good idea in any case.)

Reducing Application Memory Requirements

Let's first look at the task of reducing an application's appetite for memory.

1. If the application is running, quit it; you can't change memory requirements when a program is running.

2. In the Finder, select the application's icon and choose Get Info from the File menu.

   The Get Info window appears, with the application's memory information at the bottom of the window. (If that information doesn't appear, you aren't running under MultiFinder.)

3. If the application's Suggested Memory Size is less than the Application Memory Size, reduce the Application Memory Size value to match the Suggested Memory Size.

   — or —

3. If the Suggested Memory Size and Application Memory Size values are identical, you can try reducing the Application Memory Size to a lower value. However, the application may then run unpredictably, or it may not run at all.

4. After you alter the Application Memory Size value, click the Get Info window's close box or choose Close from the File menu. If you entered a value lower than the Suggested Memory Size value, the Finder asks if you're sure you want to change the Application Memory Size to less than the suggested minimum. Click Yes or press Return.

Finally, try running the application. If you simply reduced the Application Memory Size to match the Suggested Memory Size, the application should run without incident, although you may notice slower performance and more frequent disk accesses. And with applications that store their documents entirely in memory, you'll be restricted to smaller documents.

The Effects of Reduced Memory Sizes

What happens when you reduce the Application Memory Size to a value below the Suggested Memory Size? That depends on the application and on how much memory you give it. We conducted some informal tests using four of today's most popular applications, running under System 6.0.2. What follows are the results of our tests and some recommendations.

Microsoft Word 4.0. Word's Application Memory Size is 1024K; its Suggested Memory Size is 512K. We changed its Application Memory Size to 384K and found that the program performed reliably, though the frequency of disk accesses increased dramatically. We were able to open a 75K document, change its font and number of columns, and even switch into page-view mode to view the columns on-screen. When in page-view, however, the program was agonizingly slow when moving from one page to the next. Also, Word was unable to complete a lengthy search-and-replace operation (changing all occurrences of "e" to "#"); we received a low-memory warning about halfway through the document. With a much smaller file (9K), performance in page-view mode was still unacceptably slow. Even with the smaller file, the Repaginate command and spelling checker were very slow.

Recommendations: Word 4.0 runs with a 384K Application Memory Size, but you should avoid the page-view mode, the spelling checker, the Repaginate command (and the background repagination mode), and complex search-and-replace operations. Also, the frequent disk accesses will make performance very slow on Macs without a hard disk.

Aldus PageMaker 3.01. PageMaker's Suggested Memory Size and Application Memory Size values are both 700K. We changed its Application Memory Size to 512K, and were pleasantly surprised to find all of the program's major features still worked, if slowly. We were able to use the Autoflow mode to place a large file containing text and bit-mapped graphics, and we successfully used the Define Styles command to change style sheet formatting throughout a 20-page sample newsletter. Our success made us cocky, and we tried reducing the Application Memory Size to 400K. It didn't work; upon our trying to run the program, PageMaker displayed an insufficient-memory message.

Recommendations: PageMaker performs sluggishly with a 512K application memory size, but it does appear to run reliably.

MacDraw II version 1.1. MacDraw II version 1.1 is one of the few programs whose manual provides detailed memory-requirements information. You'll find them in the section "MacDraw II Questions and Answers" in the *New Features Guide* booklet that accompanies version 1.1. This section provides useful information on how much memory the program requires under different monitor configurations. It doesn't, however, provide guidelines for a minimum memory configuration. MacDraw II 1.1's Suggested Memory Size and Application Memory Size are both 900K. We lowered the Application Memory Size to 500K and found that the program worked well. Because MacDraw stores open documents entirely in memory, however, the size and number of documents we could open was restricted. On a monochrome Mac, we were able to open, manipulate, and print the "Floorplan #2" sample document, which contains 593 objects in four layers. We couldn't open a second document, however, as only 20K remained free. We also couldn't use the program's on line help system or spelling checker.

Recommendations: If you create relatively small drawings on a monochrome Mac (or a color Mac in its two-color mode), you can safely reduce MacDraw's Application Memory Size to 500K, but you'll sacrifice the spelling checker and on line help system.

Microsoft Works 2.0. Works' Suggested Memory Size and Application Memory Size are both 768K. We reduced its Application Memory Size to as low as 400K and still enjoyed acceptable performance. However, because Works stores all open documents entirely in memory, the number of documents we could have open simultaneously decreased significantly. We also had more trouble creating and formatting large documents. We successfully created a 35K word processor document (about 35 double-spaced pages of 12-point Geneva), but we couldn't change its font. And when we tried such basic editing functions as deleting a paragraph, Works told us there wasn't enough memory to undo the operation and asked if we wanted to proceed anyway.

Recommendations: Works 2.0 runs well when given less memory than its 768K preset. But because Works stores documents entirely in memory, a smaller memory size will limit the number and size of the documents you can open.

As these experiments show, you can often coerce an application to accept a smaller memory cubbyhole, but you pay the price in terms of performance and/or document size. But sometimes, that may be a price you're willing to pay. If you have a reasonably fast hard disk, more frequent disk accesses won't bog you down excessively, and if you have an 68020- or 68030-based Mac, performance will still be acceptable. There may be times when decreasing a few applications' memory requirements are the only way you can simultaneously run the programs you want to use. In these cases, somewhat laggardly performance is a small price to pay in return for being able to work the way you want to work.

The Effects of Increased Memory Sizes

We've seen what happens when you shoehorn a program into a smaller memory size. What happens when you give a program more memory than its Suggested Memory Size? As with the previous experiments, it depends on the application. With programs that swap documents between disk and memory (such as Word 4.0 and Aldus PageMaker), you'll notice generally better performance. With programs that store their entire documents in memory (such as Microsoft Works and Claris's MacDraw II), you'll be able to create larger documents and have more documents open simultaneously.

Microsoft Word 4.0. As noted in the previous section, Word 4.0's Application Memory Size is 1024K, but its Suggested Memory Size is 512K. After performing the reduced-memory experiment in the previous section, we restored Word's Application Memory Size to 1024K and tried performing the same lengthy search-and-replace operation that Word choked on earlier. As you might expect, the extra memory made all the difference. Word churned through the 70-page document, swiftly and successfully changing all 8,796 occurrences of "e" to "#." We were still unable to completely undo the operation, however; Word restored about half of the document, then told us there wasn't enough memory to complete the operation. The extra memory resulted in fine performance in Page View mode, even when we changed the entire document's formatting from one column of double-spaced Courier to two columns of single-spaced Optima.

Recommendations: If you perform complex tasks with large documents—tasks such as search-and-replace operations and index generation while in page-view mode—Word 4.0 benefits from a larger Application Memory Size. If you typically perform simple writing and editing tasks with small documents, however, the performance difference isn't worth the extra memory.

PageMaker 3.01. We doubled PageMaker's Application Memory Size from 700K to 1400K. Performance seemed a bit faster, but the difference wasn't significant enough to thrill us—or convince us that PageMaker could benefit from the extra 700K.

Recommendations: We don't recommend giving PageMaker more than its preset value of 700K unless you encounter low-memory error messages.

MacDraw II version 1.1. We upped MacDraw II's Application Memory Size from its preset 900K to 1400K. The benefits were dramatic. We could open numerous large documents, duplicate their objects, display the documents in color on a Mac II, and check spelling.

Recommendations: MacDraw II stores its documents entirely in memory, so more memory lets you create larger documents and have more documents open simultaneously.

Microsoft Works 2.0. We boosted Works' Application Memory Size from its 768K preset to 1400K. As with MacDraw II, the extra memory paid off. We were able to create a word processor document containing over 215 single-spaced pages, and still have enough memory left over to open a small data base and a spreadsheet.

Recommendations: Given more memory, Works lets you create larger documents and have more documents open simultaneously. If you're primarily interested in the latter, the extra memory will be well spent. But if you're interested in the former—that is, if you find yourself creating larger and larger documents—consider moving to a stand-alone word processor, database manager, or spreadsheet. Works is a "jack of all trades" program, and as such, it lacks many of the features necessary to manipulate huge documents. If you find yourself creating documents whose size causes memory error messages, you may be outgrowing Works. If that's the case, you'll be better served by a number of specialists rather than one generalist.

Conclusions. As these experiments show, you can influence a program's performance dramatically by increasing or decreasing its Application Memory Size. The best way to fine-tune your programs' memory requirements is to experiment. Adjust your programs' Application Memory Size until you reach the ideal balance between performance, reliability, and RAM efficiency. You'll get better use out of the memory you have, and you'll develop a greater appreciation for the Mac's complex memory-management capabilities.

How to Read MultiFinder's Memory Graph

We've seen the benefits and drawbacks of giving less and more memory to applications. But how much of a change should you make in an application's memory appetite? One tool for determining how much memory to give an application is MultiFinder's memory graph, which appears when you choose About the Finder from the Apple menu.

A typical memory graph display appears in Figure 9-14. Notice that each bar has a light- and dark-shaded portion. The light-shaded portion indicates how much memory has been allocated to the application (or to the System and Finder). The dark-shaded portion indicates how much of that memory is actually in use. (In technical terms, the light-shaded portion indicates the size of the application heap, or in the case of the System file, the system heap.)

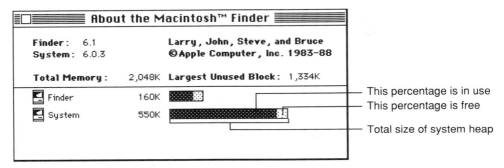

Figure 9-14: MultiFinder's memory graph.

You can gauge how an application is using memory by switching back to the Finder and choosing About the Finder. If a given application's bar contains a great deal of white space, that indicates the application isn't using all the memory allocated to it. Consider reducing that application's Application Memory Size. (Remember that you must first quit the application before you can change its memory requirements.)

To get an accurate picture of an application's memory requirements, use the About the Finder command after opening a document that represents the type of documents you usually work with, and after you've performed some tasks you usually perform. Don't simply start an application, then switch back to the Finder to display its memory graph.

An even better way to watch an application use memory is to first drag the Finder's memory graph window to the bottom of the screen, and then switch back to your application and resize its document window so that you can see the graph, as shown in Figure 9-15. With this approach, you can see the graph change as you work, and thereby get the most accurate picture of how the application uses memory. This technique is especially practical if you have a large screen monitor (or two monitors).

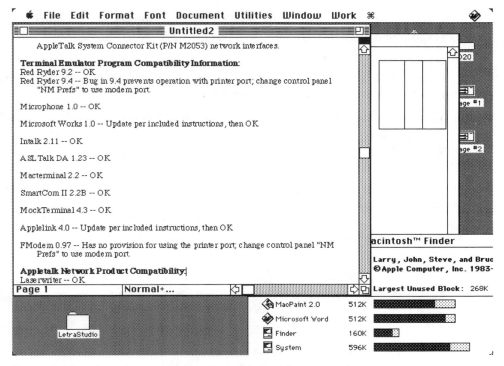

Figure 9-15: Move the memory graph to see it while you work.

Miscellaneous MultiFinder Tips

Let's wrap up our hands-on look at MultiFinder with a potpourri of miscellanous tips.

Desk Accessories and MultiFinder

Chapter 5 introduced the system file named DA Handler, which provides a "layer" in which all open desk accessories run. DA Handler has two drawbacks:

- It slows down the opening of desk accessories, since the Mac must load DA Handler's code before it can open the desk accessory you chose.

- If you have very little very memory left, DA Handler will often not be able to open a desk accessory. Instead, it displays an error message recommending that you "try closing another desk accessory or quitting an application."

You can eliminate both drawbacks by holding down the Option key while choosing a desk accessory's name from the Apple menu. This undocumented trick causes the Mac to open the desk accessory within the current application's layer.

If you have a disk- or resource-editing utility, you can modify MultiFinder so that it normally opens desk accessories in the current application layer, and opens DA Handler only when the Option key is pressed. For details, see the section "Modifying MultiFinder" in the next chapter.

Creating an Application Set

When MultiFinder is active, you can use the Finder's Set Startup command to specify that your Mac automatically start all open applications when you restart. Here's how:

1. Open the applications and desk accessories that you want to be opened automatically each time you start your Mac.

2. With the applications still open, return to the Finder.

3. Select your start-up disk icon (click it once) and choose Set Startup from the Special menu.

   The Set Startup dialog box appears, with the Opened Applications and DAs option selected, as shown in Figure 9-16.

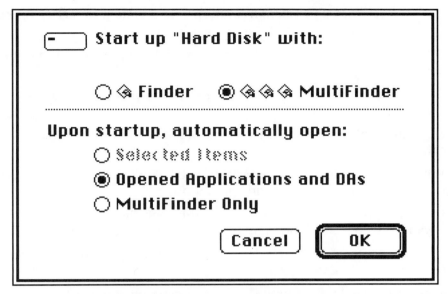

Figure 9-16: Set Startup dialog box with the Opened Applications and DAs option selected.

4. Verify that the Opened Applications and DAs option is selected, and then click OK or press Return.

From now on, when you start up your Mac, MultiFinder will open the applications and desk accessories you specified.

Creating Multiple Application Sets

MultiFinder's ability to open several applications automatically is useful, but it has a limitation: it lets you specify only one set of applications. There are times when you might want to switch between application sets. For example, you might want to create one application set containing a word processor, paint program, and desktop publishing program, and another set containing a spreadsheet and an accounting program.

Here's a tip that lets you create multiple application sets. When you use the Set Startup command, the Finder creates a file in the System Folder named Finder Startup. By renaming this file and then using the Set Startup command with a different set of applications open, you can create another Finder Startup file. You can then switch between the two sets by renaming the two files. The following steps describe how.

1. Use the step-by-step instructions in the previous section to specify your first application set.

2. Open the System Folder and drag the Finder Startup file out and onto the desktop.

3. Rename the Finder Startup file, giving it a descriptive name such as "Publishing Set."

4. Open the applications and desk accessories that will form the second application set.

5. With the applications still open, return to the Finder and use the Set Startup command to specify the second application set.

From this point on, your Mac will use this new Finder Startup file. When you want to switch to the other application set, perform the following steps.

1. Open the System Folder and drag the Finder Startup file out and onto the desktop.

2. Rename the Finder Startup file, giving it a descriptive name.

3. Rename the first start-up file, changing its name to Finder Startup.

4. Put the Finder Startup file back into the System Folder.

5. Restart your Mac.

If you don't switch between application sets often, this technique may be more trouble than it's worth. But it will save you time and effort if you frequently switch between application sets containing several applications and desk accessories.

Finder and MultiFinder Shortcuts

Table 9-11 lists Finder shortcuts that let you manage disks and directory windows more efficiently. Unless otherwise noted, these shortcuts are also available when you're running under MultiFinder.

Table 9-11: Finder and MultiFinder shortcuts.

To accomplish this...	Do this...
Bypass the warning dialog box when you discard an application or System file	Press Option while dragging the file to the trash.
Close all open directory windows	Press Option while clicking any window's close box or choosing Close commmand. — or — Press Option immediately after quitting an application (Finder only)
Move an inactive window without activating it	Press Command while dragging the inactive window's title bar (works in applications, too).
Copy a file from one folder to another instead of moving it	Press Option while dragging the file to the destination folder.
Start MultiFinder when the Finder is running	Press Command and Option while double-clicking on MultiFinder icon in the System Folder.
Quickly determine whether a file is locked or unlocked	Select the file, then move the pointer over the file's name. If the I-beam pointer appears, the file is *not* locked.
Quickly switch between applications when running under MultiFinder	Click the icon at the far right of the menu bar.
Align all icons in a window	Press Option while choosing Clean Up from the Special menu.
"Program" a directory window to close automatically when you return to the Finder	Press Option while opening the directory window (Finder only).
Rebuild a disk's DeskTop file (see Chapter 15)	Press Command and Option while inserting the disk. For hard disks, disable MultiFinder, then press Command and Option immediately after quitting an application.

You can also create your own shortcuts by using keyboard utilities such as Apple's MacroMaker, CE Software's QuicKeys, and Affinity Microsystem's Tempo II, or by using a resource-editing utility such as ResEdit. Instructions and some suggested shortcuts appear in the next chapter.

Alternatives to MultiFinder

Let's end our look at MultiFinder by examining some ways to avoid using it. The fact is, you can't always afford to donate the extra memory required to accommodate MultiFinder, especially if your Mac has only 1MB of RAM or if you run memory-hungry applications such as gray-scale or color drawing programs.

Fortunately, there are ways to get some of the benefits MultiFinder provides without having to run it:

- Use desk accessories. These handy miniprograms are always available. Desk accessories are available for most common computing tasks, including word processing, painting and drawing, disk and file management, and simple filing.

- Use integrated software. If your work involves performing relatively light-duty tasks with a variety of programs, consider an integrated program such as Microsoft Works, which provides word processing, data management, spreadsheet analysis, drawing, and telecommunications features. Orange Micro's Ragtime combines desktop publishing, word processing, and spreadsheet analysis. Neither of these programs will replace stand-alone applications such as Microsoft Word, Excel, or Aldus PageMaker, but you may not need the depth of features those programs provide.

- Use a print spooler. One of MultiFinder's benefits is that it provides background printing to PostScript printers and to the LaserWriter IISC. You can get the same benefit with print spooling software such as SuperMac Software's SuperLaserSpool, which also supports background printing to Image-Writers.

None of these alternatives provides the same flexibility as a 4MB or 5MB Mac running MultiFinder, but combined, they come surprisingly close. Put another way, you can't have your cake and eat it too, but you can at least nibble at the icing.

It's worth noting that, under System 7.0, you won't have a choice between running under the Finder or MultiFinder. Under System 7.0, MultiFinder is the only game in town.

Disk and File Management Tips

If you have a hard disk, one of the best ways to improve the Mac's performance is to organize your disk's contents efficiently. This section provides tips for managing files and keeping your hard disk running at peak performance. Although we use the term "hard disk" here, the information in this section also applies to other high-capacity storage devices such as Bernoulli Boxes.

Filing Guidelines

Our recommendations for organizing files on a hard disk boil down to two words: Use folders. Folders provide a logical way to organize your applications and documents. By grouping files into categories and then creating folders for each category, you can develop an efficient electronic filing system. Instead of having to scroll through hundreds of files to locate the one you need, you can go directly to a given folder with a few keystrokes or mouse clicks.

Equally important, extensive use of folders improves the Mac's performance. When you open a disk or folder icon, the Finder must reach out and touch every file on that disk or in that folder in order to display its name, icon, size, and other information. The more files you store within a folder, the longer this process takes. In one test we performed, a Mac SE connected to a Cirrus 40MB hard disk took 8 seconds to display the directory window of a folder containing 175 files. When we switched from the By Icon view to By Kind view, the Mac took 41 seconds to sort the files.

Then we reorganized the folder, creating 12 folders, each containing roughly 15 files. With this scheme, the Mac took only 1.2 seconds to display the folder's directory window. Switching from By Icon to By Kind view took less than a second. Table 9-12 summarizes these results.

Table 9-12: Folders improve the Finder's performance.

	Display Directory Window	Switch to By Kind view
Folder containing 175 files	8 seconds	41 seconds
Folder containing 12 folders, containing 15 files	1.2 seconds	<1 second

Similarly, if you leave the directory window of an overstuffed disk or folder open, you'll have to wait for the Finder to sort through it every time you start up your Mac or quit from an application when not running under Multi-Finder.

It's obvious that folders improve the Finder's performance. But how should you organize the files on your hard disk? We don't recommend specific filing schemes here because every Mac user performs different tasks and has his or her own style of organization (or disorganization). We will, however, provide some guidelines and suggestions that you can modify to suit your needs.

- Group your documents into logical categories. Task-oriented folder names might include Correspondence, Proposals, Budgets, Memos, Client Lists, Scanned Images, and Newsletters. Or you might prefer to group documents according to when you created them: January Work, February Work, March Work, and so on. Or you might combine both approaches: within a folder named Memos, you might create 12 additional folders: January Memos, February Memos, March Memos, and so on. Or you might mimic an alphabetized paper filing system: within the Memos folder, create 26 folders, one for each letter of the alphabet. Then file documents according to the first character of the recipient's last name.

- Group applications into logical categories. Put all your graphics-oriented applications in a folder named Graphics, all your word processors in a Word Processing folder, all your publishing programs in a Publishing Folder. If a given application uses more than one file—perhaps it uses a help file and a preferences file—give that application a folder of its own within the category folder.

- Separate applications and their documents. Don't save your word processor documents in the same folder that contains the word processor itself. Instead, create a different folder and store documents there. This approach makes it easier to back up your documents.

- Keep frequently used applications, documents, and folders on the desktop, as shown in Figure 9-17. With this approach, you won't have to open the disk's directory window to access the files you use most frequently.

- Create folders for storing miscellaneous documents and applications. Sometimes you create documents or use applications that don't fit into a specific category, or that you just don't feel like filing at the moment. Instead of leaving them at the top of the disk hierarchy, where they'll slow the Finder each time you open the disk's directory window, place them in folders named Miscellaneous Documents and Miscellaneous Applications. That isn't the most organized approach, but at least it gets them into folders, where they won't slow performance.

Finally, it's worth noting that you can nest folders approximately 12 levels deep, but navigating through more than four levels is a bit cumbersome.

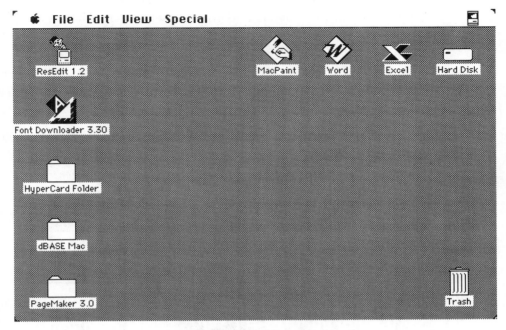

Figure 9-17: Keep frequently used files on the desktop.

What's in a Name?

Unlike most computers, the Mac lets you assign lengthy, descriptive names of up to 31 characters to both folders and files. Instead of grappling with cryptic names such as QTRBUDG.WKS and MEMO729.DOC, you can use names like "Quarterly Budget" and "July 29 Memo to Luke".

Your choice of document names can have an impact on the efficiency of your disk filing system. To determine the most appropriate naming scheme for you, answer these questions:

- Would you like to locate a file or folder within an Open dialog box by typing the first few characters of its name? If so, be sure that the file or folder contains one or more unique characters near the beginning of its name. For example, instead of naming a range of book chapters Chapter 1, Chapter 2, Chapter 3, name them 1 Chapter, 2 Chapter, 3 Chapter, or Ch1, Ch2, Ch3. The drawback of this approach is that it often leads to cryptic file names, and that's what the Mac's file system was designed to avoid.

- Are there certain files or folders that you'd like to see appear at the top of the list in the Open dialog box? If so, start their names with a punctuation character such as a comma (,), or simply begin the name with a space. When sorting file names before displaying them in the Open dialog box, the Mac places punctuation characters and spaces ahead of alphanumeric characters. Note that you can't use a colon (:) as part of a file name.

Incidentally, if you're fond of lengthy file names, be sure to include some differentiating characters early in their names. Otherwise, when you choose an application's Open command, you may not be able to tell which file is which. Figure 9-18 illustrates this pitfall and its solution.

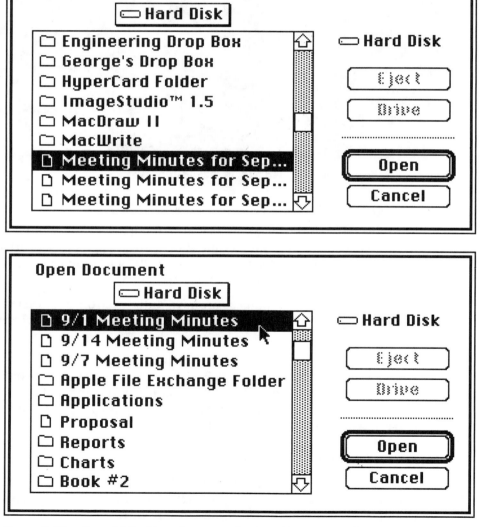

Figure 9-18: One pitfall of lengthy names (*top*) and how to avoid it (*bottom*).

Which View is Best?

We've mentioned that the Finder lets you view directory windows in six different ways (in seven ways on Macs configured for color or gray-scale displays). Which view should you use? As the following observations show, it depends on your needs.

- By Icon and By Small Icon are slowest. Because the Finder must retrieve an icon's appearance from the invisible DeskTop file (described in Chapter 5) and then draw the icon itself, the Finder takes considerably longer to display a directory window in both icon views. If you have a folder or disk containing a large number of files with different icons, you'll get better performance by using a different view.

- By Date is useful for backing up. If you want to selectively back up files that you've modified recently, use the By Date view. Files nearest the top of the list are ones that have been created or modified more recently. Because newly created or modified files appear nearest the top of the directory window, By Date is also useful for those times when you've recently created a file but forgotten its name.

- By Kind is useful for a hard disk's desktop level. It places applications first, followed by documents, followed by folders. By Kind is also useful for viewing a System Folder's contents. Because this view separates files according to their type, your start-up documents, system files, Chooser documents, cdevs, and downloadable fonts are grouped together.

- By Size is useful when you need to free up disk space. The largest files appear at the top of the list.

- By Name is useful when you're viewing the contents of a folder containing documents. In this view, files are sorted alphabetically. If you're creating a filing system that mimics an alphabetized paper filing system, By Name is the view to use.

Relying heavily on the By Color view can create problems. If you switch your Mac into gray-scale mode, you'll have trouble telling which colors are which. And if you switch it into black-and-white mode, you won't be able to tell at all. What's more, if other people use your Mac, your color scheme may be meaningless to them.

Remember that you can mix and match views as needed. You might want to use By Kind for the top level of a disk and for its System Folder, By Date for a folder whose contents you back up often, and By Name for the alphabetized folders within that Folder. The Finder remembers the viewing mode of a disk and every folder on it.

Finding Files

No filing system is perfect, and chances are you'll occasionally misplace a key document or folder. At times like those, the Mac's Find File desk accessory can help. To use Find File, type all or part of a file's name, and then press Return or click the Go button (the icon depicting a person in a frantic search). If Find File locates files whose names match what you typed, it displays their names. Click on a name, and Find File displays information about that file and shows where it's located, as shown in Figure 9-19.

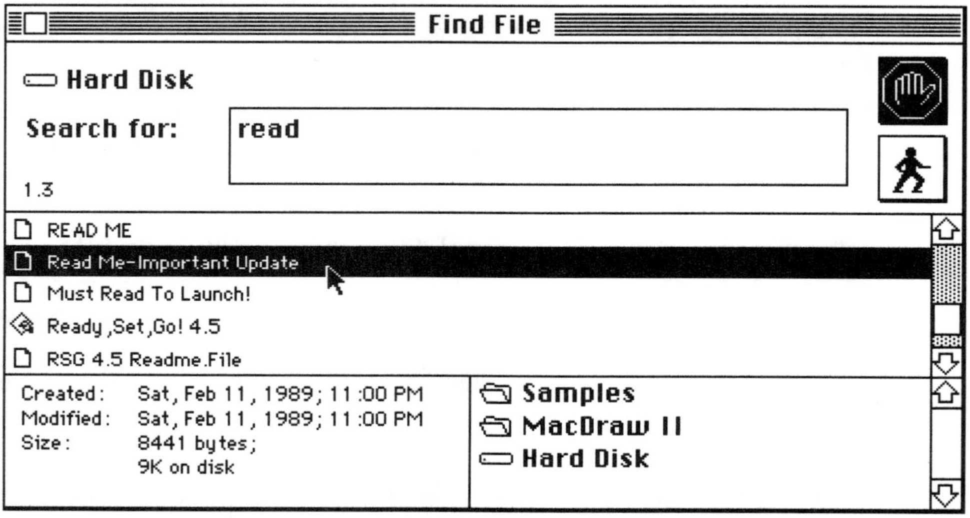

Figure 9-19:   Find File in action.

Find File is easy to use, but there are several fine points to be aware of.

- Regardless of whether you're using MultiFinder, Find File conducts its search in the background, so you can switch back to an application or open a different desk accessory while it searches. (Don't click Find File's close box to return to an application; doing so halts the search.) When Find File has searched an entire disk, it beeps and the stop sign icon is highlighted.

- Find File conducts logical AND searches; if you separate two character strings with a space, Find File searches for only those files containing both strings. For example, if you type *New Proposal*, Find File will locate files named *New Franchise Proposal*, *Proposal for New Wing*, *Newton Proposal*, and *New Proposal*. It will not locate files named *Eric's Proposal* or *New Suggestions*, since neither of those names contain both character strings.

- You can use the Search Here command in Find File's menu to specify that the desk accessory search a specific disk or folder. You might use Search Here to specify that Find File look for a document stored on a network file server. Another way to aim Find File at a different disk is to click the disk icon in the upper-left corner of Find File's window.

- You can use the Move to Desktop command to move a file or folder to the desktop for quick access. (As mentioned earlier in this chapter, this command is an easy way to disable an Init.) To restore the file or folder to its previous location, select it and choose Put Away from the Finder's File menu.

Several Inits and desk accessories are available that provide more sophisticated file-locating features than Find File. We describe them in the next chapter.

System 7.0 and File Management

The new Finder that will accompany System 7.0 will provide enhanced file-management features, including:

- File IDs that allow applications to locate documents even if you rename them or move them to a different folder. Many applications require support files such as spelling checker dictionaries, or create documents that can be linked to other documents. Many spreadsheet programs let you link worksheet documents, and many desktop publishing programs create links between publishing documents and large scanned image files. For programs like these, file IDs will be a boon, and will eliminate dialog boxes asking you to locate a file that you've moved.

- A new manager, the *Desktop Manager*, will replace the DeskTop file for keeping track of the files on a disk. The DeskTop file was effective for tracking files on floppy disks, but with hard disk capacities increasing and multigigabyte optical laser disks becoming available, the DeskTop file is showing its age. (It's the primary reason that the Finder slows so dramatically when you have hundreds of files in a folder.) The Desktop Manager will also allow applications to search for files based on their Get Info comments. Thus, Get Info comments will play a larger role in helping you manage files and disks.

- A fast disk search feature that allows applications to search entire disks for specific files according to a variety of criteria. Utilities that back up hard disks will be able to use this feature to quickly locate files that have been modified.

- A new manager, the *File System Manager*, will make it easier for developers to provide support for non-Macintosh file systems such as MS-DOS. By adding MS-DOS file system support, you could insert a 3.5-inch MS-DOS disk in a FDHD floppy disk and then view and work with its contents directly on the Finder's desktop. Presently, the FDHD floppy disk can read MS-DOS disks only through the Apple File Exchange program, unless you add additional software, such as Dayna's DOS Mounter (discussed in Chapter 11). Networking and file-exchange products are currently available that allow you to view MS-DOS disks on the desktop, but they're expensive and require their own specialized hardware. (See Chapters 11 and 12 for details on these products.)

Remember that most of these new features will lurk within the Mac's system software toolbox, and will be invisible to us until application programs are modified to take advantage of them. As new programs and new versions of existing programs appear after System 7.0's release, we Mac users will develop new, more efficient techniques for managing files.

Keeping Your Disk in Tune

As you use a hard disk, its contents become *fragmented*. Large files are scattered across the disk instead of being stored in contiguous blocks. To the hard disk, retrieving such a file is like reading an article that's scattered throughout a magazine instead of printed on contiguous pages: it takes longer. We explore the concepts behind fragmentation in Chapter 15. For now, it's enough to say that fragmentation slows a hard disk, and that there are ways to cure it.

One way to defragment a disk is to run a defragmentation utility, which reorganizes the disk's contents so that all files are contiguous. Several Macintosh disk utility packages include defragmentation utilities. Before running such a program, however, back up the entire hard disk. If a power outage or system crash occurs during the defragmentation process, you can lose files.

Another way to defragment a hard disk is to first back it up, then erase it, then copy your applications and documents back to the hard disk. When you restore the hard disk's contents, begin by copying the System Folder, then copy the applications you use most often, then your most frequently accessed documents.

Should you use a defragmentation utility or perform the task "by hand?" The manual approach requires more time, but it also gives you a chance to do some spring cleaning, purging your disk of those applications and files you no longer use. The automatic approach requires less effort, so you'll probably use it more often.

HARDWARE SETUP TIPS

The manuals that accompany the Mac and its peripherals tell you how to hook up your cables and cords, and they often provide ventilation guidelines for keeping the equipment healthy. But what about your health? Paying attention to how your hardware is physically organized can make your computing time more efficient and less of a strain on your back, neck, ears, and eyes.

Let's begin our look at hardware setup considerations by examining how to create a comfortable, reliable, and efficient working and computing environment.

Desk and Chair Height

A comfortable working environment begins with your desk and chair. The height of a desk influences the height of the keyboard and also the angle at which you view the screen. There are no carved-in-stone rules for desk and chair height, but architects and interior designers do have guidelines. According to *Interiors* magazine, the ideal height for a desk that will be used for typing is 27 inches. The seat height for such a desk should be approximately 17 inches.

If you're designing a new office, pay special attention to the issue of human-factors engineering. Two excellent sources of information are *Anthropometry for Designers* (Van Nostrand Reinhold, New York, 1981) and *Interiors* magazine (1515 Broadway, New York, NY 10036).

Monitor Viewing Angle

Many people who use compact Macs complain that the screen is too low, forcing them to unconsciously crane their necks until they ache. The solution is simple: angle the Mac upward slightly. Kensington Microware offers two stands for compact Macs that offer tilt-and-swivel bases: the $29.95 Maccessories Tilt/Swivel and the $49.95 SuperBase, which also provides storage bins. Ergotron, Inc. also offers a variety of tilt-and-swivel bases.

For a less expensive alternative, visit your local hardware store and buy a package of rubber ironing board feet roughly 1 1/2 inches long and 1 inch in diameter. Two of them placed under a compact Mac's two front feet position the machine and the screen at a far more comfortable viewing angle. The weight of the machine keeps them in place.

As for Macs with separate monitors, most monitor manufacturers offer optional tilt-and-swivel bases for their wares; some even include them with the monitor. One particularly elegant-looking monitor stand is Agio Designs' Agio

Arm, a 12 by 12-inch swiveling platform that attaches to a desk with a clamping mechanism. (The Agio Arm is available from La Cie, Ltd.; its address appears in Appendix B.)

But whether you need such a tilt-and-swivel monitor base depends in part on whether your monitor sits on top of your Mac. And that depends on where you put your Mac.

Accommodating the Biggest Macs

Many Mac II and IIx users don't want to donate half of their desks to their computers, and understandably so. The solution is to put the machine on its side, on the floor. But do observe the following precautions.

- Leave space under the machine. The II and IIx have vents on both sides of their cases that must be unobstructed. The best way to place a II or IIx on the floor without suffocating it is to use Kensington's Macintosh II Stand. Kensington also sells extension cables for the monitor, keyboard, and mouse; depending on how far apart your machine and desk are, you may not need them.

- Position the machine with the power light closest to the floor. That way, the floppy disk drives will be within arm's reach and further away from the dusty floor, and you'll be able to reach the machine's programmer's switch.

A more elaborate way to get a II or IIx out of your way is to use Ergotron's Mac II Workstation, which offers an overhead shelf for the Mac and a counter-balanced swivel arm for a monitor. Agio Designs' Agio 800SCA Workstation (distributed by La Cie, Ltd.) provides a 30 by 33-inch desk surface, a wire frame for holding a II or IIx vertically, and an overhead shelf.

Quieting Noisy Peripherals

ImageWriters and many external hard disks are whiners. If you're sensitive to noise, you can do something about it. To make a noisy printer less obtrusive, consider putting it in an *acoustic enclosure*, a large box lined with sound-absorbing material. Acoustic enclosures have openings for paper and cables, and most have see-through acrylic doors that let you visually verify that the printer is working properly. Enclosures for all three Apple ImageWriter printers are available from Global Computer Supplies and Inmac Corporation.

The best way to quiet an external hard disk is to get away from it. By using Apple's SCSI Cable Extender (Apple part number M0208), you can move an external hard disk further away from your machine. A Cable Extender is a three-foot SCSI extension cord that connects between the SCSI System Cable (the cable that attaches to the Mac) and the SCSI device. You can attach numerous SCSI Cable Extenders to each other; just be sure the total length of all your SCSI cabling doesn't exceed 20 feet. And be sure to put the drive itself in a clean, well-ventilated area that isn't prone to spilled liquids or careless footsteps.

Fighting Screen Glare

Nothing leads to eye fatigue like glare on a computer screen. The screens of compact Macs have coatings that reduce glare, but they can still produce uncomfortably bright reflections if you have a window at your back. If you have a choice, it's better to have the window in front of you; the natural light illuminates your desk, and you can periodically rest and refocus your eyes by looking out the window. If you can't avoid a window at your back, consider a glare-reducing screen filter such as Kensington's.

Incidentally, if your screen has a non-glare coating (those of compact Macs do), don't clean it using window cleaner or other strong cleaners. You'll damage the non-glare coating. Instead, wipe dust off the monitor with toilet tissue or photographic lens-cleaning tissue. (Don't use facial tissue; many brands contain softening agents that cause smearing.) If you frequently need to remove sticky fingerprints, use cleaning solutions made for computer screens. Computer supply houses such as Global Computer Supplies and Inmac Corporation sell CRT wipes—towelettes premoistened with a gentle cleaning solution that, according to their manufacturers, also helps neutralize the static that attracts dust.

A Word about External Floppy Drives

The following hardware setup tip is so well known it's practically folklore. Still, we pass it along for newcomers. If you have an external floppy disk drive and a compact Mac, avoid placing the drive to the left of the Mac. The left side of the compact Mac's case contains the machine's power supply, whose transformers generate magnetic fields that interfere with the drive's operation, causing disk errors. The Mac Plus and earlier machines are especially prone to this problem.

If you have one of these Macs, also avoid setting the external drive on top of the Mac. You'll partially obstruct the vents, and the heat given off by the Mac can cause the drive's mechanism to expand to the point where disk errors will occur. The best place for an external floppy drive is to the right of the Mac, as you face the screen.

Mouse Care and Feeding

As it rolls, the Mac's mouse picks up lint and dust. Over time, the build-up of dirt on the mouse's rollers will impair its operation. The Mac's manual recommends cleaning the rollers with a cotton swab moistened with alcohol or tape recorder head cleaner, and suggests wiping the rubber ball clean with a soft, clean, dry cloth.

The easiest way we've found to clean a mouse is to use Ergotron's Mouse 360 cleaning kit. The Mouse 360 kit uses an ingenious Velcro-covered ball that gets the mouse's internal rollers squeaky clean, and it includes cleaning solution and a chamois cloth for the mouse's rubber ball.

The mice on classic Macs have plastic feet that can wear down over time, impairing the mouse's action. If your mouse has sore feet, you can restore its vigor by attaching small felt pads to the feet. Many users also report good results using Velcro strips. Use the soft half of the Velcro pair, not the hooked half.

Surge Protectors and Power Conditioners

Many computer accessory manufacturers sell *power conditioners* such as surge protectors, which attach between the Mac's power cord and a wall outlet and, according to their manufacturers, protect your hardware from voltage surges and also filter out line noise caused by air conditioners, power tools, and other electrically noisy devices. The fact is, the Mac's own power supply provides a great deal of protection and voltage filtering. Unless your Mac is tapped into the same circuit as an air conditioner or power tool, you're unlikely to encounter problems related to noisy power lines.

A more common problem is a voltage *sag*, a momentary drop in voltage caused when a power-hungry device such as an air conditioner kicks in. Again, the Mac power supplies are fairly forgiving; the Mac II's supply, for example, can tolerate voltages ranging between 90 and 140 volts and 170 to 270 volts. Still, if you suspect that voltage irregularities are causing problems for you, consider an *uninterruptable power system (UPS)*. UPSs connect between your computer and the power source, and contain batteries that kick in within milliseconds after a power outage. Most UPSs provide between 10 and 20 minutes of standby power—more than enough time to save your work and shut down safely. UPSs also provide voltage filtering and surge protection.

Does the Mac Need Rest?

Speaking of power, you might wonder if you should turn the Mac off when you aren't using it, or if you should just leave it on all the time. If your Mac lacks a hard disk, you can leave it on all the time, but you should turn the screen brightness down to avoid burning an image of the menu bar and other screen components into the video tube's phosphor. (The original Mac manual even suggested turning the brightness down and using the dimmed screen as a night light. For people who look forward to getting away from the Mac at the end of a long day, that suggestion might seem pretty gruesome.)

If your Mac has a hard disk, you should turn it off if you aren't going to be using it for another six to eight hours. Hard disks contain bearings that can wear out over time. If you use a removeable-media drive such as an Iomega Bernoulli Box or Syquest removeable hard disk (used in drives from Mass Micro and others), consider ejecting the media if you aren't going to use your Mac for some time.

As an alternative to turning the screen brightness down to avoid burn-in, consider a *screen blanker* such as Stars (Stars II for Mac IIs), available from user's groups and on line information services. Fifth Generation Systems' Suitcase II system extender comes with a slick screen blanker called Pyro. (See the next chapter for more information on Suitcase II and screen blankers.)

Disconnecting and Connecting Add-Ons

Some users report that the Mac's ADB connectors can cause a momentary short circuit when you attach or remove them with the power on. The resulting short circuit can damage the Mac's ADB circuitry. Apple hasn't acknowledged that this potential problem exists, although it does recommend (for different reasons, described in Chapter 14) turning power off before plugging and unplugging ADB devices. Considering the added risk of hardware damage, that's good advice.

Indeed, it's a good idea to always turn off your Mac and everything connected to it before disconnecting or reconnecting any add-on. That's especially true of SCSI add-ons and external floppy disk drives.

Wiring the Mac for Sound

The Mac's built-in speaker faithfully reproduces error beeps, but high-fidelity audio is another matter. If you use HyperCard stacks that play sounds or if you use sound-oriented applications such as Electronic Arts' Deluxe Music Construction Set or Brøderbund's Jam Session, you deserve better audio quality. You can attach the Mac to an amplifier or stereo system by using inexpensive jacks and patch cords available at your local Radio Shack. Because some Macs have monaural (mono) circuitry and some have stereo circuitry, we provide separate instructions for each type.

WARNING!

The Mac can generate volume levels that can damage your audio equipment and your hearing. Attach the cables with the Mac's power off, and do not apply power until you read the section "Setting Volume Levels," after the wiring instructions.

Mac SE, Plus, and Earlier Machines

To attach a Mac SE, Mac Plus, or earlier machine to a stereo, use the following components:

- A cable with a 1/8-inch miniplug on one end, and a phono plug on the other (Radio Shack catalog number 42-2444).

- A "Y" adaptor containing a phono jack on one end, and two phono plugs on the other (Radio Shack catalog number 42-2435).

Connect the cables as shown in Figure 9-20.

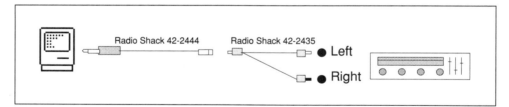

Figure 9-20: Connecting a monaural Mac to a stereo.

Do not connect the Mac to a low-level input such as one intended for a magnetic phono cartridge. Doing so can damage your stereo. Similarly, if you plan to record the Mac's audio output, connect your cables to your tape deck's Line Input jacks, *not* its microphone jack.

Mac SE/30 and II Family

To attach an SE/30 or Mac II to a stereo, use the following:

- A cable with an 1/8-inch *stereo* miniplug on one end, and two phono plugs on the other. (Radio Shack catalog number 42-2475 is a three-foot cable; catalog number 42-2481 is a six-foot cable.)

Connect the cable as shown in Figure 9-21.

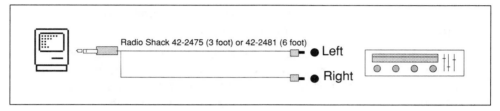

Figure 9-21: Connecting a stereo Mac to a stereo.

Do not connect the Mac to a low-level input such as one intended for a magnetic phono cartridge. Doing so can damage your stereo. Similarly, if you plan to record the Mac's audio output, connect your cables to your tape deck's Line Input jacks, *not* its microphone jack.

Setting Volume Levels

Read these instructions carefully; you can damage your audio equipment and your hearing by setting volume levels too high.

For mono Macs. Turn your stereo's volume all the way down. Next, use the Control Panel to set the volume level to 1. Turn your stereo volume up *slightly* and click on the Control Panel's volume control to produce a beep. Adjust the volume on your stereo for a comfortable listening level.

For stereo Macs. Turn your stereo's volume all the way down. Next, use the Control Panel to set the volume level to 2 or 3. Turn your stereo volume up *slightly* and click on the Control Panel's volume control to produce a beep. Adjust the volume on your stereo for a comfortable listening level.

For headphones. If you've attached headphones to the Mac as described in "Audio Alternatives" later in this section, begin with a volume control setting of 1 for both stereo and mono Macs. *For the safety of your hearing, remove the headphones when adjusting the volume control setting.*

Audio Alternatives

As an alternative to connecting the Mac to a stereo, you might consider a pair of external amplified speakers such as Radio Shack's Minimus-0.6 (catalog number 40-1259), which are designed for portable "Walkman"-type stereos. Such speakers lack the fidelity of a high-quality pair of home stereo speakers, but they certainly sound better than the Mac's speaker. You may find them adequate for your needs, especially if your Mac and your stereo aren't in close proximity.

If you opt for external amplified speakers, be careful where you place them. Speakers contain magnets that can erase disks.

You can also attach headphones directly to the Mac's audio output jack. For a stereo Mac, you can use the stereo headphones that accompany portable stereos. To use such headphones with a mono Mac, you need a mono-to-stereo miniplug adaptor (Radio Shack catalog number 274-368).

To use headphones that have standard 1/4-inch audio plugs with a stereo Mac, you need a 1/4-inch stereo-to-1/8-inch stereo adaptor (Radio Shack catalog number 274-371 or 274-367). To use such headphones with a mono Mac, you need a 1/4-inch stereo-to-1/8-inch mono adaptor (Radio Shack catalog number 274-361).

If you have a Mac II set up on the floor rather than on your desk, you may also need an extension cable for your headphones.

WARNING!

The Mac can generate volume levels in headphones that can damage your hearing. If you attach headphones to the Mac, do not put them on until you have switched on the Mac and adjusted the Mac's speaker volume to a low level. See the section "Adjusting Volume Levels" earlier in this section for guidelines on setting volume levels.

10

Customizing Tips

After you master the Mac's basic operating techniques, you start thinking of ways they could be improved to suit your working style: "If that command had a keyboard shortcut, I could choose it faster. If the Finder displayed file icons further apart, I could use long file names without them overlapping. If there was a desk accessory that allowed me to copy and delete files, I wouldn't have to switch back to the Finder all the time."

You can have all these things and more. The Mac is a malleable machine that you can sculpt to fit the way you work. To help, here's a collection of tips and techniques for customizing the way the Mac and its applications work and for changing the way the Mac interface looks and sounds.

In this chapter, we'll also take a closer look at the way the Macintosh uses resources, and we'll see how to use Apple's resource-editing utility, ResEdit, to modify applications, the Finder, and printer drivers.

RESOURCE DETAILS

Resources and ResEdit figure prominently in this chapter, so let's start out with a look at both. As you may recall from Chapter 5, resources supply the Mac and its applications with program code and/or data that the Mac or an application needs to run. The resources you're most likely to encounter when working with the System Folder are system resources such as fonts and desk accessories, Control Panel resources (cdevs), and printing resources such as the LaserWriter and ImageWriter printer drivers.

In addition to these resources, applications and documents can contain resources such as icons, menus, and dialog boxes. To understand where those resources are located, let's look at the basic structure of Macintosh disk files.

Two Forks to a File

The Mac's file structure is unique in the personal computer world in that a single disk file can actually comprise two distinct physical components: a *data fork* and a *resource fork*. Notice we said *"can* comprise." A file doesn't have to have both a data and a resource fork; whether it does is determined by its creator. If a file does contain both forks, the Mac's File Manager works behind the scenes to make these two forks appear as one file on the disk, as shown in Figure 10-1.

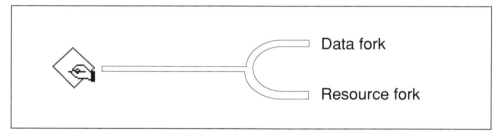

Figure 10-1: Files can contain a data fork and a resource fork.

- The data fork, as its name implies, contains data. In the case of a word processor document, the data fork may contain the text you typed using the word processor. With applications, the data fork is usually empty, at least at first; an application can use its data fork to store information.

- The resource fork, again appropriately named, contains resources. An application's resource fork generally contains everything the application needs to run: its menus, dialog and alert boxes, icons, program code, and more. As for a document, its resource fork can contain specialized resources that pertain to only that document. Claris' MacDraw II, for example, uses a MacDraw II document's resource fork to store the customized Font, Size, and Layout menu settings that you might create for that document, and also to store preferences and custom patterns that pertain to that document.

(As an aside, you may recall from Chapter 5 that the System file plays a dual role—storing RAM-based system software as well as system resources such as fonts, FKEYs, and desk accessories. That dual role takes advantage of the Mac's dual-fork file design. RAM-based software patches are stored in the System file's data fork, while system resources are stored in its resource fork.)

Resource Types

Resources are grouped into categories called *resource types*. A resource type is described by a four-character name. Table 10-1 is a partial list of common resource types and their purpose.

Table 10-1: A partial list of Macintosh resource types.

Type	Description
ALRT	Template for an alert box's appearance
BNDL	Bundle—the Finder uses BNDL resources to associate files with their icons
CDEF	Program code that creates and handles custom controls (buttons, dials, and so on)
CNTL	Control template—defines the appearance or name of a control such as a button
CODE	Contains a segment of an application's code
CURS	Cursor—defines the appearance of a pointer
DITL	Dialog item list—defines what appears in a dialog or alert box
DLOG	Template for a dialog box's appearance
DRVR	Program code for desk accessory or driver
FKEY	Function key—a Command-Shift-number routine
FOND	Font family descriptor (see Chapter 7)
FONT	Font bit map description (see Chapter 7)
ICN#	Icon list—a series of icon definitions; generally used by the Finder to show icons in various states (active, inactive, hollow); application icons are ICN# resources
ICON	Icon—a single icon definition, like that of a printer driver you see in the Chooser
INIT	Initialization information; used at startup (not to be confused with INIT documents, although these can contain INIT resources)

(continued)

Table 10-1: A partial list of Macintosh resource types. *(continued)*

INTL	International resource—contains data that an application uses to create displays appropriate to a given country (proper date formatting, currency symbols, and so on)
MBAR	Menu bar—defines all the menus in a menu bar
MENU	Defines an individual menu's commands and keyboard shortcuts
NFNT	Font in new-font-numbering-table format (see Chapter 7)
PACK	Package—contains RAM-based system software
PAT[1]	Pattern—defines a QuickDraw pattern (the patterns drawing and painting programs show in their palettes).
PAT#	Pattern list—a collection of patterns
PDEF	Contains printing software
PICT	Picture—the pictures that often appear when you choose an About command are usually PICT resources; also appear in Alarm Clock and Control Panel desk accessories
PREC	Print record—storage area for printer driver data
snd[1]	Sound resource—contains a digitally recorded sound that the Mac can play (see Chapter 14)
STR[1]	String—a series of characters that may appear in a dialog box or be used by an application; for example, in an error message
STR#	String list—a collection of strings
SIZE	Contains memory-requirements information used by MultiFinder (and Switcher)
WDEF	Window definition—describes the appearance of a window
WIND	Window template—used by the Window Manager to create a window.

[1] Name includes a space at the end. Most programming manuals list these resources within single quotes; for example 'snd' and 'STR'.

Why Resources?

Resources allow the components of an application—its program code, menus, dialog and alert boxes, icons, cursors, and so on—to be created, manipulated, and stored separately. This segregation of components adds a great deal of flexibility to the Macintosh:

- To create a foreign-language version of their software, developers need alter only the resources that contain language-specific information. For example, a developer might replace the English-language menu, dialog box, and alert box resources with new resources in French.

- If many programs use the same resources, those resources can be stored in the System file and made available to all programs. Examples of such *shared resources* include mouse pointer shapes, fonts, desk accessories, RAM-based system software components, and the templates that specify the appearance of the standard Open and Save dialog boxes.

- Because resources allow applications to be divided into small, manageable chunks, the Mac can manage its memory more efficiently by keeping in memory only those resources required at a given moment. An application developer can designate an expendable resource as *purgeable*. If the Mac needs more memory for a given task, it can use the Memory Manager to clear purgeable resources from memory. Large resources such as fonts and dialog box templates are often designated as purgeable.

What ResEdit Does

ResEdit lets you access a file's resource fork and alter its contents. By altering a file's resources, you can modify many functional and cosmetic aspects of that file.

You can buy ResEdit and its documentation through the Apple Programmer's and Developer's Association (APDA; its address appears in Appendix B). ResEdit is also widely distributed through user's groups and on line information services. However, many different versions of ResEdit are floating around within this informal distribution network; be sure you're using the latest version by selecting the file and choosing the Finder's Get Info command. At this writing, the latest *released* version is 1.2, dated Thursday, April 6, 1989. Some later versions are available in prerelease form, but are likely to be less reliable.

You can identify a prerelease version of ResEdit by the presence of a letter in its version number. Version 1.3d1, for example, indicates "development release 1" of version 1.3. Version 1.3a1 indicates the first *alpha* release, while 1.3b1 indicates *beta* release 1. Development releases are the least reliable and the most likely to change cosmetically; they're rough prototypes of the final software. Alpha software is generally cosmetically complete—the wording and appearance of menu commands, palette icons, and dialog boxes is finalized or close to it—but the software can be incomplete or buggy. Betas are closest to final, released versions; they're cosmetically complete, all commands and features have been implemented, and the final bug extermination campaign is underway. (Apple uses the "d", "a", and "b" designations for all its prerelease software; many other developers have also adopted it.)

ResEdit's documentation describes the program's operation, but the manual is often not available through user's groups or information services. Because many users obtain a copy of ResEdit through these informal distribution networks, we'll summarize the program's workings here.

WARNING!

You can damage applications, disks, and files by using ResEdit carelessly. Always make a backup copy of the file or disk you want to modify, and perform your modifications on the copy. If you have a hard disk or a floppy containing sufficient free space, you can use the Finder to make a copy of a file to be modified: select the file and then choose Duplicate from the File menu. If you're using a hard disk, consider copying the duplicate to an otherwise blank floppy disk and performing your modifications on the floppy copy.

When you open ResEdit, windows listing the contents of all the currently mounted *volumes* appear, as shown in Figure 10-2. (A volume is a unit of storage media, usually a physical disk such as a hard disk or floppy, but sometimes a RAM disk or a disk folder that's been made available to other machines on a network. These pseudo-disks are often called *logical* disks or logical volumes, as opposed to physical disks.)

As Figure 10-2 shows, the window of a volume that can be ejected (such as a floppy disk) has a close box; to eject the volume click the close box or choose Close from the File menu. If you insert a disk while ResEdit is running, ResEdit creates a directory window for the disk and adds it to the ones already on the screen.

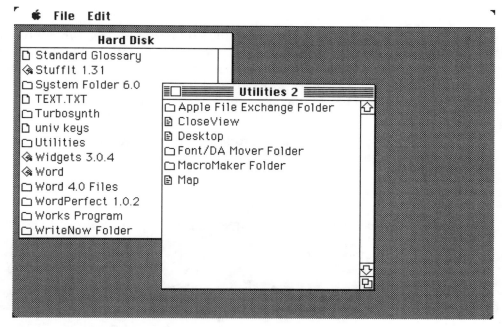

Figure 10-2: ResEdit with two open directory windows.

Here's a brief summary of how ResEdit's directory windows work:

- A directory window's display is similar to the Finder's By Name view: The volume's contents are sorted according to name, with folders, documents, and applications represented by small icons.

- Unlike the Finder's directory windows, ResEdit's directory windows also show invisible files such as the DeskTop file.

- You can select multiple files by Shift-clicking on each and by Shift-dragging across a range of files. You can also select discontinuous files by pressing the Command key and clicking on each file.

- As with the Mac's standard Open dialog box, you can select a file or folder by typing the first few characters of its name. To open a folder, double-click it or select it and choose Open.

- You can delete a file or an empty folder by selecting it and choosing Clear from the Edit menu. ResEdit asks for verification before deleting anything.

Opening a File with ResEdit

ResEdit offers three ways to open a file's resource fork: you can double click on the file's name in the directory window; you can select the file and press Return; or you can select the file and choose Open from the File menu. If the file doesn't have a resource fork, a dialog box appears asking if you want to create one. Generally, you'll click Cancel. (We'll explain why—and point out when you might want to click OK—later in this chapter.)

When you open a file's resource fork, a window appears listing the resources in that file, sorted alphabetically. Figure 10-3 shows the resource fork window for the Finder file.

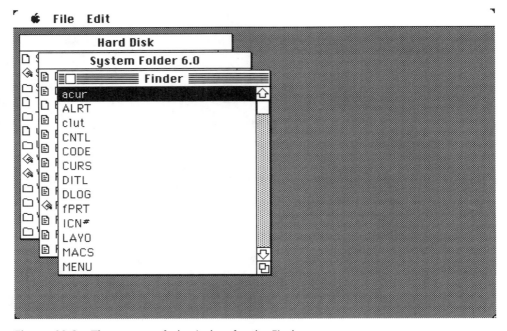

Figure 10-3: The resource fork window for the Finder.

As Figure 10-3 shows, a typical file's resource window is likely to contain standard resource types (MENUs, DLOGs, ALRTs, WINDs, and so on) as well as specialized resource types created by the file's developer. Generally, when using ResEdit to modify applications, you'll work with only standard resource types.

A ResEdit Exercise: Modifying the Finder's Menus

Because ResEdit is a complex utility, we've included the following exercise to guide you through the resource-modifying process.

This exercise shows how to modify the Finder's MENU resource to add Command-key shortcuts to the Restart and Shutdown commands. After making this modification, you'll be able to Restart your Mac by pressing Command-R, and shut it down by pressing Command-S.

To try this exercise, first open your System Folder and copy the Finder file to a floppy disk, and perform your modifications on the copy. If you have a small System file that will fit on the floppy along with the Finder, you might want to copy it to the floppy, too. This will make it easier to try the altered Finder after you modify it.

1. Start ResEdit and locate the backup copy of the Finder file. Open the Finder file by double-clicking it.

   A window appears listing the Finder's resources.

2. Locate the MENU resource and double-click it.

   A window, titled "MENUs from Finder," appears, as shown in Figure 10-4.

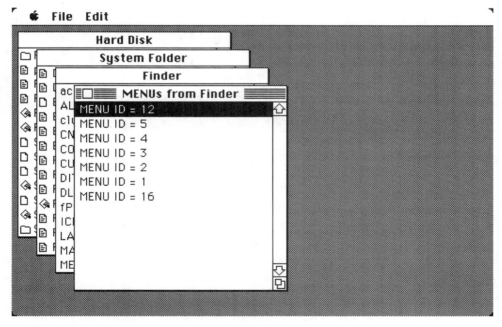

Figure 10-4: The "MENUs from Finder" window.

This window lists the resource identification numbers, or *resource IDs*, of each of the Finder's menus. (As you may recall from Chapter 7's discussion of font ID numbers, the Mac's Resource Manager uses resource IDs to refer to resources.)

3. The Finder's Special menu has an ID number of 5. To open it, double click on the entry "MENU ID=5."

A resource window appears for the Special menu, as shown in Figure 10-5. *Don't perform any modifications yet.*

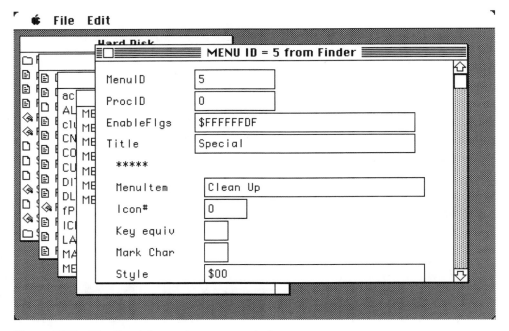

Figure 10-5: The Special menu's resource window.

This window is a *menu editor*, a window that lets you modify the characteristics of menus. ResEdit has other types of editor windows for modifying other resource types; we'll encounter several of them later in this chapter.

For this exercise, the most important component in the menu editor window is the text-editing box labeled *Key equiv*. Each menu item has a Key equiv box. To add a Command-key shortcut to a menu item, type the desired character in that item's Key equiv box. You'll do that in the next step.

4. Scroll the window until the Restart menu item is at the top. You should also be able to see the Shut Down menu item, as shown in Figure 10-6.

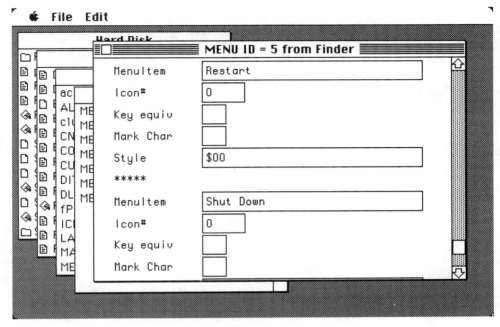

Figure 10-6: The menu item entries for the Restart and Shut Down commands.

5. Click the mouse pointer within the Key equiv box for the Restart command, and type a capital *R*. (A lowercase *r* will work too, but will make the Special menu's appearance inconsistent with that of the Finder's other menus.)

6. Click the mouse pointer within the Key equiv box for the Shut Down command, and type a capital *S*.

The menu editor window now looks like Figure 10-7.

Double-check your work, then close the menu editor window, the "MENUs from Finder" window, and finally, the Finder window itself. When you close the Finder window, ResEdit asks if you want to save your changes. Click Yes or press Return. Finally, quit ResEdit. (Tip: You don't actually have to close each window before quitting. As with other Mac applications, you can simply choose Quit and click Yes when asked to save changes. As you get more accustomed to working with ResEdit, you'll probably want to take this faster route back to the Finder.)

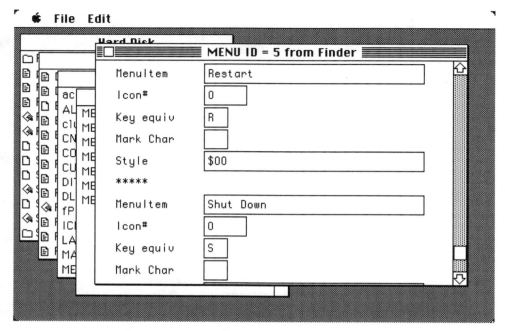

Figure 10-7: Key equivalents added to the Restart and Shut Down commands.

Trying the Modified Finder

To try your new keyboard shortcuts, the modified Finder must be on a start-up disk. As mentioned earlier, the easiest and safest way to try it is to turn the disk containing the modified Finder into a system disk by copying a System file to it. If you have a hard disk, copy its System file to the floppy. (If the file is too large to fit on the floppy—perhaps it's laden with fonts and desk accessories—you'll need to use a System file from a different disk. If that's the case, be sure the System file is from the same software release as the modified Finder file. See Chapter 5 for information on determining version numbers.)

After turning the modified Finder disk into a system disk, you need to make it the current start-up disk. If you're not running under MultiFinder, switch-launch to the modified Finder (press Command and Option while double-clicking on the modified Finder file). If you're running under MultiFinder, you won't be able to switch-launch to the disk. Instead, choose the Finder's Restart command and then insert the modified Finder disk. If you have a hard disk, you'll need to insert the disk immediately after choosing Restart to ensure the Mac doesn't start up from the hard disk.

Once the modified Finder disk is the current start-up disk, pull down its Special menu. The new Command-key shortcuts appear adjacent to the Restart and Shut Down commands, as shown in Figure 10-8. Try them if you like.

Figure 10-8:   New Command-key shortcuts for Restart and Shut Down commands.

Replacing Your Unmodified Finder

If you're pleased with the new shortcuts, you may want to copy the modified Finder file to your hard disk or frequently used floppy system disks. To do so, the disk whose Finder you want to replace must *not* be the current start-up disk. (Using a Finder that's in use to replace itself would be like trying to perform brain surgery on yourself.)

To replace an unmodified Finder, start your Mac with the modified Finder disk (or switch-launch to it), and then copy its Finder file to the System Folder of the disk containing the unmodified Finder, as shown in Figure 10-9. When asked if you want to replace the existing Finder file, click OK or press Return.

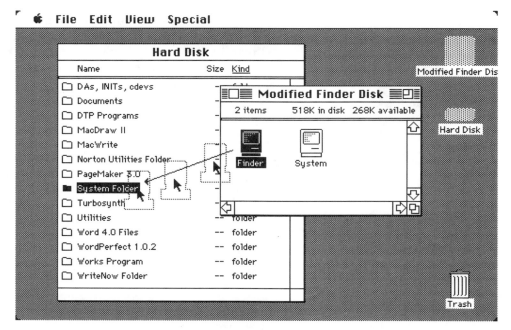

Figure 10-9: Copying the modified Finder to a different system disk.

CUSTOMIZING PROJECTS

Now you're ready to tackle some customizing projects. This section presents tips for adding Command-key shortcuts to commands that lack them, adding keyboard shortcuts to dialog box buttons and to mouse movements, modifying printer drivers to accommodate custom paper sizes, and much more.

Adding Command-Key Shortcuts

If you're fond of Command-key shortcuts, you're probably frustrated when you encounter often-used commands that don't have them. You can add Command-key shortcuts to an application in two ways:

- by using ResEdit to modify the application's menu resources

- by using a macro utility such as Apple's MacroMaker, CE Software's Quic-Keys, or Affinity Microsystem's Tempo II. (As you may recall from Chapter 5, a macro is a collection of commands or mouse sequences that you create or record for later playback.)

Each of these customizing tools has its strengths and drawbacks.

ResEdit Pros and Cons

The advantages of using ResEdit to add or modify Command-key shortcuts are:

- Your changes are saved directly in the application. If you copy the application to another disk or to another Mac, your shortcuts move along with it.

- Your shortcuts appear in the application's menus, just like the shortcuts the application's developer specified. You need not refer to a separate menu or reference screen to refresh your memory.

- You need not donate the extra memory required to accommodate the keyboard-enhancement utility.

The disadvantages of using ResEdit to modify Command-key shortcuts are:

- It's tricky. You can damage an application file if you're not careful or if the Mac crashes during the modification process.

- Some applications use special menu-handling code that prevents you from adding or changing shortcuts using ResEdit. Two examples are Microsoft Word and Ashton-Tate's FullWrite Professional (we'll list more shortly).

- Some applications provide many different menus, each of which is active at a different time. For example, Microsoft Works' menus change depending on whether you're working with a word processor, spreadsheet, database, or communications document. For applications like these, using ResEdit is either impractical or downright impossible.

Keyboard Utility Pros and Cons

Why use a keyboard utility instead of ResEdit to add keyboard shortcuts?

- You can create shortcuts that use the Control, Shift, and Option keys in addition to or instead of the Command key. ResEdit lets you use only the Command key.

- You don't risk damaging an application file by accidentally altering something you shouldn't.

- You can add shortcuts to applications whose menus don't use the standard MENU resources or Menu Manager routines, such as Microsoft Word and FullWrite Professional.

- You can use the utility to create other shortcuts that simulate mouse movements and button clicks, enter text, and more.

- You can record multiple events and assign them to one key sequence. You might, for example, create a macro that issues the Quit command, responds "Yes" to the "save changes?" dialog box, backs up the file you just saved, and then shuts down your Mac.

- Most keyboard utilities let you specify whether a given shortcut applies to only a specific application (a *local* macro), or to every application you use (a *global* or *universal* macro). If you have the Apple Extended Keyboard, you can assign macros to function keys. For example, you can record the Command-S (Save) key sequence as a global macro and assign it to the F15 (pause) key. With this shortcut, you can issue the Save command in any virtually application by pressing F15. Also, you can assign the F1, F2, F3, and F4 keys to the Undo, Cut, Copy, and Paste commands. These four keys are labelled with those command names, but the Mac's system software doesn't assign those commands to them. With a macro utility, you can.

But on the negative side:

- Your shortcuts are stored in separate files maintained by the keyboard utility. If you want to move an application to a different disk and retain the shortcuts, you must move the utility and its keyboard-shortcut file there, too. And because you're likely to create your shortcuts over time as you use various programs, you must remember to create backups of the utility's files so that you won't lose the shortcuts if the worst happens.

- Your shortcuts don't appear in the application's menus. If you forget one or more of them, you must use the utility's menus or dialog boxes to refresh your memory.

- The utility itself uses memory. If you don't plan to use the utility for other tasks, you may not want to donate precious RAM for a few keyboard shortcuts.

- Some keyboard utilities require certain menu titles and commands—File, Edit, Copy, Paste, Quit, and Shut Down, to name several—to appear in English, and therefore are unlikely to work with non-English versions of the Mac's system software.

- Because keyboard utilities modify the way the Mac responds to its keyboard, occasional incompatibilities can surface.

Creating Keyboard Shortcuts with ResEdit

To use ResEdit to add Command-key shortcuts, use the step-by-step exercise earlier in this chapter as a guide. Table 10-2 lists some applications whose MENU resources we were and were not able to modify using ResEdit 1.2. The absence of a version number after a program's name means that you can or can't modify any version of that program.

Before modifying any of the programs listed in Table 10-2, read the section, "Notes About ResEdit and Menus," following the table.

Table 10-2: A sampling of applications whose menus are and aren't modifiable with ResEdit

Modifiable	Not Modifiable
Adobe Font Downloader 3.30	DA Handler
Adobe Illustrator 1.1	FullWrite Professional
Aldus FreeHand 2.0	Microsoft Works
Aldus PageMaker 3.0	Microsoft Word[1]
Apple HyperCard 1.2.2[2]	Paracomp Swivel 3D
Apple LaserWriter Font Utility	Software Ventures MicroPhone[3]
Apple MacDraw 1.9.5	
AppleLink 4.0	
Ashton-Tate Full Impact	
Ashton-Tate FullPaint	
Brøderbund Jam Session	
Claris MacDraw II[4]	
Claris MacPaint 2.0	
Connect MacNET	
Farallon SoundEdit	
Letraset ImageStudio	
Letraset Ready,Set,Go 4.5	
Microsoft Excel 1.5 and 2.2[5]	
QuarkXpress 2.0	
Silicon Beach Super3D 2.0	
SuperMac PixelPaint 1.1	
WriteNow 2.0	

[1] In version 4.0, use the Commands command (Edit menu) to create and modify shortcuts. See the *Microsoft Word User's Guide* for details.

[2] Shortcuts you add may not work in all program modes.

[3] Use MicroPhone scripts to assign keyboard equivalents to commands.

[4] Documents may also contain MENU resources that override those within the application file.

[5] ResEdit 1.2 displays an error message when opening some MENU resources, but modifications seem to work; proceed with caution. Consider creating shortcuts using Excel macros instead.

The preceding table isn't an all-encompassing list, nor can we guarantee that every keyboard command you add will work properly. Many factors influence how an application responds to the keyboard. One shortcut may work; another may not. Experiment freely, but *only* on backup copies of your applications.

Notes About ResEdit and Menus

Here are a few odds and ends you might want to keep in mind before modifying the MENU resources of your applications.

- Avoid duplicating an existing Command-key shortcut. The Mac responds to Command-key shortcuts from right to left on the menu bar. For example, if you assign the same Command-key shortcut to a command on both the File menu and the Edit menu, the shortcut will work for the Edit menu's command, not the File menu's. You'll need to remember this point if you intend to add a Command-P (for Print) shortcut to applications such as MacWrite and MacPaint, which use Command-P to summon the plain-text style.

- Many applications contain several MENU resources for the same menu title. For example, Microsoft Excel contains several MENU resources that create the File menu, but each resource is used at a different time, depending on what kind of document is active. If you're modifying the menus of such programs, be sure to modify the alternate versions of each menu, too. Otherwise, your Command-key shortcuts won't always be available.

- Use capital letters in ResEdit's Key Equiv box. Lowercase letters will work (the Mac's Menu Manager doesn't distinguish between capitals and lowercase), but they'll look odd in the menus.

- If you have an Apple Extended Keyboard, you can generally use function keys as Command-key shortcuts, but there's a catch: The menu won't indicate which function key you should press. Instead, a hollow Apple symbol will appear next to the Command-key symbol, as shown in Figure 10-10. Worse, the Mac uses the same Apple symbol for every function key, so if you create Command-function key shortcuts for several commands, they'll all look the same.

Figure 10-10: A Command-function key shortcut in Microsoft Excel.

Macro Utilities

If you've decided that a keyboard macro utility is a more appropriate customizing tool, you need to decide which utility to use. Three macro utilities are available for the Mac: Apple's MacroMaker, which is included with the System 6.0 Update package; CE Software's QuicKeys; and Affinity Microsystem's Tempo II. (A fourth utility, Genesis Micro Software's AutoMac III, is included with Microsoft Word and some other Microsoft products.) In this section, we'll spotlight the key differences between each to help you decide which is most appropriate for you.

The primary difference between keyboard utilities concerns the methods they use to record the events you want to play back.

With MacroMaker and Tempo II, you create macros by invoking the utility's "record" mode, performing the tasks you want to record, and then stopping the recording process. While you're recording, the utility is keeping track of where the mouse pointer is when you click the mouse, and of which keys are pressed. When you play back the macro, the utility recreates those events. MacroMaker and Tempo II each add their own menu to the menu bar. MacroMaker's menu lists macros you've created; Tempo II's does not.

With QuicKeys, you create macros not by recording events, but by choosing commands from QuicKeys' menus, which appear in the Control Panel, as shown in Figure 10-11. For example, to create a macro (in QuicKeys parlance, a *quickey*) that chooses a menu command, you choose Menu/DA, choose the desired menu command, then assign a keystroke sequence to it. To create a macro that performs several events, you use the Sequences menu to chain numerous individual quickeys together. QuicKeys doesn't add a menu to the menu bar.

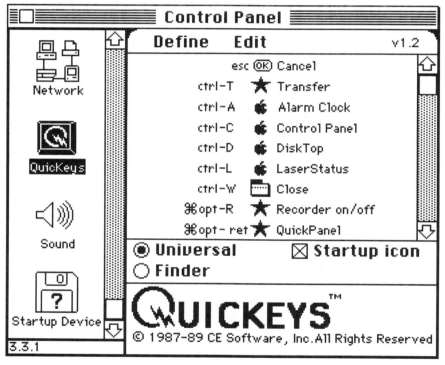

Figure 10-11: CE Software's QuicKeys.

Which approach is better? Because they record events as you perform them, MacroMaker and Tempo II are better suited to creating macros that perform task after task—such as opening a file, dragging a window, choosing a command, typing some text, then saving and quitting. Creating a multistep macro with QuicKeys can be tedious.

But QuicKeys contains many clever built-in shortcuts that Tempo II and MacroMaker lack. For example, you can define macros that insert the current time and date or true opening and closing quotes (discussed in Chapter 8).

Another built-in shortcut lets you "leaf" through the open windows on your desktop. And as we'll explain shortly, QuicKeys also contains intelligent scrolling shortcuts that lets you use the extended keyboard's navigation keys to scroll through windows. In addition to these shortcuts, QuicKeys is ideal for creating keyboard shortcuts for menu commands and dialog box buttons and for creating macros that "type" frequently used text for you.

As for AutoMac III, it offers something that MacroMaker and Tempo II lack—text *scripts* that you can edit. With MacroMaker, you can't edit macros. If, while recording, you make a typo and then correct it, MacroMaker records your typo and its correction. Tempo II lets you edit macros by stepping through them one event at a time, but the process can be difficult. With AutoMac III, you can edit the resulting script and remove the typo. However, AutoMac III's script language can be so obtuse you may find it easier to re-record a macro than to edit it.

A Closer Look at MacroMaker

Because MacroMaker is included with the Mac's system software, it's a good place to start experimenting with the power of macros. Indeed, if your macro needs involve simply creating a few Command-key shortcuts or macros that automatically type frequently used text, MacroMaker may be all you need.

But MacroMaker has some limitations that make certain types of keyboard shortcuts impossible. You can't use MacroMaker to create a keyboard shortcut that simply opens a modal dialog box (one you can't click outside of), because you can't access MacroMaker's menu in order to stop recording.

Another MacroMaker limitation is that it stores and chooses menu commands by their position within a menu, not by their name. This causes problems if you use an application in which the position of commands changes depending on what kind of document is active or what state the program is in. There is one way to work around this limitation: When choosing a command while recording a macro, use the command's keyboard shortcut, if it has one. Because this approach causes MacroMaker to record keystrokes rather than mouse movements, it doesn't require that a menu command always be located at the same position within a menu.

A third potential problem is MacroMaker's inability to record the mouse pointer's path and the time delays between events. For example, if you move the mouse across the screen and then double-click, MacroMaker doesn't record the path the mouse took or the amount of time it took to get from Point A to Point B. Instead, MacroMaker simply records that the mouse movement started at Point A and ended at Point B with a double-click. When you play back the macro, you see the mouse pointer jump abruptly from Point A to Point B.

Sometimes this isn't a problem. For example, when you're recording macros that eject disks or choose palette tools or menu commands, the mouse's path and the time it took to move are irrelevant. But if you're using a drawing program and want to record a macro that draws a shape, the mouse path becomes extremely important. Similarly, if you want to record a macro that types a few characters, waits five seconds, then types a few more characters (perhaps as part of a telecommunications sign-on sequence), the time delays between events become critical. MacroMaker isn't up to automation tasks like these.

Tempo II doesn't share MacroMaker's biggest limitations. Tempo II offers two recording modes: *real-time* and *high-speed*. With high-speed recording, Tempo II discards mouse-path and timing information, just as MacroMaker does. In real-time mode, however, Tempo II records the mouse path and the time delays between events. At playback time, events occur at the same speed as they did during recording. As we'll see shortly, Tempo II also lets you start and pause recording when a modal dialog box is open.

Macro Utility Shortcuts

In the following sections, we'll look at the different types of shortcuts you can create with a macro utility and provide some advice as to which utility can best accommodate each type of shortcut.

Menu Command Shortcuts

You can use any macro utility to create keyboard shortcuts for menu commands, but QuicKeys and Tempo II handle the task best. Both remember menu command names, not command positions, so your shortcuts will work even if your program shuffles the position of menu commands as it runs.

Dialog Box Shortcuts

Using MacroMaker to add keyboard shortcuts to a dialog box can be tricky. Because most dialog boxes are modal, you can't invoke MacroMaker's record mode while the box is open. Thus, you can't create a macro that opens a dialog box and leaves it open, since you can't stop the recording process until you okay or cancel the dialog box. With MacroMaker, the best you can do is create a macro that opens the dialog box, chooses one or more options, and then okays the dialog box.

Tempo II is ideal for creating dialog box shortcuts. With Tempo II, you can start and stop the recording process while a dialog box is open by pressing Command-comma (,). Thus, you can begin recording after the dialog box is already open, and you can stop recording before closing the dialog box. If you press Command and Option while clicking the mouse, Tempo II's menu pops up, allowing you to pause and resume recording and choose additional recording options. (This pop-up menu feature also lets you create and play macros in programs without menus, such as the Font/DA Mover.)

With QuicKeys, you can use the Buttons command in QuicKeys' Define menu to create shortcuts for the buttons in a dialog box. And CE Software's DialogKeys, a companion program included with QuicKeys, lets you "click" any dialog box button or check box from the keyboard.

Mouse Shortcuts

A third category of keyboard shortcut involves recording a mouse movement, such as clicking on a palette tool or dragging an icon or a window. MacroMaker and Tempo II both handle this task easily. However, to automate complex mouse movements that require recording of the mouse's path or the time it took to move from one point to another, you must use Tempo II. Neither MacroMaker nor QuicKeys can record the mouse's path.

Tempo II is also the best choice for creating macros that choose palette tools. Because Tempo II remembers which tool you've chosen, your macros will work regardless of the tool palette's location. You can create tool-choosing macros with QuicKeys, but the macros can fail if part of the tool palette is off the screen.

Macros that Start Programs

Most people frequently use the same programs; for them, macros that start those programs can save time, especially if the programs are buried in folders. Tempo II and QuicKeys are ideal for creating application-starting macros because they don't rely on the application residing at a specific location on the desktop. Instead, they remember the name of the application that you started.

Both Tempo II and QuicKeys also let you create *transfer macros*, which let you move to a specific application (and open a specific file, if desired) without using the Finder. When you play back a transfer macro, the macro utility "transmits" a Quit command to the active application, causing it to quit (and asking you to save changes, if necessary), and then starts the specified application. (If you're running under MultiFinder, both utilities simply start the second application without quitting the one you're using.)

Creating transfer macros is easier in QuicKeys because you need not actually transfer to the program specified in the macro. Instead, you simply choose the desired application from a dialog box that QuicKeys displays. QuicKeys also lets you create a "generic" transfer macro, which, when played back, displays a standard Open dialog box that lets you choose an application or file to open.

Macros that Enter Frequently Used Text

If you frequently type the same keystrokes—for example, your name and address—or if you frequently paste a shape or object into drawings, you can create macros that perform the task for you. Any macro program lets you easily record and play back keystrokes. Tempo II has a unique "autopaste" feature that lets you easily define and recall graphics or text. Simply select the text or graphic and choose Autopaste from Tempo II's menu. Tempo II records a macro that, when played back, retrieves whatever you selected from Tempo II's macro file, and then pastes them into the active document.

Ten Ways to Use Macros

Because macros reflect the way a person uses his or her Mac, they tend to be specialized. Still, many common tasks can benefit from automation. Here's a list of ten macro shortcuts you might find useful. In the following descriptions, we've noted when a given shortcut requires a specific macro utility. If no macro utility is mentioned, you can use any utility to create the shortcut.

Ejecting and forgetting a disk icon. Tired of reaching for the mouse to drag disk icons to the Trash? Create macros that do it for you. You might use Control-1 to eject the disk located below the start-up disk, Control-2 to eject the disk below that, and Control-3 to eject the fourth disk down. (Begin with the disk below the start-up disk, since you can't drag the start-up disk's icon to the Trash.)

Opening and closing desk accessories. With macros, you might use Control-A to summon the Alarm Clock, Control-C to call up the Control Panel, Control-R to display the Chooser, Control-F to open Find File, and Control-= (equal sign) to open the Calculator. And because few desk accessories have keyboard shortcuts for closing them, you may want to create a macro that does the job. Record a global macro that chooses the File menu's Close command and assign it to Control-W. If you use MultiFinder, record a macro that chooses the DA Handler's Quit command and assign it to Command-Q.

Changing double hyphens to em dashes. As you may recall from Chapter 8, laser-printed documents will look more professional if you take advantage of the Mac's special typographic symbols. Many applications will automatically use the Mac's typographic quotes as you type, but they won't automatically turn two hyphens (--) into an em dash (—). The solution: A macro that uses your word processor's search-and-replace feature to change all double hyphens to em dashes. Use it just before printing, and you'll never see a double hyphen again. Because this macro involves recording multiple steps, it's easiest to create with MacroMaker or Tempo II.

Using the extended keyboard's navigation keys. Word processors aside, few applications support the extended keyboard's Ins/Help, Del, Home, End, Page Up, and Page Down keys. QuicKeys' Mousies menu lets you easily put the Home, End, Page Up, and Page Down keys to work. After you've assigned one of these navigation shortcuts to a key, QuicKeys "clicks" the scroll bars in the active window to scroll to the top or bottom of your document or scroll up or down by the windowful. As for the extended keyboard's Help key, consider assigning it to a macro that chooses the Finder's Get Info command. We've also created a Finder macro that assigns the Close command to the Del key. This combination makes it easy to open and close a Get Info window. (It's also ideal for closing desk accessories.)

Switching applications under MultiFinder. Instead of reaching for the mouse to switch applications under MultiFinder, create a macro that simply clicks the application icon that appears on the right edge of the menu bar. If you also use Microsoft Windows on IBM PCs, consider assigning your switching macro to the Option-Tab key sequence. On the extended keyboard, the Option key is also labelled Alt, and Alt-Tab is Windows' application switching key sequence.

Starting often-used applications. If you keep frequently used applications on the desktop, create Finder-specific macros that start them and assign the macros to your keypad's number keys. Typing 1 might start your word processor, 2 might start your publishing program, and 3 might start your paint program. To create these macros using QuicKeys, use the Define menu's File command. Because QuicKeys' File command lists documents as well as applications, you can also use it to directly open frequently used documents.

Putting the Esc key to work. In many of Microsoft's programs, pressing Esc when a dialog box is open cancels the dialog box. That's a useful shortcut that any application can benefit from. QuicKeys is ideal for this task: Use its Button command and specify "Cancel" as the button to look for. With Tempo II, start recording while the dialog box is open, click Cancel, then stop recording. Unfortunately, Tempo II won't let you assign the macro to Esc; you'll need to combine Esc with a modifier key such as Command or Option. Save the macro as a universal macro. With MacroMaker, creating a cancel macro that works in every application is difficult, if not impossible.

Switching Set Startup options. Many users frequently switch between running under MultiFinder and running under the single Finder. If you're in this group, you can save time by creating macros that choose the Finder's Set Startup command, specify the Finder (or MultiFinder), okay the dialog box, and then choose the Restart command. For creating this multistep macro, MacroMaker and Tempo II are easier to use than QuicKeys. MacroMaker and Tempo II let you record the Restart and Shut Down commands; before the Mac restarts or shuts down, the utility's window appears, letting you save the macro. If you are using QuicKeys, use the Specials menu to specify the Restart or Shut Down commands.

Tearing off menus. HyperCard, MacPaint 2.0, and several other applications provide tool or pattern palettes in the form of *tear-off menus*—menus that you can "tear" away from the menu bar and drag anywhere on the screen, where they're always available. Generally, these applications don't remember that a menu has been torn off; each time you start the application, you must tear off the desired palette if you want to keep it available at all times. The solution: Create a macro that tears the menu off and drags it to the desired position. Because this macro involves recording mouse movements, it's easier to create in MacroMaker or Tempo II than in QuicKeys.

Pasting to the Scrapbook. Most people frequently need to paste snippets of text or graphics into the Scrapbook. Instead of manually choosing Copy, opening the Scrapbook, choosing Paste, and then closing the Scrapbook, create a macro that performs all four steps for you. Because Command-V is the standard keyboard shortcut for the Paste command, you might assign the Control-V shortcut to your paste-to-Scrapbook macro. With this macro, saving something in the Scrapbook is a matter of simply selecting it and typing Control-V.

System 7.0 and the Ultimate Macro Utility

In the end, each of these macro programs we've looked at has shortcomings, not because of its design, but because the Mac lacks a system-level mechanism for recording and playing back events. Let's look at what that involves.

In the past, the problem with all macro utilities was that they generally recorded only keystrokes and mouse movements—not the actual events that took place when keys were pressed or the mouse was moved. For example, if you recorded a macro that activated PageMaker's text tool, the macro recorder didn't record "activate PageMaker's text tool." Instead, it recorded "the mouse was clicked at screen coordinates x and y." If you dragged PageMaker's toolbox window elsewhere, the macro wouldn't work. Another example: if you started a program by double clicking its icon, the macro utility didn't record that you started a specific program; it recorded that you double clicked at coordinates x and y. If you moved the program to a different location on the desktop, the macro failed upon playback.

MacroMaker is prone to these problems, but Tempo II and QuicKeys work around many of them. Tempo II is especially "intelligent" about button clicks that activate palette tools. With Tempo II, the PageMaker macro problem just described doesn't occur. You can drag a tool window elsewhere and Tempo II will still know which tool to activate. And both Tempo II and QuicKeys let you define program-starting macros that don't depend on the application's location on the desktop.

But this degree of intelligence still can't take every event into account, and both QuicKeys and Tempo II can be tripped up. The ultimate macro recorder would record not keystrokes and button clicks, but messages, transmitted by an application, stating exactly what tasks you're performing.

Donn Denman, the Apple programmer who created MacroMaker, uses a chess program to illustrate this concept. "Say you move a pawn forward one space," he says. "None of the [current macro utilities] record that a pawn has been moved, yet that's really what should be recorded. The only thing that knows that a pawn has been moved—or even that there is a pawn—is the chess program. To me, none of these macro facilities will really be great until there's a mechanism for a chess program to say 'A pawn moved forward,' and for the macro recorder to record that."

Will the ultimate macro recorder ever exist? Perhaps. System 7.0 will provide for *inter-application communications*—the ability for applications to send messages to each other as they run. By taking advantage of this feature, applications could send messages when you perform activities. A macro utility could record these messages, and at playback time, transmit them to the application, thus recreating the events you recorded.

In order for this to occur, however, not only will we need a macro utility that can record application messages, but we'll need applications that can transmit messages to the macro recorder. In short, System 7.0 lays the foundation for the ultimate macro recorder; it's up to the architects and carpenters of the software world to build it.

Custom Paper Sizes

If you have an ImageWriter, chances are you occasionally need to print on paper whose dimensions aren't listed in the Page Setup dialog box. In this section, we'll show how to modify the ImageWriter driver to accommodate custom paper sizes. The ImageWriter driver modification applies to all recent versions of the ImageWriter and ImageWriter LQ drivers.

Coercing the ImageWriter driver into accommodating custom paper sizes involves altering one of the driver's PREC (print record) resources. You can use ResEdit to perform this task; we explain how shortly.

Before resorting to ResEdit, you might want to know about some easier ways to modify the ImageWriter driver. One way is to use an application by Bill Steinberg called PREC Manager, available free through user's groups and information services. Another is an application called Widgets, which is included with CE Software's DiskTop desk accessory, which performs Finder-like disk- and file-management tasks.

Yet another way to modify the driver is to use an application called MDL Utility. It's included with GDT Software's Mac Daisy Link, a product that lets the Mac use daisy wheel printers such as the Diablo 630. The primary purpose of the MDL Utility application is to let you modify Mac Daisy Link's driver to accommodate daisy wheel printers the driver doesn't support. But MDL Utility can also open the ImageWriter driver and modify its page size settings.

Background on PREC Resources

How does the ImageWriter driver use PREC resources to determine available page sizes? Version 2.7 of the ImageWriter driver contains three PREC resources; the one that controls which paper sizes appear in the Page Setup dialog box is PREC resource number 3. Here's what the resource contains:

- A number corresponding to the total number of page sizes defined in the resource. The Mac uses this number to determine how many radio buttons to create in the Page Setup dialog box.

- The dimensions of each paper size, expressed in units of 1/120 inch. For example, 11 inches is listed as 1320 units.

- The descriptive labels—International Fanfold, Computer Paper, and so on— that appear adjacent to each radio button.

The ImageWriter driver isn't the only place you may find a page-size PREC resource. Applications can contain their own PREC resources that override the PREC 3 resource in the ImageWriter driver. These higher priority PREC resources have a higher ID number: 4. When you choose the Page Setup command, the Mac performs the following search to find the highest priority PREC resource:

- First, it looks for a PREC 4 resource in the active printer driver. If one isn't found there, the Mac looks in the active application's resource fork. If the application doesn't contain a PREC 4 resource, the Mac looks in the active System file's resource fork.

- If the Mac doesn't find a PREC 4 resource in any of those places, it searches for a PREC 3 resource. The Mac searches in the same order: first the active printer driver, then the active application file, then the active System file.

- If the Mac doesn't find a PREC 3 resource in any of those places, a system error occurs. For this reason, be sure to always have one PREC 3 resource available. (In other words, don't remove the PREC 3 resource from the System file.)

When it finds a PREC 4 or PREC 3 resource, the Mac uses its contents to determine which sizes have been defined and to construct a radio button for each size. The dimensions of the size you choose are passed along to the application program, which uses them to set margins and perform other tasks relating to the chosen page size. At printing time, the Mac uses the dimensions to determine when to instruct the ImageWriter to advance to the next page.

Among popular applications, Microsoft Works 2.0 and Word 4.0 are two that contain a PREC 4 resource. If you use either of these applications and you want to create custom paper sizes, you'll need to modify their PREC 4 resource instead of (or in addition to) modifying your ImageWriter driver's PREC 3 resource.

Aldus PageMaker doesn't contain a PREC 4 resource, but it does override the PREC 3 resource when creating its Page Setup dialog box. This isn't a drawback, however, because PageMaker lets you specify a custom paper size in its Page Setup dialog box.

Using ResEdit to Create a Custom Paper Size

To use ResEdit to create a custom paper size, first copy your ImageWriter driver to a blank floppy disk; you'll modify this backup copy. Start ResEdit and open the ImageWriter driver backup by double-clicking on it. Doing so causes ResEdit to open the driver's resource fork and display a resource window listing the resource fork's contents. Locate the PREC entry in the resource window and double click on it. A new window appears listing the PREC resources in the ImageWriter driver.

Select the entry PREC ID=3 by clicking on it *once*. (If you accidentally double-click it, close the window that appears.) Next, choose Open as Template from the File menu. (In some older versions of ResEdit, the command reads Open As.) A dialog box appears listing ResEdit's predefined *templates*, which describe the format of a given type of resource. Use the scroll bar to locate the template with the name PRC3. When you find it, select PRC3 and click OK or press Return. ResEdit opens the PREC 3 resource and displays its contents in a new window, shown in Figure 10-12.

The window lists the resource's contents in the order described previously: the number of page size buttons, the page size dimensions of each button, and the text of the buttons themselves.

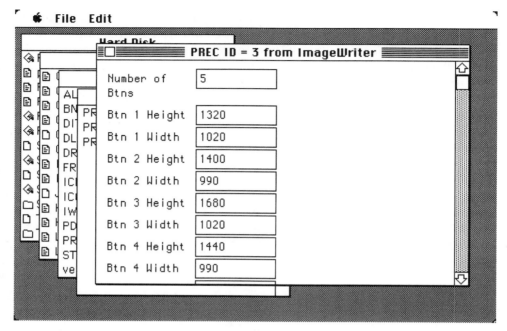

Figure 10-12: Resource-editing window for the PREC 3 resource.

The ImageWriter driver contains definitions for five paper size buttons, but the driver can accommodate six definitions. You can edit an existing definition, or create a sixth. To create the sixth definition, first replace the "5" that appears in the Number of Btns text box with 6. Next, scroll to the bottom of the window and replace the upside-down question mark (¿) that appears in the Btn 6 Name text box with a short name that describes your custom paper size, such as "Index Card."

To specify the page size, locate the Height and Width text boxes for the button you're defining. (If you're creating a sixth button, use the Btn 6 Height and Btn 6 Width buttons.) Next, calculate the dimensions of the paper by multiplying their dimensions in inches by 120. For a 3.5 by 5-inch index card, use a height dimension of 420 and a width dimension of 600. Figure 10-13 shows what the PREC 3 resource editing window looks like if you define a sixth button for index cards.

After you've edited the resource, double-check your work, then close the template window, the PRECs window, and the ImageWriter window. Or simply choose Quit and then click Yes or press Return when asked to save changes.

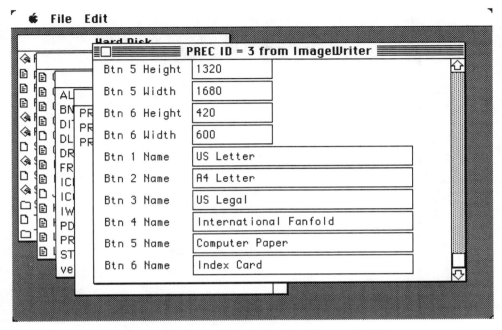

Figure 10-13: The PREC 3 window with an Index Card button definition.

Trying the New Size

After you've saved the modified driver, copy it to your System Folder. If you plan to replace an unmodified ImageWriter driver, be sure you have a backup copy of it elsewhere; if the modified driver doesn't give you the results you hoped for, you'll want to revert to the original one. Next, open the Chooser desk accessory, select the ImageWriter driver, and then close the Chooser.

The best way to try the new page size is to open an application whose document window reflects the current page size. MacDraw is ideal. Regardless of the application you use, the steps for trying the new size are the same: choose Page Setup from the File menu, select the new size, and click OK. If you're using MacDraw for this test, you'll see it update the page break lines in document window to reflect the new page size. Turn the rulers on, and you'll see that the page break lines reflect the new page size, as shown in Figure 10-14.

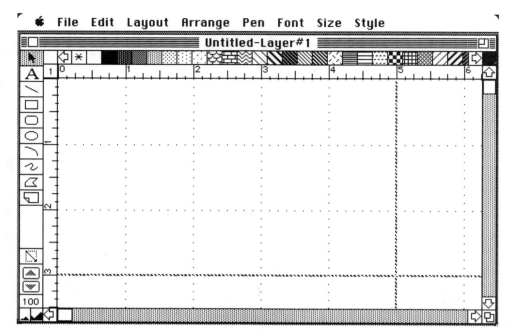

Figure 10-14: The Index Card page size at work in MacDraw II.

Many applications establish preset margins, so the rulers may not reflect the exact page size. For example, with the index card as the current page size, MacDraw II displays the page break lines at 3-inch intervals, not 3.5-inch intervals.

Here's another caveat: Some applications may not work properly with custom paper sizes. As Figure 10-15 shows, MacWrite 5.0's ruler isn't displayed properly with the index card page size. Worse, MacWrite 5.0 will not let you resize its document window to access the ruler icons for centered and justified text. (You can still choose these formatting options through the Format menu, however.) Most Mac applications are tested with only standard page sizes, so be sure to test a modified ImageWriter driver with the applications you use before replacing your unmodified driver. (And keep a backup of the unmodified driver handy—just in case.)

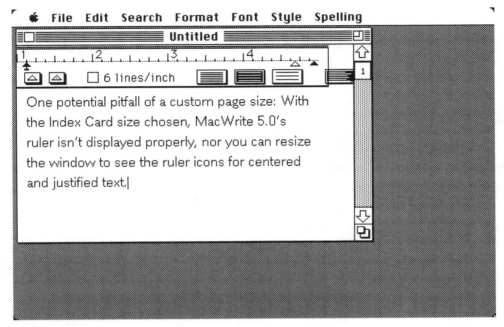

Figure 10-15:   Some applications, such as MacWrite 5.0, may not work properly with custom page sizes.

Adding a PREC 4 Resource to an Application

If you want to use a custom paper size in just one application, you can add a PREC 4 resource to that application, causing it to override the ImageWriter driver's PREC 3 resource.

Open an unmodified copy of the ImageWriter driver and open its PREC window. In the "PRECs from ImageWriter" window, select the PREC 3 resource, choose Copy from the Edit menu, then close the ImageWriter file.

Next, open the application you want to modify by double-clicking its name. When the application's resource window appears, choose Paste from the Edit menu. Next, locate the PREC entry in the application's resource window, and open it. A window, titled "PRECs from (*application name*)" opens. If a PREC 4 resource already exists in that application, remove the resource you just added by selecting it and choosing Clear from the Edit menu. Otherwise, select the "PREC ID=3" entry and choose Get Info from the File menu. A window containing information about the resource opens. In the text box labelled ID, type *4*.

After adding the new PREC resource to the application, modify its page sizes as described in the previous section. Finally, close the application's resource window, and answer Yes when asked to save changes. To try the PREC 4 resource, start the application and use its Page Setup command as described earlier.

Using ResEdit's Get Info Command to Change File Characteristics

You can get information on a file or folder by selecting it and choosing Get Info from the File menu. As Figure 10-16 shows, ResEdit's Get Info window is quite unlike the Finder's, however. ResEdit's Get Info window shows the settings of the file's *file attributes*—a collection of settings and statistics used by the Finder and applications.

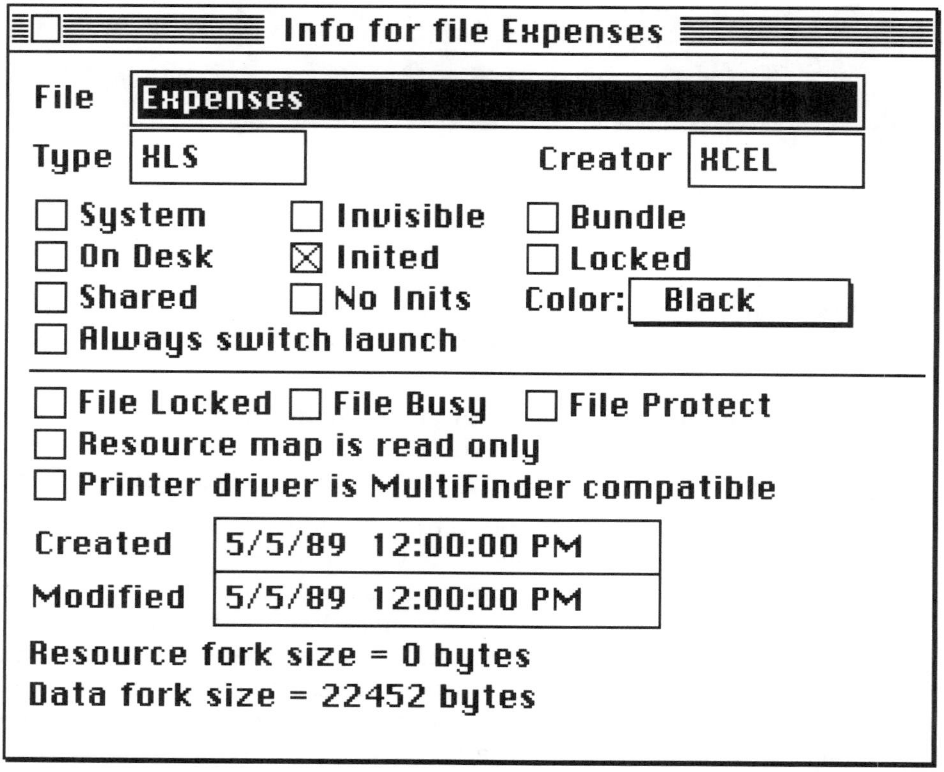

Figure 10-16: File attributes in ResEdit's Get Info window.

We'll explore the entire list of file attributes in Chapter 15. For now, let's concentrate on just one attribute: the *system* attribute. This attribute designates whether a file is a system file. The Finder uses the system attribute to determine whether to allow a file to be renamed. (Most system files must have specific names in order to operate; if the DA Handler file were renamed, for example, MultiFinder wouldn't be able to find it when you opened a desk accessory.)

You can activate the system attribute for any file or folder, and thus prevent it from being renamed. This can be especially useful if the file is used in a macro that expects to find a specific file name. Can't you prevent a file from being renamed by using the Finder's Get Info command to lock the file? Yes, but that also prevents modifications to the file. A file whose system attribute is activated can be modified or even deleted.

To activate a file's system attribute, select the file in ResEdit's directory window, choose Get Info, and click the System check box. Then close the Get Info box, and answer Yes when asked to save changes. If you need to rename the file later, simply deactivate the system attribute. Or, duplicate the file using the Finder, rename the duplicate, and throw away the original. When you duplicate a file whose system attribute is active, the Finder does not activate the system attribute in the duplicate.

Incidentally, ResEdit isn't the only tool you can use to alter file attributes. Programs that let you alter attributes include disk utilities and several file-management desk accessories.

Modifying MultiFinder

Do you frequently see out-of-memory messages when you try to open a desk accessory under MultiFinder? Are you tired of waiting for MultiFinder to open the DA Handler each time you open a desk accessory? With this customizing tip, MultiFinder 6.0's approach to desk accessories is reversed: Multi-Finder will use DA Handler only if you press Option while opening a desk accessory. Otherwise, desk accessories are opened in the current application layer. This tip is especially useful on Macs with only a megabyte or two of RAM, since they often don't have enough free memory to open DA Handler.

Performing this modification involves editing two of MultiFinder's CODE resources. Here's how:

1. Copy the MultiFinder file from your start-up disk to a blank floppy disk; you'll modify this duplicate. Also be sure you have a backup copy of the unmodified MultiFinder elsewhere.

2. Start ResEdit and open the duplicate copy of MultiFinder by double-clicking its name. ResEdit displays MultiFinder's resource window.

3. In MultiFinder's resource window, locate the CODE resource entry and open it by double-clicking it.

4. In the "CODEs from MultiFinder" window, locate and open the entry "CODE 'Main' ID=1".

   ResEdit displays the contents of the CODE resource in hexadecimal (base 16) form, and adds a Find menu to the menu bar.

5. Choose Find Hex from the Find menu.

   A window, titled "Change Hex," opens.

6. In the Find Hex text box, type *0200 0004 57c0 4400*. (We've placed spaces between each group of four characters to help you avoid losing your place as you type them. It doesn't matter if you type the spaces; ResEdit ignores any non-hexadecimal values you type in this window.)

7. In the Change To text box, type *0200 0004 56c0 4400*. As an alternative to typing the entire entry, select the values in the Find Hex box, copy them, then click in the Change To box and paste. Then edit the entry, changing the 7 to a 6.

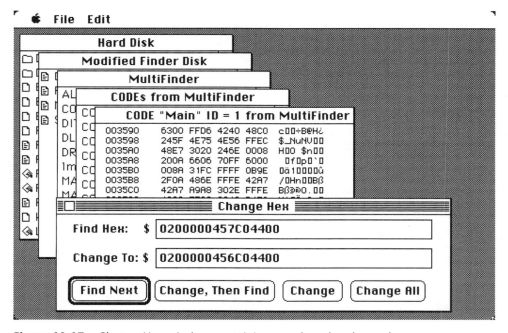

Figure 10-17:   Change Hex window containing search and replace values.

After you enter the values in both boxes, be sure the Change Hex window looks *exactly* like Figure 10-17. Don't proceed to the next step until it does.

8. When you're sure the search and replace values are correct, click the Change Hex window's Find button or press Return. If the Mac beeps, ResEdit wasn't able to find the text you specified; go over the previous steps and verify that the CODE resource named "Main" is open and that the values in the Change Hex window are correct.

9. If all went well, the Change Hex window's three Change buttons are enabled, indicating that ResEdit found the values. You might also have noticed that the "Main" resource's window scrolled slightly as ResEdit found the values and selected them. The values may be obscured by the Change Hex window; to verify that they are selected, drag the window to the top or bottom of the screen. (Don't close the window yet.)

10. Click the Change button to alter the values, then activate the CODE resource window and examine the selected values to verify that they're correct.

11. Close the "Main" resource's CODE window, but leave the "CODEs from MultiFinder" window open.

12. Open the CODE resource named "kernel_segment ID=3" by double-clicking on it.

13. Repeat steps 5 through 11 with the "kernel_segment" resource.

14. Choose Quit from the File menu, and answer Yes when asked to save changes to MultiFinder.

Trying the Modified MultiFinder

To try the modified MultiFinder, you need to copy it to your startup disk. To do so, you must not be running under MultiFinder. Restart under the Finder if necessary, and then—after verifying that you have a backup MultiFinder file elsewhere—copy the modified MultiFinder file to the System Folder of your start-up disk. When the Finder asks if you want to replace the existing Multi-Finder, answer OK.

After you've replaced the unmodified MultiFinder file, use the Set Startup command to specify that the Mac run under MultiFinder, then Restart. When the desktop appears, open a desk accessory. If the modification worked properly, the desk accessory opens in the Finder's layer. Next, open a desk accessory while pressing the Option key. This time, the Mac runs DA Handler and the desk accessory opens in its layer.

We've used this modified MultiFinder quite a bit. Sometimes a cosmetic quirk surfaces, such as part of a window not being redrawn when we switch between applications or from an application to the Finder. Otherwise, it works well.

Renaming Desk Accessories

If you have a favorite desk accessory that you'd like to move to the top of the Apple menu—or if you'd like to move a rarely used desk accessory to the bottom—this tip is for you. The list of desk accessories in the Apple menu is in alphabetical order. By renaming desk accessories, you can change the order in which they appear.

Renaming desk accessories that are already installed in the System file involves opening and editing the System file itself. If you want to rename an installed desk accessory, make a backup copy of your System file first, and modify the backup. You might prefer to simply modify a copy of the desk accessory, and then install the renamed desk accessory using the Font/DA Mover.

1. Start ResEdit and open the file (System or suitcase) containing the desk accessory to be renamed.

2. In the file's resource window, locate the "DRVR" entry and open it by double-clicking.

   A new window, "DRVRs from (*file name*)," appears. If you opened the System file, you'll see many entries, most beginning with "Desk Acc," as shown in Figure 10-18. (You'll also see some entries beginning with Driver. These are low-level routines that help the Mac communicate with the printer and other add-ons. Desk accessories and drivers share some common technical characteristics; that's why they're grouped together under the DRVR resource type.)

3. Locate the desk accessory you want to rename, and select it by clicking on it (just once), then choose Get Info from the File menu.

   ResEdit displays a Get Info window for the desk accessory.

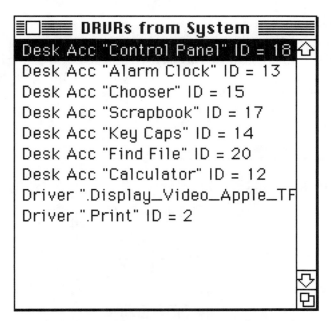

Figure 10-18: DRVR resources in a typical System file.

4. In the Name text box, edit the desk accessory's name as desired. Don't change any other entries in the Get Info window.

   To move a desk accessory to the top of the Apple menu, type a space or punctuation character before its name. Avoid using the following characters: ; ^ ! < / (. These characters denote certain menu characteristics, such as Command-key shortcuts or a disabled menu command. The Mac may not be able to create the Apple menu properly if you use them in a desk accessory name.

5. Close the Get Info window and repeat steps 3 and 4 for each desk accessory you're renaming.

6. Choose Quit from the File menu and answer Yes when asked to save changes.

   If you modified a backup copy of your System file, you'll need to replace your original System file to see the renamed desk accessory. (Remember that you can't replace the System file on the current start-up disk.) If you modified a desk accessory in a suitcase file, use the Font/DA Mover to install the desk accessory.

Altering Dialog Boxes

Another customizing job you might want to tackle is altering the appearance of the dialog boxes your applications display. The most useful dialog box modification you can make is to lengthen the text boxes into which you type values or text, and to lengthen the list boxes that allow you to choose documents to open. Both modifications will allow you to see longer file names, as shown in Figure 10-19.

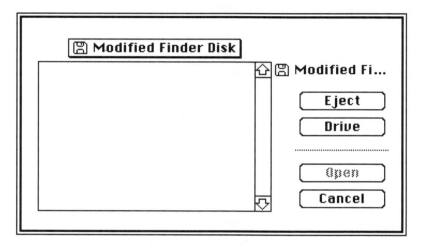

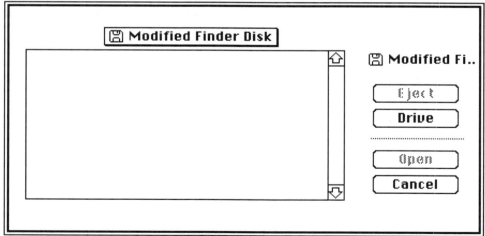

Figure 10-19: An unmodified Open dialog box (*top*) and its modified counterpart (*bottom*).

Altering a dialog box is one of the riskier ResEdit modifications you can make. Applications generally expect their dialog boxes to contain a specific number of items, and you can cause a program to crash by adding items to or removing them from a dialog box. We'll provide more guidelines and cautions at the end of this section.

Altering the Open Dialog Box

In this exercise, we'll use ResEdit to alter the Mac's standard Open dialog box to show longer file names. The resources for both dialog boxes are stored in the System file. For safety's sake, perform these modifications on a backup copy of the System file.

1. Start ResEdit and open the backup copy of the System file.

2. In the System file's resource window, locate and open the "DLOG" entry.

3. A window, "DLOGs from System," opens, listing the dialog box templates in the System file.

4. Locate the entry "DLOG ID = -4000" and open it.

A window appears showing a small facsimile of the Open dialog box, as shown in Figure 10-20.

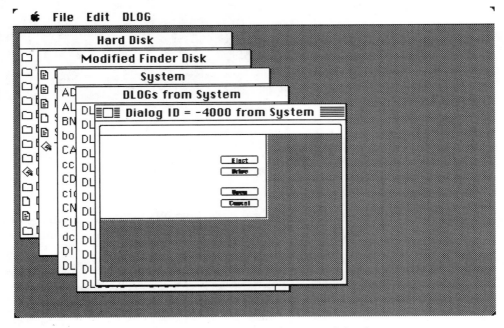

Figure 10-20: A dialog box editing window for the Open dialog box.

The first step in allowing the dialog box to show longer names is to make the dialog box wider. The extra width will provide the additional real estate needed to accommodate the wider list box. Resizing the dialog box is similar to resizing a window: first, point to its lower-right corner, then drag until the dialog box is the desired size.

5. Resize the dialog box until its width resembles the dialog box shown in Figure 10-21.

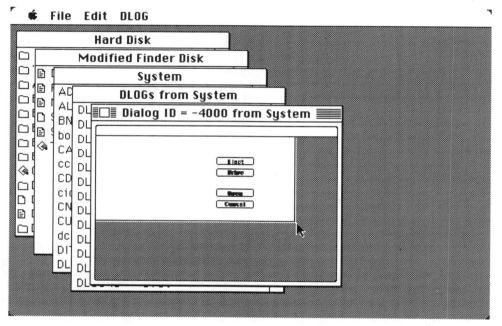

Figure 10-21:   The resized Open dialog box.

Next, you'll drag the Eject, Drive, Open, and Cancel buttons to the right. To do so, you need to edit the dialog box's DITL resource—its dialog item list.

6. Double click within the small Open dialog box.

The *DITL editor* window appears (Figure 10-22) and three menus—DLOG, Font, and Size—appear on the menu bar. Do not choose any commands from these menus.

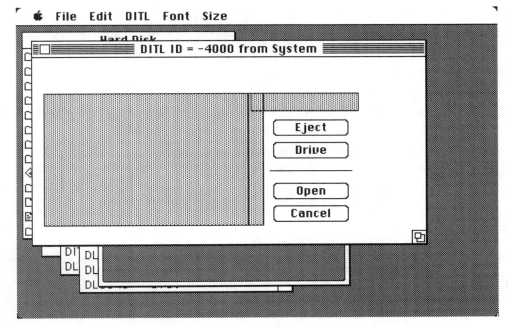

Figure 10-22:   Dialog editor for the Open dialog box.

The DITL editor shows each item of the dialog box in its actual size. The gray-shaded areas represent *user items*—items whose appearance and purpose are defined by the application or system routine that uses the dialog box. Some common user items include scroll bars, list boxes, pop-up menus, and lines that separate options. (The horizontal line between the Drive and Open buttons is a user item.)

Repositioning the Dialog Items

In the next steps, you'll reposition the buttons, moving them further to the right. To keep the dialog box neat and tidy, be sure the buttons' left and right edges align. To do so, you'll activate the DITL editor's alignment grid. The alignment grid divides the window into an invisible grid of boxes, each eight pixels square, and ensures that the boundary of any item you resize or drag rests on one of the grid's dividing lines.

1. Choose Align to Grid from the DITL menu.

2. Drag the Eject, Drive, Open, and Cancel buttons to the right until they're about a quarter of an inch from the right edge of the window. You'll need to drag the buttons one at a time; ResEdit's dialog editor, unlike many drawing

and publishing programs, doesn't let you select multiple objects. Nor can you hold a Shift key to constrain an object's movement so that it moves only horizontally.

3. Disable the alignment grid by choosing Align to Grid again.

4. Reposition the horizontal line and the gray user item that was directly above the Eject button. The horizontal line is a scant one pixel tall; you might have some trouble selecting it.

At this stage of the game, the DITL window resembles Figure 10-23. You've moved the dialog box's buttons and their corresponding user items, creating a wide gap between the buttons and the list box. In the next steps, you'll resize and reposition the list box and scroll bar user items to fill that gap.

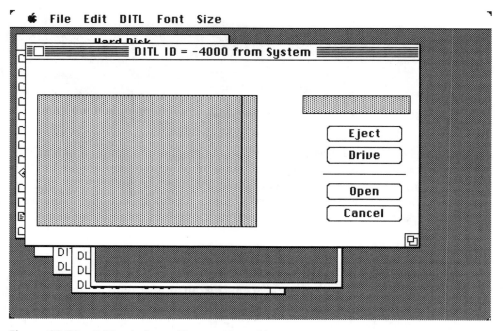

Figure 10-23: DITL window with repositioned buttons.

1. The scroll bar user item is the narrow, shaded vertical bar immediately to the left of the large shaded rectangle. Drag the scroll bar to the right until it's about a quarter of an inch to the left of the pop-up menu user item.

2. Resize the list box user item by dragging its lower-right corner to the right. Fine-tune its size until the right edge of the list box abuts the left edge of the scroll bar, as shown in Figure 10-24.

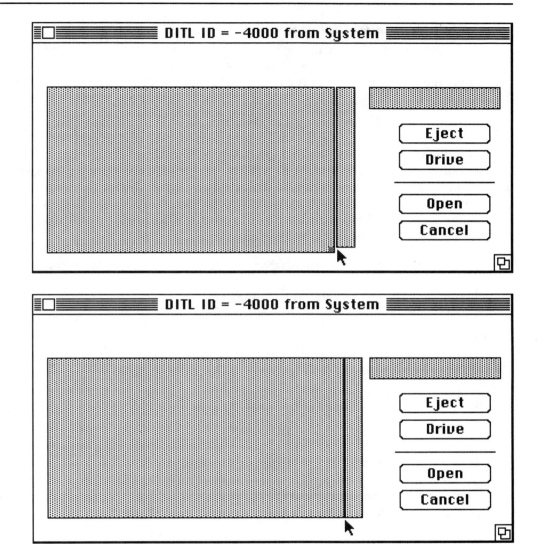

Figure 10-24: The resized and repositioned list box and scroll bar: wrong (*top*) and right (*bottom*).

3. Finished at last. Look the dialog box over and verify that it resembles the lower half of Figure 10-24, then quit ResEdit and answer Yes when asked to save changes.

Trying the Altered Dialog Box

Before taking the new dialog box out for a spin, you'll need to replace the System file on your start-up disk (after verifying that you have a backup copy elsewhere) or copy a Finder file to the floppy containing the modified System file.

To try the modified dialog box, you need to use a program that uses the standard Open dialog box. (Many programs contain DLOG resources that override the standard Open dialog box—just as some programs contain PREC 4 resources that override the ImageWriter driver's PREC 3 resource.) One program that does use the standard dialog box is Apple's TeachText, which lets you view and edit text files. In the System Update 6.0 package, there's a copy of TeachText on the System Tools disk. Figure 10-25 shows the modified Open dialog box as it's displayed by TeachText.

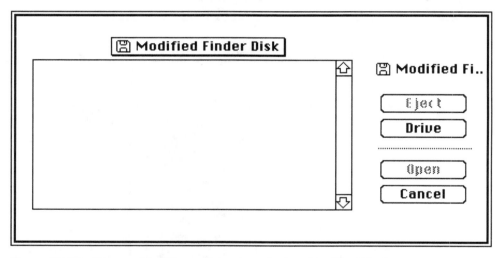

Figure 10-25:   The modified Open dialog box displayed by TeachText.

Altering the Save Dialog Box

You might also want to modify the System file's standard Save dialog box to show larger file names. You can use the same basic techniques you used to alter the Open dialog box. The Save dialog box's DLOG ID is -3999. Figure 10-26 shows how a modified Save dialog box compares to the original.

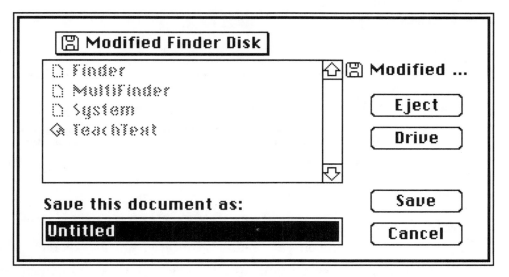

Figure 10-26: The original Save dialog box (*top*) and the modified version (*bottom*).

Remember that many programs contain DLOG resources that override the System file's standard Open and Save resources. If you want to see longer file names in such programs, you'll need to modify their DLOG resources. Table 10-3 lists the resource ID numbers of the Open and Save DLOG resources in several popular programs. The entry "none" means that the program uses the System file's standard DLOG resource; "n/a" means the program doesn't have a Save command.

Table 10-3: DLOG resource ID numbers for Open and Save commands.

Program	Open DLOG ID	Save DLOG ID
Adobe Font Downloader 3.30	-4000	none
Aldus PageMaker 3.0[1]	-358	-3999
Apple LaserWriter Font Utility	4000	n/a
Claris MacDraw II 1.1	none	3999
Claris MacPaint 2.0	-4000	-3999
Font/DA Mover 3.8	300	301
Letraset Ready,Set,Go! 4.5[2]	none	none
Microsoft Excel 2.2	258	257
Microsoft Word 4.0	-3998	256
Microsoft Works 2.0[3]	134	135
QuarkXpress 2.0[4]	none	152
T/Maker WriteNow 2.0	135	134

[1] For PageMaker's File menu's Open and Save commands; PageMaker's Place command uses DLOG ID 360.

[2] Ready,Set,Go! 4.5's Get Text command uses DLOG ID 5520; Put Text uses 5500.

[3] For Works' File menu's Open and Save commands only; Works contains many other DLOG resources for the menus' other Open and Save commands (such as the Macro menu's).

[4] QuarkXpress's Export command uses DLOG ID 167; Transfer uses ID 168; Auxiliary Dictionary uses 146.

Notes About Modifying Dialog Boxes

Here are a few comments and cautions concerning dialog box remodeling.

- Be careful to not delete any items from a dialog box. As mentioned previously, applications generally expect their dialog boxes to contain a specific number of items, and are likely to crash if they don't.

- As you experiment with dialog box editing, you're likely to encounter a special character code that begins with a caret (^) and ends with a number, as in ^0 or ^1. Don't edit these items; they're placeholders that the application will replace with text. For example, you might see a sentence reading "Save changes to ^0?" When the program is running, it will replace the code ^0 with the name of a file.

- If you double-click on a dialog box item, a window appears that lets you change its type (from check box to button, for example). Changing an item from one type to another is likely to cause a program to crash.

- The DITL menu that appears when a DLOG resource is open contains commands that let you change the order in which the dialog box's contents are drawn (Bring to Front, Send to Back), and the number of each item within the dialog box (Set Item Number). Don't use these commands when editing an application's dialog boxes.

Modifying the Finder

Versions 5.3 through 6.1 of the Finder file contain a *layout* resource that specifies a hodgepodge of Finder settings. From the customizer's viewpoint, the most interesting settings include:

- the font and size used to label icons

- the spacing of icons in directory windows

- the size of the headers and footers the Finder prints when you use the Print Directory command

- the line spacing of the Finder's text views (that is, all views except By Icon and By Small Icon)

- the view used for new directory windows

- the date format used by text views and the Get Info window

- whether the Finder displays a warning when you throw away an application file

- whether the Finder "snaps" icons that you drag to an invisible grid.

The Finder's layout resource has a resource name of LAYO. If you open the LAYO resource using ResEdit, you'll see a window similar to Figure 10-27.

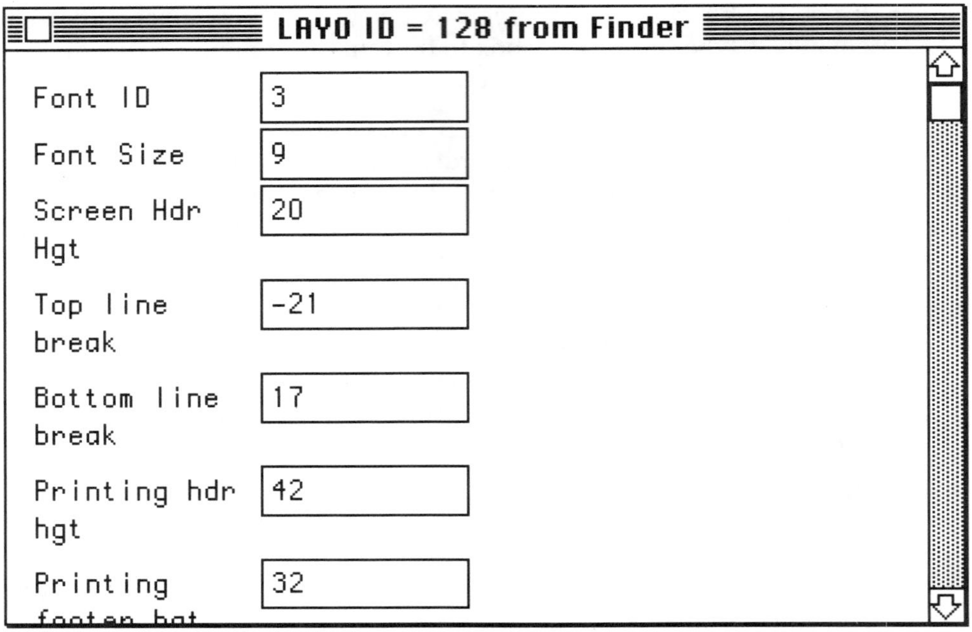

Figure 10-27: The Finder's LAYO resource.

Table 10-4 describes the contents of the LAYO resource in Finder 6.1. (If you're using an older version of ResEdit, such as 1.0, you may not see all the items described here.)

Table 10-4: Inside the Finder's LAYO resource.

Item Name	Preset Value	Purpose
Font ID	3	Font used by Finder (Geneva)
Font Size	9	Font size used by Finder (9 point)
Screen Hdr Hgt	20[1]	Size of information bar that appears at the top of directory windows
Top line break	-21[1]	
Bottom line break	17[1]	
Printing hdr hgt	42[1]	Height of header when printing directory
Printing footer hgt	32[1]	Height of footer when printing directory

(continued)

Table 10-4: Inside the Finder's LAYO resource. *(continued)*

Item Name	Preset Value	Purpose
Window Rect (top)	62[1]	Size and position of new directory windows (measured from the upper-left corner of the screen)
Window Rect (left)	14[1]	
Window Rect (bottom)	250[1]	
Window Rect (right)	418[1]	
Line spacing	16[1]	Line spacing of text views
Tab stop 1	20[1]	Position (from left) of Name column
Tab stop 2	144[1]	Position (from left) of Size column
Tab stop 3	184[1]	Position (from left) of Kind column
Tab stop 4	280[1]	Position (from left) of Date column
Tab stop 5	376[1]	Position (from left) of Time column
Tab stop 6	424[1]	(not used)
Tab stop 7	456[1]	(not used)
Column Justification	$02	Justification of text views; $02 means only Size is right-justified
Reserved	$00	(not used)
Icon Horz. spacing	64[1]	Horizontal space between icons
Icon Vert. spacing	64[1]	Vertical space between icons
Icon Vert. phase	0[1]	Staggers every other column of icons (16 is a good value)
Sm. Icon Horz.	96[1]	Horizontal spacing for Small Icon view
Sm. Icon Vert.	20[1]	Vertical spacing for Small Icon view
Default View	1	Preset view for new directory windows: 0 for by Small Icon 1 for by Icon 2 for by Name 3 for by Size 4 for by Kind 5 for by Date

(continued)

Table 10-4: Inside the Finder's LAYO resource. *(continued)*

Item Name	Preset Value	Purpose
Text view date	$0200	Date format for text views: $0200: "Mon, Apr 21, 1989" $0100: "Monday, April 21, 1989" $0000: "4/21/89"
Use zoom Rects	1	Set to 0 to disable "Open" zoom animation (Finder windows and applications open slightly faster)
Skip trash warnings	0	Set to 1 to skip trash warnings (Finder doesn't warn you if you throw away an application)
Always grid drags	0	Set to 1 for automatic clean-up (handy for keeping icons neatly aligned)
Unused 4	0	(not used)
Unused 3	0	(not used)
Unused 2	0	(not used)
Unused 1	0	(not used)
Unused 0	0	(not used)
Icon-text gap	01	Distance between icon and its text label
Sort style	4	Determine how current view is indicated in heading of directory windows: 0: plain text 1: bold 2: italic 3: bold italic 4: underline (default setting) 5: bold underline 6: italic underline 7: bold italic underline (values higher than 7 produce unattractive results)
Watch Threshold	120	Time before wristwatch hands spin (in 1/60-second units)
Unused 7	0	(not used)
Unused 6	0	(not used)

(continued)

Table 10-4: Inside the Finder's LAYO resource. *(continued)*

Item Name	Preset Value	Purpose
Unused 5	0	(not used)
Unused 4	0	(not used)
Use Phys Icon	0	When 1, shows the physical icon of a disk on the desktop (lets you quickly see which drive a floppy is inserted in)
Title Click	0	If 1, you can double-click a window's title bar to open the window of the next-higher folder in the storage hierarchy.
Copy Inherit	0	When 1, a folder copied using AppleShare has the same access privileges as the parent folder (see Chapter 12)
New Fold Inherit	0	When 1, a folder created within an AppleShare folder has the same access privileges as the parent folder (see Chapter 12)
Color Style	0	Defines which colors are available in Finder's Color menu (color Macs only)
Max # of windows	13	Maximum number of windows Finder can open

[1] This value is measured in pixels.

Altering the LAYO Resource

You can use ResEdit to alter the LAYO resource, but there are easier ways. A free program called Layout (by Michael O'Connor) lets you alter the LAYO resource by dragging icons and choosing menu commands (see Figure 10-28). Layout is available through user's groups and information services.

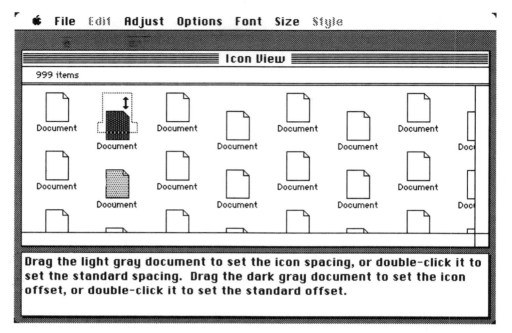

Figure 10-28: Adjusting vertical icon phase using Michael O'Connor's Layout utility.

Other ResEdit Projects

Let's wrap up our look at resource customizing with a look at a few more customizing projects you might want to try.

Altering icons. The icons an application uses for its own file and its documents are stored in an application's ICN# resource. You can edit those icons to give them a different appearance—perhaps to indicate that the application is modified, or to show its version number. As Figure 10-29 shows, ResEdit's *icon editor* works similarly to the FatBits display that most painting programs provide—the icon appears enlarged, and you can turn individual pixels on or off. An icon has two components: the icon itself and the *mask*, which the Finder uses to indicate a selected icon. After altering an application or document icon, rebuild your disk's DeskTop file to update its icon list. (Remember that you'll lose Get Info comments by rebuilding the DeskTop file.)

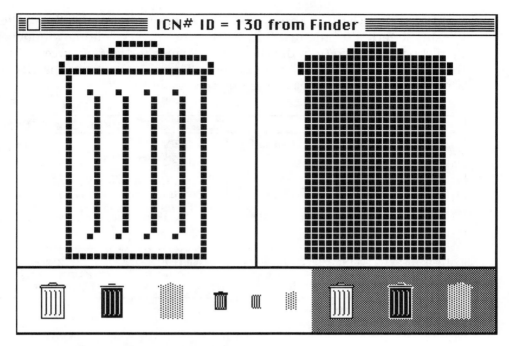

Figure 10-29: ResEdit's icon editor.

Altering cursors. The appearance of an application's pointers are stored in CURS resources. You can alter those resources to customize your cursors. ResEdit's *cursor editor* is similar to the icon editor. The CURS resource in Finder versions 5.5 through 6.1 contains seven wristwatch cursors that create the moving hands in the wristwatch. Try altering the cursor resources to create some other type of animation—perhaps a spinning beach ball, a smiling and frowning face, or an hourglass with sand running through it.

Adding version resources to documents. Most applications contain one or more *vers* resources that the Finder uses to report each application's version number in its Get Info window. You can also add a version resource to a document. You might use a version resource in a document to indicate which revision the document represents, or to add some descriptive text that people won't be able to change using the Get Info window. To add a version resource to a document, open the document using ResEdit. (If you're warned that the document doesn't contain a resource fork, read the second paragraph of this tip before proceeding). Next, choose New and select "vers" in the Select New Type list box. When the "verss from (*file name*)" window appears, choose New again. ResEdit's vers-editing window appears. Press Tab until the insertion point is in the "Get Info String" text box, then type up to two lines of text, pressing Return after the first line. Next, close the vers-editing window and then choose Get Info from the File menu. Change the vers resource's ID to 1, then close the file and save your changes. Figure 10-30 shows the Get Info windows of two documents containing vers resources.

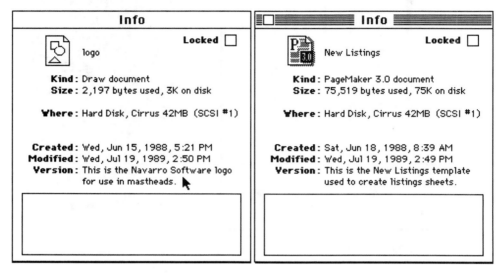

Figure 10-30:   Get Info windows for documents containing vers resources.

Some applications (including PageMaker, Microsoft Word, and Microsoft Works) create documents that lack resource forks. You can create one, however, by clicking OK when asked by ResEdit. We successfully added resource forks to PageMaker, Word, and Works documents without damaging the documents, but not all applications may be as accommodating. You might want to experiment with some backup copies of documents before adding vers resources to important ones.

Altering fonts. ResEdit's *font editor*, shown in Figure 10-31, lets you edit the FONT and NFNT resources that describe the appearance of bit-mapped screen fonts. You might, for example, replace a rarely used character with a special character such as a fraction. Remember that the Mac doesn't use these fonts to produce output on PostScript printers; changes you make will apply only to the screen and to QuickDraw printers such as ImageWriters and the Laser-Writer IISC. To edit PostScript printer fonts, you need a specialized font-editing utility such as Altsys Corporation's Fontographer.

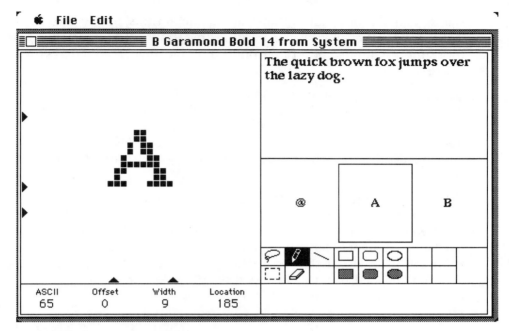

Figure 10-31: ResEdit's font-editor

CUSTOMIZING WITH ACCESSORIES

In this section, we'll look at ways to customize the Mac by using desk accessories, Inits, cdevs, and FKEYs. There isn't room to discuss every category of accessory, so we'll concentrate on customizing-oriented accessories. Many of the programs described here aren't commercial offerings, but are distributed through the Mac's remarkable "shareware" network. Before looking at specific products let's take a look at the shareware concept.

About Shareware

Shareware programs aren't sold in stores and they don't come from large commercial software firms. Instead, they're generally developed by Mac programming enthusiasts in response to requests from fellow users. The shareware concept is simple: Try the program at no charge for a week or two. If you don't like it, erase the disk or give it away. If you do like it, send the author a contribution, usually between $5 and $25. Most shareware authors encourage you to distribute their programs to others, provided that you include any documentation that accompanied the program and that the recipient understands that the program is shareware. Some authors simply give their programs away; others have some amusing "registration" requirements. One author simply requests a post card from your home town; another asks for $15 or a case of beer.

Shareware programs are generally distributed through user's groups, information services such as CompuServe and Connect, and shareware clearinghouses such as Educorp (addresses for these firms appear in Appendix B). The manuals for shareware programs are generally disk files that you print using your word processor. Some shareware authors offer printed manuals for an additional fee.

Shareware is often distributed in a *compressed* form that uses less disk space. This allows manuals to be included with the program, and it reduces the time required to transfer the software over phone lines. To *decompress* the files, you need a utility such as Raymond Lau's StuffIt, which is, itself, a shareware program. (StuffIt is also useful for "archiving" old disk files for backup purposes, since compressed files use far less disk space. And it's handy for squeezing backup copies of huge System files onto floppy disks.)

Shareware can be an economical way to expand your software library, but there are potential drawbacks. Unlike commercial software publishers, shareware programmers don't have formal testing departments; they rely on networks of friends and fellow users to test their wares and find bugs. Thus, the first releases of shareware programs often have bugs. It's common to see an update or two appear on an information service within a few days or weeks of a program's release. Also, unless a particular program becomes popular, it may not be updated as new system versions are released. Many older shareware programs don't run reliably under today's system software.

Finally, because of their informal distribution network, shareware programs can be carriers of computer *viruses*—software created by programming vandals. Viruses are designed to invade your System file or applications, where they can damage data and cause system errors. Most user's groups and information services diligently check new contributions for viruses, but that's no guarantee a program you copy will be virus-free. The chances of your system being "infected" by a computer virus are very small, but they do increase if you frequently trade shareware.

These cautions aren't intended to steer you away from shareware. A wonderful variety of programs is available through this informal and friendly distribution network, and you're encouraged to sample them. And if you do find a program you like and use, reward its author. You'll help keep the shareware system alive.

Replacing the Finder

Returning to the Finder to copy or delete files or perform other disk-management tasks can be time consuming. Even when you're running under MultiFinder, you might not feel like switching back to the Finder to rummage through disk folders and directory windows. The solution? A desk accessory that lets you start programs and manage disks and folders. Figure 10-32 shows CE Software's DiskTop, which can do almost everything the Finder can. You can even add frequently used documents and applications to DiskTop's menu, where they're just a mouse click away. DiskTop can also search for files using several criteria, including name, size, and date of creation or modification.

Another full-featured disk-management desk accessory is Electronic Arts' DiskTools II. If you're simply interested in moving from one program to another without using the Finder, consider IMI Software's SafeLaunch (shareware; $5).

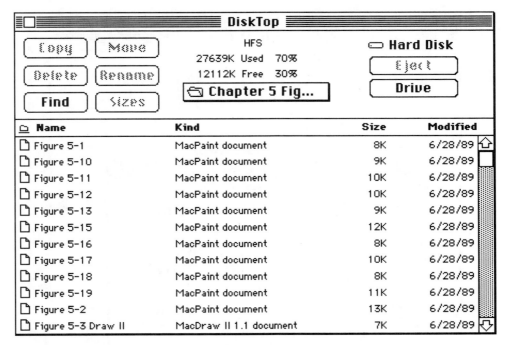

Figure 10-32: CE Software's DiskTop desk accessory.

Showing Your True Colors

As you may recall from Chapter 3, Apple takes a conservative approach to using color in the Mac's user interface. Using Palomar Software's Colorizer cdev, however, you can throw conservatism to the wind and add color to virtually every component of the user interface. As Figure 10-33 shows (in black and white), Colorizer includes a variety of preset color schemes, such as "Fourth of July," which creates a red, white, and blue theme, and "Miami Vice," which gives you pastels that Don Johnson would be proud of. You can also create your own color schemes. The Colorizer cdev also lets you create a color start-up screen that appears instead of the "Welcome to Macintosh" message.

The Colorizer package also includes an FKEY that lets you take color or grey-scale snapshots by pressing Command-Shift-5. The color snapshots are saved in a standard color file format called *PICT2*. (We'll explore this and other file formats in the next chapter.)

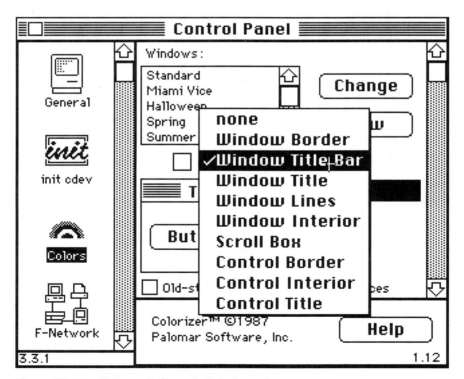

Figure 10-33: Palomar Software's Colorizer cdev.

Sounding Off

The Mac's digitally recorded alert sounds are entertaining, but you might get tired of them after a while. By adding additional sound (snd) resources to your System file, you can enlarge the Mac's audio repertoire. A vast array of prerecorded sounds is available through user's groups, or you can record your own using Farallon Computing's MacRecorder (described in Chapter 14). If you have the MacRecorder's SoundEdit software, you can use its Save As command to install a sound in the System file.

You can also use ResEdit to add snd resources to your System file. Here's how:

1. Start ResEdit and open the file containing the snd resource you want to add to the System file.

2. Locate the "snd" entry in the file's resource window and open it.

3. Locate the desired sound in the "snds from (*file name*)" window, then select it and choose Copy from the Edit menu. (You can also use the "snd" menu to play the sound if you like.)

4. Close the file and open the System file.

5. Locate the "snd" entry in the System file's window, and then open it.

6. With the "snds from System" window open, choose Paste.

7. Close the System file, saving your changes when asked.

8. Use the Control Panel's Sound option to select the new sound as the current alert beep.

Another way to copy sounds into the System file is to use a utility called The Sound Man (Tekton Software; $10 shareware fee).

As an alternative to installing sounds into your System file, you can use a cdev called SoundMaster (Bruce Tonkin; $10 shareware fee). SoundMaster plays sound files that you store in the System Folder. As Figure 10-34 shows, SoundMaster can also play different sounds when different events occur, such as when you insert or eject a disk.

Another noteworthy sound accessory is a free Init called Chime (by Robert Flickinger), which can play up to four different sounds at 15-minute intervals. The copy of Chime available on CompuServe includes a nicely recorded cuckoo clock sound.

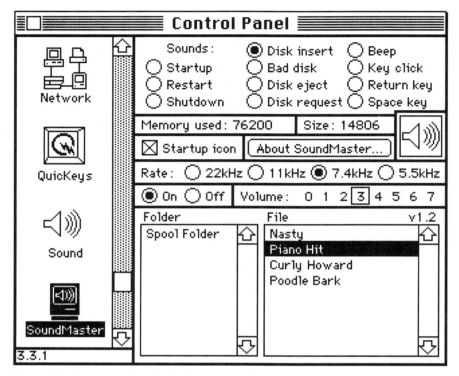

Figure 10-34: Bruce Tonkin's SoundMaster cdev.

Incidentally, if you use a system version prior to 6.0.2, you can still enjoy digitally recorded alert beeps by using a free Init and cdev package called CheapBeep (by Mark Bennett). CheapBeep works with System versions as old as 4.1.

Screen Blankers

As mentioned in the previous chapter, it's a good idea to turn your monitor's brightness down when you aren't using the Mac to prevent burning an image into the screen. Because it's easy to forget to turn the brightness down, you might prefer to use a screen blanker. Screen blankers, also called *screen savers*, replace the Mac's screen image with a continuously changing graphic pattern or moving icon that prevents image burn-in. Some screen blankers, such as the free Stars II, are desk accessories that swing into action when you choose them from the Apple menu. Others are Inits that automatically run after a specified period of inactivity. One popular Init-based screen saver is Pyro, which is included with Fifth Generation Systems' Suitcase II (described next). As its name implies, Pyro creates a fireworks-like display.

Managing Your System Resources

A fully accessorized Mac—one loaded with fonts, desk accessories, FKEYs, and sounds—is likely to have a huge System file. Backing up a colossal System file can be awkward, and adding or removing fonts and other system resources is time consuming. If you're fond of fonts and other system resources, consider using Fifth Generation Systems' Suitcase II. When you use Suitcase II, you don't have to install system resources in the System file in order to use them. You can access fonts and desk accessories stored in suitcase files, and FKEYs and snd resources in their own separate files. Suitcase II works behind the scenes to make these resources look like they're installed in the System file: desk accessories and fonts appear in the Apple and Fonts menus, and sounds and FKEYs work as they normally would. And if you press the Option key while opening a Font menu, Suitcase II displays each font in its own typeface, as shown in Figure 10-35.

Besides the Pyro screen blanker, the Suitcase II package includes two additional utilities: Font Harmony, which resolves font ID number conflicts and unclutters font menus by removing stylistic variants; and Font and Sound Valet, which compresses fonts and snd resources to use roughly half as much disk space, and then uncompresses them as they're needed. Suitcase II works with any Mac running System 4.1 or a later version. You're not likely to need it with System 7.0, however, since System 7.0 will allow you to install system resources by simply dragging them to the System file.

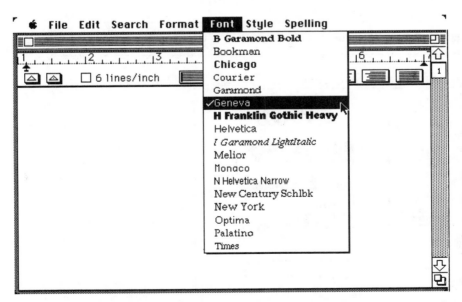

Figure 10-35: With Suitcase II, Font menu entries can appear in their own typefaces.

Managing Inits

If you have a flock of Inits in your System Folder, chances are you occasionally need to disable one or more of them to free up some memory or ferret out a troublemaker. Dragging Inits into and out of the System Folder is tedious; a better way is to use an Init-management cdev such as Init by John Rotenstein (free). When you click on Init, it lists all the Init and Chooser files in your System Folder. You can click on individual Inits to disable them. A fancier Init manager is CE Software's Aask, which is included with MockPackage, a collection of handy desk accessories, Inits, and cdevs. Unlike Init, Aask also lists how much memory each cdev uses. Figure 10-36 shows both the Init and Aask cdevs in action.

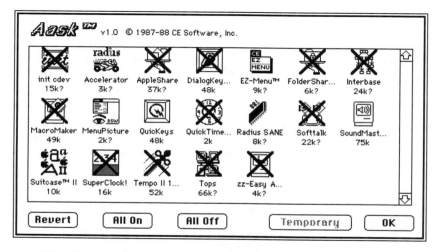

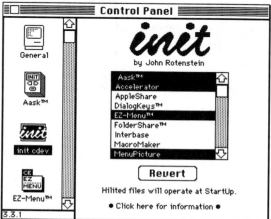

Figure 10-36: The Aask cdev (*top*) and the Init cdev (*bottom*).

CHAPTER SUMMARY

This chapter showed how you can use ResEdit and other utility programs to customize the way the Mac works, looks, and sounds. Although this chapter provided dozens of customizing suggestions and techniques, it still didn't cover the entire range of customizing options available to Mac users. A visit to a local user's group or some time spent browsing through a shareware clearing-house catalog will reveal still more ways to tailor your Mac to your working style. Some users scoff at the notion of customizing a computer, but they're missing an important point: When a machine looks and works the way you want it to, you'll feel more comfortable using it, and you're likely to use it more.

Section III

Exchanging and Sharing

11

Exchanging Data

Regardless of how you use your Mac, chances are you need to exchange data now and then. Perhaps you need to transfer a chart created in a spreadsheet program to a desktop publishing document. Or maybe you need to transfer a report you've been working on at home to a colleague in the office. And perhaps that colleague uses a MS-DOS computer such as the IBM PC.

In this chapter, we'll look at ways to accomplish all of these tasks. We'll examine:

- the fine points of the Mac's Clipboard

- common file formats you can use to exchange data between programs

- translation programs you can use to translate one kind of file into another kind

- how to transfer files between Macs and MS-DOS computers such as the IBM PC

- the enhanced data-exchange features of System 7.0.

There are two basic goals behind any data exchange endeavor: getting information from Point A to Point B, *and* retaining its formatting—its fonts, type sizes, margins, and so on. As we'll see in this chapter, retaining formatting isn't always easy.

CLIPBOARD DETAILS

The Mac's Clipboard makes it easy to move relatively small pieces of information between programs and desk accessories. As you may recall from Chapter 3, the Clipboard relies on three Edit menu commands: Cut, Copy, and Paste. The Cut command removes whatever you've selected and puts it on the Clipboard. The Copy command puts the selection on the Clipboard without removing it from the document. (Both Cut and Copy replace the Clipboard's previous contents.) The Paste command inserts the Clipboard's contents into the active document.

Pretty straightforward, right? Most of the time. But there are times when you can't retain the formatting of the data you're transferring. You might move some text from one program to another, and find that it no longer appears in its original font or size, or that you can no longer edit it. Or, you might move a graphic from MacDraw to MacPaint and find that you can't alter it as you had planned.

To understand why these formatting foibles can occur, let's step back and look at how the Clipboard handles the data that you cut and paste.

Clipboard Data Formats

When you cut or copy something to the Clipboard, your application program must store it in a specific *format*. Clipboard formats specify how the information on the Clipboard is organized. Just as the Betamax and VHS formats specify how a videocassette recorder accesses a videotape, the Mac's Clipboard formats specify how applications access the Clipboard.

The Mac provides three standard Clipboard formats:

PICT. A QuickDraw *picture*, a series of commands that allow QuickDraw to recreate an image. The PICT Clipboard format can represent monochrome or color bit-mapped and object-oriented graphics. (If you aren't familiar with the differences between bit-mapped and object-oriented graphics, see the section below, "Graphics in Two Flavors.")

styl. The styl format allows applications to place formatted text on the Clipboard. Any application that can read the styl format can accept the text with no loss of formatting information.

TEXT. A series of text characters with no formatting information. Technically speaking, the TEXT format stores only *ASCII characters*. ASCII stands for *American Standard Code for Information Interchange*, a standard that most computer manufacturers use for representing the alphabet, numerals, punctuation symbols, and certain rudimentary formatting codes such as carriage returns and tab characters. We'll encounter ASCII again later in this chapter.

Graphics in Two Flavors

If you use graphics and publishing programs extensively, it's important to understand the differences between bit-mapped and *object-oriented* graphics programs.

Bit-mapped graphics programs include Claris's MacPaint, SuperMac Software's PixelPaint, and Ashton-Tate's FullPaint, to name a few. Although these programs differ in their features and capabilities, all share a common trait: they store an image as a series of bits, each mapped to a pixel (a single dot) on the screen. You can't easily resize a shape or edit text that you've created in a bit-mapped graphics program. You must erase the old shape or text and then replace it. Bit-mapped graphics programs are often called *painting* programs or *paint-type* programs.

Object-oriented programs don't store pixel bit maps. Instead, they store QuickDraw commands that describe distinct objects—circles, lines, boxes filled with a pattern, text, and so on. It's easy to alter a shape or edit text in a drawing; when you do, the program replaces the QuickDraw commands that described the old object with ones that describe its altered version. Object-oriented programs are often called *drawing* programs or *draw-type* programs. Drawing programs include Claris's MacDraw II, Cricket Software's Cricket Draw, Deneba Software's Canvas, Adobe's Illustrator 88, and Aldus's Free-Hand.

The differences between paint programs and drawing programs are similar to the differences between bit-mapped and outline fonts. Bit-mapped images generally become distorted when they're resized, while object-oriented images can be resized without distortion. Bit-mapped images are tied to a specific resolution (generally, to the Mac's screen resolution, although some paint programs can create 300-dpi images). Object-oriented images aren't locked into a specific resolution; like outline fonts, they can take advantage of the maximum resolution a printer provides.

But bit-mapped graphics programs are generally able to render subtle shading and gray tones better than object-oriented programs; that's one reason why scanners create bit-mapped images rather than object-oriented ones. Object-oriented programs are generally better for creating precise line art; that's why they're used for architectural drawings and technical illustrations.

Private Clipboard Formats

In addition to the PICT, styl, and TEXT Clipboard formats, the Clipboard can also work with *private* Clipboard formats—data formats defined by a specific application to handle the data that application creates. Generally, applications use private Clipboard formats to enable the Clipboard to hold more formatting information than the Clipboard's standard formats allow.

For example, Aldus PageMaker 3.0 uses a private Clipboard format called ALD3 that allows PageMaker to differentiate between formatted text, images, and graphic elements such as lines and boxes. This private Clipboard format lets you copy and paste combinations of text and graphics between PageMaker documents. Without the private Clipboard format, if you copied a combination of text and graphic elements to the Clipboard and then pasted them back into a PageMaker document, PageMaker wouldn't be able to treat each element separately. It would have to treat everything as text (thereby discarding the graphics) or as a graphic (eliminating the ability to edit the text).

Some applications use more than one private Clipboard format. Microsoft Excel 2.2, for example, uses three. Each Clipboard format contains a different type of formatting information about what you cut or copied.

Why All the Formats?

When you cut or copy something, an application generally places the data on the Clipboard in its private formats *and* in one or more of the standard Clipboard formats. (Some applications, however, use only the standard formats.) By storing Clipboard data in more than one format, an application increases your chances of being able to move that information into another program while retaining its formatting information. If the program receiving the data can interpret the original program's private Clipboard format, you're in luck—you'll be able to transfer the data without losing any formatting information. (In computer jargon, the process of moving data out of a program is called *exporting*; as you might expect, bringing data into a program is called *importing*.)

If the importing program can't interpret the private Clipboard formats, it resorts to the standard Clipboard formats and reads the data as text or as a picture, depending on which format the program prefers (see Figure 11-1). For example, word processors will choose the TEXT format over PICT. Graphics-oriented programs, however, will generally choose PICT instead of TEXT.

How can you tell which Clipboard formats your favorite programs use? Manuals rarely contain that kind of information, but you can find out by using the Scrapbook desk accessory. Simply cut or copy some data from a document, and then open the Scrapbook and choose Paste. The list of Clipboard formats in which the data is stored appears in the lower-right corner of the Scrapbook window, as shown in Figure 11-2.

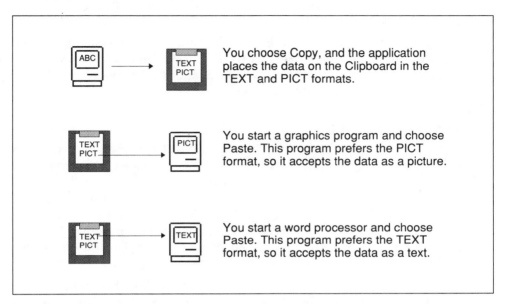

Figure 11-1: How applications donate and receive data to and from the Clipboard.

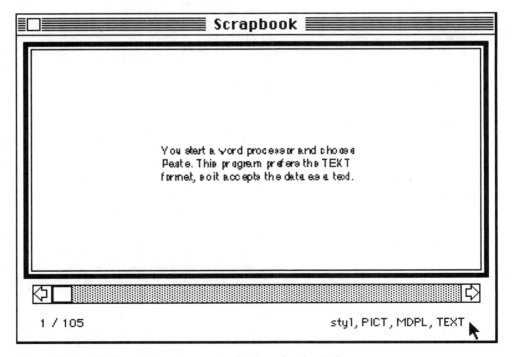

Figure 11-2: Clipboard data formats in the Scrapbook window.

Clipboard Scenarios

The best way to see how well two applications will exchange data is to put them through their paces. In this section, we'll look at how several popular programs interact through the Clipboard, and we'll provide some tips for using their Clipboard-oriented features.

Microsoft Word 4.0

When you copy text to the Clipboard, Word 4.0 stores it in two formats: TEXT and *RTF*, short for *rich-text format*. RTF is a private Clipboard format that allows text to retain all formatting information—assuming that the importing program can interpret RTF. Presently, only Word 4.0 can read the RTF Clipboard format. Microsoft Excel 2.2 will use RTF when you cut or copy spreadsheet cells, but Excel won't read RTF data when you paste text from Word. Thus, you can copy formatted spreadsheet cells from Excel to Word, but you can't copy formatted text from Word to Excel.

Tip: If you don't need to retain formatting information when you cut or copy text from Word, you can save memory by telling Word to not include RTF data in the Clipboard. Choose Commands from the Edit menu, select the "Include RTF in Clipboard" entry in the list box, and then click the Add button. These steps add the "Include RTF in Clipboard" command to the Edit menu. When you want RTF data on the Clipboard, choose the command so that it's checked. When you don't need RTF, choose the command again to uncheck it. Disabling the RTF option will also save disk space when you paste cut or copied data into the Scrapbook.

Microsoft Excel 2.2.

As mentioned above, Excel uses the RTF format when you copy or cut cells to the Clipboard. You can paste the cells into Word 4.0, where they become a table with their font, size, and style formatting intact. If you paste them into a word processor that doesn't support the RTF Clipboard format, each column of cells is separated by a tab character, and text formatting is lost.

When you copy a chart in Excel, it's placed on the Clipboard in PICT format. You can paste the chart into any application that accepts PICT data. If you paste a chart into MacDraw, you can work with each chart element (lines, bars, legends, axis, labels, and so on) separately, changing its formatting or patterns. Thus, MacDraw and Excel team up well; you might use Excel to create your original charts, and then spruce them up using MacDraw. (This also applies to charts created in Ashton-Tate's Full Impact and Microsoft Works.) You can also paste cells from Excel into a Microsoft Works spreadsheet or database document. In both cases, text formatting is lost.

Tip. You can copy one or more spreadsheet cells as a picture by holding down the Shift key and then choosing Copy Picture from the Edit menu. (When the Shift key isn't pressed, the command simply reads Copy.) If you've designed a fancy spreadsheet layout and you want to include a portion of it in another document, consider using Copy Picture. You won't be able to edit the text once you paste it into the second application, but you won't have to do any reformatting, either. (We'll look at other benefits of copying text as a picture later in this chapter.)

Microsoft Works 2.0

The Clipboard formats Microsoft Works uses depend on what you're cutting or copying to the Clipboard:

- When you cut or copy text from a word processing document, Works uses four formats: PSI2 (a private format), styl, PICT, and TEXT.

- When you cut or copy text from a database document, Works uses only the PSI2 and TEXT formats.

- When you cut or copy spreadsheet data, Works uses the PSI2, PICT, and TEXT formats.

- When you cut or copy charts or graphics drawn with Works' drawing tools, Works uses three formats: PSDR (another private format), PSI2, and PICT.

Although Works uses the styl format when it puts word processor text on the Clipboard, it doesn't *read* the styl format when you paste text into a Works document. Thus, if you paste text from MacDraw II or another program that supports the styl format, you'll lose the text's formatting.

When you paste a PICT graphic into a Works document, you can use Works' drawing tools to alter it. (Choose Draw On from the Edit menu.) If you've pasted a chart from a different spreadsheet program, you can use the drawing tools to embellish it. To work with the individual objects in the chart, select the chart and choose Ungroup Picture from the Format menu. After you've finished sprucing up the chart, you might want to group its objects together again: select all the objects by enclosing them within a selection marquee, then choose Group Picture from the Format menu.

Tip: Works provides a raft of cutting and pasting options that give you a great deal of flexibility in moving information between Works' various components. If you use Works extensively, you might want to spend some time mastering these options. They're described in detail in Chapter 20 of the Works manual.

Claris MacDraw II 1.1

MacDraw II uses a variety of Clipboard formats, depending on what you're cutting or copying. If you cut or copy a combination of text and graphics objects, MacDraw II places the items on the Clipboard in two formats: MDPL (MacDraw II's private format) and PICT. As you might expect, if you paste a combination of text and graphics into another program, they're treated as graphics.

If you cut or copy only text, however, MacDraw II puts it on the Clipboard in several formats: styl, MDPL, PICT, and TEXT. If you paste the text into a word processor, the word processor uses the styl or TEXT formats. If you paste it into another drawing program, the drawing program uses the PICT format. The way the text is treated when you paste it into a desktop publishing program, however, depends on the publishing program you use. Aldus PageMaker uses the PICT format, giving you a picture of the text. QuarkXpress and Letraset's Ready,Set,Go! 4.5, on the other hand, both accept the data as text, but discard its formatting information.

As for pasting information into MacDraw II, the program supports the styl format, so you can paste formatted text from other programs that support styl, such as Microsoft Works 2.0.

Tip: Normally, MacDraw II 1.1 removes the color information from color objects that you cut or copy to the Clipboard. If you want to retain the color information so that you can paste the colored objects into other programs that support color (such as PageMaker, QuarkXpress, and Aldus FreeHand 2.0), choose the Preferences command and select the Color Clipboard option.

Aldus PageMaker

PageMaker supports the PICT and TEXT Clipboard formats, as well as its own private format, ALD3. If you copy text from a PageMaker document, it's placed on the Clipboard in ALD3 and TEXT formats. If you paste that text into a PageMaker document, PageMaker reads the ALD3 format and, therefore, retains the text's formatting. If you paste text from a different application into a PageMaker document, PageMaker uses the TEXT format and, therefore, discards any formatting information.

There's an interesting quirk in PageMaker that can cause unexpected results when you paste text into a PageMaker document. Some programs (including MacDraw II and Microsoft Works) place text on the Clipboard in PICT format as well as in TEXT format. If you paste this kind of multiformatted text into PageMaker, PageMaker uses the PICT format, and therefore, turns the text into a graphic. To coerce PageMaker into accepting the text as text, use this workaround: Copy the text in the original application (for example, MacDraw II), and then paste it into the Notepad desk accessory, into a text-editor desk accessory such as CE Software's MockWrite, or into a word processor. Then copy the text again and paste it into the Scrapbook or into your PageMaker document. By using a text-editing program as an intermediary, you'll cause the PICT formatting to be discarded, allowing PageMaker to accept the text for what it really is.

PageMaker offers a unique Clipboard-related feature that's worth mentioning: you can import graphics directly from the Scrapbook file by choosing the Place command, and then opening the Scrapbook. This handy shortcut eliminates the need to first open the Scrapbook desk accessory, copy an image, and then paste it into the document.

Taking Pictures of Text

Generally, when you paste text into a program, you want the receiving program to treat it as text, not as a picture of text. But if you use a PostScript printer, there's a benefit to pasting text as a graphic: You can resize the graphic to create special typographic effects. The resized text won't look very good on the screen, but because of the flexibility of PostScript font outlines, the printed output will look excellent. Figure 11-3 shows two effects obtained by resizing a "text picture" in PageMaker.

Figure 11-3: Type effects created by resizing a picture of text.

Most word processors also let you resize text pictures. Simply paste the text picture into a document, then select it and drag the selection handles to resize it.

But how do you take these pictures of text? The previous section presented one technique for PageMaker users: pasting text that the original application placed on the Clipboard in PICT format. And as mentioned earlier in this chapter, Excel users can copy spreadsheet cells as a picture by selecting them, and then pressing Shift while choosing Copy Picture from the Edit menu.

If you have Microsoft Word, use this procedure: select the text that you want to turn into a picture and then press Command-Option-D. This works in Word versions 3.0 through 4.0. If you have Word 4.0, you can add a "Copy as Picture" command to the Edit menu: choose Commands from the Edit menu, select the "Copy as Picture" entry in the list box, and then click the Add button.

If you have a drawing program other than MacDraw—for example, Cricket Software's Cricket Draw or Silicon Beach Software's SuperPaint—you can also create pictures of text by typing text in the drawing program, and then copying it to the Clipboard.

Besides being useful for creating special typographic effects, text pictures can also be useful when you want a headline to fit within a specific column or margin width. Instead of laboriously experimenting with different type sizes in hopes of finding one that fits, simply turn the text into a picture and resize it until it fits exactly. Use this approach sparingly, however. Well-designed publications have a consistent typographic appearance throughout, and stretching text to different widths would destroy that consistency.

EXCHANGING DATA WITH DISK FILES

The Clipboard isn't intended to transfer huge amounts of information between programs. When you need to move large amounts of information, it's better to save the data in a disk file, and then open the disk file with the second program. Disk files have another advantage over the Clipboard: they give you more options for retaining text formatting. And for transferring data between two computers—especially between a Mac and a different computer—disk files are the data exchange medium of choice.

The key to using disk files to exchange data between programs is to use a *file format* that both the exporting and the importing program can read. A file format specifies how the information is organized within the disk file; just as a Clipboard format specifies how applications access the Clipboard, a file format specifies how applications access and interpret the contents of a disk file.

This section concentrates on exchanging text and graphics files between Macintosh programs only. Later in this chapter, we'll look at exchanging disk files between the Mac and MS-DOS computers.

Exchanging Text

There are three basic categories of text file formats:

Native files. The format that a given program normally creates when you use its Save command. A MacWrite document and a Microsoft Excel spreadsheet are two examples of native files.

Interchange files. Files saved not in a program's native format, but in data-exchange formats designed to retain some or all formatting information. Several industry-standard interchange formats exist, including SYLK, DIF, RTF, and DCA. (We'll unscramble these acronyms shortly.)

Text-only files. Files containing only ASCII text characters, retaining only rudimentary formatting information such as tabs and carriage returns.

These three file categories form a "good, better, and best" hierarchy: text-only files are a good data exchange medium, interchange files are better, and native files are best. Thus, when you need to transfer data through disk files, start by determining whether the importing program can read the exporting program's native format. If so, you'll be able to retain the original document's formatting.

If the importing program can't read the exporting program's native format, determine if there's an interchange format that both the importing and exporting programs support. (For example, Microsoft Excel and Ashton-Tate's Full Impact can both save and open files in the SYLK format.) If so, you'll be able to retain at least some of the original document's formatting.

If the exporting and importing programs don't share a common interchange format, determine whether both programs can exchange text-only files. If you're transferring spreadsheet or database information, you'll also need to consider how each spreadsheet cell or database field is separated from the others. We'll explore this important point in detail shortly.

Native File Examples

Here's a sampling of file-swapping tasks with which you can use native files. (Remember, if you aren't familiar with the types of applications discussed in this section, refer to Appendix A for some brief definitions.)

Word processors to desktop publishing programs. Most desktop publishing programs can read native files created by today's most popular word processors, including Microsoft Word, Claris's MacWrite, T/Maker's WriteNow, and WordPerfect Corporation's WordPerfect. Some desktop publishing programs, including Aldus PageMaker and QuarkXpress, can also export text in several word processor native formats. This exporting feature is useful when you've made changes to text in a desktop publication, and you want to update your original word processor files to reflect those changes.

Between word processors. Many word processors can open competing products' native files. Microsoft Word, for example, can open MacWrite documents. WordPerfect and Ashton-Tate's FullWrite Professional can open MacWrite documents as well as files created by Microsoft Word 3.02 and earlier versions.

Between outliners, word processors, and presentation programs. Symantec Corporation's MORE II outlining and presentation program can import outlines created by Microsoft Word 3.02 and earlier versions. Microsoft's PowerPoint presentation program can open MORE outlines. Symmetry Corporation's Acta desk accessory outliner can open and save MORE and ThinkTank outlines, and Aldus Persuasion can import outlines created by Acta and MORE 1.1c and earlier versions.

Between spreadsheet programs. Ashton-Tate's Full Impact, Informix's WingZ, and Microsoft Works can open spreadsheets saved by Microsoft Excel 1.5 and earlier versions.

Between programs from the same company. Many software firms design their programs so that they can read each others' native formats. Microsoft Works 2.0 can open and save word processor files created by Microsoft Word 1.05 and earlier versions. Ashton-Tate's Full Impact and FullWrite Professional can read database files created by Ashton-Tate's dBASE Mac. When you open a dBASE Mac file using Full Impact, each record in the dBASE Mac file becomes a row in the spreadsheet, and each field gets its own column. The field names appear in the first row of the spreadsheet.

More About Interchange Files

There aren't many standards in the microcomputer industry, especially where file formats are concerned. But over the years, several file formats have become unofficial standards for exchanging text between programs. The most popular include:

DCA. Short for *document content architecture*, this format was developed by IBM for exchanging word processor and other text documents. The DCA format doesn't save font and size information, but it does save bold, underline, strike-through, superscript, and subscript information. Several IBM PC word processing programs can open and save DCA files. The Macintosh and PC versions of Aldus PageMaker can also import and export DCA files. Macintosh file translation utilities (described later in this chapter) can usually interpret DCA files. The DCA format is sometimes called DCA-RFT, with RFT standing for *revisable-form text*.

DIF. Short for *data-interchange format*, the DIF file format is intended for transferring spreadsheet and database information. DIF files do not retain character formatting information.

RTF. Short for *rich text format*, the RTF format is a complex format designed by Microsoft for transferring formatted word processing documents. Unlike DCA files, RTF files can retain point size and font information. RTF files can even retain graphics and color formatting information.

SYLK. Short for *symbolic link*, the SYLK format, like DIF, is designed for transferring database and spreadsheet information. Unlike DIF files, however, SYLK files can retain a great deal of formatting information, including numeric formats, column widths, and alignment within cells.

Table 10-1 lists several popular applications that support some or all of these formats. An "R" means the application can read the format; a "W" means the application can write the format.

Table 10-1: Interchange formats supported by several popular programs.

	DCA	DIF	RTF	SYLK
Acius 4th Dimension	—	R/W	—	R/W
Aldus PageMaker	R	—	—	—
Ashton-Tate Full Impact	—	R/W	—	R/W
Claris FileMaker II	—	—	—	R/W
Informix WingZ	—	R/W	—	R/W
Microsoft Excel	—	R/W	—	R/W
Microsoft Word	—	—	R/W	—
Microsoft Works	—	—	R/W	R/W
T/Maker WriteNow	—	—	R/W	—
WordPerfect	—	—	—	—

Incidentally, if you try to use WriteNow 2.0 to open an RTF file created by Word 4.0, WriteNow displays a "Bad RTF version number" error message. To fix the problem, first use WriteNow to open the RTF file as a text-only document. When the file opens, you'll see a maze of cryptic-looking codes; they're RTF codes that describe the document's formatting. Locate the text "rtf1" (it appears at the beginning of the file) and change it to "rtf0". Finally, save the file as a text-only file (without line breaks), and re-open it as an RTF file. (WriteNow 2.0 also has trouble importing RTF files created by Microsoft Works.)

Finally, it's worth mentioning that many applications (including Page-Maker, WordPerfect, and WriteNow, to name a few) use separate files called *filters* to enable them to import and export files. Many software firms release new filters from time to time to allow their products to read and write additional file formats. If you have a program that uses filters and you need to read a specific file format, contact the program's developer to determine if a filter has been released for that format. Similarly, if you're having trouble importing or exporting documents with a program that uses filters, contact its developer to see if the filters have been updated.

The Lowest Common Denominator: The Text-Only File

If the two programs you're exchanging data between don't support a common interchange format, you may have to resort to the lowest common denominator—the text-only file. You'll lose formatting information, but you won't have to retype any text.

When you're using text-only files to swap database or spreadsheet data between programs, you need to be aware of how the exporting program separates each spreadsheet column (or data base field) and each spreadsheet row (or database record). So that the importing program can differentiate between each cell and row (or field and record), the exporting program must separate them with *delimiters*. Most programs use a tab code as a column or field delimiter, and a carriage return code as a row or record delimiter. A text-only file formatted in this way is often called a *tab-delimited* file. Figure 11-4 shows a tab-delimited text file as it's displayed by Microsoft Word 4.0 with the Show ¶ option active. The right-pointing arrows indicate tab codes.

Some programs use a different delimiting technique called *comma-separated values*, or *CSV*. A CSV file uses commas (,) rather than tabs to separate cells or fields. If a given cell or field contains a comma itself (as in "Raynak, Margaret"), the program writing the CSV file places the entire cell within quotes, as shown in Figure 11-5.

If you're using a text-only file to exchange information between database managers or spreadsheet programs, be sure that the importing and exporting programs support the same format of delimiters. If they don't, you can still move data between them by using a word processor to edit the file and using its search-and-replace feature to change the file's delimiters as necessary. Most file-translation programs can also translate between both types of delimited text-file format.

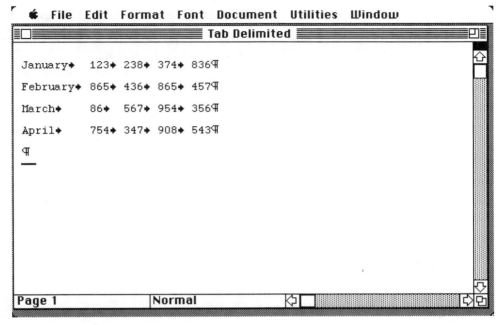

Figure 11-4: A tab-delimited text file.

Table 11-2 lists the delimited text-only formats that several spreadsheet programs and database managers can read (R) and write (W).

Table 11-2: Some programs that support tab-delimited and CSV files.

	Tab Delimited	**CSV**
Acius 4th Dimension	R/W	R/W[1]
Ashton-Tate dBASE Mac	R/W	R/W
Ashton-Tate Full Impact	R/W	—
Claris FileMaker II	R/W	R/W
Informix WingZ	R/W	—
Microsoft Excel	R/W	R/W
Microsoft File	W	—
Microsoft Works	R/W	—

[1] To import or export comma-delimited data with 4th Dimension, choose Import or Export, and then type the comma character's ASCII value (44) in the End of Field text box. This technique will not work with data containing embedded commas (as in "Campell, Amy").

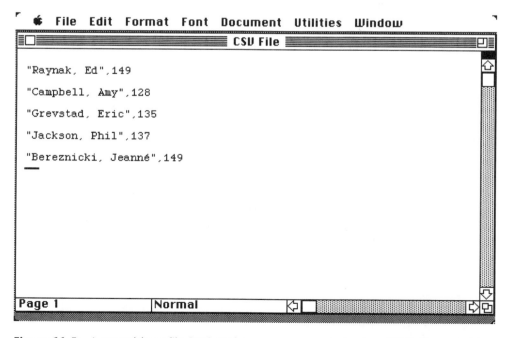

Figure 11-5: A spreadsheet file (*top*) and a comma-separated values (*CSV*) file containing its data (*bottom*).

Exchanging Graphics

Many of the same considerations you face when exchanging text between programs also apply when you're exchanging graphic images. There is one significant difference, however: you don't have the safety net of text-only files to fall back on.

Fortunately, several graphics interchange formats exist, and most are widely supported by Mac programs and by many IBM PC programs. These interchange formats include:

EPS. Short for *encapsulated PostScript*, an EPS file contains the PostScript-language instructions that describe an image's appearance. In addition to containing PostScript instructions, EPS files can also contain QuickDraw instructions that allow the importing application to display a facsimile of the image on the Mac's screen. Whether an EPS file also contains QuickDraw information depends on the application that created it. The EPS files created by IBM PC programs, for example, don't contain a QuickDraw representation of an image because the IBM PC doesn't use QuickDraw. When you import such a file, the importing program generally displays only a *bounding box*, a rectangle indicating the PostScript image's size, as shown in Figure 11-6.

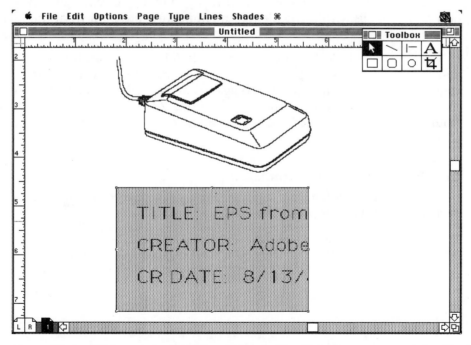

Figure 11-6: EPS images in Aldus PageMaker: with a QuickDraw representation (*top*) and without a QuickDraw representation (*bottom*).

EPS files are most commonly used to exchange illustrations created by programs such as Adobe Illustrator and Aldus FreeHand. EPS files can be used to exchange scanned images, but the TIFF format, described shortly, is better suited to this task.

PICT. This common file format is similar to the PICT Clipboard format. PICT files contain QuickDraw instructions that describe an image. PICT files can contain object-oriented graphics, bit-mapped graphics, or combinations of both. Most Mac graphics programs can create PICT files. A cousin to the PICT format, *PICT2* (also written as PICT II), stores color or gray-scale information in the form of commands for Color QuickDraw.

RIFF. Short for *raster-image file format*, the RIFF format first appeared in LetraSet's ImageStudio image-retouching program. RIFF files are designed to store gray-scale bit-mapped images, and can represent up to 256 levels of gray (eight bits per pixel).

TIFF. Short for *tagged-image file format*, the TIFF format is primarily used for exchanging bit-mapped graphics such as scanned images. TIFF files contain pieces of information called *tags* that describe an image's characteristics: its height and width, resolution, and whether it contains color and gray-scale information. TIFF files can contain bit-mapped images of virtually any resolution. Certain tags within the file tell the importing program what the image's resolution is.

MacPaint. Technically, the MacPaint file format isn't an interchange format, but because it's supported by so many programs, it can be used to exchange bit-mapped graphics. The biggest drawback of the MacPaint format is that it supports only one image resolution: 72 dots per inch. Thus, you wouldn't want to use the MacPaint format to save a high-resolution image created by a scanner.

Graphics Interchange Format Support

Table 11-3 lists which graphics file formats can be read (R) and written (W) by a variety of popular programs.

Table 11-3: Graphics interchange formats and some programs that support them.

	EPS	PICT	RIFF	TIFF	MacPaint
Microsoft Word	—	R	—	—	R
Aldus PageMaker	R/W	R	—	R	R
Aldus FreeHand	R/W	R/W[1]	—	R	R
Aldus Persuasion	R	R/W	—	—	—
Adobe Illustrator 88	R/W	R	—	—	R
Cricket Graph	—	R/W[2]	—	—	R[2]
Cricket Draw	R/W	W	—	—	R
LetraSet ImageStudio	W	R[3]	R/W	R/W	R/W
LetraSet Ready,Set,Go!	R	R	R	R	R
Microsoft PowerPoint	R	R/W[4]	—	—	R
Silicon Beach Digital Darkroom	W	R/W	—	R/W	R/W
SuperMac PixelPaint	R/W	R/W	—	—	R/W
Silicon Beach Super3D	W	R/W[5]	—	—	—
Silicon Beach SuperPaint	W	R/W	—	R/W	R/W
Silicon Beach SuperCard	—	R/W	—	R/W	R/W
Claris MacDraw II	—	R/W	—	—	—
Claris MacPaint	—	—	—	—	R/W
QuarkXpress	R	R	R	R	R

[1] To export a FreeHand image in PICT format, select it and press Option while choosing Cut or Copy from the Edit menu. Then paste the image into the Scrapbook.

[2] Cricket Graph accepts PICT and MacPaint images through the Clipboard.

[3] ImageStudio 1.5 does not read PICT files when running on a Mac Plus or SE.

[4] To save PowerPoint slides as PICT images, choose Save As, then select the "Save slides as pictures in a scrapbook" option.

[5] Super3D discards some elements of PICT files (including any bit maps) when importing them.

Opening and Saving Files in Other Formats

When you use a program's Save or Save As command, your document is saved in the program's native file format. Similarly, when you choose a program's Open command, it generally lists only its native files in the Open dialog box. (There are exceptions to this rule, particularly with word processors; they usually list text-only files as well as any other programs' native files that they can access.)

Let's look at the techniques you'll use to save documents in foreign file formats, and to open documents saved in foreign formats.

Saving Files in Foreign Formats

To save a document in a format other than the program's native format, you generally choose Save As, and then select the desired format in the Save As dialog box. With some programs, such as Microsoft Word and Works and Ashton-Tate's Full Impact, you may need to click a button to display a list of the file formats the program supports.

Some programs require other techniques. With some, such as T/Maker's WriteNow, you choose the desired format from a list box that appears in the Save As dialog box. With some database managers, you must to "print to disk" to export data. Printing to disk causes the program to sort and organize the database as if a report was going to be printed, except that the data is saved in a disk file instead of sent to the printer. Printing to disk can be an effective way to export only certain database records, or to export records sorted in a specific order. (This process differs from the PostScript print-to-disk technique described in Chapter 8; that technique creates a file containing not only data, but also the PostScript commands that specify the document's formatting.)

Because data-exporting techniques vary between programs, check your program's manuals for instructions on saving files in other formats.

Opening Documents Saved In Foreign Formats

Generally, you can't open a document saved in a foreign format by double-clicking the document's icon in the Finder. If you try, one of two things usually happens: the Finder will start the application that created the foreign file, rather than the application that you want to open the file with; or, you'll receive an error message saying "The file (*file name*) could not be opened/printed (the application is busy or missing)."

To coerce the Finder into using a specific program to open a foreign file, select both the program's icon and the foreign file's icon, and then choose Open from the File menu. Figure 11-7 shows this technique in action with a MacWrite document and Microsoft Word.

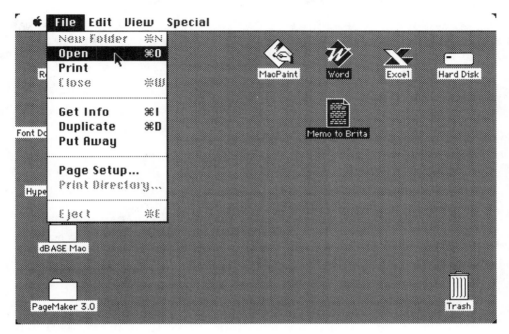

Figure 11-7: Forcing Microsoft Word to open a MacWrite document from the Finder.

To select an application and a document, both must be stored at the same level of the disk hierarchy. If they aren't, simply move both files to the gray-patterned desktop, and then select them. When you're done working with the files and you want to restore them to their previous location, select the files and choose Put Away from the Finder's File menu.

EXCHANGING FILES WITH AN MS-DOS COMPUTER

Exchanging files between Macs and MS-DOS involves many of the same file format considerations we've discussed so far, with an additional wrinkle thrown in: the task of moving the files from one computer to the other. In this section, we'll spotlight four techniques for moving files from a Mac to a PC, or from a PC to a Mac:

- You can attach an MS-DOS disk drive to the Mac, or a Macintosh disk drive to the PC. With this approach, you can directly access disks formatted for the other computer.

- If the computers are close to each other, you can connect them using a cable, and then use communications programs on both computers to transfer the files.

- If both computers have telephone modems, you can transfer files over the phone lines. You can transfer the files directly between the two computers, or you can use a communications service such as MCI Mail or Connect as an intermediary.

- You can connect the two computers to a network to allow them to share not only disk files, but also expensive peripherals such as hard disks and laser printers. We'll explore this option in the next chapter.

The Disk Drive Approach

In some ways, attaching a PC drive to the Mac or a Mac drive to the PC is the easiest file transfer approach, since you need not contend with communications or networking concepts. Equip a Mac to read MS-DOS disks, and you can access PC files using the same basic techniques you use to access Mac files. Let's spotlight several products that allow Macs to read PC disks, and vice versa.

The Apple FDHD Drive

If you have a Macintosh SE/30, IIx, or IIcx, you may already have all the file transfer hardware you need. The FDHD floppy disk drive in these Macs can directly read and write to 3 1/2-inch MS-DOS or OS/2 disks. (As mentioned in Chapter 4, an FDHD upgrade kit is available for the Mac II and SE.) Although the larger, 5 1/4-inch floppy disks have been the standard in the MS-DOS world, more and more MS-DOS machines are equipped with 3 1/2-inch drives.

You can't simply insert the PC disk in an FDHD drive and view its contents using the Finder. To access 3 1/2-inch PC disks with the FDHD drive, you must use the Apple File Exchange program, which is included with the Mac's system software. (In the System Update 6.0 package, Apple File Exchange is on the Utilities 2 disk.)

Apple File Exchange uses separate files called *translators* to convert between different file formats. Translators tell Apple File Exchange how data is organized in a specific file format. Apple File Exchange includes only one translator; it lets you convert between DCA-format and MacWrite documents. Some programs, however, include translators for their own files, and as we'll see later in this chapter, several companies sell translators for Apple File Exchange. By adding additional translators, you can extend Apple File Exchange's file-translation talents.

If you would like to be able to insert PC disks in an FDHD drive and work with them using the Finder, consider a program called DOS Mounter from Dayna Communications. This $89.95 package includes a start-up document

(Init) whose software lets you work with 3 1/2-inch DOS disks using the same techniques you use to work with Macintosh disks.

DaynaFile

Dayna Communications' DaynaFile is a hardware add-on for the Mac that can house up to two floppy disk drives; Dayna offers both 3 1/2 high-density and 5 1/4-inch high-density drives. According to Dayna, roughly 80 percent of all DaynaFile units contain 5 1/4-inch drives—a statistic that indicates the 5 1/4-inch floppy format is alive and well.

The DaynaFile connects to the Mac's SCSI port and includes a start-up document (Init) whose software allows you to view and work with MS-DOS disks directly. You can use the Finder to copy files to and from MS-DOS disks, and you access MS-DOS disks using an application's Open or Save dialog box. This makes the DaynaFile one of the easiest ways for a Mac to access MS-DOS files.

The DaynaFile's primary drawback is its cost. A DaynaFile containing only one drive costs between $650 and $850, depending on the drive you choose; a DaynaFile equipped with both a 5 1/4-inch and a 3 1/2-inch drive costs over $1,000. For less money, you can equip a PC with a network expansion board and software that will allow it and a Mac to share a hard disk. You'll have to contend with the complexities of setting up and maintaining a network, but as we'll see in the next chapter, the benefits may make the extra effort worthwhile.

Kennect Rapport and Drive 2.4

Kennect Technology offers two products of interest to Mac-and-PC file swappers. Rapport is a $295 adaptor that attaches between the Mac's external floppy drive connector and an external floppy drive and enables the drive to read from (but not write to) 3 1/2-inch MS-DOS floppy disks.

If you want to write to MS-DOS disks, connect the Rapport to Kennect's $495 Drive 2.4, a high-density external floppy disk drive. By combining Rapport with Drive 2.4, your Mac will be able to read to and write from MS-DOS, Mac, and Apple II disks. The Drive 2.4 supports 1.44MB MS-DOS and Mac formats, and includes special software that lets you format high-density Mac disks to store 2.4MB.

Apple PC 5.25 Drive

Apple offers a 5 1/4-inch floppy disk drive called the PC 5.25. The drive connects to a Mac SE or NuBus expansion board, which you purchase separately. As with the FDHD floppy drive, the PC 5.25 doesn't let you work with files directly on the desktop, as the DaynaFile does. Instead, you must use the Apple File Exchange utility to access the MS-DOS disk.

In all, you can probably find a better file transfer tool than the PC 5.25 drive. It's expensive ($399 for the drive; $129 for the NuBus or SE expansion board), and it isn't as easy to use as the DaynaFile. And the fact that it requires an expansion board is a big drawback if you have a Mac SE, which has only one expansion slot.

Copy II Deluxe Option Board

So far, we've discussed hardware that lets a Mac read MS-DOS disks. Central Point Software's Copy II Deluxe Option Board takes the opposite approach: it lets MS-DOS computers equipped with 3 1/2-inch disk drives (such as the PS/2 Models 25 and 30), read and write Macintosh disks. The $159 board includes software that lets you format Macintosh disks and copy files to and from them.

MicroSolutions MatchMaker

Here's another product that approaches file-swapping from the PC's perspective. MicroSolutions Computer Products' MatchMaker is a $149 expansion board that plugs into an IBM PC and allows you to attach an external 400K or 800K Macintosh floppy drive to the PC. MatchMaker includes software that lets you format Mac disks on the PC, copy files to and from them, delete files, and read text-only files.

Iomega Bernoulli Box II

If you need to transfer large amounts of data between Macs and PCs, you might consider Iomega Corporation's Bernoulli Box II. ("Bernoulli" is pronounced *burn-OO-lee*.) The Bernoulli Box II is a storage device that uses removeable cartridges. A single Bernoulli cartridge stores 20MB using a unique and very reliable flexible disk technology.

From the data transfer perspective, what's exciting about the Bernoulli Box II is that, when used with an Iomega program called Bernoulli File Exchange, it can read Bernoulli cartridges that have been formatted for MS-DOS. Thus, if your Mac and PC are equipped with Bernoulli Box IIs, you can transfer up to 20MB of data by swapping cartridges between the two machines.

The Cable Transfer Approach

Equipping a Mac to read PC disks (or vice versa) may provide an easy way to transfer files, but it isn't an inexpensive approach. If you need to transfer files only occasionally, you may not be able to justify spending several hundred dollars or more on specialized disk drives. If that's the case—and if your Mac and PC are close to each other—consider uniting them with a cable and using communications software to transfer files.

If you choose this approach, you have two options: making or buying a cable and using general-purpose communications software to transfer the files, or buying a cable-and-software product designed specifically for swapping files between Macs and PCs. Let's look at some products in the latter category first.

LapLink Mac

Traveling Software's LapLink is a popular product for transferring files between MS-DOS laptop computers and desktop machines. LapLink Mac is similar, except it's designed to transfer files between PCs and Macs.

LapLink Mac includes a cable and software for both the PC and the Mac. You control LapLink Mac from the PC; the Mac software simply displays a message saying "Program Active" as it communicates with its counterpart on the PC. LapLink Mac transfers data at a very swift 57,600 bits per second; a 20K file—roughly 14 pages of double-spaced text—transfers in 3 seconds.

LapLink Mac also includes a file-translator utility that can convert between MacWrite, Microsoft Word (Mac), and WordPerfect (Mac) formats and numerous PC formats, including Microsoft Word, Q&A Write, MultiMate, IBM DisplayWrite, XyWrite III Plus, WordStar, and WordPerfect.

The MacLink Series

DataViz's MacLink Plus is the latest version of the pioneering MacLink, one of the first file-transferring products available for the Mac. Like LapLink Mac, MacLink includes Mac and PC software that work together to transfer files. Unlike LapLink Mac, however, MacLink is controlled from the Macintosh. Another difference between MacLink Plus and LapLink is that MacLink Plus can also be used to transfer files over the phone lines using a modem; LapLink supports transfers over its cable only.

At this writing, the current version of MacLink Plus is version 4. This version can translate between most popular word processor formats and also supports several graphics formats, including TIFF, EPS, PICT, and PC Paintbrush (PIC) files.

If you use the Apple File Exchange utility, you might be interested in another DataViz product, MacLink Plus/Translators, a collection of translators for Apple File Exchange.

QuickShare

Compatible Systems' QuickShare takes a unique approach to transferring and translating files. QuickShare is a hardware-and-software combination; the hardware consists of a a PC expansion board that gives a PC, XT, or AT a SCSI port, and a cable that connects to the Mac's SCSI port (or, thanks to SCSI's daisy-chaining abilities, to another SCSI device attached to the Mac). The software consists of Mac and PC programs.

What makes QuickShare different is the way it transfers and translates files. Let's say you want to transfer an Ashton-Tate Framework document to the Mac. To do so, you configure Framework to print to an IBM Graphics Printer, and then you create a print-to-disk file of your document. Finally, you use QuickShare to move the document to the Mac, specifying translation options (such as the format in which the document is to be saved) in the process.

Because QuickShare intercepts formatting codes that would otherwise control a printer, it's able to recreate nearly every aspect of a document's formatting. And because it intercepts IBM Graphics Printer codes, it can translate documents created by any PC application that supports this popular printer—and most do. QuickShare's primary limitation is that it can't translate object-oriented graphics, such as those created by Micrografx Designer.

If you already have a way to move files between the Mac and PC, you might be interested in Compatible Systems' AnyText and AnyGraph, which consist of a series of Apple File Exchange translators and a program for the PC. Any-Text and AnyGraph use the same basic translation technique as QuickShare, and thus have the same drawback—they can't translate object-oriented graphics.

The Do-It-Yourself Approach

If you have communications programs for your Mac and PC, you can make or buy a cable to connect both computers and then use the communications programs to transfer files. If you already have the communications software, this approach is the least expensive. But it's trickier than simply using LapLink Mac or MacLink Plus.

To connect the two computers, you need a *null modem* cable, a cable whose wiring tricks both computers into thinking that they're connected by a telephone modem. If you have an ImageWriter I, you're in luck—its cable happens to work as a null modem cable for IBM computers and for many laptop machines. (You may need some adaptors to plug the cable in, however. For IBM machines, which have male serial connectors, you'll need a *gender changer*. For PCs and PS/2s with 25-pin male connectors, use Radio Shack's part number 26-1495. You may also need an adaptor for the Macintosh end of the cable. To attach an ImageWriter I cable to a Plus or later Mac, you'll need a DB-9 to DIN-8 adaptor, Apple part number M0199.) If you don't have an Image-Writer I cable, you can buy one from an Apple dealer (its part number is M0150), or you can order one from a computer supply house such as Inmac Corporation. (See Appendix B for its address.)

If you're comfortable with a soldering iron, you can also make your own cable. Figure 11-8 shows which pins to connect.

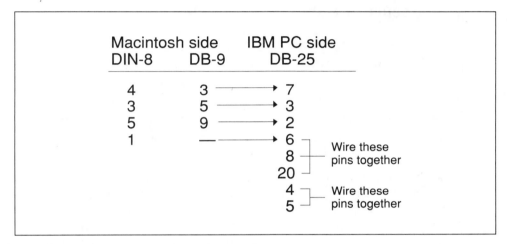

Figure 11-8: Wiring diagram for Mac/PC null modem cable.

After connecting your cable, you need to adjust both the Mac and PC communications programs to put the machines on speaking terms. Here's how:

1. First, adjust both programs' serial communications settings to match the following: 9600 baud, 8 data bits per character, 1 stop bit, and no parity. (If you're interested in knowing what these jargon terms mean, see Chapter 14.) Figure 11-9 shows these settings in one popular Mac communications program, Hayes' Smartcom II.

2. Some programs (including Smartcom II for the Mac) differentiate between a direct connection and a telephone line connection. If your programs are in this group, choose the appropriate commands to specify a direct connection. (With Hayes' Smartcom II, choose Direct Connect from the Connection menu.)

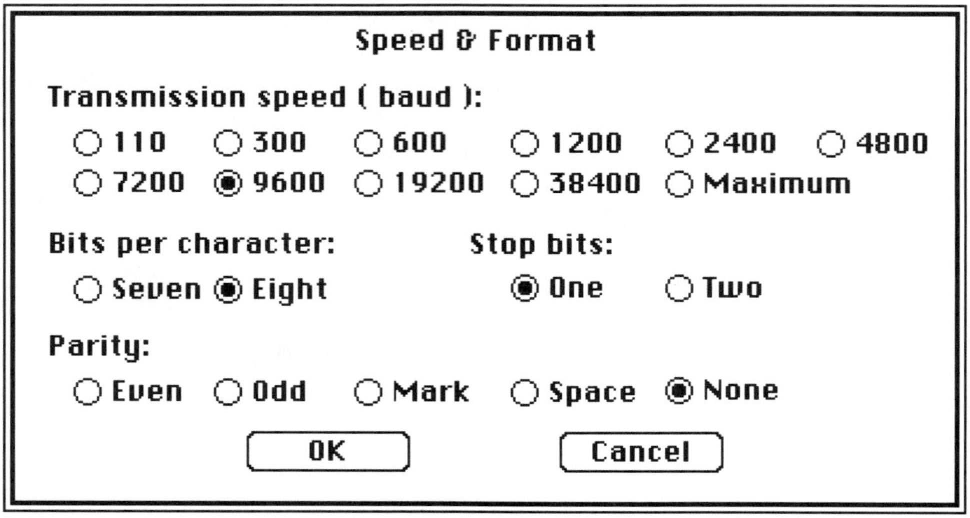

```
┌─────────────────────────────────────────────────────────────┐
│                      Speed & Format                           │
│ Transmission speed ( baud ):                                  │
│    ○ 110    ○ 300    ○ 600    ○ 1200   ○ 2400   ○ 4800        │
│    ○ 7200   ● 9600   ○ 19200  ○ 38400  ○ Maximum             │
│                                                               │
│  Bits per character:         Stop bits:                       │
│    ○ Seven ● Eight              ● One      ○ Two              │
│                                                               │
│  Parity:                                                      │
│    ○ Even   ○ Odd    ○ Mark    ○ Space   ● None              │
│         ┌──────────┐              ┌──────────┐               │
│         │    OK    │              │  Cancel  │               │
│         └──────────┘              └──────────┘               │
└─────────────────────────────────────────────────────────────┘
```

Figure 11-9: Serial communications settings in Smartcom II.

3. So that you can transfer files reliably, be sure both programs are configured to use the same *file transfer protocol*. (A file transfer protocol causes the two programs to "proofread" the data as it's being transferred to ensure that nothing is garbled.) The most widely supported transfer protocol is called *XMODEM*. Configure both programs to use the XMODEM protocol. If both programs support other protocols, such as *YMODEM* or *Kermit*, feel free to use them instead of *XMODEM*. The important thing is that both programs use the same protocol.

4. Be sure your Mac's communications program is configured to *not* use the *MacBinary* transfer option. This option allows the program to transfer Mac-specific file information, such as a file's icon. It also allows for the transfer of the file's resource fork and data fork. MS-DOS can't use this extra information, so you don't want to transfer it.

5. On both sides, turn on the program's *local echo* option. This will allow you to see what you're typing. The local echo option is usually within the program's terminal-adjustment settings.

After adjusting both programs' settings, try typing a few characters on both machines. If all is well, you'll see them appear on the other computer's screen. If you don't, look everything over for problems, starting with the communications settings, and ending with the cable itself.

If you do see the characters you type on both machines, you're ready to transfer a file. Here's how:

1. On the receiving end, choose the command that will begin receiving a file using the XMODEM protocol.

2. On the transmitting end, choose the command that transmits a file using the XMODEM protocol.

During the transfer, each program will display status messages indicating how much data it has transmitted or received.

As you can see, the do-it-yourself approach requires more effort than using a product such as MacLink Plus or LapLink Mac. Another drawback is that you don't have the benefits of those programs' file conversion features. You must rely on the conversion features of the applications you use, or on Apple File Exchange.

A Word About Mac-to-Mac Transfers

Although we're discussing Mac-and-PC file-swapping here, most of the instructions in the previous section also apply to Mac-to-Mac file transfers. The only exceptions are:

- You need a different cable. Figure 11-10 contains a diagram for a Mac-to-Mac null modem cable.

- For Mac-to-Mac transfers, activate both programs' MacBinary file transfer option. This will allow the programs to transfer all components of the files.

Macintosh		Macintosh	
DIN-8	DB-9	DIN-8	DB-9
4*	3 ⟶	4	3
6	4 ⟶	8	8
3*	5 ⟶	5	9
8	8 ⟶	6	4
5*	9 ⟶	3	5
1	⟶	2	—
2	⟶	1	—

*If you use software handshaking and short cable lengths, you need connect only these three pins.

Figure 11-10: Diagram for a Mac-to-Mac null modem cable.

The Modem Approach

If the Mac and PC (or another Mac) aren't close to each other, you can still transfer files between them, provided that both computers are equipped with telephone modems. In this section, we'll look at two ways to transfer files using modems: by transferring them directly, and by using a communications service such as MCI Mail or Connect as an intermediary.

Direct Modem Transfers

A direct modem transfer is similar to the direct cable transfer described in the previous section, except for these differences:

- Instead of using a direct cable connection, both computers use a telephone modem and the phone lines to communicate, as shown in Figure 11-11.

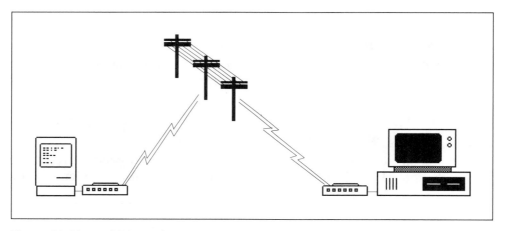

Figure 11-11:   A direct modem connection uses modems and the phone lines.

- The sending computer must dial the receiving computer; therefore, you must configure the sending computer's program to dial the phone (usually by choosing a "dial" command and then specifying the other modem's phone number), and the receiving computer's program to answer (generally, by choosing an "auto answer" command).

- Unless you have a state-of-the-art modem, you'll have to use a transmission speed slower than 9600 baud; most modems have maximum speeds of 1200 or 2400 baud.

These differences aside, the steps are similar to those described in the previous section. After the receiving computer has answered the phone, the modems will establish a connection and each user will see a message such as

"CONNECT 1200" on his or her screen. After that, you and your colleague should exchange brief typed messages to ensure that the connection is reliable and that both programs' communications settings match. If you both have a spare phone line, you might want to be talking to each other while the two computers converse. This will make it easier to troubleshoot problems, since you won't have to break the computers' connection to call each other and ask, "What went wrong that time?"

Using a Communications Service

Transferring files using the direct modem approach has some drawbacks: both computers must be on at the same time, and someone must be at each machine to choose the appropriate transfer commands and verify that the files transferred successfully. These drawbacks are especially significant if the two computers are located in different time zones. You may be ready to transmit a file at 9:00 AM in Boston, but your colleague in San Francisco may not feel like going into the office at 6:00 AM to receive it.

The solution is to use a communications service as an intermediary, as shown in Figure 11-12. You transmit the file to your colleague's electronic mailbox on the communications service, and he or she retrieves it at a convenient time.

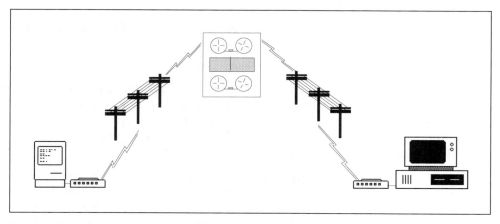

Figure 11-12: Using a communications service as an intermediary.

Two communications services are especially well-suited to Mac-and-PC file swapping: MCI Mail and Connect.

MCI Mail

MCI Communications' MCI Mail service is one of the most popular communications services. You pay a small fee to become an MCI Mail subscriber; as a subscriber, you get your own mailbox address (such as MKELLY) and a password, which helps keep your mailbox private. You can then send *electronic mail* to other MCI Mail subscribers and to FAX and TELEX machines. You can even send electronic mail to people who don't have computers: simply specify the recipient's street address, and MCI prints your letter at the service location closest to the recipient, and then mails it or delivers it by courier, depending on your preferences.

Normally, MCI Mail is a text-only service. You can send and receive text messages, but not documents containing formatted text or graphics. (These kinds of documents are often called *binary* files.) To send these types of documents, you need additional software. For the Mac, you need a program called Desktop Express, developed jointly by Apple, MCI, and Dow Jones/News Retrieval (a business information service accessible through MCI Mail). Desktop Express adds a Macintosh facade to MCI Mail's text-only interface, as shown in Figure 11-13. It also contains software that allows MCI's computers to accept binary files.

On the PC side, you need Lotus Express, a program developed by Lotus Development Corporation and MCI. Like Desktop Express, Lotus Express adds a friendlier interface to MCI Mail, and it allows you to exchange binary files with other MCI Mail subscribers who have Lotus Express or Desktop Express.

Connect

The Connect Professional Information Service, or Connect for short, hasn't been available for as long as MCI Mail, and it has fewer subscribers. But Connect has a significant advantage over the MCI/Desktop Express/Lotus Express combination: it provides software whose Mac and PC versions share a nearly identical user interface.

Connect isn't a text-only service; you can't access it using a general-purpose communications program such as Smartcom II or MicroPhone. Instead, you use Connect's proprietary software, which you purchase from a computer dealer. The PC version of Connect software runs under Microsoft's Windows/286 or Windows/386 operating environments. Both programs are shown in Figure 11-14.

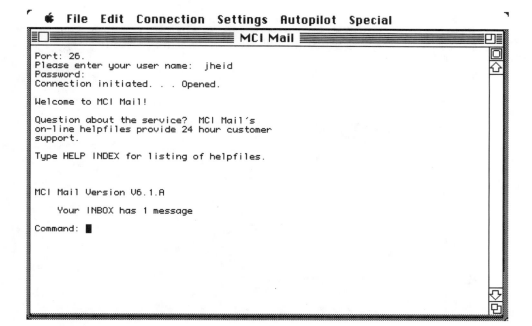

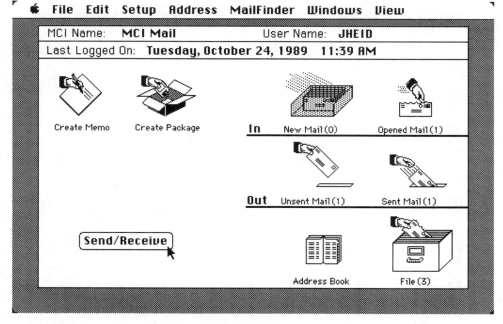

Figure 11-13: Two faces of MCI Mail: with a conventional communications program (*top*) and with Desktop Express (*bottom*).

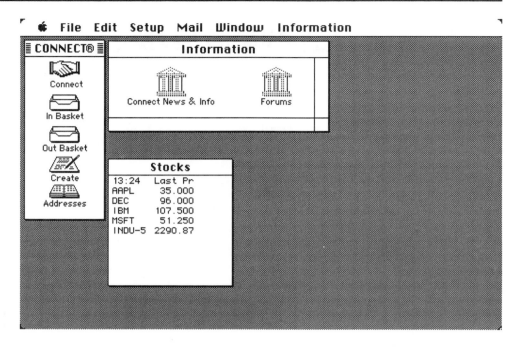

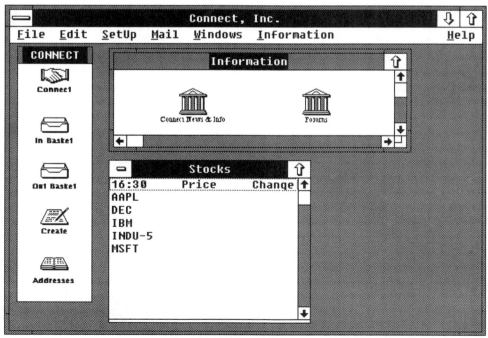

Figure 11-14: Connect for the Mac (*top*) and PC (*bottom*).

The advantage of Connect's common user interface is that you and other subscribers can move between the Mac and PC without having to learn two user interfaces. For offices that use both Macs and PCs, this can mean reduced training costs. The drawback is that you need an 80286- or 80386-based MS-DOS computer to run the Connect software. Thus, older PCs, such as the original PC and the PC/XT, are left out in the cold.

In addition to allowing you to exchange binary files with other Connect subscribers, Connect lets you send messages to MCI Mail subscribers and to FAX machines. Connect also provides specialized forums for specific products or application areas; subscribers can download free or shareware programs and exchange ideas and tips with other forum members.

USING TRANSFERRED FILES

We've seen how to move files from a Mac to a PC or a PC to a Mac; now let's look at the file format issues that you'll face after you've transferred the files.

File Formats Revisited

As you may recall from earlier in this chapter, you can use three types of files when transferring data between Mac programs: native files, interchange files, and text-only (ASCII) files. These same three levels apply to Mac-and-PC file swapping.

Native Files

Here's a sampling of Mac-and-PC file exchange applications with which you can use native files.

Between word processors. Word processors that are available for both the Mac and PC can generally read each other's native formats. Microsoft Word 4.0 can read documents created by its PC cousin, Word 5.0, and it can save documents in MS-DOS Word format. Mac Word 4.0 can also open documents created by Windows Write, the simple word processor included with Microsoft Windows. Similarly, WordPerfect for the Macintosh can read and write documents created by WordPerfect 4.2 on the PC. Ashton-Tate's FullWrite Professional can read documents created by Ashton-Tate's MultiMate 3.31, Multi-Mate Advantage, and MultiMate Advantage II. FullWrite can't save documents in these formats, however.

Between Aldus PageMaker versions. The Mac and Microsoft Windows versions of Aldus PageMaker 3.x can access each other's documents easily. After you've transferred a Mac PageMaker document to the PC, rename the document so that it ends with the file extension .PM3. (In the MS-DOS world, a *file extension* is that part of a file name that appears after a period character. MS-DOS file names can contain up to 11 characters: up to eight before the period, and up to three after it. File extensions are generally used to identify the type of file.) If the publications you're transferring contain large graphics such as scanned images, you'll need to take some special steps to transfer them. Consult your PageMaker manuals for details.

Between Aldus PageMaker and numerous word processors. The Mac version of PageMaker can read native files created by numerous PC word processors, including WordPerfect, WordStar 3.3, and XyWrite III.

Between Adobe Illustrator versions. Adobe Illustrator is also available for the Mac and for Microsoft Windows; each version can open and save files created by its counterpart.

Between Microsoft Excel versions. Microsoft Excel is another program that has Mac and Microsoft Windows versions. Version 2.2 of Excel for the Mac can open and save documents for version 2.0 of Excel for Windows, and the Windows version can open and save Mac Excel 2.2 documents.

Between other spreadsheets. Excel 2.2 and Ashton-Tate's Full Impact can open spreadsheets created by Lotus 1-2-3 and Symphony. Both can also save worksheets in two 1-2-3 formats: WK1, the format used by versions 2.0 and later of 1-2-3, and WKS, the format used by 1-2-3 version 1A. For details on how Excel treats 1-2-3 formulas and numeric formats, see the section "Lotus 1-2-3" in the *Microsoft Excel Reference* manual. Excel 2.2 and Full Impact can also read and write dBASE II (DB2) and dBASE III (DB3) database files.

Between dBASE Mac and dBASE II/dBASE III. Ashton-Tate's dBASE Mac can directly read and write to dBASE II and dBASE III data base files. dBASE Mac can't use dBASE II, dBASE III, or dBASE IV program files (PRG) files, however. If you have dBASE applications that you want to run on a Mac, consider using Fox Software's FoxBASE/Mac instead. By running unmodified dBASE applications on the Mac, you'll forego the Mac's graphical user interface, but that may be a price you're willing to pay if you have a complex dBASE application that you rely on in your business.

Interchange Formats Revisited

The interchange file formats discussed earlier in this chapter—DIF, RTF, EPS, TIFF, DCA, and SYLK—are widely supported in the MS-DOS world. Many spreadsheets and database managers can create DIF and SYLK files, and most drawing and scanning programs support the EPS and TIFF formats. Microsoft Word 5.0 (MS-DOS) can save documents as RTF files, and the MS-DOS version of Aldus PageMaker can import RTF files.

In addition to the above formats, the MS-DOS world has several popular file formats that are either directly supported by some Mac programs or are supported by Apple File Exchange, MacLink Plus, or LapLink Mac. Technically speaking, some of the formats listed below are native formats, not interchange formats. But because they're supported by several Mac programs and by some file translation utilities, they can serve as interchange formats.

CGM. Short for *computer graphics metafile*, an object-oriented file format supported by several graphics applications, including Lotus Freelance Plus, Software Publishing's Harvard Graphics, and Micrografx Designer 2.0.

DB2, DB3. The formats used for by Ashton-Tate's dBASE II (DB2) and dBASE III (DB3) database managers.

DXF. The format used by the PC version of Autodesk's AutoCAD computer-aided design (CAD) program. Several developers of Mac CAD programs offer optional translation utilities for importing DXF files.

HPGL. Short for *Hewlett-Packard Graphics Language*, HPGL files contain commands that control a plotter or printer that uses HPGL. Many graphics and drafting programs can create HPGL files, and many file translation utilities support HPGL. HPGL files often have the extension .PLT.

Lotus PIC. The format in which Lotus 1-2-3 and Symphony save charts.

Micrografx PIC. The format in which Micrografx Draw and Draw Plus (object-oriented drawing programs for Microsoft Windows) save graphics. Micrografx Designer, Graph, and Graph Plus can also create PIC files.

WKS, WK1. As mentioned earlier, the formats used by Lotus 1-2-3 Release 1A (WKS) and Release 2 (WK1).

Table 11-4 lists some Macintosh applications and file translation utilities that can read (R) and write (W) the above formats.

Table 11-4: Mac applications that support popular PC formats.

	DB2/DB3	DXF	Lotus PIC	Micrografx PIC	WKS/WK1
Apple File Exchange	(1)	—	—	—	(1)
dBASE Mac	R/W	—	—	—	—
FoxBASE/Mac	R/W	—	—	—	—
Full Impact	R/W	—	—	—	R/W
Informix WingZ	—	—	—	—	R/W
LapLink Mac	—	—	—	—	—
MacLink Plus	R/W	—	—	—	R/W
Microsoft Excel	R/W	—	—	—	R/W

(1) With appropriate translators

Converting Graphics Files

As Table 11-4 shows, support for PC graphics formats (other than TIFF and EPS, discussed earlier in this chapter) is rare in the Mac world, even among Mac file translation utilities. Fortunately, you can still convert PC graphics files to work with Macintosh applications by using one of several file translation programs available for the PC. These products include:

GCP by Kim Levitt (shareware, available through PC user's groups and the Microsoft forum on CompuServe). Formerly known as Easel, GCP is a Microsoft Windows application that can convert between the following formats: Windows Paint (MSP), GIF (described below), MacPaint, and PC Paintbrush (PCX) formats. We used GCP to convert the Connect screen in Figure 11-14 to MacPaint format; that screen image began life as a Windows Paint file.

Passport by Micrografx. Another Microsoft Windows application, Passport was in development at this writing at scheduled for release in the fall of 1989. According to Micrografx, Passport will convert between these formats: Micrografx DRW, PICT, and CGM. It will also be able to read (but not create) DFX-format files.

The Graphics Link+ by TerraVision Inc. (distributed by Harvard Systems Corp.). One of the most comprehensive PC graphics utilities available, the Graphics Link+ can convert between the following formats: MacPaint, TIFF, EPS, PC Paintbrush, DR Halo (CUT), GEM/Ventura Publisher (IMG), Lotus Manuscript Bitmap (BIT), WordPerfect Graphics Format (WPG), Windows Paint (MSP), PC Paintbrush (PCX), and CompuServe GIF. The Graphics Link+ also lets you alter images—change their size, modify their color and gray-scale information, and so on—before translating them. And it includes software that lets you save MS-DOS text and graphics screen images, a process similar to the Mac's Command-Shift-3 snapshot key sequence.

There's also a Macintosh program, Kandu Software's CADMover, that can convert between PICT formats and numerous CAD-oriented formats, including DXF and IGES (Initial Graphics Exchange Specification, a graphics standard created by the American National Standards Institute). The IGES format is common in minicomputer- and mainframe-based CAD systems.

GIF Files

In 1987, the CompuServe information service developed a file format for exchanging bit-mapped graphics called the *graphics interchange format,* or *GIF* (pronounced *jiff*). CompuServe created GIF so that its subscribers—whose computers' graphics capabilities vary widely—could display CompuServe graphics such as weather maps and stock market charts, and so that subscribers with different types of computers could exchange graphic images.

CompuServe subscribers have begun taking GIF beyond the on line confines of CompuServe and are turning it into a standard file format for swapping bit-mapped graphics between different computers. Because programs that let you view GIF images are available for both the Mac and PC, you can use GIF files to move bit-mapped graphics between the Mac and PC.

The most popular GIF viewer for the Mac is Steve Blackstock's Giffer ($20 shareware fee—or a case of beer). Several GIF programs are available for MS-DOS machines, including the Microsoft Windows utility GCP, described above. GIF viewers are also available for Amiga and Atari computers.

Using Transferred Text-Only Files

Ironically, text-only files can cause as many data exchange headaches as formatted documents. The main problem occurs with lines that end in a "hard" carriage return, such as the last line of each paragraph in a word processor document. The PC signifies a hard return with two codes—a carriage return code and a line feed code. (When creating text-only files, some PC word processors also put a carriage return code at the end of every line.)

The Mac, however, doesn't need a line feed code; it requires only a carriage return code to signify a hard carriage return. Thus, when you open a PC text-only file using a Mac word processor, you'll see a hollow box at the beginning of each line that follows a hard carriage return, as shown in Figure 11-15. (On the Mac, a hollow box signifies an "unknown" character—one that isn't part of the Mac's built-in set of characters.)

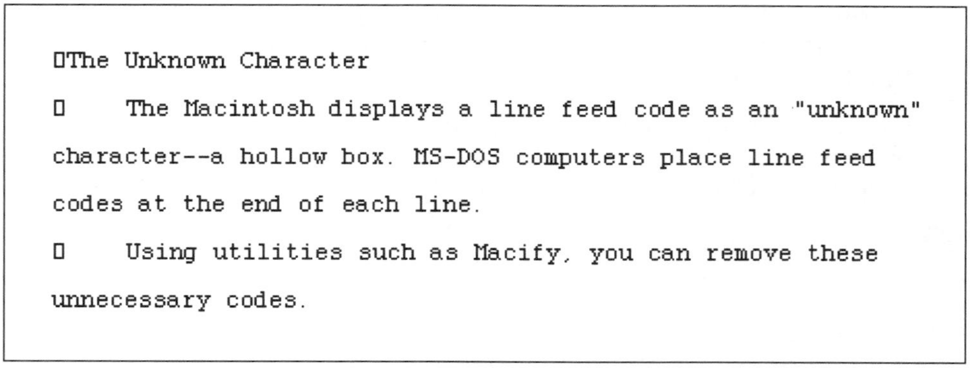

```
☐The Unknown Character

☐    The Macintosh displays a line feed code as an "unknown"

character--a hollow box. MS-DOS computers place line feed

codes at the end of each line.

☐    Using utilities such as Macify, you can remove these

unnecessary codes.
```

Figure 11-15: The Mac displays a line feed code as an unknown character.

The hard way around this problem is to use a Mac word processor to edit the transferred text file, removing the line feed codes by hand. The easy way is to use a file translation utility. Apple File Exchange is ideal for fixing PC text-only files; use its "MS-DOS to Mac" option and choose the check box labelled "Replace CR/LF with just CR," as shown in Figure 11-16.

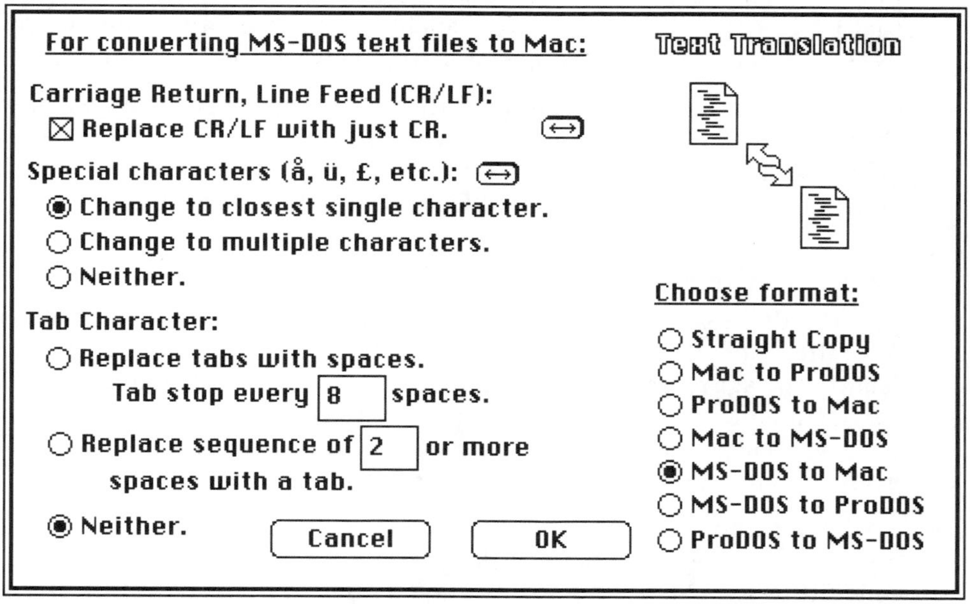

For converting MS-DOS text files to Mac: **Text Translation**

Carriage Return, Line Feed (CR/LF):
☒ Replace CR/LF with just CR.   ⟨↔⟩

Special characters (å, ü, £, etc.): ⟨↔⟩
⦿ Change to closest single character.
○ Change to multiple characters.
○ Neither.

Tab Character: **Choose format:**
○ Replace tabs with spaces.
   Tab stop every [8] spaces.   ○ Straight Copy
                                            ○ Mac to ProDOS
                                            ○ ProDOS to Mac
○ Replace sequence of [2] or more   ○ Mac to MS-DOS
   spaces with a tab.   ⦿ MS-DOS to Mac
⦿ Neither.   (Cancel)   (OK)   ○ MS-DOS to ProDOS
                                            ○ ProDOS to MS-DOS

Figure 11-16: Using Apple File Exchange to remove line-feed codes.

Another useful utility for massaging text files is Eric Celeste's Macify (shareware, $10). Macify, shown in Figure 11-17, not only lets you fix carriage return/line feed problems, it also lets you specify that single quotes be turned into true typographer's quotes and that double hyphens be turned into an em dash. And you can specify up to three character translations—a useful feature for turning asterisks (*) into bullets (•).

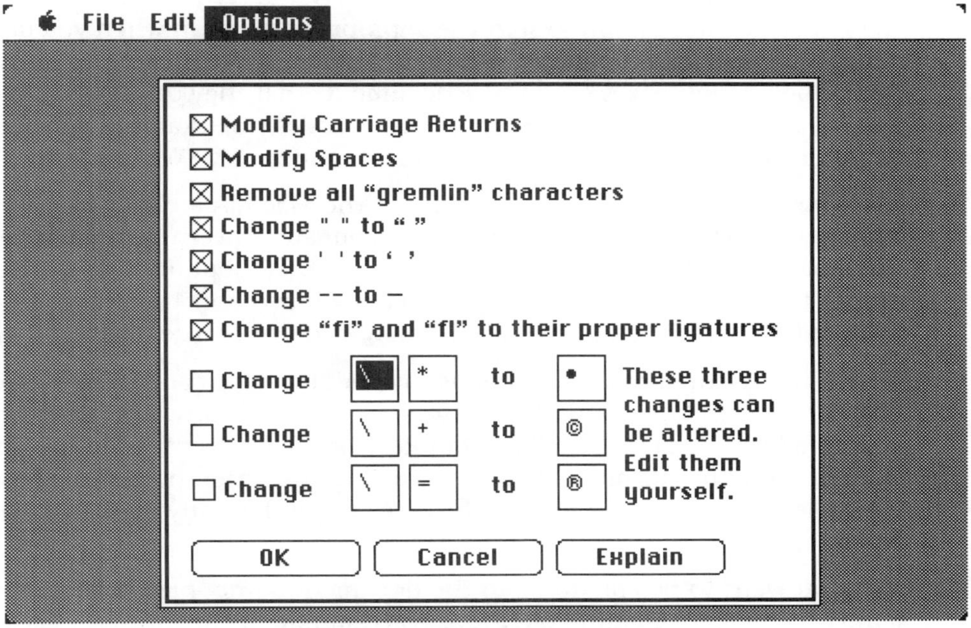

Figure 11-17: Eric Celeste's Macify utility.

A utility called Evolutions (by Kevin Hoctor; shareware, $10) can also fix carriage return/line feed problems.

Opening Transferred Files

To open files transferred to the Mac from a PC, you'll need to use the technique described earlier in this chapter. Rather than trying to open the file by double-clicking it, first start your application program, and then use its Open command to open the file. Or, select both the application and the file, and then choose the Finder's Open command.

But there are times when even these techniques won't work. For example, let's say you transfer a scanned TIFF image from the PC to the Mac because you want to alter it using Letraset's ImageStudio or Silicon Beach Software's Digital Darkroom. When you try to open the document, its name won't appear in the Open dialog box.

This problem occurs because of the unique structure of Macintosh files. Mac files contain a *signature* that specifies the file's *type* and *creator*. The Finder uses the signature information to start the appropriate program when you double-click on a document. Applications use the signature information to display in their Open dialog boxes only those documents that they can open. The type and creator entries are each four-character codes; for example, a Microsoft Word document has a type of WDBN and a creator of MSWD.

Generally, a PC file that you transfer to the Mac has a type code of TEXT. And where ImageStudio and Digital Darkroom are concerned, therein lies the rub. Both programs can open files with a type of TIFF, but not files with a type of TEXT. Thus, even though the PC TIFF file may be in the proper internal format, ImageStudio and Digital Darkroom won't recognize it as a TIFF file.

You can fix the problem by changing the file's type code using ResEdit, a disk-editing utility, or a desk accessory such as CE Software's DiskTop. To change a file's type using ResEdit, start ResEdit, then select the file and choose Get Info from the File menu. In the Info dialog box, enter the new type code in the Type text box. For a TIFF file, the type code is, logically enough, TIFF (see Figure 11-18).

If you want to be able to open the document by double-clicking it at the Finder, change its creator code, too. For example, to open a PC PageMaker document by double-clicking it, change its type to ALB3 and its creator to ALD3. You'll find a list of type and creator codes used by popular Mac programs in Chapter 15.

A Word About File Extensions

Depending on the Mac application you're using to open a PC file, you may need to add a specific file extension to the transferred file. For example, the Mac version of PageMaker can open a PC PageMaker 3.0 publication, but its name must end with the extension PM3. (This doesn't apply if you change the publication's type and creator codes as described above.) Similarly, Mac PageMaker can import several types of PC WordPerfect, WordStar, XyWrite III, and DCA format documents, but their names must end with the extensions WP, WS, XYW, and DCA, respectively.

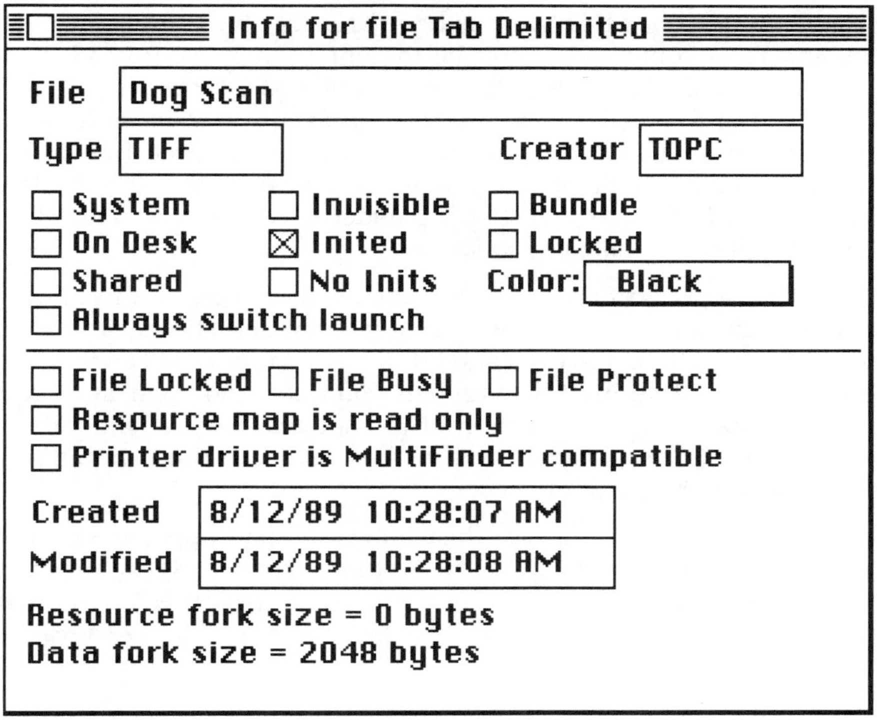

```
▤□▤▤▤▤▤▤ Info for file Tab Delimited ▤▤▤▤▤▤
```

File | Dog Scan

Type | TIFF   Creator | TOPC

☐ System   ☐ Invisible   ☐ Bundle
☐ On Desk   ☒ Inited   ☐ Locked
☐ Shared   ☐ No Inits   Color: | Black
☐ Always switch launch

☐ File Locked ☐ File Busy ☐ File Protect
☐ Resource map is read only
☐ Printer driver is MultiFinder compatible

Created | 8/12/89 10:28:07 AM

Modified | 8/12/89 10:28:08 AM

Resource fork size = 0 bytes
Data fork size = 2048 bytes

Figure 11-18: Changing a file's type code using ResEdit.

Data Exchange and System 7.0

As you may recall from Chapter 10's look at macro utilities, System 7.0 will provide for interapplication communications (IAC)—the ability for programs to communicate with each other as they're running. From a data exchange viewpoint, IAC will be the best thing to come along since the Clipboard.

Why? Consider how the present Clipboard works: When you copy a spreadsheet chart from Program A and then paste it into Program B, the chart is no longer "connected" to the program that created it. If your original data changes and you need a revised chart, you must return to Program A, change the chart, and then copy the new chart and paste it into Program B.

With IAC, you can establish "live links" between documents created by the same application or by different applications. With a live link, when your data changes in the original document, the Mac automatically updates it in other open documents in which the data appears. With the chart example, you simply return to Program A and change the chart. The Mac automatically updates the chart as it appears in Program B.

Apple has described this live-linking process as "live Copy/Paste," but the Copy and Paste commands won't be the ones you'll use. Instead, two new commands, Publish and Subscribe, will provide the gateways to live links. When you want to make some information available to other applications (even ones running on other machines in a network), select the information and choose Publish. A dialog box similar to the Save dialog box will allow you to name the information and choose a folder in which to store it. This published information is called a *publication*.

To include a publication in another document and create a live link, open that document (or switch to it with MultiFinder) and choose Subscribe. Another dialog box, similar to the standard Open dialog box, will appear showing the available publications. Select the one you want, and the data is imported and a link established. The portion of the document where the publication appears is called a *subscriber*. A new toolbox manager, the Publication Manager, handles the live-linking process.

Live Copy/Paste won't replace the Clipboard. The Clipboard will still be a useful data exchange medium for those times when a live link isn't necessary—or when one program doesn't support live Copy/Paste. As with many of System 7.0's features, applications will need to be revised to take advantage of live Copy/Paste.

CHAPTER SUMMARY

- The Mac provides three standard Clipboard formats—PICT for graphics, TEXT for unformatted text, and styl for formatted text. Many programs also provide their own private Clipboard formats for storing additional formatting information.

- When moving text between programs, if you lose formatting information, chances are it's because the importing program can't interpret the exporting program's Clipboard formats, or because the exporting program didn't use a format that can store formatting information.

- When you need to retain formatting information when transferring data between programs, choose programs that can read each others' Clipboard formats.

- Generally, you'll want to cut or copy text as text so that you can still edit it. However, cutting or copying text as a picture lets you resize it for special typographic effects.

- For moving large amounts of data between programs, use disk files instead of the Clipboard. Disk files also give you more options for retaining the data's formatting.

- You can transfer text using three types of disk files: native files, interchange files, and text-only (ASCII) files.

- When using text-only files to exchange spreadsheet or database information, it's important to use the proper delimiters so that the importing program can differentiate between each cell and row (or field and record).

- You can move files between a Mac and an MS-DOS computer by using a disk drive that reads the other system's disks, by using a cable or a telephone modem, or by using a network.

- Several file translation products are available that can convert one type of file into another type. Most translation products work with text-oriented documents such as word processor and database files, but some are also available for converting graphics files.

- System 7.0 will provide "live Copy/Paste" features that will allow you to establish live links between documents, eliminating the need to repeatedly cut and paste data to keep a document up-to-date.

12

Networking

When you work in an office, you share. You share photocopiers and other office equipment with your coworkers. You share information, relying on a central library or file cabinets that everyone uses. And you share ideas as you brainstorm with colleagues in conference rooms, on the telephone, and at each other's desks.

A *local-area network*, or *network* for short, lets you extend these same categories of sharing to your computers. In this chapter, we'll look at how networks can unite a collection of computers and their users. We'll examine:

- the benefits and potential pitfalls of networks

- networking concepts and terminology

- networking hardware and software

Finally, we'll take a hands-on, stepwise look at how you might set up a small network to share hardware and data between a group of Macs and MS-DOS computers. We'll also provide some tips and guidelines for keeping your network running smoothly.

Networking is a complex topic that would be difficult to cover fully in a single book, much less in a single chapter. This chapter will give you an idea of what to expect from a network and help you wade through the sea of jargon you'll face when shopping for network products. If you're interested in setting up a small network—perhaps a few Macs, PCs, and a laser printer—this chapter will show you how to get started. If you're planning to set up a complex network containing dozens of different types of computers, the information here will help you work with a qualified network consultant to determine your needs and choose the products that best meet them.

WHY NETWORK?

Regardless of how many computers you have, a network can provide four basic benefits:

- Your computers can share expensive add-ons such as laser printers and hard disks.

- Coworkers can communicate with each other using *electronic mail* software.

- Users can share data that everyone in the office uses, such as mailing lists, inventory data bases, and boilerplate templates for desktop publications.

- People can join forces and work on projects together, using the network to share information and ideas.

Let's take a closer look at each benefit.

Resource Sharing

Imagine if you had to buy or lease a separate photocopier, postal meter, and water cooler for everyone in your office. That's not an appealing thought, but it illustrates the dilemma microcomputer users faced until recently. If Eric in engineering had to print documents, he needed his own printer. If Amy in accounting had something to print, she needed one, too. Or she had to carry her disk to Eric's desk and interrupt him. Each person who used a communications service such as MCI Mail needed his or her own modem. The end result was either hefty hardware expenditures or inefficiency.

Networks change all that. As you'll recall from Chapter 8, PostScript printers such as the LaserWriter IINT and NTX contain hardware and software that allow them to be shared on a network. Equip an ImageWriter II or ImageWriter LQ with an optional expansion board, and you can share it on a network, too. With some additional software, you can also share hard disks and modems. Each piece of hardware that's tapped into the network—whether a computer, a printer, or a hard disk—is called a *node*.

While a network's resource-sharing benefits don't eliminate the need to buy additional hard disks or printers as your office grows, the ability to share expensive add-ons can cut costs and make it easier to justify an expensive purchase.

File Sharing

In most offices, certain people need access to the same data. A sales staff needs access to a company's product fact sheets and price lists. The legal department needs access to case histories, government regulations, and boilerplate legal text. The shipping department needs access to inventory information.

With a network, you can place this kind of information on a shared hard disk, called a *file server*, where it can be accessed by everyone—or, if you like, by only certain people. You don't need to pass files around on floppy disks, and you don't need to worry about whose version of a file is the most current. By using software designed for *multi-user* access, several people can even use the same file at once.

Depending on the programs you use—and on their developers' licensing agreements—you can even share software on a network. Instead of buying five copies of a program, you can buy only one, and then purchase additional manuals for each user.

Electronic Mail

With electronic mail coworkers can communicate with the same immediacy that the telephone provides, but without the interruptions. What's more, because electronic mail uses that endangered species—written communication—it gives you a chance to organize your thoughts, and it gives you a written record that can refresh your memory. Your communiqués can even include "enclosures"—disk files that accompany your message. And you don't have to worry about delays because of sluggish interoffice mail delivery.

Collaborative Computing

By combining resource sharing, file sharing, and electronic mail, you provide the foundation for collaborative computing, in which documents and ideas flow between workers and departments. For example, in a publishing department, a writer can send drafts to others for approval. After receiving electronically marked-up copy, he or she can make revisions and then "drop" the files in a designer's electronic "in" box, which might already contain illustrations created by an artist. The designer can combine these components into a publication, and then leave it in an "out" box where others can retrieve it for review.

What may be most exciting about networking is that all this can take place over large distances. By equipping your network for *remote access*, employees in branch offices or freelancers scattered across the country can exchange files and messages with people whose desks are next to each other. If you think it's a small world now, wait until you start copying files to a hard disk located thousands of miles away—as if it was connected directly to your Mac.

It's Not All Rosy

Before we take a closer look at networking, it's important to inject a dose of reality. A network's benefits are the result of careful advance planning. To reach the rosy world of collaborative computing, you'll need to plan your electronic work flow, then you'll need to stress to everyone on the network that it's important to work within this plan.

To keep the network running smoothly, you'll need to devote time to network-management chores such as backing up the network's hard disks and making sure all network cables are snug and tucked away from areas where people might kick them loose. Finally, you'll need to stress the importance of cooperation to everyone on the network. People need to know that they shouldn't disconnect their machines from the network without notifying others, and that they shouldn't perform tasks that will bog down the network's hard disk and prevent others from accessing it.

We'll elaborate on these guidelines throughout this chapter. But as you develop your networking plans, keep this thought in mind: Ultimately, you're not putting *computers* on a network, you're putting *people* on a network. Plan and operate your network with this in mind, and your network will serve you—instead of the other way around.

NETWORK CONCEPTS

When setting up a network, you'll need to contend with technicalities and jargon concerning:

- Network hardware, the cabling arrangements you use to physically attach each node to the network.

- Network software, which each computer attached to the network uses to communicate, and which you use to access shared resources and exchange electronic mail.

The hardware and software sides of networking are closely related. They work together to determine such factors as the network's performance, the number of nodes it can accommodate, and in many cases, its cost.

Network Hardware

To share data and hardware resources, the computers in your office must be connected by cables. Apple supports three types of networking cabling schemes for the Mac:

LocalTalk. The least expensive and most popular cabling scheme for Mac networks, LocalTalk is the cabling used to attach Macs to LaserWriters and other PostScript printers. For small networks comprising several Macs, PCs, and laser printers, LocalTalk is the most sensible choice. We'll concentrate primarily on it in this chapter. In fact, if you plan to set up a small network using LocalTalk, you may want to skim or skip the rest of this section and move on to the section "Network Software."

Token-Ring. A network standard developed by the Institute of Electrical and Electronic Engineers (IEEE), Token-Ring is especially popular in the IBM world.

Ethernet. You might recall this term from Chapter 2—it's the networking system developed at Xerox for the pioneering Star workstation. Ethernet remains a popular network standard, especially in the minicomputer and main-frame world. Digital Equipment Corporation (DEC) VAX minicomputers often use Ethernet networks.

Network Performance

As Figure 12-1 shows, these three networking media transfer information at dramatically different speeds. With Apple's LocalTalk cabling and connectors, data travels at roughly 230 kilobits per second—faster than a Mac's floppy disk, but several times slower than a fast SCSI hard disk. (Some non-Apple connectors such as Dayna's DaynaTalk can speed LocalTalk's transfer rate to 850 kilobits.) With Apple's TokenTalk NB, a NuBus board for Token-Ring networks, data travels at a swift 4 megabits per second. Ethernet can transfer data at up to 10 megabits per second.

You'll hear these performance figures tossed around often, but the fact is, they don't always reflect how well a network will really perform. A network's actual performance, sometimes called its *throughput*, isn't always easy to quantify. It depends on many factors, including the number of nodes you have and the type of demands each node places on the network.

Just how important is performance, anyway? That depends on how you plan to use your network. Tasks such as printing, sharing small document files, and exchanging electronic mail don't place heavy burdens on a network. For these applications, performance is not critical. A relatively slow network cabling scheme like LocalTalk is adequate for these light-duty needs.

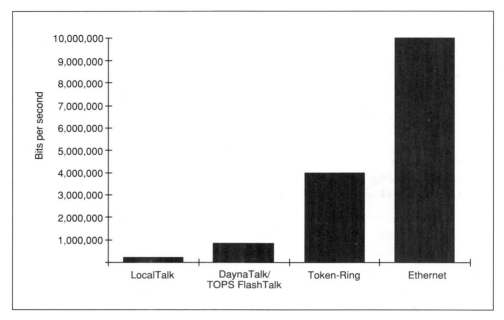

Figure 12-1: Network data-transfer speeds compared.

Speed becomes a bigger factor for multi-user software applications, such as sharing a large data base file among several users. The faster the network, the better the data base program will be able to respond to each user's requests for information.

Speed becomes most critical if you have a large network or if you plan to store applications on a file server so that all the Macs can access them. On a LocalTalk network, starting a large program stored on the file server or copying large files to and from the server can slow the network significantly, and it doesn't provide very satisfying performance. (We'll provide some guidelines for working within LocalTalk's speed limitations later in this chapter.)

Network Topologies

Topology is a buzzword if there ever was one, but it refers to a relatively simple concept: the way the cables physically interconnect the network's nodes. There are several types of network topologies:

Daisy-chain. We encountered this term when looking at the Mac's SCSI expansion bus and Apple Desktop Bus. With those buses, one device's output is connected to the next device's input. A daisy-chain network is arranged similarly, as shown in Figure 12-2. One potential drawback of a daisy-chain network is that the network can be disrupted when a node is disconnected. For example, if the Mac labeled "Eric" in Figure 12-2 is removed from the network, the ones labelled "Mary," "Denny," and "George" become disconnected, too. LocalTalk uses a daisy-chaining topology.

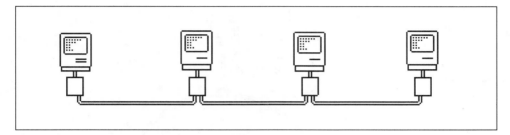

Figure 12-2: The daisy-chain network topology used by LocalTalk.

Trunk. This topology uses a central cable that each node taps into—just as the houses in a neighborhood tap into a community's cable TV system (Figure 12-3). With a bus network, you can generally disconnect one node without affecting others—just as one house's cable TV can be disconnected without affecting others. Ethernet uses the bus topology.

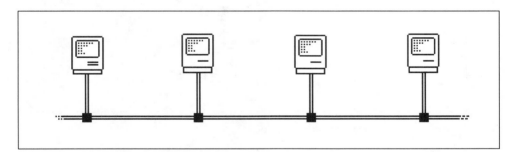

Figure 12-3: The bus network topology.

Ring. In the ring topology, the nodes are connected in a loop, as shown in Figure 12-4. A kind of electronic messenger called a *packet* travels continuously around the ring. Sometimes the messenger isn't carrying anything; other times, it's carrying information addressed to a specific node. Each node examines the packet for information addressed to it. When a node finds some, it reads the information, and then sends the empty packet along. When a node needs to send information, it waits until an empty packet arrives, then it "loads" the packet with data, addresses it, and sends it along. One drawback of the ring topology is that adding or removing a node disrupts the network, since the ring must be momentarily broken. IBM's Token-Ring network uses the ring topology.

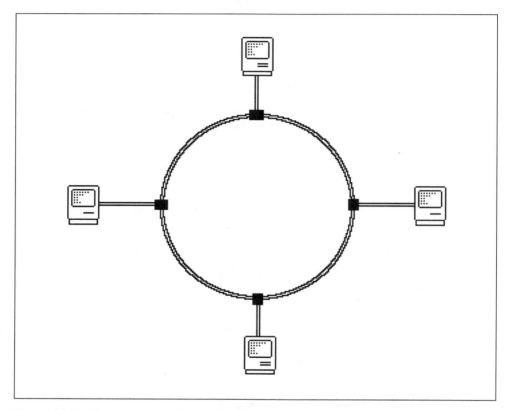

Figure 12-4: The ring network topology.

Star. With the star topology, all nodes are tapped into one central node, which controls the entire network (Figure 12-5). The telephone system is a good example of a star topology: All the phones are connected to the phone company's central switching station, and all calls are routed through that station. Farallon Computing's PhoneNet cabling system can be wired in a star configuration, and can use the spare wires in a building's existing telephone wiring to carry data between each network node. PhoneNet has become a popular alternative to LocalTalk.

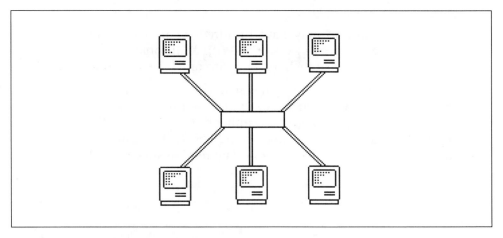

Figure 12-5: The star network topology.

The type of networking cabling arrangement you choose will depend on several factors:

The number of nodes in your network. LocalTalk, for example, is limited to a maximum of 32 nodes. (And that's a theoretical limit; because of Local-Talk's relatively slow speed, a more practical limit is 20 to 25 nodes.) Ethernet and Token-Ring can easily accommodate hundreds of nodes.

The performance you require. As mentioned earlier, LocalTalk, Ethernet, and Token-Ring each transfer data at different speeds.

The physical set up of your computers. LocalTalk has a maximum distance of approximately 1,000 feet. Farallon's PhoneNet supports network distances of up to 3,000 feet. Ethernet and Token-Ring support similarly large distances.

Your computing environment. Your choice of networking hardware may be influenced by the types of computers you want to connect your Macs to. In an IBM-oriented business, you might lean toward Token-Ring. If your business uses DEC's VAX computers, Ethernet may be a more appropriate choice.

Your networking budget. LocalTalk hardware is built into every Macintosh and every PostScript printer. To connect a device to the network, you need add only a LocalTalk cabling kit, which costs about $75. You can add a LocalTalk expansion board to an MS-DOS computer for between $200 and $350. Ethernet and Token-Ring, by contrast, require their own NuBus or SE expansion boards, which can cost between $700 and $1200 for each node.

Combining Networks

A large institution may have hundreds or thousands of computers using several different types of networks. With additional hardware, you can unite this vast array of disparate hardware into one large network, called an *internet*.

To interconnect separate smaller networks, you need a hardware add-on called a *bridge*. Bridges such as Hayes' Interbridge can be used to break up a large LocalTalk network into a number of smaller *zones*, improving reliability and performance, and working around LocalTalk's limitations of 1,000 feet of cabling and 32 nodes per network. Figure 12-6 shows two LocalTalk network zones united by a bridge.

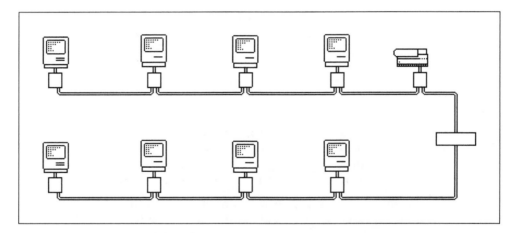

Figure 12-6: Two LocalTalk networks connected by a bridge.

A bridge connects similar networks; a *gateway* connects dissimilar ones. Figure 12-7 shows a large internet that uses gateways to unite a LocalTalk network, an Ethernet network, and a Token-Ring network. In this diagram, an Ethernet *backbone* serves as a main freeway connecting each network. One popular gateway for uniting LocalTalk and Ethernet networks is Kinetic's Fast-Path. A Macintosh equipped with appropriate boards and Apple's Internet Router software can serve as a gateway between LocalTalk, Ethernet, and Token-Ring networks.

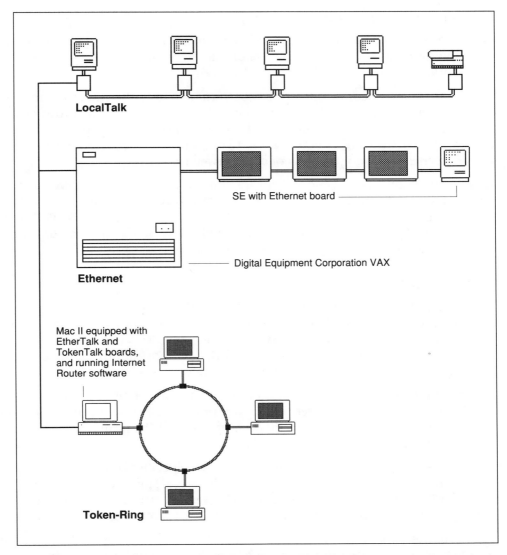

LocalTalk

SE with Ethernet board ——————————

Digital Equipment Corporation VAX

Ethernet

Mac II equipped with
EtherTalk and
TokenTalk boards,
and running Internet
Router software

Token-Ring

Figure 12-7: Three different types of networks united via gateways by an Ethernet backbone.

Network Software

A network's hardware is only a medium, a way for data to physically travel between nodes. To take advantage of that medium, we need two types of networking software:

- The fundamental software that determines how the nodes communicate with each other and how data travels on the network. Macintosh networks use a set of communication rules called *AppleTalk*. You don't see the AppleTalk software as you use a network, but it's there, working behind the scenes to govern the flow of data between nodes.

- The specialized network software you use to access a file server, send and receive electronic mail, print to networked printers, and so on. This software—the kind you *do* see—works together with AppleTalk. Put another way, AppleTalk provides the rules that allow nodes to communicate, but network software gives them a reason to do so.

AppleTalk

If a network is a freeway for data, AppleTalk is the driver's manual—it specifies the rules of the road. More specifically, AppleTalk specifies the format of the data packets that travel between nodes. AppleTalk provides several sets of rules, or *protocols*, for governing network communications, but two are especially important from our standpoint as network users:

- The *Printer-Access Protocol* (*PAP*), which specifies how the computers on a network access a printer. When you print to a PostScript printer or to AppleTalk-equipped ImageWriters, your Mac and the printer use PAP to communicate.

- The *AppleTalk Filing Protocol* (*AFP*), which specifies how the computers on the network access files stored on a file server. File server software that uses AFP is often called *AFP-compliant*. File server software that doesn't use AFP but that can coexist with software that does is often called *AFP-compatible*.

In the earlier days of Mac networking, AppleTalk also referred to the cabling and connectors that run from node to node. As Apple began developing more ambitious networking products, it changed the name of the cabling and connectors to LocalTalk to reflect their niche in small, localized networks.

The point to remember here is that AppleTalk protocols can run on a variety of cabling schemes, including Ethernet and Token-Ring. Apple's Token-Ring and Ethernet boards include the fundamental software that allows AppleTalk protocols to run with these networks. (As this book was going to press, some of Apple's Token-Ring and Ethernet products were still in development and scheduled to be available by the end of 1989.)

Several firms sell their own software that implements AppleTalk protocols on non-Apple systems. For example, LocalTalk boards for MS-DOS computers include AppleTalk driver software. On a larger scale, products such as Alisa Systems' AlisaShare, and Pacer Software's PacerShare, teach DEC's VAX minicomputers about AppleTalk protocols, and allow a network of Macs and Local-Talk-equipped PCs to use a VAX as a file server.

A NETWORK SCENARIO

Enough of concepts and jargon—let's look at what's actually involved in setting up a LocalTalk network. In this section, we'll develop a complete network step-by-step. We'll use LocalTalk to interconnect several Macs, MS-DOS computers, and a laser printer, and we'll sample some networking software.

The network that we'll set up is a typical small LocalTalk network, the kind you might see in any small business or department. It contains three Macs, an IBM PC/AT compatible, an IBM PS/2 Model 50, and a LaserWriter IINT Post-Script laser printer.

Like many businesses, we'll start out by simply sharing the laser printer. Then we'll add electronic mail service and a file server. By adding network services in phases, troubleshooting is easier.

We've broken each phase down into steps, and concluded each step with some tips and guidelines, which appear in italics. If you want a quick overview of the entire network-installation process, you might want to just read the italicized paragraphs.

Phase 1: Printer Sharing

In this phase, we'll plan the network and set it up to share the laser printer.

Step 1: Planning

The first step in setting up a network isn't attaching wires or running software installation programs. It's planning. By planning your network, you'll know exactly what hardware you need and you'll be able to lay out your cables to accommodate future network expansion.

Initially, your network will be used for printing, so advance planning involves simply deciding how many nodes you'll have and where they'll be located. So, with notepad in hand, ask yourself a few questions:

How many network nodes will you have? You'll need to know how many LocalTalk connector kits to buy. In this example, your network will have six nodes.

How many of them are PCs or PS/2s? You'll need to know how many LocalTalk expansion boards to buy. You have one PC/AT and one PS/2, so you'll need two different LocalTalk boards. For the AT, you'll use Apple's LocalTalk PC Card. (You could also choose TOPS' FlashCard or DayStar Digital's LT-200; however, you did some homework and found that neither of those boards works with version 1.1 of Apple's AppleShare PC software, which you plan to use later when you set up a file server.) For the PS/2, you'll use DayStar Digital's LT-200MC—the only LocalTalk board currently available for IBM's Micro-Channel expansion slots. The LT-200MC doesn't work with AppleShare PC 1.1, either, but it includes its own software for accessing AppleShare file servers.

What kinds of LocalTalk connectors do your nodes use? Your Macs use DIN-8 miniplugs, and so does your LaserWriter IINT. But a call to a dealer reveals that the PC and PS/2 LocalTalk boards you plan to buy use DB-9 connectors. So, you need four DIN-8 connector kits, and two DB-9 connector kits.

How many nodes might you have in the future? You plan to buy another Mac when you hire an assistant, so you'll plan your cable layout to accommodate the new machine.

Where will the nodes be located? For the computers themselves, the answer is obvious: at each desk that has a computer. But the printer is a special case. You'll want to move it to a central location, where everyone will be able to access it easily, but you'll also want to locate it so that it won't distract anyone as it churns out pages from each machine in the network.

Plan ahead. Anticipate your future needs, and verify that your present hardware purchases will be able to accommodate them. Don't overlook the little details, such as what kinds of connectors you'll need.

Step 2: Assembling the Pieces

You've visited a local Apple dealer and bought six LocalTalk Connector Kits: four with DIN-8 connectors (Apple part number M2068), and two with DB-9 connectors (part number M2065). Each connector kit includes a connection box, which plugs into a node's LocalTalk connector, a six-foot cable, and a small connector called a *cable extender* (Figure 12-8).

You also bought the the DayStar Digital LT-200MC LocalTalk board for your PS/2, and the Apple LocalTalk PC board for your AT. To have some flexibility in locating your laser printer, you bought Apple's LocalTalk Cable Kit, which includes a 30-foot LocalTalk cable and a cable extender.

Figure 12-8: A LocalTalk Connector Kit.

Try to buy all your network components from one source, preferably a knowledge-able local dealer or consultant who can help you troubleshoot problems. By purchasing locally, you can quickly exchange faulty cables and connectors or take them into the shop for testing.

Step 3: Install the LocalTalk Boards

Before you're able to wire up the network, you need to install the LocalTalk expansion boards in the AT and PS/2. Be sure the machines are turned off, and that you aren't carrying any static electricity that would damage the boards' components. Avoid shuffling across the carpet beforehand, and touch a radiator or light switch plate to discharge any static before installing the boards.

Installing the PS/2's LocalTalk board is a breeze thanks to the Micro-Channel's ability to automatically configure the system after you install a board. First, fire up the PS/2 and copy a configuration file from the floppy disk that accompanied the board to a backup copy of the PS/2 Reference Disk. Next, shut the PS/2 off, install the board, and then start the computer using the Reference Disk. Then, follow the Reference Disk's configuration menus to set up the board. Finally, copy the programs from the disk that accompanied the board to the PS/2's hard disk. These programs include drivers that implement AppleTalk protocols on the PS/2, and utilities that let the PS/2 print using LocalTalk.

Installing the AT's LocalTalk PC board is a bit trickier, since the AT's expansion slots don't offer the luxury of automatic configuration. You need to examine the other expansion boards installed in the AT to determine if any might conflict with the LocalTalk PC board. For example, let's say your AT contains a Microsoft Mouse expansion board. From consulting the LocalTalk board's manual, you learn that the mouse board could conflict with the Local-Talk board. The solution, the manual says, is to change one of the mouse board's jumpers (a small connector on the board). After doing that, run the installation program that copies the necessary driver software and utilities to the AT's hard disk.

Always follow a few basic precautions when installing expansion boards: turn the power off, discharge static electricity, and avoid touching the board's connectors or components. Check your manuals in advance for information about conflicts between boards.

Step 4: Wire the Nodes

Now every node-to-be is ready for wiring. To plan your network's wiring, you might use MacDraw to draw a simple floorplan of your office, as shown in Figure 12-9.

The first step in wiring the network is verifying that everything is shut off. Next, unpack each LocalTalk connector kit and attach the connector box to each machine. (*Be sure to plug the connector boxes into the Macs' printer ports, not their modem ports.*) Next, connect each machine using LocalTalk cables, taking care to push each cable firmly into its connector box until you hear the cable-locking mechanism click. Tuck the cables behind each desk, where they won't get tangled in someone's feet or desk chair. When you get to the desk labeled "To Be Hired," simply connect two LocalTalk cables with one of the cable extenders that came with your LocalTalk kits. When you hire that new assistant, you'll be able to add another node by simply unplugging the extender (after warning everyone in advance) and replacing it with another connector box.

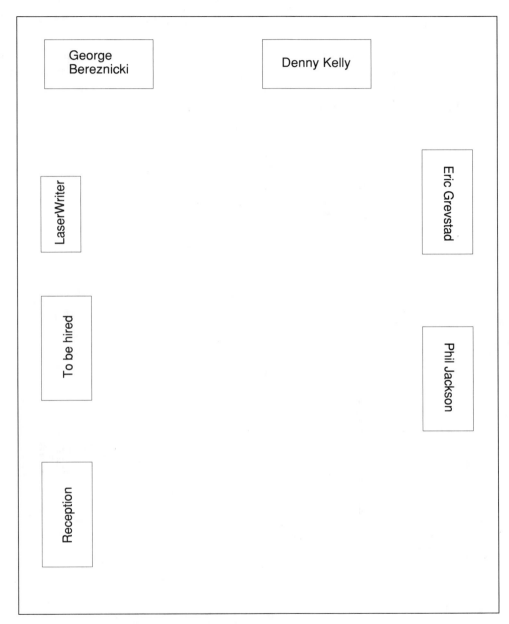

Figure 12-9: A floorplan for planning the network's layout.

When you're done, the network is wired as shown in Figure 12-10. Notice that the network's wiring doesn't form a complete circle; that is, the station named "Eric" doesn't directly connect to the station named "Phil." LocalTalk networks won't work if they're wired in a circle. If you added a wire (the dotted line) from Eric's desk to Phil's, the network would work unreliably (or not at all) because of electrical reflections within the cables.

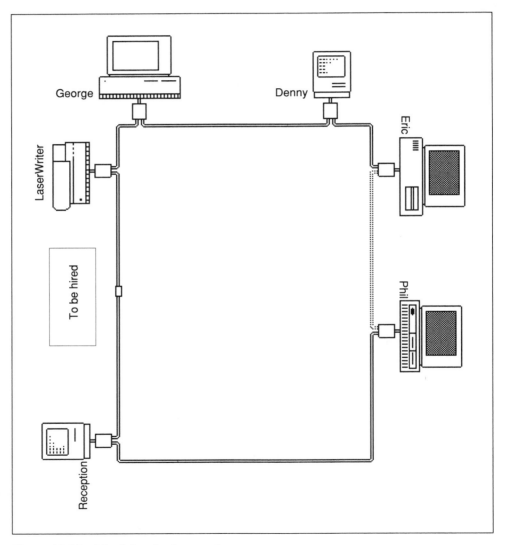

Figure 12-10: The fully-wired network.

Attach network cables firmly, pressing them into their connector boxes until you hear a click. With DB-9 connectors, tighten the thumbscrews so that the connector is snug. Position cables where they won't be knocked loose, and avoid attaching the last node in the network to the first, creating a circle.

Step 5: Check System Software

If you're the anxious type, you're probably tempted to plow right in and try to print a document. Resist the urge. Your next step should be to use the Finder's Get Info command to verify that each Mac is running the same version of the system files and LaserWriter drivers. A few minutes spent on this important task now will prevent troubleshooting headaches later. (See Chapter 5 for details on checking version numbers.)

While you're at it, use each Mac's Chooser desk accessory to activate AppleTalk, as shown in Figure 12-11. Also type a name for that workstation in the Chooser's User Name text box. If you're at someone's desk, type that person's name. If you're at a desk that different people use, choose a descriptive name that reflects the workstation's purpose, such as *Publishing Desk* or *Reception*.

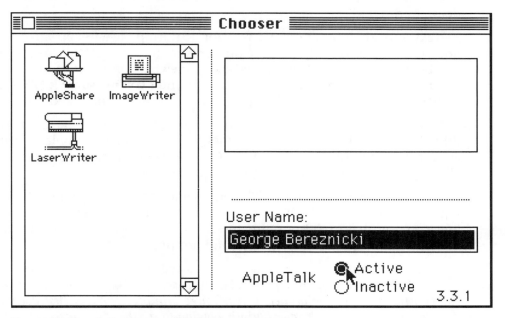

Figure 12-11: Activating AppleTalk using the Chooser.

Networks require homogeneity. Verify that all Macs are running the same version of the system software and LaserWriter drivers. During this step, you might also want to to install on each Mac the screen fonts for the LaserWriter's built-in fonts. Use the Chooser to give each workstation a descriptive name. Make a note of the names you chose so you can use them later, as you add new services.

Step 6: Fire Up the Printer

You're almost ready to print. But first, verify that the printer is configured to use AppleTalk (recall from Chapter 8 that most PostScript printers can operate in other modes, such as Diablo 630 emulation, or use other connectors, such as their RS-232C serial ports). On the LaserWriter IINT, check the printer's DIP switches against the diagram in the manual. With some PostScript printers (such as NEC's SilentWriter LC-890), you need to turn the printer on, enter its configuration mode, and then read the current mode from the printer's status display. With still other printers (including QMS' PS-810), you check the position of a rotary switch. The techniques vary between printers, but the end result is the same: By verifying ahead of time that the printer is configured for LocalTalk, you'll have one less thing to troubleshoot if the first document doesn't print.

Next, turn the printer on and wait for its startup page to appear. When it does, examine it to verify that the printer is set up for LocalTalk. You should see the word "LocalTalk" or "AppleTalk" somewhere on the startup page. (Its exact position will depend on the brand of printer you're using.) If "RS-232C" or "Parallel" appears instead, the printer isn't set up for LocalTalk.

Next, sit down at a Mac, open the Chooser, and click the LaserWriter driver's icon in the Chooser. If all goes well, the name of the laser printer appears in the right-hand side of the Chooser window. Select the printer by clicking on its name, as shown in Figure 12-12.

If you're running under MultiFinder, disable background printing by clicking the Off button in the Chooser window. To verify that the network is working, you'll want to see the status messages on the screen. Normally, those messages don't appear when background printing is active.

Check your printer's settings in advance to avoid troubleshooting hassles. When you use the Chooser to choose a printer, be sure to select the LaserWriter driver and to click on the name of the printer. When you're printing your very first document, disable MultiFinder's background printing option to see the status messages coming from the printer.

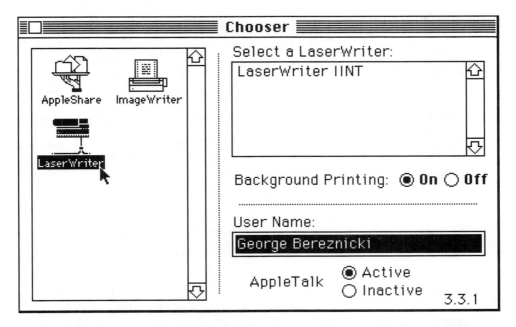

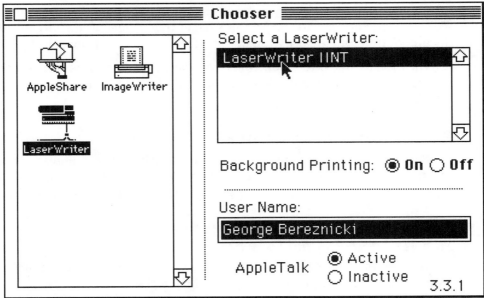

Figure 12-12: Two steps to selecting a laser printer: Choose the LaserWriter driver (*top*) and then select the printer's name (*bottom*).

Step 7: Try it!

Now you're ready to try printing a document. Start an application program and type a sentence or two. Next, choose Print and verify that the printer's name appears in the upper-left corner of the dialog box, as shown in Figure 12-13. If it doesn't, use the Chooser again and be sure to select the printer's name.

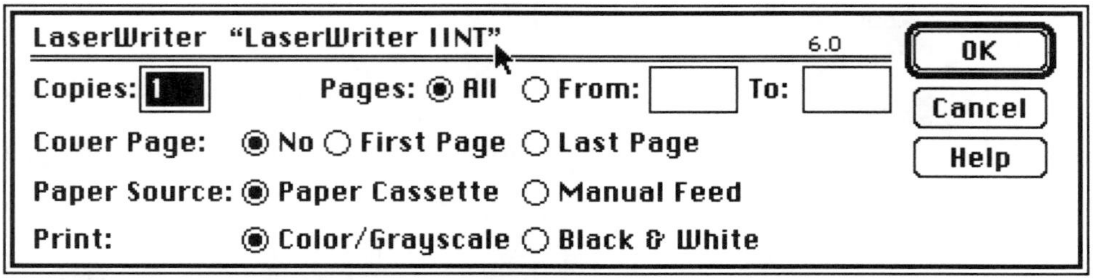

```
┌──────────────────────────────────────────────────────────────┐
│ LaserWriter  "LaserWriter IINT"              6.0  │  ┌──────┐  │
│ ─────────────────────────────────────────────────┤  │  OK  │  │
│ Copies: [1]      Pages: ⦿ All  ○ From: [   ] To: [   ] └──────┘  │
│ Cover Page:    ⦿ No ○ First Page ○ Last Page      ┌────────┐   │
│ Paper Source: ⦿ Paper Cassette ○ Manual Feed     │ Cancel │   │
│ Print:        ⦿ Color/Grayscale ○ Black & White  └────────┘   │
│                                                   │  Help  │   │
└──────────────────────────────────────────────────────────────┘
```

Figure 12-13:   The printer name in the Print dialog box.

If the printer's name does appear, click OK or press Return. In a moment, the message "Looking for LaserWriter *'printer name'*" appears. A few moments after that, a "Status: starting job" message appears. That message is followed by others, including "initializing printer" and "processing job." After a minute or so, the output appears in the printer's paper tray. After successfully printing a document from one workstation, try printing documents from the other Macs.

When you add services to a network, test them from each workstation. Take the time to test your network in advance, and you'll decrease the chances of having to troubleshoot it under pressure.

Phase Two: Printing From PCs

Now that you're successfully printing from each Mac, you're ready to tackle the next phase of the job—setting up the MS-DOS machines to access the LaserWriter. That involves installing printing software on each machine, and then testing it.

Step 1: Choose Printing Software

The type of network printing software you choose for your MS-DOS machines will depend in part on the type of MS-DOS software you run. If you use programs that support PostScript printers directly, such as WordPerfect 5.0, Microsoft Excel, and Aldus PageMaker, you'll be able to use the software that accompanied your LocalTalk boards and your software.

If you use older programs that don't support PostScript printers, you'll need additional software, such as TOPS' NetPrint. With NetPrint, you configure your old software to print to an Epson FX-80 or IBM ProPrinter. When you print, NetPrint intercepts the data and translates it into PostScript. You can even insert formatting codes into documents to access different fonts and type sizes. NetPrint doesn't let older programs take full advantage of a PostScript printer, but at least it lets them access some of its features. NetPrint also provides some goodies, including background PostScript printing, the ability to print the contents of the PC's screen on a PostScript printer, and support for LocalTalk-equipped ImageWriters. NetPrint supports the AppleTalk printer-access protocol (PAP) mentioned earlier in this chapter.

In this scenario, we're assuming you use only newer MS-DOS programs that support PostScript printers directly. So, you don't need NetPrint, but keep it in mind in case you acquire an MS-DOS program that doesn't support PostScript.

Check your MS-DOS programs' manuals to determine whether they support Post-Script printers. If they don't, you'll need software such as TOPS NetPrint or Apple-Share PC to translate your programs' output into PostScript.

Step 2: Installing the Print Software

Normally, MS-DOS programs access PostScript printers through a serial port or parallel printer port. To get a program to print over a network takes additional software, which is included with a LocalTalk expansion board. In this step, we'll install the DayStar Digital software that will allow your PS/2 to access the printer. The steps for the Apple LocalTalk PC board are similar, but we'll discuss the DayStar board here because its documentation is a bit sketchy; if you buy that board, the information in this section could save you a couple of calls to Flowery Branch, Georgia.

(If you haven't worked with MS-DOS, some of the terminology in this step might be unfamiliar. If someone in your office is more familiar with MS-DOS, consider working together with him or her when setting up your MS-DOS machines for LocalTalk printing.)

The steps needed to configure an MS-DOS computer for LocalTalk printing depend on the MS-DOS programs you'll use for printing. We've divided this section into two categories: installation for conventional DOS programs such as Microsoft Word and WordPerfect, and for Microsoft Windows programs such as Excel, PageMaker, and Designer.

Conventional DOS programs. For conventional DOS programs, you'll need two drivers from the disk that accompanies the DayStar Digital board. One is the AppleTalk driver, DTALK.EXE, which teaches the MS-DOS machine AppleTalk protocols. The other driver is called DSLPT.SYS. This driver configures MS-DOS to treat the network's printer as LPT3. To use the driver, add this line to your machine's CONFIG.SYS file:

```
device=DSLPT.SYS "Printer name"
```

In your CONFIG.SYS file, replace the text within quotes with the name of your printer as it appears in the Mac's Chooser desk accessory (leave the quotes in, however). If DSLPT.SYS isn't in your root directory, be sure to spell out its full pathname.

Because you need the DTALK.EXE driver to use the LocalTalk board, you might want to add a line to your system's AUTOEXEC.BAT file to load the driver automatically each time you start up.

After installing these two drivers and making the necessary changes to your CONFIG.SYS and AUTOEXEC.BAT files, restart your computer.

Microsoft Windows programs. To configure Windows for LocalTalk printing, you need your board's AppleTalk driver (for the DayStar Digital board, DTALK.EXE). You'll also need a Windows AppleTalk driver called APPLETLK.-DLL. This driver comes with some Windows applications, including Page-Maker. (In the PageMaker 3.0 package, APPLETLK.DLL is on the Drivers/Filters disk.) If you don't have APPLETLK.DLL, you should be able get a copy at no charge from an Aldus dealer or from Aldus Technical Support. You can also download the file from the Aldus forum on CompuServe. (Type GO ALDUS at any ! prompt.)

The APPLETLK.DLL file must be stored in the same directory as Windows' PostScript printer driver, PSCRIPT.DRV. If it's in a different directory, copy it to the proper one. Finally, if you haven't done so already, load the AppleTalk driver by typing *DTALK* and pressing Enter at the DOS prompt.

Next, you need to examine your WIN.INI configuration file to verify that it contains an entry for AppleTalk. To do so, start Windows and open WIN.INI using the Notepad application. Scroll through WIN.INI until you reach the section labeled "[ports]". This section must contain a line that reads:

```
AppleTalk=
```

If this line is missing, add it. Verify that your screen resembles Figure 12-14 and then save the WIN.INI file. Next, exit Windows and start it again. (You must exit and restart Windows for it to recognize changes in WIN.INI.)

```
[ports]
; To output to a file make an entry in this section of the form
; filename.PRN followed by an equal sign.
; The filename will appear in the Control Panel Connections dialog and
; any printer may then be connected to this file and all printing will
; be done to this file.
LPT1:=
LPT2:=
LPT3:=
COM1:=9600,n,8,1,p
COM2:=1200,n,8,1
AppleTalk=
```

Figure 12-14:   The AppleTalk entry in WIN.INI

Now you're ready to use the Windows Control Panel to set up Windows for LocalTalk printing. Start the Control Panel application and choose Connections from the Setup menu. In the Printer list box, select the PostScript printer driver; in the Connection list box, select AppleTalk. When you do, the Printer entry will read "PostScript Printer on AppleTalk," as shown in Figure 12-15.

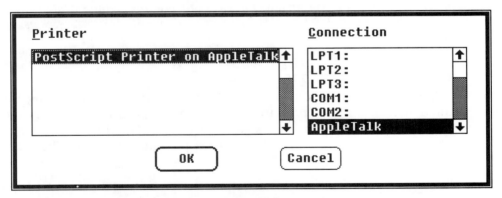

Figure 12-15:   Configuring Windows for LocalTalk printing.

Next, choose Printer from the Setup menu and double click on the "Post-Script printer on AppleTalk" entry to display the Printer Setup dialog box. When the dialog box appears, choose your model of printer from the Printer list box. Then, after verifying that your printer is on and ready, click on the button labeled AppleTalk. This displays a dialog box similar to the Mac's Chooser, as shown in Figure 12-16.

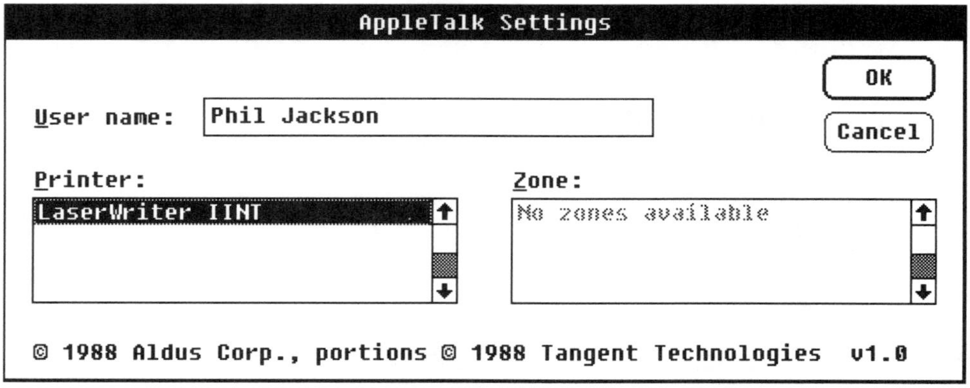

```
╔══════════════════════════════════════════════════════════════╗
║                     AppleTalk Settings                         ║
║                                                  ╭──────────╮  ║
║                                                  │    OK    │  ║
║  User name:  │Phil Jackson                    │  ╰──────────╯  ║
║                                                  ╭──────────╮  ║
║                                                  │  Cancel  │  ║
║                                                  ╰──────────╯  ║
║  Printer:                        Zone:                         ║
║  ┌───────────────────────┬─┐     ┌───────────────────────┬─┐   ║
║  │LaserWriter IINT       │↑│     │No zones available     │↑│   ║
║  │                       │ │     │                       │ │   ║
║  │                       │▓│     │                       │▓│   ║
║  │                       │↓│     │                       │↓│   ║
║  └───────────────────────┴─┘     └───────────────────────┴─┘   ║
║                                                                ║
║  © 1988 Aldus Corp., portions © 1988 Tangent Technologies  v1.0║
╚══════════════════════════════════════════════════════════════╝
```

Figure 12-16: Windows' AppleTalk Settings dialog box.

In this dialog box, type your workstation name in the User Name text box, and then select your printer in the Printer text box. Finally, click OK to confirm your entries, and then click OK again to confirm the Printer Setup dialog box.

Setting up an MS-DOS computer for LocalTalk printing requires a bit of effort and some familiarity with MS-DOS. If you're not familiar with MS-DOS, seek assistance from someone who is.

Step 3: Configuring Your Software

You've set the stage for MS-DOS LocalTalk printing by installing the required drivers. Now you need to configure your application programs to print using LocalTalk. As with the previous section, we've divided this step into separate categories for conventional DOS programs and for Windows programs.

Conventional DOS programs. The exact procedure depends on the programs you use, so we'll just outline the process. As mentioned earlier, the DayStar Digital driver configures MS-DOS to treat the network's printer as LPT3. You need to configure your applications to print to a PostScript printer via LPT3. For Microsoft Word, for example, choose Print Options, select the PostScript driver, then tab to the Setup field and press F1. In the list of ports that appears next, select LPT3:. If your program can't print to LPT3 but it can print to a disk file, configure it to print to a file named LPT3.PRN. When the DayStar Digital driver sees this file, it automatically sends it to the printer.

Microsoft Windows programs. You configured Windows for LocalTalk PostScript printing in the previous step, so you're ready to move onto Step 4: Try Printing. If you want to verify that you're configured for LocalTalk Post-

Script printing, start a Windows application, choose its Printer Setup command, and verify that the current printer entry reads "PostScript printer on AppleTalk." If it doesn't, return to step 2 and check your work.

If your LocalTalk board requires that you configure applications to print to a specific port, consult your programs' manuals to determine how to configure them. You might also consider calling their developers' technical support departments to see if they're aware of any LocalTalk printing problems or special setup techniques.

Step 4: Try Printing

At last—you're ready to see your efforts pay off. Start the program you plan to print from, type a few words, and then print the document. If you're using a text-mode program and the DayStar Digital software, you'll see status messages flash at the top of the screen. (The messages won't appear if you're using a graphics-mode program.)

If you're using a Windows program, type a few words, choose Print, and then confirm the Print dialog box. After a few moments, the Chooser-like window you saw in Step 3 appears. This gives you another chance to change printers or type a different user name. To continue with the printer you chose previously, click OK. In a moment, you'll see the "Looking for LaserWriter" message.

If your document doesn't print successfully, retrace your steps, making sure you installed the AppleTalk driver and, for non-Windows programs, the DSLPT.SYS driver. For Windows programs, be sure the APPLETLK.DLL file is in the same directory as Windows' PSCRIPT.DRV PostScript printer driver.

Configuring MS-DOS computers and MS-DOS applications for LocalTalk printing isn't always easy. We'll repeat the advice presented earlier: If you aren't familiar with MS-DOS (and with Windows, if you're using it), seek help from someone who is.

Tip: Using Downloadable Fonts

Adobe offers MS-DOS versions of its downloadable PostScript fonts, but they're designed to be downloaded via a serial or parallel connection; you can't download them over LocalTalk. However, if you have downloadable fonts in Mac format, you *can* use them in documents created by Windows programs such as PageMaker and Excel. All you need are the corresponding screen fonts in Windows format and their printer font metrics (PFM) files, which provide character-width information for the fonts. For example, if you have Adobe's Optima font in Macintosh format and you want to use it in PC PageMaker documents, you need Adobe's Optima screen font for Windows. Adobe sells its screen fonts separately; you can also download them from the Adobe forum on CompuServe.

Use Windows' Control Panel to install the screen fonts. You'll also need to edit the printer section of the WIN.INI configuration file to tell Windows that the downloadable font and its PFM file are available. Figure 12-17 shows several entries for "softfonts," the term often used in the MS-DOS world to refer to downloadable fonts.

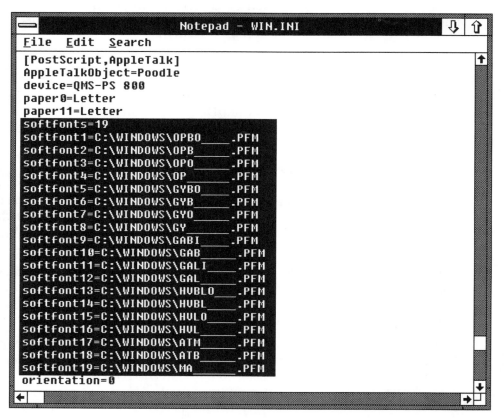

```
                        Notepad - WIN.INI
 File   Edit   Search
 [PostScript,AppleTalk]
 AppleTalkObject=Poodle
 device=QMS-PS 800
 paper0=Letter
 paper11=Letter
 softfonts=19
 softfont1=C:\WINDOWS\OPBO_____.PFM
 softfont2=C:\WINDOWS\OPB_____.PFM
 softfont3=C:\WINDOWS\OPO_____.PFM
 softfont4=C:\WINDOWS\OP_____.PFM
 softfont5=C:\WINDOWS\GYBO_____.PFM
 softfont6=C:\WINDOWS\GYB_____.PFM
 softfont7=C:\WINDOWS\GYO_____.PFM
 softfont8=C:\WINDOWS\GY_____.PFM
 softfont9=C:\WINDOWS\GABI_____.PFM
 softfont10=C:\WINDOWS\GAB_____.PFM
 softfont11=C:\WINDOWS\GALI_____.PFM
 softfont12=C:\WINDOWS\GAL_____.PFM
 softfont13=C:\WINDOWS\HUBLO_____.PFM
 softfont14=C:\WINDOWS\HUBL_____.PFM
 softfont15=C:\WINDOWS\HULO_____.PFM
 softfont16=C:\WINDOWS\HUL_____.PFM
 softfont17=C:\WINDOWS\ATM_____.PFM
 softfont18=C:\WINDOWS\ATB_____.PFM
 softfont19=C:\WINDOWS\MA_____.PFM
 orientation=0
```

Figure 12-17: Softfont entries in WIN.INI.

To print a document containing a downloadable font, first use Adobe's Font Downloader utility to download the font manually from the Mac (see Chapter 8), and then print the document from the MS-DOS computer.

We've tried this technique with Windows programs only, but it should work with any MS-DOS program that supports Adobe downloadable fonts. Check your program's documentation to find out how it recognizes and uses downloadable PostScript fonts.

Phase Three: Electronic Mail

At this stage, your network is wired and set up for printing from both Macs and MS-DOS computers. Now, you'll add electronic mail services. For these examples, we've chosen Microsoft Mail, an easy-to-use electronic mail system available for the Mac and for MS-DOS machines. It's also nicely supported by the Mac version of Microsoft Word and Excel; you can send and receive mail directly within both programs by using the Open Mail and Send Mail commands.

Microsoft Mail also has another strength: The MS-DOS version uses only about 22K of a PC's memory. As you continue adding network services, conserving memory in your MS-DOS machines will become increasingly important. As we'll see later, the MS-DOS version also has some slick features that make it easier to transfer files from PCs to Macs.

Step 1: Server Setup

Your first step in adding electronic mail is to decide which Mac will be the *mail server*, which holds mail being sent and routes it to the proper workstation. Microsoft Mail can use any Mac from a 512K Enhanced on up as a server. Microsoft Mail doesn't require you to dedicate a Mac to mail serving; you can still use the mail server for other tasks.

In this scenario, your office has a 4MB Mac IIx, a 2MB SE, and a 1MB Plus. The Mac IIx and the SE both have hard disks; the Plus has two 800K floppy drives. Any one of the three can act as the mail server; which should you use? To determine that, step back and assess each machine's capabilities and present workload:

The Mac IIx is fastest and it has the most memory. However, it also works the hardest. You use it for desktop publishing, CAD, and image scanning work—tasks that devour memory and processor time. What's more, the IIx is used by the office Mac guru, who often tests shareware and pre-release software—and therefore, falls victim to system crashes from time to time. You decide that you'd rather not burden it with another task, especially one that requires reliability.

The SE has 2MB of memory. This is not a colossal amount, but enough to accommodate the server Init (which uses 64K of memory) and still leave enough memory to run larger application programs. The SE is used for basic office tasks—word processing, spreadsheet analysis, and filing. It gets moderate but not constant use, so it's a good candidate for a mail server.

The Plus has only 1MB of memory and no hard disk. Your receptionist uses it only occasionally to write letters and memos. Because it doesn't have a hard disk, it isn't well suited to being a server. You could use it as one, but you'd get a sluggish post office and plenty of "disk full" error messages.

Based on these evaluations, you decide to use the SE as your mail server. So, you install the Microsoft Mail desk accessory in its System file and you copy two Inits to its System Folder: the Microsoft Mail Server Init and the MS Mail Init (the latter Init will let the SE send and receive mail in addition to being a server). Finally, you restart the SE to load both Inits.

When choosing which machine to use as a server, don't just consider each machine's capabilities—consider how each machine is used, too. You don't want to bog down an already hard-working machine with additional duties, nor do you want to use a Mac that may be prone to crashing. Finally, be sure the machine you choose has enough free disk space to accommodate each user's needs. As a general rule, plan on allocating roughly 500K to each user—more if they will be exchanging large disk files, less if they'll be sending only short messages.

Step 2: Mailbox Setup

After creating the server, you need to create a mailbox for each workstation. To do so, use the server's Microsoft Mail desk accessory, as shown in Figure 12-18. As you create each user's mailbox, be sure to use the exact same user name that you typed in each Mac's Chooser desk accessory when you set up the Macs for printing. You could create passwords for each mailbox at this stage, but it's better to leave that job up to each individual. That way, each person can choose a password that he or she will remember.

Next, you install the Microsoft Mail software on each node. For the Macs, that means installing the Microsoft Mail desk accessory, copying the MS Mail Init to each Mac's System Folder, and then restarting each Mac to load the Init.

For MS-DOS computers, installation involves running a setup utility that copies a few files to your PCs' hard disks. One of the files, NOTIFIER.EXE, is a terminate-and-stay-resident (TSR) program that notifies you when mail arrives, regardless of the program you're using. Another program, MAIL.EXE, is used to create, send, and receive mail.

Consistency is important in networks. Standardize user names, and use the same ones in every network service you have. Allow users to choose their own passwords; they'll be less likely to forget passwords they think of themselves.

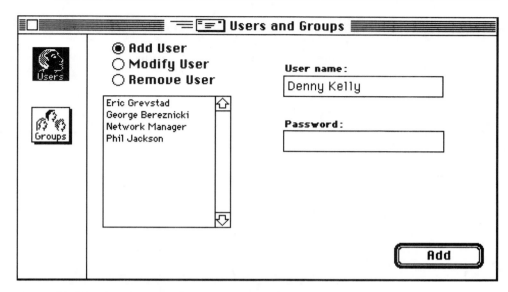

Figure 12-18: Creating a mailbox with Microsoft Mail.

Step 3: Trying the Mail Server

To try the mail server, go to a Mac and open its Microsoft Mail desk accessory. A dialog box appears asking for a user name and password. The user name previously entered in that Mac's Chooser appears in the dialog box; you can accept it or type a different name. After you enter a name and password, the Microsoft Mail mailbox window appears (Figure 12-19). This process of supplying your user name and password in order to display the mailbox window is called *signing on*. For this test, leave the mailbox window open after you've signed on.

Now, go to a different Mac and sign on to the mail server. Next, begin creating a message by double-clicking the icon labeled Note. A new window appears, shown in Figure 12-20. To address a message click the Address icon and choose the name of the recipient from the subsequent list box.

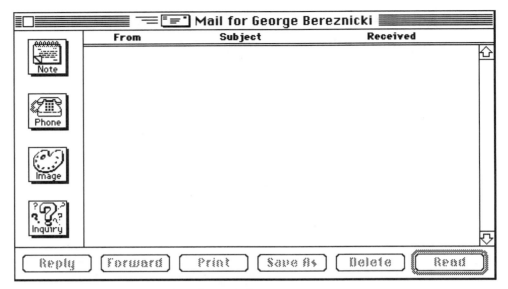

Figure 12-19: Microsoft Mail mailbox window.

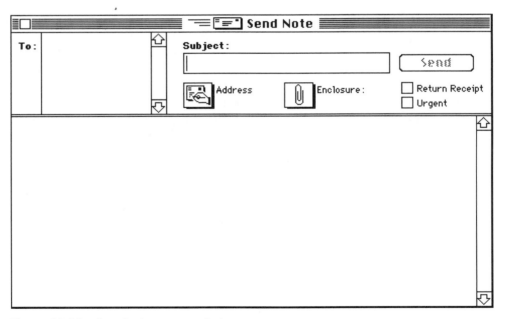

Figure 12-20: Standard message window.

Next, type a word or two in the "Subject" text box, then type a few words in the large text box at the bottom of the window. Finally, send your message by clicking Send. If all goes well, you should hear a beep and see a dialog box on the other Mac. Move to that Mac, and you should see the subject of the message you sent, as shown in Figure 12-21. Double-click it to read it.

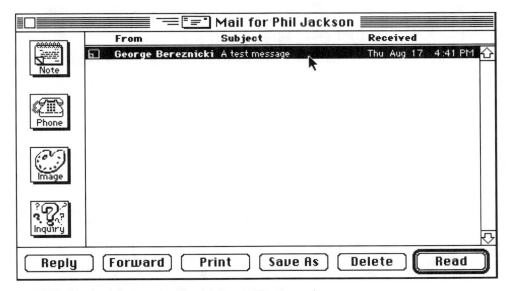

Figure 12-21:   A message received from a different node.

Repeat this testing process with each computer until you're sure that all the machines can access the mail server.

When you add a new network service, test it from each machine to make sure it's working properly.

Step 4: Basic Training

When you're sure the mail server is working and that each user can access it, make sure everyone knows how to operate the e-mail software. Show them how they can change their preferences (Figure 12-22) to tailor the way they're informed of new mail.

Also make sure each user knows about the types of messages that can be sent. Microsoft Mail, for example, lets you send text messages, graphics messages, and telephone messages (Figure 12-23). The text message (called "note") is the only type that lets you also send any disk file, called an *enclosure*.

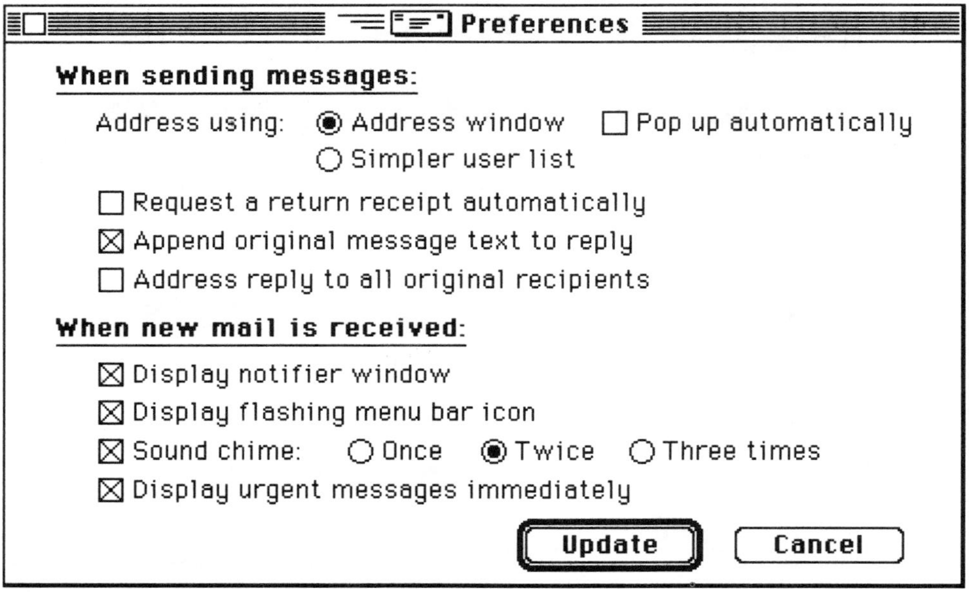

Figure 12-22: Changing preferences with Microsoft Mail.

Your network will operate more smoothly if you take the time to educate each user in its operation. Don't force people to simply "pick it up as they go along;" they'll be less likely to take advantage of the network's services, and more likely to cause problems by performing tasks improperly. Also, develop guidelines for deleting mail that's no longer needed. Messages that have been read still take up space on the mail server unless they're deleted. If users want to save messages indefinitely, they should use the e-mail's desk accessory to save them on their own hard or floppy disks, and then delete them from the server.

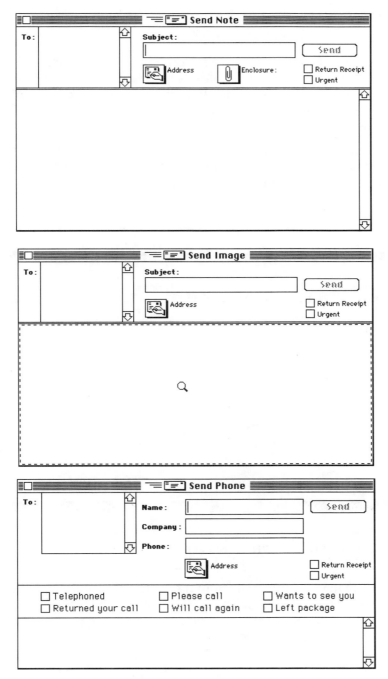

Figure 12-23: Microsoft Mail message types: Standard (*top*), Graphic (*middle*), and Telephone (*bottom*).

Microsoft Mail Tips

Here are a few tips for using Microsoft Mail.

Transferring files. If your network's users exchange files only occasionally, you may not need a network file server; simply use Mail's file enclosure feature to exchange files between machines. It's faster than swapping disks. Unlike a file server, however, it doesn't eliminate worrying about whose version of a file is the most current.

From PC to Mac. Because Mail is available for PCs, it's an ideal way to move files between Macs and MS-DOS machines. As Figure 12-24 shows, the Mac and PC versions even share similar user interfaces, so moving between the two versions is easy.

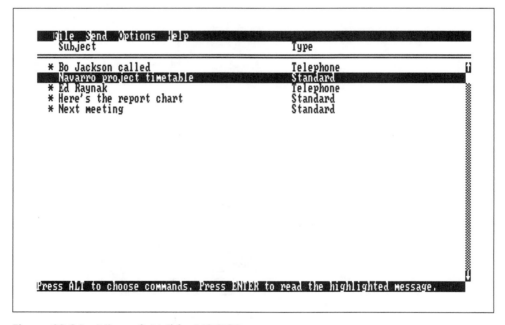

Figure 12-24: Microsoft Mail for MS-DOS computers.

When you use mail to transfer a file from the PC to the Mac, you can choose a file type for the file (Figure 12-25). When Mail transfers the file to the Mac, it adds a file signature (discussed in the previous chapter) that allows you to open the file by double-clicking it from the Finder.

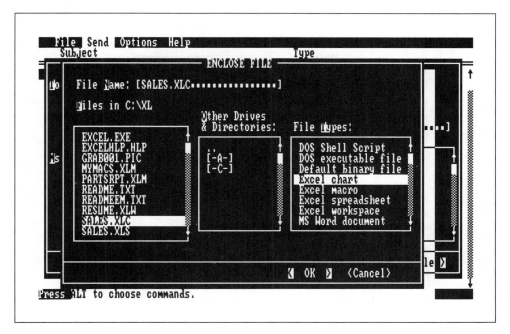

Figure 12-25: Choosing a file type in the DOS version of Mail.

Adding signatures. The DOS version of Mail uses a configuration file called MAIL.INI that stores the file-signature information shown in Figure 12-25. It isn't mentioned in the manual, but by adding additional entries to MAIL.INI, you can transfer other types of files and be able to double-click them from the Finder. As Figure 12-26 shows, the entries have four components, each separated by a colon:

1. The file extension as it appears on the PC, followed by an equal sign and a short description of that file type.

2. The file's four-character type code

3. The file's four-character creator code

4. An entry that denotes whether the file is a text file or a binary file (we looked at the differences in the previous chapter).

```
.txt=Text file:TEXT:MSWD:text
.sty=MS Word style sheet:TEXT:MSWD:binary
.wrd=MS Word document:TEXT:MSWD:binary
.doc=MS Word document:TEXT:MSWD:binary
.slk=SYLK spreadsheet:TEXT:XCEL:text
.wks=PC spreadsheet:TEXT:XCEL:binary
.wk1=PC spreadsheet:TEXT:XCEL:binary
.xls=Excel spreadsheet:XLS :XCEL:binary
.xlc=Excel chart:XLC :XCEL:binary
.xlm=Excel macro:XLM :XCEL:binary
.xlw=Excel workspace:XLW :XCEL:binary
.exe=DOS executable file::binary
.bat=DOS Shell Script:TEXT:MSWD:text
.com=DOS executable file::binary
.pm3=Pagemaker 3 publ.:ALB3:ALD3:binary
.tem=Pagemaker template:ALT3:ALD3:binary
.tpl=Pagemaker template:ALT3:ALD3:binary
.=Default binary file::binary
.???=WordPerfect 4.2 doc.:WPPC:SSIW:binary
.dbf=dBase III data file::binary
.tif=TIFF image file:TIFF::binary
PrintWidth=65
PrintLength=54
TopMargin=0
LeftMargin=0
PrintPort=COM1
COLOR=0
```

Figure 12-26: Microsoft Mail's MAIL.INI configuration file.

You might want to modify some of the existing entries in MAIL.INI. For example, if you'd prefer to open text files using WordPerfect for the Mac instead of Microsoft Word, change the text file entry's creator code from MSWD to SSIW. Similarly, if you'd prefer to open Ashton-Tate's FullImpact instead of Microsoft Excel when you double-click a transferred 1-2-3 spreadsheet, change the creator code entires for the WKS and WK1 files from XCEL to GLAS.

You can also add new entries to MAIL.INI to accommodate other types of files you might transfer. For example, if you'd like transferred TIFF files to show up in the Open dialog boxes of programs such as ImageStudio and Digital Darkroom, add the following line:

```
.tif=TIFF image file:TIFF::binary
```

Chapter 15 lists the type and creator signatures used by many popular Mac programs.

Phase 4: File Serving

In this phase, we'll add a file server to your network. We'll use file server software to turn a hard disk into a central storage area for holding files that everyone can access. In the process, we'll examine the pros and cons of the two most popular file server software packages available for the Mac: Sun Microsystems' TOPS and Apple's AppleShare.

As we'll see in this section, there are two basic approaches to file serving:

- The *distributed server approach*, in which the file-serving duties are *distributed* among several machines on the network. The TOPS networking software uses this approach.

- The *dedicated server* approach, in which one Mac and its hard disk are set aside as a file server that all other machines on the network can access. AppleShare uses this approach.

First, we'll examine the pros and cons of each file server approach, then we'll take a closer look at TOPS and AppleShare. Finally, we'll look at some other file-server options you might consider.

TOPS Pros and Cons

First, let's look at the advantages of TOPS' distributed file server approach.

It's inexpensive. The TOPS software costs $249 per Mac node, and $189 per PC node. AppleShare costs $799 for any number of nodes, but it requires a dedicated Mac and hard disk. For small networks, you might not be willing to dedicate a Mac and hard disk to file serving.

It's flexible. With TOPS, any user can make part or all of his or her hard disk accessible to other users on the network. For example, if other users need to access the files in Eric's Documents folder, Eric can *publish* that folder. When Amy needs to access the folder, she uses the TOPS desk accessory to *mount* the folder. Once mounted, the folder appears on Amy's desktop as if it were a disk. Figure 12-27 illustrates TOPS in action.

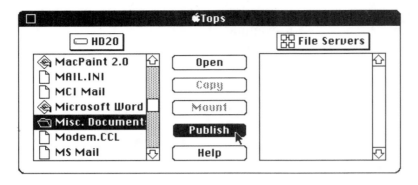

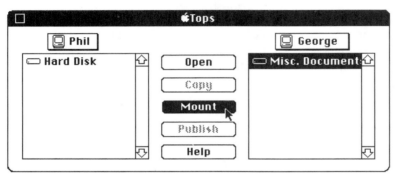

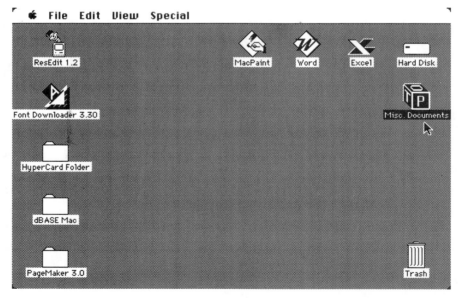

Figure 12-27: Using TOPS: Publishing a folder (*top*), and mounting it from a different machine (*middle*). At bottom, the folder as it appears on the remote machine.

It's easy. You can learn TOPS in an hour or so. Users don't need to learn new ways of accessing files or folders. The PC version provides an easy-to-use utility that uses menus to allow users to publish disks and folders and mount other users' published disks. More experienced users can publish, mount, and unmount disks by typing commands at the MS-DOS prompt.

But TOPS has some drawbacks, too:

Security is minimal. TOPS lets you assign passwords to published volumes, but it doesn't provide the security options that AppleShare does.

Anarchy is possible. Networks thrive on uniformity and consistency, and TOPS' distributed approach doesn't encourage either. Anyone can become a file server at any time. More significant, anyone can *stop* being a file server at any time. If Eric decides to *unpublish* his hard disk—or if his Mac crashes—anyone who has mounted his hard disk is in trouble. You can encourage greater uniformity by dedicating a Mac and hard disk to TOPS file serving, but at that point, you may be better off using AppleShare.

It doesn't support the AppleTalk Filing Protocol (AFP). TOPS uses its own file-access protocols, not the AFP rules that we looked at earlier in this chapter. On one level, that means you can't access TOPS servers through the Chooser desk accessory. On a more significant level, it means you can't use multi-user software that requires AFP, such as Fox's FoxBASE+/Mac. (Other multi-user data base managers, including Acius' 4th Dimension and Blythe Software's Omnis series, can work with TOPS' file-access protocols.)

AppleShare Pros and Cons

Now let's look at AppleShare's strengths.

Security is good. As we'll see later, AppleShare lets you specify several levels of *access privileges*—rules governing who can access the contents of folders on the file server.

It's elegant. AppleShare meshes well with the rest of the Mac's system software. For example, it's designed to work with the Finder to show access privileges in directory windows. And you access an AppleShare server using the Chooser desk accessory, thus reinforcing the Chooser's role as your gateway to network services.

It enforces structure. With AppleShare, you don't have to contend with the file-serving anarchy that can occur with TOPS. Everything is stored on the central file server, making it easier to enforce structure in your network and back up the contents of your file server.

But on the negative side:

It's expensive. The AppleShare software itself isn't unreasonably priced, but the fact that it requires a dedicated Mac and hard disk boosts the final cost of your file server significantly. For a small network containing only a half-dozen or so nodes, you may not be willing or able to part with at least $2000 for a dedicated Mac Plus and hard disk. For large networks, the cost per node drops, but you may need a faster—and more expensive—file server, such as a Mac SE/30 or IIcx.

It's regimented. AppleShare's enforced structure and uniformity are essential in large networks, but may be overkill for small, informal ones in which people swap files only occasionally.

A Closer Look at TOPS

For your small, fledgling network, you decide that TOPS is the more appropriate—and more affordable—choice for file server software. So, you purchase three copies of TOPS for the Macintosh (one for each Mac), and two copies of TOPS/DOS for the MS-DOS machines. In this section, we'll take TOPS for a spin, and we'll provide some guidelines and tips for using TOPS effectively.

Installation

Installing TOPS for the Mac is easy: Simply run the TOPS installation program, which copies the TOPS startup document (Init) and several other files to the System Folder of your choice, and then installs a TOPS desk accessory in your System file. You perform this task on each Mac, using a separate TOPS installer disk for each. (Each disk installs a unique serial number; during startup, TOPS checks to see if any other nodes are using the same serial number. If it finds one that is, it won't load.) Finally, you restart each Mac to load the TOPS software.

Installing TOPS/DOS is equally straightforward: type *INSTALL* and press Enter, and an installation program creates a TOPS subdirectory on your hard disk and copies several files to it. Finally, the installer asks if you want it to modify your CONFIG.SYS and AUTOEXEC.BAT files. If you answer yes, it increases the number of files and buffers specified in CONFIG.SYS to 20, and it adds the TOPS directory to the AUTOEXEC.BAT file's PATH statement.

Using TOPS for the Mac

Many file-serving programs (including AppleShare) need to analyze and often rearrange the contents of a file server's hard disk. Not TOPS. You can use it immediately after installing it.

In our network scenario, your receptionist uses a Mac Plus without a floppy disk. You'd like her to be able to store the correspondence and memos she writes on your SE's hard disk. That way, you'll be able to access them when you need to, and you'll be able to back them up more conveniently.

The key to controlling TOPS is the TOPS desk accessory, shown in Figure 12-27. The disks attached to (and inserted in) your Mac appear in the left-hand list box.

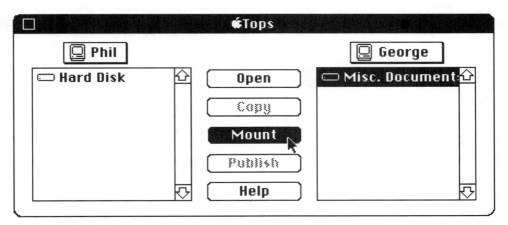

Figure 12-28: The TOPS desk accessory.

To make an entire disk available to other machines on the network, select its name and click the Publish button. As Figure 12-29 shows, TOPS indicates when you've published a disk or folder by displaying a small network icon next to the disk or folder's name.

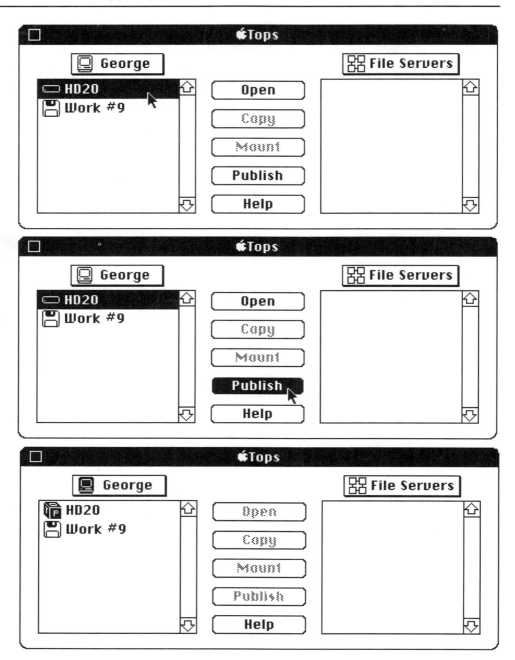

Figure 12-29: Publishing a TOPS volume: Select the disk name (*top*) and click the Publish button (*middle*). TOPS indicates the published volume with a network icon (*bottom*).

In this example, you don't want to publish the entire SE's hard disk. Instead, you want to publish a single folder named Correspondence. So, you create the folder using the Finder's New Folder command, then you open the TOPS desk accessory, and double click on your disk's name to view its contents, as shown in Figure 12-30.

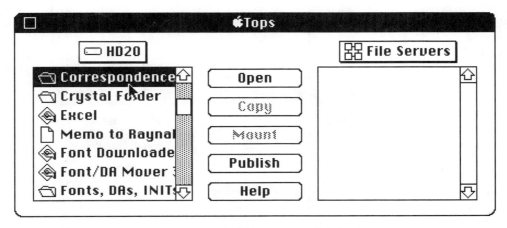

Figure 12-30: The TOPS desk accessory with an opened disk volume.

Once you've opened the disk, you scroll through the list box to locate the Correspondence folder, then you publish it by selecting the folder and clicking Publish. TOPS indicates that you've published the folder by displaying the network icon next to its name. At this point, the SE is a file server.

To access the server—or, in TOPS lingo, to become a *client* of the server—your receptionist opens the TOPS desk accessory on her machine. The right-hand list box shows the names of the file servers on the network. To mount the Correspondence folder, she double-clicks the server's name. Then, she selects the Correspondence folder and clicks the Mount button, and the folder appears on her desktop as if it were a disk. Figure 12-31 illustrates the process.

At this point, the receptionist can work with the Correspondence folder as if it were a disk installed in her own machine. She can copy files to and from it using the Finder, she can throw away documents, and she can open and save documents by using her programs' Open and Save commands. When she's done with the folder, she can unmount it by dragging its icon to the Trash.

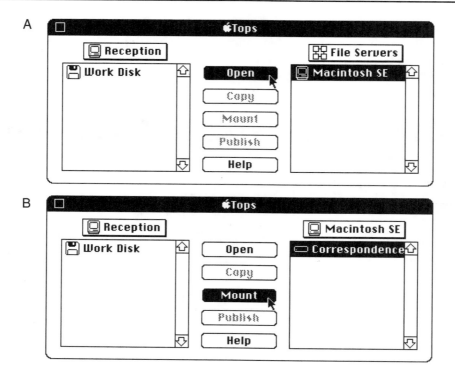

Figure 12-31: Accessing a TOPS server: Opening the server (*A*) and mounting the folder (*B*), which appears on the desktop (*C*).

In network parlance, a volume located on a different machine is called a *remote volume* or a *network volume*. A volume connected directly to your machine—such as your floppy drives and any SCSI hard disks—is a *local volume*.

Using TOPS/DOS

With TOPS/DOS, the users of your MS-DOS machines can access published volumes from the Mac or other MS-DOS machines, and they can publish their disks or subdirectories to make them available to the other machines on the network.

Let's say that Denny, who uses the PS/2, has just finished working up a spreadsheet in Microsoft Excel, and wants Eric on the Mac II to look at it. To make the file available to Eric, Denny will publish the subdirectory that contains it; Eric will then mount that directory and open the file using the Mac version of Excel.

Since Denny is just starting out with TOPS, he'll use the menu-driven TOPSMENU program to publish his volume. He starts TOPSMENU, and chooses the Server Utilities command. In the next menu, he chooses Publish a Volume. Then, he types the name of the subdirectory he wants to publish (in this case, XL), and gives it an *alias*, a name that will appear in the TOPS desk accessory instead of the subdirectory's real name. (Unlike DOS subdirectory names, aliases can be up to 16 characters long and can contain spaces.) Finally, he specifies that other users should be able to write to the volume as well as read from it. Figure 12-32 illustrates this process.

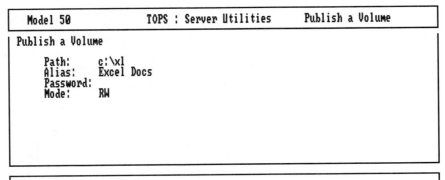

Figure 12-32: Publishing a volume with TOPSMENU.

After Denny has published the subdirectory, Eric uses his TOPS desk accessory to mount it. Then he starts Excel, opens the spreadsheet using the Open command, makes some changes, and saves the file.

TOPS Guidelines

As we've seen in this section, TOPS lets anyone turn his or her machine into a file server with only a few steps. It's quick and easy, but potentially dangerous, too. For example, if Denny shuts down his PS/2 while Eric is working with the Excel spreadsheet, Eric will lose the work he did on the file. Similarly, if your SE crashes while your receptionist is using the Correspondence folder, she's likely to lose work.

A TOPS network works best when each user observes a few guidelines:

After you've published a disk or folder, avoid performing time-consuming tasks on your machine. Examples of time-consuming tasks include initializing a disk, copying files (especially to or from floppies), installing fonts or desk accessories with the Font/DA Mover, and transferring files over a telephone modem. Tasks like these all but monopolize your machine's CPU, preventing TOPS from allowing others to access your published volumes. If someone's machine is accessing one of your published volumes and you begin a time-consuming task, his or her machine will appear to have "locked up"—it won't respond to typing or other commands. After a minute or so, they're likely to see an error message saying that TOPS is attempting to connect to the server. Sometimes, however, TOPS simply locks up, requiring you to restart your computer.

Back up often. One of the drawbacks to TOPS' distributed file serving approach is that an office is likely to have important files scattered across several machines, instead of stored in a central server. This makes it imperative that all users back up their hard disks frequently. But because backing up certainly qualifies as a time-consuming task, no one should back up a hard disk that's being used as a server by a remote machine.

After you publish a volume, use your Mac carefully. Don't perform tasks that might cause it to crash, such as running untested shareware or pre-release software. Don't perform any system-modifying tasks, such as installing fonts or desk accessories or modifying something with ResEdit.

Avoid publishing floppy disks. TOPS will let you publish a floppy disk, but it isn't a good idea to do so. Its performance as a server will be abysmal.

Think twice about running large applications stored on a remote volume. If a file server volume that you've mounted contains applications, you can run them, but because of LocalTalk's speed limitations, they'll start rather slowly. Table 12-1 shows the time required to start Microsoft Excel 2.2 from a local hard disk and from a published TOPS volume. (We performed the tests on a 2MB Mac II equipped with an Apple HD20SC hard disk.)

Table 12-1:   Time required to start Excel from a local hard disk and from a mounted TOPS volume.

	Local Hard Disk	Network Volume
Start Microsoft Excel	13 seconds	31 seconds

As the table shows, it can take more than twice as long to start a program stored on a remote volume. This performance gap can grow even larger if the user who published the volume is performing tasks while the application is loading. For these reasons, you're better off not running large applications stored on a remote disk, especially if that server is being used for other tasks.

Notice that last guideline began with "think twice," not "don't ever." There are few carved-in-stone rules where file serving is concerned, especially with TOPS and its distributed operating style. Depending on the size of your network and on how you use its nodes, it may be perfectly acceptable to run a large application from a remote server volume. As a general rule, if a given server isn't being used locally and if it isn't being accessed by more than two nodes, you can run a large application from it. However, if a server is being used locally, or if it's being accessed by several nodes, each node should use the server for storing document files only.

TOPS Tips

Here's a collection of tips for using TOPS and conserving memory with TOPS/DOS.

A quick way to transfer files. You don't have to mount a file server volume to transfer a file between two nodes. An faster way is to use the TOPS desk accessory to transfer the file. First, publish one node's disk or folder, then open the other node's TOPS desk accessory. Next, double-click the server volume until it opens to the file level, as shown in Figure 12-33. Then, repeat this procedure with your own disk to open it to the file level. Finally, to transfer the file, select it, and then click the Copy button. You can also create a text-only version of the file by pressing Option while clicking the Copy button. For details on these procedures, see Chapter 4, "Copying Files Over a TOPS Network," in the TOPS manual.

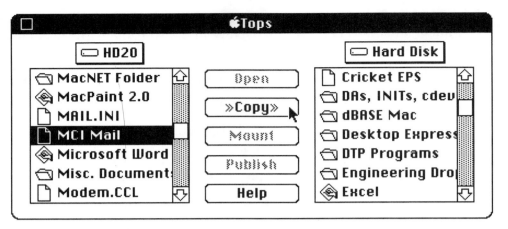

Figure 12-33:   Opening a volume to the file level.

Remembering server and client options. If you hold down the mouse button while pointing at TOPS' Mount button, a pop-up menu appears reading "Mount...". If you choose this command, a dialog box appears containing a check box labeled Remember. If you select this check box, TOPS will mount that volume the next time you start your Mac. To tell TOPS to forget about the volume, press Option while clicking the Unmount button, and then deselect the Remember check box.

Using server-access options. If you hold down the mouse button while pointing to the Publish button, a pop-up menu containing a "Publish..." command appears. If you choose Publish a dialog box appears whose options let you specify how your published volume can be accessed (Figure 12-34). The Password text box lets you specify a password that users must supply before they can mount the volume. The Write-protected button lets you publish a volume so that clients can read from it, but not write to it. Don't use the Write-protected option if you're publishing a folder for the first time. When a client mounts that folder, his or her Finder needs to create a DeskTop file for keeping track of its contents. (The DeskTop file is discussed in Chapter 3.) If you publish a folder as write protected, the Finder won't be able to create a DeskTop file for that folder.

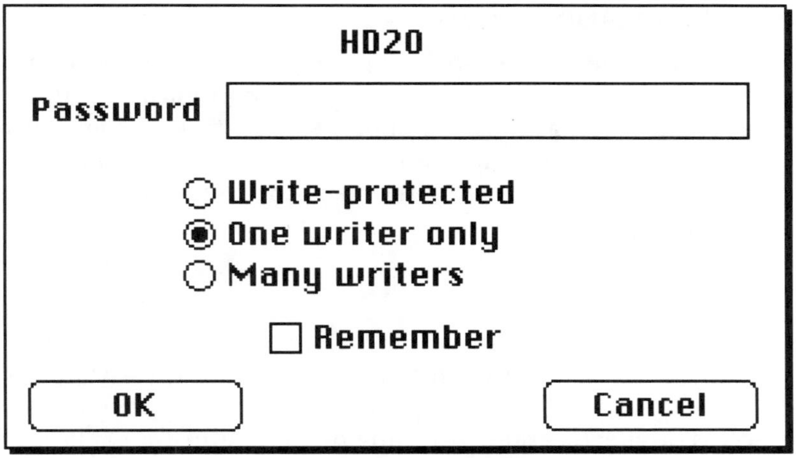

Figure 12-34: TOPS' volume-publishing options.

Dedicating a server. TOPS doesn't require you to dedicate a Mac or PC as a server, but there's no reason why you can't do so. If you dedicate a Mac as a server, you can improve the server's performance by using the Control Panel to create a disk cache. For a 1MB machine, try a 256K disk cache. For faster, more reliable operation, TOPS recommends that you leave the dedicated server's TOPS desk accessory open at all times.

Deleting TOPS files you don't need. If your network doesn't have any TOPS/DOS nodes, you can delete the Interbase and PC Icon files from each Mac's System Folder.

Conserving memory with TOPS/DOS. One problem with TOPS/DOS is that it uses roughly 200K of memory, and that doesn't include the memory required by your LocalTalk board's drivers. In many cases, you may not be able to run TOPS/DOS and memory-hungry applications such as the Windows versions of Excel or PageMaker. The solution? Configure TOPS/DOS for client-only operation. You won't be able to publish any volumes, but you'll reduce TOPS/DOS' memory requirements to about 120K. Another way to reduce TOPS/DOS' appetite is to edit the TOPSKNRL.DAT file, which contains TOPS/DOS configuration options. For details on editing TOPSKRNL.DAT, see Appendix A, "Setting Configurations," in the TOPS/DOS manual.

A Closer Look at Appleshare

Let's leave the flexible, do-your-own-thing world of TOPS to examine the more regimented, centralized file-serving approach of AppleShare. In this section, we'll set aside your hard disk-equipped Mac SE to be a file server, and we'll show how you might use AppleShare's security options to govern who has access to the server's contents. We'll wrap up the section with some AppleShare tips and guidelines.

Installation

Installing AppleShare is a multi-step process. First, you need to install the server software, then you need to install the workstation software on each computer. Finally, you need to configure the server by suppling user names, specifying access privileges, and performing other administrative tasks.

The word "administer" is an important one in the AppleShare world. The person in charge of setting up and maintaining the server is the *administrator*. The administrator uses a program called AppleShare Admin to perform these tasks.

To install the AppleShare server or workstation software, you use Apple's Installer utility. AppleShare comes with two server installation disks and three workstation installation disks: One for the Mac Plus and later machines, one for Apple IIs equipped with LocalTalk boards, and one for the 512K Enhanced—the oldest Mac AppleShare supports. The Mac installer disks also include scripts for updating each Mac's system software to the latest version recommended for that Mac.

The server's installer script modifies the Mac's hard disk, renaming the System Folder to "Server Folder," and altering its contents so that the server runs automatically upon startup instead of the Finder. The workstation installer scripts add an AppleShare file to the System Folder, and a desk accessory called Access Privileges to the System file. The AppleShare file's icon appears in the Chooser and lets you access the server. Access Privileges lets you control who can see and alter the contents of the folders you create on the server—more about that shortly.

Creating Users and Groups

For most networks, the AppleShare administrator's first job is to create a list of *registered users*, people who will be accessing the server, and a list of *groups*, collections of users who will be able to share information. The users within a group can use AppleShare's security options to set up folders that each group member can access, but that members of other groups can't. Figure 12-35 shows the relationship between users and groups.

Group	Users
Engineering	Eric Grevstad Joe Smith Amy Johnson Duncan Kelly
Testing	John Raynak George Bereznicki William Arthur Peter Remy
Sales	Travis Montgomery Tina Buchanan Robert Ewing Jack Campellone

Figure 12-35: Users belong to groups.

You use AppleShare's Admin program to create users and groups. Creating a registered user (or *user*, for short) is easy: Choose Create User from the Users menu, and supply the user's name in the New User window (Figure 12-36). You can also supply a password for new users, but it's often better to let them come up with passwords on their own.

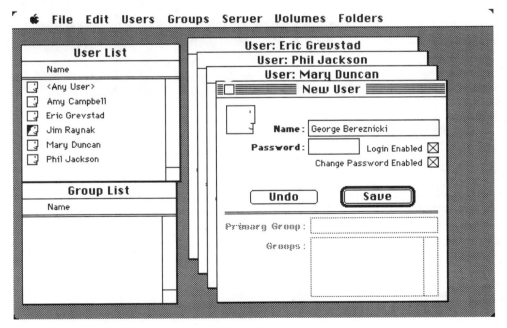

Figure 12-36: Creating a new user with Admin.

Creating a group is similarly easy: Choose New Group and type a name for the group, and click the Save button. Depending on how you're organizing the network, your group names may be departments (Production, Engineering, Testing, and so on), or they may reflect certain projects that each group works on (Newsletter, Catalog, Manuals, and so on). After creating a group, you specify its members by dragging their user names to the Group window's Members list box, as shown in Figure 12-37.

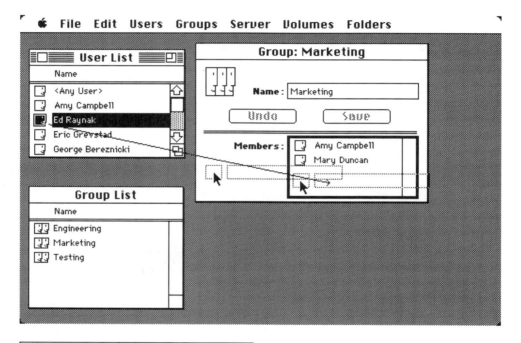

Figure 12-37: Adding a user to a group.

It's worth mentioning that you don't have to specify a list of users. If you don't, the users in your network will access the server as *guests*. A guest can't *own* a folder—that is, he or she can't create a folder and then specify security options for it. However, guests can still create folders. If your office doesn't require AppleShare's security options, you may just want to operate your server in guest-only fashion.

Similarly, don't feel obligated to divide your workforce into groups. If everyone in the network performs similar tasks, you might want to create a list of registered users, but no groups. With this approach, registered users will still be able to own folders, but they won't be able to create "communal" folders that only a certain group of people can access.

This stage of AppleShare set up sounds complex, but it isn't. It simply involves determining how users work together in real life, then implementing that working style on the server.

Setting Access Privileges

Users and groups are only half of the AppleShare security picture; *access privileges* are the other half. Access privileges govern what a registered user or a guest can do with a given folder. There are three categories of access privileges:

- *See Folders*—the privilege to see any folders within a given folder.

- *See Files*—the privilege to see and open documents or applications within the folder.

- *Make Changes*—the privilege to modify the folder's contents, including moving icons and creating or deleting files.

You can assign these access privileges in any combination to three categories of network user:

- *Owner*—the folder's owner, usually (but not always) the user who created a given folder. When the Owner check box is selected for a given privilege, only the folder's owner has that privilege.

- *Group*—the collection of users associated with a specific folder. When Group is checked for a given privilege, only members of that group have that privilege.

- *Everyone*—anyone with access to the server, including guests. When Everyone is checked for a given privilege, anyone who accesses the server, whether a registered user or a guest, has that privilege.

The administrator can set access privileges for any folder by using the Admin program. Registered users can view privileges and set privileges for their own folders by selecting a folder and choosing Get Privileges from the Finder's File menu. This displays the Access Privileges window, shown in Figure 12-38. (If they're running a program, they can use the Access Privileges desk accessory.)

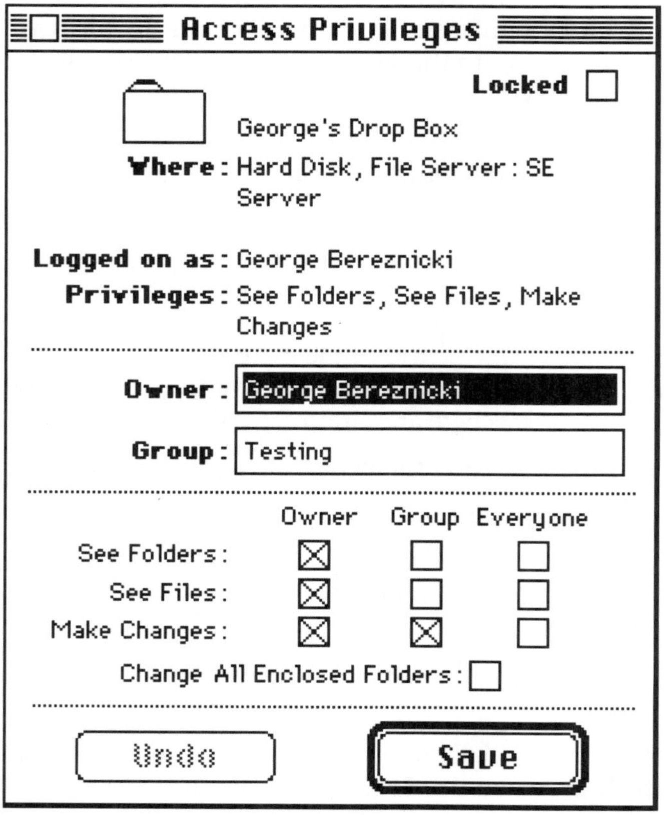

Figure 12-38: Access Privileges window.

In Figure 12-38, the owner of the folder—George Bereznicki—has all three access privileges. The members of the group George belongs to, Testing, can copy files into the folder, but they can't open the folder to see its contents. Thus, for the group members, this folder serves as an electronic drop box—users can "drop" files into it, but only George can retrieve them. Finally, because none of the privileges is selected in the "Everyone" column, anyone who isn't in the Testing group can't open the folder or copy files to it.

Once you've set up your server and, if necessary, created your user and group lists, you're ready to put the server into action. To do so, you restart the SE. When it starts up again, AppleShare loads and runs automatically. After a few status messages appear, the SE's screen looks like Figure 12-39.

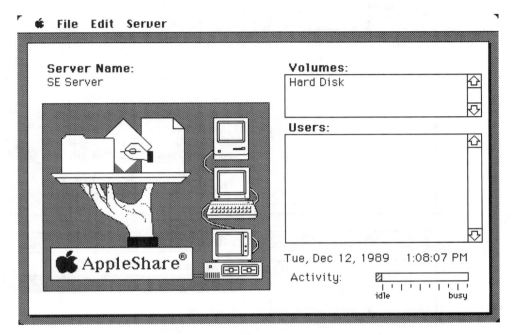

Figure 12-39: The AppleShare server screen.

Accessing the Server from a Mac

You access—or, in AppleShare lingo, *log on* to—the file server using the Chooser desk accessory. First, select the AppleShare icon to display a list of file servers. Next, select the file server you want by double-clicking it. Finally, select the server volume (or volumes) you want to mount, click OK, and the volume appears on the desktop. Figure 12-40 shows the entire process.

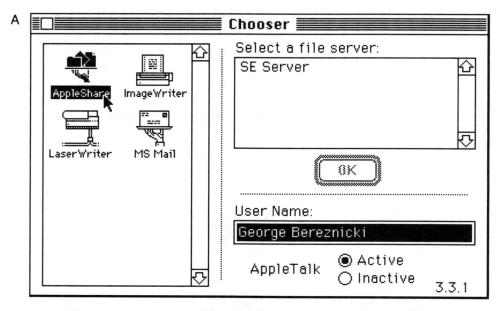

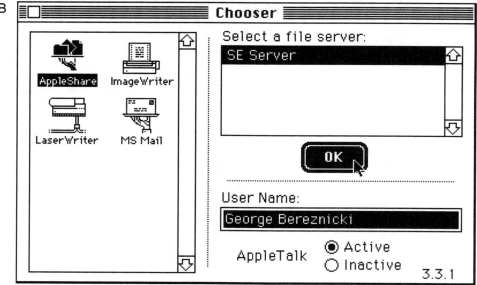

Figure 12-40: Logging onto AppleShare: Selecting the AppleShare icon (*A*), selecting the desired file server (*B*), and selecting the volumes to be mounted (*C*). The mounted volume appears on the desktop with an AppleShare icon (*D*).

C

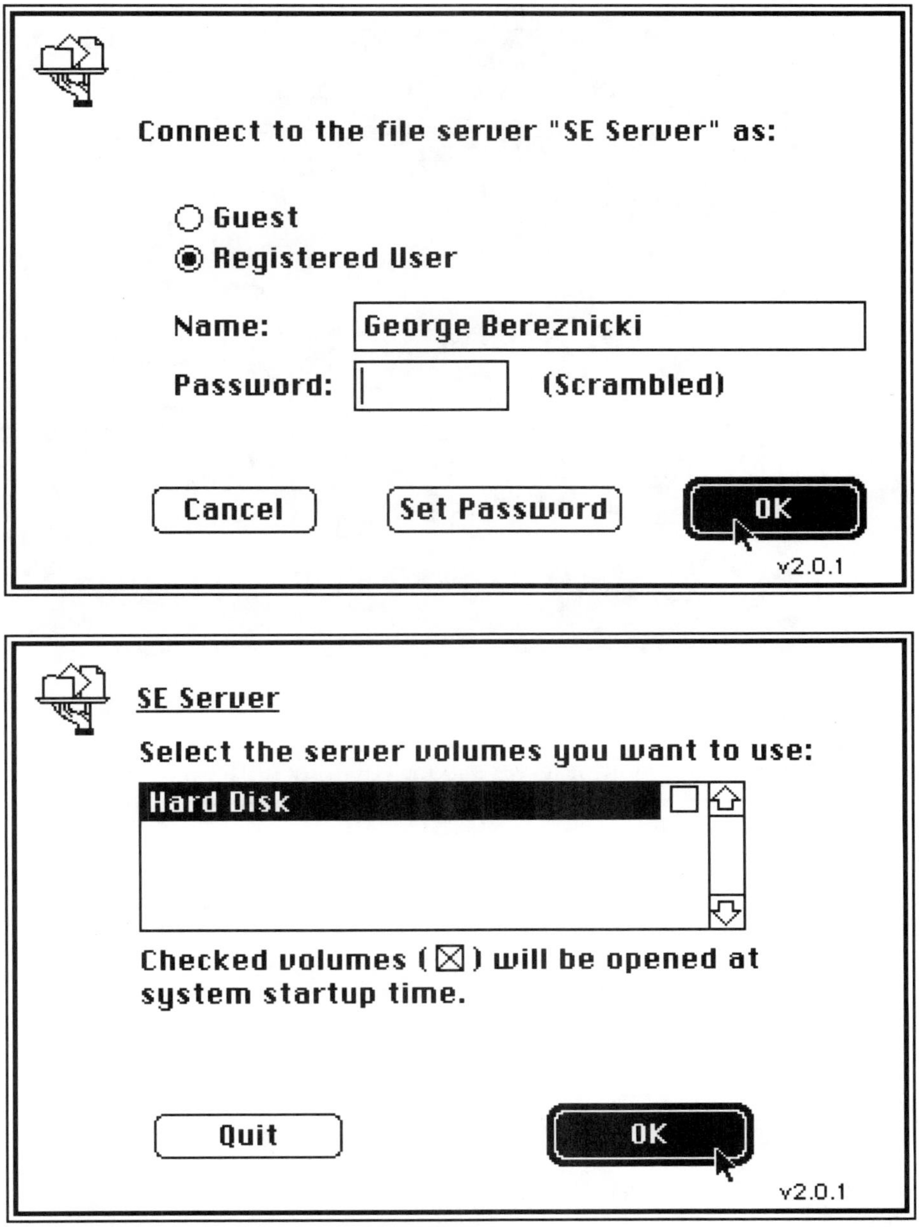

Connect to the file server "SE Server" as:

○ Guest
◉ Registered User

Name: George Bereznicki

Password: (Scrambled)

Cancel   Set Password   OK

v2.0.1

SE Server

Select the server volumes you want to use:

Hard Disk   ☐

Checked volumes (☒) will be opened at system startup time.

Quit   OK

v2.0.1

Figure 12-40: (*continued*)

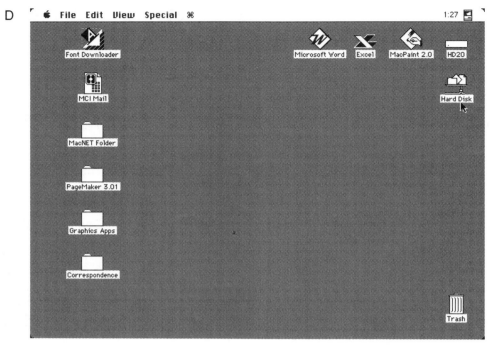

Figure 12-40: (*continued*)

When you open the server's icon, you may notice a different appearance to certain folders. That's AppleShare's way of visually indicating what your access privileges are. Similarly, when you open a folder's directory window, access privilege icons appear in its upper-left corner. Figure 12-41 shows the types of folder icons you might see and describes the privileges associated with each.

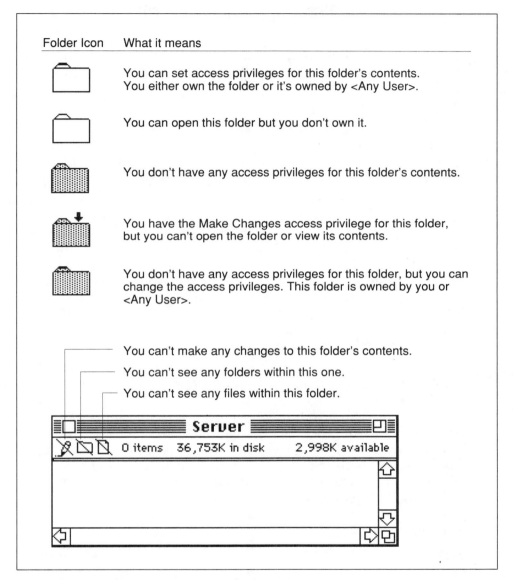

Figure 12-41:   Folder icons and their associated privileges.

Accessing the Server from the DOS Machines

To log on to the server from your IBM AT compatible, you use AppleShare PC, a software package that includes drivers for Apple's LocalTalk PC expansion board, and a variety of programs that let you access the server.

The AppleShare PC server-access program is modeled after the Mac's Chooser desk accessory; it's even called "the desk accessory" in the AppleShare PC documentation. The AppleShare PC desk accessory lets you select a file server, view and modify access privileges, and mount and unmount server volumes. When you mount a server volume, you assign a drive letter to it. After that, you can access it in the same way that you access local disks.

You can also specify that the AppleShare PC desk accessory remain resident in memory (as a TSR program), allowing you to open it from within any application by pressing Alt-Enter. When the desk accessory is memory resident, AppleShare PC uses between 190K and 215K of memory. When the desk accessory isn't memory resident, AppleShare PC uses 127K. (As an aside, it's worth noting that the AppleShare software on a Mac workstation uses only 10K of memory—the remaining code required to access the server is already available in the AppleShare Chooser driver and in the System file's AppleTalk code resources. This illustrates a point made earlier in this chapter—AppleShare is tightly integrated into the Mac's system software.)

As mentioned earlier, AppleShare PC version 1.1 works only with Apple's LocalTalk PC board. (According to Apple, AppleShare PC version 2.0, scheduled to ship in late 1989, will work with other firms' LocalTalk boards.) To access the server from your PS/2, you use several programs that accompanied your DayStar Digital LocalTalk board. A program called MOUNT lets you access a server volume, while one called UNMOUNT lets you "eject" it. Unfortunately, the DayStar Digital board doesn't include software for viewing or modifying access privileges. And the mounting utilities themselves are spartan compared to AppleShare PC's nicely designed desk accessory. Until AppleShare PC 2.0 becomes available, PS/2 users can't take full advantage of an AppleShare server.

Because MS-DOS file names are limited to only 11 characters (including the extension), AppleShare automatically creates a short name for files or folders whose names exceed MS-DOS' length limits. Shortened names always begin with an exclamation mark (!). For example, a Mac file named "AppleShare Tips" appears as "!APPLESH.ARE" on the MS-DOS machines. If you plan to share certain Mac files with PCs, you may want to name those files with MS-DOS' file name restrictions in mind to begin with. You can probably come up with more descriptive 11-character file names than AppleShare can.

AppleShare Tips

We'll conclude our look at AppleShare with a collection of tips.

Back up your Users & Groups file. AppleShare's Admin utility creates a file called Users & Groups that stores the user and group names you've created. Each time you alter your user and group specifications, you should make a back up copy of the Users & Groups file. If you switch hard drives or if something happens to your old file server, you can copy the backup Users & Groups file to your new server and be spared the chore of recreating all your user and group names. To back up the Users & Groups file, start the Admin program and choose Save Users & Groups As from the File menu. Next, insert a floppy disk and press Return. Keep your back up in a safe place—preferably in the same safe place you use to store your server backups.

Avoiding "hidden" windows. A strange thing can happen if some users on your network have large-screen monitors and others don't: If someone with a large monitor drags the directory window of a folder he or she owns too far from the upper-left corner of the screen, users with small screens may not be able to see that folder's window when they log on to the server. The moral? Users with large-screen monitors should be sure to position directory windows closer to the upper-left corner of the screen, not closer to the Trash can.

Fine-tuning the server. If your server's hard disk was used as a local disk drive before you turned the Mac into a server, consider using a defragmentation utility to defragment its contents as described in Chapter 9. You'll get better performance if the server's files are contiguous.

Choose backup software carefully. We've already stressed the importance of backing up a server's contents. When choosing backup software for this important task, be sure the software you buy retains AppleShare's access privileges information. Otherwise, you'll need to respecify all access privileges when you restore the server's contents. Two backup programs that retain access privilege information are SuperMac's Network DiskFit and Personal Computer Peripherals Corporation's HFS Backup 3.0.

Combining AppleShare and TOPS. AppleShare and TOPS can coexist on the same network. You can even publish an AppleShare volume that you've mounted. For example, let's say Eric on the PS/2 doesn't have AppleShare PC, but he does have TOPS/DOS. Let's also assume that George on the Mac II has both AppleShare and TOPS installed. To make the AppleShare server available to Eric, George logs in to the server on his Mac II, and then he uses the TOPS desk accessory to publish it. After that, Eric can use TOPS/DOS to mount the server. George's Mac II then acts as a intermediary between AppleShare and TOPS.

While this technique works, you do need to observe a few precautions. First, do not install TOPS on the file server Mac. AppleShare uses its own techniques to keep track of what's stored on the server's hard disk, and it expects to have complete control over how the disk's contents are modified. If other nodes used TOPS to mount the server hard disk and modify it, AppleShare wouldn't be aware of the modifications.

Second, TOPS doesn't recognize AppleShare's folder access privileges. When George publishes the AppleShare volume, any TOPS user who mounts that volume will have the same access privileges as George.

Finally, because AppleShare and TOPS use different file-access protocols, no one should mount a published AppleShare volume through both AppleShare and TOPS. This would cause the volume to appear twice on the desktop—once as an AppleShare volume, and once as a TOPS volume. The resulting clash of file-access protocols could cause a crash or damage data on the server.

Network Miscellany

We'll wrap up our tour of Mac networking by looking at:

- file-server options that don't require a dedicated Mac
- using a modular Mac as an AppleShare server
- how to share a modem on a network
- choosing software to run on your network.

Other AFP Server Options

In the AppleShare scenario that we played out in this chapter, we turned your hard disk-equipped Mac SE into a server. Most AppleShare users follow this path of setting aside a Mac and its hard disk for file serving. But there are other ways to create a file server that uses the AppleTalk Filing Protocol (AFP). With these alternatives, you don't need to buy the AppleShare server software. You simply install the AppleShare workstation software that's included with the Mac's system software. (In the System 6.0 Update package, the AppleShare Workstation installer script is stored in the Special Installer Scripts folder on the Utilities 1 disk.)

Two non-Mac file server options are:

- **Using an MS-DOS computer.** You can turn an MS-DOS machine into a dedicated AFP file server using DayStar Digital's FS100 file-server software. This software includes an MS-DOS equivalent to the Admin utility that you use to create and specify access privileges. Unless you're using a fast 80286- or 80386-based MS-DOS machine, however, the server's performance is likely to be slower than a Mac-based server.

- **Using DirectServe.** Jasmine Technologies' $1,299 DirectServe is a small box containing AFP file server software, 1MB of RAM (expandable to 4MB), a microprocessor, and a SCSI port for external hard disks. You control the server by running an administrator's utility from any Mac on the network. You need to add a hard disk to use DirectServe, but even so, the total cost may be less than a hard disk-equipped Mac Plus and AppleShare software. If you don't already have a suitable Mac to turn into a file server, you might consider DirectServe.

The Modular Mac Server

A Mac II, IIx, or IIcx makes a high-performance server that can accommodate heavy network traffic. You can cut the cost of using a modular Mac as a server by about $1000 if you don't buy video hardware or a keyboard for that Mac. To set up the server, use the video hardware and keyboard from a different Mac II in your office. After setting up the server, turn it off, remove the video hardware and disconnect the keyboard, then start the server up again.

To perform maintenance on the server or run the Admin utility, you'll need to reinstall the video hardware and keyboard. To avoid that chore—or if you don't have another Mac II whose video hardware and keyboard you can steal for a while—consider using Farallon Computing's Timbuktu software, which lets you control one Mac from a different Mac. Equip the server and the remote Mac with Timbuktu, and you can run the AppleShare Admin utility from the remote Mac.

Modems and Networks

If more than one person on your network uses communications services such as MCI Mail or CompuServe, you can eliminate having to buy multiple modems (and pay for multiple phone lines) by using a network modem such as Shiva Corporation's NetModem. You attach the NetModem to your Local-Talk network, and then run an installation program on each Mac that needs access to the modem. After installing the NetModem software, the Mac can access the modem as if it were attached directly. The NetModem even uses the Mac's speaker to recreate the scratchy, squealing sounds that modems make when connecting. The NetModem is a 2400-baud modem, and it responds to industry-standard Hayes modem commands, so you can use it with virtually all communications software.

Another benefit to the NetModem is that it allows other users to dial in to your network and become *remote nodes*. A Mac connected to your network through the NetModem can do everything that a local Mac can—send and receive electronic mail, access a file server, and even print documents on a PostScript printer. It's an excellent way for branch offices or employees on the road to remain linked to the home base.

Shiva's remote access software is called Dial-In Network Access. To use it, you simply open the Control Panel, choose the Network cdev, and then connect, as shown in Figure 12-42. Shiva also sells an MS-DOS program called DOS Dial-In that lets MS-DOS machines dial in to a LocalTalk network. DOS Dial-In could be of special interest to people who use laptop MS-DOS computers and want to exchange documents and e-mail with remote networks.

Although remote Mac can do anything a local Mac can, it can't do it as quickly. You wouldn't want to run an application program stored on a remote file server, and you probably wouldn't want to print a large document, either. Even for sending and receiving electronic mail and exchanging small files, the NetModem's 2400-baud speed is barely adequate.

You can get better remote-node performance by using a faster modem, such as Hayes' SmartModem 9600. In one test we performed, it took over two minutes to copy a 20K file from remote AppleShare server when communicating at 2400 baud. At 9600 baud, however, the same test took 39 seconds. (Copying the file from a local AppleShare server took only 4 seconds.) To use a faster modem for dial-in access, you'll need to attach it to your network with Shiva's NetSerial, a hardware add-on that lets you share virtually any serial device on the network.

Select Network cdev and click Dial-In Access button.

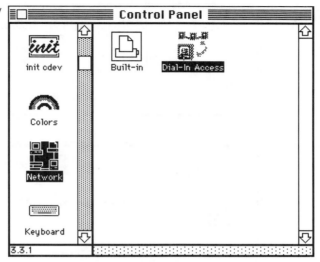

Click Connect button to dial and connect to remote network.

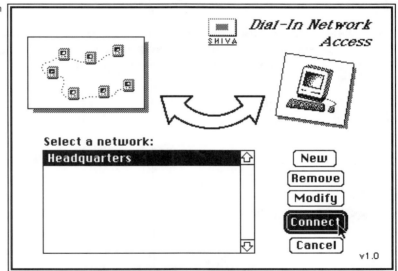

Figure 12-42:   Connecting to a remote network using Shiva's Dial-In Network Access.

The Mac dials the
remote network...

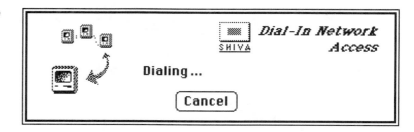

...and then connects
to it.

Figure 12-42: (*continued*)

Figure 12-43 shows two ways to set up your network for remote access: one using NetModem for 2400-baud remote access, and the other using NetSerial and a Hayes Smartmodem 9600 for 9600-baud remote access.

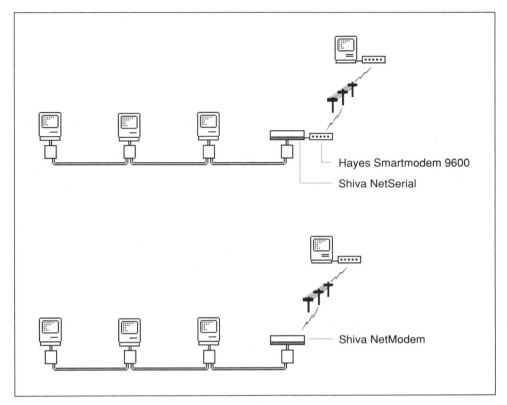

Hayes Smartmodem 9600

Shiva NetSerial

Shiva NetModem

Figure 12-43:   Two ways to set up a network for remote access.

Network Software Issues

It's likely that you'll be storing application programs—word processors, publishing programs, data managers, and so on—on your network's file server, where everyone will be able to access them. Some users may also run applications directly from the file server (although as mentioned earlier, performance will always be better if programs are stored and run from a local hard disk). Storing and running programs on a server introduces technical and legal issues that you may need to consider when shopping for software.

From the technical standpoint, you need to determine whether the software is designed to operate from a shared volume. If it is, then several people can run the same program at once. If it isn't, then only one person can run the program at once.

Two things can prevent a program from working properly in a shared environment:

- Saving information such as your working preferences in its own resource or data fork as it operates.

- Creating temporary work files that always have specific names.

A program that does either of these things is likely to cause unexpected results or crash completely if two people try to run it at the same time. Apple has published specific recommendations for developers to enable them to create software that operates in a shared environment. One such recommendation is that a program store working preferences in a separate file located in the startup disk's System Folder, not in the folder where the program is stored.

Programs that behave properly in a shared environment are often described as being *AppleShare-aware*. Some programs that Apple has certified as being AppleShare-aware are listed in Table 12-2. The presence of a version number after a product name means that version or a later version is AppleShare-aware.

Table 12-2:   A partial list of applications that are AppleShare-aware.

Program	Publisher
4th Dimension	Acius
FileMaker Plus	Claris
InBox 2.0	Symantec
Insight Expert 2.0	Layered, Inc.
Insight Professional 3.0	Layered, Inc.
MacProject	Claris
MacWrite 5.0	Claris
Microsoft Excel 1.04	Microsoft
Microsoft Mail 1.41	Microsoft
Microsoft Word 3.01	Microsoft
Microsoft Works 1.1	Microsoft
MORE 1.1	Symantec
Omnis III Plus 3.25	Blythe Software
PageMaker 2.0	Aldus
PictureBase	Symmetry Corp.
PowerPoint 1.0	Microsoft
Ready,Set,Go! 4.0	Letraset

Note that this isn't a complete list; check with your dealer or with a developer's technical support staff to determine if a program that isn't on this list is AppleShare-aware.

Another factor you should consider when shopping for network software is whether you're legally permitted to use a program on more than one machine at a time. Every software developer has a license agreement whose terms you accept when you open the disk package. Generally, these license agreements state that you're allowed to run the program on only one machine at a time. In order to run the software on several machines at once, you'll need a special licensing agreement, often called a *site license*. When you purchase a site license, you can also purchase additional copies of a program's documentation for each user.

CHAPTER SUMMARY

- With a network, a group of people can share expensive peripherals, access programs and documents stored on a file server, and exchange ideas with electronic mail.

- Each computer and peripheral attached to a network is called a node.

- Several different schemes, or topologies, exist for interconnecting the nodes on a network.

- Several network cabling options are available to Mac users, with each offering different data-transfer speeds and options for connecting to other types of computers.

- Network protocols such as AppleTalk specify how data travels on a network.

- When setting up a network, add services in phases to eliminate troubleshooting nightmares.

- When equipped with LocalTalk expansion boards and appropriate software, MS-DOS computers can print using LocalTalk and access Macintosh file servers.

- The two most popular file-server software packages, TOPS and AppleShare, take different approaches to file serving. TOPS is a distributed file server; it lets any machine become a server and still be used locally. AppleShare is a dedicated file server; it turns a Mac and its hard disks into a central server that other machines on the network can access.

- With network hardware such as Shiva's NetModem and NetSerial, remote users can dial in and access your network. Remote access works best, however, when your network and the remote machines are equipped with fast modems.

- When purchasing software that will be used by network members, it's important to choose programs designed to operate in a shared environment, and to evaluate the program's licensing agreement to determine if it permits the program to be run on a network.

Section IV

How the Mac Works

13

Hardware Details

A dizzying array of events takes place within the Mac. Data travels between the central processor, memory, and disk drives at the speed of light. Another circuit constantly updates the contents of the Mac's RAM chips while painting an image on the video screen. And through it all, the Mac is on the alert for keystrokes and mouse movements. This is the precisely choreographed dance between hardware and software that we mentioned in Chapter 1. And it must go off without a hitch. If one member of the team steps on another's toes, the result is usually a system crash—and lost work.

In this chapter, we'll peer under the hood for a look at the Mac's hardware to examine:

- the basic hardware concepts around which the Mac and most other microcomputers are built

- how data travels within the Mac

- the key components in the Mac and where they're located

- how the Mac's RAM and ROM chips operate

- the expansion slots in the Mac SE, SE/30, and II family

- the 68000 family of microprocessors and the key differences between each member

- what happens when you switch on your Mac.

If you're worried about slogging through a course in electronics theory, rest easy. This chapter does get a bit technical, but we'll concentrate less on theory and more on the basic concepts that will help you understand how the Mac works—concepts that will help you choose hardware add-ons, diagnose difficulties, and give you a greater appreciation for the Mac's design.

HARDWARE CONCEPTS

Most microcomputers have certain design traits in common:

- The tasks they perform are governed by an internal heartbeat generated by a *quartz crystal*.

- They use *interrupts* to allow the central processor to respond to outside events such as keystrokes and mouse movements.

- Data travels within the computer on electronic freeways called *buses*.

Let's explore these concepts as they relate to the Mac.

The Internal Clock

In order to have a dance—even one between hardware and software—you have to have a beat. In the Mac, the beat is provided by a quartz crystal that vibrates millions of times per second when stimulated by electric current. This crystal and the circuitry that supports it form the Mac's *internal clock*. (Don't confuse the internal clock with the clock that keeps track of the time and date. They're separate beasts. To avoid confusion, the Mac's time-and-date clock is often called the *real-time clock*. In this book, we've used the term *alarm clock* to refer to the real-time clock, in honor of the Alarm Clock desk accessory.)

Many of the Mac's circuits use the internal clock. The circuitry that controls the Mac's RAM uses it to periodically refresh the contents of each RAM chip. The video display circuitry uses clock ticks to time the painting of the video screen. The CPU uses the clock as a metronome to time its accesses to RAM, ROM, and peripherals.

After reading that last point, you might infer that the speed of a computer's internal clock plays a big part in determining the computer's overall performance. You're right. The more times per second a computer's metronome ticks, the faster the pace of its internal dance.

The speed of a computer's internal clock is called its *clock rate*. As we saw in Chapter 4, the original Macs, the Mac Plus, and the SE share the same clock rate: 7.8336 million cycles per second. Cycles per second are measured in Hertz, so 7.8336 million cycles per second equals 7.8336 megahertz, or 7.8336 MHz for short. The Mac SE/30 and the II family have 15.6672 MHz internal clocks. (In this book, we've rounded these values up to 8 MHz and 16 MHz, respectively, in the interest of brevity.) That faster clock rate allows them to access memory and peripherals more quickly, and to load and execute program instructions faster.

Did you notice that clock rates of the SE/30 and Mac IIs are exactly twice the clock rates of other Macs? In the Mac, as in all microcomputers, the quartz crystal whose oscillations govern the internal clock actually vibrates many times faster than the actual clock rate. The computer uses a series of *divider chips* to arrive at the final clock rate. In Mac IIs, the divider circuitry simply doesn't divide the original oscillations as many times as the divider circuitry in an 8MHz Mac.

Interrupts

Even when it's just sitting idle, the Mac is hard at work, painting the image on its video screen, keeping the contents of its RAM chips fresh, and remaining alert for mouse movements or keystrokes. When you start a program, open a document, or access a disk in some other way, the Mac works even harder, performing all those jobs even as it accesses the disk.

It may seem that the Mac is performing all these tasks at the same instant. It isn't. In reality, it's switching from one task to the next under the control of *interrupts*. Interrupts are signals sent to the CPU by a device or component that needs the CPU's attention. When you press a key or move the mouse, the keyboard or mouse generates an interrupt, in effect saying to the CPU, "Listen up! I have some data for you."

The CPU acknowledges the interrupt, and then turns control over to an *interrupt handler*—a routine whose job is to respond to, or *service*, that particular kind of interrupt. The interrupt handler then does its job. In the case of a keystroke, that means determining which key was pressed and storing its corresponding character. The interrupt handler then returns control of the CPU to the program you're running.

The whole process works much like a phone conversation: the device generates an interrupt (the phone rings), the CPU acknowledges it (you answer the phone), and the interrupt handler services the interrupt (the conversation takes place). Afterwards, the CPU resumes what it was doing beforehand (you resume watching *Dallas*).

Interrupt Priorities

Anyone who watches *Dallas* knows that some interruptions are more important than others. The Mac also has its own priorities where interrupts are concerned. Some kinds of interrupts must be serviced before others. For example, the interrupt the mouse generates has a lower priority than the interrupt a disk drive generates, because the disk drive transmits far more data in the same amount of time than the mouse. The Mac can temporarily ignore mouse movements in order to respond to the disk drive without losing any important data or impairing performance. However, if it were to ignore data being sent from the disk drive in order to respond to the mouse, information would be lost—or disk performance would slow to a crawl—each time you moved the mouse during a disk access.

You can see the results of this priority scheme by moving the mouse while the Mac is accessing a floppy disk: you'll see the mouse's pointer movement become jerky as the CPU divides its attention between the higher priority disk interrupts and the lower priority mouse ones.

Catching the Bus

The roadways upon which data and program code travel are called *buses*. Buses are the link between the CPU and the components that serve it—and ultimately, between the CPU and the Mac's keyboard, mouse, printer, hard disk, and other add-ons.

All Macs have two primary buses: the *address bus* and the *data bus*. The address bus carries memory addresses from the CPU; these signals specify the location in memory where data is to be stored or retrieved. The data bus carries the data itself. The two buses work together like a taxi dispatcher and a taxi: the dispatcher specifies where data is to be delivered or picked up, and the data bus carries the data itself. These buses are often called *external buses* because they're outside of the Mac's CPU chip, which contains its own address and data buses, called *internal buses*. Unless otherwise noted, the following descriptions refer to the external buses.

With both the address and data buses, speed is of the essence. Thus, both transfer their data in parallel—with the bits that form each byte traveling alongside each other, instead of in single-file, serial form.

A computer bus is often described in terms of its *width*. Bus width refers to how many bits of data a bus can carry at once. Just as some freeways have more lanes than others, some buses are wider than others, and therefore, can carry more data in the same amount of time.

Generally, the wider a bus, the better. But the specific advantage of a wider bus width depends on the type of bus you're dealing with. Let's look at the impact bus width has on an address bus and a data bus.

Address Bus Width: The Wider the Bus, the More Memory

With an address bus, greater width means the computer can access a larger amount of memory. Why? Think back on Chapter 1's discussion of bits and binary: The more bits you lump together, the greater the range of values you can represent. Consider the taxi analogy we just used: having a wider address bus is like having a more powerful dispatcher's radio that can reach a wider area of addresses.

The 68000 chip in the Mac Plus and SE has a 24-bit address bus, which, in theory, would allow these machines to access a maximum of 16MB of RAM. However, because of the way the Plus' and SE's address lines are used, these machines are limited to accessing a maximum of 4MB of RAM.

Macs containing 68020 or 68030 processors—the SE/30 and the II family—have 32-bit address buses. In theory, a 32-bit address bus allows access to up to four *gigabytes* (GB) of memory—4096 megabytes. In practice, however, System 6.0 and earlier versions of the Mac's system software are unable to access more than 8MB. System 7.0 will, however, support *32-bit addressing*, opening the memory frontiers to the full 4GB that 32-bit address buses allow.

Data Bus Width: The Wider the Bus, the Faster

Because an address bus carries addresses, a wider bus width allows a computer to access a greater range of memory addresses. But a data bus carries data, so a wider data bus has no effect on how much memory a CPU can address. With a data bus, greater width means greater speed, because more data can be transferred across the data bus in the same amount of time—just as an eight-lane freeway can move more cars per hour than a four-lane one.

68000-based Macs have 16-bit data buses. 68020- and 68030-based Macs have 32-bit data buses, allowing these Macs to internally move twice as much data at a time. Their wider bus and their faster clock rates are two of the factors that make these high-powered Macs so much faster than their predecessors. (Another reason is that the 68020 and 68030 microprocessors are faster and more efficient than the 68000; more about that later.)

It's important to realize that a computer's overall speed is determined by many other factors, including the speed of its disk drives, the software it's running, and the internal structure, or *architecture*, of its microprocessor. The width of a computer's data bus is only one factor that influences performance.

Control and Interrupt Lines

The CPU gains access to the data bus by sending out a signal. That signal travels along a *control line*, a specialized internal roadway that carries not addresses or data, but status and control information.

The Mac contains numerous control lines, and uses them for such diverse tasks as:

- gaining control of the data or address bus
- turning a disk drive's motor on or off
- selecting between the floppy disk drives in Macs equipped with more than one drive
- carrying clock signals that other components use to time their operation.

In the next section, we'll look at the chips that are connected to the Mac's buses and control lines.

UNDER THE HOOD

In this section, we'll set the stage for our look at the Mac's hardware by looking under the hood to see what's located where.

Inside the Compact Macs

If you use a modular Mac, you may have ventured inside the case to install an expansion board. But most users of compact Macs—the Plus, SE, and SE/30—will never see inside their machines' cases. Compact Macs are tightly sealed boxes, intended to be opened, in the words of the case, "by qualified service personnel."

And even a qualified service person has to work to "crack" the case. A half-dozen or so odd-looking screws bond its two halves together. Finding the tool—a Torx T-15 screwdriver with a six-inch blade—that fits these screws can be like shopping for surgical tools for a brain transplant. When you finally do succeed in extracting the screws, the case's two halves remain tightly married. To separate them without marring either half, you need an exotic instrument called a *Mac cracker*. Various forms of Mac crackers are available through computer mail-order firms specializing in Mac products.

Fortunately, a small Mac's case doesn't need to be opened often. Aside from when the hardware breaks, the only times you'll need to crack an SE's defenses are to install more memory, an expansion board, or an internal hard disk. (These same three installation jobs apply to the Plus and earlier machines, too, although expansion boards and internal hard disks are less common.)

The Mac Plus and earlier machines share a similar internal layout with the SEs. For that reason, we've grouped them together in this section, while noting the significant differences between each.

As Figure 13-1 shows, compact Macs contain two printed circuit boards: the *analog board* and the *digital board*, also called the *logic board*.

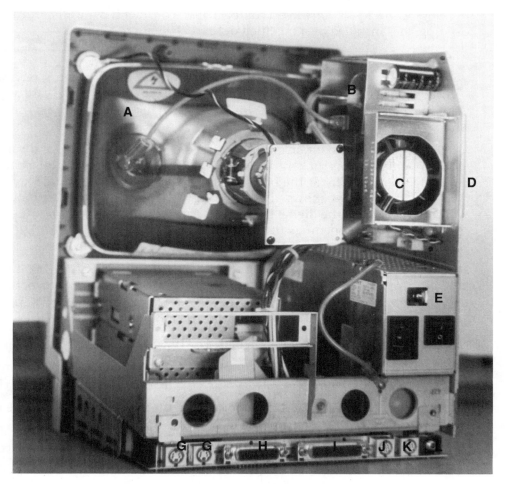

Figure 13-1: Inside a Mac SE. A: Video tube, B: Video, C: Fan, D: Analog board, E: Power supply, F: Logic board, G: ADB, H: External Floppy, I: SCSI, J: Printer port, K: Modem port, L: Audio out.

WARNING!

There are potentially fatal voltages inside the Mac, and they can be present even when the power is switched off. If you open your Mac's case, don't touch any components on the analog board or any of the wires leading to the video tube. Moreover, opening the case will void your warranty. If you have a compact Mac, consider having all hardware upgrades installed by a qualified dealer.

The analog board contains the circuitry for the Mac's video screen and power supply, and is mounted vertically along the left side of the case as you face the screen. The Mac's power switch is located here, and protrudes through a hole in the rear half of the case.

The digital board contains the CPU, the RAM and ROM chips, and various support chips, many of which we'll describe shortly. The digital board is mounted horizontally at the bottom of the case, below the cathode-ray tube (CRT). As Figure 13-1 shows, the connectors for the Mac's ports are mounted on the rear edge of the digital board. Like the power switch, these connectors protrude through openings in the back of the Mac's case. Left to right, the connectors on an SE are as follows:

- Two Apple Desktop Bus ports for the keyboard and mouse. The ADB ports are four-pin female connectors similar to those used on some videocassette recorders. (The Mac Plus and earlier Macs lack the two ADB ports; in their place is one female DB-9 connector for the mouse.)

- The external disk drive port, a female DB-19 connector.

- The SCSI port, a female DB-25 connector (128K, 512K, and 512K Enhanced Macs lack a SCSI port).

- The printer port, a female DIN-8 connector (on pre-Plus Macs, a female DB-9 connector).

- The modem port, also a female DIN-8 connector (a female DB-9 connector on pre-Plus Macs).

- The audio-output jack, a female 1/8-inch phono connector.

Incidentally, the DB designation refers to the number of pins in the connector: a DB-25, for example, has 25 pins or, in the case of a female connector, pin receptacles.

The back of the SE and SE/30 cases also contain a plastic *knock-out*—a rectangular piece of plastic you can remove by breaking the plastic tabs that connect it to the rest of the case. Once the knock-out is removed, you can mount new connectors from optional internal expansion boards in its place.

The Analog Board and Power Supply

The power supply's job is to convert the 110-volt alternating current (AC) power coming through the power cord into the 12 volts and 5 volts of direct current (DC) that most of the Mac's integrated circuits require. The power supply also creates other voltages used by the Mac's video tube and other components. And because the AC power in most buildings tends to fluctuate and can also carry electrical "noise" from appliances, power tools, and air conditioners, the power supply contains a variety of filters that smooth voltage irregularities and provide an electrically clean, consistent power source. The Mac's power supply is quite forgiving of fluctuations in incoming voltage; the Mac can operate on any incoming voltage between 85 and 135 volts. The power supplies in the SE and SE/30 are even more agile, able to sense and adapt to 110-volt and 220-volt power.

There are some significant differences between the power supplies in a Mac Plus, SE, and SE/30.

- The Mac Plus' power supply can deliver a maximum of 46.8 watts of power; the SEs' heavier duty power supply can deliver a maximum of 76 watts. (Wattage refers to the quantity of power used by an electric device. If you imagine electricity as water flowing through a hose, the voltage corresponds to the water pressure, while the wattage corresponds to the quantity of water flowing through the hose.) Its stronger power supply allows the SE and SE/30 to electrically accommodate an expansion board.

- The SEs' power supplies are encased in a metal box that traps electrical interference and helps keep careless hands away from dangerous voltages. The Mac Plus' power supply components are mounted directly on the analog board.

- Because of the extra heat generated by the heavy duty power supply (and by any expansion board you may have installed), the analog board in the SE and SE/30 contains a cooling fan.

In addition to the power supply, the analog board houses circuitry that drives the compact Mac's video screen. As Chapter 6 described, the video circuitry controls the horizontal and vertical motion of the video tube's electron beam.

Another part of the video circuitry's job is to provide the very high voltage required by the video tube. This voltage is produced by a large *flyback transformer*. In a Mac SE, the flyback transformer is located near the fan; in a Mac Plus or earlier machine, it's near the top of the analog board, just below the cooling vents. A thick wire extends from the flyback transformer to the video tube itself.

Power Supply Woes in Compact Macs

Power supply problems are common in the air-cooled Mac Plus, 512Ks, and 128K. Indeed, service technicians we've talked to say that, in their experience, analog board replacements are the most common repair performed on all Mac models. The most common power supply problem is a burned-out flyback transformer, although other components can sometimes fail, too.

If you have an air-cooled Mac whose screen image is jittery or seems to have shrunk, chances are its flyback transformer or another power supply component is about to fail. You may also hear humming or clicking sounds coming from within the Mac's case. What can you do? An Apple dealer will replace the entire analog board for approximately $200. As an alternative, you might want to have your Mac's existing analog board repaired; Total Systems Integration of Eugene, OR (800/874-2288) rebuilds Mac power supplies, and offers a heavy-duty rebuilding option that you should consider if your Mac contains a memory upgrade or accelerator board. You may be able to find other firms in your area by asking around at local user's group meetings.

If your air-cooled Mac is still healthy, you can do two things to keep it that way:

• Keep it clean. The dust that collects on electronic components acts as a blanket that traps heat. Cover the Mac with a dust cover when it isn't turned on, especially if you work in a dusty environment. (Never put a dust cover on a Mac that's still on.) Dust covers are available from several firms; visit a local dealer or check the advertisers index in Macintosh magazines. If your Mac is a few years old and it hasn't been covered, consider taking it to a dealer for a thorough cleaning. The dealer can check out its power supply at the same time.

• Keep it cool. Don't obstruct the ventilation slots located on top of the Mac and at its base. Allow several inches of space around them so that air can circulate. If you're working in a hot environment, you may want to switch the Mac off if you won't be using it for several hours. Avoid turning it on and off too frequently, however; that can stress the power supply, too. You might also consider adding a fan such as Kensington's System Saver. If the inside of the Mac is dusty, however, a fan is unlikely to help.

Although the Mac SE's power supply has a much better track record than that of the air-cooled Macs, some early SEs are prone to screen jitter and their fans are annoyingly loud. If your SE's serial number precedes F749xxxx, you can have its power supply (and fan) replaced at no charge by an authorized Apple dealer.

The Compact Mac Digital Boards

The analog board supplies the brawn to make the Mac work; the digital board provides the brains. Crammed into the digital board are the chips and circuits that form the Macintosh. Figure 13-2 shows the digital board from a Mac SE. Where appropriate, we'll note the differences between the SE's digital board and that of other compact Macs. In Macs other than the SE, the components described here are in different places than they are on the SE's digital board.

The key players on the SE digital board include:

A. The 68000 microprocessor (in the SE/30, the 68030)

B. Two ROM chips (in the SE/30, four ROMs mounted on a SIMM)

C. RAM chips. In the 512K and 512K Enhanced Macs, 16 RAM chips are soldered directly to the digital board. In the SE and Plus, the RAM chips are installed on small circuit boards called single in-line memory modules, or SIMMs. By plugging in additional SIMMs, you can expand the RAM in an SE or Plus to a maximum of 4MB, and the SE/30's to a maximum of 8MB.

D. A floppy disk-controller chip, called the *Integrated Woz Machine* (*IWM*), in honor of Apple cofounder Steve Wozniak, who was also the primary designer of the Apple II. When designing the Apple II's disk controller board, Wozniak devised a clever technique for encoding data on floppy disks. Apple adapted that technique to the Macintosh, and shrunk Woz' circuitry to fit on a chip. The primary function of the IWM chip is to convert between the serial data-storage method that disks use and the parallel transmission method that the Mac's data bus uses. The SE/30 uses an updated version of the chip, which we'll examine when we look at the Mac IIx, since it also uses the updated chip.

E. A serial port controller chip, the Zilog Z8530 Serial Communications Controller (SCC). The SCC chip controls the Mac's modem and printer ports, discussed in the next chapter.

F. A SCSI interface chip, the NCR 5380. The SCSI chip controls the high-speed parallel data transmission of the SCSI port, also discussed in the next chapter. (Macs preceding the Plus lack this chip.)

Figure 13-2: The Mac SE digital board.

G. The Versatile Interface Adapter (VIA). The VIA chip provides control lines for the Mac's floppy disk drive, video, SCSI, serial port, and sound circuits. In the Mac SE, a custom VIA designed by Apple also serves as an interface between the digital board and the real-time clock and Apple Desktop Bus ports (used by the mouse and keyboard, and described in the next chapter). In the Mac Plus and earlier machines, a Rockwell International 6522 VIA performs these same tasks, but because these Macs lack ADB ports, the VIA deals directly with the keyboard and mouse.

H. A custom chip that works with the video circuitry and also controls the speed of the floppy disk motors and works with the Sony sound chip to produce audio. In the Mac SE, this chip is named the Bob Bailey Unit (BBU), in honor of its designer. In the Mac Plus and earlier machines, sound, disk speed, and video control is provided by a number of other custom chips.

I. A sound chip, built to Apple's specifications by Sony. The sound chip works together with other chips to allow the Mac to produce simple sounds (such as alert beeps) as well as complex synthesized sounds. The SE/30, which provides stereo audio circuitry, contains two Sony sound chips as well as the Apple Sound Chip.

J. An expansion connector that lets you plug in optional boards. In the SE, the connector contains 96 pins and is connected directly to the SE's address and data buses. The SE/30 contains a 120-pin expansion connector, which provides access to the SE/30's 32-bit buses. The Mac Plus and earlier machines lack this connector.

Other Components in the Compact Mac

The remaining components inside a compact Mac are mounted on the same metal chassis that holds the digital and analog boards. These components include:

- The video screen, which measures 9 inches diagonally and provides an image size of approximately 4 3/4 inches by 7 inches.

- A speaker, 2.25 inches in diameter. In the SEs, the speaker is at the front of the machine, near the Apple logo. In earlier compact Macs, the speaker is mounted on the analog board.

In all Macs, the speaker is too small to produce acceptable fidelity. You can connect the Mac to an external amplifier or stereo system by using inexpensive audio patch cords available at Radio Shack. For instructions—and an important caution—see the section "Wiring the Mac for Sound" in Chapter 9.

- One or two floppy disk drives. The Mac Plus and earlier machines and the SE/30 can accommodate one floppy drive; the SE can house two, with one stacked above the other. The Mac's floppy disk drives are built to Apple's specifications by Sony, which invented the 3.5-inch, hard-cased microfloppy disk format.

- A hard disk (optional). The Mac SE and SE/30 are designed to accommodate an internal hard disk. In the SE, a hard disk takes the place of one floppy disk drive. Apple offers a variety of hard disk configurations, and many drives are available from developers of Mac hardware. Some of these drives are sold in do-it-yourself form, and require no soldering and only a few tools for installation.

Inside the Mac II and IIx

The Mac II and IIx share similar internal layouts, so we've grouped them together here and noted the differences between each.

Figure 13-3 shows a Mac II with the case removed. The significant components include:

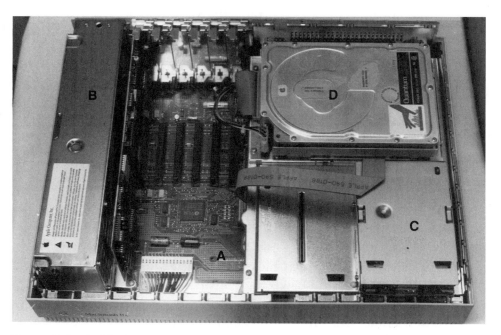

Figure 13-3: Inside the Mac II.

A. The *main logic board*, also called the *motherboard*. The Mac II contains one main circuit board, not two as in the compact Macs.

B. The power supply, which can deliver up to 132 watts (compared to the 46.8 watts in the Mac Plus and earlier machines, and 76 watts in the Mac SE). The heavier duty power supply is required to power the six expansion boards a Mac II can house. Like that of an SE, the Mac II's power supply is encased in a metal enclosure and cooled by a fan.

C. Floppy disk drive (or drives). The floppy disk drives in the original Mac II are identical to those in the SE and Plus. The IIx uses Apple's FDHD floppy drives, each of which can store 1.4MB, nearly twice their predecessor's capacity. Unlike the compact Macs and the Mac IIcx, the II and IIx do not support an external floppy disk drive.

D. An internal hard disk (optional). A Mac II's hard disk, if installed, sits between the floppy drives and the rear of the case. The internal hard disk connects to an internal SCSI connector.

E. A video card. Unlike small Macs, a Mac II does not include any video display circuitry on its main circuit board.

The Mac II and IIx Logic Board

Figure 13-4 shows the logic board of a Mac IIx. The key components on the board include:

Figure 13-4: The Mac IIx logic board.

A. The 68030 microprocessor (in the Mac II, the 68020)

B. A *floating-point numerics coprocessor*, a microprocessor dedicated to performing math operations. The Mac II uses the Motorola 68881; the IIx uses the newer, faster 68882. We'll look at both chips later in this chapter.

C. SIMM-mounted RAM chips. All Mac IIs can house up to 8 megabytes of SIMM-mounted RAM using 1MB SIMMs. When 4MB SIMMs become widely available (and affordable), the II and IIx will be able to accommodate up to 32MB of RAM. (Both Macs can also accommodate RAM installed on NuBus expansion boards.)

D. Four ROM chips. In the Mac II, the chips are plugged into sockets; in the IIx, they're mounted on a SIMM for easier replacement.

E. A floppy disk-controller chip. The Mac II uses the same IWM chip as the SE (described in "Compact Mac Digital Boards," earlier in this chapter). The Mac IIx and IIcx use an updated version of the chip called the *super Wozniak integrated machine*, or SWIM. The *SWIM* chip supports these Macs' high-capacity floppy disk drives, and allows them to read and write disks in non-Macintosh formats such as Apple II ProDOS, MS-DOS, and OS/2.

F. A serial port controller chip, the Zilog Z8530 Serial Communications Controller (SCC). This is the same SCC chip as is used in the small Macs; it controls the Mac's modem and printer ports, discussed in the next chapter.

G. The NCR 5380 SCSI interface chip. Again, the Mac II family uses the same SCSI controller chip as the compact Macs.

H. Two Versatile Interface Adapter (VIA) chips. One VIA performs the same jobs as the single VIA in a Mac SE: it provides control lines for the Mac's floppy disk drive, video, SCSI, ADB, serial port, and sound circuitry. The other VIA performs functions specific to the Mac IIs, including monitoring the NuBus expansion slots and shutting off the power supply when you choose the Finder's Shut Down command or press the power switch.

I. A custom chip called the *GLUE* chip, which handles a potpourri of tasks, from refreshing the contents of the Mac's memory chips to decoding the address space for RAM, ROM, and NuBus cards.

J. An Apple Sound Chip, which gives the II and IIx their stereo audio capabilities.

Not shown in Figure 13-4 is a socket for a specialized chip called a *paged-memory management unit*, or *PMMU*. The PMMU socket is present in the original Mac II only. When a PMMU chip is plugged into this socket, the Mac II is able to use the virtual memory features that System 7.0 will provide. The Mac II is designed to accommodate Motorola's 68851 PMMU. As we'll see later in this chapter, the 68030-based Mac IIx lacks a PMMU chip because its 68030 already contains built-in paged-memory support.

Inside the Mac IIcx

Electronically, the petite Mac IIcx has much in common with the II and IIx, but because the layout of its case and logic board are so different, we'll look at it separately. Figure 13-5 shows a Mac IIcx with its cover removed.

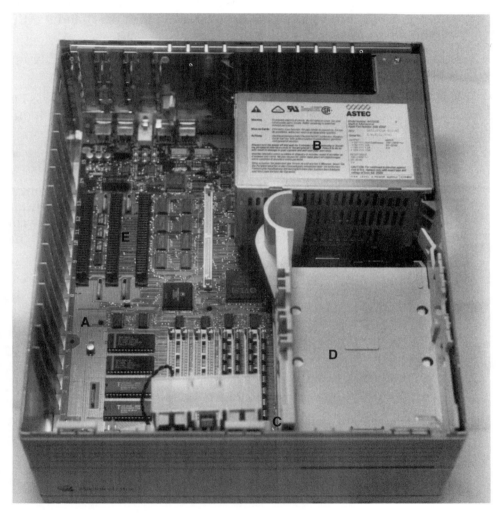

Figure 13-5: Inside the Mac IIcx

The key components are:

A. The main logic board.

B. The power supply, self-adjusting to 110 or 220 volts.

C. One FDHD floppy disk drive. Unlike the II and IIx, the IIcx can accommodate just one internal floppy drive. But also unlike the II and IIx, the IIcx offers an external floppy drive connector.

D. An internal hard disk (optional). A IIcx's hard disk lives directly upstairs from the floppy drive.

E. A video card. Like the larger member of the II family, the IIcx lacks built-in video. You choose the video card that meets your needs and plug it into one of the computer's three NuBus expansion slots.

The Mac IIcx Logic Board

Figure 13-6 shows the logic board of the Mac IIcx. The IIcx uses many of the same components as the II and IIx. For that reason, we won't repeat each component description here. For information on the workings of each component, see the section "The Mac II and IIx Logic Board," earlier in this chapter.

A. 68030 microprocessor

B. 68882 math coprocessor.

C. SIMM-mounted RAM chips.

D. Four ROM chips. In the Mac IIcx, the chips are soldered to the logic board; the IIcx logic board also contains a socket for SIMM-mounted ROMs.

E. SWIM floppy disk-controller chip.

F. Serial port controller chip, the Zilog Z8530.

G. NCR 5380 SCSI interface chip.

H. Two Versatile Interface Adapter (VIA) chips.

I. GLUE chip.

J. Apple Sound Chip

K. Three NuBus slots.

Figure 13-6: The Mac IIcx logic board.

MEMORY DETAILS

We've discussed the Mac's RAM and ROM chips in general terms; now let's get into specifics. If you plan to expand your Mac's memory, read this section for an introduction to memory concepts. We'll concentrate on RAM in this section, but most of the concepts also apply to ROM.

RAM Basics

Like most microcomputers, the Mac uses dynamic RAM chips, or *DRAMs* (pronounced *dee-ram*). In order to retain their contents, DRAMs require a periodic *refresh signal*, an electronic prodding that keeps the RAM chip's electronic switches in position. The other primary category of RAM, *static RAM*, doesn't require this constant prodding. Static RAM tends to be more expensive and electrically complex than dynamic RAM, and plays a relatively small role in microcomputing.

In compact Macs, the DRAMs are refreshed 60 times per second by the video display circuitry. As we've said in previous chapters, the Mac uses a bit-mapped display in which each dot on the screen corresponds to a bit in memory. The area of memory that holds this screen data is the *screen buffer*. The Mac's video circuitry must scan the screen buffer at regular intervals as it labors to keep the contents of the screen current.

Because the screen buffer requires regular scanning and because DRAMs require regular refreshing, Apple's engineers devised a kill-two-birds-with-one-stone technique in which the video circuitry refreshes the RAM chips and updates the screen display (for details, see the section below, "Understanding Blanking Intervals"). This scheme simplifies the compact Mac's hardware. But it also slows memory-access performance, since the CPU must often wait for the video circuitry to finish painting a line on the screen before it can access RAM.

The Mac II family works differently. In these Macs, the screen buffer isn't part of the Mac's main RAM, but is located on a separate video card. In Mac IIs, the GLUE chip refreshes the DRAMs every 15.6 milliseconds. Except for these fleeting interruptions, the CPU has uninterrupted access to RAM.

Where RAM is concerned, the SE/30 straddles the fence between the SE and the II family. Like the II family, the SE/30 provides dedicated video RAM; it doesn't use part of the machine's main memory for video. But like the SE, the SE/30 requires CPU cycles for refreshing.

The bottom line: the II can transfer data within RAM far faster than a compact Mac. For example, the original Mac II has an average RAM access time of 12.53 megabytes per second. By contrast, the Mac SE's average access time is only 3.22 megabytes per second. The Mac Plus is slower still, averaging about 2.56 megabytes per second. And all of this illustrates a point made earlier in this chapter: Many factors influence a computer's overall performance.

Understanding Blanking Intervals

The periods of time when the video tube's electron beam switches off because it's reached the right edge of a scan line or the lower-right corner of the screen are called *blanking intervals*. The horizontal blanking interval occurs after each scan line is drawn; the vertical blanking interval occurs only once per frame, when the beam reaches the lower-right corner of the screen. Both blanking intervals are important, especially in compact Macs. In compact Macs, the vertical blanking interval is the period when the video circuitry refreshes the Mac's DRAM chips.

During each vertical blanking interval, the Mac's VIA chip generates an interrupt called the *vertical blanking interrupt*. By using a Toolbox manager called the *Vertical Retrace Manager*, Mac software can take advantage of this interrupt to specify that certain tasks be performed each time a vertical blanking interrupt occurs. The Mac's system software itself uses the vertical blanking interrupt for several tasks, including checking whether a floppy disk has been inserted and updating the pointer's position to reflect recent mouse movements.

DRAM Density

The amount of information a DRAM chip can hold is determined by the chip's *density*, which is measured in kilobits. One kilobit, or *Kbit* for short, equals 1024 bits. (Notice that we're talking about *bits* here, not *bytes*.)

These days, the most common DRAM chip densities are 64-Kbit, 256-Kbit, and one-megabit. You can determine how many bits a chip can store by multiplying its density by 1,024. For example, by multiplying 1,024 by 256, we learn that one 256-Kbit DRAM chip contains a total of 262,144 electronic switches—each of which can be on or off, storing a value of one or zero. A one megabit chip contains a staggering 1,048,576 electronic switches.

Cramming over a million bits on a single chip is impressive, but remember that bits are combined into larger, more versatile units—bytes. To get one megabyte of RAM, you must tie together 32 256-Kbit DRAMs or 8 1-Mbit DRAMs.

The key concepts to remember here are:

- Individual RAM chips store *bits*, not *bytes*.

- The density of individual chips is measured in kilobits (Kbits) or megabits (Mbits).

- Because the byte is the workhorse when it comes to representing programs and data, and because there are eight bits to a byte, the Mac uses RAM chips in groups of eight.

DRAM Access Time

Memory chips store and supply data quickly, but even within their microscopic world, things take time. The time required for for the Mac to successfully read from or write to a DRAM chip is called its *access time*. The Mac Plus and the SE require DRAMs with an access time of 150 nanoseconds (ns—one billionth of a second). The faster Mac IIs and the SE/30 require 120-ns DRAMs. When shopping for Mac memory upgrades, look for chips whose access time equals or is faster than that required for your Mac.

You can use DRAMs with a faster access time than your Mac requires—for example, 120-ns DRAMs will work fine in a Mac Plus—but doing so will not increase your Mac's performance, since the Mac's circuitry is designed for the timing of 150-ns DRAMs. According to Apple, future Macintosh models may be able to sense and adapt to faster DRAMs. Current Macs, however, assume a specific access time for their DRAM chips, and can't take advantage of faster ones.

Mac 128K and 512K DRAM Configurations

In 1983, during the final days of the Mac's design, 256-Kbit DRAM chips were just completing the journey from research lab to production line. 256-Kbit DRAMs weren't available in the quantities Apple needed; as a result, the pioneering 128K Mac used 64-Kbit DRAMs. (It's also worth noting that, in the early 80s, 64-Kbit DRAMs were considered the state of the art. The original IBM PC used 16-Kbit DRAMs.) The 128K Mac contained 64-Kbit DRAMs, and the 512K and 512K Enhanced Macs used 256-Kbit DRAMs. In all three Macs, the DRAMs are individual chips soldered into the logic board.

Mac Plus and SE DRAM Configuration

With the Mac Plus, Apple began using SIMMs for the Mac's DRAM chips. Each SIMM contains eight 256-Kbit DRAM chips mounted on a small circuit board, as shown in Figure 13-7. Some IBM PC expansion boards use SIMMs containing nine chips, with the ninth chip used for an error-checking scheme called *parity checking*. According to Apple, nine-chip SIMMs will also work in a Mac, provided that the DRAMs themselves meet Apple's access-time specifications.

A one-megabyte Mac Plus, SE, or SE/30 contains four SIMMs, with each SIMM containing eight 256-Kbit DRAM chips. You can expand the Plus' and SE's memory to 2, 2.5, or 4 megabytes. Here's how the SIMMs are configured for each upgrade:

- The 2MB configuration uses two 1MB SIMMs. In this configuration, two of the logic board's SIMM slots are vacant.

- The 2.5MB configuration uses two 1MB SIMMs and two 256-Kbit SIMMs.

- The 4MB configuration uses four 1MB SIMMs.

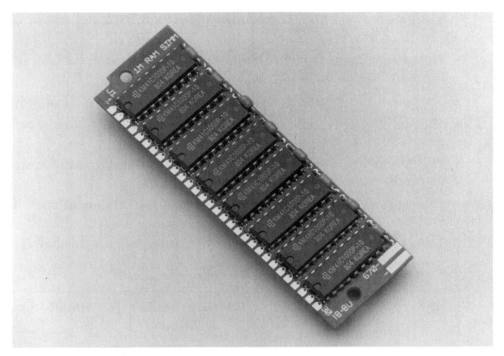

Figure 13-7: A Single In-line Memory Module (SIMM).

It's worth mentioning that the Plus and SE require additional components called *RAM size resistors* to be installed in various combinations, depending on how much RAM the machine contains. Adding a RAM upgrade to a Plus or SE requires installing or removing certain RAM size resistors and making minor adjustments in the Mac's power supply to accommodate the new DRAM chips. This is another reason we recommend you have Plus and SE upgrades performed by a qualified technician.

Mac II Family and SE/30 DRAM Configuration

As with the Plus and SE, you can expand the memory in the Mac II family and the SE/30 in incremental stages. Unlike the Plus and SE, however, these machines can accommodate a maximum of eight megabytes—their logic boards contain not four SIMM slots, but eight. Each set of four slots is called a bank; the two banks are named *bank A* and *bank B*.

There are five possible SIMM configurations for the Mac II, IIx, IIcx, and SE/30:

- The one-megabyte configuration uses four SIMMs, each containing eight 256-Kbit DRAMs. Bank B is vacant.

- The two-megabyte configuration fills Bank B with four 256KB SIMMs.

- The four-megabyte configuration uses four 1MB SIMMs in bank A; bank B is empty.

- The five-megabyte configuration uses four 1MB SIMMs in bank A, and four 256KB SIMMs in bank B.

- The eight-megabyte configuration uses four 1MB SIMMs in bank A, and four 1MB SIMMs in bank B.

Table 14-1 summarizes the SIMM configurations in the Mac family.

Table 14-1: Macintosh family SIMM configurations.

Model	Total RAM	SIMMs in Bank A	SIMMs in Bank B
Plus, SE	1MB	4 256KB	—
	2MB	2 1MB	—
	2.5MB	2 256KB, 2 1MB	—
	4MB	4 1MB	—
II family,	1MB	4 256KB	empty
SE/30	2MB	4 256KB	4 256KB
	4MB	4 1MB	empty
	5MB	4 1MB	4 256KB
	8MB	4 1MB	4 1MB

SIMMs for 68030 Macs

Incidentally, some of the SIMMs used in 68030-based Macs will not work in 68000- and 68020-based Macs because certain timing-related signal lines are reversed from their position in previous SIMMs. These SIMMs are stamped "030 ONLY" on the back. 68030-based Macs contain additional ROM code that recognizes and adapts to these SIMMs.

Where are the DIP Switches?

If you've ever installed memory in an IBM PC or compatible computer, you've probably struggled with *DIP switches*—those infuriatingly small switches on the PC's motherboard that you set to tell the computer how much memory you've installed. If you upgrade your Mac's memory, you'll be spared that chore. When you switch the Mac on, ROM-based diagnostic software tests the RAM and determines how much is installed. This diagnostic routine stores a value in RAM that corresponds to the amount of memory your Mac contains. The Finder and other parts of the Mac's system software can access this value to find out how much memory your Mac contains.

A Word About ROM

Although this section concentrates on RAM, some of the concepts we've discussed also apply to ROM. ROM density—the capacity of a ROM chip—is described in the same way: in kilobits or megabits. And as with RAM chips, multiple ROM chips are electrically tied together. Table 14-2 shows the ROM configurations in each member of the Mac family.

Table 14-2: ROM configurations in the Macintosh family.

Mac Model	Number of ROMs	Density	Total ROM
128K	two	256-Kbit	64K
512K	two	256-Kbit	64K
512K Enhanced	two	512-Kbit	128K
Plus	two	512-Kbit	128K
SE	two	1-Mbit	256K
SE/30	four[1]	512-Kbit	256K
II	four	512-Kbit	256K
IIx	four[1]	512-Kbit	256K
IIcx	four	512-Kbit	256K

[1] ROMs are mounted on a SIMM.

One DRAM concept that doesn't apply to ROMs is that of a regular refresh cycle. Because a ROM's contents are electrically frozen at the factory, a ROM chip doesn't require a refresh signal at regular intervals. Simply put, ROMs don't forget.

EXPANSION SLOTS

The expansion slots in the Mac SE, SE/30, and the II series provide direct access to these machines' data and address buses. If the bus is a freeway, then a slot is a set of on-ramps and off-ramps. When you plug an expansion board into a slot, you connect its circuitry directly to the Mac's main freeways. Because an expansion board is connected directly to the internal bus, it has fast, direct access to the CPU and other components. Put another way, when performance counts, ride the bus.

We spotlighted the key categories of expansion boards in Chapter 4. Now let's take a look at how the Mac family's expansion slots work.

The Mac SE Expansion Bus

The Mac SE contains a single expansion slot that uses a Euro-DIN 96-pin male connector. 40 of the 96 pins on the expansion connector lead to the SE's 24 address lines and 16 data lines. The remaining pins provide access to clock signals, interrupt lines, and numerous control lines. Several of the pins also carry juice from the power supply to an expansion board's components.

Three control lines on the SE expansion bus allow an expansion card to gain full control of the SE's address, data, and control lines. These three lines allow accelerator and coprocessor boards to supplement or supplant the SE's CPU.

A board installed in the SE's expansion slot can access RAM at the same speed as the 68000 microprocessor itself: at 3.22 megabytes per second. An SE can physically accommodate a board as large as 4 by 8 inches, although most expansion boards are smaller. As we saw earlier in this chapter, the rear of the SE's case contains a plastic knock-out that, when removed, reveals an opening that can accommodate the connectors or cables an expansion board might use. Boards that provide their own connectors and cables include networking boards and specialized video boards.

The Mac SE/30 Expansion Bus

The SE/30's 030 Direct Slot provides many of the same basic signals as the SE's slot. Unlike the SE's slot, however, the 030 Direct Slot provides direct (hence its name) access to every signal line that the 68030 provides. Also, the 030 Direct Slot is a full 32-bit slot—a necessary characteristic for accommodating 24- and 32-bit video cards.

NuBus Expansion Slots

The members of the Mac II family provide a far more sophisticated expansion bus. Their expansion slots are based on NuBus, a bus standard developed in the 1970s at the Massachusets Institute of Technology and refined in 1985 by a standards committee comprising engineers and representatives from MIT, AT&T, Texas Instruments, Apple, and other firms. Like many computer- and electronics-related standards, NuBus was born under the auspices of the Institute of Electrical and Electronic Engineers (IEEE, pronounced *eye-triple-e*).

Two primary factors make NuBus a more sophisticated expansion bus.

- NuBus supports multiple processors. The Mac II's NuBus slots are designed to coordinate the workings of up to seven processors, including the CPU on the main logic board. If your work involves specialized tasks such as real-time animation or sound processing, you can equip your Mac II with the appropriate coprocessor boards to perform those tasks more quickly.

- NuBus boards configure themselves. In the IBM PC world, installing an expansion board often means the DIP switch dance—fussing with the settings of DIP switches in an attempt to get all your expansion boards to coexist. With NuBus, DIP switches are relics of the past. All NuBus boards are self-configuring: you plug them in, switch on your Mac II, and go.

Let's take a closer look at the technicalities behind these strengths.

Sharing the Bus

NuBus provides a scheme that allows an expansion board to become a *bus master*. As its name implies, the bus master is a board that has control of the bus. Under normal operation, the Mac's logic board is the bus master; however, thanks to special NuBus control signals, a NuBus board can say, "I'm the boss now," and take over the bus to become the new bus master. Accelerator boards use this feature to disable the Mac II's CPU. More significant, coprocessor boards can use this feature to work with the CPU—taking over when a specialized task arises, and then returning control to the CPU when their work is done.

NuBus provides a *fair arbitration* scheme of bus arbitration. That simply means that each card installed in the machine has the same chance of becoming a bus master as the card next to it—no slot has a higher priority than another; all slots are considered peers.

Automatic Configuration

The self-configuring nature of NuBus boards allows you to fill a Mac II with boards without worrying about them conflicting with each other. Each NuBus board contains a *configuration ROM*, a ROM chip that tells the Mac what the board can do: control a video monitor, perform graphics calculations, provide additional memory, and so on.

A configuration ROM may also contain other items, including (but not limited to):

- Driver software the board can load into the Mac's memory upon startup to activate the board's features

- Text information about the board, such as its name and version number, that might appear in a cdev (a Control Panel device) or application program

- A serial number. To thwart software pirates, a company selling a combination hardware-and-software product might use this feature to write software that runs only when its matching board is installed.

Two components of the Mac's system software, the *Slot Manager* and the *Start Manager*, work together with a NuBus board's configuration ROM. As its name implies, the Start Manager orchestrates the Mac's start-up process. Part of that job involves using the Slot Manager to check for NuBus cards and to load any special software from their configuration ROMs into the Mac's memory. The Start Manager performs this check-and-load routine just prior to loading any Init resources that may be in your start-up disk's System Folder.

Variations from the NuBus Standard

In the microcomputer world, standards aren't always standard. That's the case with Apple's implementation of NuBus in the Macintosh. NuBus wasn't designed with personal computers in mind; for that reason, Apple adapted the original draft of the standard in several areas. These changes eventually became part of a revised NuBus standard. A few of the more significant adaptations include:

Different physical dimensions for boards. The NuBus standard calls for boards to measure approximately 11 by 14 inches. Obviously, accommodating such large boards would require a huge case. Moreover, few microcomputer expansion boards need that much real estate to hold their circuitry. Apple created an alternate board size of approximately 4 by 13 inches.

An additional signal line for interrupts. The NuBus standard provides no provision for simple interrupts. Instead, a board that needs the CPU's attention must become a bus master. And that means equipping the board with the circuitry necessary to handle NuBus' bus arbitration techniques. That kind of sophisticated circuitry is overkill for relatively simple cards such as internal modems or cards that provide additional serial ports. To allow a board to get the CPU's attention without becoming a bus master, Apple added a new signal line named NMRQ, short for *non-master request*.

An enhanced power-fail warning signal. The NuBus standard specifies a signal line named PFW, short for *power fail warning*. The original NuBus standard intended the PFW line to be used as a way of warning a board that power to the system was about to be removed. Apple enhanced the workings of the PFW line so that it can not only warn of an impending shutdown, but also actively turn the power off or on. Thus, a NuBus board can use the PFW line to control the Mac's power. A modem board and communications program might use this feature to turn the Mac on at a specified time, sign on to an electronic mail service to retrieve waiting mail, and then turn the Mac off.

THE MAC'S MICROPROCESSORS

A computer's hardware is like a ship's crew: every crew member is needed, but one member is especially important. On a ship, it's the captain; in a computer, it's the CPU. This section is an introduction to the CPUs used in the Mac family. We'll provide an overview of how a microprocessor operates, and we'll spotlight the key characteristics of each Mac's CPU chip.

What's in a Number?

Most introductions begin with an exchange of names, so let's start there. The Mac family uses the MC68000 series of microprocessors designed and manufactured by Motorola. The matriarch of the family is the MC68000, introduced in 1979.

The Mac wasn't the first microcomputer to use the 68000, but it was the Macintosh that gave the 68000 the prominence it enjoys today. The Mac 128K, 512K, 512K Enhanced, Plus, and SE all use the 68000.

Just as computer companies compete by introducing ever-faster machines, microprocessor makers are always at work creating faster, more efficient versions of their best-selling chips. Indeed, computer companies and chip makers have a symbiotic relationship: computer makers' constant desire to create faster machines drives the progress of the microprocessor industry. Or perhaps the progress of the microprocessor industry inspires computer makers to take advantage of faster chips. In either case, when a computer company wants to create a faster machine, it turns to the newest generation of microprocessors.

In 1984, Motorola introduced the 68020, the CPU used in the Mac II. The 68020 offered faster performance while remaining compatible with the 68000. The Mac II, unveiled in 1987, uses the 68020. Accelerator boards containing the 68020 are available for the Mac Plus and SE.

In 1987, Motorola unveiled the 68030. This chip doesn't provide the leap in performance that the 68020 provided over the 68000, but as we'll see shortly, it is slightly faster and, more important, it offers other advantages that will become significant when System 7.0 is released. The Mac IIx, IIcx, and SE/30 use the 68030. Accelerator boards containing the 68030 are available for the Mac II, as is a IIx upgrade kit.

In the interest of brevity, the 68020 and 68030 are often referred to as the 020 and 030, respectively. If you're concerned about pronunciation, here's the way to name drop:

- 68000—sixty-eight-thousand

- 68020—sixty-eight-oh-twenty, or oh-twenty for short

- 68030—sixty-eight-oh-thirty, or oh-thirty for short

Common Denominators

While there are some significant differences between the 68000 and its successors, all three chips—and, for that matter, all microprocessors—share a great deal of common ground. The primary components of the 68000 and its successors include:

- A number of internal storage areas called *registers*. Registers are similar to memory, in that they can store data and program instructions. Unlike a computer's main memory, however, registers are built into the CPU chip itself, and they provide a very limited amount of storage space. Some registers serve as small scratchpads where the CPU can store the results of calculations or a set of numbers to be calculated or compared. Other registers perform behind-the-scenes tasks, such as storing the currently executing instruction and keeping track of which instruction is to be executed next.

- *The arithmetic and logic unit*, or *ALU*. The ALU is the part of a microprocessor that performs arithmetic and decision-making operations. The ALU swings into action when a calculation needs to be performed or when two values need to be compared to determine which is greater.

- The *instruction decoder*. When a program instruction has been transferred from memory into the CPU's *instruction register*, the instruction decoder deciphers the instruction and causes the chip's internal timing circuits to produce the sequential signals necessary to perform the events that the instruction specifies.

- Internal address and data buses. Don't confuse these buses with the address and data buses that traverse the Mac's logic board. A microprocessor's address and data buses exist within the processor's subminiature world, and connect to the computer's address and data buses.

The 68020 Difference

The 68020 provides several distinct advantages over the 68000:

- It's a true 32-bit microprocessor. The 68000 provides a 32-bit internal bus, but a 16-bit external bus: the chip can manipulate data in 32-bit chunks, but transfers data to and from the Mac's data bus in 16-bit chunks. By discarding this hybrid approach, the 68020 can move twice the data in the same amount of time.

- It contains a 256-byte *instruction cache*, a small area of high-speed, on-chip memory that stores the most recently used instructions and supplies them to the CPU if they're needed again. According to Motorola, the instruction cache boosts performance by 40 percent by allowing near-instantaneous access to recently used instructions.

- It can accommodate faster clock rates. The 68000 can accommodate clock rates of up to 16.67 MHz. The 68020 can run at up to 33 MHz.

The 68030: Moving Toward Tomorrow

The 68030 represents the further evolution of the 68000 family. The 68030's primary improvement is its built-in *paged memory management unit*, or *PMMU*. The PMMU in the 68030 works along with Apple's A/UX version of the UNIX operating system to provide AU/X's *paged memory* (also called *virtual memory*) features. An operating system that provides paged memory is able to treat a hard disk as an extension of the computer's memory by tricking the CPU into thinking that the hard disk is actually part of the computer's main memory. By swapping chunks, or *pages*, of memory between the hard disk and RAM chips, the computer can run much larger programs and run more programs at the same time. As we've mentioned previously, System 7.0 will also provide virtual memory features.

On the Mac II, you must add a separate PMMU chip—Motorola's 68851—to run AU/X, or to use virtual memory under System 7.0. System 6.0 does not provide paged memory features, and therefore doesn't require a PMMU. When System 7.0 is released, however, the 68030's built-in memory management unit will be ready for it.

The 68030's other improvements include:

- A 256-byte *data cache*, which holds 256 bytes of the most recently used data, and supplies the data to the CPU if it's needed again, eliminating the need for the CPU to retrieve it from main memory or from disk. The 68030 also retains the 256-byte instruction cache found in the 68020. (These caches aren't related to the Mac's disk cache, which we looked at in Chapter 9.)

- Two internal 32-bit address and data buses. These buses operate in parallel, allowing the CPU to perform multiple tasks simultaneously, thus boosting performance. For example, the 68030 can simultaneously access its instruction cache, its data cache, and external memory. The 68030 was the first microprocessor to have two internal address and data buses. This parallel bus design first appeared in some mainframe computer CPUs, and is called the *Harvard-style bus architecture*.

Math Coprocessors

The 68020 and 030 also have the ability to *off-load* instructions to a different microprocessor; that is, they can turn certain instructions over to a different processor instead of executing them themselves. The Mac II family and the SE/30 take advantage of this feature by providing math *coprocessors*, specialized microprocessors designed to calculate and store *floating point* values—numbers with decimal portions—faster and more accurately than a general-purpose microprocessor. Because math coprocessors specialize in floating point calculations, they're often called *floating point coprocessors*.

The CPU and a math coprocessor work together: when the CPU encounters a complex calculation, it says to the math chip, "This is your job; I have other things to do." The coprocessor performs the calculation and transfers the result to the CPU, which, by then, is ready to perform the next program instruction. The result of this joint effort is that a coprocessor-equipped Mac can perform calculations roughly 200 times faster than other Macs.

The Mac II uses Motorola's 68881 math chip. The IIx, IIcx, and SE/30 use the faster and newer 68882. According to Motorola, the 68882 is two to four times faster than the 68881. Two primary factors combine to give these chips their number-crunching skills.

- Both contain special circuits that can store and process information in 80-bit (10-byte) chunks. This allows the processor to accurately calculate values with up to 18 digits after the decimal point. Without a coprocessor, the Mac's calculations are accurate to a maximum of 14 digits.

- Both contain many built-in *constants* (values that don't change, such as 0, 1, and pi) as well as transcendental and non-transcendental functions for performing trigonometric and logarithmic calculations. These constants and functions are part of the coprocessor's hardware; without a coprocessor, the CPU must tie up memory and time by using software routines to perform the calculations.

The 68000 doesn't have a built-in coprocessor interface; however, it does provide bus-arbitration signal lines that allow a math coprocessor to gain control of the internal bus in order to do its work. Accelerator boards containing math coprocessors are available for the Mac Plus and SE.

THE START-UP PROCESS

Sometimes it seems like the Mac takes a long time to start up. Like the Concorde supersonic jet, the Mac works pretty quickly, but it takes a while to get off the ground.

The fact is, a remarkable number of events takes place between the time you switch on the Mac and the time the Finder's desktop appears. When you switch the Mac on, it appears that the machine simply beeps and asks for a disk. Behind the scenes, however, the Mac performs a series of tests and tasks before the beep is sounded. Let's look at what happens when you switch on your Mac.

Phase 1: Initialization

The first part of the Mac's start-up process is the *initialization process*. The initialization process sets the Mac's hardware and software components to known states. The process occurs when you switch the power on or restart the Mac by pressing the programmer's switch or choosing the Finder's Restart command.

Here's what happens:

1. A set of diagnostic routines test both versatile interface adaptors, the serial communications controller, the Integrated Woz Machine, the SCSI controller, and the Apple Sound Chip. If no problems are detected, the Mac's start-up tone is sounded and the hardware components are initialized.

2. Memory is tested. If you've just switched the machine on, the Mac performs a complete memory test; if you're restarting, a faster, less extensive test is performed.

3. The Start Manager determines which CPU is installed and the clock rate at which it's running. The results of these tests are stored in memory where the operating system and application programs can access them to find out about your hardware. If the 68020 or 030 is installed, their instruction caches are enabled during this step.

4. Key memory values used by the operating system and its various managers are initialized, that is, set to specific values and known states.

5. On 32-bit Macs, the system is placed in 24-bit mode to retain compatibility with the current Mac operating system. (This step will be unnecessary in System 7.0.)

6. A small amount of memory, called the *system heap*, is set aside for the operating system's use.

7. Several ROM-based managers are initialized.

8. On the Mac II, IIx, and IIcx, the Slot Manager is initialized and the configuration ROM of each installed NuBus card is read. If the configuration ROMs contain any initialization code for their boards, the code is executed.

9. The ADB Manager, which controls the Apple Desktop Bus, is initialized.

10. On the Mac II, IIx, and IIcx, the Start Manager looks for a video board to use as the primary video display. During this process, QuickDraw is initialized and the grey desktop is drawn.

11. The SCSI Manager, Disk Manager, and Sound Manager are initialized.

12. The arrow pointer appears.

Phase 2: System Startup

A great deal has happened, but so far, all we have is a gray desktop with an arrow pointer on it. Phase 2 of the startup process involves starting the Macintosh from a disk and turning control over to the Finder. Here's how it happens:

1. The drive number of the internal SCSI hard disk (if one is installed) is obtained from the Mac's battery-powered parameter RAM. The Start Manager pauses for up to 30 seconds to allow the hard disk to spin up to speed.

2. The Start Manager looks for a start-up device. First, it checks the floppy disk drives for a disk. If no disk is found, the Start Manager uses the drive you specified as the start-up device (using the Control Panel). If you never specified a start-up drive, or if that drive is disconnected or otherwise unavailable, the Start Manager looks for drives attached to the SCSI port.

3. Once the Start Manager has located a start-up drive, it reads the system start-up information from that drive. On a Mac II, IIx, and IIcx, a NuBus board can intercept the start-up process at this point and take over the system.

4. The System file on the current start-up drive is opened and the Mac's Resource Manager, System Error Handler, and Font Manager are initialized.

5. The "Welcome to Macintosh" message is displayed.

6. If it's present on the disk, the system *debugger*, a software utility used by programmers to ferret out bugs, is loaded. Unless you've configured your system to load a debugger, this step won't occur on your system.

7. ROM patches are loaded from the System file into memory.

8. On Macs equipped with the Apple Desktop Bus, all ADB-related routines are loaded from disk and executed.

9. The Mac begins to track mouse movement.

10. Driver software corresponding to installed NuBus boards may be loaded and executed, depending on the nature of the boards.

11. The RAM cache specified in the Control Panel is created, and an area of memory for holding applications, the application heap, is set aside and initialized.

12. All Init files in the current System Folder are loaded and executed, in alphabetical order.

13. The size of the system heap (created in Step 6 of the initialization process) is adjusted as needed.

14. If you specified one or more start-up applications using the Finder's Set Startup command, those applications are started. Otherwise, the Finder starts.

Finally—the Macintosh is up and running.

CHAPTER SUMMARY

- Within the Mac, an oscillating quartz crystal acts as a steady metronome whose clock ticks govern accesses to memory and the internal bus.

- As a general rule, the faster a computer's clock rate—the more times per second a computer's clock ticks—the faster the computer.

- All computers contain address and data buses—freeways upon which data travels between memory, the CPU, and other components.

- The number of bits the computer's data bus carries at once also influences performance. The wider the data bus, the more bits the computer can move during one bus access.

- Because an address bus carries memory addresses, the wider the address bus, the more memory the computer can access.

- Compact Macs contain two circuit boards—an analog board containing the power supply and video circuitry, and a digital board (also called a logic board), which contains the CPU, RAM, ROM, external ports, and their support chips.

- The Mac II contains one large circuit board called the logic board. The Mac II's logic board contains no video circuitry; instead, you buy a separate video board that installs in one of the machine's NuBus slots.

- Macs use dynamic RAM chips, or DRAMs, which require a regular refresh signal to retain their contents.

- DRAM chips are available in different capacities, or densities. The most common DRAM densities are 64 Kbit, 256 Kbit, and one megabit.

- A DRAM chip's access time refers to the time required to successfully read from or write to the chip. You must use DRAMs whose access time meets or exceeds Apple's specifications for your Mac.

- With the Mac Plus, Apple began using plug-in SIMMs (single in line memory modules), to hold DRAM chips. Each SIMM holds eight RAM chips.

- The Mac SE and II families provide expansion slots that allow boards to connect directly to the internal buses. Slots allow these Macs to easily accommodate hardware such as accelerator boards, coprocessor boards, and optional video boards.

- The slots in the Mac II family are based on NuBus, a bus standard developed by Texas Instruments and refined by an IEEE standards committee. NuBus provides for automatic board configuration and provides a bus-arbitration scheme that allows multiple processors to share the bus.

- The Mac family uses the 68000 series of microprocessors from Motorola. The 68020 and 030 are true 32-bit microprocessors (instead of being 16- and 32-bit hybrids), and they contain other improvements that make them faster and more efficient than the 68000.

14

Input and Output

As essential as the Mac's buses, RAM and ROM chips, slots, and CPU are, they're worthless unless you can get information into and out of the computer. That's where the keyboard, mouse, video screen, and external ports come in.

We looked at Macintosh video, font, and printing concepts in earlier chapters. In this chapter, we'll examine the rest of the Mac's input and output features, including:

- how the Mac's keyboard and mouse operate

- how the Mac produces sound

- how the Mac's SCSI bus operates and how to connect SCSI devices

- how the Mac's serial ports operate.

THE KEYBOARD AND MOUSE

You may recall from the previous chapter that the Mac uses interrupts to maintain a constant vigil for keystrokes and mouse movements. Let's take a closer look at how the keyboard and mouse operate.

The Mac Plus and earlier Macs use a different keyboard and mouse than the SE, the II family, and other Macs equipped with the Apple Desktop Bus, or ADB. For that reason, we'll discuss the keyboards and mice for non-ADB Macs separately from those used by ADB-equipped Macs.

The Non-ADB Keyboards

Keyboards for the original Macs come in two flavors—the original keyboard, which lacked cursor keys and a built-in numeric keypad (a detached keypad was optional); and the Mac Plus keyboard, which offers a keypad and cursor keys. Internally, all non-ADB Mac keyboards operate in the same way. The keyboard contains its own microprocessor, which receives power from one of the four wires that connects the keyboard to the Mac. The microprocessor contains a small amount of RAM and ROM dedicated to watching for keystrokes and communicating with the Mac.

As for the other three wires, one carries data between the keyboard and Mac. The keyboard's *data line* is a serial line; data travels from the keyboard to the Mac (and vice-versa) in serial fashion. Another wire carries a clock signal that times the transmission of data from the keyboard to the Mac. The fourth wire is connected to *ground*. (In any electrical circuit, ground is a common point of connection.)

Where communicating with the Mac is concerned, the keyboard is at the Mac's mercy. That is, the keyboard never initiates communication with the Mac; instead, the reverse occurs. The Mac's keyboard driver software sends an *inquiry* command to the keyboard four times per second. This inquiry command performs two primary jobs: It allows the Mac to verify that the keyboard is still connected, and it allows the keyboard to tell the Mac that a key has been pressed or released.

When a key has been pressed or released, the keyboard transmits a code corresponding to the key's position to the Mac's Versatile Interface Adapter (VIA) chip. The VIA then generates an interrupt to the CPU, and the CPU uses the Mac's data bus to retrieve the key code from the VIA.

Those last two paragraphs were laden with jargon, so let's clarify things by describing the keyboard's operation in conversational terms. Four times per second, the Mac says to the keyboard, "Hey, are you there?" If no key has been pressed since the last inquiry command, the keyboard responds by saying, "Yes, but nothing's new." If a key has been pressed—let's use the *T* key for this example—the keyboard responds, "Yes, and the *T* key has been pressed since the last time you checked."

If you press a key before releasing a different key, the keyboard interprets both keystrokes in their proper sequence. This feature is called *two-key rollover*.

Keyboard Mapping

In the mock conversation above, the keyboard told the computer that the *T* key had been pressed. Actually, the keyboard never describes a key by what's printed on top of the key. Instead, the keyboard transmits a code that corresponds to the key. Every key transmits a unique code, or number. Within the Mac's keyboard driver software, every key code is assigned, or *mapped*, to a given character. When the driver software receives a key code, it consults the *keyboard map* to learn the character that corresponds to that code. The driver then translates that code into the appropriate character.

This may seem like technical trivia, but it's a significant point. By replacing part or all of the keyboard map, you can *remap* the keyboard—change the workings of some or all of the keys on the keyboard. You might want to remap only a few keys—to more conveniently access opening and closing quotes, for example—or you might want to create an entirely different keyboard layout such as the Dvorak Simplified Layout, a more efficient layout developed by August Dvorak in the 1940s. Two keyboard-remapping programs are CE Software's QuicKeys (examined in Chapter 10) and Avenue Software's MacKeymeleon.

The Mac Plus Mouse

The Mac Plus' mouse contains a rubber-coated steel ball that touches two *capstans*, each connected to a slotted wheel called an *interrupter wheel*, as shown in Figure 14-1. Each interrupter wheel is sandwiched between a light-emitting diode (LED) and a light-sensitive transistor called a *phototransistor*.

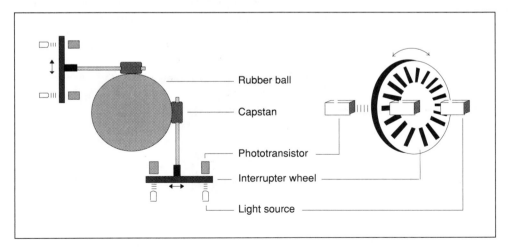

Rubber ball

Capstan

Phototransistor

Interrupter wheel

Light source

Figure 14-1: Inside a Mac Plus mouse.

When you move the mouse, the ball rolls and turns the interrupter wheels. Horizontal motion turns one of the wheels, while vertical motion turns the other. Each slot in each interrupter wheel allows light from the LED to reach the phototransistor. The phototransistors respond to the pulses of light by generating signals corresponding to the wheel's movement. A mouse that combines a mechanical roller ball with optical measuring techniques is often called an *opto-mechanical* mouse.

The signals from the mouse's phototransistors travel through the mouse cable to the Mac's serial chip and to its VIA chip. The signal that travels to the serial chip simply tells the Mac that the mouse has moved. The signals that travel to the VIA indicate the direction of movement. The serial chip generates an interrupt for the CPU, and the Mac's mouse driver software consults the VIA to determine what direction the mouse is moving.

What about the mouse button? Beneath the button is a small switch (a *microswitch*) that, when pressed, completes a circuit. The Mac checks the state of the mouse button each time the video circuitry finishes painting a complete screen image. That occurs roughly 60 times per second—fast enough to catch the most fleeting press of the mouse button.

The Apple Desktop Bus

As we saw in Chapter 4, Apple created ADB in order to have a standard interface for input devices on all of its computers, thus eliminating the need to manufacture several different types of mice and keyboards. But the bus also has an advantage for us: it can accommodate multiple input devices. You can attach several input devices to your Mac by daisy-chaining them—connecting one device's output to another device's input, as shown in Figure 14-2.

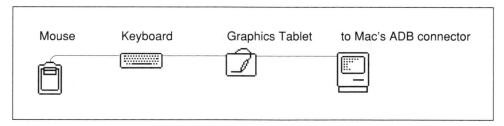

Figure 14-2: Daisy-chaining input devices.

ADB's ability to accommodate daisy-chained devices allows you to attach more than two input devices to a Mac. An architect or draftsperson might want to use a graphics tablet in addition to the keyboard and mouse. A foreign-language translator might want to use a foreign-language keyboard along with the English-language keyboard. Technically, ADB can accommodate up to 16 devices, but Apple recommends against daisy-chaining more than three because ADB signals can weaken as they travel through the devices' wiring.

How ADB Works

ADB is a *single-master, multi-slave serial bus*. That's a mouthful, but it translates into a few simple concepts.

- Single-master. The Mac is always in control of the Apple Desktop Bus. When a device needs to send data to the computer, it transmits a service request signal to the Mac, which acknowledges the request and then reads the data.

- Multi-slave. We've touched on this point already; ADB can accommodate up to 16 devices. When the Mac starts up, it assigns each device its own address. The Mac uses these addresses to identify each device on the bus.

- Serial. ADB transmits the bits that comprise each byte of data in serial fashion (with one bit following the next). ADB is limited to a maximum data-transmission speed of about 4,500 bits per second (bps). That's slow for a computer interface, but remember, ADB was designed for input devices; 4,500 bps is fast enough to keep up with the fastest typists and mouse movers.

Every ADB device contains an *ADB transceiver chip*, a microprocessor that transmits and receives (*transceives*) data to and from the Mac. Communications between the Mac and an ADB device is a joint effort between these chips.

The ADB Keyboards

At this writing, Apple offers two ADB-equipped keyboards—the Apple Keyboard and the Apple Extended Keyboard—for use in English-speaking countries. (A number of foreign-language keyboards are also available.) Both ADB keyboards work similarly. When you press a key, its corresponding code is stored in the keyboard's ADB transceiver, and then transmitted to the Mac's ADB transceiver. The ADB transceiver forwards the data to the VIA, and the ADB Manager transfers control to the Mac's keyboard driver software, which interprets the code and makes it available to applications.

Like the original Mac keyboards, both ADB keyboards provide two-key rollover.

The ADB Mouse

The ADB mouse (in Apple's terms, the *Apple Standard Mouse*) sports a sleek design that fits the hand more comfortably than the original Mac mouse. Underneath, the ADB has large Teflon feet that help the mouse move smoothly. The original Mac mouse, by contrast, has molded plastic feet that can wear after extensive use, hampering the mouse's movement. (For some tips for making the original Mac mouse roll more smoothly—and for cleaning all Mac mice—see "Mouse Care and Feeding" in Chapter 9.)

Internally, the ADB mouse works in much the same way as the original Mac mouse. The signals generated by the ADB mouse's interrupter wheels travel to the mouse's ADB transceiver chip, which communicates with the ADB transceiver in the Mac. The Mac's ADB transceiver forwards the mouse information to the VIA, and ROM routines translate the information into on-screen pointer movement.

Two Fine Points About Mice

Before leaving the Mac's input devices to discuss its sound features, let's look at two mouse-related details:

• The difference between relative and absolute motion pointing devices

• Mouse tracking, how it affects pointer movement, and which tracking settings you might want to use.

The following points apply to all Mac mice.

Relative Versus Absolute Motion

The Mac's mouse is a *relative-motion* pointing device. That is, it doesn't report where it is—for example, two inches from the edge of your desk, or at the upper-left corner of the screen. Instead, the mouse reports only how far it has moved and in which direction.

For most applications, that's all you need. It can be a drawback for some graphics-oriented applications, however, particularly for drafting applications that involve tracing original artwork. For such applications, you might prefer an *absolute-motion* pointing device such as a graphics tablet, which does report the location of its stylus relative to the tablet's surface area. We discussed graphics tablets briefly in our discussion of mouse-tracking options in Chapter 5, "System Folder Details."

About Mouse Tracking

You may remember from Chapter 5 that the Mouse cdev lets you specify how the mouse's physical speed relates to the speed of the on-screen pointer. This ratio of mouse speed to pointer speed is called *mouse tracking* or *mouse scaling*.

The Mac's designers knew that users would sometimes need a great deal of pointer precision (when using a drawing or desktop publishing program, for example), but that they would also want to be able to zip the pointer from one end of the screen to the other in a hurry—for example, to move to a scroll bar or up to the menu bar. To accommodate both requirements, they gave the Mac a mouse tracking feature. With the slowest tracking settings, the mouse needs more desk space to move the pointer. With faster tracking settings, the Mac senses when you're moving the mouse quickly, and zips the pointer across the screen.

To illustrate the difference, we created a mouse dragstrip by clamping a ruler to the edge of a desk. Next, we made sure that the mouse pointer was at one end of the screen, and then we butted the flat edge of the mouse against the ruler. Finally, we moved the mouse as quickly as possible and measured how much desk space was required to move the pointer from one end of a 13-inch Mac II screen to the other. We performed this test with each of the Control Panel's tracking settings. Table 14-1 shows the results. As the table shows, with the faster tracking settings, the mouse needs far less desk space to move the pointer across the screen.

Table 14-1: Tracking settings and how they affect pointer movement.

Tracking Setting	Desk Space Needed (inches)
Very Slow	9
Slow	4
Second-to-slowest	3
Second-to-fastest	2 1/2
Fast	less than 2

Which tracking settings should you use? That depends on three factors:

- Your mouse proficiency. If you're new to the Mac and haven't quite gotten the hang of mousing around, you might prefer the slower tracking settings at first.

- The size of your monitor. If you have a 13-inch or larger monitor, you'll probably prefer the faster tracking setting for general-purpose navigation tasks such as scrolling, choosing menu commands, and dragging.

- What you're using the mouse for. If you're using a publishing or drawing program, and you want extra pointer precision, consider using the slower tracking settings. Slower settings won't actually increase the mouse's precision (it registers roughly 90 units of movement per inch regardless of the tracking setting), but they'll make it easier to move objects in single-pixel increments.

SOUND DETAILS

We've examined how sound fits into in the Macintosh world, how to attach your Mac to an audio amplifier, and how to customize your Mac's alert sounds. In this section, we'll explore the technicalities behind the Mac's audio capabilities. We'll look at:

- how the Mac produces simple music and sound

- how the Mac digitally records and plays back sound

If you're unfamiliar with such sound-related terms as *waveform*, and *frequency*, you'll find some background in the next section, "Sound Basics." Otherwise, you might want to skip on to the section "The Sound Manager."

Sound Basics

Sound is formed by variations in air pressure. When you speak, your vocal cords vibrate, causing "ripples" in the air around them, just as a stone plopping into a pond causes ripples in the water. When these atmospheric ripples, or *sound waves*, reach your ears, they cause your eardrums to vibrate accordingly. The eardrums generate minute electrical pulses that the brain receives and interprets as sound. Loudspeakers and microphones mimic the workings of the vocal chords and ear, respectively: a speaker uses a vibrating paper cone to recreate variations in air pressure, while a microphone uses a small, eardrum-like *diaphragm* to sense variations in air pressure and generate corresponding electrical pulses.

Sound waves generally follow a repeating pattern that can be displayed visually, as shown in Figure 14-3. In these *waveform* displays, the vertical axis represents the sound's loudness, or *amplitude*, while the horizontal axis represents time. The peaks in a waveform display correspond to regions of higher air pressure; the valleys, or *troughs*, represent lower air pressure; the center line represents normal air pressure. The more vibrations that occur per second, the more often a soundwave completes a cycle, and the higher the sound's pitch, or *frequency*. For example, a soprano singer's vocal cords vibrate more times per second than those of a baritone.

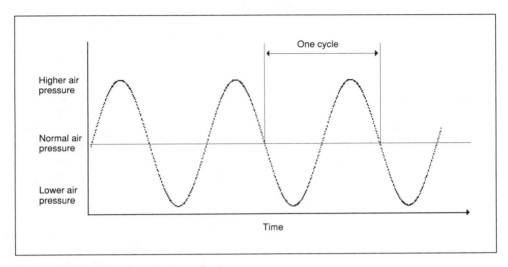

Figure 14-3: A simple waveform display.

The Sound Manager

Until the release of System 6.0 in 1988, the Mac II had more sophisticated sound-generating software than other Macs. Prior to System 6.0, compact Macs used a ROM-based device driver called the *Sound Driver* to produce sound. For the Mac II, however, Apple created a more sophisticated set of sound routines called the *Sound Manager*. Apple created the Sound Manager in order to meet the increasing demands of developers and users of music and game software, and to take advantage of the superior sound features of the Apple Sound Chip. We encountered the Apple Sound Chip briefly in the previous chapter.

With System 6.0 and later versions, the Sound Manager is patched into the RAM of a Mac Plus or SE during startup. Thus, when running System 6.0 or a later version, every Mac from the Plus on up has the same sound-generating software. (However, because older Macs lack the Apple Sound Chip, newer Macs still have more sophisticated sound *hardware*.) Because all but the oldest Macs now use the Sound Manager, we won't discuss the Sound Driver here.

Sound Manager Synthesizers

The Sound Manager produces sound by using *synthesizers*. These synthesizers aren't music keyboards like the kind you see on music videos. Instead, they're sets of software routines that interpret Sound Manager commands and control the Mac's audio circuitry accordingly.

The Sound Manager provides four standard synthesizers:

- The *note* synthesizer produces alert beeps and can also produce simple monophonic (one note at a time—no chords) melodies.

- The *wave-table synthesizer* can produce sounds with far more complex timbres. However, it's up to individual programs to create the data that represents these timbres; the wave-table synthesizer doesn't provide any preset sounds. Instead, the program stores in memory a complete description of the sound, which it then sends to the Sound Manager. Unlike the note synthesizer, the wave-table synthesizer can produce polyphonic (more than one note at a time, as in a chord) melodies, playing up to four sounds, or *voices*, simultaneously.

- The *MIDI synthesizer* provides a standard way for applications to control external music synthesizers (the kind you do see in music videos) that are equipped with the Musical Instrument Digital Interface (MIDI)—a standard method of connecting synthesizers to each other and to computers and other music-oriented hardware. (We'll look at MIDI in a moment.) Unlike the Sound Manager's other three synthesizers, the MIDI synthesizer doesn't produce sound through the Mac's speaker; instead, it sends MIDI commands that tell an external instrument which notes to play.

- The *sampled-sound synthesizer* lets the Mac play digitally recorded sounds using techniques similar to those of a compact disc player. Because it plays back digitally recorded sounds instead of synthesized sounds, the sampled-sound synthesizer can produce the most realistic audio effects.

MIDI Basics

Like SCSI, MIDI is a standard that specifies the physical wiring of cables and connectors as well as the format in which signals are transmitted and received. MIDI cables contain five wires and use five-pin DIN connectors. The MIDI protocol transmits data serially at a rate of 31.25 kilobits per second—fast enough for a chord to still sound like a chord, even though the instrument actually receives each note separately, one after the other. MIDI data itself comprises two categories of *message*s: *channel messages*, which convey note information (such as which key was pressed and how hard it was pressed); and *system messages*, which can control instrument settings.

To connect a MIDI instrument to the Mac, you need a *MIDI adaptor*, a hardware add-on that connects to the instrument and to the Mac's modem or printer port. Apple offers a simple MIDI adaptor with one MIDI In and one MIDI Out connector. More sophisticated MIDI adaptors are available from Opcode Systems, Passport Designs, and Southworth Music Systems, among others. These firms' adaptors include multiple MIDI In and MIDI Out connectors and have features that allow you to synchronize the playback of a MIDI sequence to an audio recording or to the audio track of a film or videotape.

The MIDI specification allows data to be transmitted on up to 16 channels. If you attach multiple MIDI instruments to the Mac, you can specify that each one respond to notes transmitted on a specific channel.

Once you've attached one or more MIDI instruments to the Mac, what can you do with them? That depends on the music software you use. *Sequencer* programs let you record and play back MIDI data. When you play the instrument, it transmits MIDI data that the sequencer stores in the Mac's memory. You can edit the data—correcting misplayed notes or transposing the key, for example—and then play it back. During playback, the sequencer transmits the MIDI data to the instrument, thus turning it into a kind of digital player piano. If you have multiple instruments or an instrument that can play different sounds, you can create complete arrangements by recording new tracks while playing back existing ones. Another popular software category includes *patch editors*, which let you store and manipulate your synthesizer's sound settings. Using them, you can tailor your instrument's sounds to your musical requirements.

Sampled Sound Details

Sampled sound is becoming increasingly popular in the Macintosh world. You can hear it in many games and HyperCard stacks. In an arcade-style game called Airborne (from Silicon Beach Software), you hear the wash of helicopter blades and the scream of fighter jets. In a HyperCard stack called Bird Anatomy II (by Yale University's Patrick Lynch), you hear recordings of bird songs. In Bright Star Technology's HyperAnimator, you can synchronize the lip movements of on-screen characters to digital sound.

In this section, we'll take a closer look at how the Mac stores and plays back digitally recorded sound. But first, let's lay the foundation for our discussion by examining two concepts that play a vital role in digital audio: analog-to-digital and digital-to-analog conversion.

Analog versus Digital

Webster's dictionary defines *analog* as "being or relating to a mechanism in which data is represented by continuously variable physical quantities." We live in an analog world. The Earth rotates continuously; it doesn't pause for a minute, then move, then pause again. Ice skaters glide continuously across the rink; they don't move in fits and starts. Sound is also an analog phenomenon. The variations in air pressure that comprise a sound are continuous variations.

But computers are digital devices; their world is one of ones and zeros. To recreate an analog phenomenon such as sound, a computer must first convert the analog data into digital data. This process is performed by a circuit called an *analog-to-digital converter*, or *ADC*. The Mac lacks an ADC for recording sound. To record, you need additional hardware, such as Farallon Computing's MacRecorder. MacRecorder also includes software that lets you alter sounds and save them as snd resources in your System file or in HyperCard stacks.

When digitally recorded sound is played back, another circuit, a *digital-to-analog converter (DAC)*, turns the digital data back into analog data. All digital audio circuitry—whether in a compact disc player or a Macintosh—performs a digital-to-analog conversion in order to play back recorded sound.

Sampling: Snapshots of Sound

The term *sampling* comes from the process that occurs when audio is converted to digital data. As a digital device, the Mac can't store the continuous variations in air pressure that comprise a sound. However, by using a digital-to-analog converter to examine, or *sample*, the sound at periodic intervals, the Mac can create a reasonably accurate digital representation of the sound, as shown in Figure 14-4.

One way to understand the concept of sound sampling is to consider another form of sampling: the motion picture. A movie camera takes a sample of its subject 24 times per second. When those samples are played back, the illusion of smooth, analog motion is created.

But the ears are less forgiving than the eyes. To accurately represent sound, digital recording equipment must take thousands of samples each second. Each sample represents the state of the sound at the moment the sample was taken, just as each frame of a movie represents the action at the moment the frame was photographed.

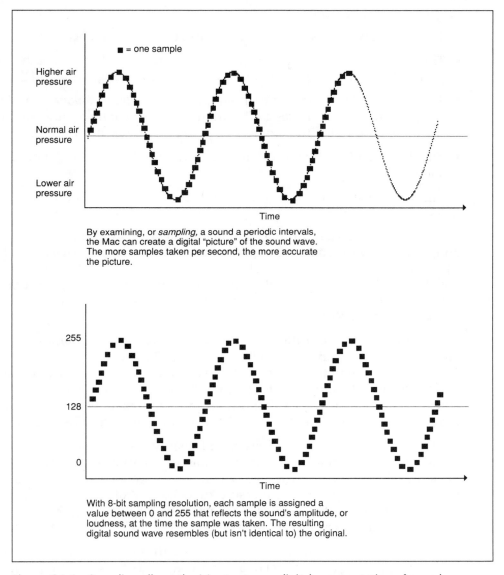

By examining, or *sampling,* a sound a periodic intervals, the Mac can create a digital "picture" of the sound wave. The more samples taken per second, the more accurate the picture.

With 8-bit sampling resolution, each sample is assigned a value between 0 and 255 that reflects the sound's amplitude, or loudness, at the time the sample was taken. The resulting digital sound wave resembles (but isn't identical to) the original.

Figure 14-4: Sampling allows the Mac to store a digital representation of sound.

Sound Quality Issues

Three primary factors influence the sound quality of digital audio:

- The number of samples taken each second—the *sampling rate*. Faster sampling rates provide a more accurate snapshot of the original sound.

- The number of bits used for each sample—the *sampling resolution*. A higher sampling resolution makes each sample a more accurate representation of the original sound at the moment the sample was taken.

- The design and quality of the audio circuitry used to filter and amplify the sound.

This isn't an audio book, so we won't discuss the third factor here. Instead, let's concentrate on the first two.

Professional digital recording equipment takes over 44,100 samples per second; technically speaking, this equipment uses a *sampling rate* of 44.1 *kilohertz* (thousands of cycles per second, abbreviated KHz). The sampling talents of the Mac Plus and SE fall short of that; their maximum sampling rate is approximately 22.255KHz (the rate is usually stated as simply 22KHz). All faster Macs can sample at 44.1KHz.

The sampling rate also affects sound quality because it determines the highest frequency that can be accurately recorded. To accurately record a given frequency, the sampling rate must be twice that frequency. For example, to accurately record sounds up to 10KHz, the sampling rate must be at least 20KHz. This upper frequency limit (in the preceding example, 10KHz) is called the *Nyquist frequency*, after the scientist who discovered this phenomenon.

The sampling resolution affects sound quality because it determines how accurately the computer can detect dynamic variations—changes in loudness—in the sound being sampled. The more bits you assign to each sample, the more accurately you can measure the sound. Professional digital audio equipment uses 16-bit sampling resolution, allowing it to recognize and reproduce thousands of different loudness levels.

All Macs use 8-bit sampling resolution, and thus can discern 256 dynamic levels. When the dynamic level of a given sample lies between two points, it's rounded to the nearest point. This rounding process, also called *quantization*, results in sampling errors that you hear in the form of noise.

If you have a Mac II, SE, or SE/30, you can boost your Mac's sampling rate and sampling resolution to professional levels by adding a board such as Digidesign's Sound Accelerator, which contains a Motorola 56001 *digital signal-processing* (*DSP*) chip.

Incidentally, if you'd like to hear examples of various sampling rates and digital audio effects, you can do so with a HyperCard stack called Jim Heid's Sound Stack. It's available through many user's groups and communications services such as CompuServe.

Sound and System 7.0

System 7.0 will provide significant sound-oriented enhancements that will allow audio to play an even larger role in the Macintosh world. These enhancements fall into three categories:

- **Sound Manager improvements.** The enhanced Sound Manager will be able to load and play multiple channels of sound simultaneously. Using this feature, an application or HyperCard stack will be able to play sampled narration while background music plays. With the Sound Manager in System 6.0 and earlier versions, the Mac can play only one sampled sound at a time; a second sound can't play until the first one completes. Another Sound Manager enhancement will allow applications to specify how much CPU time the Mac should allocate to each sound channel.

- **Audio compression and expansion.** One drawback of sampled sound is that it uses disk space with a vengeance. For example, just one second of sound sampled at 22KHz uses 22K disk space. Storing 45 seconds of sound requires a megabyte of disk space. System 7.0 will lessen the amount of disk space required to accommodate sounds by allowing sound to be *compressed*—encoded to use less disk space—by either a 3-to-1 or 6-to-1 ratio. At playback time, the Mac will *expand* the sound in real-time; that is, as the sound is being played. Apple calls this compression-and-expansion feature *MACE*, short for *Macintosh Audio Compression/Expansion*.

- **MIDI enhancements.** Application developers will be able to use a new MIDI Manager as a standard interface to the Mac's MIDI capabilities. Thus, individual developers will be spared the task of writing their own MIDI driver software. Other MIDI enhancements will allow numerous applications running under MultiFinder to share the same MIDI data.

All of these features will work on any Macintosh capable of running System 7.0.

SCSI DETAILS

In this section, we'll take a detailed look at how the Mac's SCSI bus operates. We'll provide some tips and guidelines for setting up SCSI devices, and we'll describe some free and shareware programs that let you tinker with and learn about the SCSI bus and the devices attached to it.

First, let's briefly review some SCSI basics.

- The SCSI bus provides high-speed parallel data transmission, and is typically used to connect to hard disks, tape-backup drives, scanners, and certain printers.

- The Mac Plus provides a single SCSI connector, a DB-25 located at the back of the case. The SE and II families provide two SCSI connectors: a rear-panel DB-25, and an 50-pin ribbon connector located inside the case to accommodate internal hard disks.

- The SCSI bus lets you daisy-chain up to seven devices to the Mac. The Mac differentiates between devices by using the devices' addresses. You can change a SCSI device's address, usually by setting switches on the device, but sometimes by running an utility program that comes with the device.

- A SCSI device's address also specifies its priority on the bus. When two devices vie for the Mac's attention at the same time, the device with the higher priority wins.

- The Mac always has a SCSI address of 7 (the highest possible address, and the one with the highest priority). When a Mac has an internal hard disk, the hard disk's address is always 0.

SCSI Cables

As you set up your SCSI devices, you may work with three types of cables:

SCSI System Cable. This cable attaches between the Mac's SCSI port and the first SCSI device; it has a male DB-25 connector on one end, and a 50-pin connector on the other.

Peripheral Interface Cable. This cable lets you daisy-chain one SCSI device to the next. Apple's Peripheral Interface Cable (part number M0207) is 1 meter (about 3 feet) long.

Cable Extender. This cable, also about 3 feet long, is a SCSI extension cord that gives you more flexibility in positioning your SCSI devices. (It's great for getting a noisy hard disk out of earshot.) The part number of Apple's Cable Extender is M0208.

Figure 14-5 shows a few ways you might use these three cables. Notice that you can attach several Cable Extenders together, as long as the total length of all the SCSI cabling in your system doesn't exceed 20 feet. Beyond that distance, SCSI signals deteriorate, causing unreliable operation. And be sure to use the cables' metal clamps and thumbscrews to establish a tight, reliable connection.

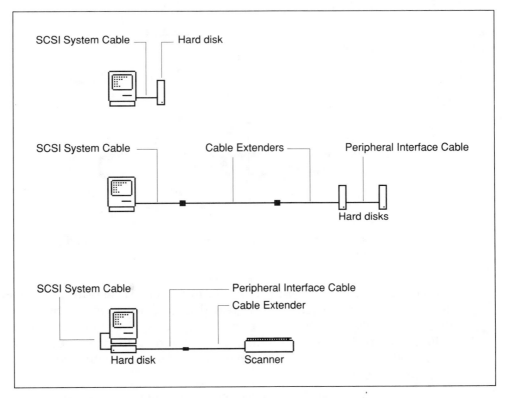

Figure 14-5: Some typical SCSI cabling setups.

SCSI Termination

When attaching a SCSI device to the Mac, you may need to contend with one of the trickier aspects of SCSI: *termination*. In order for the Mac to know where the SCSI bus begins and ends, the bus needs special components called *terminators*, which absorb the SCSI signals at the end of the bus, preventing them from "bouncing" throughout the SCSI cabling. That causes electrical noise in the cabling that can lead to disk errors and other problems.

Reliable operation is one good reason to ensure your SCSI bus is properly terminated; keeping your Mac healthy is another. As we'll see shortly, incorrect termination can damage the Mac's SCSI circuitry.

Terminators come in two varieties: internal and external. An internal terminator is located within a SCSI device's case. An external terminator is located outside the case, and clamps between the SCSI cable and the device's connector, as shown in Figure 14-6.

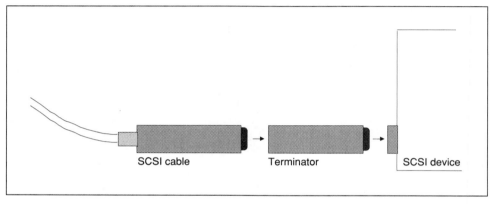

SCSI cable   Terminator   SCSI device

Figure 14-6: An external terminator attaches between a SCSI cable and a SCSI device's connector.

Some SCSI devices contain internal terminators, while others use external ones. Unfortunately, there isn't a great deal of consistency in the industry. Internal hard disks use internal terminators, but so do some external drives. Similarly, some SCSI scanners use internal terminators, but others don't. You'll need to check your devices' manuals to determine which kind of terminators they use.

As a general rule of thumb, your SCSI bus should have two terminators, one at each end of the SCSI bus. But there are exceptions to this rule. Figure 14-7 shows several SCSI connection and termination schemes that Apple recommends. You'll find more examples in your Mac's manual and in the manual, *Apple SCSI Cable System*, which comes with Apple's SCSI System Cable.

Finally, remember the first rule of SCSI installation: Turn off your Mac and everything attached to it before attaching or removing a device.

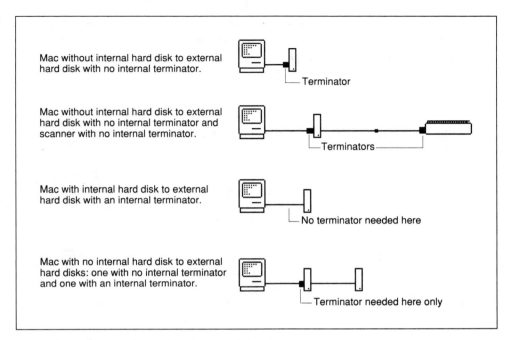

Figure 14-7: A sampling of SCSI connection schemes.

Setting SCSI Addresses

As mentioned earlier, the Mac uses addresses to differentiate between each SCSI device on the bus. Generally, you'll want to assign the higher priority addresses (those closer to 7) to high priority devices such as hard disks. Use lower-numbered addresses for lower priority add-ons such as tape backup drives or scanners.

You don't need to number devices sequentially. You can, for example, use addresses 6, 3, and 1, and skip over 5, 4, and 2. What *is* important, however, is that you don't give two devices the same address. That causes an *address conflict*, which often results in the Mac not being able to recognize either device. If you've just added a SCSI device to your system and you've found you can't start up your Mac, there may be an address conflict between your hard disk and the new SCSI device. If that's the case, turn everything off, adjust the SCSI switches to give each device its own address, and then power up again. (If your device requires that you run a utility program to change the address, you may need to disconnect the first SCSI device in order to allow the Mac to recognize the new one. This illustrates one drawback of SCSI devices that require software to set their addresses.)

Incidentally, if your SCSI devices use thumb switches or pushbutton switches to set addresses, be careful where you position the devices in your work area. Take care to not place the devices where you might accidentally change their addresses by bumping them.

Tinkering with SCSI

Several free or shareware programs are available that can help you work with and learn more about SCSI devices. They include:

- SCSI Tools (by Paul Mercer; $5 contribution to Unicef requested). SCSI Tools is a Control Panel device (cdev) that lets you determine which addresses your SCSI devices are using (Figure 14-8). It also lets you access a SCSI drive that wasn't turned on when you started up your Mac.

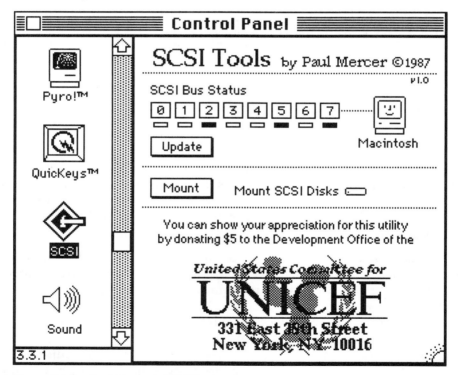

Figure 14-8: Paul Mercer's SCSI Tools cdev.

- SCSI Identifier (by Laurie Gill of Dantz Development; free). This simple application scans your SCSI bus and displays information about each device it finds. It's especially useful to find out who manufactured your hard disk. (Only a handful of companies actually manufacture hard disk drives; most hard disk companies buy drives from these firms and package them with their own power supplies and cases.)

- SCSI Evaluator (by William A. Long; shareware, $20). This program, shown in Figure 14-9, is the most complex of the bunch. SCSI Evaluator lets you measure the performance of a SCSI drive and the data-transfer rate of your Mac's SCSI bus. You can also use it to determine how your hard disk is physically constructed (how many read/write heads it has, whether it uses its own internal disk cache, who manufactured it, and so on). Registered users receive a 100-page manual that details the program's operation.

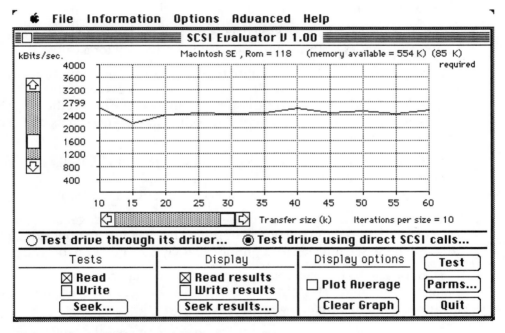

Figure 14-9: William Long's SCSI Evaluator utility.

SCSI Technicalities

For the technically curious, we've included some details on how the SCSI bus operates. In this section, we'll describe how the Mac communicates with SCSI devices, and we'll look at how different SCSI communication techniques affect how quickly the Mac can exchange data with a SCSI device.

You don't need to know this information to connect and use SCSI devices. If you aren't interested in SCSI technicalities, feel free to skip this section.

SCSI Communications

Because the SCSI bus can accommodate numerous peripherals, it requires a communication scheme that allows the Mac to address the correct peripheral. In the SCSI world, the device that instigates communication on the bus is called the *initiator*. The device the initiator addresses is called the *target*. In the Mac world, the Mac itself usually plays the role of initiator, while a hard disk is the most common target.

The SCSI bus uses seven different operating modes called *phases*, which allow initiator and targets to communicate with each other. As the following descriptions of each phase show, SCSI communications compares to the process of making a telephone call.

Bus-free phase. When no SCSI device is using the bus, the bus is in bus-free phase. The phones are hung up, and the lines are ready for a call.

Arbitration phase. Before an initiator can begin a communications session with a target, it must gain control of the bus. This process compares to picking up the phone and hoping no one else in the house is already on the line. Once a initiator has "picked up the phone," no other device—regardless of its priority—can interrupt it.

Selection phase. After the initiator picks up the phone, it dials the number—that is, it selects the target device. This phase ends with an acknowledgement from the target device—it "answers the phone," so to speak.

Command phase. At this point, the initiator and the target are talking to each other. In the command phase, the target receives instructions from initiator—it's the SCSI equivalent of a phone caller saying, "I'd like to order a pizza."

Data phase. In the data phase, the transfer of data occurs between the initiator and the target. The initiator says, "I'd like a large with everything except anchovies." (SCSI devices hate anchovies.)

Status and message phases. In these final two phases, the target sends two bytes of status and message information to complete the data transfer. If the transfer was successful, it might say, "OK, thanks for your order." If a communications error occurred, it might say, "Sorry, could you repeat that?"

SCSI Data Transmission

As mentioned previously, the SCSI bus uses parallel, rather than serial, data transmission. The Mac's SCSI chip can operate in two modes: *normal mode* and *pseudo-DMA mode*. (DMA stands for *direct-memory access*, an efficient data-transmission technique by which data is transferred between a peripheral and memory without requiring the CPU to be involved in every step of the process.)

In the SCSI chip's normal mode, the Mac's SCSI driver software manages the communication process between the Mac and the SCSI device. Because normal mode uses software to manage this handshaking process, it imposes demands on the Mac's CPU, slowing the machine's performance. In the pseudo-DMA mode, the internal logic circuits within the SCSI chip handle the handshaking process, freeing the Mac's CPU for other tasks.

The Mac uses both operating modes to transfer data. First, the CPU uses the normal mode to initiate the data transfer, then it uses the pseudo-DMA mode for the actual transfer itself. In conversational terms, the CPU says to the SCSI chip, "I'll get things started, then you take over." Once the transfer is underway, the SCSI chip uses one of its internal registers (the Bus and Status register) to indicate when it has received a byte of data from, or sent a byte to, the peripheral.

But the CPU can't completely remove itself from the process. It must still supervise the transfer. It does so by checking the SCSI chip's Bus and Status register to verify that data was received or written.

The CPU can use one of two ways to check the Bus and Status register: With the *polling* method, the CPU checks it before each byte is read or written. With the *blind transfer* method, the CPU checks it only once, before a block of bytes is read or written. Again, to put things in conversational terms, the polling method involves the CPU saying to the device, "I want to know each time you're ready to receive or send a byte." With the blind transfer method, the CPU says, "I want to know when you're ready to receive or send this chunk of data. After that, you can deal with my assistant, the SCSI chip."

As you might expect, the polling method requires more effort on the part of the CPU; thus, using it means slower performance. In the Mac SE, for example, the maximum transfer rate for polled transfers is 172K per second; with blind transfers, it jumps to 656K per second. The Mac II family is faster still; with blind transfers, they can shuttle 1.4MB per second across the SCSI bus.

THE SERIAL PORTS

We'll wrap up our look at the Mac's input and output features by examining its modem and printer ports. This section describes:

- serial communications terminology

- how the Mac's modem and printer ports operate

- the differences between the two ports

Serial Jargon

The serial communications world has its own jargon, and if you plan to use communications software and telephone modems, you'll encounter this jargon frequently. In this section, we'll define the terms you're most likely to encounter.

Start, Stop, and Parity Bits

As you may recall from Chapter 1, with serial transmission, the bits that form each byte travel in single-file, with one bit behind another. In many cases, some additional bits travel along with each byte. Two such specialized bits—*start bits* and *stop bits*—mark the beginning and end of each byte. Figure 14-10 illustrates how start and stop bits serve to frame each byte. (Although this figure shows just one stop bit, two are often used.) To return to our automotive analogy, if you imagine each byte as a presidential motorcade, the start and stop bits compare to the police escorts at the beginning and end of the motorcade.

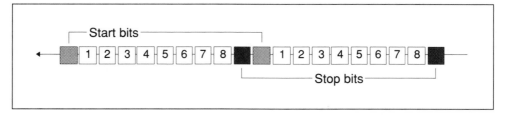

Figure 14-10:   Start and stop bits frame each byte.

Another specialized bit in serial communications is the *parity bit*. A parity bit serves as a data proofreading device: it allows the receiving device to verify that it has accurately received a given byte. With parity checking, the transmitting device processes the bits in a given byte according to a formula, and then sets the parity bit accordingly. When the receiving device receives a given byte, it processes its bits according to the same formula, and then verifies that it comes up with the same result. If it doesn't, it can tell the transmitting device to send the byte again.

In working with communications software, you'll encounter three possible parity settings:

Odd. With odd parity, the transmitting computer always sends an odd number of 1 bits (bits with a value of 1). When a given byte contains an even number of 1 bits, the sending device adds an additional bit. The receiving device then verifies that it received an odd number of bits.

Even. With even parity, the transmitting computer always sends an even number of 1 bits. When a given byte contains an odd number of 1 bits, the sending device adds an additional bit. The receiving device then verifies that it received an even number of bits.

None. With this setting, no parity bit is transmitted or expected on the receiving end. This is the most common setting in microcomputer communications.

When a parity bit is used, it's positioned before the stop bit that marks the end of a given byte.

Asynchronous versus Synchronous

Start and stop bits make possible a form of communications called *asynchronous communications*. The word *asynchronous* means "without synchronization." In the computer world, it means that two devices are not communicating under the control of rigid timing signals. Instead, they use start and stop bits to denote the beginning and end of each byte. Asynchronous communication is a very flexible method of data transmission; the transmitting device can send data as it's ready, and as long as the two devices are set up to send and recognize the right combination of start and stop bits, the message will get through.

But asynchronous communication has a drawback, too: it's inefficient. Start and stop bits don't carry actual data; they simply go along for the ride, telling the receiving device when to expect the actual data. This excess baggage effectively reduces the overall transmission speed; time that could be used exchanging data is wasted sending and receiving start and stop bits. Think back to our presidential motorcade analogy, and consider how much roadway all those motorcycles require.

Synchronous communication solves this inefficiency problem by using a timing clock to regulate the transmission of data. With synchronous communications, data is transmitted in chunks (typically containing 256 bytes) called *frames* or *packets*. Each frame is preceded by timing information that tells the receiving device how many characters to expect in a given amount of time. The receiving device then uses this timing information to count off incoming characters. Start and stop bits aren't required, and as a result, the two communicating devices can exchange more data in the same amount of time.

In the personal computer world, asynchronous communication is far more common than its synchronized counterpart. Synchronous communication is generally used in mainframe computers and in local-area networks (including AppleTalk).

Most low- to medium-speed modems (those providing speeds up to and including 2400 bits per second) use asynchronous communication. Many of today's high-speed modems, such as Hayes' Smartmodem 9600, also support synchronous communication.

Full Duplex versus Half Duplex

Another consideration in serial communication involves whether both devices can transmit and receive simultaneously, or whether only one device can transmit at a time. The former is called *full duplex* operation; the latter is *half duplex*.

Both types of communication have parallels in the non-computer world. Full duplex operation compares to telephone calls: both people on the line can speak and listen at the same time. Half duplex operation compares to two-way radio: Only one person can talk at a time, and must signal the other person when it's his or her turn to speak.

Personal computer communication almost always uses full-duplex mode.

Handshaking

When two serial devices are communicating, the receiving device may occasionally need to tell the transmitting device to pause momentarily. For example, when you're printing to an ImageWriter, the printer's internal memory may fill periodically, and the printer must tell the Mac to stop sending more data, lest some characters get lost. When the printer is ready to resume receiving data, it needs a way to tell the Mac to continue. Similarly, if you're connected to an information service and you're saving incoming data on disk, the Mac must periodically tell the transmitting computer to pause while it accesses the disk.

This wait-and-resume is called *handshaking*, or *flow control*. Two forms of handshaking exist:

Software handshaking, in which the receiving device transmits a software code to the sender. The most common form of software handshaking is called *X-on/X-off*. When the receiving device requires a pause in data transmission, it sends an X-off code. When it's ready to resume receiving, it sends an X-on code. When using a communications program, you can often send X-off code by typing Control-S, and an X-on code by typing Control-Q. Some programs may use the Command key instead of the Control key.

Hardware handshaking, in which the receiving device changes a voltage on a signal line in order to pause transmission.

Software handshaking is generally used in remote communications applications, such as when you're connected via modem to an information or electronic mail service. Hardware handshaking is common in links between a computer and a serial add-on, such as a printer (although software handshaking can be used here, too).

The Mac's Serial Ports

As we've mentioned previously, all Macs provide two serial ports, called the modem and printer ports, labeled on the Mac's case by telephone handset and printer icons. In some technical documentation, the ports are referred to as ports *A* and *B*. Port A is the modem port; port B is the printer port.

Figure 14-11 shows the pin configuration and signal assignments for the Mac family's serial ports.

The Mac's serial ports are controlled by the Zilog Z8530 Serial Communications Controller (SCC) chip and by a ROM-based device driver called the *Serial Driver*. The Serial Driver automatically configures both serial ports to communicate at 9600 bits per second (bps), with eight data bits, no parity bit, and two stop bits. The Mac uses these settings when communicating with an ImageWriter printer.

While the ports are initially configured for 9600-bps communications, they can operate at speeds of up to approximately 230K bps using the internal clock. (LocalTalk operates at this speed.) When driven by an external clock signal, the ports can operate at speeds of up to 1M bps. Both ports support both hardware handshaking and X-on/X-off software handshaking.

Female DB-9
(Mac 512K Enhanced and earlier)

Female DIN-8
(Mac Plus and later)

1	Chassis ground
2	+5 volts
3	Signal ground
4	Transmit data +
5	Transmit data −
6	+12 volts
7	Input handshake or external clock
8	Receive data +
9	Receive data −

1	Output handshake
2	Input handshake or external clock
3	Transmit data −
4	Signal ground
5	Receive data −
6	Transmit data +
7	Clock input (see note below)
8	Receive data +

Note: Pin 7 clock input available on modem port only of SE, II, and later machines. On the Mac Plus, this pin is not connected.

Figure 14-11: Serial port pin-outs and signal assignments.

Serial Port Differences

There are some important differences between the modem and printer ports:

• The modem port has a higher interrupt priority in the Mac's serial chip, making it the preferred port for high-speed communication.

• In the SE and II families, the modem port provides a second incoming line for handshaking. This line allows these Macs to support the external timing clocks used by synchronous modems.

• If you use a LocalTalk network, you must connect the LocalTalk connector to the printer port—not because the printer port has special LocalTalk-oriented hardware, but simply because the Mac's AppleTalk Manager is configured to use the printer port.

• In the Mac 512K, 512K Enhanced, and 128K, the modem and printer ports provide lines that supply +5 and +12 volts from the Mac's power supply. Many early peripherals, including the ThunderScan scanner and several MIDI interfaces, used these voltages to operate. Some peripherals, however, placed too large a load on the Mac's power supply, and as you'll recall from the previous chapter, the early Mac's power supplies never won any awards for robustness. Beginning with the Plus, power was no longer available at the serial ports. ThunderWare, makers of the ThunderScan, devised a clever workaround: its PowerPort connects to the Mac's external floppy drive port, and taps into its +5- and +12-volt power lines.

CHAPTER SUMMARY

- The Mac's keyboard and mouse communicate with the Mac serially. The keyboard and mouse in the SE and II families uses the Apple Desktop Bus.

- The mouse measures relative, rather than absolute, motion. You can change the mouse tracking by using the Control Panel.

- The Sound Manager, present in all Macs running System 6.0 or later versions, allows the Mac to create four-voice synthesized sound and also to play back digitally recorded, or sampled, sounds. To record sampled sound, you need to add additional hardware containing the necessary analog-to-digital converter.

- Three factors influence the sound quality of digital audio: the sampling rate, the sampling resolution, and the design and quality of the audio circuitry used to process the sound. The Mac Plus and SE have a maximum sampling rate of 22KHz; all faster Macs can sample at up to 44.1KHz. All Macs provide 8-bit sampling resolution.

- The Mac II family and the SE/30 contain the Apple Sound Chip, whose internal memory replaces the old sound buffer and whose hardware implementation of ROM routines imposes fewer demands on the Mac's CPU. These Macs also have stereo sound circuitry; they provide two Sony sound chips.

- The SCSI port lets you daisy-chain up to seven devices to the Mac. Each device has a unique address, which allows the Mac to differentiate between devices. A device's address also specifies its priority on the bus.

- Hooking up several SCSI devices requires using the proper number of terminators (never more than two) and making sure each device has its own address.

- The SCSI bus uses seven different operating modes called phases, which allow initiator and targets to communicate with each other.

- All Macs from the SE on support SCSI hardware handshaking and contain faster SCSI drivers, allowing them to transfer data more quickly than the Mac Plus.

- The Mac's modem and printer ports work together with the Serial Driver to provide serial communications. Both ports support hardware and software handshaking, but there are some other differences between the two. On all Macs from the SE on, the modem port supports synchronous modems as well as asynchronous ones.

15

Disk Details

Fast microprocessors and megabytes of memory are great, but ultimately, the Mac's capabilities are determined by the capacity, speed, and reliability of its mass-storage devices. Storage capacity is important if you have a large software library or you're working with sounds or color and grey-scale images. Speed is significant because it determines how quickly the Mac can load programs and access documents. And reliability is important for obvious reasons.

Fortunately, disks fare well in all three categories. In this chapter, we'll examine:

- how floppy and hard disks operate
- other types of storage devices
- factors to consider when shopping for storage devices
- how to interpret hard disk performance specifications
- how the Mac keeps track of what's on a disk
- how to diagnose and fix disk problems
- programs that let you explore the contents of disks

We'll also provide some tips for choosing disks and taking care of them.

DISK BASICS

In Chapter 2, we said that breakthroughs in user interface design allowed computers to become more interactive. These software breakthroughs couldn't have occurred without advances in hardware. The video screen was one such advance. Another was in the area of mass-storage. Punched paper cards—the kind you couldn't fold, spindle, or mutilate—surrendered to a faster, more reliable storage medium: magnetic tapes. You've probably seen these spinning back and forth in science-fiction movies. Soon, magnetic tapes gave way to magnetic disks.

Disks offer a significant advantage over tapes and cards: they're a *random-access* medium. A computer can quickly access any portion of a disk without having to read through the entire disk's contents. It's similar to the difference between phonograph records and cassette tapes: You can access a specific song on a record in a fraction of the time it would take to locate it on tape.

Inside a Floppy Disk

How do disks provide their random-access benefits? Within the plastic shell of a 3-1/2-inch disk is a circle of flexible plastic, as shown in Figure 15-1. This flexible—or floppy—plastic disk is coated with invisible particles of iron oxide—a material not too different from everyday rust. When it's being read from or written to, the disk spins at a rate of between roughly 390 and 600 revolutions per minute.

When the Mac is writing to the disk, a pair of *read/write heads*, one for each side of the disk, moves across the surface of the disk as shown in Figure 15-2. Each head generates magnetic fields that rearrange the disk's iron oxide particles into patterns representing the bits being written. When the Mac is reading from the disk, the particles recreate those magnetic fields in the heads. The heads then send electrical impulses to the Mac's disk-controller circuitry, which interprets the impulses and sends the resulting bits to the CPU.

Figure 15-1: A disassembled floppy disk.

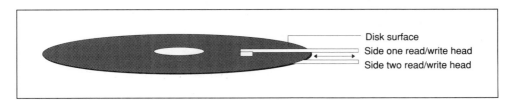

Figure 15-2: Inside a floppy disk drive.

What Initializing Does

Any storage system requires some structure and organization, and a brand new disk doesn't provide either. Its surface is simply an array of randomly arranged microscopic magnets. When you insert a new disk, the Mac tells you it's unreadable and asks if you want to *initialize* it. During the initialization process, the Mac uses the disk drive's read/write heads to create magnetic divisions that will provide the structure needed to store files.

The most basic of these magnetic divisions are *tracks* and *sectors*. Tracks are concentric circles—like the rings of a tree. Each side of a disk contains 80 tracks. The tracks closer to the outer edge of the disk are physically longer than the ones closer to the hub, and thus can store more information. To take advantage of the greater capacity of these longer tracks, the disk spins more slowly when the outermost tracks are being accessed.

Sectors are smaller magnetic divisions created within each track, as shown in Figure 15-3. Each sector of a floppy disk stores 512 bytes. The number of sectors in each track depends on the track's location on the disk. The outermost tracks of an 800K disk have 12 sectors each; the innermost ones have 8 sectors each.

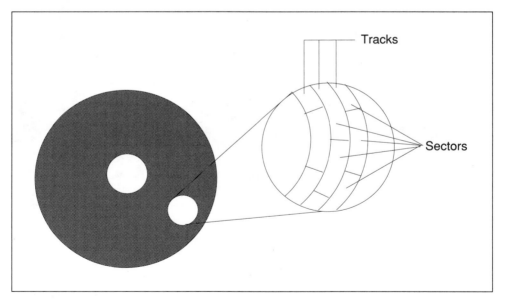

Figure 15-3: Sectors are divisions within each track.

High-Density Differences

The 1.4MB high-density disks used by the FDHD drive (sometimes called the *SuperDrive*) work slightly differently. Each side of a high-density disk still contains 80 tracks, but each track—regardless of its location on the disk—contains 18 sectors. Also, high-density disks always spin at 300 revolutions per minute when they're being accessed. Table 15-1 summarizes the differences between 800K and 1.4MB disks.

Table 15-1: 800K and 1.4MB disk specifications compared.

	800K Disks	1.4MB Disks
Bytes per sector	512	512
Sectors per track	8-12	18
Tracks per side	80	80
Capacity per side (bytes)	409,600	737,280
Capacity per disk (bytes)	819,200	1,474,560
Rotation speeds (rpm)		
Tracks 0-15	394	300
Tracks 16-31	429	300
Tracks 32-47	472	300
Tracks 48-63	525	300
Tracks 64-79	590	300

The 400K disks used by the 128K and 512K Macs have the same basic specifications as 800K disks, except that they record information on one side of the disk only. If you click the Single Sided button when asked if you want to initialize a disk, the Mac formats the disk on one side only. (One reason you might want to do this is to create a disk that can be accessed by a Mac that has only 400K drives.)

Incidentally, the "capacity per disk" entries in Table 15-1 reflect the disk's *total* capacity. That entire amount isn't available for storing applications or documents. As we'll see later in this chapter, the Mac requires some space for storing information about the disk's contents.

Tips for Floppies

Floppy disks are an extremely reliable storage medium, provided that you follow some common-sense shopping and storage guidelines.

- *For 800K drives, buy disks tested for double-sided operation.* Disk manufacturers don't have separate factories or assembly lines for single-sided and double-sided disks. Instead, all new disks are tested on each side, and those that fail the test on side two are packaged and sold as single-sided disks. But these disks can often be initialized as double-sided disks. Thus, some people try to economize by buying single-sided disks and initializing them for double-sided use. It's false economy. The second side of the disk may initialize properly, but quickly develop problems that can cause lost data. Disks are inexpensive, especially compared to recreating lost work. Always buy high-quality disks that are certified for double-sided use.

- *For FDHD drives, buy certified high-density disks.* High-density disks have a hole in the upper-left corner of their housing that identifies them as high-density, as shown in Figure 15-4. An FDHD drive will not create a 1.4MB disk unless the disk contains this hole. This contrasts sharply with many high-density drives in the MS-DOS world, which will let you initialize an ordinary double-sided 3 1/2-inch disk to store 1.4MB. Many users save money—but risk data—by doing just that. (We'll take a closer look at high-density disk issues shortly.)

- *Always eject disks properly.* Drag a disk's icon to the Trash when you're done using it, and always choose the Finder's Shut Down command before shutting the power off. (On Mac IIs, that's easy, since Shut Down also turns off the power.) Ejecting a disk properly enables the Mac to update its invisible DeskTop file and perform any other necessary tidying tasks.

- *Don't open a disk's metal shutter by hand and touch the disk surface inside.* We know you wouldn't do that, but an inexperienced colleague or child might.

- *Don't use a cold or hot disk (or disk drive).* If you've just brought a new box of disks or your Mac in from a hot car or cold winter day, wait until the disk or drive has reached room temperature before using it.

- *Watch those disk labels.* If a disk's label becomes loose, it may hang up in the drive, preventing you from ejecting the disk. Be sure labels are securely attached to the disk, with no large air bubbles or lifting edges that could catch on the drive's mechanism. When you're peeling an old label off a disk, be sure it doesn't tear and create dusty paper fragments. Instead of struggling to remove an old label, consider simply applying a new one directly over the old.

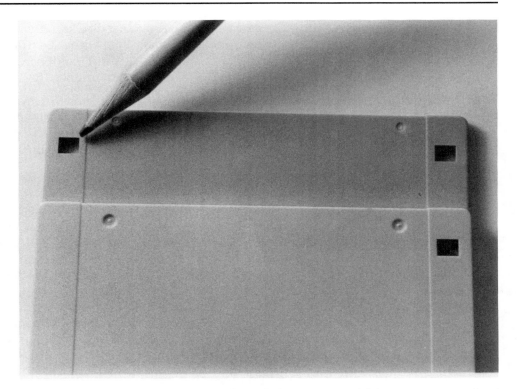

Figure 15-4: A high-density disk (*top*) has a hole in its upper-left corner; a conventional disk (*bottom*) doesn't.

- *Erase a disk you want to recycle.* Don't simply throw its files in the Trash. When you use the Erase Disk command, the Mac checks the disk to verify that it's in good working order. If an "Initialization failed!" message appears, consider throwing the disk away. You might be able to successfully initialize it on the second or third try, but chances are it's near the end of its useful life.

- *Use the drive spacers when you ship your Mac.* To keep your disk drives in proper alignment, insert the plastic drive spacers when you ship your Mac or carry it in a car. If you threw the spacers out, use unneeded disks instead.

- *Store and ship disks carefully.* Keep them in a cool, dry place. Don't leave them locked in a hot car or in the sun, and don't set them on your desk, where they might get soaked by spilled coffee. Don't set them near devices that generate magnetic fields, such as loudspeakers, high-intensity or halogen desk lamps, and appliances containing electric motors. And as mentioned in Chapter 9, avoid setting up an external floppy disk drive to the left of a Mac Plus or SE.

Because the edges of the disk's case aren't sealed against dirt, keep them in a covered box when they aren't in use, and don't mail them without extra protection against dust and bending. For mailing disks, use a cardboard disk mailer such as Dennison's Mini Floppy Disk Mailer (order number 18-275).

As for airport x-ray machines, the x-rays themselves don't pose a threat to a disk's contents, but the machines can contain transformers that generate magnetic fields. Generally, airport security equipment isn't a threat to disks, but to be on the safe side, you may want to request that your disks be inspected by hand.

Mixing High-Density and 800K Disks

After the FDHD drive was released, some people complained about problems occurring when high-density disks were used in 800K drives. The problems trace back to the fact that high-density disks are physically different than 800K, double-sided disks. In addition to the extra hole mentioned earlier, a high-density disk has a thinner magnetic coating and smaller magnetic particles. The thinner coating means that the magnetic force needed to alter the particles doesn't have to be as strong as it does in an 800K drive. The smaller particles allow data to be packed more tightly on the disk—they help make it possible for a high-density disk to have 18 sectors per track.

If you use an 800K drive to initialize a high-density disk, the drive will create an 800K disk that will appear to work properly—until you insert the disk into an FDHD drive. At that time, the drive will notice the extra hole and attempt to read the disk as a high-density disk. Because the disk isn't in high-density format, a dialog box will appear asking if you want to initialize the disk.

So, if you need to exchange files between 800K and FDHD drives, don't use high-density disks to do it. Instead, format an 800K disk and use it to exchange the files.

HARD DISKS

Conceptually, hard disks are very similar to floppies. They use read/write heads to change the patterns of the magnetic particles representing bits and bytes, and their surfaces are magnetically divided into tracks and sectors.

Physically, however, hard disks are quite different. Instead of using a flexible circle of plastic to hold magnetic particles, they use one or more rigid disk surfaces called *platters*. Each platter in a hard disk has its own set of read/write heads, as shown in Figure 15-5.

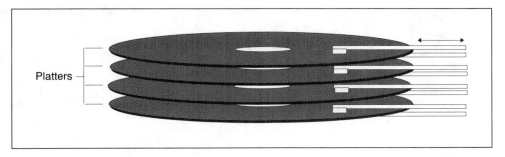

Figure 15-5: Inside a hard disk drive.

These platters are machined to very precise tolerances, allowing their magnetic particles to be packed more closely together, thus providing more storage capacity. Most floppy disks can accommodate a maximum of 135 tracks per inch, but hard disks can have several hundred or more tracks per inch.

Unlike the heads of a floppy disk, a hard disk's heads don't touch the disk surface, but ride a hair's width above it, "floating" on a thin layer of air. If a speck of dust lands on a spinning disk platter and hits the head, it can cause the head to bounce up and down on the platter. That undesirable occurrence is called a *head crash*. In the early days of hard disks, a head crash could permanently damage the disk's fragile magnetic coating. Today's hard disk platters are much more durable; a head crash can cause a momentary loss of data—a *soft error*—but it's less likely to permanently damage the platter. In any event, because dust is a significant threat to a hard disk, its platters are sealed in a dust-free chamber.

Hard disks also spin much faster than floppies—generally at about 3600 revolutions per minute, or about ten times faster than floppies. What's more, hard disks spin continuously; floppies spin only when they're being accessed. A hard disk's faster rotation speed and tighter data packing are two of the factors that help hard disks transfer data so much faster than floppies. (We'll examine other speed issues shortly.)

REMOVEABLE-MEDIA DRIVES

Several drives are available that combine the warehouse-like capacity of a hard disk with the removeable nature of floppies. In a *removeable-media* drive, often simply called a *removeable drive* for short, the magnetic medium is enclosed in a cartridge that slips into and out of the drive, as shown in Figure 15-6. In this day of grey-scale and color graphics, digital sound, and programs that come on five floppy disks, removeable-media drives are becoming increasingly popular.

Figure 15-6:   A removeable-media drive and cartridge.

Removeable-media drives have several advantages over conventional hard disks:

- Convenience. If you frequently need to move megabytes of data from one machine to another, you can simply buy two drives and swap cartridges between them as needed.

- Security. You can store a removeable cartridge in a safe at the end of the day or pop it into your briefcase and carry it home.

- Capacity. No matter how large a hard disk you buy, chances are you'll fill it someday and need to throw away old files to make room for new ones. With a removeable-media drive, when you fill one cartridge, you can replace it with another.

- Flexibility. A removeable-media drive not only works well for day-to-day storage, it makes a wonderful backup device for a hard disk, since you don't have to feed it floppy after floppy to backup your work.

A Removeable Drive Sampler

Let's spotlight the three most popular removeable-media drives available for the Mac.

Iomega Bernoulli Box. Iomega Corporation's pioneering Bernoulli Box was the first practical, reliable removeable media. Original Bernoulli cartridges were bulky affairs that held a mere 10MB; today's Bernoulli Box drives store 44MB on compact (5 1/4-inch) cartridges. Inside the cartridge, a flexible disk spins within a cushion of filtered air that draws the disk toward the drive's read/write head—just as a shower curtain is drawn inward by the difference in air pressure between the shower and the rest of the room. (These principles of fluid dynamics were discovered by an eighteenth-century mathematician named Daniel Bernoulli.) In a Bernoulli cartridge, if a dust particle works its way between the disk and head, the disk simply flexes to make room for it, while the filtered air blows it away. Thus, Bernoulli Boxes are virtually immune to head crashes.

Syquest removeable hard disk. Syquest's removeable hard disk drives haven't been available for as long as Bernoulli Boxes, but they've become popular and have proven themselves reliable. Several companies sell Syquest-based drives, including Mass Micro Systems (DataPak), Peripheral Land (Infinity 40 Turbo), La Cie (Cirrus 45), Relax Technology (Mobile 42 Plus), DPI (DPI 44), and Crate Technology (ExpandaCrate, shown in Figure 15-6). The Syquest cartridges contain a single hard disk platter that holds 44MB. The platter spins at 3280 rpm, almost as quickly as a conventional hard disk.

Kodak/Verbatim floppies. The Verbatim division of Eastman Kodak offers an ultra-high-density floppy drive that stores 20MB. A Verbatim disk cartridge contains a 5 1/4-inch disk that looks similar to the disks IBM PCs use. The way the drive accesses the disk, however, is quite different. Special *servo* signals are recorded on the disk at the factory that allow the drive to monitor the exact position of its heads and adjust them with extreme accuracy. This allows a Verbatim disk to provide 333 tracks per inch, versus the 135 tracks per inch a Mac floppy provides. (In a conventional floppy drive, the drive's electronics have no way of knowing exactly where the heads are located on the disk; thus, the tracks must be wide enough to allow for some positioning error.)

And the Verbatim disk spins at 600 rpm, making it considerably faster than a floppy. However, the drives are much slower than a hard disk or Bernoulli drive. You probably wouldn't want to use a Kodak/Verbatim drive as your main storage device, but one would be ideal for backing up a large-capacity hard disk. Companies selling Kodak/Verbatim drives include Jasmine Technologies (the MegaDrive 20) and Mirror Technologies (the RM20).

Finally, it's worth stressing that the same care-and-storage guidelines we presented for floppies also apply to removeable-media cartridges—in spades. Losing the contents of an 800K floppy disk is bad enough; losing an entire 40MB worth of data can be traumatic enough to send you over the edge. Don't carry a cartridge for long distances without backing up its contents first.

Tomorrow's Removeable Media—Today

The Bernoulli, Syquest, and Kodak/Verbatim drives are the three most popular removeable-media drives currently available for the Mac. In the future, these drives are likely to supplemented—or supplanted—by optical storage media that use lasers and compact-disc technology to store hundreds of megabytes.

Two primary types of optical drives are already available: *WORM* drives and *erasable optical drives*. WORM is an unflattering acronym for *write-once, read many times*. In a WORM drive, a laser "burns" pits that represent binary ones and zeros into the surface of the disk. As the name implies, once you save something on a WORM drive, you can't delete it. With between 400 and 800MB available, however, that may not be a real drawback. A few of the companies selling WORM drives for the Mac include Giga Cell Systems (Data WORM 800), Laserdrive (Model 820), Laser Optical Technology (Optical WORM), and Colby Systems (Colby WORM).

An erasable optical (EO) drive, also called a *magneto-optical* drive, offers the cavernous capacity of a WORM drive, but with the erase-and-reuse flexibility of magnetic media. Indeed, EO disks use minute magnetic particles embedded in the surface of the disk. A laser and electromagnet orient these magnetic particles to create the binary ones and zeros that represent what you're storing. The laser uses a high-powered beam when writing to the disk, and a low-power one when reading from it. Firms offering EO drives for the Mac include Pinnacle Micro (REO-650), Jasmine Technologies (DirectOptical), Personal Computer Peripherals Corporation (OER600), and Racet Computers (Cosmos 600). All of these firms sell the same basic Sony-, Ricoh-, or Maxtor-built drives, which store between 290 to 325MB per side, depending on how they're formatted. To access the second side of one of these disks, you must flip it over—just as you flip a record over to play its second side. This somewhat inconvenient "flippy disk" style of operation is likely to be eliminated as EO technology matures.

SHOPPING FOR STORAGE

In Chapter 9, we mentioned that a hard disk or other high-capacity storage device should be one of your first hardware purchase priorities. The Mac's system software is growing larger, as are commercial programs. Gray-scale or color graphics and digital sound devour disk space. The bottom line is that unless you use a Mac for extremely simple tasks, you need a high-capacity storage device.

But what kind of device should you buy? In this section, we'll provide some guidelines to help you decide.

What Do You Need and Want?

Before you shop for storage, you need to assess your needs and your preferences:

- How much storage do you want? These days, the smallest-capacity hard disks you can buy store 20MB. That used to be more than enough for most users, but today, it's barely adequate. You might want to consider a 30MB or 40MB unit instead; they don't cost much more, but they do store much more.

- Do you want an internal or external drive? Internal drives are convenient if you frequently carry your Mac with you, and they don't require you to clutter your work area with SCSI cables and power cords. But if an internal drive breaks, your Mac must go to the shop along with it. Internal drives also add heat to the inside of the Mac. For these reasons, many users prefer external drives. Another benefit of an external drive is that it's easy to move it to another Mac. They tend to cost more than internal drives, however, since they require their own cases and power supplies.

- Should you buy a conventional hard disk or a removeable-media drive? Conventional hard disks tend to cost less than removeable drives, but keep in mind that their storage capacities are finite. After you fill a hard disk, you'll need to throw away old files to free up space. With a removeable drive, you can simply add new cartridges.

- How important is speed? Any high-capacity drive is delightfully fast compared to floppy disks, but there can be significant differences in performance between drives. For example, Bernoulli Boxes and Kodak/Verbatim removeable drives are slower than hard disks, as are optical drives. And some hard disks are faster than others. In the next section, we'll provide more guidelines for assessing drive speed, and we'll demystify some of the technical terms you'll encounter when shopping for storage.

But whether speed is critical depends on how you'll use your drive. If you tend to spend a lot of time in one program before starting another, differences in drive speeds aren't very important. On the other hand, if you routinely switch between programs under MultiFinder or if you'll be using a drive with a file server, a drive speed's becomes critical. A fast hard disk will also be important if you plan to take advantage of System 7.0's virtual memory feature, described in previous chapters.

Technical Factors to Consider

Shopping for storage is like shopping for a stereo: You'll encounter a lot of technical specifications, many of which were born in a laboratory or marketing department and don't really relate to the real world. But you can learn something about a drive by evaluating its technical specifications, so we'll take a brief look at the most common—and most important—specs you're likely to encounter.

- Data transfer rate. A drive's *data transfer rate* specifies how quickly the drive can send data to the Mac. The higher the value, the better—to a point. As we saw in the last chapter, slower Macs such as the Plus can't accept data over the SCSI bus as quickly as a Mac II.

- Average access time. The average amount of time it takes for the drive's heads to reach a given track is called the *average access time*. The lower the value, the faster the drive's heads can locate a given track. A value of more than 60 milliseconds is considered rather slow; 40 to 60 is better; 20 to 40 is very good; and under 20 is excellent. Many of the fastest drives use *voice coil actuators* to move the drive's heads. In addition to providing faster access times, voice coil actuators are quieter and often more reliable than the other common head-positioning mechanism (and the one used in floppy drives), the *stepper motor*.

- Mean time between failure. Drive manufacturers often rate the reliability of their products by assigning a *mean time between failure (MTBF)* rating to them. Like laser printer engine-life ratings, MTBF ratings don't relate very well to the real world. Still, they can be useful, especially if you're purchasing a drive that will be used by a file server. Such a drive will see more constant use than a workstation drive. With MTBF ratings, the higher the value, the better.

A Word About Interleave Ratios

Another technical phrase you'll hear tossed around is the *interleave ratio*. The interleave ratio describes how the sectors in each track are organized, as shown in a Figure 15-7. A one-to-one (1:1) interleave means the sectors are numbered sequentially and that the Mac can read each one in turn. With a 2:1 interleave, the Mac must read every second sector, so it takes two revolutions of the disk to read an entire track. With a 3:1 interleave, the Mac reads every third sector.

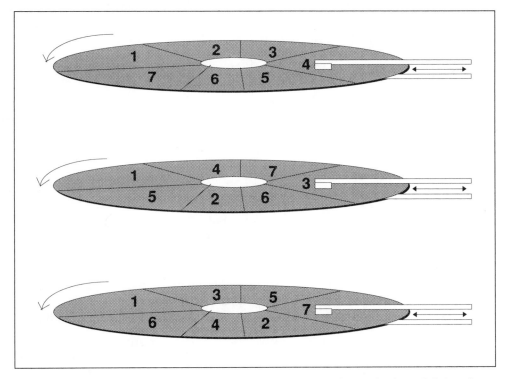

Figure 15-7: How sectors are organized with a 1:1 interleave (*top*), a 2:1 interleave (*middle*), and a 3:1 interleave (*bottom*).

Generally, a 1:1 interleave is best—provided that your Mac can accept the data that quickly. The SE/30 and II family can, but the SE requires a 2:1 interleave, and the Plus, a 3:1 interleave. Use a drive formatted for a 1:1 interleave on one of these Macs, and performance will actually be slower.

However, some drive manufacturers supply their own SCSI drivers that allow a slower Mac to use a 1:1 interleave. Other drives include built-in *track caches*, which store an entire track in a small amount of memory contained in the drive. Should the Mac need subsequent sectors from a given track, the drive supplies them from its cache, thus boosting performance.

A drive's interleave ratio isn't a fixed value like its access time or MTBF ratings. Many drives include utility software that lets you change the interleave ratio. (Note that doing so requires you to reinitialize the drive.)

The ins and outs of interleave ratios can be summarized in one sentence: When you buy a drive, be sure that its interleave ratio either matches that required by your Mac, or that you can change the ratio if it doesn't.

Other Factors to Consider

As you may recall from Chapter 8, many laser printers are available for the Mac, but most use engines made by only a few manufacturers. There's a parallel in the mass-storage world: A couple of dozen companies offer hard disks and removeable drives for the Mac, but only a few firms actually manufacture drives.

Still, there are factors that differentiate one drive from the next. For example, many mass-storage vendors include utility software that adds extra value to their products. You might find utilities for backing up the drive, locating files, testing and formatting the drive, encrypting files so they can't be read, partitioning the drive into numerous logical volumes, and *parking* the drive's heads—moving them to a safe, unused portion of the disk so they can't damage its surface if the drive is jostled while being moved. (Many drives automatically park their heads when you turn their power off.) When you're shopping, determine which types of utilities a company includes with its drives.

It's also important to evaluate a company's warranty and customer-support policy. How long is the drive guaranteed? Does the company have a customer-support hotline? You may also want to talk with members of a user's group to determine if they've had good or bad experiences with the company. Have they been able to get through to the technical support department, or have they left messages that are never returned? If they've had to return a drive, does a replacement arrive promptly? These issues are especially important if you plan to buy a drive through the mail rather than at a local dealer.

If you'll be using a drive in a quiet office, you'll also want to determine how loud it is. All drives make some noise, but some are louder and more grating than others. And if you plan to move a drive around with you, you'll want to assess its portability and ruggedness. Many manufacturers provide *g-force* ratings that measure how well their drives stand up to physical abuse such as being dropped. With g-force ratings, the higher the value, the better.

Hard Disk Tips

Here are several tips for keeping your hard disk healthy. Although these tips apply specifically to hard disks, many of them also apply to removeable-media drives.

- Don't move it when it's turned on. Doing so is an invitation to a head crash. Always turn the power off and wait a minute for the disk platters to stop spinning. If the drive includes a head-parking utility, run it before moving the drive.

- Avoid drastic temperature changes. If you've just brought a hard disk (or removeable cartridge) in from a hot or cold car, give it a couple of hours to adjust to its new surroundings before using it.

- Keep its files contiguous. As you'll recall from Chapter 9, you can defragment a hard disk's contents by using a utility program such as ALsoft's DiskExpress, or by backing up the disk, erasing it, and then restoring its contents. Keeping a disk's files contiguous does more than just optimize its performance; it prolongs the life of the drive's head actuator mechanism by reducing the need to constantly move the heads from one track to another in order to piece together fragmented files.

- Let it breathe. Be sure to give the hard disk plenty of ventilation space. If you're using SCSI cable extenders to move a noisy drive out of earshot, be sure the location you choose for the drive is well ventilated and clean. Don't banish it to the dusty floor of a hot closet—it will get its revenge sooner or later (probably sooner).

HOW THE MAC SAVES FILES

We've looked at the physical characteristics of various storage media, and we've presented some guidelines for taking care of floppies and shopping for high-capacity drives. Now let's journey into the world of tracks and sectors to examine how the Mac stores data on disks. Some technical background on how the Mac accesses disks can help you diagnose disk difficulties—a subject we'll look at next.

Reserved Disk Areas

The key to understanding how the Mac accesses disks is to understand that not all of a disk's tracks and sectors are available to hold files. During the initialization process, the Mac sets aside certain areas of the disk to hold information that allows it to keep track of the disk's contents. These reserved sections of a disk are extremely important; if something happens to them, you can lose files.

In this section, we'll look at these "reserved seating" sections. We won't explore every nook and cranny of each reserved area; instead, we'll provide an overview of the jobs each area performs. These descriptions apply specifically to disks that use the Hierarchical File System (HFS)—that includes 800K and 1.4MB floppies, and all hard disks. At the end of each section, we'll note any differences in the structure of 400K disks, which use the original Macintosh File System (MFS). (If you'd like a refresher on the differences between HFS and MFS, refer to Chapter 3.)

The Directory: A Table of Contents

Tracks and sectors are like the page numbers of a book: They provide the underlying structure needed to locate something quickly. But a book's page numbers aren't very useful without a table of contents. Similarly, a disk needs a table of contents to allow it to keep track of where files are located.

A disk's table of contents is called the *directory*. When the Mac needs to read a file, it consults the directory to determine which tracks and sectors contain that file, then it moves the disk's read/write heads accordingly. When you save a file for the first time, the Mac adds an entry to the directory for that file, then it saves the file using sectors that aren't in use by other files.

On HFS disks, the directory actually comprises two separate files: the *Catalog B-Tree* file and the *Extents B-Tree* file. Both files can grow or shrink as you add or remove data from a disk.

The Catalog B-Tree file contains an entry for each file and contains information that describes the hierarchical filing structure you've set up for that disk. Each file's entry contains the file's four-character type and creator codes, the file's name, its attributes, and information specifying where the file is located on the disk. (We'll examine these entries again later in this chapter.) Unless a file grows particularly large, all the information for it can be stored in the Catalog B-Tree file.

When a file grows large and becomes fragmented across physically non-contiguous files on the disk, the Extents B-Tree file comes into play. This file contains information about where each file fragment is located on the disk. Figure 15-8 shows what a fragmented file might look like if you were able to see it by looking at a disk.

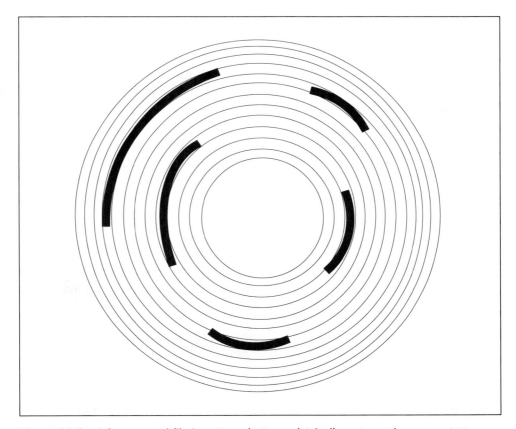

Figure 15-8: A fragmented file is scattered across physically non-contiguous sectors.

On MFS-format disks, the directory is located at a specific area of the disk (sectors 4 through 15). The fact that the directory is fixed in size has an important ramification: A large number of small files on a disk can fill the directory and, therefore, prevent you from adding more files, even though the disk may still contain free sectors. (This won't occur on HFS disks, since their Catalog B-Tree and Extents B-Tree files can grow as needed to accommodate more files.)

The Volume Bit Map: A Seating Chart

When it's writing to the disk, the Mac uses another reserved area, the *volume bit map*, to determine which sectors are free and which are in use.

The volume bit map is like the seating chart that a restaurant host or hostess uses. When a large group of diners arrives, the host first checks the seating chart to make sure enough tables are free to accommodate them. Then, the host seats the diners and makes notations on the seating chart to indicate that those tables are taken.

Similarly, when the Mac needs to save a file, it first checks the volume bit map to determine if enough free sectors are available to hold the file. Then, while saving the file, it makes notations in the volume bit map to indicate which sectors are no longer free.

On MFS disks, an area called the allocation block map keeps track of free and used sectors. The allocation block map also lets the Mac piece together files that are fragmented across the disk. On HFS disks, the latter job is performed by the Catalog B-Tree and Extents B-Tree files, as described earlier.

What Happens When You Delete a File

When you delete a file by dragging it to the Trash and then choosing the Empty Trash command, the Mac removes that file's directory entry and updates the volume bit map to indicate that the file's sectors are available again. There's an important subtlety here: The Mac doesn't actually delete the file's contents, it simply removes its directory entry and updates the volume bit map to free up its sectors. Disk utility programs such as the Norton Utilities can resurrect a file that you've deleted by recreating its directory entry and restoring the volume bit map to indicate that the file's sectors are again in use.

But there's a catch. Because the volume bit map indicates that a deleted file's sectors are available, it's possible for a newly added or expanded file to use up some of those sectors, making it impossible for a disk utility to resurrect the entire file. To return to the restaurant analogy, imagine that our group of diners have paid their bill and have strolled out into the parking lot, but then decide to go back and have desert. If any new diners have entered the restaurant since the old ones left, there's a chance that some or all of the original diners' tables will no longer be available.

The moral? A deleted file's sectors are free game for any newcomers. If you delete a file by mistake, don't make any modifications to that disk until you resurrect the file.

Volume Information

A disk's *volume information block* contains a collection of details about the disk, including the date and time that the disk was initialized, and the date and time that the disk was last modified. The Finder's Get Info command uses these pieces of information. Other data in the volume information block indicates how many times the disk has been written to, and specify the size of other reserved areas of the disk.

The Boot Blocks

The Mac uses another reserved disk area, the *boot blocks*, when starting up. The boot blocks get their name from the computer term *boot*, which refers to system start-up process, during which the computer "pulls itself up by its *boot-straps*." Both HFS and MFS disks use the same basic boot blocks.

The boot blocks contain information such as the name of the System file, the name of the application to run after you quit a program (usually "Finder"), and values that specify the initial size of the system heap, the reserved area of memory that holds Inits and other system software. As we'll see later, if the Mac ejects a disk during startup and displays the frowning Mac icon, one possible cause could be damaged boot blocks.

(Here's a trivia question for Mac historians: the first two bytes in the boot blocks contain the ASCII values for the letters "LK." Whose initials are those? The answer is at the end of this section.)

Summary of Reserved Disk Areas

We've waded through a few technicalities in this section, so let's step back and summarize the reserved areas of the disk that we've looked at. They include:

- The directory, an electronic table of contents that contains an entry for each file. On MFS disks, it's a fixed area, and that limits the number of files you can store on the disk. On HFS disks, it's comprised of two files, the Catalog B-Tree file and the Extents B-Tree file. Both files can grow or shrink as you alter a disk's contents.

- The volume bit map, a "seating chart" that indicates which sectors are free and which are in use.

- The volume information block, which contains various details about the disk, such as the date and time it was initialized and last modified.

- The boot blocks, which contain information used at start-up time. (And here's the answer to the trivia question: The initials "LK" belong to Larry Kenyon, the principal designer of the Mac's original file system.)

Some Common File Signatures

In previous chapters, we've seen that the Mac uses four-character file signatures to identify the type and creator of a file. These signatures work together with the DeskTop file's application list to enable the Finder to start the appropriate application when you double-click on a document.

Generally, you don't need to know the type and creator codes for your program's documents. However, having this information has its advantages. For example, as we saw in Chapter 11, if you transfer a file from an MS-DOS computer, you can change its type and creator code to be able to open it by double-clicking it from the Finder.

Table 15-2 lists the type and creator codes for numerous popular applications. You can determine a file's type and creator codes for yourself by using ResEdit: Select the file (click on it once) and then choose Get Info from the File menu.

Table 15-2: A sampling of common type and creator codes.

Type of file	Type Code	Creator Code
Any application	APPL	varies
Any text file	TEXT	varies
HyperCard Stack	STAK	WILD
MacDraw II document	DRWG	MDPL
MacPaint document	PNTG	MPNT
MacWrite document	WORD	MACA
Microsoft Excel document	XLBN	XCEL
Microsoft Word document	WDBN	MSWD
PageMaker 2.0 document	PUBF	ALD2
PageMaker 3.0 document	ALB3	ALD3
QuarkXpress document	XDOC	XPRS
SuperPaint document	SPTG	SPNT

(continued)

Table 15-2: A sampling of common type and creator codes. *(continued)*

Type of file	Type Code	Creator Code
System-Related Files		
System file	ZSYS	MACS
Finder	FNDR	MACS
DeskTop file	FNDR	ERIK
Startup focument	INIT	varies
Control Panel device	cdev	varies
Chooser document	RDEV	varies
FKEYs	FKEY	varies
TeachText document	TEXT or ttro	ttxt
ResEdit file	rsrc	RSED

DISK TROUBLESHOOTING

Floppy and hard disks are generally very reliable, especially if you observe the guidelines presented earlier in this chapter. Still, problems can arise. In this section, we'll look at some of the problems that can occur with disks, and at some remedies you might try. But remember, no remedy is as effective as a current set of backup disks. The best way to avoid losing work is to keep at least one set of backup disks current at all times.

What Can Go Wrong

The programs and data that reside on disks face many threats, which fall into several general categories:

- Physical damage. Someone in your office might use a floppy disk as a Frisbee or run over it with an office chair. Your external hard disk might fry in a sun-baked car or be jostled during shipping. Or, a section of the disk's magnetic coating may become damaged or dislodged by dirt or old age. You may be able to recover data from a disk suffering from minor physical problems, but there's little hope for a disk doused with spilled soda.

- Magnetic damage. As mentioned earlier, many appliances and other devices generate magnetic fields that can partially erase a disk's contents. If some of the disk's track and sector boundaries are obliterated by a strong magnetic field, even a disk-recovery program isn't likely to help.

- Logical damage. If a problem such as a system error or power glitch occurs while you're saving a file, the portion of the disk being accessed may contain invalid information. If a file was being accessed, some of its contents may appear scrambled. If the directory or other reserved area was being accessed, the problems could be more serious, since they're likely to affect more than one file. Computer viruses can also damage disks and files.

- Operator error. Everyone makes mistakes. You might accidentally throw away a file. Or, you might switch off your Mac without choosing the Shut Down command or waiting for the "You may now switch off your Macintosh safely" dialog box to appear.

What Can You Do?

First, always keep a set of current backups handy. (Yes, we're hammering this point into the ground, but it warrants the treatment.)

Second, invest in at least one disk-utility and file-recovery program. A few of the disk utilities available at this writing include 1st Aid Software's 1st Aid Kit, Central Point Software's PC Tools, and Symantec's Symantec Utilities for Macintosh (SUM). A simple but often-effective disk utility called Disk First Aid is also included with the Mac's system software.

We recommend investing in more than one recovery program. Each of the aforementioned programs includes a different mix of features for recovering information, repairing disks, and just making your Mac easier or more enjoyable to use. (1st Aid Kit, in particular, has an excellent manual packed with troubleshooting tips, many of which go beyond the category of disk errors.) All are inexpensive, especially compared to the time it takes to redo your work from scratch. When disk illness strikes, you'll be glad you had a well-stocked doctor's bag.

Finally, if you frequently run untested public-domain software or shareware, you might want to invest in a *virus-detection program* such as HJC Software's Virex, 1st Aid Software's Anti-Virus Kit, or Symantec's Symantec AntiVirus for Macintosh (SAM). These programs look for the specific viral "strains" that were circulating when the product was released, and they monitor activity on your disk and warn you when an attempt is made to alter your System file or other system resource.

Many people strongly recommend virus-detection programs, but we're more conservative. Viruses are like earthquakes in California: Everyone worries about them, but your chances of being victimized by one are extremely small. And because a new virus can appear at any time, no virus-protection program can guarantee complete protection.

How Disk Utility Programs Work

Disk utilities provide a few defenses against lost data:

- They can help you resurrect an accidentally deleted file. Most recovery programs include a startup document (Init) that creates an invisible file on each disk you use. This invisible file contains a record of the modifications you perform on that disk. If you delete a file by mistake, the recovery program can use the information in its invisible file to recover the file (assuming that a newly saved file hasn't taken over its sectors, as described earlier in this chapter).

- They can directly access any part of a disk. The Finder and application programs expect disks to be healthy, with directories and other reserved areas intact. When that isn't the case, error messages, system crashes, or data loss can result. Disk utility programs, however, make few assumptions about a disk; instead, they take it at face value, and therefore can display the contents of any sector that isn't magnetically or physically damaged. If a program's automatic recovery features don't work, you may be able to "manually" recover at least some information by locating it using the utility's track-and-sector display mode, and then retyping what you find into a text-editing desk accessory or word processor.

- They can automatically repair certain areas of the disk. Most utilities can quickly repair damaged boot blocks, and many can repair damaged directories or files by scanning the disk's contents.

Troubleshooting Common Problems

This section is a guide to troubleshooting common disk-related problems. We won't provide details on using specific disk recovery programs, since each program works differently. Instead, we'll describe the types of problems or error messages you might encounter, then we'll provide some general guidelines for recovering from them.

Symptom: When you start up from a floppy disk, the Mac ejects the disk and displays an "X" over the disk icon.

What's wrong: This is an easy one: the disk isn't a startup disk; that is, it doesn't contain the System and Finder files.

What to try: Either turn the disk into a startup disk by copying a current System Folder to it, or start your Mac with a disk containing a System Folder.

Symptom: During startup, the Mac displays the "Welcome to Macintosh" message, but crashes shortly after that.

What's wrong: If your System Folder contains more than one Init, the Inits may be conflicting with each other. Or one or more Inits may be damaged. Or, the System and/or Finder files may be damaged.

What to try: Restart the Mac, and watch the bottom of the screen carefully. Most Inits display an icon when loading; by watching to see which Inits have successfully loaded, you may be able to track down the offender. If the Mac always crashes just before a specific Init loads, try starting up the Mac with a different startup disk, and then renaming the offending Init to change its loading order. (Remember that the Mac loads Inits alphabetically.)

If that doesn't fix the problem, one or more Init may be damaged. Restart the Mac with a different disk, and then replace any damaged Inits with fresh copies from their original disks.

If these remedies fail, try reinstalling the disk's system software by using Apple's Installer utility, described in Chapter 5.

Symptom: You can't start the Mac from a hard disk that was previously working.

What's wrong: The hard disk's boot blocks or its System and Finder files may be damaged. The hard disk's driver software may be corrupted. Or, the contents of the Mac's parameter RAM, which stores (among other things) the currently selected startup device, may be corrupted. Or, if you've just attached a new SCSI peripheral, you may have a SCSI address conflict or a problem with your cabling or terminators.

What to try: Try repairing the disk's boot blocks. If the drive came with a utility that lets you reinstall its driver software, run it and do so.

To reset the Mac's parameter RAM, press Command-Shift-Option while opening the Control Panel. A dialog box appears warning that you're about to "zap the PRAM" and asking if you want to continue. Click Yes. After clearing the parameter RAM, you may need to readjust your basic Control Panel settings, such as the keyboard repeat rate and double-click speed.

If you've just attached a new add-on, check your SCSI addresses, cabling, and terminators. (See Chapter 14 for more details on SCSI cabling and termination.)

Symptom: When you insert a disk, the Mac says it's unreadable and asks if you want to initialize it.

What's wrong: The disk may be magnetically or physically damaged, or it may not be seated properly in the drive. Or it may be that you inserted a double-sided disk into a single-sided drive, or a high-density disk into non-FDHD drive. Or, the disk may be blank or formatted for a different type of computer.

What to try: First, eject the disk. Examine it to verify that it's the one you really wanted to insert, and that it's compatible with your Mac. If it is, try inserting the disk again. (Use a different floppy drive, if possible—the first drive you tried may be misaligned or damaged.)

If that doesn't work, try using a disk utility program to recover as much of the disk's contents as possible.

Symptom: When you insert a disk while the Finder is active, the Mac says it needs minor repairs and asks if you want to repair it.

What's wrong: The disk's DeskTop file is probably damaged or inconsistent.

What to try: Click OK to tell the Finder to rebuild the DeskTop file. When the DeskTop file is rebuilt, you'll lose any Get Info comments you specified for that disk's contents.

If this remedy doesn't work, you may still be able to easily recover the disk's contents. First, start your Mac under the Finder (not MultiFinder). Next, start an application, choose its Open command, and then insert the troublesome disk and attempt to open its documents. By not inserting the disk with the Finder running, you bypass the bad DeskTop file. If this technique works, immediately save any files you're able to open to a different disk.

You might also consider using ResEdit or a disk utility to rename the DeskTop file. After doing so, you can insert the disk at the Finder, and the Finder will create a new DeskTop file.

Symptom: The Mac is unable to open a document when you double click on it. Instead, a message appears saying the application is busy or missing.

What's wrong: You may not have the application that originally created the document. Or, the document may not be intended to be opened from the Finder (for example, perhaps you accidentally double clicked on a program's spelling checker dictionary or preferences file). Or, the disk's DeskTop file may be damaged.

What to try: If the application that created the document is missing, copy it to your hard disk or startup floppy disk in order to open the file. If you don't have the application (for example, MacWrite) but you do have an application that can read the document (for example, Microsoft Word), start the application you do have and then use its Open command to access the document.

If you do have the original application, try rebuilding the disk's DeskTop file. For floppy disks, insert the disk while pressing the Command and Option keys, then answer OK when asked if you want to rebuild the desktop. For hard disks, restart the Mac and press the Command and Option keys before the menu bar appears.

Symptom: When you're using the Finder or MultiFinder, an error message appears saying, "The disk is so full that the folder changes couldn't be recorded."

What's wrong: The disk is so full that the Finder isn't able to record your changes to a folder's viewing mode or icon arrangement in the disk's DeskTop file. Or, the DeskTop file itself may be corrupt.

What to try: If the disk is full or nearly full, free up some space by removing unneeded files or copying some files to another disk.

If there's plenty of room on the disk, try rebuilding its Desk-Top file.

Symptom: When you try to delete a file or folder, the Finder reports that the item is locked or busy and can't be removed.

What's wrong: You may have tried to throw away a file that the Mac is currently using. (For example, the Finder file, or an application or document that's currently open under MultiFinder.) Or, the file may be locked. Or, a bug in a program or a recent system crash may have simply caused the Mac to *think* the file is in use.

What to try: First, verify that the file you're trying to delete isn't currently open. The current startup disk's System and Finder files can't be thrown away, nor can the MultiFinder file when you're running under MultiFinder. If you want to throw away these files, restart the Mac with a different startup disk. Or, if you aren't running under MultiFinder, simply switch-launch to a different startup disk as described in Chapter 3.

If you really want to throw away an application or document, quit or close it first. If you're running under MultiFinder and you want to delete a document you just closed, you may also need to quit the document's application in order for the Finder to "know" that the document is no longer in use.

To throw away a locked file, use the Finder's Get Info command to unlock it. Or simply press the Option key while dragging the file to the Trash.

If these techniques fail, restart the Mac and try again. If the problem was caused by a program bug or temporary inconsistency in the Mac's memory, restarting should clear the problem.

Symptom: A message saying "Please insert the disk *disk name*" appears.

What's wrong: Probably nothing; chances are the Mac simply needs to access a disk that you've ejected by using the Finder's Eject command, by clicking the Eject button in the Open or Save dialog box, or by using the Command-Shift-1 or Command-Shift-2 FKEYs. One time you might see this message is if you eject a disk and then double-click its dimmed icon in order to view its contents.

What to try: Insert the disk that the Mac is looking for. If you've double-clicked a dimmed icon and you don't want to insert the disk, press Command-period. The Finder displays an error message saying, "The folder/disk *'disk name'* couldn't be opened."

If the Mac asks you to swap between two disks over and over, there might be a temporary problem with memory or an application program. First, humor the Mac by swapping the disks a few times. The Mac may really need to alternately access the disks. If this floppy disk shuffle goes on for more than a half-dozen or so swaps, however, chances are there's a problem. Try pressing Command-period to break out of the disk-swap loop. Depending on why the Mac was asking for the other disk, however, this technique may cause a system crash. If Command-period seems to work, save all open documents and restart the Mac to clear its head.

To avoid these problems, it's always best to eject disks by dragging their icons to the Trash. Note, however, that you can't use this technique to eject a disk containing an open document or application.

Symptom: When you're copying files, the Finder reports that a file couldn't be written (or read) and was skipped.

What's wrong: A disk error is preventing the Finder from successfully writing to (or reading from) a disk.

What to try: If the problem disk is a floppy, try ejecting and reinserting it. The disk may not have been seated properly in the drive, or the drive may be slightly out of alignment. If this fixes the problem but it occurs again with different disks, have the drive serviced.

If the problem disk is in an external disk drive, be sure the drive isn't located to the left of the Mac or near a high-intensity or halogen desk lamp. It may be that a strong magnetic field is causing disk errors (or worse, that it magnetically damaged the disk).

With floppy or hard disks, try copying the files one at a time. If the Mac is having a problem writing to a disk, try using the Finder's Duplicate command to duplicate a small file on that disk. This will cause subsequent files to be written on different sectors. If this works, back up the problem disk immediately and, if it's a floppy, stop using it. If it's a hard disk, consider having it serviced.

You may also want to use a disk utility to verify the disk's contents. During verification, the utility scans the disk for errors and inconsistencies.

CHAPTER SUMMARY

- Disks use patterns of magnetic particles, oriented by read/write heads within the disk drive, to store the binary ones and zeros that form your programs and data.

- When you initialize a disk, the Mac records magnetic divisions on its surface called tracks and sectors. Tracks are concentric circles; sectors are divisions within each track. Both provide the foundation needed to store and locate files.

- Mac floppy disks offer capacities of 400K, 800K, and 1.4MB. 400K disks are single-sided, while 800K and 1.4MB disks are double-sided. 1.4MB disks contain finer particles that allow each track to contain 18 sectors, versus the 8 to 12 sectors that the tracks of 400K and 800K disks contain.

- Hard disks are conceptually similar to floppies, but use rigid platters that spin faster and pack data more tightly. Removeable-media drives combine the high capacities of hard disks with the convenience and security of floppies.

- The Mac uses reserves certain areas of a disk for its own use, storing information about where files are located on the disk and about the disk itself.

- Disk utility programs can often recover information from damaged disks, but they aren't a substitute for a careful, faithfully followed backup routine.

A

Appendix

In this book's introduction, we mentioned that we don't describe specific application categories. From the beginning, we've assumed that you have at least a basic familiarity with the kinds of programs available for the Mac.

But even a seasoned Mac veteran may not be familiar with every application area. For that reason, we've included this glossary of the most common ways Macs are used. With each definition, we've mentioned some (but not all) of the programs available in that application category. Use these definitions as starting points for further investigation.

Accounting   Managing financial information: payrolls, accounts receivable, accounts payable, maintaining a general ledger, and tracking expenses. Accounting programs include Survivor Software's MacMoney, Layered's Insight series, and SoftView's MacInTax. Many data base managers can also be used for accounting applications.

Animation   Combining sequences of images that, when played back, provide the illusion of motion. Macintosh animation programs include MacroMind Director and VideoWorks II, Beck-Tech's MacMovies, and Bright Star Technology's HyperAnimator.

Business graphics   Creating charts that visually depict trends or relationships between values. Business graphics programs can generally create numerous types of charts; examples include pie charts, bar charts, and line charts. Most spreadsheet programs provide built-in graphing features; you can also choose stand-alone graphing programs such as Computer Associates' Cricket Graph or Fox Software's FoxGraph.

Computer-aided design (CAD)   Creating architectural drawings, mechanical drawings, and circuit schematics. CAD programs provide sophisticated features for automatically measuring the components in a drawing and for retrieving often-used shapes from *symbol libraries*. CAD programs include VersaCAD, MiniCAD, and Claris CAD.

Data base management   Storing, editing, organizing, and retrieving information, generally organized in a rigid format comprising *fields* (pieces of information, such as a person's first name, last name, and address) and *records* (a collection of fields pertaining to one entry, such as one person's complete name and address). Many Macintosh data base managers can also store graphic images. Data base programs include Claris' FileMaker II, Acius' 4th Dimension, and Ashton-Tate's dBASE Mac. Most spreadsheet programs also provide limited data-management features.

Desktop publishing   Preparing final artwork, generally by combining text and graphics created in other programs, for documents that will be printed and distributed. Desktop publishing programs generally have sophisticated text-formatting features that give you more control over character and line spacing than word processors provide. Examples of desktop publishing programs include Aldus PageMaker, QuarkXpress, and Letraset's Ready,Set,Go!.

Drawing   Creating graphic images by using an object-oriented program, in which images are comprised of distinct shapes (circles, lines, polygons, and so on). Drawing programs include Claris MacDraw II, Computer Associates' Cricket Draw, Adobe Illustrator 88, and Aldus FreeHand. See also *painting*.

HyperCard   The application category that defies simple definitions. Apple calls HyperCard "system software," but more accurately, it's a programmable data base that lets you establish links between on-screen buttons and pieces of information. In a HyperCard stack about Mozart, for example, you might click on one button to read a biographical sketch, another button to view a picture of Mozart's home town, and a third button to listen to a musical passage. HyperCard's programming language is called *HyperTalk*. HyperCard documents are called *stacks*.

Image processing   Analyzing and altering the appearance of graphic images, usually those created by a scanner. Image processing programs let you electronically retouch images, removing spots or imperfections and changing brightness, contrast, or color balance. Most programs provide tools that correspond to real-world retouching tools, such as airbrushes and pencils. Two popular image processing programs are Silicon Beach Software's Digital Darkroom and Letraset's ImageStudio.

Optical-character recognition (OCR)   Interpreting the text in a scanned image and creating a editable text file containing its characters. Without OCR software, scanning a page of text is like photocopying it—you can't edit the results. OCR programs include Caere's OmniPage and Olduvai Software's Read-It.

Painting   Creating graphic images, generally by using pencil and paintbrush-like tools that "apply" black pixels to an electronic canvas. Painting programs create bit-mapped images, which can show excellent shading and detail, but can become distorted when resized. Painting programs include Claris' MacPaint, Electronic Arts' Studio/1 and Studio/8, Silicon Beach Software's SuperPaint, and SuperMac's PixelPaint.

Presentation graphics   Preparing presentation visuals such as overhead transparencies, slides, and hand-outs. Presentation programs generally combine built-in outlining features to help organize your thoughts with drawing features that let you create your visuals. Presentation programs include Aldus Persuasion, Microsoft PowerPoint, and Symantec's MORE II.

Project management   Analyzing and refining the steps in a project by supplying a list of required tasks, the time each takes to complete, and the resources available to complete it. Project management programs let you visually depict the workflow of a given project and claim to help you allocate resources and schedule appropriately. Claris' MacProject II is the best-known project manager for the Mac.

Spreadsheets   One of the mainstay applications of the business world, spreadsheet programs let you enter values in a grid-like array of *cells*, specify relationships between the cells, and then perform calculations based on the relationships. Change a value in one cell, and the spreadsheet program recalculates other cells to show the result. Using this technique, you can play "what if?" games: What if sales rose 10 percent instead 15 percent? What if costs were cut in half? What if interest rates rise next year? Spreadsheet programs include Microsoft Excel, Ashton-Tate's FullImpact, and Access Technologies' Trapeze.

Telecommunications   Literally, "communicating at a distance." Specifically, connecting to other computers using the phone lines and telephone modems. With a modem and communications software, you can tap into the computers of information services such as Connect and CompuServe. These offer a vast world of free software, shareware, technical insights and advice (from fellow users and from hardware and software firms), stock quotes, weather forecasts, travel information, and much, much more. You can also send electronic mail to other computer users who have modems. Chapter 12 contains more information on telecommuncations. Some popular communications programs include FreeSoft's Red Ryder, Hayes' Smartcom II, and Software Ventures' MicroPhone.

Word processing   The final definition in this appendix, but the most popular application in the microcomputer world. Word processors turn the Mac into a sophisticated electronic typewriter that lets you enter and revise text and then commit it to paper. Word processors offer *search and replace* features that let you make wholesale revisions in one swoop—changing all occurrences of "Mac" to "Macintosh," for example. Some word processors can also automatically compile indexes and tables of contents. Many of today's Mac word processors have features that encroach on desktop publishing territory, such as fine control over line and letter spacing, the ability to combine text and graphics, and features for creating multiple-column pages. Word processors include Microsoft Word, T/Maker's WriteNow, Claris' MacWrite II, WordPerfect Corporation's WordPerfect, Ashton-Tate's FullWrite, and Paragon Concepts' Nisus.

B

Appendix

Manufacturer	Products Discussed
1st Aid Software 42 Radnor Rd. Boston, MA 02135 800/843-3497	Disk 1st Aid
Acius 20300 Stevens Creek Blvd. Cupertino, CA 95014 408/252-4444	4th Dimension
Adobe Systems PostScript fonts 1585 Charleston Road Mountain View, CA 94039 415/961-4400	Adobe Illustrator 88, Adobe Type Library
Affinity Microsystems, Ltd. 1050 Walnut St., Suite 425 Boulder, CO 80302 303/442-4840, 800/367-6771	Tempo II

Manufacturer	Products Discussed
Aldus Corp. 411 First Avenue South Seattle, WA 98104 206/622-5500	PageMaker, FreeHand, Persuasion
Alisa Systems 221 E. Walnut St., Suite 175 Pasadena, CA 91101 818/792-9474	AlisaShare
ALsoft Box 927 Spring, TX 77383 713/353-4090	Font/DA Juggler
Apple Computer, Inc. 20525 Mariani Ave. Cupertino, CA 95014 408/996-1010	Apple Macintosh computers, AppleShare, Apple File Exchange, Apple PC 5.25 drive, LaserWriter IINT, NTX, SC
Apple Programmer's and Developer's Association (APDA) Apple Computer, Inc. 20525 Mariani Ave. Cupertino, CA 95014 800/282-APDA	ResEdit, Technical literature
Ashton-Tate Corp. 20101 Hamilton Ave. Torrance, CA 90502 213/329-8000	FullWrite Professional, FullImpact, dBASE Mac
Bitstream, Inc. Athenaeum House 215 First Street Cambridge, MA 02142 617/497-6222	FontWare fonts
Bright Star Technology 14450 NE 29th, Suite 220 Bellevue, WA 98007 206/885-5446	HyperAnimator

Manufacturer	Products Discussed
Casady & Greene 26080 Carmel Rancho Blvd. #202 Carmel, CA 93923 800/331-4321	ImageWriter and PostScript fonts
CE Software, Inc. 1854 Fuller Rd, PO Box 65580 West Des Moines, IA 50265 515/224-1995	QuicKeys, MockPackage
Central Point Software 15220 N.W. Greenbrier Pkwy #220 Beaverton, OR 97006 503/690-8090	Copy II Deluxe Option Board, PC Tools
Claris Corp. 5201 Patrick Henry Drive P.O. Box 58168 Santa Clara, CA 95052 408/727-8227	MacWrite, MacPaint, FileMaker II, MacDraw II
Compatible Systems Corp. P.O. Drawer 17220 Boulder, CO 80308	QuickShare, AnyText, AnyGraph
Compugraphic Corp. 90 Industrial Way Wilmington, MA 01887 800/622-TYPE	PostScript fonts
CompuServe Information Service Box 20212 Columbus, OH 43220 800/848-8199 Ohio: 614/457-8600	Information service; shareware, public-domain software, support forums, electronic mail
Computer Associates International, Inc. 10505 Sorrento Valley Rd. San Diego, CA 92121 800/531-5236	Cricket Draw

Manufacturer	Products Discussed
Connect Inc. 10101 Bubb Rd. Cupertino, CA 95014 408/973-0110	Information service; shareware, public-domain software, support forums, electronic mail
Crate Technology 6850 Vineland N. Hollywood, CA 91605 818/766-4001	ExpandaCrate
Custom Applications, Inc. Building Eight 900 Technology Park Drive Billerica, MA 01821 508/667-8585	Freedom of Press
Dataproducts Corp. 6200 Canoga Ave. Woodland Hills, CA 91365 818/887-8000	LZR-2665
Dataviz, Inc. 35 Corporate Drive Trumbull, CT 06611 203/768-0030	MacLink Plus
Dayna Communications, Inc. 50 S. Main St., 5th Floor Salt Lake City, UT 84144 801/531-0203	DaynaFile, DOS Mounter
DayStar Digital 5556 Atlanta Hwy. Flowery Branch, GA 30542 404/967-2077	LT-200MC LocalTalk board, FS100 file server software
Deneba Software 7855 NW 12th St., Suite 202 Miami, FL 33126 800/6-CANVAS 305/594-6965	Canvas, LaserQuotes

Manufacturer	Products Discussed
Digidesign, Inc. 1360 Willow Rd., Suite 101 Menlo Park, CA 94025 415/327-8811	Sound Accelerator
DPI 40 Corning Ave. Milpitas, CA 95035 800/825-1850 408/945-1850	DPI 44
Edco Services, Inc. 12410 North Dale Mabry Hwy. Tampa, FL 33618 800/541-2255 813/962-7800	LetrTuck
Ergotron Box 17013 Minneapolis, MN 55417 800/328-9829 612/854-9116	MacWorkstation furniture, Mouse360 cleaning kit
Eric Celeste 358 North Parkview Columbus, OH 43209	Macify
Farallon Computing, Inc. 2201 Dwight Way Berkeley, CA 94704 415/849-2331	PhoneNet, MacRecorder, Timbuktu
Fifth Generation Systems 11200 Industriplex Blvd. Baton Rouge, LA 70809 800/87-FIFTH 504/291-7221	Suitcase II, FastBack
Fox Software 118 W. South Broadway Perrysburg, OH 43551 419/874-0162	FoxBASE+/Mac

Manufacturer	Products Discussed
GCC Technologies 580 Winter St. Waltham, MA 02154 617/890-0880	Personal LaserPrinter, Business LaserPrinter
Genesis Micro Software 106 147th Ave. SE, #2 Bellevue, WA 98007 206/747-8512	AutoMac III
Global Computer Supplies 45 South Service Rd Dept. 92 Plainview, NY 11803 800/845-6225	accessories, supplies, cables
Harvard Systems Corp. 1661 Lincoln Blvd., Suite 101 Santa Monica, CA 90404 213/392-8441	The Graphics Link+
IBM 1133 Westchester Ave. White Plains, NY 10604 800/IBM-2468	Personal Page Printer II
ICOM Simulations 648 S. Wheeling Rd. Wheeling, IL 60090 312/520-4440	MacKern
Informix Software, Inc. 16011 College Blvd. Lenexa, KS 66219 913/492-3800	WingZ
Inmac Corporation 2465 Augustine Dr. P.O. Box 58031 Santa Clara, CA 95052 Outside CA: 800/527-8523 Inside CA: 800/527-8522	accessories, supplies, cables

Manufacturer	Products Discussed
Iomega Corp. 1821 West 4000 South Roy, UT 84067 800/777-6654 801/778-1000	Bernoulli Box II
Jasmine Technologies, Inc. 1740 Army St. San Francisco, CA 94124 415/282-1111	DirectPrint, MegaDrive, DirectShare
Kennect Technology 271 E. Hacienda Ave. Campbell, CA 95008 Outside CA: 800/552-1232 Inside CA: 408/370-2866	Rapport, Drive 2.4
Kensington Microware 251 Park Ave. South New York, NY 10010 800/535-4242 212/475-5200	System Saver, various accessories
Kim Levitt Synergistic Enterprises 8033 Sunset Blvd., Suite 975 Los Angeles, CA 90046	GCP
Kiwi Software 6546 Pardall Rd. Santa Clara, CA 93117	Kiwi Envelopes
La Cie, Ltd. 1400 NW Compton Dr. Beaverton, OR 97006 503/690-1400	Hard disks, Panther PDX laser printer, Agio Designs furniture
Letraset USA 40 Eisenhower Dr. Paramus, NJ 07653 800/634-3463 201/845-6100	ImageStudio, Ready,Set,Go!, LetraStudio

Manufacturer	Products Discussed
Mass Micro Systems, Inc. 550 Del Rey Ave. Sunnyvale, CA 94068 800/522-7979 408/522-1200	DataPak
MCI Mail P.O. Box 1001 1900 M St. NW Washington, DC 20036 800/624-2255	Electronic mail, FAX services
Micrografx 1303 Arapaho Richardson, TX 75081 800/272-3729 214/234-1769	Passport, Designer
Microsoft Corp. 10611 NE 36th Way Box 97017 Redmond, WA 98073 206/882-8080	Microsoft Word, Mail, File, Excel, Works
MicroSolutions 132 W. Lincoln Hwy. DeKalb, IL 60115 815/756-3411	MatchMaker
Pacer Software 7911 Herschel Ave., Suite 402 La Jolla, CA 92037 619/454-0565	PacerShare
Palomar Software 2964 Oceanside Blvd. Oceanside, CA 92054 619/721-7000	Colorizer
Peripheral Land, Inc. 47800 Westinghouse Dr. Fremont, CA 94538 415/657-2211	Infinity 40 Turbo

Manufacturer	Products Discussed
Personal Computer Peripherals Corp. 6204 Benjamin Rd. Tampa, FL 33634 813/884-3092	HFS Backup
Peter Norton Computing, Inc. 100 Wilshire Blvd. Santa Monica, CA 90403 213/453-2361	The Norton Utilities
QMS, Inc. One Magnum Pass Mobile, AL 36618 800/367-7561	PS-800, PS-810 laser printers
Quark, Inc. 300 S. Jackson, Suite 100 Denver, CO 80209 800/543-7711 303/934-2211	QuarkXpress
RasterOps 2500 Walsh Ave. Santa Clara, CA 95051 408/562-4200	ColorBoard/104, Colorboard/264
Relax Technology 3101 Whipple Rd., #22 Union City, CA 94587 800/848-1313 415/471-6112	Mobile 42 Plus
Shiva Corporation 155 Second St. Cambridge, MA 02141 617/864-8500	NetModem, NetSerial, DOS Dial-in
Silicon Beach Software 9770 Carroll Center Rd. San Diego, CA 92126 619/695-6956	SuperPaint, Airborne

Manufacturer	Products Discussed
Software Shop 516/785-4422	Kern Rite
Sun Microsystems 950 Marina Village Parkway Alameda, CA 94501 415/769-9669	TOPS, NetPrint, FlashTalk
SuperMac Technologies 295 N. Bernardo Ave. Mountain View, CA 94043 415/962-2900	PixelPaint, Network DiskFit, SuperLaserSpool, Spectrum/24 video board
Symantec Corp. 10201 Torre Ave. Cupertino, CA 95014 408/253-9600	More II, SUM, SAM
T/Maker Corp. 1973 Landings Dr. Mountain View, CA 94043 415/962-0195	WriteNow for Macintosh
Traveling Software 18702 North Creek Parkway Bothell, WA 98011 800/662-2652 206/483-8088	LapLink Mac
Varityper 11 Mt. Pleasant Ave. East Hanover, NJ 07936 800/631-8134 NJ: 201/887-8000, ext. 999	VT600, VT600W printers
WordPerfect Corp. 1555 N.Technology Way Orem, UT 84057 801/225-5000	WordPerfect

Index

A

accelerator boards, 89
accent marks, 76–78
accessories
  for customization, 369–376
  desk. *See* desk accessories
ADB (Apple Desktop Bus), 542–544
  devices, 309
  keyboard, 103–105
Alarm Clock desk accessory, 72. *See also*
  desk accessories
Alto computer, 24–26
analog boards, 508, 509
AppleShare, 138, 467–468, 478–490. *See*
  also file servers
AppleTalk, 438–439, 490–491
applications. *See also* particular application
  choosing from menu, 63
  definition, 13–14
  in DeskTop file, 59
  display on desktop, 60
  macros and, 337
  managing, 51–52
  opening, 51
  organizing, 51
  selection techniques for specific,
    263–264
  sets, 292–294
  shortcuts for specific, 269
  switching between, 63–65, 337
asynchronous communications, 563–564
audio. *See* sound

B

Backgrounder file, 129
backing up data, 135, 271–272
bit map smoothing, 234

C

bit-mapped display, 32–35
  character display versus, 146–147
  fonts, 172–175, 186–187
  graphics, 383
bits
  definition, 5
  as measurement of power, 7–8
  start, stop, and parity, 562–563
boards. *See* particular board
boot blocks, 589
bugs, 12–13
buses, 504–505, 526–529
  Apple Desktop Bus. *See* ADB (Apple
    Desktop Bus)
  SCSI. *See* SCSI bus
bytes, 5

C

cables
  exchanging data with, 404–409
  in networking, 432–435
Calculator desk accessory, 72. *See also* desk
  accessories
cdevs, 115–129
central processing unit, 4–5, 8–9
chair height, 305
characters, foreign, 76–78
chips, 4, 529–533
Chooser desk accessory, 73–75. *See also*
  desk accessories
chunky (packed pixel) architectures,
  160–161, 162–163
Clipboard, 71
  data formats, 382–385
  Excel and, 386–387
  MacDraw and, 388
  PageMaker and, 388–389

Word and, 386
Works and, 387
clock, 72, 125–126, 502–503
CloseView cdev, 118, 127
color
    adjusting, 119
    architectures, 160–163
    boards, 142–143
    Colorizer package, 82, 372
    compatibility and, 158–159
    gray scale and, 151
    limitations, 157
    look-up tables, 153–156
    in Macintosh interface, 81–82
    memory and, 157–158
    storing and representing, 152–153
Color Disk update, 142–143
Command-key shortcuts, 127, 268–269,
    326
communications
    boards, 89
    services, 411–415
    synchronous and asynchronous,
        563–564
computers, 3–14
    forerunners of Macintosh, 21–26
    interacting with, 18–21
    numbering systems and, 5–7
Connect Professional Information Service,
    412, 414, 415
Control Panel desk accessory, 75. See also
    desk accessories
control panel devices (cdevs), 115–129
coprocessor boards, 89
Copy command, 71, 79–80
Copy II Deluxe Option Board, 404
CPU, 4–5, 8–9. See also hardware
cursors, 47, 367
Cut command, 71, 79–80

D

DA Handler file, 131
daisy-chaining, 432–433
dashes, 244–245
data
    backing up, 135, 271–272
    computer treatment of, 5–8

exchanging, 381–425
    with cables, 404–409
    with Clipboard, 382–390
    with disk files, 390–415
    graphics, 397–400
    with modems, 410–415
    with MS-DOS computers, 401–424
    with SCSI bus, 561
    System 7.0 and, 423–424
    text, 391–397
forks, 314
selection of. See selection of data
storage, 10. See also disks
data base management, 264, 602
data-acquisition boards, 89
DaynaFile, 403
dBASE Mac, 416
desk accessories, 71–81
    DA Handler file, 131
    extenders, 135
    Font/DA Mover utility, 141, 185
    macros and, 336
    MultiFinder and, 292
    renaming, 350–351
desk height and space requirements,
    305–306
desktop, 35–36
DeskTop file, 59–60
desktop publishing programs
    definition, 602
    exchanging data, 391–392, 415–416
    shift-clicking in, 258
dialog boxes, 44–47
    directory, 55–59, 269–270
    modifying, 352–361
    shortcuts, 334–335
digital boards. See logic boards
digitally recorded sounds, 82
DIP switches, 525
directory
    dialog boxes, 55–59, 269–270
    windows, 36, 37
disk caches, 275–277
disk drives
    drive spacers, 575
    erasable optical (EO), 580
    exchanging data with, 402–404
    FDHD, 402–403, 573, 574

floppy, 307
hard. *See* hard disks
PC 5.25, 403–404
technical factors, 582
WORM, 580
disk utility programs, 593
disks. *See also* memory
    backing up, 271–272
    boot blocks, 589
    directories, 585–591
    displaying contents of, 49–50, 60
    ejecting with macros, 336
    error messages, 594–598
    floppy. *See* floppy disks
    gauging storage requirements, 581–585
    hard. *See* hard disks
    interleave ratios, 583–584
    management, 297–304
    saving files to, 585–591
    start-up, 67–68
    storage of data, 10
    switching, 270
    system, 66–70
    tracks and sectors, 572, 585–588
    troubleshooting, 591–599
    unreadable, 595
    volume bit map, 585
    volume information blocks, 589
dithering, 149
document windows, 37
documents, 51–52. *See also* files
dot matrix printing, 203–204
double clicking, 35, 48, 265–267
dragging text, 35, 48
DRAM chips, 519–524
Drive 2.4, 403
drive spacers, 575

E

Easy Access Init, 127–128
electronic mail, 429, 455–465
em and en dashes, 244–245
erasable optical (EO) drives, 580
Esc key and macros, 337
Ethernet networks, 431. *See also*
  networking
Excel. 396–387, 416. *See also* spreadsheet
  programs

expansion
    boards, 88, 89
    slots, 88, 526–529

F

FDHD drives, 402–403, 573, 574
file extensions, 422
file servers, 465–490
    AppleShare, 467–468, 478–490
    combining, 489–490
    modular, 491
    TOPS, 465–467, 468–477, 489–490
FileMaker II, 264
files. *See also* folders
    changing characteristics, 346–347
    converting, 418–419
    exchanging data
        between programs, 390–401
        with MS-DOS computers, 401–415
    finding, 302–303
    formats
        foreign, 400–401
        graphics, 397–399
        text, 391–396, 415–421
    GIF, 419
    how Macintosh deletes, 588
    how Macintosh saves, 585–591
    interchange, 391, 392–394, 416–418
    locating via dialog boxes, 269
    locked, 597
    Macintosh filing system, 55–60
    managing, 51–52
    naming, 299–300
    native, 391–392, 415–416
    opening transferred, 421–422
    opening with ResEdit, 320
    organizing, 297–298
    selecting multiple, 53–54
    sharing via networks, 429
    signatures, 590–591
    structure, 314
    suitcase, 176–177, 181–185
    System 7.0 and, 303–304
    text-only, 391, 394–396, 419–421
    transfer, 462, 475
    unreadable, 598
    viewing directories, 301

Find File desk accessory, 76, 302–303. *See also* desk accessories
Finder, 35–36, 49–54. *See also* System Folder
  description, 49
  evolution, 136–140
  menus, 321–325
  MiniFinder, 137
  modifying, 361–365
  MultiFinder. *See* MultiFinder
  replacing, 371
  shortcuts, 294–296
  Startup file, 130
firmware, 4
FKEYs, 113–114. *See also* resources
floppy disks, 570–576
  care of, 574
  description, 10, 570, 571
  ejecting, 574
  erasing, 575
  high-density, 573, 574, 576
  initializing, 572
  labels, 574
  mixing high-density and 800K, 576
  recommendations, 574
  storage, 575
folders, 36. *See also* files
  accessing, 56–59
  displaying contents of, 49–50, 60
  locked, 597
  naming, 299–300
  opening and closing, 270
FOND font-handling resource, 189–190. *See also* resources
font, caching, 228–229
Font/DA Mover utility, 141, 175–185
fonts, 33, 34, 167–195. *See also* printing; type
  adding, 175–180
  altering, 368–369
  bit-mapped, 172–175, 186–187
  boldface, 187–188
  conflicting, 192–193
  downloading, 225–228
  extenders, 135
  Font Manager and, 186–187
  handling resources, 189–190
  ImageWriter printing modes and, 208
  italics, 187–189
  memory and, 227
  monospaced, 171–172
  multi-bit, 190
  outline, 172–75, 193–194
  PostScript printers and, 224–232
  proportional, 171–172
  purchasing, 209
  QuickDraw and, 186–187
  removing, 175–177, 180–181
  Resource Manager and, 186–187
  screen versus printer, 200–202
  SCSI and, 230–231
  sharing on a network, 242
  suitcase files, 176–177, 181–185
  typefaces versus, 168–169
  width and spacing, 191

G

GCC Business LaserPrinter. *See* PostScript, printers
GCP (graphics conversion program), 418
gender changers, 406
Get Info command, 346–347
GIF files, 419
glare from screen, 307
Graphics Link+, 418–419
graphics, 601–603. *See also* data
  bit-mapped. *See* bit-mapped display
  exchanging, 397–400
  object-oriented, 383
  palettes, 153–156
  programs, 258, 383
gray scale, 149–151
grid-fitting, 229–230

H

halftones, 235
handshaking, 564–565
hard disks, 576–585
  care of, 585
  defragmenting, 304
  description, 10
  head crash, 577
  keeping files contiguous, 585
  noise reduction, 306–307
  removeable-media types, 577–580

hardware, 501–537
    analog boards, 508, 509
    basic computer, 8–11
    buses, 504–505, 526–529
    central processing unit, 4–5, 8–9
    control lines, 506
    customization accessories, 369–376
    definition, 3
    DIP switches, 525
    DRAM chips, 519–524
    expansion slots, 526–529
    handshaking, 565
    internal clock, 502–503
    interrupts, 503–504
    logic boards. *See* logic boards
    memory and, 519–525
    microprocessors, 529–533
    networking, 431–437
    power supply, 509–511
    ROM. *See* ROM
    set-up, 305–312
    SIMMs, 524
    of specific Macintosh models. *See*
      particular model
    start-up process, 533–535
head crash, 577
Hierarchical File System (HFS), 55–60
hierarchical menus, 43–44
high-density floppy disks, 573, 574, 576

I

I-beam pointer, 47–48
IBM computers. *See* MS-DOS computers
IBM Personal Page Printer II. *See*
  PostScript, printers
icons, 35–36, 60, 366
Illustrator, 416
ImageWriter printers, 202–211
    custom paper sizes and, 209
    driver for, 114
    fast printing, 209
    fonts and, 208–209
    for PostScript proofing, 210
    print modes, 204–206, 208–210
    ribbon use, 211
    Tall Adjusted option and, 208
information. *See* data

initialization
    floppy disk, 572
    Macintosh, 533–534
initialization resources (Inits),126–127,
    251–252, 376
input devices, 10–11
insertion point, 47–48
Installer utility, 132–133, 134, 135
integrated circuits, 4, 529–533
interfaces, user, 18–21. *See also* Macintosh,
    interface
interleave ratios, 583–584
interrupts, 503–504

J

Jobs, Steve, 27–29

K

Kay, Alan, 23, 24
kerning, 191
Key Caps desk accessory, 76–78, 131. *See*
    also desk accessories
Key Layout file, 131
keyboard(s), 103–105. *See also* selection of
    data
    ADB, 543
    adjusting, 120, 127–129
    equivalents (for commands), 42
    macro utilities, 128–129, 331–339
    mapping, 541
    operation of, 539–544
    shortcuts, 328–330
    utilities, 327–328

L

LapLink Mac, 405
Laser Prep file, 115, 241
laser printers, 211–248
    controllers, 219–248
    drivers for, 113–114, 139–140, 142–143
    engines, 212–219
    fonts and, 224–232
    halftoning capabilities, 235
    imaging methods, 215
    PostScript. *See* PostScript, printers

print quality, 216–217
QuickDraw. *See* QuickDraw, printers
resolution, 214–215
toner, 213
typographic capabilities, 231–232
LaserWriter
    IINT. *See* PostScript, printers
    IINTX. *See* PostScript, printers
    IISC, 247–248
launching the Macintosh, 52, 67–78
LAYO (layout) resource, 361–365. *See also*
    resources
leading, 191
line spacing, 170–171
Lisa computer, 27–29
local-area networks. *See* networking
LocalTalk networks, 431. *See also*
    networking
logic boards, 508
    Mac II and IIx, 515–516
    Mac IIcx, 518
    Macintosh Plus and SE, 511–513

M

Mac II series, 97–102
    special hardware features, 514–519,
        523–524
    upgrade, 108
    video, 151–159
MacDraw, 287, 289, 388
Macintosh. *See also* computers
    basic features, 91
    buying discontinued models, 107
    continuous use, 309
    customizing. *See* accessories, for
        customization; ResEdit utility
    desk space requirements, 306
    development of, 27–30
    display. *See* bit-mapped display
    forerunners of, 21–26
    hardware. *See* hardware
    interface, 31–83
        Clipboard. *See* Clipboard
        color. *See* color
        commands, 39–44
        desk accessories. *See* desk accessories
        filing system, 55–60
        Finder. *See* Finder

fonts. *See* fonts
    menus. *See* menus
    mouse. *See* mouse
    MultiFinder. *See* MultiFinder
    sound. *See* sound
    system disk, 66–70
    launching, 52, 67–68
    microprocessors, 4, 529–533
    models, 85–108. *See also* particular
        model
    navigation techniques, 257–272
    performance tips, 273–280
    software. *See* software
    upgrades, 108
Macintosh 512K and 512K Enhanced,
    106–108, 522
Macintosh 128K, 105–106, 108, 522
Macintosh Plus, 92, 96
    mouse, 541–542
    special hardware features, 506–513,
        522–523
Macintosh SE series, 92–96
    special hardware features, 506–513,
        522–524, 526
    upgrade, 108
MacLInk series, 405
macro utilities, 128–129, 331–339
MacroMaker Init, 128–129
magneto-optical drives, 580
Mail (electronic mail system), 455–465
Map cdev, 125
marquees, 259
MatchMaker, 404
math coprocessors, 94, 532–533. *See also*
    microprocessors
MCI Mail communications service, 412,
    413
memory
    addressing and accessing, 8–9
    allocating with MultiFinder, 61
    color and, 157–158
    fonts and, 227
    fragmented, 282–284
    gauging storage requirements, 581–585
    hardware and, 519–525
    management with MultiFinder, 66
    measurement of, 9–10
    MultiFinder and, 280–292
    RAM. *See* RAM

ROM. *See* ROM
saving by altering system Folder, 251–257
specific application requirements, 284–290
virtual, 90, 256–257
menu command shortcuts, 334
menus, 20, 39–43
hierarchical, 43–44
pop-up, 45–46
ResEdit and, 321–325, 330, 331
tear-off, 338
microprocessors, 4, 529–533
MIDI, 548–549, 553
MiniFinder, 137
modems, 410–415, 491–495
monitors. *See also* video
multiple, 156
switching between, 124
viewing angle, 305–306
motherboards. *See* logic boards
Mouse Keys feature, 127
mouse, 34–35. *See also* selection of data
ADB, 544
adjusting, 121, 545–546
care of, 308
keypad replacing, 127
operation of, 541–546
shortcuts, 335
MS-DOS computers
file exchange with Macintosh, 401–424
file servers and, 473–474, 477, 488
printing in network, 448–454
TOPS and, 473–474
MultiFinder, 60–66, 112–113
alternatives to, 296
application sets, 292–294
desk accessories and, 292
memory and, 280–292
modifying, 347–350
removal to save memory, 255–256
shortcuts, 294–296
multitasking, 62–63

N

naming files and folders, 299–300
navigation techniques, 257–272

networking, 428–498
advantages of, 428–430
applications and, 495–497
combining networks, 436–437
electronic mail and, 455–465
file servers. *See* file servers
hardware, 431–437
modems and, 491–495
operation scenario, 439–468
printers and, 439–454
printing MS-DOS files, 448–454
software, 438–439, 495–497
topologies, 432–436
Windows programs, 450–453
NFNT font-handling resource, 189–190. *See also* resources
nodes, 428, 442–445
noise reduction, 306–307
Note Pad desk accessory, 80. *See also* desk accessories
NuBus slots, 527–529

O

object-oriented graphics, 383
operating system, 12–13
Option key, 267–268
output devices, 10–11

P

Page Setup command, 199–200
PageMaker. *See also* desktop publishing programs
Clipboard and, 388–389
exchanging data, 391–392, 415–416
memory requirements, 287, 289
special selection techniques, 263
Palo Alto Research Center (PARC), 23, 24
paper
choice of, 243–244
custom sizes, 209, 339–346
handling by PostScript printers, 236
parallel ports, 11
parity bits, 562
Passport (graphics conversion program), 418
Paste command, 71

PC 5.25 drive, 403–404
PCs. *See* MS-DOS computers
peripheral noise, 306–307
pixels, 32, 148–149
planar architectures, 161, 162
ports, 11, 562–567
PostScript, 220–245
    advantages and disadvantages, 223–224
    description, 220
    dictionary, 142
    font use, 228–229
    printers. *See also* laser printers
        clones, 237–239
        differences between, 233–237
        emulation modes, 236
        fonts and, 224–232
        LocalTalk and, 236
        non-PostScript fonts and, 240
        operation, 221–223
        paper-handling features, 236
        SCSI drives and, 230–231
        tips for use, 239–244
        typographic capabilities, 231–232
    versions, 233
power conditioners, 308
power supply, 509–511
PREC (print record) resources, 339–346.
    See also resources
Precision Bitmap Alignment option,
    241–242
Print Monitor file, 130
printer(s). *See also* printing
    dot matrix, 203–204. *See also*
      ImageWriter printers
    drivers, 114–115, 198–200
    fonts, 200–202. *See also* fonts
    ImageWriter. *See* ImageWriter printers
    laser. *See* laser printers
    name change, 241
    noise reduction, 306–307
    ribbons, 211
    sharing via networks, 439–454
    switching between, 73–75
printing, 197–250. *See also* fonts; printers
    background, 129
    drivers, 139, 140, 142–143
    envelopes, 242–243
    increasing speed of, 209

    monitoring, 130
    MS-DOS files in network, 448–454
    overview, 197–202
    paper choice, 243–244
    print files, 240–241
    start-up page, 239–240
    System 7.0 and, 248–249
Puzzle desk accessory, 81. *See also* desk
accessories

Q

QuarkXpress, special selection techniques,
    264. *See also* desktop publishing
    programs
QuickDraw, 32, 142, 186–187
    printers, 245–248. *See also* laser printers
QuickKeys. *See* macro utilities
QuickShare, 406
quote marks, 244–245

R

RAM, 9–10, 519–520
    cache, 117
    disks, 275, 277–280
raster display, 147
read-only memory. *See* ROM
reference cards, 270–271
ResEdit utility, 317–376
    advantages and disadvantages, 327
    changing file characteristics, 346–347
    Command-key shortcuts, 326–327
    creating custom paper size, 341–345
    cursor altering with, 367
    description, 317–319
    editing resources, 317–326
    font altering with, 368–369
    icon altering with, 366
    keyboard shortcuts, 328–330
    keyboard utilities versus, 327
    menus and, 330, 331
    version resources and, 367–368
resources
    editing, 317–326
    explanation and types, 313–317
    font-handling, 189–190
    LAYO, 361–365

managing, 375
PREC, 339–346
version, 367–368
ring networks, 433–434
ROM, 9–10, 12–13, 525
configuration, 156, 528

S

sampled sound, 549–553
Scrapbook desk accessory, 79–80, 338. *See also* Clipboard; desk accessories
screen blankers (or savers), 309, 374
screens. *See* video
SCSI bus, 554–561
cables, 554–555
communications, 560
data transmission, 561
explanatory programs, 558–559
font storage and, 230–231
ports, 91–92
setting addresses, 557–558
termination, 555–557
Select All command, 259
selection of data
cancelling, 264–265
combining techniques, 260–265
selection marquees, 259
specific software packages, 263–264
spreadsheets, 261–262
strategies, 257–259
serial ports, 11, 562–567
Set Startup command, 52, 337
shareware, 369–370
shift-clicking, 35, 48, 258
shortcuts
application-specific, 269
Command-key, 127, 268–269, 326
directory dialog boxes, 269–270
Finder, 294–296
keyboard, 328–330
macro utility, 334–339
menu command, 334
mouse, 335
MultiFinder, 294–296
SIMMs, 91, 524
68000 microprocessor, 5, 27, 529–531
68020 microprocessor, 530, 531

68030 microprocessor, 530, 531–532
software
application, 13–14
customization accessories, 369–376
definition, 4
handshaking, 565
networking, 436–437
operating system, 12–13
printing MS-DOS files, 448–449
shareware, 369–370
system, 12–13, 445–446
sound, 546–553
adjusting, 122
analog versus digital, 550
audio compression and expansion, 553
enhancing, 309–312
in Macintosh interface, 82
MIDI, 548–549, 553
modifying, 373–374
quality, 552–553
sampled, 549–553
Sound Manager, 547–548, 553
System 7.0 and, 553
speed of processing, 86–88
spreadsheet programs. *See also* particular program
definition, 603
exchanging data, 392, 416
selection techniques, 261–262
star networks, 434–435
start bits, 562–563
start-up
disk, 67–68
documents, 251–252
options, 52
problems with, 593–594
process, 533–535
Startup Device cdev, 123
Sticky Keys feature, 127
stop bits, 562–563
storage of data, 5, 10. *See also* disks
suitcase files, 176–177, 181–185
surge protectors, 308
Switch-A-Roo, 274
switch-launching, 69–70
synchronous communications, 563–564
System 7.0. *See also* System Folder
exchanging data and, 423–424

file management and, 303–304
macros and, 338–339
outline fonts and, 193–194
printing and, 248
sound and, 553
virtual memory and, 90, 256–257
system disk, 66–70
System file, 110–114. *See also* System
  Folder
System Folder, 67–79, 109–143. *See also*
  System 7.0
  choosing between versions, 133–134
  contents, 112–128
  evolution, 135–143
  setting up, 251–257
  streamlining, 253–257
  updating, 131–135
  version numbering, 110–112
System resources. *See* resources
system software, 12–13, 445–446
system start-up, 135, 534–535
System Tools 5.0, 139–140

T

Tall Adjusted option, 208
tear-off menus, 338
Tempo II. *See* Macro utilities
Tesler, Larry, 24, 28
text. *See also* data
  boxes, 46–47
  entry, 47–48
  exchanging, 391–397
  macros and, 336
  selecting, 48–49
text-only files, 391, 394–396
Token-Ring networks, 431. *See also*
  networking
TOPS, 465–467, 468–477, 489–490. *See also*
  file servers
transferring data. *See* data, exchanging
trunk networks, 433. *See also* networking
type. *See also* fonts
  accent marks, 76–78
  character components, 169–170
  kerning, 191
  leading, 191
  measuring, 170–171

print quality, 216–217
typefaces versus fonts, 168–169

U

upgrades, 108
user interfaces, 18–21. *See also* Macintosh,
  interface

V

version resources, 367–368
video, 145–164. *See also* monitors
  adjusting view, 118, 127
  basic description, 146–151
  bit-mapped display. *See* bit-mapped
    display
  boards, 89
  color. *See* color
  features, 89–90
  gray scale, 149–151
  Mac II, 151–159
  matching mode to task, 273
  memory and, 157–158
  pointer, 34–35
  resolution, 148
  screen glare, 307
  switching modes, 274
virtual memory, 90, 256–257
volume bit maps, 585
volume information blocks, 589
volume levels, 311

W

Windows programs, 450–453
windows, 35–39, 60
word processing programs. *See also*
  particular program
  definition, 604
  exchanging data, 391–392, 415–416
Word. *See also* word processing programs
  Clipboard and, 386
  memory requirements, 286, 288–289
  special selection techniques, 263–264
WordPerfect, 263. *See also* word processing
  programs
Works, 287–288, 289, 387
WORM drives, 580

About the Author

Jim Heid has been working with and writing about the Macintosh since 1983 when, as Senior Technical Editor for *Microcomputing* magazine, he previewed the computer before its introduction. For the past five years, he's been a Contributing Editor of *Macworld* magazine and has written its popular monthly "Getting Started" column since 1986. He's been working with microcomputers since the late 70s, when he computerized his home-built ham radio station with one of the first Radio Shack Model I computers. A native of Pittsburgh, Pennsylvania, Jim now lives in Northern California with his wife and toy poodle. He is a member of the Author's Guild.